BRITISH SECRET PROJECTS

BRITISH SECRET PROJECTS

2

Jet Bombers since 1949

TONY BUTTLER

Crécy
www.crecy.co.uk

Crécy Publishing Ltd

www.crecy.co.uk

British Secret Projects Volume 2
Jet Bombers since 1949
Tony Buttler MA AMRAeSp

First published in 2000 by Midland Publishing
Second edition published in 2018 by Crécy Publishing

A CIP record for this book is available from the British
Library

Printed in Slovenia by GPS Print

ISBN 978 1910809105

Crécy Publishing Ltd
1a Ringway Trading Estate, Shadowmoss Rd
Manchester M22 5LH
Tel (0044) 161 499 0024
www.crecy.co.uk

FRONT COVER ART – Specially commissioned artwork
from Daniel Uhr showing how the Armstrong Whitworth
AW.56 might have looked had it entered service as one
of the RAF's V-Bombers. *Daniel Uhr*

REAR COVER

TOP An RAF Harrier GR.Mk.5 with a full weapon load.

MIDDLE Artist's impression of the single-engine Vickers
Type 571 strike aircraft.

BOTTOM Model made by John Hall of the Avro 730.
John Hall

FRONT FLAP

TOP Avro long range OR.230 bomber study.
Avro Heritage

BOTTOM Original manufacturer's model of the
Armstrong Whitworth AW.168. *Ray Williams*

Contents

Introduction to the First Edition

This book follows my first major work with Midland Publishing, *British Secret Projects: Jet Fighters since 1950*, and forms a natural companion to it. Here the design and development of the British Bomber since the end of the Second World War is examined in similar depth with particular emphasis placed on the tender design competitions between projects from different companies. The subtitle date, 1949, relates to the first flight of the English Electric Canberra, Britain's first jet bomber, but of course studies were under way several years prior to this.

Once again extensive use has been made of previously unpublished primary source material held by museums and record offices and in company and private collections, much of it recently declassified. Consequently, it is again possible to reveal more of the Government's side of events than has probably ever been included before in a publicly available book, and give an insight into a secret world where few people had any idea of what was happening. Some of the factors and arguments that led to certain types either being cancelled or chosen for production and service are also reported, often for the first time.

This book brings together many little-known projects within a full narrative of bomber development. Plenty of bomber projects have been drawn by British companies over the last fifty years, particularly before the formation of the British Aircraft Corporation and Hawker Siddeley Aviation, but few were turned into hardware and little has been previously published about most of them. Bombers were more expensive than fighters and 'paper plane' competitions were crucial to acquiring the best aircraft yet, such were the advances in aerodynamics in the years after the end of the Second World War, four competing medium bombers were actually built and flown to give Britain the V-Force. The main lines of design absorb by far the majority of this book but space is also devoted to less obvious types such as the anti-submarine aircraft.

Most of the projects shown here would have been tunnel tested but it is impossible to say from the evidence available if they would have worked (although any design sent to the Air Ministry would be expected to fly). Few designs that did not at least reach wind tunnel testing are worthy of historical attention. Project data throughout this book is the manufacturer's estimates. If submitted to the Ministry, the figures would normally be re-assessed by specialists and often changed (the weights in particular would increase regularly) but using company data as much as possible provides a common factor to presenting figures.

I think it is correct to say that few, if any, large bomber designs (medium and upwards) have been produced in Britain since TSR.2; an interdictor strike aircraft such as Tornado was about the biggest programme the country could afford to take on. From about 1960 onwards there has been a great deal of effort towards producing multi-role aeroplanes with both fighter and bomber capability. Often it has been difficult to find a demarcation line because there was so much overlap and, consequently, one has to decide if a project should be in a fighter or bomber volume. By the time AST.396 was reached one or two projects were under way, such as Brough's P.153, that were indeed more fighter than bomber but they have to be included in this volume for completeness. In fact, because they were integral to both stories, the Hawker P.1154 and Supermarine Scimitar feature here and in the companion *British Secret Projects: Fighters*.

The bomber is perhaps one of man's most unpleasant creations but many times they have proved to be a vital element within his armed forces. Technically and politically they can be captivating subjects while certain examples can inspire affection on a remarkable scale (witness the popularity of the Avro Vulcan at air shows); indeed why is it that some of man's most beautiful creations are killing machines? Regardless of such arguments, it has been fascinating to write about them and I hope those of you who sample this book enjoy reading it as much as I have enjoyed writing it.

Introduction to the Second Edition

In the decade and a half that has passed since the first edition of this book was published there has been little sign of any new pure bomber aircraft types coming from the British aircraft industry. The 'conversion' of the Eurofighter Typhoon to a full 'swing role' multi-role aircraft is the major development to have taken place. As this is written the Royal Air Force is conducting an enhancement programme known as Project Centurion that has the objective of integrating, besides the Meteor air-to-air missile, both the MBDA Storm Shadow cruise missile and the MBDA Brimstone air-to-surface missile into the Typhoon's inventory. This programme is to be completed in December 2018 and will provide the aircraft with the weapons and capability of the Panavia Tornado GR.Mk.4 before that aircraft is finally retired in 2019. What will follow is anyone's guess, but with such work progressing today it is sometimes easy to forget that once upon a time Britain could produce so many bomber types of its own.

With the acquisition of the Midland/Ian Allan back catalogue by Crécy Publishing this revision of *British Secret Projects: Jet Bombers since 1949* forms the second stage in the updating of my books in the Secret Projects series. The original fighter volume had quite a few missing projects and the second edition of that book was able to fill in most of the gaps for what I had considered to be the most important projects and proposals. The design coverage in the first edition of bombers was overall rather more complete but here there is still a good supply of previously unpublished drawings and additional information. The opportunity has also been taken to replace as many of the photographs as possible with new images, in some cases rare colour shots that collectors have so kindly made available for me to use.

I would like to thank all of you who contributed to making the first edition of *Jet Bombers* the success that it was. I hope readers who are familiar with the original will feel that the revision undertaken here is worthy of the contents, and also that any readers new to this title and subject will be as stimulated by the extraordinary designs presented here as I was when I first discovered them. In many cases that is now more than twenty years ago!

Tony Buttler MA AMRAeS
Bretforton, January 2018

Acknowledgements

I am greatly indebted to many people who helped to bring this work together. The lists of unbuilt projects in the Putnam series on Aircraft Manufacturers, and other titles listed in the bibliography, provided a framework for my research. After that I must thank the following for allowing me to raid their archives for information, drawings and photographs, and for permission to publish material.

Wg Cdr Ron Allen; Peter Amos; the late Fred Ballam (Westland Archive); Peter Collins (Rolls-Royce Heritage, Derby); Sir George Cox; Peter Elliot, Gordon Leith, Simon Moody & Andrew Whitmarsh (RAF Museum); Ken Ellis; Steve Gillard and the staff of BAe Brough Heritage; the late Harry Fraser-Mitchell (Handley Page Association); the late Peter Green; Duncan Greenman; Barry Guess (BAe Farnborough); Bill Harrison; Bob Hercock (Rolls-Royce Heritage, Filton); George Jenks and the staff of Avro Heritage; Roff Jones and Don Tombs of Jet Age Museum (Gloster Aircraft); Brian Kervell; Ian Lawrenson and the staff of North West Heritage Group (BAe Warton); Roger Lindsay; Paul McMaster (Ulster Aviation Society); Thomas Muller; the staff of the British National Archives at Kew; the late Jim Oughton; Barry Pegram; Brian Riddle (Royal Aeronautical Society/National Aerospace Library); Tony Roden (Westland Cowes); the late Ray Sturtivant (Air-Britain); Julian Temple (Brooklands Museum), who also gave permission to photograph some 1/24th scale models on loan from BAE Systems; Les Whitehouse (Boulton Paul Archive) and Ray Williams (Armstrong Whitworth Archive).

I am particularly grateful to Chris Farara (Brooklands) for checking the Harrier text, the late Bob Fairclough (North West Heritage) for checking the TSR.2, Jaguar and Tornado text, Joe Cherrie and John Hall for providing models that filled gaps in my illustrations and Phil Butler for supplying the contract details. Special thanks go to the late Eric Morgan for making available his archives to me and Clive Richards (formerly of MoD Air Historical Branch) for information describing Britain and NATO's nuclear policies.

For this second edition I must add Terry Panopalis to the list for once more providing me with some incredibly rare colour images from the 1950s. And as ever my thanks go to Jeremy Pratt, Gill Richardson, Rosanna Farrell and the team at Crécy for asking me to undertake this revision and for putting it all together, and to Daniel Uhr for the superb cover artwork.

Chapter One
Mosquito Replacement

Britain's First Jet Bomber: 1944 to 1951

In 1945 Great Britain possessed a huge and immensely powerful strategic bomber force that had shown itself to be capable of all manner of bombing operations, from near wiping out complete cities to delivering 10-ton bombs from great height to hit pinpoint targets with great accuracy. As a weapon of war this was of immense strategic value. However, during the last year or so of the Second World War both Allied and Axis air forces had put jet-powered fighter aircraft into service, which meant that the piston-powered Avro Lancaster and its sisters would become obsolete pretty quickly. Britain was still to field

replacement piston bombers in the shape of the Avro Lincoln and American B-29 Washington but, once the new power source began to offer better range (early jet engines were notoriously heavy on fuel), then jet bombers had to be the way forward.

The replacement of the strategic force machines would lead to the V-bombers but there was another handy chap also made obsolescent by jet fighters that needed replacing. This was the de Havilland Mosquito, which could accurately be described as the world's first multi-role aircraft. Designed as a very fast unarmed

ABOVE An English Electric Canberra B.Mk.1 prototype displays at Farnborough.

bomber, its speed and performance had ensured it found service as a fighter, bomber, fighter-bomber, anti-shipping aircraft, photo-reconnaissance type and, after retirement from the front line, many other secondary duties. Therefore, quite naturally, Britain also concentrated on finding a replacement 'Jet Mosquito' and this was also to prove so successful that many different versions were produced, although initially it was considered to be more of a strategic bomber.

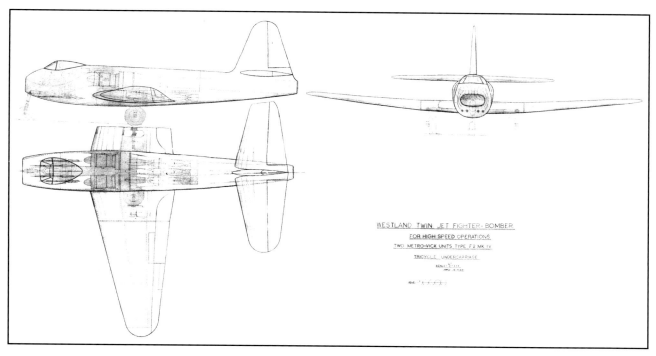

Westland P.1056, P.1057 and P.1061

ABOVE Westland P.1061 (18.4.44). *Jet Age Museum, adapted by Chris Gibson*

When the English Electric Canberra made its first flight in May 1949 it became the first jet bomber to be built and flown in the UK. The work leading up to it, however, had begun over five years earlier, not in the north of England but in the south-west in Somerset. In March 1944 Westland Aircraft's Technical Director, W. E. W. Petter, had completed a private venture design study for a high-speed, twin jet-powered fighter-bomber in two (or three) versions. This step had followed discussions between the company and two members of the Ministry of Aircraft Production (MAP) – Sir Wilfrid Freeman and N. E. Rowe (DTD).

The principal difference between the two main projects lay in their undercarriage; P.1056 had the tailwheel arrangement used by most piston aircraft whereas P.1061 introduced a tricycle undercarriage with a nosewheel. Power was supplied by a pair of Metropolitan Vickers (MetroVick) F.2/4 Beryl axial jet engines mounted side-by-side in the upper centre fuselage and fed by a large nose intake. To avoid the tailwheel the P.1056 ejected its exhaust

through holes in the side of the fuselage ahead of the tailplane but the tricycle gear meant P.1061 could have a more effective single pipe at the very end of the fuselage serving both engines. Both single and twin fins were examined. Each version had two crew seated side-by-side in a cockpit placed close to the nose to provide an excellent view, four 20mm cannon mounted in the lower forward fuselage and a large internal bomb bay situated beneath the engines and exhaust pipes.

BELOW AND OVERLEAF Model of the Westland P.1056 project, which was similar to the P.1061 except for its tailwheel undercarriage. *Joe Cherrie*

Detail drawings have been seen showing alternative loads for the P.1056, which included nine 500lb (227kg) bombs, three 500lb and three 1,000lb (454kg), three 500lb plus eight 90lb (41kg) rocket projectiles, or two 2,000lb (907kg) blockbuster bombs or mines. Another alternative was six 500lb (227kg) plus two 6lb (2.7kg) guns (with the 20mm omitted), and additional fuel could also go in the bay instead of some of the weaponry. Finally, if eight rocket projectiles were carried then the 20mm fitting could be increased to six (the six-pounder guns and the blockbuster bombs required additional fairings outside the lines of the lower fuselage). With such loads the aircraft had ranges between 790 and 1,000 miles (1,271km to 1,609km). One more drawing showed similar weapon loads for another associated project called the P.1057 but no further details were available.

The idea generated much interest and a mock-up was built of the nose and central fuselage, while Petter had a scale model on his desk complete with bombs, engines and other internal fittings. This project died when the designer left Westland but he took the jet bomber idea with him. It appears Petter had become frustrated with the direction that his company was moving (it had started work on a large naval fighter that later became the Wyvern) and in September 1944 he joined English Electric at Preston (with Westland's agreement). Anthony Furse's book *Wilfrid Freeman* claims that 'Freeman rescued the project by arranging for Petter to join the new English Electric aircraft team as Chief Designer'.

Westland P.1061 (18.4.44)	
Span	56ft 4in (17.17m)
Length	45ft 5in (13.84m)
Gross wing area	550sq ft (51.2sq m)
Gross weight	32,000lb (14,515kg)
Powerplant	two MetroVick F.2/4 Beryl 3,500lb (15.6kN)
Maximum speed/height	520mph (837km/h) at 25,000ft (7,620m)
Armament	four 20mm cannon, typical load 3,000lb (1,361kg) bombs

English Electric High-Altitude High-Speed Unarmed Bomber (single engine)

After his arrival at English Electric, Petter moved the bomber concept towards a preliminary specification, based on the requirements of the Air Staff, to replace the Mosquito bomber. The fitting of defensive guns was dropped and on 2 February 1945 he told Rowe: 'The company welcomes the opportunity to carry out design investigations of a high-speed unarmed bomber.' A preliminary study had been completed by 8 March and Petter reported that he 'believed a machine weighing not more than 40,000lb (18,144kg) can comply with the specification'. The full design brochure was ready on 1 June 1945 to the following specified limits:

i). Cruise speed of 500mph (805km/h) at an altitude of between 35,000ft and 45,000ft (10,668m and 13,716m).

ii). Still air range of 1,600 miles (2,574km).

iii). Bomb load of 6,000lb (2,722kg).

iv). Two crew.

The specified cruising speed was, in fact, so high that at 40,000ft (12,192m) it corresponded to about three-quarters of the speed of sound (Mach 0.75), so very special consideration had to be given to all drag excrescences, wing thickness and the intersection between body and wing and tail. The 40,000lb (18,144kg) weight was confirmed but this would require 12,000lb (53.3kN) of jet thrust to obtain a speed of 500mph

BELOW Model of the EE high-altitude bomber. *Joe Cherrie*

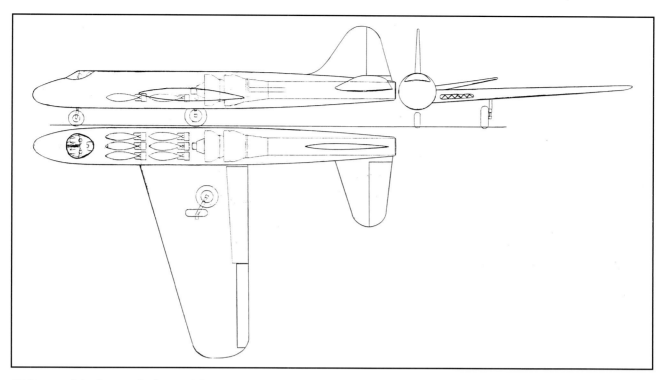

ABOVE English Electric's high-speed, high-altitude bomber (16.5.45). Note the monster centrifugal engine and six 1,000lb (454kg) bombs. *North West Heritage Group*

(805km/h), and that would need a fuselage with a large cross-sectional area to accommodate two or even three existing type engines, each at least 4ft (1.22m) in diameter. Hence, the multi-engine arrangement had a frontal area governed by the engines and this came to more than would be necessary for just crew and load.

Consequently, the discussions looked at what thrust could be obtained from a single engine, without exceeding the size of forgings and other parts that could be manufactured from present equipment. Consultations with Rolls-Royce concluded that an engine of 66in (168cm) diameter appeared to be feasible and that such an engine in two-stage form could produce the required 12,000lb (53.3kN) thrust. This offered very considerable savings in items such as jet pipe weight, fuel and control systems while, further, a single engine would cut drag and provide even better performance, thus reducing the likelihood of interception. It was to be housed in a circular-section fuselage that offered low drag at the wing and tail intersections. The proposed engine was

of the two-stage centrifugal type producing 12,500lb (55.6kN) static thrust and was more than 12% more efficient than existing types in its use of fuel (the document gives no designation to the proposed engine but it was almost certainly the RB.43). Air was fed through two wing ducts and, due to the aircraft's fairly large size, it had been possible to arrange these very efficiently. The jet pipe was made in light Inconel (nickel-chromium-base) alloy sheet.

The body between the crew's pressure cabin and the engine was divided into upper and lower compartments by a 'floor'; the upper for fuel and lower for a long bomb bay. All fuel was housed in the fuselage (space was available in the wings for any additional capacity that might be required) and, although the front bombs were forward of the CofG, it was felt that the aircraft was so disposed that even with bombs gone there was still an ample margin of stability. It was not anticipated that any difficulty would be experienced with CofG shift should all bombs be dropped simultaneously but it was proposed to undertake a simple

flight test on an existing aircraft to prove this point.

The cabin pressure provided for the crew would give an equivalent of not more than 25,000ft (7,620m) at all times (Petter had considerable experience of high-altitude aircraft pressure cabins after his work on the Westland Welkin piston fighter). Semi-monocoque construction was used for the centre (and rear) fuselage with the upper portion filled by a 1,165gal (5,297lit) self-sealing bag fuel tank. The bomb bay beneath could accommodate, as typical loads, six 1,000lb (454kg) bombs, one 4,000lb (1,814kg) or a combination of two 1,000lb and eight 500lb (227kg) bombs. Another 500gal (2,273lit) bag fuel tank was placed in the forward part of the rear fuselage, while the fin was made integral with the rear fuselage structure.

The tailplane was made in two halves and was to have electrically actuated variable incidence, while the flying controls were horn-balanced with spring tabs. A single main spar was used in the low-position wing and it was planned to combine simple

ABOVE Model of the EE high-altitude bomber. *Joe Cherrie*

construction with a complete absence of spanwise joints in the plating as far back as 40% chord from the leading edge. The nose plating consisted of special sheets 3ft (91cm) wide and up to 15ft (4.57m) long wrapped around the leading edge from top to bottom spar boom. Aspect ratio was 5.4. The main wheels retracted into the wings but the nose leg needed to rotate through 90° to comfortably sit horizontally beneath the cockpit.

Maximum weight was 43,800lb (19,868kg), of which 19,500lb (8,845kg) comprised bombs and fuel, and at this weight maximum speeds were 533mph (858km/h) at sea level, 541mph (870km/h) at 10,000ft (3,048m) and 504mph (811km/h) at 40,000ft (12,192m); sea level rate of climb was 4,260ft/min (1,298m/min) rising to 7,370ft/min (2,246m/min) when the machine was light at 28,000lb (12,701kg). At these weights times to 10,000ft were 2.7 and 1.6 minutes respectively; to 40,000ft 18.9 and 9.8 minutes, and service ceiling (100ft/min [30.5m/min] climb) 43,500ft (13,259m) and 48,500ft (14,783m). Take-off wing loading was 42.0lb/sq ft (205kg/sq m). Petter confirmed that every endeavour had been made to keep the machine as small and as fast as possible, consistent with the very high cruising altitude.

English Electric High-Altitude High-Speed Unarmed Bomber (two engines)

On 9 July 1945 Petter informed MAP: 'Since sending our drawing we have heard from Rolls-Royce that they have progressed with a very efficient axial flow engine'. Petter had discussed this with Hives at Rolls-Royce the previous week and he could report that 'in consequence we are working out two alternative proposals – although both have approximately the same performance and size, the alternative may possess advantages that you may prefer'. A second brochure appeared later in the month using two Rolls-Royce

English Electric High-Altitude Bomber (1.6.45)	
Span	75ft 0in (22.86m)
Length	63ft 0in (19.20m)
Gross wing area	1,040sq ft (96.7sq m)
t/c ratio	12% root, 9% tip
Gross weight	43,800lb (19,868kg)
Powerplant	one RR RB.43 12,500lb (55.6kN)
Maximum speed/height	544mph (875km/h) at 10,000ft (3,048m) combat power, 28,000lb (12,701kg) weight
Weapon load	one 4,000lb (1,814kg), six 1,000lb (454kg) or mix of bombs

Small Diameter (Axial) Jet Engines giving 6,500lb (28.9kN) of thrust each. The rapid development of this type, over just a few weeks, made it possible for Rolls-Royce to confidently offer new units that, for a given thrust, were of smaller diameter, about 30% lighter and with a fuel consumption 5–10% better than the best previously envisaged. This was due to the perfection of high-speed axial flow compressors in place of the centrifugal type. Petter and his team had automatically re-examined his original design and produced an alternative and improved proposal.

The narrower engines meant they could be housed almost entirely within the wing roots, an arrangement previously considered near impossible on account of the large engine diameters. Situated here they had very short and direct high-speed entry ducts and tail pipes, while twin-engine reliability was also provided. This arrangement also offered rather more flexibility in regard to future engine developments, although to 'bury' the engine the wing section thickness had been blown up to 15% overall at the root. The main wheels had been moved much closer to the centreline and within the fuselage the changes were very beneficial.

The disappearance of the fuselage engine and raising of the wing made possible a long uninterrupted bomb bay on the CofG 6ft (1.83m) wide, 24ft (7.32m) long and a maximum 3ft (0.91m) deep. This made for extreme flexibility in the choice of bomb load, ranging from a large number of small bombs up to one 8,000lb (3,629kg) bomb, but including the specified six 1,000lb (454kg). For the same reasons, the fuel tanks above the bomb bay were simplified, brought closer together and reduced in size, by reason of the lower consumption, to a total of 1,500gal (6,820lit) of internal fuel. Elimination of the fuselage jet pipe made possible a simpler and lighter adjustable tailplane and saved considerable weight aft, and as the engine weight had also moved forward the balance could be maintained with a shorter front fuselage. The compressor at the front of the engine projected through the wing spar so the unit would be withdrawn rearwards and downwards.

These changes, together with a reduced engine and fuel weight, had cut the gross weight by more than 10% to 39,300lb (17,826kg) (including six 1,000lb bombs and 11,500lb [5,216kg] fuel) while the wing area came down to 950sq ft (88.4sq m) without increasing the wing loading. The aspect ratio was slightly reduced to 4.9. After discussions with radar specialists, the pressure cabin layout had been improved with the navigator–radar operator now seated behind the pilot, facing forward. The radar scanner was housed entirely within the lower half of the nose, while the twin nosewheel had been moved so it would retract vertically behind the pressure cabin bulkhead.

At maximum take-off weight (39,300lb) maximum speeds were 542mph (872km/h) at sea level, 547mph (880km/h) at 10,000ft (3,048m) and 506mph (814km/h) at 40,000ft (12,192m); sea level rate of climb was 4,800ft/min (1,463m/min) rising to 7,950ft/min (2,423m/min) when the machine was light at 24,900lb (11,295kg). At these weights times to 10,000ft were 2.3 and 1.5 minutes respectively; to 40,000ft 15.6 and 8.4 minutes, and service ceiling (100ft/min [30.5m/min] climb) 44,700ft (13,625m) and 50,300ft (15,331m). Take-off wing loading was 41.4lb/sq ft (202kg/sq m). In reply, Rowe confirmed that a 'big improvement has been obtained compared with the original layout using one large engine housed in the body. In particular the bomb bay is not restricted and can be made to carry a wide variety of bombs of the latest design'.

A second alternative layout used wing sweepback. A sweep angle of about 30° at the quarter chord line had attractive features such as raising the 'critical speed' at 40,000ft (12,192m) by about 35mph (56km/h). However, difficulties such as early tip stalling, which was at the time proving troublesome in sweptback tailless layouts, were anticipated and there would be an increase in wing structure weight. Since the cruising and even maximum speeds were not very seriously affected by compressibility effects with the present available thrust, English Electric did not yet consider it essential or even, at this stage, desirable to adopt the sweptback form. However, this was considered to be a most promising development and one that, with the same basic aeroplane, made possible a further big step forward in conjunction with an improved engine later on. An all-moving tail unit might also be introduced at the same time.

In discussion with the author, British Aerospace at Warton suggested that the original centrifugal engine was not very practical for this type of aircraft. The first arrangement with essentially a much uprated Nene in the mid-fuselage position near the wing trailing edge was perhaps the worst place to put the engine because it was in the CofG, where the payload should really go. The axial engine was much better and it also offered growth potential, so when Rolls-Royce proposed the early model Avon Petter put two in the wing roots. Wing sweep was not worthwhile here since the required Mach number did not need it and such a modification would have increased the structure weight. Three months later, Petter moved the engines into neat and tidy wing nacelles as a final solution, leading to the machine we all know today as the Canberra.

English Electric High-Altitude Bomber (7.45)	
Span	68ft 0in (20.73m)
Length	61ft 0in (18.59m)
Gross wing area	950sq ft (88.4sq m)
t/c ratio	15% root, 9% tip
Gross weight	39,300lb (17,826kg)
Powerplant	two RR AJ.65 6,500lb (28.9kN)
Maximum speed/height	549mph (883km/h) at 10,000ft (3,048m) combat power, 24,900lb (11,295kg) weight
Weapon load	one 8,000lb (3,629kg), six 1,000lb (454kg) or mix of bombs

BELOW The revised English Electric swept wing design had two AJ.65 axial jets.
North West Heritage Group

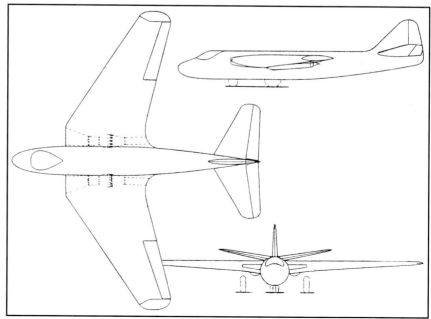

English Electric A.1 Canberra

ABOVE **The first Canberra prototype is seen in flight on 23 August 1949.**
RAF Museum

The first draft of AST.199 was produced in September 1945 and the first issue of the full OR.199 was released in January 1946 with specification B.3/45 to cover it drafted the previous November. Intended to be a replacement for the unarmed Mosquito, it would be 'complementary to a long-range high-speed armed bomber' also currently being discussed (Chapter Two). A contract for the design and construction of four prototypes of the English Electric A.1 to B.3/45 was awarded in December 1945, A.1 being derived from the SBAC numbering system; later versions of the aircraft would have been the A.2 and A.3 but the name Canberra was used instead. The first public reference to 'a twin-engined jet bomber' was made in March 1949 but without specifying the type or manufacturer, and the first prototype made its maiden flight on 13 May.

The aircraft was seen as a considerable advance, both in speed and operating height, over any existing type. By 1947–48 it was intended that the high-altitude light strategic A.1 would be an interim replacement for Bomber Command's Main Force of piston aircraft pending the introduction

of the greater-range types. A blind bombing aid was needed for this role and the entirely new H2S Mk.9/NBC (Navigation and Bomb Computer) Mk.2 was specified. In July 1949 it was reported that this equipment had been delayed to a date when it would be required simultaneously by both the Canberra B.Mk.1 and the Vickers B.9/48 medium-range bomber (later the Valiant). As only one type of blind bomber was required and since the production date of the B.9/48 compared favourably with that of the fully equipped Canberra, the development effort for H2S/NBC was, therefore, fully devoted to the B.9/48 and further development of Canberra Mk.1 was cancelled. ACM the Hon Sir Ralph Cochrane, Vice Chief of the Air Staff (VCAS), decided that since B.3/45 H2S could not be ready before the B.9/48, the former 'is no longer an Air Staff requirement' and production of English Electric's blind bomber was not required. With the entire nose taken up with H2S and its scanner the type could not be used for visual bombing. Fortunately for the makers, other versions were on their way.

In February 1947 the Air Staff stated a requirement for a tactical day bomber variant to replace the de Havilland Mosquito and Bristol Brigand tactical day bombers in the RAF's Middle East and Far East Air Forces. To evade enemy defences this was to rely on high speed, good manoeuvrability and a rearward warning device. Specification B.5/47 and OR.235 were written around the type in November 1947. Maximum speed at 20,000ft (6,096m) was not to be less than 440 knots (815km/h) with cruise speed not less than 390 knots (723km/h). Range was to be at least 1,000nm (1,852km) and maximum bomb load 7,500lb (3,402kg), with delivery by a Visual Automatic Computing Sight. The aircraft would have three crew and no defensive weapons.

Cochrane wrote that there had been 'a tendency to look upon the Canberra as a long-range high-flying bomber' when 'it was generally accepted that [it] is a short-range tactical bomber [and] that there is no equipment which will enable it to hit a small target from 45,000ft' (13,716m). As early as April 1948, before B.3/45 was cancelled, it

was realised that the tactical B.5/47 would be in production first. As the B.Mk.2 the new type entered RAF Service in May 1951, the prototype (the fifth Canberra) having flown on 23 April 1950. The original concept had been scaled down and its weapons

comprised one 5,000lb (2,268kg), two 4,000lb (1,814kg), six 1,000lb (454kg) or mixtures of smaller bombs. The much larger aircraft to be described in Chapter Two was expected to become the RAF's primary bomber but it would be clearly uneconomic to use this for many expected short-range tasks, so the smaller Canberra type was still an important addition to the service (in the event, a greater proportion of the RAF's bomber force was to equip with Canberras than with V-bombers).

A photographic reconnaissance

PR.Mk.3 variant was built to PR.31/46 and OR.223 while the next bomber variant was a target marker to Specification B.22/48 and OR.263 to replace the pathfinder Mosquito B.Mk.35. Although the requirement called for a primary role of visual target marking at low level, it did say that the aircraft should have a secondary role as a light bomber. Operating height was to be between sea level and 40,000ft (12,192m) with maximum and cruise speeds at the upper level again 440 knots (815km/h) and 390 knots

ABOVE The second prototype VN813 was first flown on 9 November 1949 powered by two Rolls-Royce Nene engines, which necessitated larger sections to the forward part of each nacelle. *Rolls-Royce via Terry Panopalis*

English Electric Canberra B.Mk.2 (flown)

Span	63ft 11.5in (19.495m)
Length	65ft 6in (19.96m)
Gross wing area	960sq ft (89.3sq m)
t/c ratio	12% root, 9% tip
Gross weight	46,000lb (20,866kg)
Powerplant	two RR Avon RA.3 6,500lb (28.9kN)
Maximum speed/height	570mph (917km/h) at altitude
Weapon load	six 1,000lb (454kg), one nuclear or mix of bombs

(723km/h) respectively. Up to 2,000lb (907kg) of target indicators or 6,000lb (2,722kg) of bombs were to be carried. The prototype flew on 6 July 1951 but no orders for this variant, the B.Mk.5, were forthcoming. Instead versions followed to cover the interdictor and reconnaissance roles.

Progress with the aircraft's engines did not go to schedule either. It was not until 25 March 1947 that the AJ.65 (Avon RA.1) first ran on the bench and then at well below the specified 6,500lb (28.9kN) rating. Such were the delays in getting it flight worthy that the second prototype, VN813, was adapted to take centrifugal Rolls-Royce Nene

engines to enable flight testing to begin on time. Studies were made in July 1948 comparing the AJ.65 with an 'interim' Avon of 5,500lb (24.4kN) thrust, the Nene II at 5,000lb (22.2kN) and a re-rated Nene at 5,500lb. Respective cruising speeds for the four types were 435, 420, 360 and 400 knots (806, 778, 667 and 741km/h), and cruise altitude at 40,000lb (18,144kg) weight 40,500ft, 36,500ft, 31,500ft and 33,000ft (12,344m, 11,125m, 9,601m and 10,058m). Still air range with normal fuel and bombs fell from 1,800nm (3,335km) for the AJ.65 to 1,290nm (2,390km) for the Nene II. Clearly the Nene was much inferior but

in the event the first flight was made using Avon power. In 1948 the modified RA.2 gave 6,000lb (26.7kN) of thrust and was cleared to fly in the A.1 in January 1949 (VN813 flew with Nenes on 9 November 1949).

BELOW The Canberra B(I).Mk.8 interdictor variant. Note the off-centre canopy.

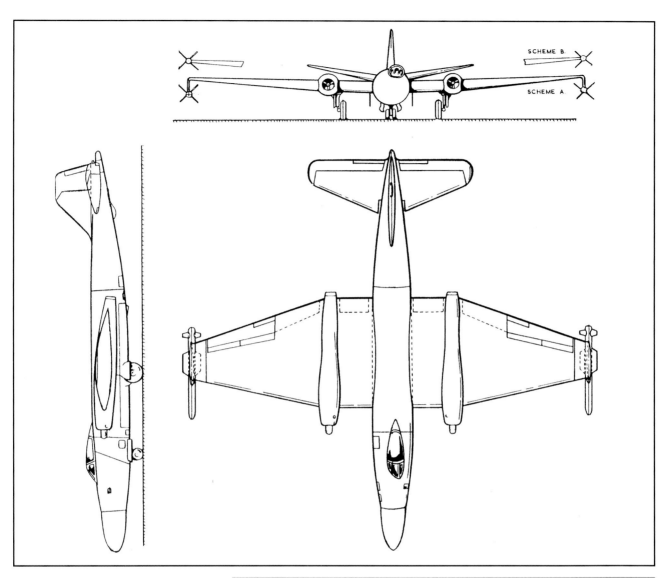

ABOVE The English Electric P.12 all-weather fighter development of the B(I).Mk.8 Canberra (5.3.56).
RIGHT Model of the EE P.12. *Joe Cherrie*

English Electric P.12

English Electric appraised its new aeroplane on 25 July 1947. 'Known initially as the "Mosquito Replacement", the development of this larger and faster aircraft had shown considerable similarity to the Mosquito in some respects and it is apparent that the production of a high-speed aircraft of medium range and a useful carrying capacity, in which defence depends upon provision of the best possible performance, lends to many uses in directions other than those originally

ABOVE **Canberra B.Mk.5 prototype VX185 pictured at Farnborough in 1951.**
Terry Panopalis collection

contemplated. Already, in addition to the strategic high-altitude bomber, a photo reconnaissance, a low-altitude tactical bomber and a trainer are being built or are already investigated, and it seems certain fighter roles could also be filled by this aircraft.'

It is worth taking a quick look at a proposed fighter Canberra. In June 1949, with just twelve hours of test flying completed, test pilot Wg Cdr R. P. Beamont had written that 'with only minor modifications to the existing design a night fighter variant could be produced for Squadron Service … which would compare favourably in performance with the proposed interim types [de Havilland Vampire and Gloster Meteor], and would most probably exceed them in rate of climb,

BELOW **Canberra B.Mk.2 WD933 powered by Sapphire engines was displayed at the Farnborough Show in 1954.** *Terry Panopalis collection*

ABOVE VX185 also returned to Farnborough in 1954 as the Canberra B(I).Mk.8 prototype. *Terry Panopalis collection*

endurance, operational ceiling and firepower'.

The P.12 all-weather fighter was dated 5 March 1956 and made use of the B(I).Mk.8 interdictor's basic fuselage. It had 11,250lb (50kN) Avon RA.24s (though 13,500lb [60kN] RB.126 units were directly interchangeable), AI.18 radar and was armed with two Vickers Red Dean air-to-air missiles carried under the wing tips. This study was made with General Electric at Stanmore and with Vickers, while Boulton Paul would be responsible for the installation work. Somewhat surprisingly, the study revealed an interception performance equal or superior to any aircraft that could operate this system before it was superseded. This was due to the high performance intended for Red Dean and the ability of Canberra to carry the complete system to an adequate speed, just short of buffet and other transonic problems, without suffering the endurance, stowage and other difficulties of a supersonic aircraft. In addition, the all-round scan of the missiles mounted at the wing tips would be very important for a fighter that may have to attack targets faster than itself. A fully equipped prototype would be ready in March 1958. Span was 67ft 3in (20.50m), length 68ft 7in (20.90m), gross weight with two Red Dean plus guns 41,771lb (18,947kg), maximum level cruise Mach 0.9 above 11,000ft (3,353m) to 50,000ft (15,240m), sea level rate of climb 12,500ft/min (3,810m/min) (17,500ft/min [5,334m/min] for RB.126), and time to 40,000ft (12,192m) 5.1 minutes (3.6 minutes for RB.126). This project was never taken up but it suggests that the variant could easily have dealt with the type of target that Canberra itself presented as a bomber.

Incredibly, Canberra stayed in RAF service in its PR.Mk.9 form until 2006, fifty-seven years after its maiden flight. This chapter, covering Canberra only, is relatively short. Just like the Mosquito it replaced, the type was a superb aircraft and its roles became very diverse. However, this success was to create something of a problem because from the mid-1950s onwards the RAF had the task of finding its successor. The search for a 'Canberra Replacement' was to cause quite a bit of bother and fills a much bigger chunk of this book.

Chapter Two
Vital Bombers

Building Britain's V-Force: 1945 to 1955

ABOVE **Vulcan B.Mk.2 XJ824 first flew in April 1961.** *Crown Copyright via Phil Butler*

My earliest recollection of aeroplanes must have been when I was about four or five years of age. We lived in a very old cottage in Broad Marston, Worcestershire, which, apart from the arrival of electricity in 1952, the telephone and some cars, had changed relatively little since the early years of the century. The peace and tranquillity of village life was now often interrupted (shattered!) by the roar of four Avons as a Vickers Valiant passed slowly overhead at quite low level making its way back to Gaydon. I think it is fair to say that the general mechanisation of British farming had hardly started in the late 1950s, so the arrival of these advanced jets, as part of the immensely rapid progress in aviation under way at that time, made for

a great contrast between the old and the new. A lovely memory and happy days.

The main portion of the Second World War piston bomber fleet was to be replaced by the new medium-range jet bomber, a programme that was to give rise to the Valiant and the rest of the V-Force. A big influence was the new atomic bomb, which was to become the driving force behind the development of heavy and medium bomber aircraft and so, from now on, Britain's future bombers would be configured as nuclear weapon delivery systems. But what direction would the jet-powered replacements for the piston Lancaster and Lincoln take? This

chapter reveals some of the background to what were to become primary elements of Britain's nuclear deterrent – the Valiant, Vulcan and Victor bombers. There were two main issues: how large should the new aircraft be since it was the desire of the Air Staff to have a long-range bomber, and would defensive armament be fitted?

Short S.A.4

On 16 February 1945 Short Brothers at Rochester was asked by the Air Ministry to undertake a study to see if a 5,000 mile (8,045km) range could be attained by a jet-propelled high-speed bomber. The resulting 'Design

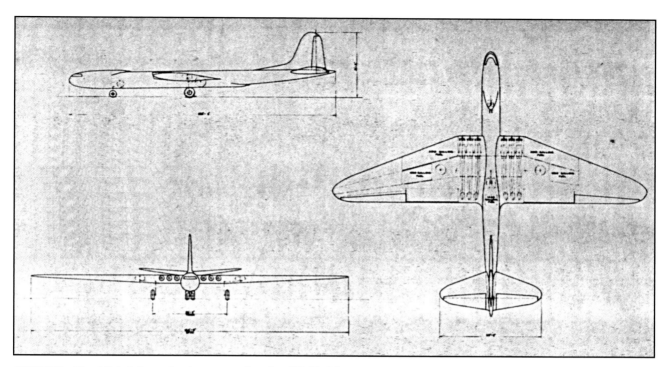

ABOVE **The Short S.A.4 six-engine long-range bomber (16.12.45).**
BELOW **The smaller four-engine S.A.4 (26.4.46).**

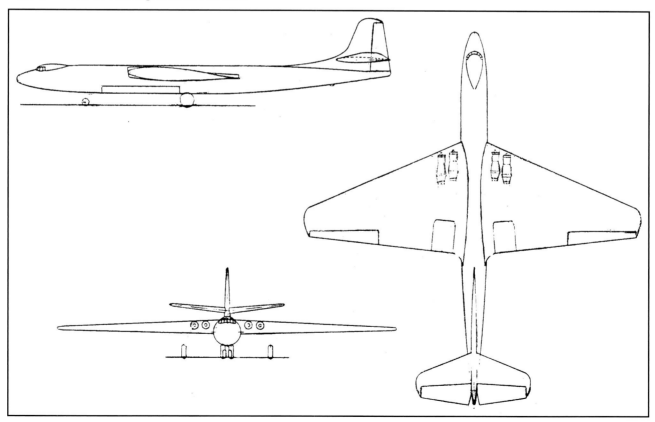

Appreciation', finished in November and submitted on 16 December, considered the job could be done without any revolutionary changes in the methods of aircraft design. Shorts' work drew on German wartime research and the opinions of its consultant, Professor Geoffrey Hill, the assumption being that the bomber was to be capable of 500mph (805km/h) at 40,000ft (12,192m). The result was an enormous machine with a four-man crew housed in a cockpit that filled the nose beyond the front wheels. Two 30mm cannon were housed directly behind on top of the fuselage and two more were beneath the fuselage behind the wing. The main undercarriage comprised a two-wheel leg that folded into the centre of the fuselage and two more single wheels just outside the engines retracting into the wings. A large bomb bay filled most of the lower fuselage between the nose and centre gear. Six of the newly proposed Rolls-Royce AJ.65 (Avon) axial 'pure' jets were housed three per side in the inner wings. With 6,000gal (27,281lit) of fuel the take-off wing loading was 44.0lb/sq ft (215kg/sq m) and still air range 5,000 miles (8,045km).

Soon afterwards the company was asked to consider reducing the machine's size, the suggestion being that four AJ.65s rather than six would make for a much smaller design without, perhaps, giving too great a penalty in range or performance. This investigation, for an aircraft that had no guns, was completed on 26 April 1946 but, in regard to speed and range, Shorts felt that it was a disappointment when compared to the original. Both designs were designated S.A.4.

The guns had now been taken out of the first design but some additional equipment, such as self-sealing fuel tanks, more than counterbalanced the weight saved. Furthermore, Rolls-Royce reported a big increase in the estimated weight of its engine while Shorts had finished a more detailed study of the structural aspects for this type of aircraft, with the result that the estimates for mainplane and tail unit weight had also gone up. Much of the latter stemmed from an assumed maximum dive speed of Mach 0.95 when a figure of Mach 0.85 would give a much smaller increase. With four AJ.65s and 4,800gal (21,825lit) of fuel the range was 3,800 miles (6,114km). The undercarriage arrangement and bomb bay were unchanged and at 115,000lb (52,164kg) weight the wing loading was 42.8lb/sq ft (209kg/sq m). The margin on the cruise speed of the

six-engined aircraft came from an uncertainty as to the onset of compressibility drag, the economical cruise speed for long range being determined by this. On the four-engine layout speed was limited by engine power and came below the speed where compressibility drag was likely to occur.

Shorts felt the four-engine project was still a practical proposition and that the engines could still be buried in the wings. However, to put them there it would be necessary to employ a disproportionately large root chord and choose between an unnecessarily large wing area or an undesirably short span. A higher altitude, which would give a longer range, could only be achieved by increasing the span and wing area with a consequent reduction in cruising speed. All of these factors had to be taken into account and close study of these concepts by the Air Staff revealed there was no hope of adding defensive armament without a prohibitive penalty in weight and drag, fuelling again an ongoing and very strong guns/no guns debate. Nevertheless, a Draft Operational Requirement was forthcoming.

By summer 1946 the Air Staff had forwarded a fairly detailed outline for a long-range bomber, the type that it really

Short S.A.4 (six engines)	
Span	154ft 0in (46.94m)
Length	128ft 6in (39.17m)
Gross wing area	3,615sq ft (336.2sq m)
t/c ratio	12%
Gross weight	158,890lb (72,073kg)
Powerplant	six RR AJ.65 6,500lb (28.9kN)
Maximum speed/height	475mph (764km/h) at 50,000ft (15,240m) - revised 4.46 to 480-500mph (772-805km/h)
Weapon load	2,120lb (962kg) total weight

Short S.A.4 (four engines)	
Span	112ft 0in (34.14m)
Length	123ft 0in (37.49m)
Gross wing area	2,685sq ft (249.7sq m)
t/c ratio	12%
Gross weight	115,000lb (52,164kg)
Powerplant	four AJ.65 6,500lb (28.9kN)
Maximum speed/height	465mph (748km/h) at 40,000ft (12,192m)
Weapon load	2,120lb (962kg) total weight

wanted. This had to be capable of delivering a 10,000lb (4,536kg) bomb load to a target 2,000nm (3,706km) from a base situated anywhere in the world (i.e. a range of 4,000nm [7,408km]). Such an aircraft would have to attack targets well into enemy territory and, to help avoid destruction from ground or air-launched weapons, it must have a continuous cruising speed at all heights from sea level to 50,000ft (15,240m) of 500 knots (576mph/927km/h) or Mach 0.875, whichever the lower, and be capable of reaching 50,000ft (15,240m) with the maximum fuel/bomb load combination inside two hours from take-off. Two more companies offered designs and Avro also made a study.

Bristol Type 172

Far more advanced than the S.A.4, the Bristol Type 172 from May 1946 featured swept wings, a swept 'butterfly' tail and four Bristol jet engines buried in the wing roots and exhausting through the trailing edge (almost certainly the BE.10, which would evolve into the Olympus). The range with a 10,000lb (4,536kg) bomb was given as 5,000 miles (8,045km). However, the original design had a high wing loading, which led to a lower cruising altitude, so by October 1946 Bristol had redesigned its Type 172 with a high-position wing and thinner root, but with the V-tail and wing root engines retained. Bristol estimated that this later aircraft could carry one 10,000lb (4,536kg) bomb over a range of 4,350 nautical miles (8,060km) at a cruising speed of 520 knots (964km/h) and at between 43,000ft and 51,000ft (13,106m and 15,545m).

A brochure was issued in October 1946 and described an aircraft that, with swept wings and a smooth surface finish, had the potential to reach Mach 0.91. It was to this end that a V-tail had also been adopted to raise the tailplane above the jet cones and avoid the interference and drag from the fin and tailplane produced by a conventional tail at high speeds (speed and altitude were relied upon in this aircraft for protection since no defensive armament was to be

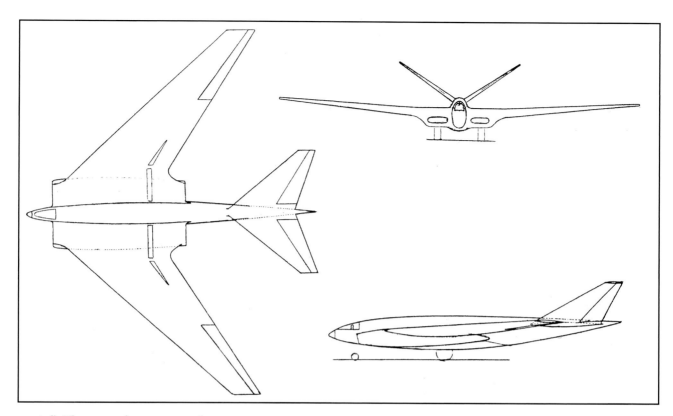

carried). There were four crew members and the four Bristol jets were mounted in the leading edge of the centreplane forward of the main wing with the jet pipes passing through the wing and discharging at the trailing edge. As a result, the centreplane was untapered and had no sweep. The tapered outer wings were swept 45° at quarter chord and in principle the wing structure was similar to that developed for the Bristol Type 167 Brabazon airliner. Front and rear shear webs, together with thick skin stabilised by extruded stringers, formed a torsion box, to which were attached the leading and trailing edge sections. The thick skin and extruded stringers would take nearly all of the end loads due to bending, thus avoiding the use of concentrated spar-booms, which were uneconomical in a thin wing. It was the thick skin that also lent itself to the production of a smooth surface finish, and boundary layer suction was envisaged for the wings. According to the best available data, landing flaps were ineffective on swept-back wings and so were not provided. And electrically operated powered flying controls were to be used.

ABOVE Bristol Type 172 at 28.5.46.
Duncan Greenman, Bristol AIRchive

RIGHT The version of the Bristol Type 172 covered by the October 1946 brochure.
Rolls-Royce Heritage, Filton

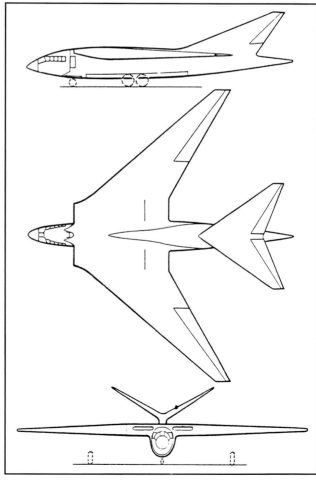

The body employed normal monocoque construction with stressed skin, stringers and frames. The pressure cabin occupied the first section, the main section had the wing in its upper half with the bomb cell beneath (with reinforcing longerons for the wing and bomb door attachments), and aft of this came the tail unit that, on account of its sweepback, occupied an unusually large portion of the fuselage. The V-tail surfaces were also swept back to 45°, they were of similar construction to the wings and were raised above the body on a short 'stalk' in order to provide ample clearance for the inboard jets. The body was finished off with a conical fairing behind the stern frame that could be removed and replaced by a radar scanner of the same diameter. The bomb doors were opened by rotating them upwards into the body, where they would be completely protected from the airstream at high speeds.

The undercarriage was of the tricycle type with sideways retracting main units and a backwards retracting nose unit. The fuel load was considerable; a total permanent fuel capacity of 6,450gal (29,328lit) was available, with 2,850gal (12,959lit) in the wings and 3,600gal (16,369lit) in the forward and centre fuselage, while a further 1,700gal (7,730lit) could go in detachable long range tanks inside the bomb bay; another 1,600gal (7,275lit) could also go in the bomb cell when the aircraft was used for photo-reconnaissance work. For a normal bomb load of 10,000lb (4,536kg) with fuel in part of the bomb bay the take-off weight was 160,000lb (72,576kg), but for a full 36,000lb (16,330kg) load without extra fuel the take-off weight came to 171,830lb (77,942kg); in the former case the take-off wing loading was 71lb/sq ft (347kg/sq m). Alternative conventional loads included a single 22,000lb (9,979kg) bomb, two 12,000lb (5,443kg), three 8,000lb (3,629kg) or six 6,000lb (2,722kg) bombs. The brochure envisaged the building of a half-scale model aircraft to assess the 172's flying characteristics and this is described in the next chapter.

Bristol 172	
Span	110ft (33.53m)
Length	100ft (30.48m)
Gross wing area	2,250sq ft (209.25sq m)
t/c ratio	13.5% root, 10% tip
Gross weight	171,830lb (77,942kg)
Powerplant	four Bristol turbojets 9,000lb (40.0kN)
Maximum speed/height	600mph (965km/h) Mach 0.91 at 40,000ft (12,192m)
Weapon load	Maximum 36,000lb (16,330kg) bombs

Handley Page HP.72A/HP.80

Handley Page's HP.72 project was a heavy piston engine transport to Specification C.15/45 that was abandoned around the end of 1945. The HP.72A designation was introduced early in 1946 as a general cover to screen designer Godfrey Lee's work on a large jet bomber, initiated after he had visited Germany immediately after the war as part of a commission to look at German research. This was ahead of any requirement. Lee's first ideas had centred on a civil transatlantic transport but, after a memo from Sir Frederick Handley Page had asked the Design Department to look at a jet-propelled Lincoln replacement, he moved on to a bomber.

When presented in its preliminary form in June 1946 the bomber project had been renumbered HP.80. It was powered by four scaled-down Rolls-Royce AJ.65 axial jets because the standard Avon was felt to be larger than was ideal (these gave 86% of the standard AJ.65 thrust at corresponding heights and speeds and were 86% of the weight). Range for a 10,000lb (4,536kg) load was 5,000 miles (8,045km) when flying at 520mph (837km/h) and between 45,000ft and 50,000ft (13,716m to 15,240) altitude. This speed gave only a small difference between the bomber and possible enemy fighters that, when coupled with the short time spent over enemy country, meant it would be difficult for any interceptions of the bomber to be made. Consideration had been given to the fitting of rear defence with a limited field of fire, but such fitments increased drag unduly in what

had to be a relatively perfect streamlined airframe form; consequently the aircraft was unarmed. The presence of the body in this design had a good effect when compared to a pure all-wing design, where the beneficial effect of sweepback in raising the critical Mach number was inevitably reduced at the centreline.

The HP.80 had its wing swept back at 45° at the leading edge, the engines and main part of the tricycle undercarriage were buried in the centre wing roots aft of the main spar, and when the latter was retracted the aircraft had a perfectly clean external surface with low drag conditions maintained at least forward of the spar. The centre wing with its engine installation and nose undercarriage came in a single unit with the centre fuselage. Both front and rear sections of the fuselage were separate units attached to this main centre unit and the rear fuselage structure was faired to complete the fuselage shape. The latter carried a small tailplane that was used to trim out the aerodynamic moments due either to the operation of the flaps or changes in the centre of pressure in a high-speed dive. Fore and aft lateral control was obtained by power-operated elevons extending over the outer rear part of the wing and bag-type fuel tanks were housed – for balance – in the wing torque box between the main spar web and the wing skin. The maximum fuel capacity was 4,600gal (20,916lit).

The HP.80 would have an all-metal stressed skin structure with aluminium alloy sheet and extrusions. The wing weight had been estimated in some detail but the weight of the other major components had been estimated statistically on the basis of the company's experience with the piston-powered Halifax bomber and Hastings transport. The primary radar was H2S Mk.9, whose radome was placed below the flight deck, and the crew's cabin was pressurised to simulate conditions at 25,000ft (7,620m) when flying at the operating height of 50,000ft (15,240m). The HP.80's service ceiling at climb thrust from a take-off at maximum gross weight was 46,500ft (14,173m), the maximum rate of climb at sea level in climb thrust was 3,200ft/min

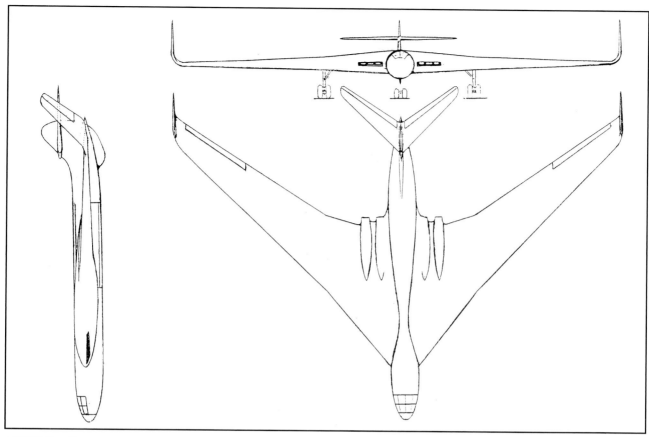

ABOVE Handley Page HP.72A/HP.80 long-range bomber (6.46). *Handley Page Association*
BELOW Artist's impression of the HP.72A/HP.80. *Handley Page Association*

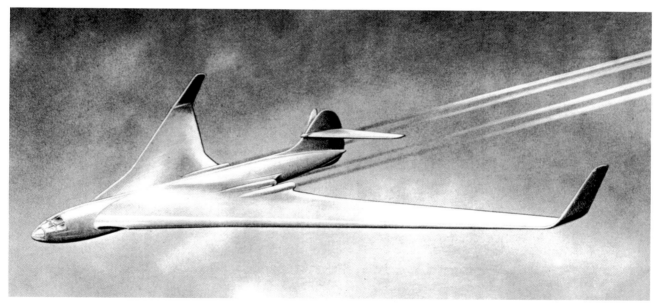

(975m/min) and time to 45,000ft (13,716m) 38.5 minutes.

An alternative 90,000lb (40,824kg) layout with a front 'rider-plane' was similarly screened as the HP.75A but swiftly rejected in favour of the HP.72A/HP.80. This had swept wings and tip rudders but with a small swept tail so the elevators could counteract any nose-down pitching, a problem expected from high-speed compressibility or lowering the flaps at low speed.

Despite their weaknesses, the Bristol 172 and HP.72A/HP.80 were remarkable for their day and show how some British companies were ready to experiment with new aerodynamic shapes.

Handley Page HP.72A/HP.80

Span	122ft 0in (37.19m)
Length	92ft 0in (28.04m)
Gross wing area	2,100sq ft (195.3sq m)
t/c ratio	16% root, 9% tip
Gross weight	90,000lb (40,824kg)
Powerplant	four RR scaled AJ.65 5,600lb (24.9kN)
Maximum speed/height	520mph (837km/h) Mach 0.79 at 50,000ft (15,240m)
Weapon load	10,000lb (4,536kg) bombs maximum

In July 1946 RAE Farnborough reported that the estimated structure weights of all three projects at that stage were probably optimistic, the two high-sweepback designs being difficult to assess in this respect since the effect on structure weight from such a configuration had yet to be explored. Both had high top speeds and any estimates would have to depend on very scanty data of air load distributions for swept wings at high Mach numbers. Each design's cruise speed, particularly the Bristol 172 (in its original form), was very near that for compressibility drag rise if not beyond it, and extensive tunnel testing would be needed to minimise the problem. For the 172, however, the Farnborough high-speed tunnel was not capable of exploring the speeds needed. Both Bristol and Handley Page had thickened the wings of their projects at the root, a step considered inadvisable aerodynamically since it was in this region that the favourable effects of sweepback were least applicable.

Avro Long Range Bomber

Before moving on it must be noted that Avro also produced a Long Range Bomber study that was really a scaled up version of the Type 698 discussed below. A covering report was completed in July 1947 just two months after the original 698 brochure had been submitted, when the design team found that the OR.229/B.35/46 project could achieve the range called for in OR.230 at 20% overload. As such the 698 would have a gross weight of 124,000lb (56,246kg) and it would fly at a lower altitude over the target, but with the same speed of Mach 0.88, 500 knots (576mph/927km/h). However, Avro wanted to know what size of delta wing aircraft would be required to meet OR.230 in full, in other words to raise the operating altitude over the target from the calculated 46,500ft (14,173m) up to 50,000ft (15,240m).

BELOW Avro's OR.230 study had three bomb bays, flight control surfaces on the trailing edge of the wing and four engines stacked in two pairs in a very similar format to the Avro 698. *Avro Heritage*

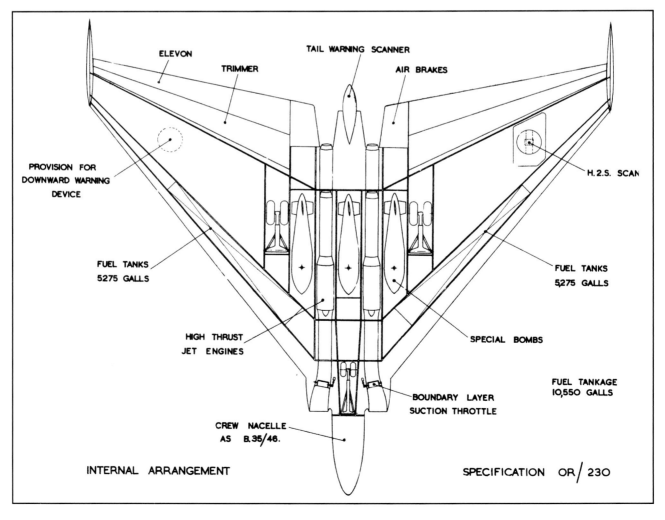

The answer proved somewhat startling because the gross weight actually rose to 190,000lb (86,184kg), a heavy price to pay for an increase in altitude of just 3,500ft (1,067m) over the target. Also, the OR.230 aeroplane would require four jet engines of 15,000lb (66.7kN) thrust each compared with the 698's 9,140lb (40.6kN) units. An advantage of the OR.230, however, would be its ability to carry 30,000lb (13,608kg) of bombs as against 20,000lb (9,072kg) on the smaller type, since the larger aircraft had three bomb bays of the same capacity as the 698's two. This unnumbered OR.230 study had a span of 129ft (39.32m), its length was 120ft (36.58m) and wing area 5,940sq ft (552.4sq m). Fuel load was 10,550gal (47,970lit) housed entirely in wing leading edge tanks.

At first the Air Staff had only intended to issue a long-range bomber requirement, but by December 1946 it was realised such an aircraft would be very expensive and financial stringency made it unlikely that any but a few squadrons could be equipped with it. The severe requirement (now designated OR.230) would need an exceedingly heavy load of fuel and some studies suggested that the final gross weight could reach 200,000lb (90,720kg). Coupled with swept wings, this represented too great an advance in design to be entertained at present while any project would also probably need half-scale flying models. As the majority of targets could no doubt be reached by an aircraft having about 75% of the original range, requirements were now prepared for an advanced medium-range bomber, a step that crystallised into OR.229 and Specification B.35/46. However, this too would be difficult to meet since it would still need swept-back wings and other, as yet untried, features, so an interim bomber was also introduced as a back-up.

Investigations had also now shown that it did not pay to have defensive armament if a speed of about 500 knots (576mph/927km/h) could be reached at high level. If defensive armament was introduced, speed and altitude would be

lost and the resulting aircraft would likely be no more than an improved Boeing B-29 with reciprocating engines. It was also thought impractical to devise adequate armour to counter new fighters firing controlled rockets at a range of 2 to 4 miles (3.2 to 6.4km). The medium bomber requirement visualised a high-speed, high-altitude, unarmed aircraft built around the atomic bomb, and weight would be critical.

Short B.14/46

By November 1946 the four-engine S.A.4 had been chosen as the interim insurance bomber, and Specification B.14/46 (possibly reserved at the start for the long-range OR.230 bomber) and OR.239 were prepared around it. The cruise speed between 35,000ft and 45,000ft (10,668m to 13,716m) was to be 450mph (724km/h) and, with a 10,000lb (4,536kg) bomb load, the radius of action was 1,500nm (2,780km). Maximum load was 20,000lb (9,072kg).

At the end of January 1947, David Keith-Lucas of Shorts finished a study for a propeller-turbine (turboprop) S.A.4 capable of 500mph (805km/h) at 40,000ft (12,192m) at an gross weight of about 110,000lb (49,896kg). This showed that eight Bristol Proteus engines were needed in four coupled pairs, instead of the four AJ.65s, and the effects of this were not good. The total weight for eight Proteus against four AJ.65s was 24,800lb (11,249kg) against 7,800lb (3,538kg) which, despite a reduced fuel volume, meant an increase in gross weight of more than 13,000lb (5,897kg) and a drop in range of well over 1,000 miles (1,609km) compared to a jet-powered type of similar structure, equipment and bomb load. The results were checked using published figures for the Armstrong Siddeley Python turboprop, which showed to rather less advantage than the Proteus. This work confirmed Keith-Lucas's July 1945 findings when a pure jet, propeller turbine, ducted fan and mixed pure jet/propeller turbine had all been reviewed. Four jets offered a much neater layout.

Agreement for ordering two S.A.4s

was reached in late February 1947, at which point it was planned to house the four AJ.65s side-by-side in two underwing nacelles. However, in mid-February 1949, after tunnel testing at RAE Farnborough, Keith-Lucas confirmed that two engines in a single vertical nacelle above and below each wing had been adopted instead of the previous arrangement or an alternative with four single underwing nacelles. Rolls-Royce's experience on a design with twin engines mounted side-by-side had indicated that the aerodynamic forces on the cowl were very large and needed a heavy structure. Engines arranged horizontally in a nacelle suspended below the wing by a slim faired strut had also been suggested (and were favoured by RAE), but Shorts rejected this because it presented several structural problems and would be difficult to accommodate without undertaking an extensive redesign of the wing. And the construction of the prototype had just begun.

B.35/46 (and Operational Requirement OR.229)

Issued on 7 January 1947, Specification B.35/46 called for a bomber able to hit a target up to 1,500nm (2,778km) away at a continuous 500 knots (576mph/927km/h) cruise at 45,000ft to 50,000ft (13,716m to 15,240m) altitude. Its maximum speed had to be as high as possible but exceeding the cruise speed was not essential. Still air range with a 10,000lb (4,536kg) bomb load was to be 3,350nm (6,208km) and the cruise ceiling of 50,000ft (15,240m) must be reached within two and a half hours from take-off. Maximum performance was the ultimate aim and was not to be sacrificed unduly for ease of maintenance, while flight had to be possible in all weather conditions.

Gross weight was not to exceed 100,000lb (45,360kg) and the maximum 20,000lb (9,072kg) bomb load included the following alternatives: two 10,000lb (4,536kg) concrete-piercing, two 10,000lb HC (High Capacity), four 5,000lb (2,268kg) HC, twenty 1,000lb (454kg) MC

(Medium Capacity), twenty 1,000lb incendiary and fragmentation clusters or one Special (nuclear) gravity bomb (to OR.1001 – this was later called Blue Danube). No defensive armament was to be fitted, only warning devices, and the crew comprised two pilots, two navigator/bomb aimer/radar operators and one wireless/warning and protective device operator. This requirement was put out to tender in January 1947 and six submissions were forthcoming.

Armstrong Whitworth AW.56

This design dispensed with a tailplane since Armstrong Whitworth (AWA) felt the various problems presented by sweptback wings were easier to solve with a tailless aircraft. In addition, little was known about the behaviour of a tailplane in the downwash of a heavily swept wing working at high Mach numbers. By careful manufacture and the provision of boundary layer suction, AWA was confident that it was possible

to maintain laminar flow over the first 30% of the wing chord while suction further reduced the effects of shock stall at high speed and improved the low-speed stalling characteristics; range was dependent on a smooth laminar airflow over the wing since it reduced drag. Wing suction was to be employed at all speeds and achieved through a series of slots located at 0.15 chord over 77% of the span; it also gave a high critical Mach number. Continuous suction at high engine speeds was maintained by an auxiliary axial flow fan driven by the engines. Leading-edge slats were rejected because they damaged the smooth airflow and increased drag; semi-Fowler type flaps were placed well forward of the main chord.

Using an orthodox two-spar structure on large-span swept wings made it difficult to obtain the aeroelastic requirements so the AW.56 utilised box spar construction combined with cellular-type wing covering, which testing had proved to be highly efficient and almost twice as

stiff as the usual two-spar system. Consequently, practically all of the wing ribbing was eliminated, which simplified the wing's production by allowing plenty of prefabrication prior to assembly. The structure comprised a metal sandwich of a fairly thick outer skin reinforced by a second corrugated skin and a third thin inner skin riveted to the bottom of the corrugations to provide strength and stiffness. The corrugations supported the outer skin at very close intervals, thus providing and maintaining the smooth accurate wing surface required for laminar flow. This method of assembly had been used in exactly the same way on the then nearly complete AW.52 research aircraft being built to Specification E.9/44. Experiments on this type of skin had shown that buckling did not occur until just before the ultimate factor.

AW.52 experience had revealed that one of the most difficult problems in the design of high-speed tailless aircraft, or indeed any sweptback wing, was the provision of adequate flexural

BELOW The five-engine Armstrong Whitworth AW.56 as tendered to Specification B.35/46 (4.47).

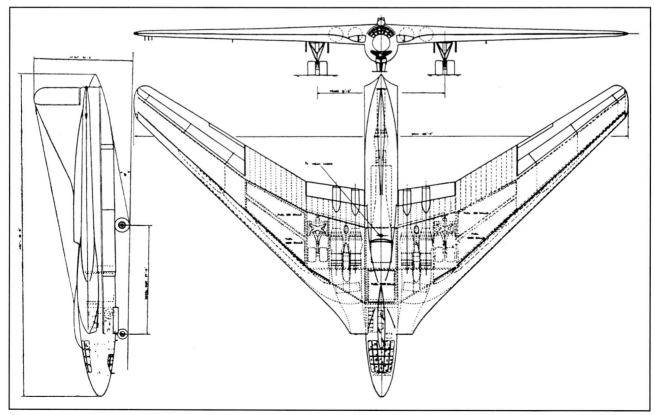

THIS PAGE **Model of the original AW.56.**
Ray Williams Collection

and torsional stiffness to prevent aileron reversal and wing-aileron flutter. The bending stiffness of a swept wing was vitally important since pure bending distortions produced changes in incidence, something that did not occur with a normal unswept wing.

Longitudinal and lateral control was achieved using two surfaces in tandem on each outer wing called the 'corrector' and 'controller'. Also used on the AW.52, the corrector was the forward surface and its function, under power operation, was to provide the

pilot with a coarse-trimming device capable of counteracting major changes of longitudinal trim such as occurred when the landing flaps were lowered. The controller acted as an elevator and aileron, and was hinged behind the corrector. A tricycle undercarriage had

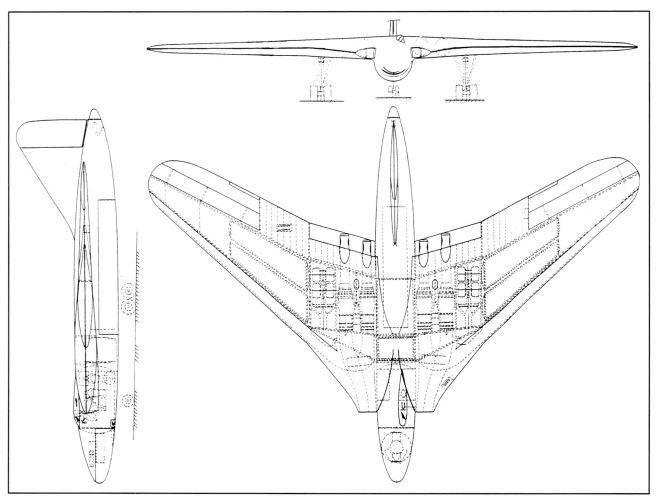

ABOVE The revised AW.56 with four engines (late 1947).

main wheels of long vertical travel to allow the aircraft to glide unchecked on to the ground, a capability thought to be helpful in poor visibility. Investigations showed that the AW.56 was controllable and stable in all conditions and about all axes but the control surfaces were provided with pressure-sealed balances, again tried on the AW.52, to give the pilot a measure of manual control if needed.

Four Avons were mounted in the wing roots and a fifth in the fuselage rear with its own intake on the upper fuselage. At 36,000ft (10,973m) and 90,000lb (40,824kg) weight the top speed was estimated to be 640mph (1,030km/h) Mach 0.97. When the aircraft was fully laden the sea level rate of climb was 4,180ft/min (1,274m/min). A normal flight plan would comprise a climb to 40,000ft (12,192m), cruise for

105 minutes and then a further climb to 50,000ft (15,240m), this height being reached after two and a half hours' flying. The brochure stated that the maximum cruise speed at 50,000ft (15,240m) and 80,000lb (36,288kg) weight would be 580mph (933km/h) Mach 0.88 without compressibility drag, 545mph (877km/h) Mach 0.825 with compressibility drag. However, an Air Staff document gave 501mph (806km/h) at 50,000ft (15,240m), which suggests they had doubts.

All bomb loads (nuclear or small or large conventional) were held in the fuselage. The bomb bay doors divided transversely in the centre, the sections sliding fore and aft to prevent any serious effect on speed and trim. Internal fuel, in fuselage and wing tanks, totalled 5,620gal (25,554lit) and the maximum wing loading was 43.3lb/sq ft

(211kg/sq m); range was 3,350nm (6,204kg) with 10,000lb (4,536kg) of bombs. Completion of detail design from ITP was predicted to take a hundred weeks with the first flight taking another twenty weeks. MetroVick F.9s could substitute the Avons without major changes and, for two reasons, these offered a considerable reduction in the fuel required for the specified range. First, they had a lower fuel consumption when cruising, and second their greater thrust allowed a direct climb to 50,000ft (15,240m) with no intermediate cruise. The fuel saving came to about 6,700lb (3,039kg) for a take-off weight of 106,000lb (48,082kg).

After the Tender Design Conference a revised AW.56 was proposed to meet the Air Staff's relaxed intermediate bomber requirements (below) which used a new Rolls-Royce 7,500lb (33.3kN) 'Avon Replacement' bypass engine. This was the RB.77 and was Rolls' first bypass engine prior to the RB.80 Conway. RB.77 was physically interchangeable with the Avon and was expected eventually to supply 8,000lb (35.6kN) thrust as the BJ.80 (bypass jet, 8,000lb). Four units were fitted, which permitted the deletion of the tail motor and its intake for a more streamlined shape. The pilot now had a fighter-type canopy offset to port with the rest of the crew hidden in the fuselage and, overall, the aircraft was a touch smaller. Climb rate at ground level with RB.77s was 4,475ft/min (1,364m/min), fuel capacity 4,630gal (21,052lit). A further alternative had just the four Avons for a maximum weight of 97,200lb (44,090kg) and a cruise speed of 547mph (880km/h).

Armstrong Whitworth AW.56

Span	120ft 0in (36.58m)
Length	80ft 0in (24.38m)
Gross wing area	2,611sq ft (242.8sq m)
t/c ratio	13% root, 10% tip
Gross weight	113,000lb (51,257kg)
Powerplant	five RR Avon AJ.65 6,500lb (28.9kN)
Maximum speed/height	582mph (936km/h) at 36,000ft (10,973m)
Weapon load	one 10,000lb (4,536kg) special, two 10,000lb HC, three 6,000lb (2,722kg) or nineteen 1,000lb (454kg) bombs

Armstrong Whitworth AW.56 Revised Brochure (B.35/46 Relaxation)

Span	102ft 0in (31.09m)
Length	75ft 0in (22.86m)
Gross wing area	2,250sq ft (209.25sq m)
t/c ratio	13% root, 10% tip
Gross weight	101,150lb (45,882kg) or with four AJ.65 97,200lb (44,090kg)
Powerplant	four RR RB.77 7,500lb (33.3kN) or four RR Avon AJ.65 6,500lb (28.9kN)
Maximum speed/height	575mph (925km/h) at 36,000ft (10,973m) or with four AJ.65 547mph (880km/h) at 40,000ft (12,192m)
Weapon load	one 10,000lb (4,536kg) special, two 10,000lb HC, three 6,000lb (2,722kg) or fourteen 1,000lb (454kg) bombs

Avro 698

In 1947 the new problems faced by the designers of advanced aircraft were many. In order to fly economically there had to be the minimum possible drag, and in order to keep drag down at speeds approaching the speed of sound (as these machines were) it was necessary to sweep the wings back at a very pronounced angle to the fuselage. In addition, wing thickness had to be kept as low as possible; that is to say, whatever the wing chord was at any particular point along its span, the thickness should be kept to 10% or even less. Furthermore, if one wanted to fly at a high true air speed and go as far as possible with an economical fuel load, it was known that the aircraft must go as high as possible where the air was less dense.

BELOW The original Avro 698 (5.47).

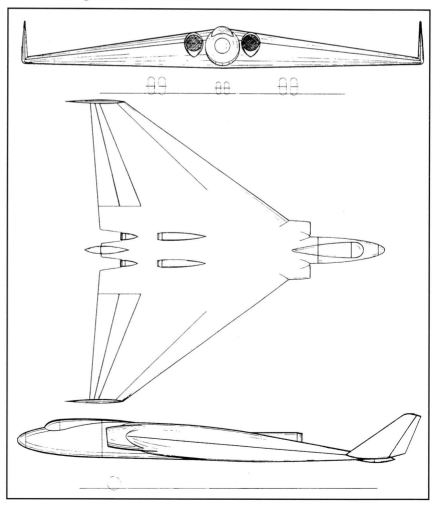

Unfortunately, the speed of sound falls with increasing altitude and so, with designs intended to fly higher, not only must the designer take the steps mentioned already but in addition he must keep the angle between the wing and the flight path low (known in 1947 as the angle of incidence but more recently the angle of attack), otherwise the drag would rise very rapidly. In order to keep the angle of incidence low it was necessary to keep the wing loading low, or in other words for a given weight of aircraft the wing area must be larger than had previously been the case. Another factor was that on a long-range bomber, or commercial aircraft, if one wanted to fly long distances then wings of high aspect ratio must be used; that is, the span would be large relative to the

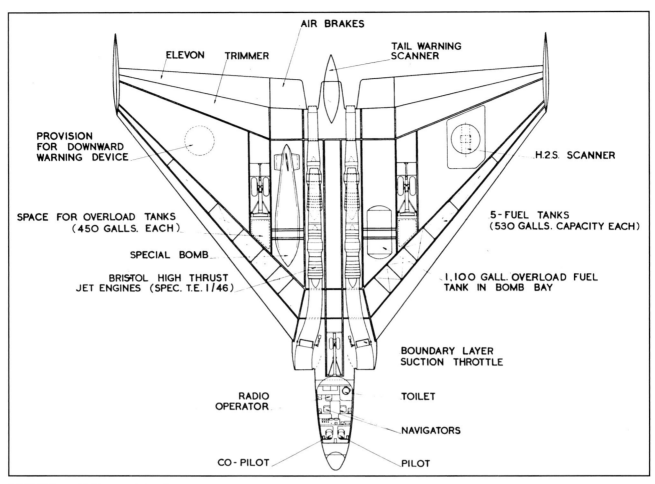

ABOVE Avro 698 internal detail.

chord, the ratio varying from perhaps 9 up to 14. This was necessary to keep down induced drag (the drag penalty from wing lift). This broad picture was what the designer of a large, load-carrying, long-range aircraft was faced with. If he wished to fly at speeds comparable with the speed of sound he had, at one and the same time, to sweep the wings back, make them thinner, increase the area and keep up the span. This posed very great structural problems. (The above section is based on text from a Avro report *The Case for the Delta* written by Chief Designer Stuart Davies in April 1951).

Avro realised that B.35/46 could not be met by present types of aeroplane since the high speeds called for the use of all known aerodynamic improvements, much new research into aerodynamics and the development of much more powerful jet engines than

those currently available. The 500 knot (526mph/927km/h) requirement between 36,000ft and 50,000ft (10,973m and 15,240m), when the speed of sound was 574 knots (661mph/1,064km/h), implied that the critical Mach number must be greater than 0.872; this made a thin wing of high-speed section and large sweepback a necessity. Preliminary investigations using all available British and German reports compared a conventional swept wing/swept tail design, a tailless swept wing aircraft and a delta wing and concluded that only the delta could meet the speed, range, load and gross weight limits laid down. It appeared impossible to meet B.35/46 with a conventional arrangement at any gross weight while the tailless machine weighed in at 137,500lb (62,370kg), it had a span of 138ft (42.06m) and wing area of 4,540sq ft (422.2sq m).

Avro felt that the delta provided a neat

solution to B.35/46. Whilst admitting that it was still largely an unknown quantity, the company was confident that, both aerodynamically and structurally, it would be less difficult to develop the delta wing than either of the other options. Control and stability were no more difficult and structurally there were enormous advantages since it was simple in form and, even with a low t/c, it was inherently adapted to take care of both flexural and torsional loadings through its great depth of wing section. In addition, it automatically provided a great internal volume for powerplant, equipment, fuel and bombs. At its centre the 698's wing was 7ft 9.5in (2.37m) deep and Avro noted that the delta would give the lowest possible structure weight of any form of aeroplane. In comparison, the piston Avro Lincoln had a span of 120ft (36.58m) as against the 698's 91ft 6in (27.89m), yet at the centreline the

THIS PAGE This relatively new model of the original Avro 698 was professionally made using the original drawings.
George Cox

Lincoln's wing depth was just 2ft 10.5in (0.875m).

The only excrescence were the air intakes, the jet pipes and an extension of the nose for the crew nacelle. Two pairs of stacked superimposed engines, expected to be Bristol 'High Thrust Jet Engines to TE.1/46' (later the BE.10 Olympus), were completely buried in the wing very close to the centreline so that the offset thrust in the event of an engine failure was very small and easily controlled. The top 'forward' pair exhausted above the centre wing upper surface, the lower 'rear' pair through a cut-back section of the trailing edge, and they were fed by two big circular pitot intakes. All the fuel was carried in ten tanks in the leading edge. Thanks to the low wing loading, just 29.7lb/sq ft (145kg/sq m), there were no landing flaps.

Longitudinal control and trimming were effected by a trimming 'controller' and by differentially operated elevons at the wing trailing edge. Wing tip fins and rudders gave directional control but it was thought that after further research these might be deleted. High-speed tunnel evidence indicated slightly better stability characteristics at high speed for the delta layout but the effects of the tip fins on these high-speed characteristics were unknown. Boundary layer suction was provided over the span covered by the ailerons via a large valve in the air intake just ahead of the point where it bifurcated, the valve only operating during take-off and landing.

ABOVE Well-known photos of an original Avro model of the 698 with cut away sections. *Avro Heritage*

Since there was no fuselage as such, the bomb bay was split in two either side of the engines. Each side could take eight 1,000lb (454kg) conventional bombs or, when in atomic 'mode', the port bay took the nuclear store while more fuel was housed in the starboard bay, although each compartment was capable of carrying two of the large 'special bombs'. It was proposed to suppress all external aerials and the H2S scanner, mounted inside the port wing, had a suitable area of the bottom plating made in wood to give the necessary visual angles. The tricycle

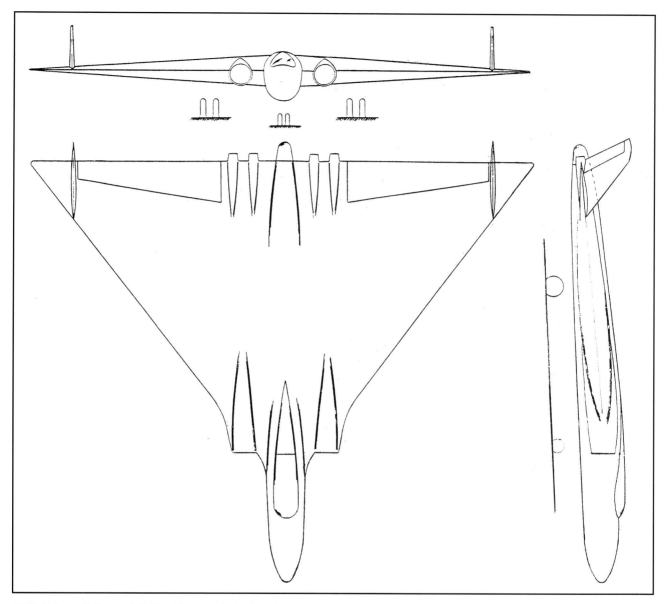

ABOVE Avro 698 as at 6.4.48 with extended wing tips. *Avro Heritage Centre*

undercarriage had its main gears outboard of the weapons bay. Avro stated that the aircraft would be simpler to build than existing types bar the wing leading edge up to 25% of the chord, which would have to be of laminar flow construction requiring considerably more care in manufacture than had been customary in the past. This point, of course, would apply to all future high-speed aeroplanes and the laminar flow construction was based on the lines developed by Armstrong Whitworth.

At 50,000ft (15,240m) the maximum cruise speed was 576mph (927km/h), at 20,000ft (6,096m) it increased to 632mph (1,017km/h), rate of climb at sea level was 5,900ft/min (1,798m/min) and the fuel totalled 5,030gal (22,871lit). The 698 met all the performance requirements except that the altitude over the target would be 49,000ft (14,935m) instead of 50,000ft (15,240m) and the gross weight rose to 104,000lb (47,174kg), not 100,000lb (45,360kg). If Bristol engines were not ready for the prototype it could be flown with Rolls-Royce Avons or MetroVick F.9s (later the Armstrong Siddeley Sapphire), although these would reduce both the mean altitude and cruise speed. Design

completion from ITP would need 156 weeks, and 208 weeks were quoted from ITP to first flight. The brochure was dated May 1947.

Avro 698	
Span	91ft 6in (27.89m)
Length	92ft 0in (28.04m)
Gross wing area	3,364sq ft (312.85sq m)
t/c ratio	12% root, 12% tip
Gross weight	104,000lb (47,174kg)
Powerplant	four Bristol BE.10 9,140lb (40.6kN)
Maximum speed/height	584mph (940km/h) at 49,000ft (14,935m)
Weapon load	two 10,000lb (4,536kg) special or HC, four 6,000lb (2,722kg) or twenty 1,000lb (454kg) bombs

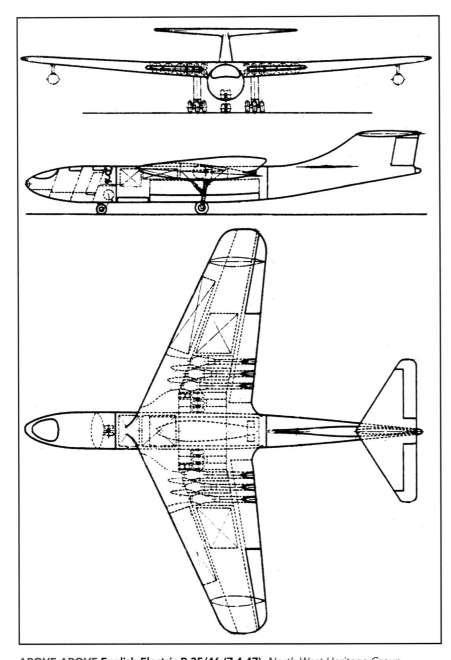

ABOVE ABOVE English Electric B.35/46 (7.4.47). *North West Heritage Group*
BELOW Model of English Electric's submission to B.35/46 (29.3.47).
North West Heritage Group

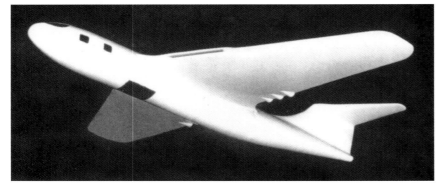

English Electric B.35/46

This relatively conservative project, dated 7 April 1947, offers a good contrast to the Avro 698; something of a surprise when one considers the radical designs Petter had produced at both Westland and English Electric (EE). However, the study was treated as an attempt to provide a high cruising altitude and low gross weight at the expense of equipment and cruise speed and was designed to meet both medium and long-range requirements within the same airframe but with increased internal and jettisonable fuel tanks. After careful consideration of seventeen alternative combinations of aerodynamic and engine layouts, EE stated that its project met both OR.229 and OR.230 in the great majority of respects; the only exception was performance. While appreciating the need for the highest possible cruise speed to avoid interception, the company considered that the difference in the layout required between 450 and 500 knots (518/576mph, 834/927km/h) was of a revolutionary character.

With present knowledge it was not a practical proposition to design a 100,000lb (45,360kg) class aeroplane having a cruising speed of 500 knots (927km/h). EE believed this must be approached in stages and hoped that the B.3/45 (Canberra) would contribute much to this end. The high Mach number was the biggest unknown and, until satisfactory flying qualities were obtained in level flight by at least a fighter-class design, without the limits of size and range, EE felt it would be most imprudent to promise the full combination desired. In addition, it was unlikely that those fighters in service in the next eight years would have any margin of speed and ceiling to intercept and outmanoeuvre this proposal flying at 450 knots (834km/h) and 50,000ft (15,240m). The company was hopeful that a speed of 475 knots (547mph/880km/h) would be possible following high-speed tunnel tests using information from work conducted by Göthert in Germany on improved wing sections, but a more conservative 450

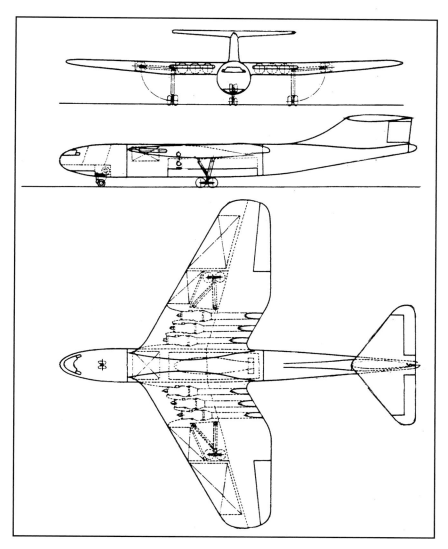

ABOVE Revised English Electric B.35/46 (29.10.47). EE's final brochure in January 1948 had variable leading-edge sweep but otherwise appears to have been very similar. *North West Heritage Group*

knots (518mph/834km/h) was used for the brochure performance estimates.

To back this up, the specified cruising altitude had been exceeded while the aircraft's size was kept within reasonable limits. The latter was achieved four ways. Firstly, evidence from the USA supported the view that structure weight could be of a low order provided the limiting dive speed was strictly controlled. The speed proposed was 403mph (648km/h) EAS, which meant considerable restrictions both in level and diving flight at low altitude, but this ceased to have an effect over 27,000ft (8,230m). Secondly, new and more fuel-efficient engines were expected that would reduce the

volume of fuel to be carried. Thirdly, the engines and undercarriage were completely buried in the wing and by using six engines, and keeping protuberances to a minimum, this provided a drag reduction that reduced the coefficient by 10% from the B.3/45. Finally, every effort was made to keep down equipment weight. EE had discovered that 1.5lb (0.7kg) of fuel was burnt in each sortie for each pound (0.45kg) of equipment carried, so detailed control was essential.

The wings were of two-spar construction with the three-wheel main gears and three engines per side mounted between the spars. The outer wings contained large integral fuel tanks and all

control surfaces were power operated. To achieve the long-range OR.230, the standard machine was overloaded with drop tanks and additional internal fuel, yet at 96,310lb (43,686kg) its weight was still under OR.229's limits. In the medium-range case the fuel load was 3,600gal (16,357lit), for long range 5,000gal (22,718lit) and the equivalent ranges for cruise at 518mph (833km/h) were 3,400nm (6,297km) and 4,400nm (8,149km). Top level speed was 593mph (954km/h) at 24,000ft (7,315m), the service ceiling at 90,000lb (40,824kg) weight was 50,000ft (15,240m) and at 50,000lb (22,680kg) it was 62,000ft (18,898m), and the maximum rates of climb were 5,600ft/min and 10,300ft/min (1,709m/min and 3,140m/min) respectively. Full wing loading was 42lb/sq ft (205kg/sq m).

The Mk.9 H2S navigation equipment gave the biggest installation job; it profoundly affected the aircraft's layout and, after EE had considered various positions, this equipment was placed at the rear of the bomb bay. Six axial jets of 4,850lb (21.6kN) thrust were specified, either Napier E.131 or Armstrong Siddeley, mounted in the wing roots and arranged with the compressors partly projecting through the front spar. A maiden flight was predicted at 182 weeks from ITP. Further investigations demonstrated that it was possible to carry two 10,000lb (4,536kg) MC bombs situated one above the other with the bomb bay doors partly open and the lower store projecting outside the fuselage contour for about a third of its width.

On request this project was revised, in a brochure dated 29 October 1947, to accommodate Avon or F.9 (Sapphire) engines that were already well on the way to development. The use of four Avons or F.9s was feasible for the range only if a reduced cruising speed of 489mph (787km/h) and a large altitude reduction were accepted; in fact EE felt that this aeroplane was underpowered. Fitting six units pushed the performance up to the specified figures and slightly improved on the original design with cruise now at 547mph (880km/h). The sweep angle at one-quarter chord had been increased from 20° to 30° but the gross weight rose to 111,150lb (50,418kg) with Avons or 111,350lb (50,508kg) with F.9s. Both versions offered a range of 3,400nm (6,297km) and a height of 51,000ft (15,549m) over the target. Internal fuel totalled 5,850gal (26,580lit) and the H2S was moved to the nose.

English Electric B.35/46

Span	100ft 0in (30.48m)
Length	97ft 0in (29.57m)
Gross wing area	2,000sq ft (186.0sq m)
t/c ratio	14% root
Gross weight	84,000lb (38,102kg)
Powerplant	six Napier/Armstrong Siddeley jets 4,850lb (21.6kN)
Maximum speed/height	518mph (833km/h) at 49,000ft (14,935m) to 60,000ft (18,288m)
Weapon load	one 10,000lb (4,536kg) special/HC, three 6,000lb (2,722kg) or eighteen 1,000lb (454kg) bombs

English Electric Revised Brochure (B.35/46 Relaxation)

Span	100ft 0in (30.48m)
Length	108ft 0in (32.92m)
Gross wing area	?
t/c ratio	?
Gross weight	111,150lb (50,418kg)
Powerplant	six Avon AJ.65 6,500lb (28.9kN)
Maximum speed/height	547mph (880km/h) at 51,000ft (15,545m)
Weapon load	?

BELOW The first crescent wing. Handley Page HP.80 to B.35/46 (5.47).

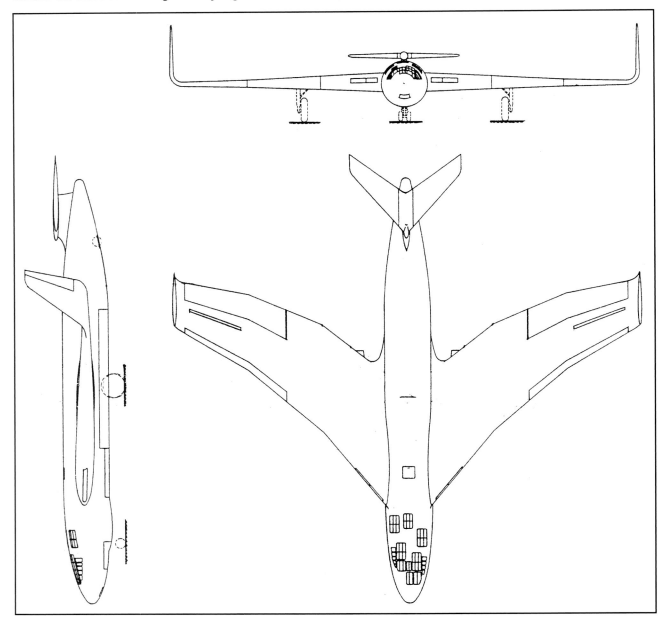

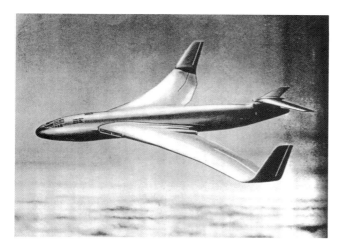

ABOVE Artist's impression of the tip-finned HP.80.

ABOVE Artist's impression of the revised HP.80 with conventional tail and single fin (1.48).

Handley Page HP.80

The original HP.72A/HP.80 was revised for B.35/46, the main external differences being a very short stub fin and the introduction of a second kink in the wing to give what HP called the 'crescent' wing. The HP.72A's wing had a small single kink outboard of the engines, with the remainder tapering to the tip fins. The crescent had evolved from extensive wind tunnel research and the relationship between sweepback and t/c ratio, varied progressively along the wing, was designed to give a high and approximately constant critical Mach number along the span with freedom from shock wave formation (so delaying the drag rise). It gave a low structure weight and avoided the tip stalling and loss of longitudinal stability inherent in the retention of high sweep at the tips.

HP stated that without sweepback the wings would be so thin that the structure weight would be prohibitive and the undercarriage, engines and fuel could not be housed in them. The crescent wing had its semi-span divided into three near-equal parts, the quarter chord lines of which were swept back at 48.25°, 37.5° and 26.75° to give the greatest sweepback at the structurally important centre section and the least at the tips where the section was thinnest. Thin wings with small sweepback, or large uniform sweepback, would either be excessively heavy or have poor stalling properties. The wing had flaps and leading-edge slats over the outer 50% of its semi-span in conjunction with rear slots at 60% of the chord. This combination of slots controlled the boundary layer on the outer wing so that flow breakdown, normally associated with a large sweepback, was delayed until the general stalling angle was reached. On a straight wing of equivalent sweepback, leading-edge and rear slots were found to be inadequate to prevent premature tip stalling; only through the combination of slots and a crescent planform could a satisfactory stalling behaviour be obtained.

All of the flying controls were fully power operated with complete duplication and no mechanical feedback or mass balancing. The tip fins and rudders were made structurally integral with the wings, the junction being carefully faired. Tests of the crescent planform with and without tip fins had shown that the fins offered a reduction in drag without any detriment to the tip stalling properties. The wing structure consisted of a single spar with concentrated light alloy flanges and a torque box with front and rear webs and closely spaced ribs. Forward of the spar the skin was of sheet sandwich construction while aft single skinning was used, a method adopted to ensure the best possible surface for laminar flow. There were no spanwise stringers.

A small slab tailplane, rotatable about a spanwise axis to provide variable incidence (all-moving), gave additional damping in pitch and provided longitudinal trimming at cruising and climbing speed without recourse to trimming the elevons. Trimming by elevon alone distorted both chordwise and spanwise loading and thus impaired the retention of laminar flow over the outer wing. The tail also made the problem of balancing the nose-down moments during flap operation much easier and was a powerful control to deal with large changes of longitudinal trim near the transonic region. There was a tricycle undercarriage and, like all B.35/46 projects, the crew cabin was jettisonable as a unit. A shallow streamlined 'blister' in the lower fuselage just rearward of the cabin housed the H2S scanner. Much of the fuselage was to be built conventionally with alloy hoop frames and stringers but some of the skinning was made of resin-impregnated glass fibre sandwich with onozote filling. Four MetroVick F.9 axial engines were placed two per side adjacent to the fuselage and mounted between strong tail ribs carried from the wing spar. The intakes were in the wing leading edge, and the jet pipes were faired into the trailing edge and, in the case of the inboard engines, also into the wing root fillet. Rolls-Royce AJ.65s would become an alternative when they had been developed sufficiently to give the same thrust and specific fuel consumption. By the time the brochure was submitted, the design of a one-third scale glider to check the low-speed flight characteristics had commenced (but noted in pencil on an MoS copy of the brochure as a 'bit premature').

The sea level rate of climb at maximum gross weight was 6,200ft/min (1,890m/min) and with a 10,000lb (4,536kg) bomb the still air range was 3,350nm (6,208km). Normal fuel capacity was 3,092gal (14,059lit) with another 1,240gal (5,638lit) available in auxiliary tanks. Full load wing loading was 47.5lb/sq ft (232kg/sq m). Based on a programme start date of 1 October 1947, a 'flying shell' prototype was expected to fly in March 1952 with a fully equipped machine following in September 1952.

Handley Page HP.80

Span	100ft 0in (30.48m)
Length	91ft 6in (27.89m)
Gross wing area	2,000sq ft (186.0sq m)
t/c ratio	14% root, 8% tip
Gross weight	95,000lb (43,092kg)
Powerplant	four MetroVick F.9 7,500lb (33.3kN)
Maximum speed/height	576mph (927km/h) at 50,000ft (15,240m)
Weapon load	one 10,000lb (4,536kg) special, two 10,000lb HC, three 6,000lb (2,722kg) or twenty-one 1,000lb (454kg) bombs

Short S.B.1

Shorts considered this tailless aircraft to be the optimum for B.35/46 and it incorporated much of the experience gained with the B.14/46 S.A.4 'Interim Bomber'; in fact in many ways it was a direct development. Nevertheless, it had been found impossible to meet the range and altitude requirements with an aircraft of this size unless the equipment weight could be substantially reduced; a larger machine with six or more engines would be necessary to meet the performance in full and this would be well over the required weight. Shorts' weight estimates owed much to the detailed structural investigations made for the B.14/46.

The fuselage arrangement and bomb bay were very similar to B.14/46 with the jettisonable forward section, including the pressure cabin and H2S scanner, practically identical. However, whereas the conventional straight wing interim type could cruise at 500mph (805km/h), the sweptback S.B.1 could cruise at 575mph (925km/h), which at 50,000ft (15,240m) gave a Mach number of 0.87 and thereby necessitated a large sweep angle of about 40° to delay

the onset of compressibility. With so much sweepback a tailless design became practical immediately and, for a number of reasons, was preferred to a conventional tail. This flying wing with a central fin was intended to remove the parasitic drag of a normal tail.

Preliminary schemes had been prepared both with and without tails. Among the arguments for not having a tail were:

1. The tailless type would have a small advantage in structural simplicity, weight and drag over that with a tail.

2. When a tail was fitted it was necessary to ensure that it still provided good control up to and beyond the speed at which the wing became shock stalled. A large sweep angle was therefore required on the tailplane, which would result in a serious loss of elevator effectiveness.

3. On a swept wing it was quite easy to put the flaps where flap deflection caused little or no change of pitching moment on the wing, and therefore no change of trim on a tailless aircraft. Once a tail was

BELOW Short S.B.1 (5.47).

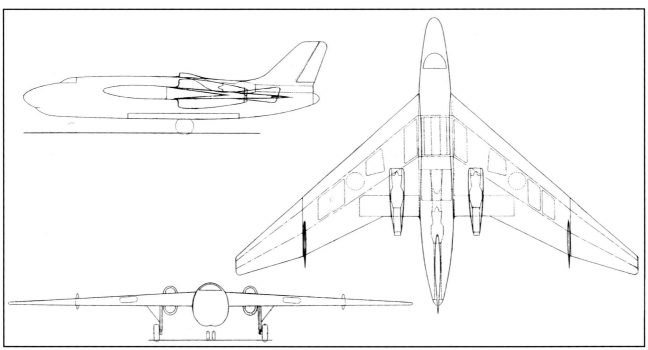

introduced the balance was upset by the downwash on the tail and could only be restored by moving the flaps a long way aft of the wing or by extending them to the wing tips (the S.B.1 had split flaps).

4. On this particular design it was desirable to fit at least one engine and a rear warning scanner in the end of the fuselage; a tail would create structural complications.

Longitudinal and lateral control and the prevention of tip stalling were the next problems. The control problem was complicated not only by the high Mach number but also by the aeroelastic effects, which were particularly troublesome on a swept wing. It had recently become increasingly evident that on conventional high-speed aircraft it was essential to provide adjustment of the tailplane incidence, otherwise violent variations in stability might occur with increasing speed due to torsional deflection of the tailplane. In fact, the tailplane incidence had to be so adjusted that the elevator setting was very nearly neutral at high speed. This problem applied even more forcibly to a tailless design because the torsional rigidity of a wing was obviously likely to be less than that of a tailplane.

One solution was to fit a small trimming tail but this introduced a weight penalty and other complications. A more direct solution was to fit the equivalent of an all-moving tail, namely all-moving wing tips or 'controllers', so designed that as the wing bent they were able to twist just sufficiently to preserve the correct incidence. This had been advocated by Professor Geoffrey Hill and flown on his Westland Pterodactyl aircraft in the 1930s. Such wing tips provided control, freedom from tip stalling and the avoidance of aileron reversal. Good control could be obtained up to higher Mach numbers than was the case with conventional surfaces because the tips operated at a lower incidence than the rest of the wing and therefore shock stalled later. Extended over the outer third of the span, they could be moved together for elevator control and

differentially for aileron control. It was essential that they were power operated. Shorts noted that the simplicity of the scheme had much to recommend it over any other system yet devised. Structural factors were an obvious objection but the company felt that the problem was similar to the wing fold on quite a small naval aircraft. This feature was later termed the 'aero-isoclinic' wing. The fin and rudder were mounted on the fuselage but small auxiliary fins were also placed just inboard of the controllers to prevent cross flow at the controller hinge, to provide further help in preventing tip stalling and to increase the directional stability.

Five AJ.65 Avons powered the S.B.1, a six-engined design having been rejected because the gross weight was too high. It had been hoped that three engines could be mounted in the rear fuselage but this was found to be impractical, so one unit only was housed in the fuselage with two in each wing mounted in pairs one above the other aft of the rear spar. This arrangement offered low frontal area and was unlikely to affect the critical Mach number to any extent. The difficulty would be to provide satisfactory intake orifices, a problem inherent in wing engines on a swept wing.

At 115,000lb (52,164kg) gross weight the S.B.1's combat speed was 628mph (1,010km/h) at sea level and 595mph (957km/h) at 40,000ft (12,192m); the equivalent cruise speeds were 544mph and 578mph (875km/h and 930km/h) and a maximum 638mph (1,027km/h) was possible at 12,000ft (3,658m). It was estimated that the specified cruise speed in B.35/46 could just be achieved without any compressibility drag rise but this required maximum cruising thrust from all five engines. If the bombs were carried 'all the way' the range was 2,730nm (5,056km), and 2,930nm (5,426km) if they were dropped halfway. Sea level rate of climb was 3,740ft/min (1,140m/min) and the service ceiling 47,500ft (14,478m). The internal fuel totalled 4,720gal (21,461lit) and take-off wing loading was 48.2lb/sq ft (235kg/sq m).

Short S.B.1	
Span	114ft 0in (34.75m)
Length	86ft 3in (26.29m)
Gross wing area	2,385sq ft (221.2sq m)
t/c ratio	13% root
Gross weight	115,000lb (52,164kg)
Powerplant	four RR Avon AJ.65 6,500lb (28.9kN)
Maximum speed/height	576mph (927km/h) at 47,000ft (14,326m)
Weapon load	one 10,000lb (4,536kg) special, two 10,000lb HC, two 6,000lb (2,722kg) or twenty-one 1,000lb (454kg) bombs

Vickers B.35/46

The Vickers' B.35/46 project did not embody highly advanced aerodynamic features, which the firm knew would necessitate years of research work and the construction of flying models. This would save time and would be a key element in getting the new bomber into service quickly. Vickers stated in its brochure that 'the aircraft design submitted … is the outcome of an exhaustive investigation of the B.35/46 specification during which some 20 projects were made'. To meet the 500 knots (576mph/927km/h) cruise requirement would require the employment of advanced aerodynamic features, such as highly swept back or delta wings of extreme thinness, and Vickers considered that the successful resolution of the problems associated with such features could not be accomplished in time to have the aircraft in service by the end of 1952. The importance of this timetable had been emphasised by both the Air Ministry and MoS and was, therefore, allowed to influence the whole Vickers design.

The proposal offered, therefore, was a mid-wing aeroplane of relatively orthodox lines employing 25° of sweep back and a conventional fuselage–tail combination with the single fin and rudder carrying the tail clear of the jets. This would meet the specification in general except that the cruising speed over the target was 484 knots (557mph/897km/h) at 45,000ft (13,716m) instead of 500 knots (576mph/927km/h) at 50,000ft

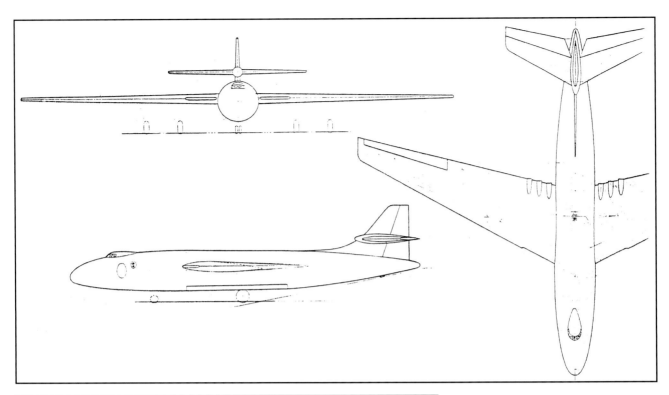

ABOVE Vickers B.35/46 (5.47). Note the four main undercarriage wheels.
LEFT Artist's sketch showing the Vickers B.35/46 project.

(15,240m), or 460 knots (530mph/852km/h) at the required height. To raise the aircraft's performance to the B.35/46 level would require an gross weight approaching 170,000lb (77,112kg), but in order to use existing heavy bomber runways the weight would need to be considerably less than this. Vickers noted that an aircraft employing an orthodox tricycle undercarriage should not weigh more than 100,000lb (45,360kg), but with this design an gross weight of 115,000lb (52,164kg) was possible by using four main undercarriages each with a single wheel, in a fashion similar to that employed successfully by the firm's wartime Windsor piston bomber prototype; there was a twin-wheel nose unit.

The design's H2S scanner was placed in the nose and the powerplant was three Napier E.131 engines buried in each inner wing (alternative choices were six Armstrong Siddeley AS.45C or, if this and the E.131 were unavailable, four Rolls-Royce Avon or MetroVick F.9). Normal ram air would enter through a slot at the leading edge of the wing and was then directed via ducting to its appropriate engine. The structure of this aircraft was to be stressed skin throughout and a fuselage of conventional construction would use stringers and circular-section frames of high-tensile light alloy to stabilise a thin-clad sheet covering. The wing structure was basically a thick skin stabilised as fully as possible by means of span-wise stringers, but where there were cut-outs for engines and undercarriage the wing loads would be taken by leading and trailing edge spars. The tail unit was also conventional stressed skin construction. There was a pressurised nose cabin and a midships bomb compartment, and the internal fuel totalled 4,875gal (22,166lit). Wing loading was 49lb/sq ft (239kg/sq m), sea level rate of climb 4,000ft/min (1,219m/min), range with a 10,000lb (4,536kg) bomb 3,350nm (6,208km) and service ceiling 52,000ft (15,850m).

A period of 178 weeks was predicted from receipt of order to completion of drawings and 195 weeks to the first flight, so from a late 1947 go-ahead flight could be expected in September 1951 with production deliveries commencing early in 1953. Vickers added that, once the aerodynamics had been proved, a further development of the aircraft would be provided by sweeping the wings back to 40° and this would meet the specification in full.

Following the Tender Conference, Vickers became the third company to submit a revised design to incorporate some changes and relaxed requirements suggested by the Air Staff (detailed later). As modified, four Avons or F.9 Sapphires replaced the six Napier units (the latter following a verbal request from the DMARD, J. E. Serby, to fit them). The aircraft's appearance now came closer to the eventual Valiant bar its overall size, a narrow cockpit and a bullet tail fairing, but the fundamental concept of the original design and the programme timescale were retained. The wing root was now swept 37°, the outer section 20° and with a curved leading edge blending the two sections together. Increased sweep at the root delayed the onset of compressibility while the satisfactory stalling and handling properties associated with low sweepback were retained by the outer plane. It was generally recognised that the ineffectiveness of the sweepback at the root caused only half the theoretical compressibility gain to be obtained in practice; with this planform the full theoretical gain should be obtainable near the tip. Thus the proposed wing was as effective in delaying compressibility as a straight-tapered wing swept back at an angle of 29°.

These changes increased the 'over target' cruise speed with four Sapphires to 570mph (917km/h) at 45,000ft (13,716m); range was 3,350nm (6,208km) and ceiling 51,000ft (15,550m). Sea level climb rate was 5,230ft/min (1,594m/min) and for the Avons 3,320ft/min (1,012m/min). At about 85,000lb (38,556kg) weight the top speed with Sapphires was 599mph

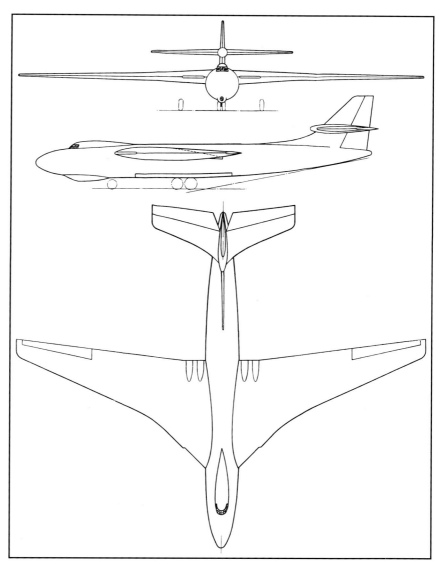

ABOVE **The revised Vickers B.35/46 (late 1947). This design had a more conventional main undercarriage.**

BELOW **Impression of the revised Vickers project to the relaxed B.35/46 requirement.**

(964km/h) at 30,000ft (9,144m), with Avons 584mph (940km/h). The concession to reduce the maximum bomb load to one 10,000lb (4,536kg), two 6,000lb (2,722kg) or eighteen 1,000lb (454kg) permitted a smaller fuselage of 11ft 3in (3.43m), diameter down from 13ft (3.96m) and saved 5,000lb (2,268kg) in weight. A tandem-wheel tricycle undercarriage was now used.

Further development would be possible by fitting the 7,500lb (33.3kN) 'Avon Replacement' RB.77 bypass engine. By adding 1,730gal (7,866lit) of internal fuel for an gross weight of 124,600lb (56,519kg), Vickers predicted that the long-range OR.230 demands could be met with a cruise speed of 553mph (890km/h) at 48,500ft (14,783m) over the target. It was emphasised, however, that no features of the basic B.35/46 design had been influenced by this version; in all respects the design offered was the optimum for the medium-range requirement.

RAE Farnborough commented on each project. No design was considered entirely satisfactory but all bar Vickers and EE reached the specified cruising speed, this pair opting for a lower figure in order to obtain more height over the target. It was clear there were important gaps in the knowledge of stability and control at high speeds that made it impossible to declare that a particular design would be satisfactory without extensive tunnel testing. It was, for instance, not possible to say whether or not a tailplane was necessary. In present form the HP.80 was considered the best but the Avro delta had several potential advantages that could be exploited with some redesign. However, limited experience with delta wings gave doubts as to what critical Mach number might be achieved.

The Shorts isoclinic wing was likely to remain effective above Mach 0.90 but needed a great deal of research before a satisfactory scheme could be developed. AWA's system would also need work for control to be satisfactory at high speeds and this machine's best cruise speed was likely to be its critical Mach number of 0.87. The Vickers project was expected to have a maximum usable cruising speed of Mach 0.79 (520mph/837km/h), not the Mach 0.84 (553mph/890km/h) quoted by the company, and RAE felt the cruising height and range must be reduced in order to reach this speed.

EE's and Vickers' designs were described as semi-conventional projects when the others all used advanced aerodynamics. The MoS felt that the current knowledge of aerodynamics, and to some extent powerplants, was not sufficient to enable any of the advanced types to be constructed with any degree of confidence, although it seemed that one of them was more likely to meet the objective than the less advanced layouts. In addition, the long-range Bristol 172 had also been considered and was thought sufficiently promising to justify the construction of a half-scale model (the Type 174 in Chapter Three). The 172 was no more advanced than some of the B.35/46 submissions and it was felt reasonable to consider it in any general planning programme. If a long-range bomber was to be in operational use by 1958 the design of a prototype must begin not later than 1952.

The Tender Design Conference, held at the Ministry of Supply on 28 July 1947, was chaired by Stuart Scott-Hall, PDTD(A). He began by saying that Bristol had proceeded with a design study (the Type 172) to the original long-range requirement, but it was realised there would be great difficulties in meeting it and so no specification was raised and no order placed. However, flying models were planned.

Of the six medium-range tenders, the Shorts, AWA, HP and Avro schemes represented aerodynamic conceptions as advanced as the Bristol 172 while the semi-conventional EE and Vickers did not meet B.35/46 in full. In addition, Shorts had been working for more than two years on a bomber of conventional aerodynamic layout (the B.14/46) and early in 1947 it had been agreed to place an order for this design as an insurance against the more ambitious B.35/46. The EE and Vickers designs bore comparison with the Short B.14/46 and so the meeting was to consider two different aspects:

a). Selection of the best type or types from Short, AWA, HP and Avro;

b). Whether any change to the B.14/46 order was necessary in the light of the EE and Vickers tenders.

In the event it was agreed that the Short S.A.4 should continue as ordered except for possible improvements to the engine layout. AVM Boothman, ACAS(TR), explained that a bomber having the greatest possible chance of penetration was vital to national defence and there should be no hesitation in proceeding boldly with the most promising design, even if development risks were incurred. It was agreed that a prototype of any design must be available in five years

Vickers B.35/46	
Span	137ft 0in (41.76m)
Length	111ft 0in (33.83m)
Gross wing area	2,350sq ft (218.6sq m)
t/c ratio	13% root, 12% tip
Gross weight	115,000lb (52,164kg)
Powerplant	six Napier E.131 5,055lb (22.5kN) or Armstrong Siddeley A.S.45C
Maximum speed/height	(mean weight 92,300lb/41,867kg) 570mph (917km/h) at sea level, 591mph (951km/h) at 20,000ft (6,096m)
Weapon load	one 10,000lb (4,536kg) special, two 10,000lb HC, three 6,000kg (2,722kg) or twenty-four 1,000lb (454kg) bombs

Vickers Revised Brochure (B.35/46 Relaxation)	
Span	136ft 3in (41.53m)
Length	114ft 6in (34.90m)
Gross wing area	2,490sq ft (231.6sq m)
t/c ratio	12%
Gross weight	either engine 110,000lb (49,896kg)
Powerplant	four AS Sapphire 7,500lb (33.3kN) or four RR Avon AJ.65 6,500lb (28.9kN)
Maximum speed/height	Sapphire 570mph (917km/h) at 45,000ft (13,716m), Avon 553mph (890km/h) at 45,000ft (13,716m)
Weapon load	one 10,000lb (4,536kg) special or HC, two 6,000kg (2,722kg) or eighteen 1,000lb (454kg) bombs

while flying models should be built in parallel with the prototypes. The results from such models would be available more than a year before prototype completion, which would allow any necessary major alterations to be made in time.

There were difficulties in assessing the stability and control of the four proposals. High-speed tunnel testing on a model of the de Havilland DH.108 research aircraft with conventional ailerons showed that control power vanished at Mach 0.9. Full-span elevons were also tested on the Boulton Paul Delta (P.111) research machine and here control power for small control angles was lost at Mach 0.93. The bomber projects were all cruising close to their critical Mach number and increases in thrust could not therefore improve performance. It was noted that Avro's delta had plenty of room available for extra equipment or fuel when none of the other three could be similarly overloaded except by adding external tanks.

It was thought the Shorts all-moving wing tip would be effective up to the full Mach number of its project but the only real flight experience on such a feature was on the original Pterodactyl, an aircraft that was only lightly loaded. Reference was made to the greater weight and lower manoeuvrability of this design compared to the others, and also to its higher tyre pressure, which affected runway design, so on these grounds it was agreed that the S.B.1 could be eliminated from further discussion. The AW.56 would be simpler, cheaper and quicker to manufacture than the other two, but the Avro delta was a practical manufacturing design. There was a need for flying models with both HP and Avro projects since they involved a technical risk that was not entirely removed by wind tunnel tests; HP's in particular involved a totally untried wing planform. Avro's 698 was clearly the most promising, the HP.80 second and AW.56 third. Objections to the latter were the greater fuel load and gross weight, lesser manoeuvrability and inferior radar layout.

It was agreed that an order should be placed for the Avro 698 and for a flying model to be designed and built in parallel. RAE Farnborough would undertake priority high-speed tunnel tests on the HP crescent wing, following which a choice would be made between this and the AW.56; if the HP.80 was chosen then a parallel model was also wanted. There were to be no changes in the plan to have flying replicas of the Bristol 172. In due course crescent wing tunnel testing gave promising results that indicated satisfactory stability and trim up to Mach 0.93, so clearing the way to proceed with the HP.80.

After the conference the Air Staff and MoS agreed that the importance of the medium bomber was such that a further type must be ordered between the two extremes of B.35/46 and B.14/46, which was the reason why AWA, EE and Vickers were invited to produce revised brochures (above). It was recognised that the Avro and HP bombers were very advanced designs with many unknowns and the new work was prompted by some relaxations from B.35/46. Briefly, the Air Staff would be content with the carriage of a single 10,000lb (4,536kg) bomb and its accurate delivery at a radius of 1,500 miles (2,413km) while accepting a speed limitation below an altitude of 25,000ft (7,620m). Thus, an aircraft of better performance than the B.14/46 should result but taking less risk than the B.35/46s and requiring less-prolonged development and testing.

A Design Study Conference was held on 15 January 1948, where the revised AW.56 was immediately ruled out since it was a tailless design and relied on suction to achieve adequate lift at low speed and to preserve lateral control, features that placed it beyond the interim class now envisaged. However, AWA had by this time informed Scott-Hall it was changing its policy and would like to submit a new design with a tail but H. M. Garner, PDSR(A), felt the company would not put serious effort into this and so no formal invitation was made for a resubmission. Scott-Hall stated that on broad aerodynamic grounds the EE approach was correct by RAE standards,

the Vickers incorrect, but in regard to items such as equipment and crew layout the Vickers design appeared much better. There was also the need to keep Vickers employed while EE was fully loaded with Canberra work. Scott-Hall thought the issue of retaining Vickers in the industry was of paramount importance. It was essential to order this bomber with the minimum delay since the Lincoln was by present standards completely out of date, so both companies were to be advised of the objections to their designs and asked to resubmit with the utmost urgency.

In fact, by early February 1948 all three companies had submitted further 'intermediate bomber' brochures. EE modified the wing of its earlier aircraft to have 30° leading-edge sweep at the root with reduced sweep further out. AWA's had a constant 30° sweep but now featured a tail. T. V. Somerville, assessing them as part of the RAE's Advanced Bomber Project Group, concluded that both the EE and Vickers designs would be much heavier than estimated, EE's offering few, if any, compensating advantages, so it must be rejected. Nothing was gained from using six engines bar the extra weight, while the limitation to its diving speed also counted against the EE project. Though admittedly experimental, AWA's smooth wing skin based on the AW.52 was relatively inefficient from a weight point of view.

AWA's and Vickers' designs were similar in performance and it appeared impossible to choose between them on technical grounds. Both were good compromise designs for an interim bomber and the final selection might depend on the design ability and productive capacity of the companies concerned. The Vickers project was in due course the one chosen for production and B.9/48 was raised in July 1948 to cover it. By accepting a drop in performance over B.35/46 it was hoped to avoid the lengthy development period of the advanced designs but the anticipated performance was expected to be better than the Short B.14/46. Cruise for B.9/48 was to be 535mph (861km/h) at 35,000 to 45,000ft (10,668 to 13,716m).

Intermediate Bomber 2.48 - Final Brochures ('B.9/48' - OR.229)

Armstrong Whitworth (with tail)

Span	100ft 7in (30.66m)
Length	101ft 4in (30.89m)
Gross wing area	2,120sq ft (197.2sq m)
t/c ratio	11%
Gross weight	104,350lb (47,333kg)
Powerplant	four RR Avon AJ.65 6,500lb (28.9kN)
Maximum speed/height	541mph (870km/h) at 44,800ft (13,655m)
Weapon load	?

English Electric

Span	100ft 0in (30.48m)
Length	108ft 0in (32.92m)
Gross wing area	2,500sq ft (232.5sq m)
t/c ratio	12%
Gross weight	111,150lb (50,418kg)
Powerplant	six RR Avon AJ.65 6,500lb (28.9kN)
Maximum speed/height	547mph (880km/h) at 51,000ft (15,545m)
Weapon load	?

Vickers

Span	113ft 4in (34.54m)
Length	101ft 6in (30.94m)
Gross wing area	2,320sq ft (215.8sq m)
t/c ratio	12%
Gross weight	107,000lb (48,535kg)
Powerplant	four RR Avon AJ.65 6,500lb (28.9kN)
Maximum speed/height	535mph (861km/h) at 45,000ft (13,716m)
Weapon load	?

Sperrin, Valiant, Victor and Vulcan

Go-ahead for four medium bombers was now approved but the production plans for the S.A.4 were finished by the Vickers B.9/48. In March 1950, the Treasury was informed by the MoS that there was no longer any justification in spending money on the S.A.4 as an operational aircraft and cancellation of the contract had been considered. There was still a desire, however, to complete two prototypes for flight test work to expedite by eighteen months the readiness for service of the V-bombers. Estimates indicated a further £0.87m were needed to complete the two aircraft following the £1.15m already spent, the Ministry indicating that about one third of the extra money would have to be spent anyway in order to keep the contractor occupied until other work

became available. Accordingly, the Treasury agreed to the completion of both S.A.4s.

There was also the need to avoid damaging Shorts' design team and on 13 March 1950 F. C. Musgrave, US(Air), proposed to continue the contract until another, for a large flying boat to Specification R.2/48, provided an alternative. Musgrave declared that R.2/48 'would be placed with the company', but in fact the Saunders-Roe P.162 Duchess project would win that competition. The first S.A.4 flew on 10 August 1951, but after it was unveiled at that year's Farnborough Show *Flight* magazine reported some general criticism that the aircraft was 'conventional' rather than being more 'characteristic of the 'jet era' with sweepback, buried engines and so forth'. (Shorts had favoured fitting a swept wing in order to improve the speed).

In May 1950 it was agreed to complete the second machine as a flying laboratory for ballistic research work and H2S/NBC development. Shorts disliked the 'flying laboratory' designation, preferring 'research aircraft', and on 19 September offered the name Stormont. The MoS would not agree to either title so B.14/46 was retained until in 1954 the S.A.4 was named Sperrin. Both machines were successfully employed on trials and research, a role that included dropping dummy Blue Danube bombs and replacing the lower Avon in each nacelle with the far more powerful de Havilland Gyron for a combined total thrust of 53,000lb (235.6kN). In the meantime, Shorts had examined an S.B.1 with four Rolls-Royce Conways and another design with a delta wing and four engines in the roots.

In February 1948 Vickers put forward a design study for a thinner-winged aircraft but an MoS meeting held on 23 March concluded that this had several disadvantages and might take an extra two years to develop, so becoming a competitor to the Avro and HP projects. It was agreed to order the aircraft with the original wing and Vickers received instructions to

proceed with two prototype B.9/48s on 16 April 1948. With a deterioration in the situation regarding the Soviet Union, particularly after the Blockade of Berlin in 1948, there was increased urgency to get the aircraft into the air. The first Type 660 flew on 18 May 1951, ahead of the S.A.4 and seven months ahead of schedule. A production order was placed in February 1951 and in June the aircraft was named Valiant (Vickers had wanted Vimy but the Air Ministry refused this). The first squadron was formed in February 1955.

The overall HP.80 design was approved in December 1947 following an ITP on 19 November for both flying model and full-scale aeroplane, but there were concerns about the effects of flutter on the tip fins and rudders. In January 1948 these were deleted and replaced by a more conventional central fin and rudder that increased the span to 110ft (33.53m) and added 500lb (227kg) in weight, but it helped with the flying model's construction. Contracts for two HP.80 prototypes were placed in March 1949 and the first production order followed in June 1952. Production specification B.128P was raised in September and the prototype flew on 24 December 1952. Service deliveries began in November 1957.

Despite Avro's 698 being declared best project at the Tender Conference, contract placement was held up until the MoS was satisfied that the technical strength of the Avro team was sufficient to handle the programme. Two prototypes, a mock-up and flying models were cleared for ordering in December 1947. On 6 April 1948 Avro released a Design Development brochure that highlighted a number of changes made to the original configuration in order to solve the numerous problems that had arisen. RAE high-speed tunnel tests had revealed a need to retain adequate control at air speeds exceeding Mach 0.9 and the solution was the addition of all-moving pointed wing tips outside the tip fins. This caused a considerable aft movement of CofG that necessitated

ABOVE AND RIGHT **The first Short S.A.4 Sperrin carried the serial VX158.** *Shorts via Terry Panopalis*

a complete redisposition of equipment. The wing t/c ratio was also cut from 12% to 10% to increase the critical Mach number to 0.88 and reduce low-speed profile drag, which meant the engines could no longer be stacked but were mounted side-by-side. It was also found preferable to use a single bomb bay on the centreline instead of two outside the engines. Span rose to 99ft (30.18m), length dropped to 86ft 9in (26.44m), the gross weight was now 101,764lb (46,160kg) and sea level rate of climb 6,900ft/min (2,103m/min).

The first 698 prototype flew on 30 August 1952, by which time, like the HP.80, the tip fins had been dispensed with and replaced by a central fin and rudder; production specification B.129P was raised on 25 September after an initial production order was made in July. Avro considered the name Ottawa (to reflect its Avro Canada connections) but this was turned down. The MoS discussed a host of alternatives but the CAS wanted V-names to go with the Valiant,

offering Vulcan (for Avro) and Victor (HP) on 3 October 1952; this was agreed on 4 December, thus creating the V-Force. The RAF received its first Vulcans in January 1957.

During the latter part of 1951 and early in 1952 the Air Ministry was led to believe that the MoS was preparing an appreciation to show which of the B.35/46s should be bought in quantity

ABOVE This nose angle view of VX158 shows its original twin-Avon engine nacelles very nicely. *Shorts via Terry Panopalis*

BELOW Later in its career VX158 carried more powerful de Havilland Gyron engines in the lower bay of each engine nacelle, which necessitated an enlargement of the casing.

ABOVE The first Vickers Valiant prototype WB210 seen at the Farnborough Show in September 1951 with an impressive range of aircraft behind. Note the original air intakes. *MoS Photo*

BELOW The second Valiant prototype WB215 had redesigned air intakes, which can be seen clearly here as the aircraft takes off.

ABOVE **Two Valiants fly together. The nearest is serial XD858.**
OPPOSITE **The Valiant's relatively conventional wing shape is displayed by early production B.Mk.1 WP204.**
BELOW **Valiant XD866 of No.138 Squadron pictured at Leconfield on 3 September 1960.** *via Terry Panopalis*

ABOVE Imposing view of the Handley Page Victor prototype's nose.

LEFT The second prototype Victor WB775 was displayed at the 1955 Farnborough Show in an attractive blue colour scheme. *via Terry Panopalis*

BELOW The first Victor production aircraft was XA917. Early V-bombers were painted silver rather than the more well-known white.

ABOVE Victor XA928 shows off the type's beautiful crescent wing.
BELOW Avro Vulcan prototype VX770 at Farnborough. *via Terry Panopalis*

ABOVE The second Vulcan VX777 makes a slow pass at Farnborough with what looks like some of the Avro 707 scale model research aircraft following in the distance.

for the RAF. At the end of this period it seems no one was prepared to commit themselves in favour of one type or the other and many reasons, political and otherwise, were put forward to justify a production order for both the Avro and HP aircraft. Thus by July 1952, although neither of the prototypes had flown, a production order was placed for twenty-five of each series aircraft.

B.35/46 was a bold specification and perhaps the most illuminating point from these designs is the mix of advanced wing shapes then under consideration; they make a fascinating series and, at the time, must have appeared quite extraordinary. Many have written that Britain's aircraft designers were slow to adopt the advanced aerodynamic shapes that became available after the war, with so much German data to back them up. Yet in spring 1947, just two years after war's end, British designers were offering swept wings, a delta wing, a crescent

wing and two flying wings to one of the most important requirements so far. With fifty years of hindsight it seems to have been a huge waste to build four different bombers, and put three into production, all to satisfy the same need. However, documents from both industry and Ministry suggest a degree of nervousness towards these shapes and their capabilities that made a strong case for back-up insurance types. In the event all four bombers performed well and so providing such insurance may now seem unnecessary, but perhaps that was just good fortune since the concurrent day fighter programmes suffered far worse with major development problems for both the Hawker Hunter and Supermarine Swift.

In 1978 Air Marshall Sir Geoffrey Tuttle, formally DOR and ACAS(OR), wrote in *RAF Quarterly* that the [HP] crescent and [Avro] delta wing types were 'regarded by the Ministry of Supply as rather a technical gamble,

and an insurance was taken out in the form of an aircraft which emerged as the Valiant. It is not easy to see why such a plethora of machinery was produced, but I believe the real reason was that the effect of the atom bomb on war had not got through to the Ministry of Supply, which wanted a big industry to fight another big and long war … Korea kept the ball rolling and Mr Attlee [the Prime Minister] had a defence budget of £4,700m for three years. So all the projects went ahead'. Finally, despite their improved performance the V-bombers were still classed in the medium bomber category because America had by now built its huge B-36 and B-52 bombers, which took the term 'heavy bomber' up to an altogether different level.

ABOVE In its early form the Vulcan wing was a pure delta, as shown by early production aircraft XA890. Later it would be enlarged and have a more complex shape.

BELOW XA890 again, on this occasion at RAF Abingdon on 14 September 1963. Here still painted silver, this aircraft spent its entire career on trials programmes. *via Terry Panopalis*

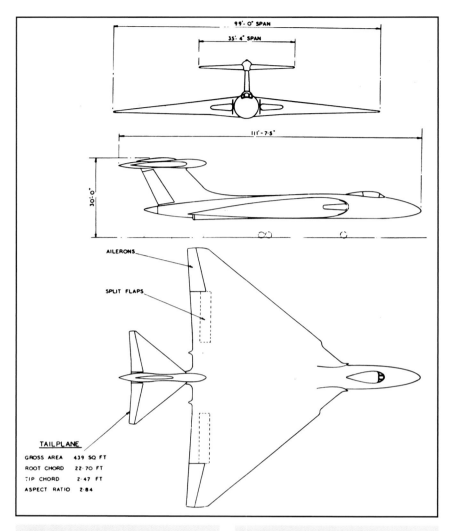

LEFT In mid-1951 Avro conducted a private study into fitting a tailplane to the 698, the present design of which was at the time considered the optimum. The 698's span was unchanged at 99ft 0in (30.18m) but the length rose to 111ft 7.5in (34.02m). The advantages proved not to be great. The modification would, for example, improve the aircraft's flying qualities and steadiness as a bomb aiming platform, but the direct weight penalty for fitting the tail and enlarging the fin came to 2,180lb (989kg). The tailplane version had an estimated take-off gross weight of 145,230lb (65,876kg), a reduced range and a lower height over the target. Tailplane span was 35ft 4in (10.77m). *Avro Heritage*

de Havilland DH.111

There is one final design to B.35/46 that falls outside the main story. de Havilland (DH) did not tender to the specification but on 27 May 1948 completed a brochure for a military adaptation of its DH.106 Comet airliner called the DH.111. The company had been invited by the MoS to produce such a project some months earlier. DH.111 did not fully meet B.35/46, falling short in cruise speed and maximum permissible Mach number, but de Havilland felt it represented the most advanced aeroplane that could be ready in a reasonable time with a certainty of success, when the extremely unorthodox bombers now proposed might take very much longer to develop than presently estimated. And the DH.111 was based on an aircraft being built when all the rest still only existed on paper.

It was proposed to make a new fuselage of much smaller cross-section than the DH.106 but leave the rest almost unchanged except for the centre section across the fuselage; the wing was mid-set rather than the Comet's low position. The prototype DH.106 was expected to fly in about a year, which meant, since the control and performance characteristics would be known from the civil prototype, virtually a prototype of the bomber would be flying several years earlier

Short S.42/S.A.4 Sperrin (B.14/46-OR.239 – First Prototype)

Span	109ft 1in (33.25m)
Length	102ft 2in (31.14m)
Gross wing area	1,897sq ft (176.4sq m)
t/c ratio	12%
Gross weight	115,000lb (52,164kg)
Powerplant	four RR Avon RA.2 6,000lb (26.7kN)
Maximum speed/height	564mph (907km/h)
Weapon load	one Blue Danube nuclear bomb or conventional weapons

Avro Vulcan B.Mk.1 (B.129/OR.229/3)

Span	99ft 0in (30.18m)
Length	97ft 1in (29.59m)
Gross wing area	3,554sq ft (330.5sq m)
t/c ratio	12.3% root, 8% tip
Gross weight	170,000lb (77,112kg)
Powerplant	four Bristol Olympus 101 11,000lb (48.9kN)
Maximum speed/height	620mph (998km/h) at height
Weapon load	Nuclear or twenty-one 1,000lb (454kg) bombs

HP Victor B.Mk.1 (B.128/OR.229/3)

Span	110ft 0in (33.53m)
Length	114ft 11in (35.03m)
Gross wing area	2,406sq ft (223.8sq m)
t/c ratio	16% root, 6% tip
Gross weight	180,000lb (81,648kg)
Powerplant	four Armstrong Siddeley Sapphire 202 11,050lb (49.1kN)
Maximum speed/height	645mph (1,038km/h) at height
Weapon load	Nuclear or thirty-five 1,000lb (454kg) bombs

Vickers Valiant B.Mk.1 (B.9/48/OR.229)

Span	114ft 4in (34.85m)
Length	108ft 3in (32.99m)
Gross wing area	2,362sq ft (219.7sq m)
t/c ratio	12% root, 9% tip
Gross weight	175,000lb (79,380kg)
Powerplant	four RR Avon 201 10,000lb (44.4kg)
Maximum speed/height	567mph (912km/h) at height
Weapon load	Nuclear or maximum twenty-one 1,000lb (454kg)

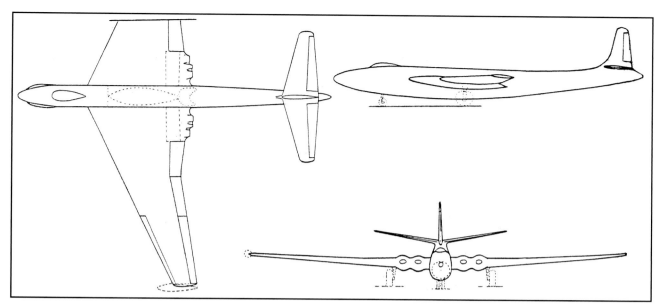

ABOVE The de Havilland DH.111 bomber project was based on the Comet airliner (27.5.48).

than would normally be the case. From a production point of view the wing, empennage (slightly altered to suit the smaller fuselage), main undercarriage, control surfaces and flaps were identical, along with the advantage of jigs and tools already in existence. The bomb bay was designed for a single 10,000lb (4,536kg) or eighteen 1,000lb (454kg) bombs but providing stowage for the specified alternative loads would entail a much larger fuselage. The huge H2S scanner was housed in the nose and needed 'swollen cheeks' in the fuselage to fit. In true Mosquito fashion, DH left out any unnecessary equipment to save weight, and reduced the crew from five to four.

Power came from four DH Ghost engines and a 15% increase in take-off thrust was being explored by the use of water or water-methanol injection. For military service de Havilland Engines expected that using improved hot area materials would allow an appreciable increase over present engine ratings in four to five years' time. A total of

2,400gal (10,913lit) of fuel was in the fuselage and 3,950gal (17,960lit) in the stub wing to give a still air range of 3,720nm (6,893km); take-off wing loading was 51.9lb/sq ft (253.4kg/sq m). Split flaps were used inboard, plain flaps outboard of the engines out to the ailerons, and wing tip leading-edge slats were fitted. The bomb release height when using full engine power was 50,000ft (15,240m).

The RAE and the MoS studied the DH.111 closely and fully re-estimated the weight and performance figures. It was not certain all the equipment could be stored in the proposed body, and stowage of the 10,000lb (4,536kg) special nuclear bomb might lead to difficulties. de Havilland had assumed a streamlined form for the bomb and even then could only stow it by introducing a bend in the rear spar. If provision was needed for the full cylinder, then a deeper fuselage and longer undercarriage might be needed together with engine nacelles and a consequent reduction in the

de Havilland DH.111	
Span	115ft 0in (35.05m)
Length	95ft 0in (28.96m)
Gross wing area	2,024sq ft (188.2sq m)
t/c ratio	11.5%
Gross weight	105,000lb (47,628kg)
Powerplant	four DH Ghost 5,700lb (25.3kN)
Maximum speed/height	518mph (833km/h) at 50,000ft (15,240m) (maximum power)
Weapon load	one 10,000lb (4,536kg) special or HC, two 6,000lb (2,722kg) or eighteen 1,000lb (454kg) bombs

performance. It was estimated that the first DH.111 would not fly inside two and a half years, i.e. about the same time as the Short B.14/46. Initially the MoS considered that this design might make a useful insurance to the other B.35/46 projects, but at the end of September 1948 Air Cdr T. G. Pike, DOR(A), noted that, as there were already five bombers being developed and there was no good advantage in this proposal, he did not consider 'that we should go any further' with it.

ABOVE This view from a rather wet SBAC Farnborough Show in 1957 shows white Vulcan prototype VX770 nearest, a silver production Vulcan alongside, a white Victor behind that and a de Havilland Comet airliner at the end of the row.

BELOW Smartly painted Short Sperrin prototype VX158 at Farnborough in 1951. *Terry Panopalis collection*

ABOVE Views of the first Vickers Valiant prototype WB210 taken at Farnborough in 1951. *Terry Panopalis collection*

ABOVE The all-white colour scheme of Vulcan VX770 contrasts beautifully with the clear blue sky seen at Farnborough in 1954. *Terry Panopalis collection*

BELOW Handley Page Victor B.Mk.2 XL164 displays at Farnborough in 1961. *Terry Panopalis collection*

Chapter Three
V-Bomber Encore

Test Aircraft and Further Developments: 1947 to the 1960s

What were the factors and effects of designing bombers powered by the newly introduced jet engine? Air Cdr G. R. C. Spencer, recently the Commandant of the Central Bomber Establishment, considered these in his March 1948 report, *Implications of the Jet Bomber*. The main limitations with early jet engines were restricted conditions for efficient operation and a high fuel consumption, especially at low altitude. The jet could be comparatively efficient provided it was working under its own conditions of high speed and great height. Although the thrust decreased with height, aircraft drag decreased in greater proportion and both the thermal and overall efficiency of the engine increased appreciably.

Fuel consumption at maximum height for an engine of 6,500lb (28.9kN) thrust was 200gal (909lit) per hour, which meant that a lot of fuel was needed to fly a long way; one problem was that throttling back did not appreciably reduce the consumption. A range of 4,000 to 5,000 miles (6,436km to 8,045km) would need a very big aircraft to hold the large volume of fuel required, about one-third of the total weight, and the bomb load would be a relatively small proportion of this weight. Spencer calculated that a bomber having a bomb load of 20,000lb (9,072kg) and a total engine thrust of 26,000lb (115.6kN) would need 7,500gal (34,102lit) of fuel to achieve a range of 4,500 miles (7,241km); its maximum weight would be about 160,000lb (72,576kg).

From a flying point of view, it was the primary aim of every designer to produce a bomber with as high a Mach number as possible. This gave a good engine efficiency and the lowest possible difference in speed between the bomber and its opposing fighters, thus reducing the chances of interception. If the bomber could get close to the sonic barrier, the fighter could not get much nearer unless it passed through the barrier (a capability that in 1948 was seen to be some time away) and a margin kept within 40mph to 50mph (64km/h to 80km/h) invalidated much of the case for arming the bomber. Removing the defensive armament made the designer's job easier but achieving a high Mach number (0.9 was the objective) brought extra complication to the design, such as the need to use swept wings.

To get the maximum range from a jet aircraft, it would need to climb at full thrust, as steeply as possible, to its operational height. It would then climb gradually to maintain the operational height, which increased as the aircraft became lighter through the consumption of its fuel. Since it was necessary to keep as high as possible for as long as possible, the gradual climb due to decreasing weight had to be maintained on the return flight until it was time to lose height preparatory for landing. Besides these aerodynamic aspects, introducing jet bombers also brought far-reaching, long-term changes in ground organisation and airfield design

The V-bomber story did not end with the entry into service of the types described in Chapter Two; there were also more advanced developments and the scale model test aircraft described in this chapter. Several replica aircraft were built to assist the bombers' development programmes and aviation research overall. As far as possible it was hoped that aerodynamic development problems could be solved in the wind tunnel but, at this time, there was no equipment available in the UK or elsewhere capable of solving every difficulty. Some could only be answered in flight and, in general, it was felt that this could be done at less expense and more quickly by using flying models.

Bristol 174 and 176

The Bristol Type 172 described in Chapter Two was never ordered, but the design was thought sufficiently promising to justify the construction of a scale model. The October 1946 brochure that detailed the bomber had also devoted some space to the Type 174 research model. Judging by past experience of large military aircraft the document noted that the design and construction of the full-scale Type 172 might well occupy two to three years. A considerable time would then be needed for flight trials and development, so a period of four to five years would elapse before the design could be cleared for production. Bristol considered that much time, money and labour could be saved by constructing a half-scale flying model at the outset. This would employ wooden construction and a single Rolls-Royce Nene engine, and it would be used to investigate the design's stability, controllability and manoeuvrability in advance of the full-scale machine. It would carry no military equipment and a mock-up conference would not be required, enabling construction to start immediately drawings were available. Flight trials could commence within twelve months of starting the design and the preliminary results from the model could be available at about the time of the 172 Mock-Up Conference. Any major design changes found necessary by the model could then be introduced at the mock-up stage.

Externally the 174 model was geometrically similar to the full-size Type 172 and the use of wood would facilitate the attainment of a highly polished surface. The Nene was placed amidships in the body with dual intakes in the leading edge of the wing and dual jet pipes discharging at the trailing edge. Both intakes and jet pipes were located in the same positions as the full-scale machine to enable the same aerodynamic conditions to be set up around the centreplane and tail. However, the effective thrust from this installation was rather less than the model would require to reach the full-scale speed, but this deficiency could be made up by diving. The flying controls would be electrically operated and the engine could be removed from the aircraft by using doors in the belly, for

BELOW When the V-bomber programme began AWA already had a flying wing scale model test vehicle under way for bombers and large aircraft in general. The first AW.52, serial TS363, flew on 13 November 1947 and this view shows the aircraft in slow flight with everything down. The AW.52 was a beautiful aeroplane. *Phil Butler*

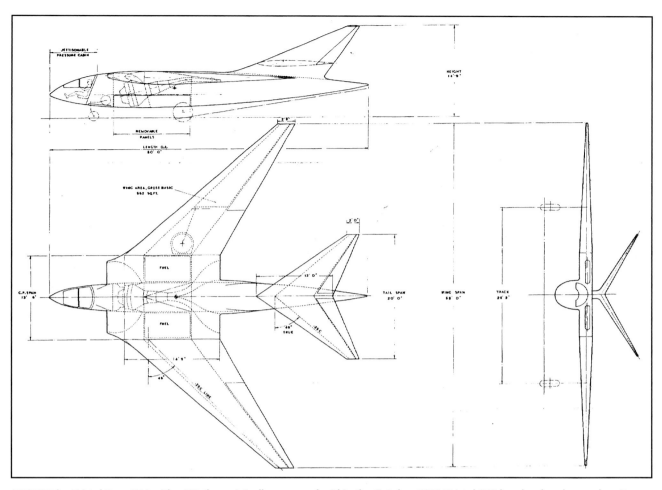

ABOVE The Bristol Type 174 with a V-tail as originally proposed within the October 1946 Bristol 172 bomber brochure, when it was just called the 'Bomber Scale Model (23.10.46). Note the angle at which the Nene engine is positioned. *Rolls-Royce Heritage, Bristol*

which it would be necessary to place the aircraft over a pit. Owing to its much lower weight, the 174 did not require the tandem wheels used by the 172, a conventional tricycle undercarriage being fitted with single main wheels retracting sideways and a single nosewheel retracting backwards. The scale machine was to have 574gal (2,610lit) of internal fuel and the initial plans called for an orthodox swept tail and fin, but a 172-style swept V-tail would be introduced later. It was also proposed to investigate at a later date the effect of boundary layer suction on the model. Wing sweep angle was 45° and a further objective was to obtain more high- and low-speed swept wing knowledge overall.

Two Type 174 four-tenths scale flying models, serials VX317 and VX323, were ordered in May 1947 to Specification

E.8/47 and OR.250, possibly the first contract to be placed in regard to OR.229 and OR.230. Work began at Bristol in 1947 and reached the stage of loft plates and tooling, and a shop was allocated for manufacture, but the effort was halted when the wing/body junction shape was found to be unsatisfactory. The project was eventually replaced by a second aircraft called the Type 176. The efficiency of the 174's powerplant installation, with the sharp angles needed to get the intake air to the Nene, has been questioned.

The later Type 176 three-tenths scale model was to be powered by one of the first production Rolls-Royce Avons and had a limiting Mach number of 0.92. E.8/47 was raised to Issue II in May 1948 to cover the airframes, the first having provision for alternative wing tips, an all-moving tail

and at least 360gal (1,637lit) of internal fuel. In time Bristol saw this project more as a pure research aircraft in its own right and gave little further thought to putting the Type 172 into production, despite the opinion of T. G. Pike, DOR(A), that a limited number of 172s should be built if the model proved its worth. The designer in charge of the 176 project was Barry Laight and the aircraft's purpose became quite simply to fly an aeroplane with swept wings. The Swept Wings Advisory Committee met industry and research representatives at the Royal Aeronautical Society to discuss progress nationally and reported that Bristol's role was to obtain some practical flight experience.

The 176's layout was the simplest arrangement for flying these swept wings, the nose intake was split around

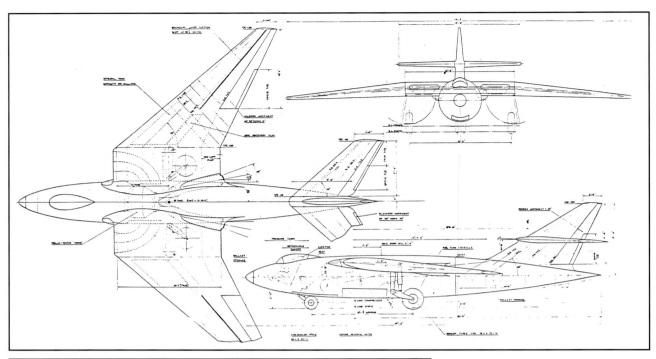

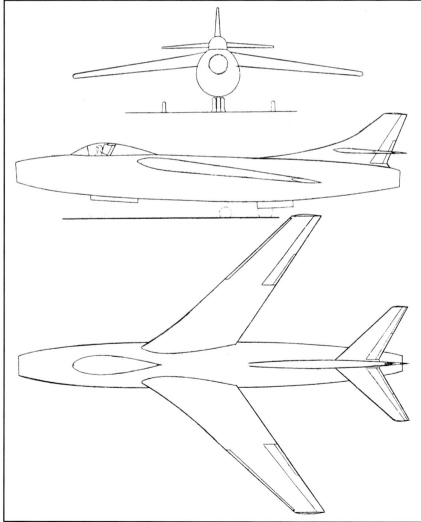

ABOVE In its final form the Bristol 174 had acquired a fighter-type canopy and anhedral to the outer wings (4.11.47). The span here is 45ft 9in (13.94m), wing area wing 442sq ft (41.1sq m), wing t/c ratio 12.5%.

LEFT Bristol Type 176 (5.1.48). A drawing dated 1 January 1948 showed a deeper fuselage to house an additional small Armstrong Siddeley Adder jet for boundary-layer suction. *Duncan Greenman, Bristol AIRchive*

the single-seat cockpit, and because of the limited wing thickness a bicycle undercarriage had to be used. Take-off wing loading would be 56.3lb/sq ft (274.8kg/sq m). Work stopped after the Mock-Up Conference in October 1948 and the project was cancelled in 1949 to release funds for other developments. A memo from C. B. Baker at the MoS, dated October 1953, noted that Bristol had 'lost interest and the project was cancelled at the company's request'. Barry Laight told the author that the 176 had possibly overcooked the sweep at 45° when the planform, section, twist and tip foils, and the effects of flaps, ailerons and spoilers, were all new and uncharted areas of design.

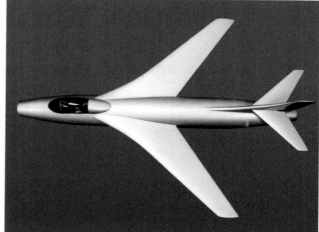

ABOVE Display model of the Bristol 176.
RIGHT Close up nose detail for the Type 176 model.

Bristol Type 174 (10.46)	
Span	45ft 9in (13.94m)
Length	47ft 2in (14.38m)
Gross wing area	435sq ft (40.5sq m)
t/c ratio	12.5%
Gross weight	26,000lb (11,749kg)
Powerplant	one RR Nene 5,500lb (24.4kN)
Maximum speed/height	High subsonic
Weapon load	None

Bristol Type 176	
Span	33ft 0in (10.06m)
Length	46ft 0in (14.02m)
Gross wing area	217sq ft (20.2sq m)
t/c ratio	?
Gross weight	12,200lb (5,534kg)
Powerplant	one RR Avon 6,500lb (28.9kN)
Maximum speed/height	Mach 0.92
Weapon load	None

Short S.B.1 and P.D.10

Despite Shorts' S.B.1 being rejected, the company persevered with its 'aero-isoclinic' wing studies and constructed a one-third scale glider, which also was designated S.B.1. Designer Keith-Lucas was satisfied that there was much to commend Geoffrey Hill's wing proposal but realised the research to prove it must be planned carefully. The glider was towed into the air on 14 July 1951 but crashed on its second flight. Rebuilt with Turboméca Palas jets, it became the S.B.4 Sherpa and first flew under its own power on 4 October 1953.

In July 1953 a follow-on high-speed transonic research vehicle called the P.D.10 was proposed using a Supermarine Swift fighter fuselage fitted with a set of aero-isoclinic wings and all-moving tip controls. This was to have been built for general research but was also directly relevant to jet bomber proposals from Short Brothers. A flight trials programme would verify a number of claims made for this type of wing and Shorts also felt this aircraft might prove to be a very useful fighter with outstanding manoeuvrability and performance at high altitude. The estimated time from ITP to first flight was given as seventy-eight weeks and a mock-up would comprise one full-size wing plus part of the fuselage at the wing attachment. An angle of 47.5° of sweep at the leading edge was slightly more than had been built into any British aeroplane so far but, apart from cropping the tailplane span, the Swift fuselage was to be altered as little as possible. Powerplant was a single afterburning Avon RA.7R and the P.D.10 was expected to reach Mach 1.2 in a 30° dive; its predicted sea level rate of climb was 6,560ft/min (2,000m/min). The P.D.10 was not ordered.

BELOW Shorts' scale model glider for its B.35/46 S.B.1 bomber project also began life with the S.B.1 designation. It first flew on 14 July 1951.

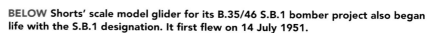

ABOVE AND RIGHT The S.B.1 was rebuilt as the S.B.4 Sherpa with two small jets and flew again on 4 October 1953. It is seen on display at the September 1954 Farnborough Show. The airborne view shows the wing tip controllers to advantage. *Terry Panopalis*

LEFT Artist's impression of the P.D.10. *Shorts*

BELOW General arrangement of the Shorts P.D.10 high speed aero-isoclinic wing research proposal (7.53). *Shorts*

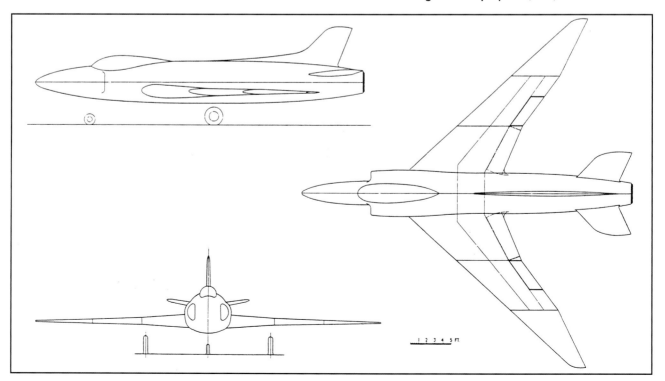

Short P.D.10	
Span	43ft 0in (13.11m)
Length	41ft 6in (12.65m)
Gross wing area	317sq ft (29.5sq m)
t/c ratio	root 13.6%, first kink 10%, second kink 9%, tip 6%
Gross weight	17,000lb (7,711kg)
Powerplant	one RR Avon RA.7R
Maximum speed/height	716mph (1,152km/h) Mach 0.97 at 10,000ft (3,048m), 677mph (1,089km/h) Mach 1.0 above 30,000ft (9,144m)
Weapon load	None

Handley Page HP.88 (Flown)	
Span	40ft 0in (12.19m)
Length	39ft 10in (12.14m)
Gross wing area	286sq ft (26.6sq m)
t/c ratio	14% root, 5% tip
Gross weight	13,197lb (5,986kg)
Powerplant	one Nene R.N.2 5,000lb (22.2kN)
Maximum speed/height	c. Mach 0.85
Weapon load	None

Handley Page HP.88

In April 1948 a contract was issued for Handley Page to build two two-fifths scale models of its bomber called the HP.88. This became very much a combined effort by several companies and followed the abandonment of the HP.87 one-third scale glider. Since HP had insufficient drawing office capacity, the detail design was sub-contracted to General Aircraft, where the type was called the GAL.63. Soon afterwards General merged with Blackburn and the aircraft was retitled Y.B.2, the design work moving from Feltham to Brough. One example was cancelled on 14 October 1949 for economy but the second, VX330, was completed to Specification E.6/48. HP's Reg Stafford visited Supermarine's design office at Hursley Park, where it was agreed to use an Attacker fighter's fuselage for the HP.88, but late in February 1948 this was changed to a modified type similar to Supermarine's Type 510 because the fuel tanks were compatible with swept wings (Supermarine called the project the Type 521). VX330 first flew on 21 June 1951, but broke up in the air during a flight on 26 August.

Avro 710 and 707

Avro's B.35/46 Development Brochure of 6 April 1948 (Chapter Two) gave the first details of delta flying scale models. To investigate the remaining aerodynamic problems surrounding the operation of the delta aircraft at the Mach numbers and altitude required (in particular control and drag reduction at high speed), it was proposed to build a half-scale model called the Avro 710. This would enable a check on performance, control and stability to be made and, using the maximum continuous cruise power of its twin Avon powerplant, this aircraft was expected to be capable of cruising at the bomber's specified speed of 575mph (925km/h) at up to 60,000ft (18,288m) if required. The 710 would be a true model (with certain minor deviations) and had the all-moving pointed wing tips outside the fins introduced to the 698 at this stage. Sea level climb rate was predicted to be 8,250ft/min (2,515m/min) using a constant EAS of 224mph (360km/h) but much higher climb rates, particularly near sea level, would be possible by using higher speeds. The 710 had 820gal (3,728lit) of fuel in the wings and would fly twenty-one months from its start date.

Simulating the full-scale aircraft much less closely, a smaller one-third scale Avro 707 would assess the equivalent problems at low speeds and altitudes. If any low-speed and low-altitude control and stability problems could not be overcome, then the high-speed qualities of the 698 were of no practical significance. The idea was to make the 707 far easier to produce than the all-metal 710 by using mostly wood construction together with existing standard items such as the undercarriage and controls, and in such simple form it would not be designed to high-speed parameters. Using a Rolls-Royce Derwent V engine, the performance was expected to be 400mph (644km/h) at up to 10,000ft (3,048m), enabling all preliminary aerodynamic investigations

BELOW The Handley Page HP.88 flew on 21 June 1951 but tragically crashed two months later. It was painted royal blue with the roundels and lettering outlined in silver. This is one of the very few air-to-air photos taken of the aircraft. *BAE SYSTEMS, Brough*

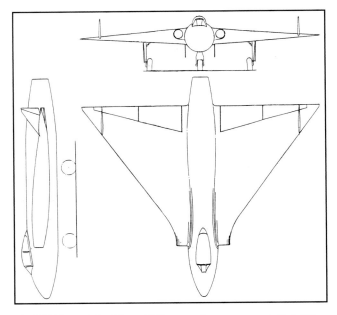

ABOVE The original Avro 707 general arrangement (6.4.48).

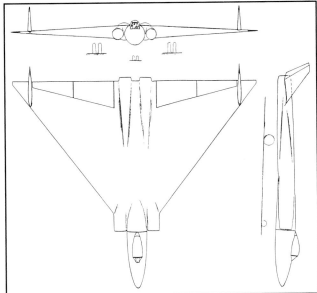

ABOVE Avro 710 (6.4.48).

ABOVE Avro 707 prototype VX784 seen in September 1949.
BELOW The Avro 707A prototype WD280 replaced the Type 710 as a 'high-speed' scale model test aircraft.

ABOVE Blue-painted Avro 707B VX790 was used to investigate the low-speed stability of delta wings. It was first flown in September 1950 and is seen here at the 1954 Farnborough Show. *Terry Panopalis*

to be undertaken in flight, particularly the problems concerning the landing of the delta aircraft. A first flight was expected in about a year.

By 6 April 1948 Avro had begun work on both models. This lengthy programme of development using flying scale aircraft was felt to be justified because it enabled knowledge to be gathered as quickly as possible that was not obtainable by any other means. There would be no mock-ups of these scale models. J E Serby was enthusiastic about the rapid-build 707 since it offered knowledge quickly and would push enthusiasm for the delta bomber, which was a very revolutionary design. An ITP was given for both models on 8

June with serials VX799 and VX808 allocated to the 710s and VX784 and VX790 to the 707s, and a contract letter was sent to Avro on 6 July for two 707s (and two 698 prototypes).

However, in July RAE suggested that the 710 design job would be nearly as big and as difficult as a proposed full-size 'flying shell' 698,

ABOVE **WD280 in orange in a view taken in September 1954. Note the wing root intakes.** *Terry Panopalis*

and both scale models were useless from the structural standpoint. They considered that the 710 should be dropped and on the 26 Serby wrote to Avro suggesting it was quicker to do just the one model – did Avro agree? Avro's W. S. Farren gave his support to this move on 14 September and suggested increasing the 707s to three by adding a high Mach number machine with a different intake and stiffer structure. There were insufficient staff to handle all the projects simultaneously, the 710 would seriously delay the full

prototype, while developments on the 698 made it more difficult to reproduce certain essential features sufficiently closely, or at all, on the 710. In fact, Farren felt the move would advance the full 698 prototype by a year and the new plan was accepted. Avro designer J. G. Willis had prepared the additional one-third scale 707 by 26 October 1948 and explained that the aircraft seemed quite strong enough to operate to the same Mach number limits as the 698. Serby agreed this change to the programme would save time, though

the half-scale machine was not finally cancelled until 15 February 1949. The 'flying shell' 698 (to E.11/49) was also dropped. Specification E.15/48 was raised to cover the two original 707s, the first flying on 4 September 1949 with a single fin, and E.10/49 covered three further examples that were eventually built.

Returning to the three V-bombers themselves, further variants were proposed to fulfil a specific role or to give more general improvements in capability. Some of these were built but others stayed on the drawing board.

BELOW **VX790 pictured in flight. This aircraft had its air intake positioned over the rear fuselage.**

ABOVE The Avro 707s were famous for their vivid colour schemes. Here from left to right we have VX790 (blue), WD280 (red) and WZ736 (orange) pictured at Farnborough. *Terry Panopalis*

Avro 707 (at 6.4.48)	
Span	33ft 0in (10.06m)
Length	30ft 0in (9.14m)
Gross wing area	not given
t/c ratio	not given
Gross weight	7,972lb (3,616kg)
Powerplant	one RR Derwent
Maximum speed/height	400mph (644km/h) up to 10,000ft (3,048m)
Weapon load	None

Avro 710 (at 6.4.48)	
Span	49ft 0in (14.94m)
Length	44ft 9in (13.64m)
Gross wing area	not given
t/c ratio	not given
Gross weight	19,651lb (8,914kg)
Powerplant	two RR Avon 6,500lb (28.9kN)
Maximum speed/height	575mph (925km/h) up to 60,000ft (18,288m)
Weapon load	None

Avro 707 (VX784 flown)	
Span	33ft 0in (10.06m)
Length	40ft 2.25in (12.25m)
Gross wing area	366.5sq ft (34.1sq m)
t/c ratio	not given
Gross weight	8,600lb (3,901kg)
Powerplant	one RR Derwent 5 3,500lb (15.6kN)
Maximum speed/height	403mph (648km/h)
Weapon load	None

BELOW The final Avro scale model was 707C WZ744, which was painted silver and here is pictured at RAF Coltishall in October 1964. This aircraft was a two-seater. *via Terry Panopalis*

Vickers Type 673 Pathfinder

The Valiant B.Mk.1 was the only variant of the type to reach a squadron but in September 1948 Vickers proposed a target marker version intended to fly over its target at low level (5,000ft [1,524m]) and high speed. At the time this was a very forward-looking idea since bombers were expected to fly at ever higher altitudes. Due to the structural loads involved with flight at sea level the Valiant Mk.1 was limited to 414mph (666km/h), whereas the 673 would be stressed to fly much faster. In August 1949 the company proposed a bicycle undercarriage for this aircraft but it was not adopted. OR.285 was raised for the Pathfinder in July 1950, for introduction into service concurrently with the other V-bombers, and specification B.104D was issued along with the first prototype order in November. The aircraft was to perform both target marking and bombing and became the Valiant B.Mk.2. Carriage of the Blue Boar guided bomb was stated in January 1952 having been added to OR.229 in February 1950.

In January 1949 Vickers reported that the first Valiant Mk.1 prototype was to have Avon engines, the second Sapphires, the nacelles in both aircraft being capable of taking either type without modification. There was the possibility of replacing them later with the Bristol Olympus or Rolls-Royce Conway. In April 1951 it was agreed that the first Mk.2 should have Avon RA.14s and a contract for twenty-four Mk.1 aircraft and seventeen Mk.2s was placed in October. The major changes on the Type 673 B.Mk.2 from the B.Mk.1 were a considerably strengthened wing and load-bearing structure for higher speeds, a new undercarriage, an extended forward fuselage for extra equipment and a revised bomb aimer's blister (a later long-range version would have extended wing tips and Conway engines). It was the undercarriage that showed the most obvious external difference to the original with its four-wheel main gears retracting backwards into underslung pods outboard of the jet pipes.

The programme seemed to be progressing smoothly but in September 1952 the Air Ministry withdrew OR.285 on economy grounds, though it was agreed to finish the Mk.2 prototype (which was 60% complete) to assist Mk.1 clearance and to convert the Mk.2 order into B.Mk.1s. A dedicated photo reconnaissance Valiant to OR.279 with larger wings and Conway engines was also dropped and replaced by a simple modification to the B.Mk.1. Ironically, a submission was made to the Treasury the following month for another fifty-six B.Mk.1s; this was granted in April 1953 but as fifty-three B.Mk.1s and nine B(PR).Mk.1s. The requirement to carry Blue Boar in any Valiant was cancelled in August 1953 but the B.Mk.2 prototype, WJ954, flew on 4 September and in the following August began RATO trials in support of the Mk.1. It was scrapped in August 1958.

ABOVE **WJ954 taxis out for a test flight.**

A paper dated 27 April 1956 considered the Valiant as a specialised low-level bomber and concluded that the B.Mk.1 did not approach the Air Staff's requirements in any respect. The Valiant 2 had the required speed at low level with a performance approximating closely to the requirements but its range was only 50% of the stated limit, while the carriage of the new 'powered inertia bombs' (Blue Steel) would necessitate a major redesign. However, such a development would give a 30% saving in cost over a more specialised aircraft and the report recommended that a small number of Valiant 2s should be ordered to improve the low-level threat.

This plan was never implemented.

However, due to the introduction of SAMs and other advanced enemy defences, most bombers were eventually forced to fly at low level and the Valiant was no exception. In 1964 those still serving in the strike role were switched to low-level operations, but by mid-year fatigue cracks had been discovered in both the front and rear spars of some aircraft. Any rebuilding was rejected and the decision was taken in January 1965 to scrap almost the entire fleet, including tanker conversions. It has always been assumed that had the order for Valiant B.Mk.2s been completed this situation would not have arisen, but in

Vickers Valiant B.Mk.2 Pathfinder (Flown)	
Span	114ft 4in (34.85m)
Length	108ft 3in (32.99m)
Gross wing area	?
t/c ratio	12% to 8%
Gross weight	196,492lb (89,129kg)
Powerplant	four RR Avon RA.14 10,000lb (44.4kN)
Maximum speed/height	552mph (888km/h) at sea level
Weapon load	one 10,000lb (4,536kg), two 5,000lb (2,268kg), twenty-one 1,000lb (454kg) bombs, one 10,000lb Blue Boar or two 5,000lb Blue Boar

fact the planned order for the B.Mk.2 was just seventeen aeroplanes and so sufficient low-level Valiants would not have been available anyway.

BELOW **The gleaming Black Valiant on the runway at Farnborough in 1954.** *Terry Panopalis*

Vickers Low-Level and Supersonic Valiant Developments

There were proposals for supersonic versions of each V-bomber. In January 1952 Vickers undertook a combined preliminary investigation for two separate Valiant developments, a dedicated low-level bomber and a supersonic bomber.

The former would operate at relatively low level throughout and carry 10,000lb (4,536kg) of bombs at Mach 0.85 over 4,300nm (7,964km). It was designed around the Valiant Mk.2 but had modified mainplanes and a 10ft (3.05m) extension to the forward fuselage to make room for more fuel. The wing sweep was increased to improve the critical Mach number and a larger tail was necessary to cope with the increased main chord. Any engine from the current 9,000lb to 12,000lb (40kN to 53.3kN) class could be accommodated but the maximum take-

off weight was 250,000lb (113,400kg) when the range needed a weight of 306,000lb (138,802kg), so the extra fuel would be taken from a tanker after take-off. Cruise speed at top weight with drop tanks was 600mph (965km/h) and without tanks over the target at 200,000lb (90,720kg) it was 652mph (1,049km/h). To reach these speeds needed a total thrust of 28,000lb (124.4kN) which was just possible using four Avon RA.14s, but the Conway's unfavourable thrust/speed characteristics would currently only develop about 21,000lb (93,3kN). The initial rate of climb was 1,050ft/min (320m/min) at 306,000lb (138,802kg) weight and 3,320ft/min (1,012m/min) at 200,000lb (90,720kg).

The long-range, high-altitude Valiant development was capable of sustained supersonic speed. With four Conway Co.3s, 2,000°K reheat and take-off at 177,000lb (80,287kg) weight it could reach Mach 1.41 at 50,000ft (15,240m) or Mach 1.2 at the absolute ceiling of 58,000ft (17,678m). Still air range at

Mach 0.95 cruise was 3,640nm (6,741km) giving an over-the-target height of 41,000ft (12,497m). If 500nm (926km) was flown supersonically this reduced the range to 1,930nm (3,574km), but drop tanks would increase these figures to 4,440nm (8,223km) and 2,630nm (4,871km) respectively while reducing the maximum Mach number to 1.43 at 36,000ft (10,973m). The engines were cantilevered from the rear spar and fed by intakes that passed under the wing to leave the primary structure unbroken. If maximum rpm was used without reheat for a take-off at 177,000lb (80,287kg), then 700mph (1,126km/h) Mach 0.99 would be possible at 20,000ft (6,096m) and 672mph (1,082km/h) Mach 1.02 at 36,000ft (10,973m).

These projects were prepared as a result of informal discussions between Vickers and the Air Staff and represented preliminary examinations without detail work. The Ministry felt both were indicative of the type of aircraft that could be produced to meet

BELOW Vickers Low-Level Bomber (1.52).

BELOW Vickers Supersonic 'Valiant' (1.52).

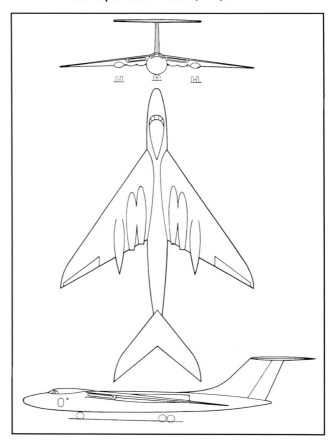

these roles and the low-level bomber in particular was considered a practical proposition. However, Air Commodore G. Silyn-Roberts described them both as 'very sketchy'.

Vickers Low-Level Valiant

Span	81ft 0in (24.69m)
Length	124ft 6in (37.95m)
Gross wing area	2,150sq ft (200.0sq m)
t/c ratio	Not given
Gross weight	306,000lb (138,802kg)
Powerplant	See text
Maximum speed/height	652mph (1,049km/h) between 2,500ft (762m) and 7,500ft (2,286m)
Weapon load	one 10,000lb (4,536kg) or various smaller

Vickers Supersonic Valiant

Span	85ft 0in (25.91m)
Length	130ft 0in (39.62m)
Gross wing area	2,000sq ft (186.0sq m)
t/c ratio	5%
Gross weight	177,000lb (80,287kg), or 207,000lb (93,895kg) with tanks
Powerplant	four RR Conway Co.3
Maximum speed/height	1,013mph (1,630km/h) Mach 1.33 at sea level, 979mph (1,575km/h) Mach 1.48 at 36,000ft (10,973m)
Weapon load	one 10,000lb (4,536kg) or various smaller

Vickers Type 722 Valiant Mk.3

In May 1952 the company proposed a Mk.3 Valiant as a replacement for the Mks.1 and 2. Essentially a standard Mk.1, it had a more highly swept wing and a Mk.2 chassis, and could fulfil the bomber, reconnaissance or Pathfinder roles. It was designed for a diving speed of 449mph (722km/h) EAS but, due to compressibility losses at sea level, this figure became 501mph (806km/h) when acting as a Pathfinder. On the level at 124,200lb (56,337kg) weight it could reach 564mph (907km/h) at 45,000ft (13,716m). The normal built-in tankage gave a range with a 10,000lb (4,536kg) bomb of 5,100nm (9,450km) and with drop tanks this rose to

RIGHT **Vickers Type 722 Valiant Mk.3 (5.52).**

6,440nm (11,933km). Sea level rate of climb at 132,700lb (60,193kg) weight was 4,900ft/min (1,494m/min) and service ceiling 48,000ft (14,630m).

Vickers Valiant Mk.3

Span	108ft 9in (33.15m)
Length	108ft 2in (32.97m)
Gross wing area	2,270sq ft (211.1sq m)
t/c ratio	12% root, 8.45% tip
Gross weight	188,541lb (85,522kg)
Powerplant	four RR Conway 11,500lb (51.1kN)
Maximum speed/height	501mph (806km/h) at sea level, 616mph (991km/h) at 20,000ft (6,096m)
Weapon load	10,000lb (4,536kg) normal, up to 41,000lb (18,598kg) with reduced fuel

Victor and Vulcan B.Mk.2s

By 1954 the Air Staff had become increasingly concerned about the vulnerability of the V-bombers and so asked the manufacturers to study seriously to what extent the aircraft could be developed. Little in the way of improvement in speed was likely so the effort concentrated on improving the height performance. Developing the Victor involved increasing the span by 10ft (3.05m), increasing the chord and the centre section of the wing, and increasing the size of the engine intakes to cater for more powerful engines so that thrusts up to 17,500lb (77.8kN) could be fully absorbed. Handley Page called this the Phase 2A wing and the type entered service as the B.Mk.2, the first aircraft flying on 20 February 1959.

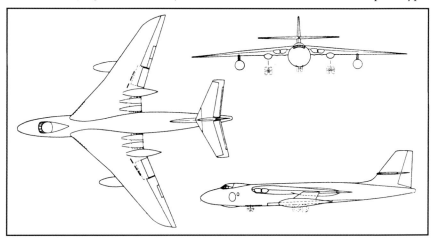

An April 1956 report looked at fitting the Bristol Olympus 6 (16,000lb [71.1kN]), Olympus 7 (17,300lb [76.9kN]), Rolls-Royce Conway Stage 2 (14,500lb [64.4kN]) or Conway Stage 3 (16,500lb [73.3kN]) to both Mk.2 Victors and Vulcans; the Olympus gave a slight edge with height, the Conway in range. There was a long debate regarding the merits of each engine since installing greater power in the V-bombers meant plenty of redesign to accommodate them (the two engines are discussed later). The decision to fit Conways in the Victor, instead of the Sapphire 9, was made in December 1955 along with a ruling that the new wing should be developed and introduced as soon as possible. The units fitted were 17,250lb (76.7kN) Conway.Mk.103s but engine surge problems postponed the first flight from its August 1958 schedule. Deliveries began on 1 November 1961 and later aircraft had 20,600lb (91.6kN) Conway 201s.

Improving the Vulcan B.Mk.2 involved extending and cambering the wing leading edge, thinning the outer wing and increasing both chord and span. This enabled local airflow velocities to be kept subsonic up to a higher aircraft Mach number, thereby delaying the separation and consequent buffeting as lift was increased. Engine thrusts up to 17,500lb (77.8kN) could then be fully absorbed. Avro called this the Phase 2C wing, it was proposed in August 1955 and the manufacturer turned the second Vulcan prototype,

ABOVE Vulcan prototype VX777 was from 1956 fitted with the larger wing to be used by the B.Mk.2. As the Mk.2 aerodynamic prototype it first flew in this form on 31 August 1957.

VX777, into a Mk.2 aerodynamic test vehicle, flying it on 31 August 1957 with the new wing and Olympus jet pipes. The first production aircraft flew on 30 August 1958 with 16,000lb (71.1kN) Olympus 200s that were selected for the type in June 1957, while later machines had the 17,000lb (75.6kN) Mk.201 or 20,000lb (88.9kN) Mk.301. The earliest Vulcan had been designed to reach Mach 0.95 in a shallow dive but Phase 2C was stressed to cover Mach 1.0.

The Vulcan and Victor programmes were split into Phases. Vulcan Phase 1 was the basic airframe as exemplified by the second prototype and early production aircraft and Phase 2 had a drooped 20% chordwise extension to part of the outer wing, giving maximum improvement for minimum structural alteration. This was tested on an Avro 707 and showed increased lift coefficient at the buffet threshold, but as more powerful engines became available a more extensive modification was required. Further modifications called Phase 2A and 2B were superseded by Phase 2C. Phase 3 would have had an entirely new and thinner outer wing constructed of honeycomb sandwich, a new main undercarriage capable of operating at take-off weights up to 220,000lb (99,792kg) and increased fuel capacity. It was proposed in February 1955 along with either Olympus 6 or 7s, Super Sapphires or a Conway 5 development; gross weights were 100,494lb, 101,143lb, 100,449lb or 98,553lb (45,584kg, 45,878kg, 45,564kg or 44,704kg) respectively (the proposed 'Super' Sapphire offered 50% more thrust at 50,000ft [15,240m] and 575mph [926km/h] than the Sa.9). Phase 3's weakness was the amount of redesign required and so Phase 2C was adopted to give the same improvement in buffet threshold but without the severe structural modifications. The altitude performance was very similar to Phase 3 but the latter's outstanding range was lost.

ABOVE Handley Page Victor Mk.2 XL512 with a Blue Steel round on board. Note the fairings on the wing trailing edge.
Crown Copyright

The transition to the Victor and Vulcan B.Mk.2s was helped by limited improvements made to each B.Mk.1 as B.Mk.1As. An improved ceiling would be valuable for survival against current fighter developments while the modest increase in range, a mere 200 to 350nm (370 to 648km), actually increased the number of targets that could be attacked by 25%. In 1957 it was predicted that by 1960/61 the Soviets would have surface-to-air guided weapon (SAGW) defences and so the V-bombers would then need to carry the Blue Steel stand-off bomb to hit targets from outside SAGW range; later on the longer-range Blue Steel Mk.2 powered bomb to OR.1159 was to be introduced (which in fact was never carried). The extra weight of these weapons and other planned equipment would require engine thrusts of around 20,000lb (88.9kN). Carriage of Blue Steel was proposed for B.Mk.1 Vulcans in February 1957 but the centre section front spar was not cranked on these aircraft, which made it impossible to submerge the missile beneath the

fuselage as much as on Mk.2 aeroplanes. This had an adverse effect on performance and drag and so the weapon was carried on the later mark only, becoming operational in 1963.

In September 1956 the Air Staff discussed removing either Vulcan or Victor B.Mk.2 from the RAF programme, depending on the size of the V-Force that could be afforded after the forthcoming Defence Policy Review. After April 1957 the extra equipment fitted in Mk.2 V-bombers would bring substantial increases in expenditure but more money was expected to be available after that year's Defence White Paper had cancelled most of Britain's fighter projects. However, twenty-five of the fifty-seven Victor B.Mk.2s on order were cancelled in July 1960, although South Africa did consider buying Mk.2s in October 1961 to use up components made redundant by the smaller order.

This reduction came from the adoption of the American Skybolt as Britain's principal deterrent weapon instead of the Blue Streak ballistic missile,

a major change to defence policy announced by the Minister of Defence, Harold Watkinson, on 13 April 1960. It was felt that the Mk.2 Vulcan would technically make a better Skybolt carrier and this became policy in July, though Handley Page told the MoA on 15 July that the Victor Mk.2 could 'carry two Skybolt missiles without modifications to the aircraft or missile to improve ground clearance'. An easy Phase I conversion could permit a Victor Mk.2 to carry two missiles for fourteen hours, while Phase II modifications would increase the load to four with the same duration and gain CA Release by 1964/65. A satisfactory take-off performance up to 285,000lb (129,276kg) gross weight would be provided by reheated 20,000lb (88.9kN) thrust Conway 17s, while two Spectre rockets could be added to permit even higher weights.

The Skybolt Vulcan was proposed in May 1960 as the Phase 6 and was basically a package of modifications designed to be applied retrospectively to the Mk.2. It would use Olympus 21 or

Avro Vulcan B.Mk.2 (Flown)	
Span	111ft 0in (33.83m)
Length	105ft 6in (32.16m)
Gross wing area	3,964sq ft (368.6sq m)
t/c ratio	10% root, 5% tip
Gross weight	204,000lb (92,534kg)
Powerplant	four Bristol Olympus 201 17,000lb (75.6kN)
Maximum speed/height	640mph (1,030km/h) at height
Weapon load	one Blue Steel or twenty-one 1,000lb (454kg) bombs

Handley Page Victor B.Mk.2 (Flown)	
Span	120ft 0in (36.58m)
Length	114ft 11in (35.03m)
Gross wing area	2,597sq ft (241.5sq m)
T/c ratio	?
Gross weight	233,000lb (105,689kg)
Powerplant	four RR Conway 103 17,250lb (76.7kN)
Maximum speed/height	645mph (1,038km/h) at 40,000ft (12,192m)
Weapon load	one Blue Steel or thirty-five 1,000lb (454kg) bombs

2½ engines with reheat, the existing intakes and bay installation and carry four GAM-87A Skybolt missiles on underwing pylons (2½ had the larger turbine of TSR.2's Olympus 22 to give the same performance as the later engine). Other changes included a new wing with greater area and span, an integral tank outboard and bag tanks inboard in the wing, new inner elevons with the existing outer elevons, a dorsal fuel tank behind the canopy, local stiffening of the centre section, fin height increased by 3ft (91cm) and a new main undercarriage with a four-tyre bogie to meet the higher gross weight. With Olympus 21/2s, 21,940gal (99,759lit) of fuel and four missiles the gross weight would be 339,168lb (153,847kg). Span was 121ft 0in (36.88m), length 99ft 11in (30.46m) and wing area 4,215sq ft (392sq m).

Skybolt was 38ft (11.58m) long and weighed 12,000lb (5,443kg).

A Vulcan/Skybolt modification programme, with OR.1187 covering the weapon, was prepared in October 1960 and the first aircraft was to be delivered in March 1963. However, by July 1961 this had still not been agreed between the Air Ministry and MoA, and Treasury approval was still limited to £1m. The first flight of a Vulcan B.Mk.2 carrying two captive mechanical Skybolts was successfully completed on 29 September 1961 with the first successful dummy drops following in December. Eventually, through development problems and rising costs, the Americans cancelled Skybolt and Britain was forced to do the same in December 1962. It was replaced by the submarine-launched Polaris ballistic missile.

Further Vulcan Development Proposals

The Vulcan Phase 5 of November 1956 carried the proposed Avro W.107 powered missile to OR.1149. Missile weight was 23,000lb (10,433kg) and take-off weight with either 20,290lb (90.2kN) Olympus Ol.21s or 20,000lb (88.9kN) Conway Co.31s came to either 223,535lb (101,395kg) or 225,000lb (102,060kg). Some Ministry documents suggest that V-bombers carrying the OR.1149 missile would have presented a deterrent superior to the Avro 730 (see Chapter Six).

A November 1961 brochure described the Vulcan carrying two, three or four advanced W.140 missiles, an Avro long-range stand-off weapon to OR.1182. This had a slim body 37ft 3in (11.35m) long with a 6ft 6in (1.98m) span delta wing, all-moving elevons for control aft of the wing and a Rolls-Royce RB.153-17 jet. Its launch weight would be 8,550lb (3,878kg) and the Vulcan's gross weight 247,828lb (112,415kg) but take-offs were limited to 210,000lb (95,256kg). If the weapon was launched at Mach 0.84 and 45,000ft (13,716m) then a range of 1,550nm (2,871km) was possible, but this fell to 950nm (1,759km) if the missile flew the last 100nm (185km) at Mach 1.5

BELOW Avro Vulcan Phase 6 with Olympus 21/2 engines and four Skybolts (5.60). *Avro Heritage Centre*

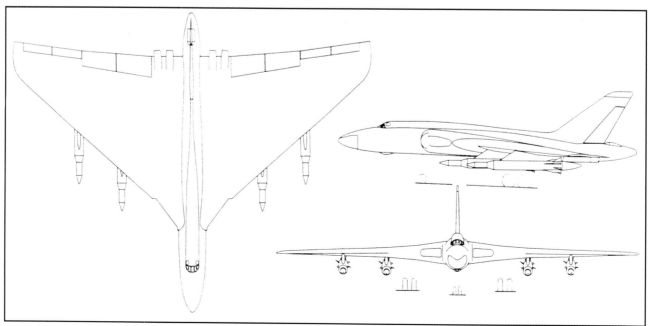

at sea level. W.140 would cruise at Mach 3 at 70,000ft (21,336m).

Anticipating the likely cancellation of Skybolt, in November 1962 the Air Staff considered the procurement of the BAC X-12, which was also known as Pandora. Work on this ramjet-powered weapon had been initiated by the Guided Weapons Division of Bristol Aircraft prior to the formation of BAC in 1960. Proposals dated 3 January 1963 showed a Vulcan carrying two X-12s on hefty pylons just outboard of the main wheels. Designed to meet OR.1182, this low-level stand-off bomb had a slim 50ft (15.24m) long fuselage of just 3ft 2in (0.97m) diameter and small delta wings 15ft (4.57m) long and 6ft (1.83m) span. The latter, and a semi-integrated BS.10-13 ramjet optimised for Mach 2.5, were mounted around the rear fuselage, a 28ft (8.5m) mid-fuselage section housed the fuel and the nose contained the warhead and guidance. At 20,000lb (9,072kg) weight X-12's range would have been at least 1,000nm (1,852km), its maximum ceiling was expected to be 70,000ft to 76,000ft (21,336m to 23,165m) and, initially, a cruising speed of Mach 4 had been planned. The projected in-service date was 1966.

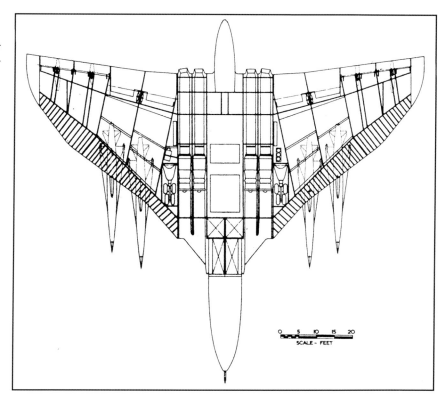

ABOVE Avro Vulcan B.Mk.2 adapted to carry four W.140 missiles (11.61).

BELOW This proposed Vulcan B.Mk.2 development had a fuselage spine to provide extra fuel and extended range (10.57).

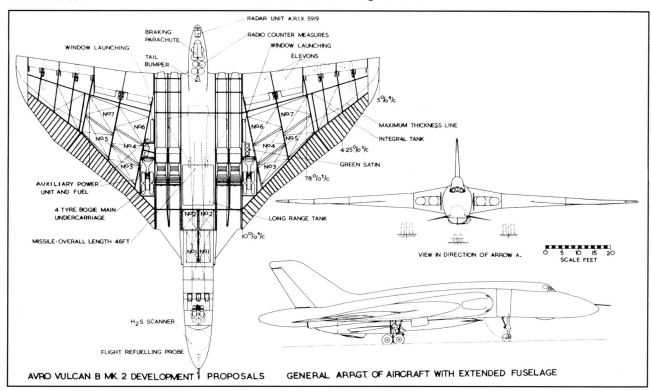

AVRO VULCAN B MK.2 DEVELOPMENT PROPOSALS   GENERAL ARRGT. OF AIRCRAFT WITH EXTENDED FUSELAGE

Another modification to the basic Vulcan suggested fitting two extra engines, cold Olympus 3s, on small nacelles two-thirds of the way out on the wing to provide more thrust, but this also reduced the range and increased drag. An alternative was to bury them behind and below the four normal power units which, coupled with thinner outer wings of 5% t/c, it was predicted would increase the drag rise Mach number by at least 0.02 from 0.87.

Finally, an October 1957 brochure suggested a way of keeping Vulcan operational until the 1970s. This had enlarged intakes, a four-wheel undercarriage to allow gross weights up to 225,000lb (102,060kg) and the nosewheel retracting vertically to make room for more weapons. Extra fuel and 17,250lb (76.7kN) Olympus Mk.200s gave a range of 5,000nm (9,260km). In addition to the basic 9,290gal (42,241lit), another 3,300gal (15,005lit) was housed in the bomb bay, 800gal (3,638lit) in a new dorsal spine and 1,250gal (5,684lit) in the wing. The take-off weight with a Blue Steel plus rear fuselage ECM gear was given as 221,047lb (100,267kg) and it was found desirable to provide fuel forward of the CofG to counter-balance the extra fuel in the integral wing tanks. Recent tunnel tests had shown that the existing Vulcan canopy was responsible for an undesirable drag increment so a revised shape was proposed. The opportunity was then taken to extend this new canopy aft and fair it into the existing dorsal fin so that extra fuel could be carried without an increase in frontal area or a reduction in critical Mach number. This aircraft would have cruised at Mach 0.873.

Avro Type 732

Efforts to produce a supersonic 'Vulcan' came under the Type 732 project number, although not all of the designs drawn would necessarily have been supersonic. Four confirmed 732 drawings have been found, the first two of which are labeled IPD 1120 and IPD 1122 and both are dated August 1956. The second of these is clearly based around the Vulcan airframe while the first has in essence retained the wing shape, but information on dimensions and powerplant and any performance data is lacking for both. IPD 1120 was described as a Supersonic Vulcan Development and was to be powered by four large engines, two each in extended wing nacelles with the drawing showing alternative configurations for the port and starboard sides. There was a central cockpit canopy, each main undercarriage had four wheels, the nose leg two, and the wing t/c ratio was 4%. The IPD 1120 drawing did not indicate if this version was to be supersonic but it had some impressive features, not least eight engines stacked in four pairs around the fuselage centre. Here each main undercarriage had eight wheels in four bogies, the nose leg once more had twin wheels, and the pilot's cockpit and canopy were offset to port. Both designs had a large delta-winged guided missile beneath the fuselage but it is assumed that neither progressed so far as a full brochure.

There was also an IPD 1125 (drawn in fact in July 1956) that had a Vulcan B.Mk.2-type wing, a small delta-shaped canard and four engines ranged around the upper rear fuselage in a form that, from the nose angle, reminded one of the bullet chambers in a hand revolver.

The fourth drawing, IPD 1124, shows another supersonic development of the Vulcan from 1956 that shared the latter's general delta wing layout with a single fin and no tail. The fuselage was streamlined with an appearance suggesting 'high speeds' and power was to be supplied by eight de Havilland Gyron Junior engines, probably with a thrust rating of about 7,000lb (31.1kN) to 7,500lb (33.3kN). The engine arrangement looked quite complex with four engines laid in pairs side-by-side in the mid/rear centre fuselage and fed by what appears to be individual intakes arranged one above the other at the sides of the fuselage. The other engines were housed in pairs in underwing pod nacelles. Housing engines in such pods would permit them to receive air undisturbed by the fuselage body or the wing, and it would allow a much slender wing giving less drag compared to engines buried in the wing roots (wing thickness/chord ratio was 4%). The tricycle undercarriage again had twin wheels on the nose leg with twin bogies and eight wheels on each main leg, the latter retracting forwards into a bay just outboard of the intakes. The underfuselage weapon is unidentified but may have been a theoretical design by RAE; it appears to have two engines and its lower fins would have been folded when the aircraft was on the ground. Here some handwritten notes give the aircraft's span as 94ft (28.65m), length 102ft (31.09m), wing area 3,875sq ft (360.4sq m) and leading-edge sweep angle 50°. No predicted performance details are available.

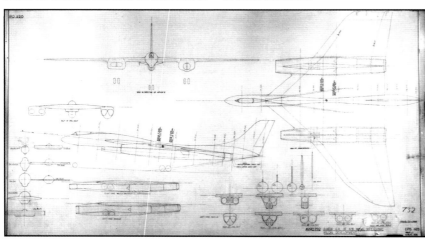

LEFT Version of the Avro 732 project covered by drawing IPD 1120. *Avro Heritage Centre*

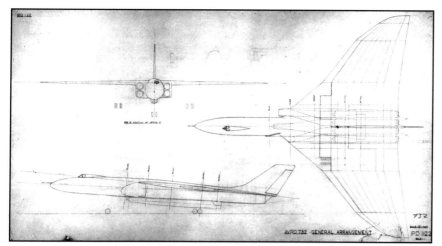

LEFT Avro 732 project covered by drawing IPD 1122. *Avro Heritage Centre*

BELOW This detailed drawing, IPD 1124, shows another version of the Avro 732.

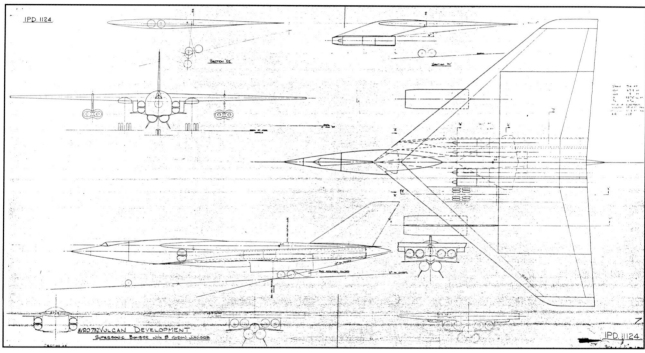

Handley Page Victor III

Either side of the development of the Victor B.Mk.2 Handley Page produced brochures for several enlarged or developed versions. The Victor III of July 1954 presented a stretched airframe with a larger span and bigger Rolls-Royce Conway 6 engines. The Mk.1's outer and intermediate wings, its rear fuselage, the bomb bay, nose and cabin were all retained and joined to an extended centre wing and two fuselage extensions. There would be little change to the wing sweep and aspect ratio so the Victor's good low-speed characteristics would be preserved, and the thickness/chord ratios across the wing were also identical, which enabled a similar critical Mach number to be obtained. Despite the normal take-off weight rising to 190,000lb (86,184kg) from the Mk.1's 160,000lb (72,576kg) (the figure quoted in the brochure), it would not be necessary to alter or strengthen any of the Mk.1's major components. The take-off performance would be improved, the developed aircraft would fly rather higher than the Mk.1 for the same range and bomb load (maximum bombing height was 55,500ft [16,916m]), and when flying at the same height the range was improved by some 800nm (1,480km). A still-air range of 7,620nm (14,120km) was predicted for an overload weight of 225,000lb (102,060kg) and the estimated sea level rate of climb at normal gross weight was 5,150ft/min (1,570m/min). The same brochure also described a 'Victor II' fitted with Sapphire 9 engines rather than the present Sapphire 7s. In due course the Victor III was revised as the Victor B Phase 3 below.

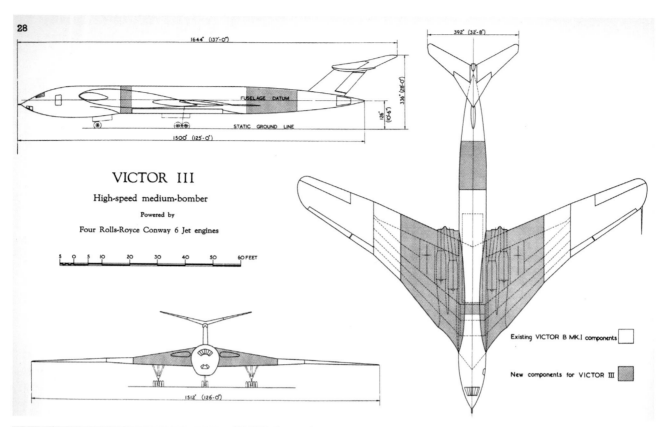

VICTOR III

High-speed medium-bomber

Powered by

Four Rolls-Royce Conway 6 Jet engines

Existing VICTOR B MK.I components

New components for VICTOR III

ABOVE General arrangement drawing of the Victor III proposal (7.54). The white areas depict the existing Victor B.Mk.1 airframe to be used in the new version and the shaded areas represent new sections. *Handley Page Association*

Handley Page Victor III	
Span	126ft 0in (38.40m)
Length	137ft 0in (41.76m)
Gross wing area	?
t/c ratio	16% root, 6% tip
Gross weight	190,000lb (86,184kg)
Powerplant	four RR Conway 6 15,000lb (66.7kN)
Maximum speed/height	Unknown but similar to B.Mk.1
Weapon load	one 10,000lb (4.536kg) nuclear or conventional or thirty-five 1,000lb (454kg) bombs

Further Victor Developments and the HP.104

A Handley Page Pathfinder high-speed target marker called the HP.98 was proposed in November 1951 and this was aerodynamically and structurally identical to the HP.80 as built, complete with the same bomb bay, to allow it to easily revert to the standard bomber role. Its normal take-off weight was estimated to be 145,000lb (65,772kg), overload 175,000lb (79,380kg) and cruise speed 576mph (926km/h). Radar-sighted,

remotely controlled tail guns were fitted for low-level operations and the favoured power unit was the Conway 3 ahead of the Sapphire 4 and Olympus 3, but the Air Staff preferred the Valiant B.Mk.2.

To satisfy the Air Staff's desire for more height over the target Handley Page offered the Phase 2 and Phase 3 developments of spring 1955. Phase 2 had improved 14,000lb (62.2kN) Sapphire 9s and a span of 115ft (35.05m) while Phase 3 was pretty well an all-new design called the HP.104. It possessed the same speed/range/bomb load as the B.Mk.1 from which it was developed and could cruise over the target at 58,000ft (17,678m). Emphasis was placed on retaining the Mk.1's excellent flying qualities so no attempt was made to increase the critical Mach number or the buffet boundary beyond the Victor prototype's limits. The improved cruising altitude was achieved through extra thrust and wing area, the most powerful engines currently envisaged (Olympus

Ol.7s) being fitted. Standard Victor components would be used bar a new centre wing section to house the larger engines plus a longer rear fuselage to provide better missile stowage and to accommodate two 30ft (9.14m) sideways-looking aerials. Phase 2 and 3 were replaced in October by Phase 2A, which became the Victor B.Mk.2. The HP.114 Victor Phase 6 was a proposed missile carrier of August 1958.

Handley Page HP.104	
Span	137ft 0in (41.76m)
Length	136ft 0in (41.45m)
Gross wing area	3,267sq ft (303.8sq m)
t/c ratio	15% root, 10% 1st kink, 8% 2nd kink, 5.7% tip
Gross weight	210,000lb (95,256kg)
Powerplant	four Bristol Olympus Ol.7 17,160lb (76.3kN)
Maximum speed/height	576mph (926km/h) at height
Weapon load	one 10,000lb (4,536kg) special, one 12,000lb (5,443kg) Tallboy or one 22,000lb (9,979kg) Grand Slam bomb

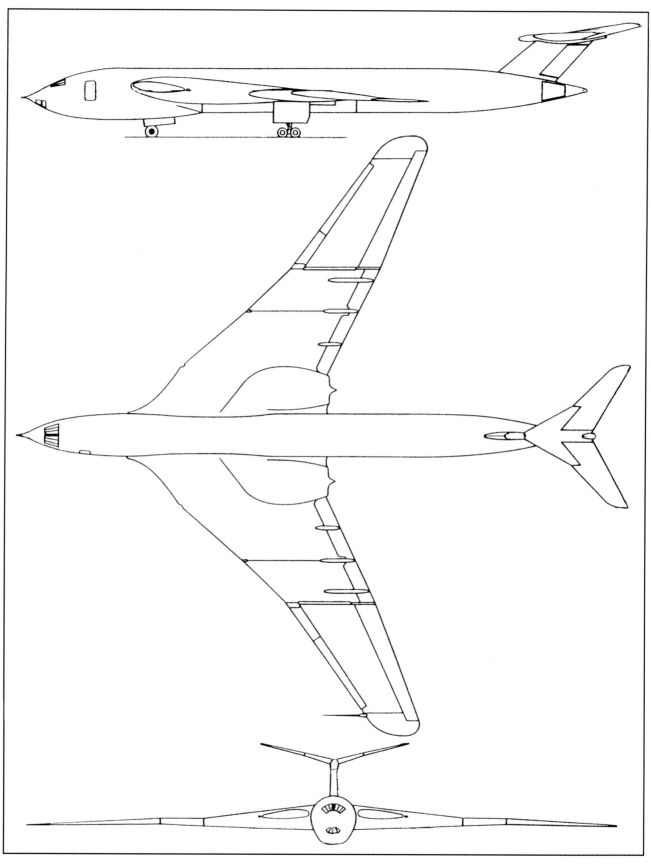

ABOVE Handley Page HP.104 Victor Phase 3 (28.4.55).

Handley Page Supersonic Victor

The Phase 4 Victor resulted from studies of the B.Mk.1 and 2's supersonic capabilities. Applying area rule showed that the Victor closely approximated to the optimum shape for minimum compressibility drag in supersonic flight, so the supersonic Phase 4 introduced a redesigned fuselage incorporating area rule and also reheat; the existing Mk.2 wings and tail were retained. With a take-off at 170,000lb (77,112kg) weight, Phase 4 cruised at Mach 1.06 (702mph [1,130km/h]) at 65,000ft (19,812m) over the target while subsonically it had a range/load/height performance comparable to the Mk.2 with an optimum cruise speed of Mach 0.9 (593mph [954km/h] TAS). An

BELOW Handley Page Supersonic Victor Phase 4 (10.56).

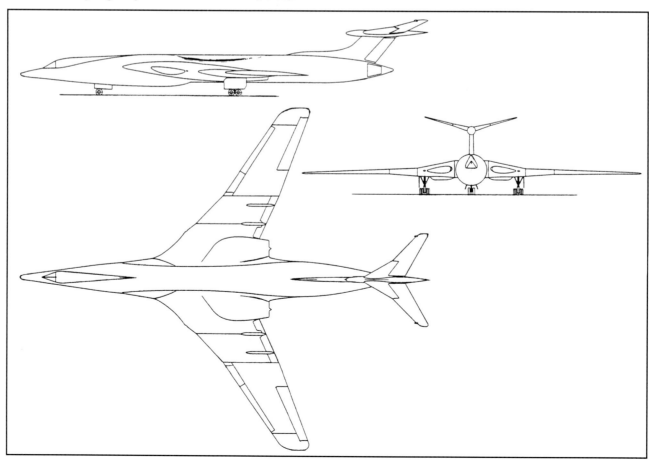

ABOVE & RIGHT The recently produced model of the Supersonic Victor Phase 4 was professionally made using the original drawings. *George Cox*

intensive supersonic wind tunnel programme was proposed to check the aerodynamics along with flight tests using a Mk.1.

HP's philosophy for the supersonic Victor indicated that by 1960–63 a subsonic bomber, flying over heavily defended areas at about 55,000ft (16,764m), might be unacceptably vulnerable to developments in defensive guided weapons. The successful development of air-to-ground missiles, enabling the V-bomber to avoid such areas, would provide a partial solution but possible setbacks to this policy included delays with these missiles, particularly in the problem of guidance. HP felt the Phase 4, with its ability to cruise at 65,000ft (19,812m) during a supersonic spurt, offered an effective insurance. It should be reasonably invulnerable over heavily defended areas during bomb dropping or reconnaissance and fully so when launching a guided missile over less heavily defended spots. Its potential for rapid increases in altitude and speed from the cruise condition should also provide adequate protection against attack from defensive fighters. The aircraft's normal internal fuel capacity was 11,750gal (53,426lit).

HP felt that the aircraft had a high degree of operational flexibility in speed, height, range and alternative roles and it provided an essential link in the development chain for the critical period 1960–66, when subsonic V-bombers might well be unacceptably vulnerable

Handley Page Supersonic Victor	
Span	120ft 0in (36.58m)
Length	145ft 0in (44.20m)
Gross wing area	2,672sq ft (248.5sq m)
t/c ratio	15% root, 10% kink, 8% kink, 5.6% tip
Gross weight	long range 200,000lb (90,720kg), medium range 170,000lb (77,112kg)
Powerplant	four RR Conway 31 20,000lb (88.9kN) dry; reheat gave 4,000lb (17.8kN) at 60,000ft (18,288m) and Mach 1.05
Maximum speed/height	Mach 1.1 at 36,000ft (10,973m)
Weapon load	one 7,000lb (3,175kg) conventional store, one 2,000lb (907kg) nuclear store or one 15,000lb (6,804kg) stand-off weapon

and fully supersonic types were not yet available. However, the Handley Page Association has suggested to the author that developing Phase 4 could have been difficult since relatively little was then known about body waisting, and it also might have suffered from severe drag.

The engines specified for the V-bombers also first appeared in the late 1940s. Project design for the first Olympus was completed in 1949 and it was intended to be more powerful than any axial turbojet previously built in Britain. It was the first two-spool engine in the world having compound or twin-spool axial compressors in series, each driven by its own turbine, giving the advantage that the overall pressure-ratio could be higher than anything possible using a

single-spool unit. Olympus was developed into many versions and power ratings and when the Olympus 6 appeared it was the most advanced mark so far, and its first bench test took place on 14 December 1954. Olympus 7 was first proposed in 1953 and by May 1958, with reheat and a convergent–divergent nozzle, it was giving 22,400lb (99.6kN) of thrust for supersonic flight speeds.

The first RB.80 Conway of December 1948 was based on the RB.77 bypass engine noted in Chapter Two. RB.77 was essentially a brief study against the Avon. A bypass engine or turbofan is a turbojet where part of the air from the main compressor does not pass through the combustion chambers but, instead, re-joins the hot gases in the exhaust pipe. The bypass ratio (bpr) is calculated by dividing the volume of air not passing through the core by the volume that does. This allows a designer to make an engine that can run at a higher temperature and give more energy from the burnt fuel, which then cuts the fuel consumption and makes a lighter engine possible (but there are penalties). The Conway could be thought of as having an oversize front compressor capable of passing more air than is required for combustion with the surplus bypassed around the outside of the combustion zone. This formula was seen as ideal for a strategic bomber but on the Conway the bpr was eventually only about 0.6 maximum so, in the end, there was not that much difference to a pure turbojet. Initially the RB.80

Conway was rated at 9,000lb (40kN) thrust but it was lighter than the Olympus. The two engines competed against one another throughout the 1950s and the reheated RCo.16R offered 31,360lb (139.4kN) thrust.

In November 1955 the Air Staff recommended that both Olympus and Conway should both be available for the V-bomber force as an insurance against failure of either and that the Conway should go into the Victor and Olympus into the Vulcan to fit in with their new wings. As of 25 June 1956 the Olympus held a lead over the Conway due to its higher recorded thrusts on the bench and longer running times. The basic bomber Olympus started at 16,000lb (71.1kN) and was developed straightforwardly to the Ol.21 at 16,500lb+ (73.3+kN). The Conway began at 13,000lb (57.8kN) and was developed straightforwardly to 16,500lb (73.3kN), but thereafter the Stage 4 (18,500lb [82.2kN]) was virtually a redesigned engine and there were doubts whether it would be interchangeable.

The detonation of atomic bombs over the Japanese cities of Hiroshima and Nagasaki in August 1945 brought the Second World War to an abrupt conclusion. They also marked the beginning of a profound shift in strategic thinking. During the immediate post-war period advocates of air power in the USA and the UK perceived the unprecedented destructive power of atomic weapons as having changed the nature of war. Future conflicts, it was argued, would be fought from the outset using atomic weapons delivered over vast ranges, and the possession of a nuclear arsenal became the hallmark of great power status.

Policy leaders in the UK were quick to grasp the implications of this new strategic environment. The Labour Government that came into office in 1945 was committed to maintaining Britain's status as a major power and leading figures in the new government, including the Prime Minister, Clement Attlee, and the Foreign Secretary, Ernest Bevin, quickly came to regard the development of an independent atomic

capability as vital to the UK's standing in the world. This conviction was reinforced by the passage of the McMahon Act by the US Congress on 6 November 1946 that banned all overseas access to US atomic secrets and brought to a halt wartime co-operation between the US and UK in this field. Convinced that Britain could no longer call upon the unqualified support of America, in January 1947 the Attlee Government formally committed the UK to develop an atomic weapon. Work also started on the new range of bombers capable of carrying such weapons over long ranges at high speeds and altitudes.

However, the development of atomic weapons and the means to deliver them continued to form only one element of the UK's defence posture. Britain remained committed to the defence of the Commonwealth and the maintenance of Britain's position overseas, and non-nuclear forces formed the core of that commitment. Additionally, the UK played an important role in the creation of an alliance structure to secure Europe in the face of a perceived Soviet threat, culminating with the signing of the North Atlantic Treaty in Washington on 4 April 1949. The outbreak of the Korean War in 1950 was feared by many to be the opening round of a Third World War and spurred the rapid expansion of the West's conventional forces. In February 1952 a NATO Council meeting in Lisbon agreed the force goals to be met by each member of the Alliance. Policy statement MC 14/1 outlined a plan for no fewer than ninety-six army divisions within thirty days of mobilisation, the target for the UK being set at between nine and ten regular and territorial divisions (later revised to nine regular and nine territorial divisions).

Changes in UK defence policy during the early 1950s were to move the UK independent deterrent to the forefront of British strategy. By the middle of 1952 it had become clear in London that the force goals embodied in MC 14/1 were completely unrealistic. From a British perspective the demands of rearmament threatened to boost defence spending to 10% of the gross national product (GNP)

and such a crippling economic burden could not be sustained. Moreover, it was reasoned that in the event of an atomic war with the Soviet Union most of the West's conventional forces would be of little practical value. Meeting at Greenwich in the summer of 1952 the UK Chiefs of Staff hammered out a policy document (the 'Global Strategy Paper') that eschewed large numbers of expensive soldiers, sailors and airmen and their equipment. Deterrence lay at the heart of this approach. Soviet aggression would be met not with NATO forces but with a nuclear attack on the Soviet homeland; all that would be required were sufficient ground, naval and air forces to keep the Russians in check while the atomic offensive launched by the West's strategic air forces, the US Air Force's Strategic Air Command (SAC) and Royal Air Force Bomber Command, would wreak havoc.

Although viewed initially in Washington as an attempt by the British to renege on their existing commitments, the Global Strategy Paper actually foreshadowed changes to American defence policy introduced by the Eisenhower administration in 1954 (the 'New Look'). In 1957 the concept of massive retaliation was formally accepted as the keystone of NATO's defensive posture in the form of policy document MC 14/2. In this new strategy conventional forces were reduced to the role of a 'tripwire' to test Soviet intentions. Should NATO be faced with an all-out onslaught on the part of the USSR and its Warsaw Pact allies, NATO would rapidly resort to the arsenal of tactical and strategic nuclear weapons held by member states. The emergence of the Soviet nuclear arsenal during the 1950s led to the establishment of an uneasy status quo; by the end of that decade it had become clear that any aggression by East or West could lead to a devastating exchange.

By the early 1960s, therefore, NATO had become a nuclear alliance, and British nuclear forces played a vital role within this structure. A series of agreements concluded in 1957 enabled British and US nuclear strike planning to be closely co-ordinated, and from 31 December 1959 nuclear-armed Valiants were committed to the Supreme Allied Commander Europe (SACEUR) as the Tactical Bomber Force. Nevertheless, despite the intimate relationship between RAF Bomber Command and SAC, successive British governments remained committed to the concept of an independent deterrent under the sole control of the Prime Minister. One aspect of Britain's adherence to the concept of massive retaliation was the 1957 Defence White Paper. Military personnel levels were cut from 690,000 regulars and National Servicemen to an all-regular force of 375,000 men and women; conventional forces were reduced, with emphasis being placed on weapons and equipment for use in a short 'spasm war', culminating in an all-out nuclear exchange.

Although offering both NATO and the Warsaw Pact every incentive to avoid a serious confrontation in Europe, by the early 1960s many in Washington had come to question the utility of massive retaliation. In the aftermath of confrontations with the Soviet Union in Berlin (1961) and Cuba (1962), the Kennedy and Johnson administrations began to search for options that would enable NATO to respond to a Soviet attack in Europe or elsewhere without plunging the world into nuclear war. Such an approach appeared rather less attractive from the European perspective. Despite Britain's small nuclear arsenal, NATO's defensive posture was almost wholly reliant upon extended deterrence – the notion that US strategic nuclear forces could deter a Soviet nuclear attack on European targets. However, any move on the part of the United States to find options short of an all-out nuclear exchange raised fears in the mind of many European theorists and politicians that the superpowers could fight a 'limited' war in Europe with conventional and nuclear weapons – a war that might be limited in global terms, but which would be as devastating for Europe (and particularly for Germany) as any worldwide conflict.

Despite European concerns, in 1967 NATO formally adopted the doctrine of 'flexible response' in the shape of MC 14/3. No longer was the defence of the NATO alliance dependent upon the early release of nuclear weapons. Rather, any Soviet thrust into Western Europe would be met by conventional forces. Only in the event of a Soviet breakthrough, or in retaliation for the use of Soviet tactical nuclear weapons, would tactical nuclear weapons be used, with the US and British strategic nuclear arsenal preserved as a last resort. Flexible response was to form the core of NATO strategy throughout the 1970s and 1980s.

In their heyday the V-bombers were strategic weapons systems designed to deliver nuclear weapons following a high-level penetration to the target. Development of the first atomic weapons to be used by the V-Force was undertaken by a team led by Dr William Penney, a leading member of the UK contingent at Los Alamos during the development of the first US atomic weapons (the Manhattan Project). Work progressed quickly, and on 3 October 1952 the UK joined the 'atomic club' when a 25-kiloton (kt) atomic device was detonated below the River class frigate HMS *Plym* then at anchor in the Monte Bello Islands off Australia's north-western coast (Operation *Hurricane*).

Subsequently the RAF's initial atomic weapons were delivered to the Bomber Command Armament School at RAF Wittering in November 1953. Britain's initial atomic bomb was given the codename Blue Danube. Designed to operational requirement OR.1001, Blue Danube had a nominal yield of 20kt and was contained inside a casing derived from the 12,000lb (5,443kg) 'Tallboy' bomb. Following extensive trials the RAF demonstrated that it possessed a credible deterrent on 11 October 1956 when a Valiant of No 49 Squadron dropped a live Blue Danube Mk.1 round at Maralinga, Australia, one of four detonations carried out as part of Operation *Buffalo*. Only a small number of Blue Danube bombs were produced prior to withdrawal of the

weapon from service in 1962.

The first tactical nuclear weapon to enter the UK arsenal was Red Beard. A fission bomb some 12ft (3.66m) long and weighing 2,000lb (907kg), the development of Red Beard commenced in 1954 in response to operational requirement OR.1127 for a tactical weapon to be carried by the RAF's Canberra force and by the Scimitars and later the Buccaneers of the Fleet Air Arm. Sources suggest that Red Beard had a variable yield of 5–20kt. Red Beard served with the RAF between 1961 and 1970 but modifications to the weapon to enable it to be safely stowed aboard the Royal Navy's aircraft carriers and carried externally by the Scimitar delayed delivery of the first examples to the Fleet Air Arm until 1962. The naval variant was phased out in 1971.

Development of Britain's first hydrogen weapon (employing the fusion rather than fission of atomic nuclei) commenced during the 1950s (the H-bomb was more powerful than an atom bomb). On 15 May 1957 a No 49 Squadron Valiant (XD818), operating from Christmas Island in the Pacific, dropped a test round about a mile (1.6km) from the southern tip of Malden Island; although heralded as Britain's first H-bomb trial, it is now believed that this device may not have been a two-stage thermonuclear weapon. Subsequently, on 28 April 1958 Valiant XD825 of No 49 Squadron dropped a fully-fledged hydrogen bomb in the *Grapple Y* test.

The first example of an interim megaton (mt) weapon for the RAF, codenamed Violet Club, was delivered to the Bomber Command Armament School in March 1958. This bomb was rapidly superseded by Britain's first truly operational megaton-range thermonuclear weapon, Yellow Sun. Yellow Sun Mk.1 bombs, weighing 7,000lb (3,175kg), were introduced to arm the Vulcan B.Mk.1 and Victor B.Mk.1 in 1960. Later, the Yellow Sun Mk.2 was introduced weighing 7,250lb (3,289kg) and with a yield of 1mt; Yellow Sun formed the backbone of the RAF's free-fall nuclear arsenal during the 1960s.

Not all of the air-delivered nuclear weapons carried by RAF bombers during the 1960s were of British origin. Following the co-ordination of British and US strike planning in 1957, from 1958 a number of US nuclear bombs were made available to RAF Bomber Command (and subsequently to the RAF Canberra squadrons in Germany) under a programme codenamed Project 'E'. When carried by RAF aircraft these weapons remained under USAF control. Bombs provided to the RAF included the 6,000lb (2,722kg) Mk.5 and the 1,900lb (862kg) Mk.28 for the V-Force, the 1,650lb (748kg) Mk.7 for the Canberra, and the 2,100lb (953kg) Mk.43, which was carried by both the Valiant and the Canberra. Bomber Command's Vulcan and Victor squadrons ceased to employ Project 'E' weapons in March 1962. US bombs continued to be used in conjunction with the Valiants of the Tactical Bomber Force until the aircraft was withdrawn from service in 1965, and by RAF Germany until 1969.

The first atomic and hydrogen bombs used by the RAF were free-fall weapons. However, the rapid improvement of Soviet air defences during the 1950s spurred the development of new weapons that would not require the carrier to pass over the target. An early attempt to afford RAF bombers with a weapon offering both a stand-off capability and increased accuracy came in the form of the Vickers Blue Boar TV-guided glide bomb, development of which commenced in 1947 to OR.1059. However, Blue Boar was limited to the range of its guidance system and was cancelled in 1954 to be replaced by the much more ambitious Avro Blue Steel air-launched guided weapon. Developed to meet AST/OR.1132 and specification UB.198, Blue Steel was designed to be carried under the fuselages of the Vulcan and Victor. The result was a large weapon that was 35ft (10.67m) long, had a span of 13ft (3.96m) and weighed 14,640lb (6,641kg). The RAF's first

Vulcan/Blue Steel squadron, No 617, became fully operational with the missile in February 1963.

Blue Steel could be launched using a variety of attack profiles. Although the maximum range of the missile was in the region of 200 miles (322km) at Mach 0.8–0.9, a high-level launch might involve a release from 50,000ft (15,240m) some 100nm (185km) from the target. After release its 16,000lb (71.1kN) Armstrong Siddeley Stentor HTP/kerosene engine would accelerate the missile to a speed of Mach 2.5 at 70,000ft (21,336m). A small sustainer would then propel it for the remainder of its four-minute flight, at the end of which it would pitch over to dive in at an angle of 40° and a speed of Mach 1.5–1.8 towards the detonation point. Blue Steel carried the Red Snow megaton-range warhead, the operational requirement for which (OR.1141) had been issued in January 1956.

During the early 1960s it became clear that Blue Steel's stand-off range would not be sufficient to guarantee that Victors and Vulcans could reach their launch positions at high level before falling foul of Soviet fighters and surface-to-air missiles. In response to this threat, following a successful series of low-level firing trials at Woomera the Blue Steel force was switched from high to low level in 1964. In this new attack profile release ranges were reduced to 25 to 30 miles (40km to 48km) and the missile would then zoom climb to an altitude of 17,000ft (5,182m) before diving onto its target. The last RAF squadron to be equipped with Blue Steel (No 617) flew its last sortie with this weapon on 21 December 1970.

In 1957 work commenced on a long-range, ramjet-powered version of Blue Steel to meet operational requirement OR.1159 and specification UB.200. Blue Steel Mk.2 was expected to weigh in at between 22,000lb and 25,000lb (9,979kg and 11,340kg) and to enter service in 1969. However, its development was cancelled on 1 January 1960 in favour of the Douglas Skybolt air-launched ballistic missile, which in turn was cancelled by the

Kennedy administration (as described earlier). Prior to Skybolt's entry into RAF service, it had been projected that Blue Steel would be replaced in 1963–64 by a powered bomb with a range of 1,000nm (1,825km). Covered by an operational requirement (OR.1149), this weapon's specification was prepared by the Air Staff and tenders were submitted by several companies that included Avro's W.107 and Handley Page's HP.106.

As well as the OR.1182 weapons described earlier, other options considered by the Air Staff for the V-Force included the US Hound Dog missile, enhanced versions of Blue Steel Mk.1, an unpowered momentum bomb or new low-level, lay-down bombs; alternatively, the V-Force could be replaced by Minuteman inter-continental ballistic missiles. The momentum bomb was proposed in 1962 for carriage by the V-bombers, Buccaneers or TSR.2 and would have had a range of 6 miles (9.7km) at low level and 40 miles (64km) at height. The primary version was to be nuclear but there would also be a high-explosive version. Configurations were analysed with either folding wings plus a canard or with a slim wing running alongside most of the body's length. The latter appeared to be the more promising but the weapon was abandoned because it was expected to fly too slowly to make an effective attack. In the event the decision by the British Government to procure the Polaris missile system signalled the end of the manned bomber as the UK's primary strategic deterrent system. The continued development of the X-12 Pandora as a hedge against the failure of Polaris was rejected by the Air Staff at the end of 1962.

When discussing nuclear weapon carriage, early bomber brochures often refer to a 'special bomb', Target Marker Bomb or other discreet terms. This was because the aircraft manufacturers had yet to receive any concrete information about the weapon. For example the projects to B.35/46 described in Chapter Two were intended to take a 10,000lb (4,536kg) 'special bomb', which was

ABOVE Model of a momentum bomb.

actually Blue Danube (for authenticity this brochure description has been retained in the data tables). Such bogus names were euphemisms to help conceal the atomic weapons' existence, but they also made it easier to discuss them.

Chapter Four
Low-Level Introduction

Initial Low-Level Bomber Studies: 1952 to 1954

ABOVE Artist's impression of the Short P.D.9 in flight. The intakes for the fuselage-mounted Sapphires were to be faired over for cruising flight. *Short Brothers*

During the Second World War much the greater part of the heavy bombing campaign undertaken over Germany by the RAF and USAAF was made at height, except for selected operations such as the Dams raid. That particular operation took place in moonlight, requiring flight to and from the target at 200ft (61m) or less to help avoid detection by radar and attack by fighters and flak. Such practice would become essential within the next fifteen to twenty years. The greater speeds made available by jet propulsion allowed high-level bombing to continue for a period after the end of hostilities, but eventually the advent of combined and co-ordinated radar, surface-to-air missiles and interceptor fighters suddenly made this a far more difficult and dangerous proposition. A solution was high-speed, low-level penetration but this produced much greater loads and stresses on an airframe, with a consequent reduction in its fatigue life.

The argument for a Low-Altitude Bomber (LAB) was first mooted by the Air Staff on 26 June 1951, two and a half years before the first flight of a production Vickers Valiant (all the V-bombers were designed for high-level bombing). Current bomber developments saw a restriction in operations for these machines, except at short range, to a comparatively narrow height band from 40,000ft (12,192m) upwards, casting away the full three-dimensional advantage hitherto available to the attacker in air war. From early 1952 until September 1954 the Air Ministry and MoS considered the desirability of developing a high-speed, low-altitude bomber to supplement the V-bombers. The V-force had two potential limitations – it was expected that the enemy (the Soviet Union) would soon concentrate his defensive effort on the band above 40,000ft (12,192m) while, at the same time, the force would become increasingly vulnerable to ground-launched missiles as they were developed. A low-altitude bomber would not suffer these limitations and its use with the V-bombers would force the enemy to considerably extend his defence effort.

A LAB Working Party set up in December 1952 concluded that for a maximum range of 4,500nm (8,339km), an aircraft of about 200,000lb (90,718kg) would be required with a very high wing loading of up to 300lb/sq ft (131kg/sq m). The weapons, electronics and engines needed were all examined closely (a minimum of three engines was felt necessary for agreeable failure safety) but the overriding factor governing the introduction of a LAB into service was the development of a winged stand-off missile. This dictated a service entry of 1962/63, which accordingly became the target for the MoS. In-flight refuelling was felt to be particularly desirable and a 30mm Aden cannon in a rear turret was, for a period, a clear requirement (manned if possible but remotely controlled if the former gave an excessive weight penalty). Long before the Working Party had completed its studies, an Operational Requirement was raised and it was envisaged that designs made to the eventual OR.324 requirement would entail as great an advance in aircraft design as had been necessary to produce the V-bombers.

B.126T

Specification B.126T and the accompanying OR.314 were approved on 5 May 1952 (OR.314 was later superseded by OR.324). Many points were left open so that designers could forward their opinions; for example, either turboprops using supersonic propellers or turbojets could be used, though it was acknowledged that no such propeller was then under development. Investigations would consider new problems such as low-altitude navigation, low-level bombing and the physiological effects arising from long periods at low altitude and high speed. The machine's role was to attack targets deep in enemy territory from low level, either as a diversion and complement to high-altitude operations or, should the latter's losses become prohibitive, as the main bomber effort. The whole operation was to be carried out at low level to reduce the warning

available to enemy radars of the bomber's approach and to minimise the effect of guided missiles, interceptors and anti-aircraft gunfire.

A 10,000lb (4,536kg) bomb load was to be taken to a target 2,500nm (4,633km) away but, if a good proportion of development time could be saved, a minimum operational radius of 1,500nm (2,780km) would be acceptable initially. The operational height was to be 500ft (152m), or less for 80% of the outward journey, and the cruising speed was to be at least Mach 0.85, together with short bursts at a higher speed if possible for evasion. This was later quantified as Mach 0.95 for ten minutes over the target. In-flight refuelling was requested and external bomb stowage was accepted. The bomb was originally described as a propelled controlled air-to-surface missile to be released between Mach 0.85 and the aircraft's maximum speed, while the avionics included both forward and sideways-looking radars. On 4 June 1952 Avro, Bristol, de Havilland, Folland, Handley Page and Shorts were all asked to supply a design study and four of these firms had submitted proposals by the end of December 1952.

Avro 721

Avro felt that its Type 721 fulfilled B.126 completely and its construction could proceed at once without the need for fundamental aerodynamic or structural research. It utilised Avro's growing experience with delta wings following the Vulcan and 707 family, but in appearance the aircraft looked more like a short-haul airliner. An outstanding feature was its very low aerodynamic drag, achieved essentially by a reduced wing area, and each component was designed for minimum drag; for example, a fuselage of circular section and moderate fineness ratio gave the smallest surface area necessary to enclose the three crew members, an atom bomb, the operating equipment and most of the huge volume of fuel.

Described as a tail-first aircraft, the 721 had a small wing and large fuselage. The outer wing t/c ratio was 6%, rising

to 7% at the kink and 11% at the body-side, while at the same time the maximum thickness was moved forward. This was an extension of the method of controlling the effective sweepback at high subsonic Mach numbers developed by RAE and used on the Vulcan. Critical Mach number was 0.9. An advantage of the delta was its inherent stiffness (essential at the high air speeds for which the 721 was designed), which permitted the spars to be at right angles to the line of flight, and this also removed the weight and complexity of cranked and jointed spars. A straight trailing edge gave maximum lift from the Fowler flaps, supplemented by a split flap under the fuselage. The wing structure was continuous across the fuselage and contained a 600gal (2,728lit) fuel tank, while the main wheels retracted into the forward wing. The fuselage housed fuel tanks of 11,300gal (51,371lit) total capacity.

Following a comprehensive study of various layouts, the 'tailplane' had been placed ahead of the wing, which helped to increase lift on take-off and landing, improve tail efficiency (and therefore reduce tail size and drag) and to accommodate trim changes. It was particularly suited to carrying the bomb in the extreme tail of the fuselage. The Type 721 was intimately bound up with the bomb's size and shape, the methods of its release and travel to target. After studying possible bombing techniques to allow the 721 to be at a safe distance when the bomb exploded, Avro felt this was best achieved by using a winged rocket-propelled weapon. Dropping the weapon at high speeds from a bomb bay was deemed impossible so it was stored in the rear fuselage and ejected backwards through opening doors; this permitted its carriage with the minimal loss of performance and disturbance on release. Other types of bomb could be carried here, or externally below the fuselage (the rear fuselage also contained built-in rocket motors for take-off assistance). Ejecting the bomb from a mid-fuselage bay had been studied but this was found to reduce the range. There were no defensive guns.

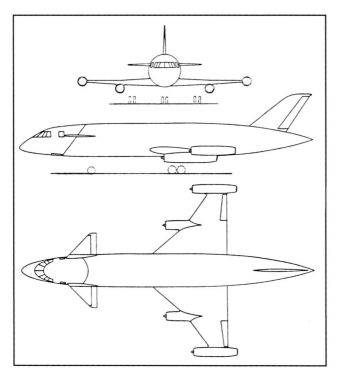

ABOVE Avro 721 with four Napier NP.172 ducted fans (12.52).

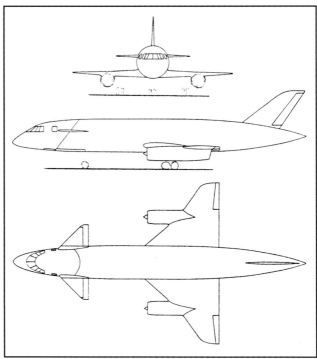

ABOVE Alternate Avro 721 with two Rolls-Royce Conways (12.52).

BELOW Same-scale size comparison of Avro 721 and early Avro Vulcan.

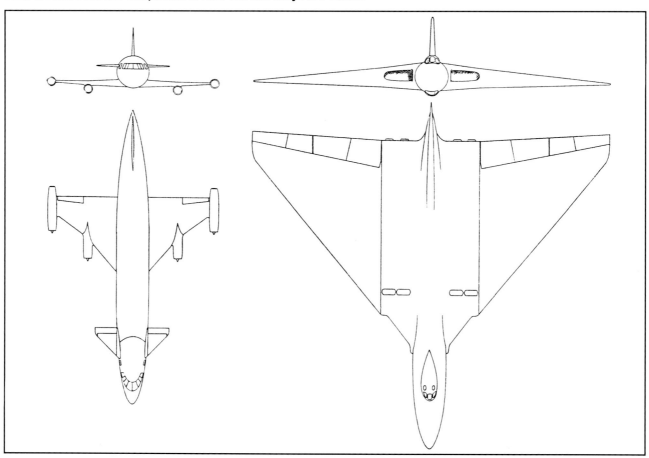

ABOVE Artist's impression of the Avro 721.

ABOVE Avro model of the Type 721, which carries the 'serial' XL985. *Avro Heritage Centre*

A ducted fan engine was necessary for good specific fuel consumption (1.0lb/lb/hr under these conditions rather than the current best of 1.1lb/lb/hr). Specific schemes had been prepared by Napier and Rolls-Royce but, as proposed, the Type 721 had four 5,440lb (24.2kN) Napier NP.172 ducted fans that gave enough power for flight to be sustained in the target area without one engine. Another advantage was that one or two units could be stopped under reduced speed conditions to conserve fuel. Alternatively, the 721 could use two 11,500lb (51.2kN) Rolls-Royce Conways modified to give a greater bypass ratio, which reduced the span by 3ft (0.91m), but the Conway lacked sufficient power for flight under engine-cut conditions except at very light weights. In truth, a unit of about 12,700lb (56.5kN) was required so a study was made using two Napier NP.172s scaled up by a factor of 2.34 to

the required 12,700lb. However, even this 'Napier high thrust engine' gave problems for single-engine flight.

The Type 721 had a high wing loading and, consequently, a normal unassisted take-off was impossible except at very light weight. To carry enough fuel for a 3,350nm (6,208km) range the take-off could be rocket assisted or at minimum weight followed by flight refuelling, hence the two 10,000lb (44.5kN) rockets mounted in the rear fuselage. To provide a range of 5,500nm (10,193km), which was 20% over specification, a take-off would have to be made with the fuel for the 3,350nm (6,208km) sortie and using RATO, followed then by air refuelling. The take-off weight for the 5,500nm (10,193km) mission was 90,400lb (41,005kg). For a full weight departure a proposal was included for mounting four 20,000lb (89kN) rocket motors (developed from the Armstrong Siddeley Screamer or de Havilland Spectre) beneath the fuselage

and inclined 30° down. An alternative envisaged the use of a 'slip-plane', which was in fact another aircraft powered by four jet engines to supply additional thrust and wing area. The 721 and the slip-plane would take-off as a composite aircraft before separating at a safe height.

An appreciation of the 721 could be gained by comparing it to the current Vulcan. With the same bomb load the latter flew at Mach 0.87 and 50,000ft (15,240m) for a range of 5,000nm (9,266km). Air density at sea level is six times that at 50,000ft (15,240m) and, to obtain a reasonable value of air miles per gallon of fuel at the same true air speed, the 721's drag had to be correspondingly reduced. Although the Mach numbers of the two aircraft were similar, the greater temperature at sea level resulted in a further 69mph (111km/h) air speed. Maximum level speed for the Type 721 at 80,000lb (36,287g) weight was about Mach 0.94 at 15,000ft (4,572m) with its design dive speed reaching Mach 1.0. Reheat would push the level speed up to Mach 0.97 but that needed more fuel and hence gave a larger and heavier aircraft.

Avro 721	
Span	47ft 0in (14.33m)
Length	80ft 0in (24.38m)
Gross wing area	600sq ft (55.7sq m)
t/c ratio	11% root, 6% tip
Gross weight	124,400lb (56,427kg) for maximum range
Powerplant	four Napier NP.172 5,440lb (24.2kN) plus two rockets 10,000lb (44.4kN)
Maximum speed/height	Mach 0.94 at 15,000ft (4,572m)
Weapon load	two 5,000lb (2,268kg) bombs, one internal, one external, or four 1,000lb (454kg) bombs internal

BELOW Bristol 186 (19.12.52).

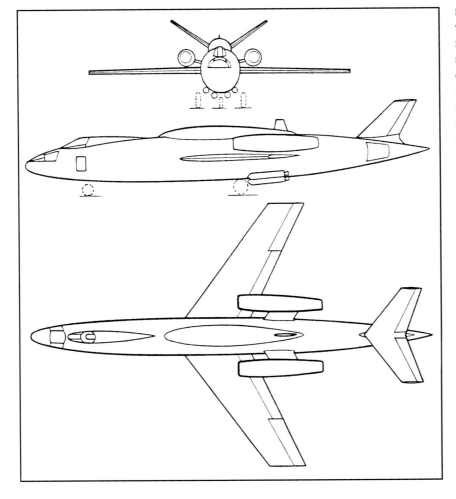

Bristol Type 186

The Bristol 186 offered the unusual approach of engines mounted on struts above and to the side of the rear fuselage. The multi-spar wing's take-off loading was 136lb/sq ft (61.1kg/sq m), at the gross weight it was 250lb/sq ft (112.2kg/sq m), and the wing housed 2,150gal (9,774lit) of fuel. Hydraulically operated single-slotted trailing-edge flaps were provided together with unbalanced ailerons, which were power-operated through duplicate units. A V-tail with 35° of dihedral was chosen to minimise any disturbance from the bomb release and this was adjustable in flight through 6°. When moved in the same direction the tail's trailing-edge flaps acted as the elevators, and when moving in opposite directions they became the rudders.

The body had an elliptical cross-section and, excepting the cut-outs for the bomb-cell, undercarriage units and wing, contained 14,500gal (64,613lit) of fuel from aft of the cockpit to the tailplane front spar. Its construction was conventional using light alloy skins, stringers and frames. The undercarriage was a normal tricycle with all units folding forward and upward into the body, and the crew comprised a pilot and navigator/bomber, with the latter housed in the extreme nose; an extra crewman was provisionally proposed. The engine pods housed two 11,000lb (48.9kN) modified Bristol Olympus 101s while around the lower fuselage just behind the main landing gear were four RATO motors that would give a total of 14,700lb (65.4kN) of extra thrust for thirty-two seconds.

The single streamlined 10,000lb (4,536kg) bomb was carried half-buried in a recess on the top fuselage, above the wing roots between and slightly forward of the engine pods. With its wings and horizontal tail surfaces folded down, this gave a relatively smooth compound shape that reduced drag during the flight to the target area. For release it was raised on a support until the folded wings were clear of the parent aircraft. These were then unfolded as the propulsion unit was started up, the support then extended further out to present the bomb to the airstream at an attitude suitable for release, and as this happened a door would cover the now empty stowage slot in the fuselage. The bomb's form was an approximation of the specified weapon but suited to fit the 186's body; its diameter was 5ft 0in (1.52m) and length 31ft 11in (9.73m) and it had thin, low aspect ratio, constant chord wings. Control in flight was provided by

OPPOSITE MIDDLE The Bristol 186's bomb elevating mechanism.

OPPOSITE BOTTOM The two streamlined bombs designed to fit on the Type 186's body. The larger weapon was 31ft 9in (9.68m) long and had a span of 11ft 1in (3.38m), the smaller was 21ft 2in (6.45m) long with a span of 9ft 4.5in (2.86m).

ABOVE Two views of a model of the Bristol 186, the first showing a 10,000lb (4,536kg) winged bomb partially housed within the fuselage and the second with this weapon raised for launch with wings and tail surfaces extended.

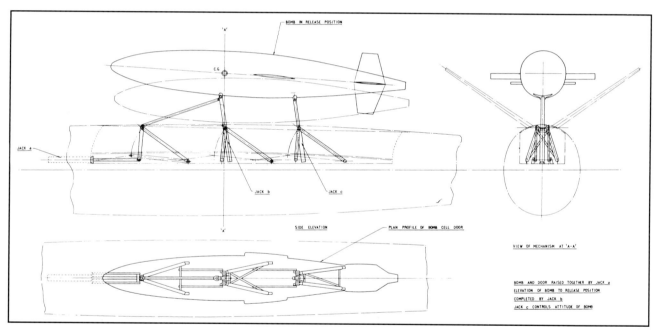

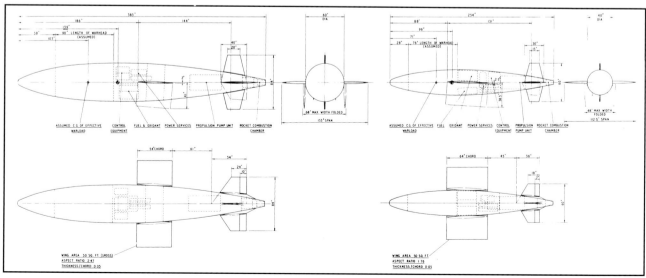

a cruciform tail with the upper vertical surface exposed during the whole flight. After launch it was assumed that free flight would last about sixty seconds with propulsion provided by a rocket in the rear body that would maintain the speed at between Mach 0.8 and 0.9. The guidance system would be fed with information up to release and manoeuvres after release might involve turns, climbs and dives at up to 3g.

Since flight refuelling was felt necessary, the take-off weight was less than the gross weight; the undercarriage was designed for a take-off maximum of 97,000lb (43,998kg). Gross weight was 180,000lb (81,647kg), of which 128,000lb (58,060kg) was fuel. Still air range with the bomb dropped at half range was 5,000nm (9,266km) at sea level and 5,170nm (9,581km) at 1,000ft (305m), and the cruise speed was Mach 0.85, which at 1,000ft (305m) was

Bristol 186	
Span	58ft 6in (17.83m)
Length	92ft 0in (28.04m)
Gross wing area	720sq ft (66.9sq m)
t/c ratio	9%
Gross weight	180,000lb (81,647kg)
Powerplant	two Bristol Olympus 101 11,000lb (48.9kN) plus four rockets 3,675lb (16.3kN)
Maximum speed/height	Mach 0.9+ at height
Weapon load	one 10,000lb (4,536kg) bomb

645mph (1,038km/h). A 30mm cannon was provisionally mounted in the rear fuselage with a defence radar pod in the tail root, but no defensive armament was planned in the long term.

BELOW Handley Page HP.99 (1.53). Note the weapon beneath the fuselage. *RAF Museum*

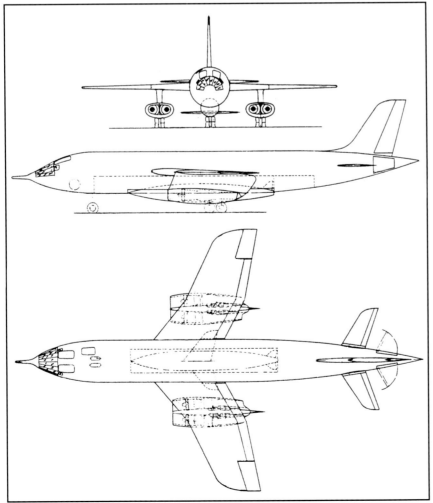

Handley Page HP.99

Handley Page completed its HP.99 brochure in January 1953 and reported that it was possible to design a small aircraft to meet the short-range requirement (1,500nm [2,780km] radius), but it needed to carry very large drop tanks in order to reach the 2,500nm (4,633km) limit and the resultant wing loading then became too high to be practicable. These conclusions had led to the adoption of a larger aircraft able to carry a substantial bomb load over a range approaching 4,500nm (8,339km) at sea level. Reductions in engine fuel consumption and fully laden weight would increase this to 5,500nm (10,193km).

Long range at low altitude demanded that aircraft drag must be kept to a minimum and three methods for reducing drag had been explored:

a). Reducing wing area at the expense of wing loading.

b). Employing boundary layer control to improve propulsive efficiency.

c). Reducing wetted area in flight.

For (b) a study was made using gas turbines to apply suction to the whole surface of the aircraft (wings, tail and fuselage), which was ejected aft at approximately the flight speed. This gave an increase in propulsive efficiency and a consequent saving of some 15% in gross weight but, although providing the most efficient design, it would have to be a long-term project. Method (c) involved retractable or jettisonable wings, jettisonable tanks (both attached to and towed behind the aircraft) and external and towed bomb containers, but the resulting complexity and extended development time gave no saving in cost.

The chosen wing plan followed an examination of many alternatives and showed good landing and stalling characteristics, a low rate of descent in an engine-out situation and a satisfactory rate of climb after a baulked landing. It was a compromise to allow a cruise of Mach 0.85 with an aspect ratio

ABOVE Artwork showing the HP.99. This low-altitude bomber project had its four Avon RA.14 engines paired in low-slung underwing pods. *RAF Museum*

high enough to ensure ample reserve power on the approach without penalising low-speed control at the stall. A satisfactory performance had been confirmed in the wind tunnel. An aircraft designed for supersonic bursts had been considered and rejected because the severe restrictions imposed by supersonic flight prejudiced its high subsonic performance and greatly restricted its range, bomb and missile capacity. Therefore, the HP.99 was designed for cruise at high subsonic speed (Mach 0.85) although future investigations were planned using wings designed for Mach 0.9 cruise. The maximum Mach 0.92 at sea level was limited to five minutes.

The HP.99 had three crew, Handley Page noting that fatigue would be reduced by having two pilot-navigators and one radio navigator. Fatigue from the bumps usually associated with high-speed, low-altitude flying would be moderated by the aircraft's high wing loading, which would nullify the effects of gusts. HP.99 had a total fuel capacity of 22,700gal (103,196lit) and a flight refuel probe was fitted in the nose. Four Avon RA.14s were installed in pairs in pods beneath the wing, in preference to

buried engines that HP felt would have had a relatively large adverse effect on the wing characteristics because of the surface's small area and thin root-section. The undercarriage main gears were mounted in the engine pods.

Maximum take-off weight using water injection and rocket boost was 160,000lb (72,575kg) while maximum laden weight following a mid-air transfer of 13,000gal (59,099lit) of fuel was 260,000lb (117,934g). At 260,000lb (117,934g), complete with a single 10,000lb (4,536kg) bomb, the range for a speed of Mach 0.85 at sea level throughout was 4,440nm (8,228km); with 80% of the mission flown at sea level and 20% at optimum height this figure became 5,020nm (9,303km) and for the entire flight performed at optimum height it was 7,350nm (13,621km). At 160,000lb (72,575kg) weight the equivalent ranges were 1,925nm, 2,405nm and 4,450nm (3,567km, 4,457km and 8,247km). The wing loading for a normal take-off was 145lb/sq ft (65.1kg/sq m).

To achieve effective results without the aircraft being endangered, bombing at low altitude required the solving of many problems. It would be necessary

to retard the bomb by parachute after dropping it or to replace it by a powered self-controlled winged missile that, after release, would fly to the target. The missile could be mounted either above or below the aircraft but the lower position was chosen for the HP.99 to make it available for normal bombing operations if required. The winged missile was installed by replacing the non-structural sides of the bomb bay with suitable fairings and ample space was available for the powered ejection of bombs. Very little equipment existed for navigating a bomber at low altitude so, for daylight operations, it was assumed that the main approach for the HP.99 would be visual observation matched with synchronised moving maps.

Handley Page HP.99	
Span	70ft 6in (21.49m)
Length	104ft 6in (31.85m)
Gross wing area	1,100sq ft (102.2sq m)
t/c ratio	10% root, 7% tip
Gross weight	260,000lb (117,934kg)
Powerplant	four RR Avon RA.14 9,500lb (42.3kN) plus optional rockets
Maximum speed/height	Mach 0.92 at sea level, Mach 0.92+ at height
Weapon load	one 10,000lb (4,536kg) bomb

Short P.D.9

Shorts' preliminary studies showed that the biggest problem of low-altitude bombing was to achieve the required range without going to an unreasonably high weight and wing loading. Four ideas were reviewed – the 'straightforward approach' with delta wing and four Olympus (two mounted forward and two aft); a similar short-range version with three Sapphire Sa.3s; an 'aero-isoclinic wing' design and a curious 'partly expendable aircraft' that progressively reduced its weight and drag in flight as fuel was consumed. The idea was to shed the undercarriage after take-off (flexible deck landing), shed wing area and perhaps some of the engines as weight decreased, and finally the bomb cell with its fuselage after dropping the bomb. A relatively small piloted aircraft formed the upper component of a

composite, the lower part carried the bomb load and was jettisoned after the drop to leave the piloted machine to return to base.

For its P.D.9 design Shorts concluded that it was theoretically possible to build a twin-engined aircraft to fulfil the specification, but for safety felt that nothing less than four engines would be acceptable. The result was a conventional design with moderate sweepback and a tail that the company thought represented a straightforward and practical solution from both the constructional and operational aspects, with minimum time required before service entry. P.D.9 was orthodox in appearance and embodied no major structural or aerodynamic problems. The ailerons were power operated, the all-moving tail was set high on top of the fin and the undercarriage comprised two main units in tandem, both retracting into

the fuselage, with tip outriggers which folded into the engine pods. The front main leg had four wheels on a single axle, the rear four wheels on a bogie.

The two-man crew comprised pilot and navigator with the pilot station offset to port under a canopy modelled along fighter lines to keep its size to a minimum. This feature had an incidental but important advantage, namely it would be less vulnerable to bird impacts that, although a known hazard, were now expected to assume greater importance on low-flying aeroplanes. The exact nature of the equipment to be installed in terms of radar and navigation was still unknown. With the exception of the equipment areas, weapon and undercarriage bays, the fuselage was filled almost entirely with 16,280gal (74,010lit) of fuel. Another 2,470gal (11.229lit) were housed in the wings and a further 'jettisonable' 15,000gal (68,191lit) made for a total fuel load of 33,750gal (153,431lit).

The bomb cell was arranged within the fuselage underside to provide stowage for a 'small size' 10,000lb (4,536kg) bomb delivered by toss-bombing. A 'large' version or several normal bombs could be accommodated instead (the former replacing some fuel) and a radar-controlled cannon was mounted in the extreme tail for defence. Four 11,000lb (48.9kN) Armstrong Siddeley Sapphire Sa.7s were fitted, two in wing tip pods and two more adjacent to the fuselage sides under and ahead of the wing. The latter were to be used primarily for take-off only, being shut down and faired over once airborne to leave the tip-mounted units for cruising. In addition, two 10,000lb (44.5kN) retractable rocket motors were installed in the sides of the rear fuselage to assist with the take-off.

The maximum take-off weight was 144,000lb (65,317kg) and the operational gross weight for a still air range of 3,750nm (6,949km) (i.e. a 1,500nm [2,780km] radius of action) was 195,000lb (88,450kg), so reaching maximum weight would again require

BELOW Short P.D.9. *Short Brothers*

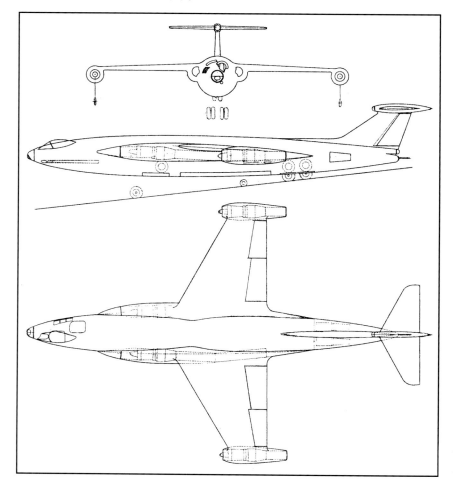

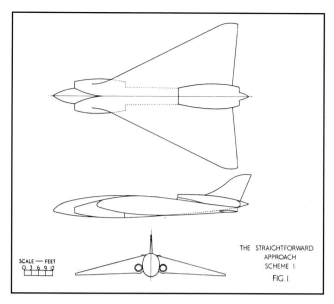

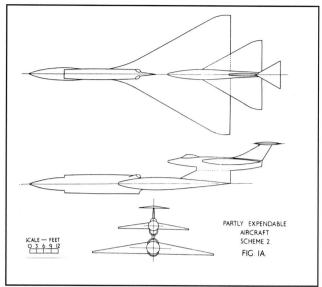

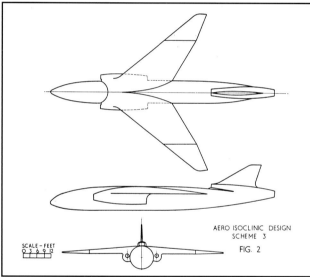

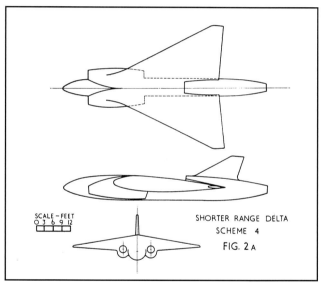

ABOVE The four basic preliminary designs or configurations assessed by Shorts prior to moving on to the P.D.9. They present a straightforward approach using a delta wing and four Olympus engines with two mounted forward and two aft; a partly expendable aircraft where the smaller piloted upper section only would return to base; an 'aero-isoclinic wing' design, and a similar short-range straightforward delta using just three Sapphire Sa.3 engines. *Short Brothers*

in-flight refuelling once the aircraft was airborne. The range was achieved by cruising at Mach 0.85 and 500ft (152m), but the specified full operational radius of 2,500nm (4,633km) could not be reached in this configuration. Top speed using the extra 20,000lb (89.0kN) of rocket thrust was 737mph (1,186km/h), dropping to 715mph (1,151km/h) on jet power alone. Wing loading with full fuel was 195lb/sq ft (87.6kg/sq m).

After considering its preliminary studies, Shorts envisaged a stage-by-

stage approach to achieve B.126 in full. The P.D.9 would be Stage 1, while Stage 2 would increase the gross weight to 230,000lb (104,326g) by adding fuel for a radius of action of 1,880nm (3,484km), but this depended on the development of take-off techniques at high wing loading and the availability of more powerful rockets. Stage 3 deleted the undercarriage and filled the bays with additional fuel for a 2,070nm (3,836km) range (the tandem wheels made this possible) and the take-off would employ

a jettisonable undercarriage or a 'soft trough' catapult with landing on a flexible deck. Finally, Stage 4 envisaged the installation of new jet or ducted fan engines specifically designed for low-altitude operation – with a small increase in gross weight this aircraft could achieve the full operational radius of 2,500nm (4,633km). Shorts felt the big advantage was that Stage 1 involved a conventional machine (P.D.9) that relied on existing RATO and flight refuelling techniques, so it could be built immediately.

Shorts P.D.9	
Span	63ft 6in (19.35m)
Length	96ft 6in (29.41m)
Gross wing area	1,000sq ft (92.9sq m)
t/c ratio	7%
Gross weight	195,000lb (88,450kg)
Powerplant	four AS Sapphire Sa.7 11,000lb (48.9kN) plus two rockets 10,000lb (44.4kN)
Maximum speed/height	Mach 0.96 at sea level, Mach 0.96+ at height
Weapon load	one 10,000lb (4,536kg) bomb

The principle objective for these studies was to obtain and assess different approaches before putting together a draft Operational Requirement, which in due course appeared as OR.324. In February 1953 RAE Farnborough produced Technical Note Aero 2193, called *Problem of the Low Altitude, High Speed, Long Range Bomber*, which was based on B.126T and highlighted two main difficulties:

i). The functions of the low-altitude requirement – defence, bombing, vision.

ii). Situations where high wing loadings were an important factor – take-off and landing and control behaviour in gusts.

The conclusions were that the many and varied problems could be solved. The perception that gust effects made the aircraft unflyable over long periods was examined using present knowledge (could pilots tolerate it?) and the report recommended that research into gust alleviation should continue as a high priority.

On 9 July 1953 the Ministry's V. H. E. Cole reported on some of the project's political aspects. To begin with, it had been assumed throughout the Ministry and Air Staff that work would start with an initial outlay of £4m and was to be tackled by just one company only, with no question of an insurance type being considered. Two companies undertaking the project had been a possibility but the hallowed practice of many years, to ensure top priority projects on which the whole offensive power of the RAF would

depend, was not needed for the low-altitude medium bomber (the practice usually took the form of a fairly conventional development proceeding in parallel with an advanced or unconventional development).

This bomber was viewed as a complementary weapon system and, although very important, was not one on which the Air Staff were staking their all. If sufficient basic knowledge existed for the project to proceed without delay then the insurance policy was unnecessary, particularly as the Air Staff's emphasis on speed suggested waiting to make a choice from competing developments was a luxury that could not be afforded. In addition, the present financial circumstances made the doubling-up of provisional estimates to allow two companies to proceed difficult to justify.

For most preceding programmes the accepted view was that design study contracts were issued by the MoS with a view to writing a specification, which was then put out to an industry tender design competition. The Ministry was not necessarily bound by this course for the LAB but it was more than twelve months since design studies had been requested and a point had now been reached where the traditional bomber companies were running out of work, and Cole felt that other companies might like to tender designs. After all, LAB development would take six to seven years and possibly longer if it embodied a new engine such as the Armstrong Siddeley Project X, a proposed 15,000lb (66.7kN) unit.

Cole also noted that the Ministry believed it was essential for one team to handle the design of both the aircraft and the guided bomb it was to carry, which limited the number of companies that could be considered. Both Avro and Handley Page were seeking work and the former was particularly anxious to enter the sphere of guided weapons. There was every indication that Bristol had its hands full with civil and guided weapon commitments and the company was understood to be likely to seek outside help if the Canadians required

the Britannia airliner as a maritime reconnaissance aircraft. It was also probable that an imminent future review might show that the Ministry could no longer maintain a total of ten design companies, which raised the question of whether they needed to maintain in existence so many design teams specialising in large military aircraft. Finally, Cole indicated that the OR could use existing engines since a relatively small production order was expected that would not justify developing an expensive new engine for this aircraft alone.

On 24 September 1953 J. E. Adamson minuted L. J. Dunnett, (US[Air]), to propose seeking immediate Ministerial approval to proceed with the LAB since the Air Staff attached much importance to it. The LAB was considered to be no more than the next step in bomber development and its airframe should be no more expensive to produce than the V-bombers. Dunnett's reply indicated doubts that the project was within current electronics and aircraft design resources. From inception it had been recognised that both airframe and missile would need to be very closely integrated within the overall design because the normal bomb bay stowage system did not apply.

On 28 October an invitation for new tenders was close but the situation remained confused as discussions continued. OR.324 (dated 30 October 1953) had now superseded OR.314 and the whole flight to and from the target was now to be made at an average height of 1,000ft (304m) or less; unrefuelled range was now 5,000nm (9,266km). The aircraft would carry one of three types of special OR.1125 winged, powered and inertia-controlled bombs per sortie, similar in size and weight to Blue Danube, or several smaller stores (a redesign of Blue Danube was proposed). The alternatives were:

a). A large subsonic 14,000lb (6,350kg) bomb, 45ft (13.72m) long, 5ft 2in (1.58m) in diameter.

b). A small supersonic 11,000lb

(4,990kg) bomb, 35ft (10.67m) long, 2ft 9in (0.84m) in diameter.

c). A small subsonic 7,500lb (3,402kg) stand-off bomb, 35ft (10.67m) long, 2ft 9in (0.84m) diameter.

A meeting was held at St Giles Court on 11 February 1954 to decide how the LAB should be handled, the project now being viewed as a complete weapon system, but a decision to proceed was never to be made.

By September 1954 thoughts had turned towards discontinuing the LAB in the list of requirements, and on the 17th OR.324 was cancelled together with the OR.1125 weapon. The full background was described by the Controller Aircraft, John W. Baker, to the Minister of Defence on 4 October. As the assessment of the design studies and draft OR by the MoS and Air Ministry proceeded, the difficulties for such an aircraft became alarmingly apparent. The high speeds required at low altitude raised serious structural problems, the bomb would be very complex and expensive, new navigational techniques and equipment would be required, the integration of the total design effort presented great problems of organisation, and if any

one of the systems necessary for the carriage and dropping of the bomb should prove unsuccessful, the whole aircraft would be useless.

Such was the magnitude of these problems that the total cost of development was estimated to be £12m to £15m. With the danger that the required technical effort and resources could only be concentrated at the expense of other, more important projects, and the fact that the huge sums of money involved had to be found within a limited Defence Budget again at the expense of other projects, the Air Ministry decided to cancel its requirement for a low-altitude bomber. The item was now deleted from the research and development programme.

In truth, B.126 was an information-gathering exercise to bring together the many new aspects and problems associated with high-speed, low-altitude flight. For example, the Institute of Aviation Medicine examined airsickness and the methods needed to counter it since fast flight in rough air at that time simply made the crew ill. Also, much greater stresses were exerted on the airframe by rough, bumpy airflows and these had to be accommodated with care, a problem best illustrated by their effect on the

Vickers Valiant when this bomber was switched from high- to low-level operations in 1963 (see Chapter Three). Within a year cracks had been found in both front and rear spars of many Valiants because the fatigue resistance of these vital parts, designed for high-level flight only, was far short of that needed for prolonged low-level work.

This low-altitude requirement explored much new ground but it had several weaknesses. For example, meeting the range needed the carriage of a phenomenal amount of fuel (all four design studies were essentially flying fuel tanks) while accurate navigation and terrain clearance for these aircraft would have been tough because the relevant equipment had still to be created. The absence of such technology raises an interesting point – jet engine development had made such tremendous strides that it enabled these aircraft to fly close to the speed of sound at low level, yet the design studies still included visual observation with synchronised moving maps. In the event, B.126T only created great volumes of paper, but the knowledge gained helped pave the way for the Buccaneer, TSR.2, Jaguar and Tornado.

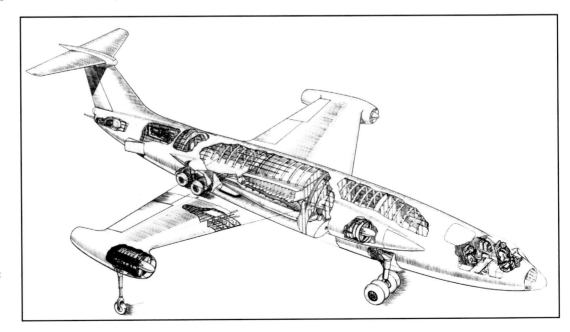

RIGHT Drawing of the P.D.9 that presents some internal detail. *Short Brothers*

Chapter Five
Fleet Air Arm Pirate

Naval Strike Aircraft: 1954 to 1958

ABOVE Buccaneer S.Mk.1 XN928 of 809 Squadron at Yeovilton in June 1964. *Alan Trent*

The need for combat aircraft to fly at low level to satisfactorily accomplish the penetration of defended airspace without losing most or all of the force was recognised and acknowledged by the Admiralty ahead of the RAF. While the latter conceived and then rejected the Low-Altitude Bomber (Chapter Four), the Admiralty got to grips with turning its thoughts on the subject into its own requirement, although the task must have been made a little easier by the fact that the sea is usually flat. Hills, mountains and electric pylons don't make a habit of turning up in the middle of an ocean.

M.148T (and NR/A.39)

Dated 27 March 1954, Specification M.148T defined a two-seat naval strike aircraft well in advance of current types. Naval Requirement NR/A.39 (or NA.39) had been drafted the previous October, stimulated by the Soviet Union's new and impressive *Sverdlov* class cruisers, and the aircraft's primary targets were both shore installations and warships. A mix of weapons would be carried but with the gross weight and size kept within the limits set by its carrier. These comprised one target marker tactical nuclear bomb (TMB) of about 2,500lb (1,134kg) weight, one Green Cheese anti-ship homing bomb, four Red Angel (Special M) bombs, 24 air-to-surface OR.1099 rockets, up to four mines, two 2,000lb (907kg) armour-piercing (AP) or four 1,000lb (454kg) standard MC bombs, or a four-gun 30mm Aden pack. The avionics would include a monopulse radar, lightweight Doppler and a search radar.

After cruising at altitude, low-level bombing was preferred with a high-speed, low-level dash to and from the target from beyond radar range, but the Green Cheese attack against large ships was to be 'blind' at medium altitude using the search radar. The maximum possible sea level speed was required, at least 550 knots (633mph/ 1,019km/h) but more if possible, with a minimum radius of action of 400nm (741km) at low level and 800nm (1,483km) for high attack and search. Flight refuelling was required together with a pack installation to make the aircraft itself suitable for tanker duties. The dimensions when folded were 51ft (15.54m) long and 20ft (6.10m) wide. The aircraft would have two engines and was to be in service by 1960.

At the end of March 1954 Armstrong Whitworth, Blackburn, Fairey, Shorts and Westland were invited to tender for ten or twenty development aircraft; there would be no prototypes. In addition, Percival Aircraft expressed considerable interest and asked permission to tender, which was granted on 13 April. However, after studying M.148T at greater length, Percival's representatives visited the MoS in mid-June to explain that the firm felt unable to produce a complete design for such a complex aircraft, with all the necessary engineering detail, in the available time. Instead, the meeting agreed that Percival should investigate a 'novel scheme' around a 'ghost' aircraft to meet M.148T that would show a method of generating and deploying engine compressor air to aerodynamic advantage (this was a development of an idea already proposed in a Percival helicopter design). The 'ghost' airframe would be schemed to suit the specification requirements but not developed from an engineering point of view.

In September 1954 the five companies plus Hawker Aircraft tendered their designs. Hawker did not make an official tender with a full breakdown of costs and delivery dates but instead, at a late stage and as an afterthought, sent in a project brochure and drawings. Sydney Camm had shown little interest in the requirement because it called for a bomber, essentially outside the company's favoured area of fighter design, and he only went ahead after the Admiralty had

made a personal approach. In addition, there was no Rolls-Royce engine on hand of an appropriate size to power a twin-engined aeroplane such as this. This lack of interest by Hawker was to be reflected in the design's poor showing against the competition.

Armstrong Whitworth AW.168

AWA felt that the most difficult part of M.148T was to limit the normal take-off weight to 40,000lb (18,144kg) since experience showed that this component increased quickly once the project had become hardware. So weight saving became a fundamental part of the AW.168 study and keeping down the

span was important because it reduced structure weight and avoided a second wing fold, with the associated mechanisms that generated. The process proved effective since it allowed enough additional fuel within the 40,000lb (18,144kg) limit to increase the low-level operational radius with the heaviest store by more than 25% to 510nm (945km).

Alternative layouts had been considered, all of which suffered from a very large central mass. One had two engines immediately adjacent to the fuselage as per the Gloster Javelin and Avro CF-100 and this was attractive in regard to its single-engine performance and full effectiveness of sweepback. But the need for a large bomb bay relative to

BELOW Armstrong Whitworth AW.168 (9.54). *Ray Williams Collection*

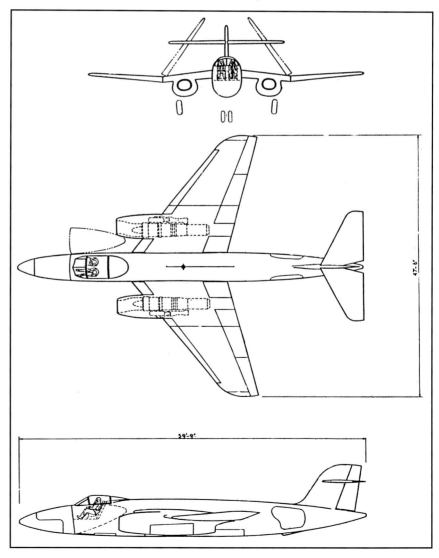

ABOVE The original manufacturer's AW.168 model in Royal Navy livery, a very attractive project that might easily have found itself lining up on the decks of Britain's carriers. *Ray Williams Collection*

the aircraft's size prevented the engines being 'tucked in' to the fuselage unless they were mounted above bomb bay level, and as such they encroached on the internal fuel capacity. Hence, this arrangement was discarded though its high-speed drag characteristics proved to be very good. Another had underslung nacelles mounted on the inner wing with the main undercarriage placed just inboard, but the retraction method pushed the nacelles too far out along the wing, which led to unsatisfactory single-

engine characteristics at low speeds. The weight was also prohibitive.

AWA felt big advantages would come from a system bleeding off compressor air and ejecting it at high speed over the flap upper surfaces to prevent airflow breakaway. These included a reduced landing speed or an increased landing weight, reduced wing area, a decrease in the deck incidence required to prevent 'sink' on leaving the catapult, and a steeper angle of climb when required. Blown flaps

were particularly advantageous for landing and entirely justified on a naval aircraft, but they gave nothing to the take-off performance. Hence, a deflected jet was also fitted to further augment the lift, AWA believing that this, in conjunction with blown flaps, would give all the required lift with minimum extra weight.

Jet deflection would make an aircraft behave as if it had a lower weight than was really the case and was usually effected by pointing the jet pipe downwards to increase lift. On the AW.168 the jet deflection consisted of a simple cowl lowered from above the jet-stream to produce a downward local jet angle of 45°. The wing had full-span drooped leading edges working in conjunction with the plain blown flaps. AWA felt that blowing should be used only briefly to boost the lift immediately after the catapult launch, then the need was for maximum thrust because a twin-engined aircraft usually attained a measure of safety from a rapid acceleration along a near horizontal path – if an engine failed, having the flaps and undercarriage up gave the least possible drag and half thrust would allow flight to continue. In contrast, a single-engine type would achieve safety directly after take-off by a modest increase of attitude at the earliest possible moment, while a shore-based aeroplane, instead of accelerating, would initially climb steeply to surmount a 50ft (15m) obstacle; no such limitation existed when flying from a carrier.

The AW.168's gross weight with a Target Marker Bomb was 37,000lb (16,783kg), this became 38,500lb (17,463kg) at maximum weapon load (4,320lb [1,960kg]) and 40,000lb (18,144g) at full load; take-off wing loading was 70lb/sq ft (342kg/sq m). This aircraft had a simple straightforward layout and structure. Its two-spar wing had just the single fold and two de Havilland Gyron Junior engines were slung underneath the inboard fixed portion of the wing with a simple forward-retracting undercarriage contained in the outer nacelle; the folded span was 23ft (7.01m). The controls were power operated and all the fuel was carried internally, mostly in the fuselage above the bomb bay but also in two inboard wing tanks, and a total of 1,690gal (7,683lit) pushed the estimated range as noted to 510nm (945km). Another 500gal (2,273lit) was provided in two plastic underwing tanks while flight refuelling could be incorporated by the fitting of a nose probe and small additions to the fuel system.

The fuselage had a conventional longeron, skin and stringer assembly. The nose housed the radar and could be folded to cut the AW.168's length by 8ft 9in (2.67m) for carrier stowage, while the crew sat side-by-side to further reduce the overall length. An all-moving tail was placed high on the fin and the bomb bay had been specially designed to take and deliver the large mix of weaponry. An Aden or Hispano four-gun pack could fit in the bay as an alternative armament, in which case bombs were then slung on the outer wings to make up the service load. Considerable drag testing was undertaken in AWA's wind tunnel facilities and a full mock-up was assembled complete with a folded wing and nose. AWA proposed that the first two aircraft should be 'flying shells' with a fixed wing and nose and no bomb bay, pressure cabin or jet deflection. The next would have the deflected jets and the fourth and all subsequent aircraft would be fully equipped to operational standard. First delivery would be thirty months from date of contract, with the twentieth and last aircraft following fourteen months later.

Armstrong Whitworth AW.168	
Span	47ft 6in (14.48m)
Length	59ft 9in (18.21m)
Gross wing area	555sq ft (51.6sq m)
t/c ratio	8.5%
Gross weight	40,000lb (18,144kg)
Powerplant	two DH PS.43 Gyron Junior 7,000lb (31.1kN)
Maximum speed/height	674mph (1,084km/h) at sea level
Weapon load	Green Cheese (GC), TMB, Red Angel (RA), bombs or air-to-surface rockets in bomb bay or under wings

Blackburn B.103

The first B.103 design had a 'big' wing, large air intakes and no area rule, Blackburn having rejected a machine powered by a single Avon. Many changes were made before the company completed its brochure and area rule was added at a late stage to give a high maximum level speed. Blackburn's objective had been to find the best

solution to the requirement as a whole rather than to emphasise any particular aspect. With new developments such as blown flaps reaching a level of practical application, Blackburn felt it had an aircraft of exceptional flexibility of weapon load and range combined with a performance well beyond that requested in M.148T.

The B.103 could take either of two new engines, although the brochure performance figures were based on a scaled down de Havilland Gyron Junior called the PS.43 of lower thrust (7,000lb [31.1kN]) than the original PS.37's 8,000lb (35.6kN); besides being the first available, PS.43 also showed a 6% improvement in fuel consumption. Supersonic performance was anticipated from more powerful Gyron Juniors or by using the alternative engine, a new 11,400lb (50.7kN) Bristol unit of very similar dimensions called the BE.33. The gross weight came well inside the 40,000lb (18,144kg) limit with a substantial margin for development and the engines were placed adjacent to the body. Engines further out along the wing had been rejected due to the increase in transonic drag and poor asymmetry, while placing them through the wing reduced frontal area and drag and gave the best air flow around the wing, nacelles and body.

The B.103's structure represented something of a new departure for Blackburn. To give structural strength, two huge machined steel spars were used in the inner wing plus integrally stiffened machined skins on both the highly loaded thin wings and the all-moving tail surfaces; a notch was cut in the wing but did not survive into hardware. Fuselage structure was conventional and the engines were mounted adjacent to the fuselage with the main undercarriage retracting sideways into spaces below them. A folding nose housed the radar and a novel rotating and lowering bomb bay door was proposed; in fact, the homing bomb was soon cancelled, which allowed this rotating door to be simplified.

All the specified weapon loads were carried internally but extra weapons

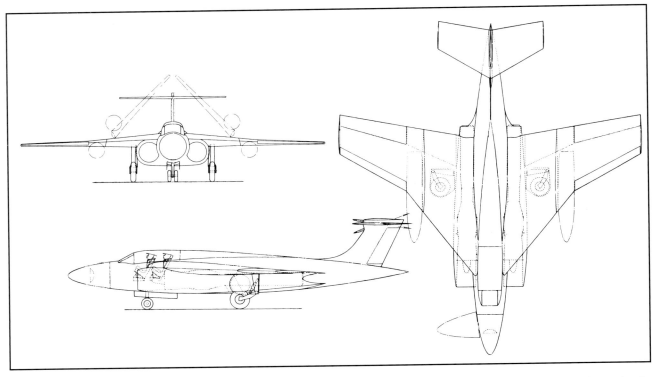

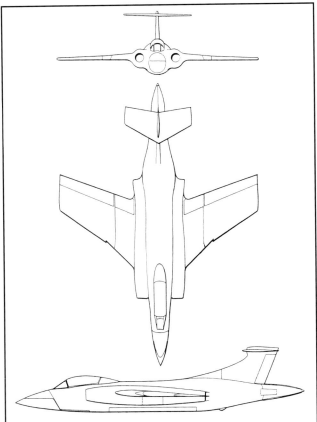

ABOVE The very first Blackburn B.103 drawing. This is clearly a Buccaneer ancestor but is some way from the finished article (1953). *BAe Brough Heritage Centre*

ABOVE Model of the B.103 to M.148T. *BAe Brough Heritage Centre*

BELOW Manufacturer's sketch artwork showing the B.103. *BAe Brough Heritage Centre*

ABOVE The B.103 as submitted to M.148T (9.54). This arrangement originally lacked the area-rule bulges and a close examination will show that several modifications are still required to turn this into an S.Mk.1 Buccaneer. *BAe Brough Heritage Centre*

could be carried under the wings inboard of the fold. Fuel was housed in the upper fuselage but there was provision for underwing drop tanks and fixed bomb bay tanks. When the B.103 carried Aden guns in the front half of its bomb bay, more fuel could be loaded in the rear. At overload, weapons and fuel could be interchanged and the range extended to twice the specified limit to give tremendous flexibility (a 1,115nm [2,066km] radius of action). This could be further extended to 1,300nm (2,409km) by completely filling the bomb bay with fuel, which was to be the arrangement when the aircraft flew as a flight refuelling tanker. Service ceiling was 35,000ft (10,668m).

High-speed air from the engine compressors was blown over the flaps and ailerons, the outer wing upper surface from just aft of the leading edge, and the tailplane, to give remarkable low-speed characteristics. This arrangement increased the available lift, gave good stalling characteristics and full lateral control down to the stall. The air was bled from the engine compressor and test results showed that the project would satisfy all of the carrier operation take-off and landing demands. In fact, the team at Blackburn, under the leadership of Barry Laight and Roy Boot, had examined bleeding of hot high-pressure air in much more depth than anyone else and the results transformed the aircraft and set new standards. Blackburn considered the B.103 offered the prospect of a clear lead over contemporary aircraft, provided it was brought into service at the earliest possible time, and in no way was it inferior to a land-based aircraft designed for similar duties.

It was intended to have the first aeroplane flying thirty-three months from date of contract with the tenth and last development aircraft ready just under two years later. If twenty machines were ordered, the programme would be accelerated. The first two or three airframes would be 'flying shells' without folding wings or nose, radar and navigation equipment, bomb bay doors, pressure cabin and weapons. Blackburn's drawing office was at the end of large-scale work for the Beverley transport and its staff could be rapidly transferred to the B.103 for a 'flying start' to the programme.

Blackburn envisaged using a BE.33-powered B.103 as a carrier-borne, all-weather fighter that offered a much improved performance and extended the scope for different roles. The engine would also be more adaptable for supplying air for boundary layer control but none would be available for the B.103 prototypes. For an increase in weight of about 1,500lb (680kg), a BE.33/B.103 could achieve a level Mach 1.05, cruise at 45,000ft (13,716m), have a greater rate of climb (22,500ft/min [6,858m/min] at sea level and 40,000lb [18,144kg] weight) and 15% more range. The company also briefly considered a third engine, the Armstrong Siddeley P.151N, which was broadly similar to the Gyron Junior but its future was uncertain. Gyron Junior was expected eventually to give 10,000lb (44.4kN) of unreheated thrust and a maximum Mach 1.03. As built the S.Mk.1 Buccaneer lacked power and would have benefited from the BE.33's

Blackburn B.103	
Span	42ft 6in (12.95m)
Length	61ft 6in (18.75m)
Gross wing area	535sq ft (49.7sq m)
t/c ratio	9% to 6%
Gross weight	39,308lb (17,830kg), maximum overload 46,000lb (20,866kg)
Powerplant	two DH PS.43 Gyron Junior 7,000lb (31.1kN)
Maximum speed/height	737mph (1,186km/h) at sea level, Mach 0.97 to 0.98 at all heights up to 30,000ft (9,144m)
Weapon load	GC, TMB, four RA, 4,000lb (1,814kg) of bombs or twenty-four RPs in bomb bay; two GC, four RA, 4,000lb (1,814kg) of bombs or twenty-four RPs under wings

additional thrust; this problem was not addressed until the S.Mk.2 arrived with Rolls-Royce Speys.

Fairey M.148

Fairey felt it would be difficult to meet most or all of M.148's requirements and numerous and extensive studies were made of various configurations before

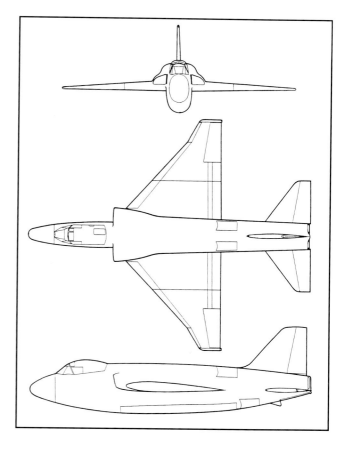

RIGHT **Fairey M.148 (9.54).** *Bill Harrison Collection*

TOP LEFT Manufacturer's artwork showing the Fairey M.148.   **ABOVE Model of the Fairey M.148.**

the design to be submitted, which represented the best compromise, was selected. It incorporated some advanced aerodynamics and structure and would be maintained easily. Because of the large fuel load a big problem had been to keep within the size limits, but the delta wing did allow a reduced t/c ratio to give the same structure weight as a conventional swept wing plus a better high-speed performance. The result had a multi-spar wing, deep fuselage and low-set, all-flying tailplane, design experience with the firm's Delta 2 supersonic research aircraft providing the background information for the choice of wing. There was a single wing fold and the main undercarriage, positioned just inside the fold, retracted sideways into the wing centre section. All controls were power operated.

Single, twin and multi-engine installations were investigated before Fairey chose two Gyron Juniors mounted side-by-side on top of the wing

centre section. Originally Fairey had been biased against de Havilland's engine and had pushed the Ministry to 'urge Rolls-Royce to make a lightweight Avon'. The sea level rate of climb was 5,010ft/min (1,527m/min) at take-off weight and the climb at altitude was expected to be ample for the high-level dropping of Green Cheese. The dive bombing requirements were met using the dive brakes, which could hold the aircraft at 500 knots (576mph/927km/h) EAS in a 60° dive from 20,000ft (6,096m) at a weight of 35,000lb (15,876kg). Top speed at 30,000ft (9,144m) was 578mph (930km/h).

The fuselage used conventional light alloy semi-monocoque construction throughout. Its bomb bay was situated under the wing centre section, the doors retracting into the bay with front and rear fairings provided to assist the airflow. Fairey explained that some lowering gear would be required for the Green Cheese and 'push off' equipment for the Target Marker Bomb. For

additional lift at low speeds the machine had leading-edge slats and double-slotted flaps with supersonic blowing over the flaps (a system described by a Ministry assessor as half-hearted, stating 'the firm supplied no details for the blowing system which had clearly not been thought out'). At normal landing weights and with flaps extended (but without blowing) the approach speed for carrier landings was estimated to be 140mph (225km/h); with blowing the approach speed was 129mph (208km/h). Fuselage and wing tanks gave a range of 1,660 miles (2,672km), but this could be increased to 2,130 miles (3,428km) by fitting two 300gal (1,364lit) overload tanks for a gross weight of nearly 45,000lb (20,412kg).

Fairey estimated it would need three years to deliver the first aircraft and sixty-nine months to complete the twentieth, but the brochure lacked specific build details and the assessor could only assume that the first would be built to a full naval standard but

Fairey M.148	
Span	42ft 0in (12.80m)
Length	51ft 0in (15.54m)
Gross wing area	500sq ft (46.5sq m)
t/c ratio	9% inner wing, 5.3% tip
Gross weight	39,500lb (17,917kg)
Powerplant	two DH PS.43 Gyron Junior 7,000lb (31.1kN)
Maximum speed/height	658mph (1,059km/h) at sea level
Weapon load	Mix of Green Cheese, TMB, Red Angel, 4,000lb (1,814kg) of bombs or RPs in bomb bay or under wings

initially unequipped. The brochure offered as an alternative one RA.24 Avon with the design's span increased to 45ft (13.72m) and wing area to 550sq ft (51.2sq m), but its sea level speed would drop to 645mph (1,038km/h) and rate of climb to 3,855ft/min (1,175m/min). Except for the engine installation, this aircraft was essentially the same and had a gross weight of 38,500lb (17,464kg).

Hawker P.1108

As noted earlier, Hawker had shown little interest in M.148T and its P.1108 project was put together at the last minute. Nevertheless, it still displayed some typical Kingston curvature, particularly in the wing. As Rolls-Royce had no suitable engine for a twin-powerplant configuration (Hawker favoured the Derby company) the choice settled on a unit still on the drawing board. This was the small 20in (508mm) diameter RB.115 and four were placed in pairs under the inner wing. The single wing fold began just outboard of the engines but was then angled outwards to make room for a leading-edge slat on the inner wing. A fixed tail with movable elevators was located near the bottom of the fin and the P.1108 had a tricycle undercarriage with the main gear folding into the side fuselage. Its two crew were seated side-by-side while the nose with its radar could be folded to reduce the length by 7ft (2.13m). The bomb bay was designed to partially enclose the Green Cheese nuclear weapon for semi-buried carriage. Since this was not an official tender there were no estimated delivery dates.

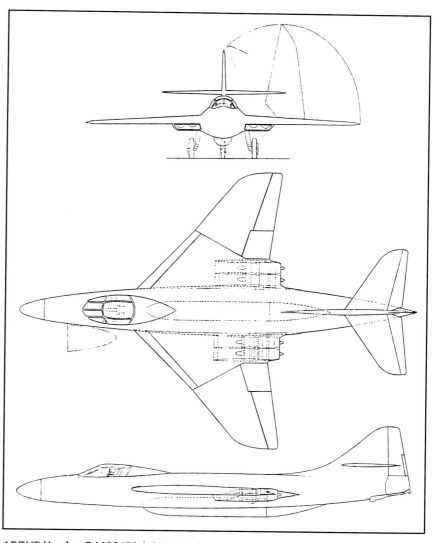

ABOVE Hawker P.1108 (30.9.54). *British Aerospace*
BELOW Impression of the P.1108 showing the small powerplants and semi-buried Green Cheese weapon. *BAE SYSTEMS*

Hawker P.1108	
Span	40ft 0in (12.19m)
Length	58ft 0in (17.68m)
Gross wing area	510sq ft (47.4sq m)
t/c ratio	7%
Gross weight	?
Powerplant	four RR RB.115
Maximum speed/height	?
Weapon load	Mix of Green Cheese, TMB, Red Angel, bombs and RPs in bomb bay or under wings

Short P.D.13

Shorts noted that M.148T could be met with a conservative design with a top speed of 630mph to 690mph (1,014km/h to 1,110km/h) but felt that a much better performance was desirable. If a naval strike aircraft was to have a long life on first-line duty then it should not fear an encounter with anything but the first-line fighters of the major air powers. Hence, a target of Mach 1 in level flight was set coupled with a very high degree of manoeuvrability. However, the low wing loading normally required by deck-landing aircraft was not conducive to attaining transonic speeds and so the solution chosen by Shorts was to use high power to augment lift at low speed, a move that also substantially reduced the wing area, structure weight and drag. The method chosen was to deflect the jet pipe itself to give a measure of direct lift and it was found that the saving in fuel and structure weight was sufficient to offset the weight of the more powerful engines. As such the design offered a high performance and no weight penalty over the conventional lower performance alternative (Shorts had examined a delta with two 10,500lb [46.7kN] Avon 27s).

The P.D.13 had a highly swept 'V' wing similar to that of the experimental Short S.B.5 so that the jet efflux at the root of the wing trailing edge could be deflected downwards without producing a change of trim. With such a large angle of sweepback there was no need for a tailplane, the control, stability and damping in pitch being satisfactory throughout the speed range. Moreover, a low tail could not be used with jet deflection and a high tail had been shown to be unsatisfactory, especially at the stall. The P.D.13 was therefore tailless and featured Geoffrey Hill's 'aero-isoclinic' wing with tip controllers. All-moving wing tips, equivalent to the all-moving tail on conventional high-speed aeroplanes, were considered essential for control at high speeds on a tailless aircraft. And on this machine the usable rate of roll would be determined by the pilot's ability to withstand acceleration, not by the limits of aileron effectiveness; hence, at Mach 0.85 at 5,000ft (1,524m) the theoretical maximum rate of roll was around 800°/sec. At low speed the controls had to be particularly effective and here again the all-moving tips were eminently suitable.

BELOW Short P.D.13 (9.54). *Short Bros*

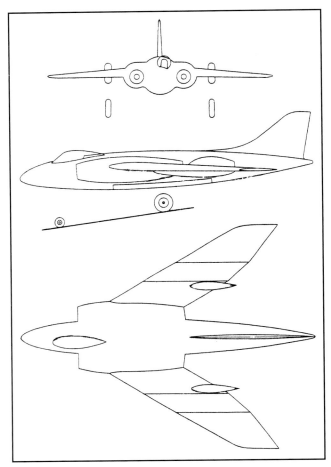

BELOW Installation of the jet pipe on the P.D.13. *Short Bros*

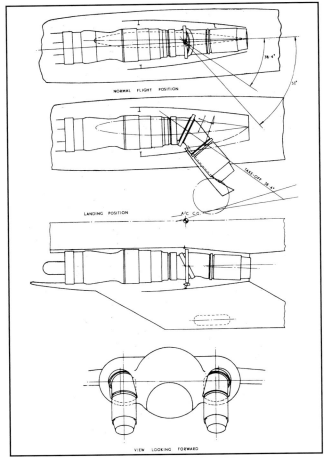

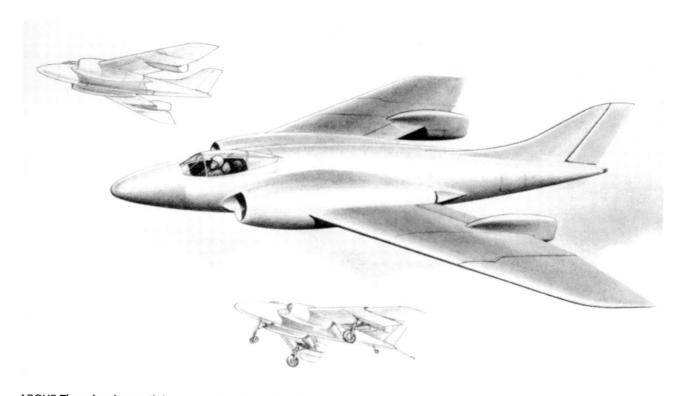

ABOVE These lovely pencil drawings of the Short P.D.13 were specially produced for the proposal brochure. *Short Bros*

BELOW AND OVERLEAF Model of the Short P.D.13. Note the raised pilot's and enclosed navigator's cockpits, the jet deflection, main undercarriage wing nacelles, and the 'isoclinic' wing tip controllers. *Short Bros*

The resulting configuration was not unlike Shorts' S.B.4 Sherpa experimental aircraft and the excellent handling qualities of that aeroplane had given the company the confidence to produce this design, which it was felt could be undertaken without any further development programme to prove the control system. P.D.13's performance figures substantially exceeded those demanded by M.148T and it was capable on emergency power of supersonic speeds at height. The best sea level rate of climb was 24,000ft/min (7,315m/min), although a take-off at 39,600lb (17,963kg) cut this to 11,800ft/min (3,597m/min), and the operational ceiling was 34,800ft (10,607m).

The two-spar wing had a single fold. Inside this the main wheels folded rearwards into their own trailing-edge nacelles while the nosewheel could be extended by the pilot on the deck to put the aeroplane into catapult attitude. Wing construction was semi-orthodox in that, owing to the breaks at the controller and fold, most of the bending and torsion would be taken by the spars. Integral fuel tanks were placed in the inner wing forward of the spar with the rest of the fuel carried above the bomb bay; there was no in-flight refuelling. The fuselage used standard frame and stringer construction with a

rotating bomb bay door and a lowering bomb bay floor. The cockpit had tandem seating (to reduce drag) and an ASV.21 search radar was carried in the non-folding nose. Two Avon RA.19 engines with full jet deflection were mounted close to the fuselage. Gross weight with the TMB was 40,000lb (18,144kg), rising to 40,520lb (18,380kg) with Green Cheese. The first delivery would take thirty months with the twentieth in just under five years.

Short P.D.13

Span	38ft 1in (11.61m)
Length	51ft 0in (15.54m)
Gross wing area	482sq ft (44.8sq m)
t/c ratio	10% root, 7% tip
Gross weight	40,520lb (18,380kg)
Powerplant	two RR Avon RA.19 12,500lb (55.6kN)
Maximum speed/height	758mph (1,220km/h) at sea level, 709mph (1,141km/h) at 30,000ft (9,144m)
Weapon load	Mix of Green Cheese, TMB, Red Angel, bombs and RPs in bomb bay or under wings

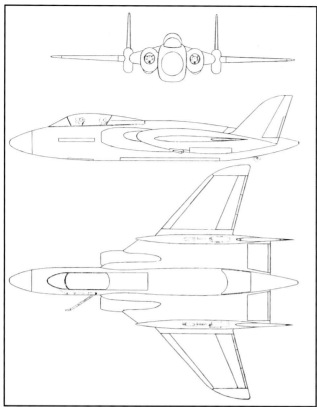

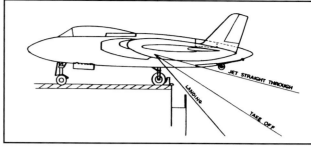

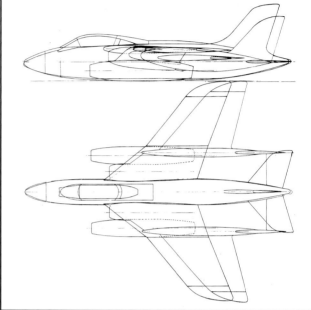

ABOVE **Westland M.148 (9.54).** *Westland*

ABOVE RIGHT **The angles of jet deflection possible on Westland's M.148 design.** *Westland*

ABOVE **For much of its M.148 study Westland compared its proposed design with a more orthodox layout which had two engines in underwing pods. This drawing has the two layouts on top of one another with, at this stage, the semi-delta having a (net?) wing area of 700sq ft (65.1sq m) and the orthodox type 450sq ft (41.85sq m).** *Westland*

Westland M.148

One aircraft to be replaced by M.148T was the Westland Wyvern and its manufacturer offered a successor to the specification; in fact, the firm declared that it was anxious to maintain the continuity of its naval strike development work. Over and above the technical problem of designing to the requirements, Westland stated that the governing condition was that the aircraft was required in service by 1960. If the new type was to follow the sequence of prototype design and development, extended trials and then a production order, then it would be impossible to meet this date. However, if it was intended to place prototype, pilot production and tooling contracts all at the same time, amounting to say twenty aircraft in all, then the firm could meet the date.

This proposal was a two-seat, twin-jet, semi-delta aircraft mounted on a four-wheel undercarriage and with a number of special features that would help the Navy to operate a strike aircraft of this size and weight using the same facilities as smaller types. An artificial high-lift device was required over and above that obtained on a conventional aircraft by the use of slots and flaps, and for this Westland had selected the method of jet deflection using the information the firm had obtained from trials with a converted Gloster Meteor fighter (serial RA490). Jet deflection was attractive because of the direct result it gave from a simple installation, all the high-lift generating devices were gathered together in the

powerplant without extensive 'plumbing', and the engine thrust was not impaired by losses in the compressor. Increases of power also gave smooth and effective changes in the rate of descent without change of trim, the aircraft being immediately responsive to rate of descent with throttle movement and without inducing fore and aft acceleration.

The brochure stated how 'taking the conditions at full power as the aircraft leaves the catapult, depending on the jet deflection angle down, the aircraft stalling speed at the end of the catapult can be lowered from about 120 knots (138mph/222km/h) to between 96 and 106 knots (111mph/178km/h and 122mph/196km/h). If the same stalling

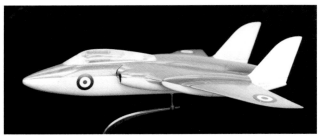

ABOVE AND LEFT Westland's M.148T two-seat naval strike aircraft had a distinctive twin-fin configuration. The underside view shows the rotating jet pipes and the small tailwheel.

speed is accepted, the weight can be increased from around 40,000lb (18,144kg) to between 47,000lb and 51,000lb (21,319kg and 23,134kg), which for emergency overload conditions represents a very great increase in the load carried. Considering the approach to land and assuming 54% maximum thrust is used, the stalling speed can be lowered from 102 knots to about 90 knots (117mph/189km/h to 104mph/167km/h), depending on the jet deflection angle and varying with the maximum thrust'. It added later that the stalling speed was reduced by about 12 knots (14mph/22km/h) for 7,000lb (31.1kN) of engine thrust and by about 30 knots (35mph/56km/h) for 11,000lb (48.9kN). The propelling nozzle was deflectable between the angles of 11° and 45° and it was anticipated that a suitable setting for take-off would be 28° and for landing 45°.

The two de Havilland Gyron Juniors were placed either side of the fuselage and mounted forward of the main structure in the root leading edge. However, the official choice of engine for the M.148 brochure was considered to be a handicap. The Gyron Junior was shown as the powerplant in the document and it would enable flight development work to proceed, but for the proper operational development of the aircraft a jet turbine with a high five-minute thrust rating for take-off and combat would give a rich dividend in overall performance. Such an engine would be the Bristol BE.33.

The proposed design had, in fact, been developed in parallel with a conventional tailed version that had engines in underwing pods and supersonic blowing over the flaps. After carrying out a full comparison of the two types it was also found that the semi-delta aircraft was superior in meeting the specification and it offered greater scope for future developments (in parallel with developments in engine thrust). The semi-delta plus the use of jet deflection for take-off and landing had resulted in a compact aircraft with a good performance at both high and low level. At the same time these two elements also gave good manoeuvring qualities because of a more moderate wing loading and this would enable very tight turns to be made in the target area at low altitude (thereby keeping the time spent in this region to a minimum). Also, the two-position undercarriage provided a nose-down attitude for landing and a tail-down attitude for catapult take-offs.

The semi-delta with wing fences at the wing fold joint gave a good approach for dealing with the problems of stiffness and structure. The worry of airframe heating due to the jet deflection was to be countered by the use of steel sheeting in close proximity to the jet nozzle, and titanium on the under surface of the aircraft aft of the jet nozzle. In the same way the rear fuselage and centre wing areas affected by jet heat when the 'high speed' jet

pipe setting was in use were to be covered by titanium.

The forward fuselage would employ conventional monocoque construction and housed the crew and the rearwards retracting nosewheel. The centre wing and its portion of the fuselage formed the aircraft's 'backbone', to which were attached the front fuselage and at the aft end the twin fins, rudders and elevators. Since this unit also included the main undercarriage and an auxiliary tail wheel it was capable of being transported on its own wheels. The main spars with extruded booms and plate webs spanned the centre wing and supported the outer folding wings on two hinges. Fences that housed the main undercarriage were then extended aft to support two fins and rudders and they also formed end plates that increased the effectiveness of the elevators. The brake flaps came in two parts, on the top and bottom of the rear fuselage just aft of the bomb bay rear bulkhead, while the outer wings saw the continuation of the main spars and supported both the ailerons and drooped leading edges (the latter had been found necessary to prevent wing tip stalling at high incidence between 15° and 20°). All the control surfaces were metal covered and fully power controlled.

All the internal fuel was carried in the upper portion of the fuselage centre section and in the inner wing (with the bomb compartment in the lower centre fuselage) and a folding flight refuelling probe was placed to

ABOVE **Artwork showing the upper surfaces of the Westland M.148.** *Westland*

ABOVE **Three Westland naval strike aircraft are shown flying in formation.** *Westland*

the port side of the cockpit. The bomb doors were designed to withstand the maximum diving speed and the weapons were all carried internally on a bomb beam; this retracted into the roof of the bay for carriage and was then lowered to the open doors for delivery. Because the project was short and stocky there was no need for the nose to fold. Design dive speed was 660 knots (760mph/1,223km/h) and the sea level rate of climb at 30,500lb (13,835kg) weight was about 8,300ft/min (2,530m/min). A mock-up of the design was built and Westland's timetable (for a contract placed in January 1955) was for the first flight of an aerodynamic test aircraft in spring 1957, with the batch of twenty aircraft fully operational by December 1959. Thus the first squadron could form in 1960.

Westland M.148	
Span	43ft 0in (13.11m)
Length	50ft 10in (15.49m)
Gross wing area	863sq ft (80.3sq m)
t/c ratio	none given
Gross weight	40,915lb (18,559kg)
Powerplant	two DH PS.42 Gyron Junior 6,830lb (30.4kN)
Maximum speed/height	674mph (1,085km/h) at sea level, 564mph (907km/h) at 35,000ft (10,668m)
Weapon load	one GC or TMB, four RA, 8,000lb (3,629kg) of bombs (overload), mines or twenty-four RPs in bomb bay

Saunders-Roe P.178

In the period up to the issue of M.148T Saunders-Roe completed two naval strike aircraft designs that seem to fit closely to the requirement, but the drawings mention no specification and no brochures were submitted. They do, however, show a TMB in an internal bay. Both had side-by-side seats, twin Gyron Junior PS.37 engines, a gross weight of 40,000lb (18,144kg) and a 4,000lb (1,814kg) bomb load. P.178/1 had engines in pods above the rear fuselage and its span was 37ft 6in (11.43m), length 48ft 9in (14.86m), wing area 470sq ft (43.7sq m), thickness/chord ratio 8% and wing loading 85lb/sq ft (415kg/sq m). P.178/2 had PS.37s in pods above the wings with a span of 39ft 0in (11.89m), length 51ft 0in (15.54m), wing area 520sq ft (48.4sq m), t/c 8% and wing loading 77lb/sq ft (376kg/sq m).

Before the Design Conference took place the suitability and workloads of the companies and their varying design experience were assessed. AWA was currently engaged on Sea Hawk development and production and, apart from the AW.52 high-speed tailless aircraft and Apollo airliner, had a design staff that in recent years had worked solely on aircraft designed by other Hawker Siddeley companies (the Meteor NF.Mk.11 and Sea Hawk). Its most recent tender, however, the Mach

2.5 AW.166 research aircraft to ER.134T, had been a very close second to the Bristol 188. The team was young and of good quality, borne out to some extent by the detailed M.148 brochure.

Blackburn's work on the Beverley freighter was expected to diminish by the end of the year. The company had a naval background through its Firebrand and GR.17/45 aircraft and in recent years had strengthened its top design staff. But its only recent high-performance design was the HP.88 crescent wing research aircraft sub-contracted from Handley Page, though its B.89 naval fighter to N.114T had tied with Westland on technical merit. B.103 would be more difficult to design and build than the AW.168, chiefly through the introduction of machined skins and large complex centre section forgings.

Fairey was fully occupied on Gannet modifications and development, Rotodyne and ultra-light helicopter design, and the flight development of the Delta 2 research aircraft, so its design capacity would be fully employed until mid-1956. Recruiting enough additional staff was impossible and Fairey's proposal to sub-contract the M.148 or other existing work was not considered feasible. It was felt that, in spite of the company's acknowledged experience in naval and high-performance aircraft, if the Gannet's

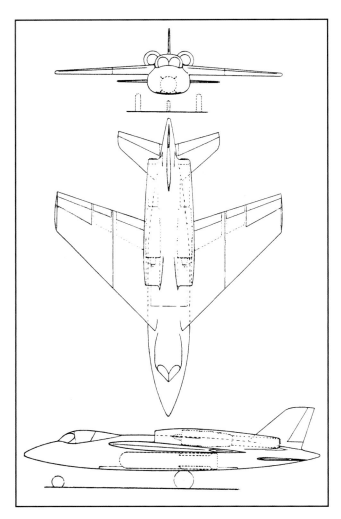

ABOVE Saunders-Roe P.178/1 (20.1.54). *Westland*

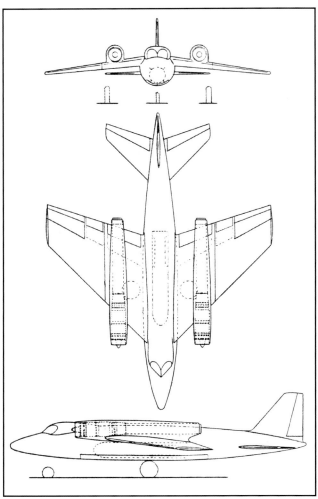

ABOVE Saunders-Roe P.178/2 (2.4.54). *Westland*

development was to proceed unhindered then M.148 should not go to Fairey on the grounds of a complete lack of design capacity. Shorts was engaged only on the Seamew and the experimental vertical take-off S.C.1 projects and had ample staff available for M.148. The company had a naval design background (Sturgeon and Seamew) and recent low-speed, swept-wing experience (S.B.5 and Sherpa), while its design administration was excellent and considered to be without equal in the industry. The lack of a tail on the P.D.13 made for a simpler design and construction task, but the time saved might be lost by the extra flight testing required to develop the controller and jet deflection.

Hawker and Westland were not assessed in detail. Hawker was

considered short of manpower because of its Hunter fighter work – basically it was a single-seat fighter company but with naval and high-performance experience and it was yet to tackle a project of this size. It was also understood that the availability of the proposed RB.115 would not match the official MoS programme for M.148. Westland was a relatively small company that had designed the jet deflection Meteor and had recent naval experience with the Wyvern, and its current work included Wyvern modifications and Whirlwind helicopter development. But the company was very short of design capacity and needed either to recruit at least a hundred extra staff or sub-contract about 60% of M.148 detail design; in fact its brochure admitted

this deficiency. Westland's programme proposals were regarded as well conceived but the quoted flight dates were felt to be optimistic by some nine months, particularly in view of the design staff situation. J. R. Webber (of RD Projects Department) completed this assessment on 18 November 1954.

The Tender Design Conference took place at the home of the MoS, St Giles Court, on 3 December 1954. At the outset both Hawker and Westland were rejected, the former by reason of no formal tender submitted, the latter because its proposal had little merit with a performance appreciably less than required; Westland was also considered to have insufficient capacity. All the survivors had a comparable performance in the dive but Shorts just failed the high-altitude cruise limits and Fairey missed them by some margin. AWA, Blackburn and Fairey all proposed a degree of sonic blowing but did not depend on this to meet the performance requirements, but the Shorts project totally depended on its jet deflection to meet them. The AWA and Shorts submissions were somewhat on the heavy side.

Blackburn's B.103 was a progressive design on which the company had done much tunnel work; the project held great promise and the sonic blow scheme seemed satisfactory, but more tunnel testing was desirable for handling purposes. With its jet deflection and wing tip controllers Shorts' P.D.13 was also very advanced, but more doubtful in achieving the performance due to the many unknowns associated with the design. The configuration was logical for a Mach 1.4 aircraft but the gain for a Mach 1.0 type was not so obvious, making the uncertainties of the tip controller unjustified. Shorts' jet deflection proposals were also regarded with some doubt. Everyone had been attracted by this novel design, but no tailless aircraft had so far proved satisfactory in service and it seemed unwise to choose the configuration for the most difficult case of all in deck landing. Considering the various companies' different ways to increase lift it was agreed that, despite a lack of experience, the use of blowing showed great promise.

Operationally, the chosen aircraft would be in service beyond the mid-1960s and would need adequate development potential. Blackburn's project was considered the best from all operational considerations such as equipment installation and ease of maintenance. It was felt that the company had made a welcome advance with its integral construction technique and there was every reason to suppose it would prove satisfactory, but the need for new machine tools would extend the development time. RAE preferred the simpler AWA proposal but there were doubts about its weight estimates. The AW.168 was the only

aircraft likely to meet the 1960 in-service date and AWA's high quality of production made it a clear first choice here. Neither Shorts nor Blackburn could be relied upon to meet the date and Fairey was definitely out due to lack of design capacity. Blackburn had little past experience on high-speed aircraft and its current manufacturing reputation was poor, but the Naval Staff said it would prefer the B.103 in 1961 rather than the AW.168 in 1960. Fairey's tender was the least satisfactory and was not considered further.

The order of merit was:

1. Blackburn. The B.103 appeared to offer the Naval Staff what it required, it should have reasonable development potential and remain useful well beyond its date of entry into service (nobody could have predicted this would mean the 1990s). It offered slightly more risk than AWA's design and seemed to represent the best compromise between the technical quality likely to be obtained and the certainty of obtaining it.

2. Armstrong Whitworth. This was a more conventional design that could be relied upon to enter service by 1960, but with a relatively short useful life. It was heavier than the other two and offered the most predictable and certain development but, technically, the smallest advance; there was little promise of further development.

3. Short Bros and Harland. A greater gamble than choosing Blackburn through the uncertainties over the wing tip controllers. The degree of risk was very high.

Ordering two types, the B.103 and AW.169, was considered with one to be halted after a year when wind tunnel and initial design work would indicate which was superior. But it was agreed that it might still be difficult to choose between them and so on 9 December 1954 recommendations were made that the B.103 should be the only aircraft ordered to M.148. Blackburn's B.103 was christened Buccaneer and the first aircraft took to the air on 30 April 1958. Forty S.Mk.1 Buccaneers were built with Gyron Junior turbojets but a lack of sufficient thrust, particularly in hot conditions, made them operationally inadequate. The first S.Mk.2 with more powerful Rolls-Royce RB.168 Spey turbofans, a military version of the RB.163 civil engine, flew on 17 May 1963 and showed great improvements.

The Buccaneer was rejected several times by the RAF, often in vitriolic fashion, but eventually politics, cancellations and circumstance combined to give the RAF no choice but to take it as the S.Mk.2B. Later chapters will show how the RAF lost its TSR.2, F-111K and AFVG, which presented a potentially catastrophic situation when one considers the capability of the Soviets. However, the Buccaneer was so ahead of its time that

BELOW XK489 was the first fully-navalised Buccaneer and this aircraft is seen in Malta in around 1960 during the type's trials flying programme.

ABOVE AND OPPOSITE TOP Two further photos of Buccaneer development aircraft. The first shows XK527, again in Malta and undergoing preparations for a test flight. Note the relatively small diameter air intakes for the de Havilland Gyron Junior jets. The second view shows XK526 after its conversion to a Mk.2 prototype with Rolls-Royce Spey engines. The most noticeable visual difference is the larger intakes.
AE Hughes via Ray Sturtivant

Blackburn Buccaneer S.Mk.2 (flown)	
Span	42ft 4in (12.9m)
Length	63ft 5in (19.3m)
Gross wing area	508.5sq ft (47.3sq m)
t/c ratio	9.25% to 6%
Gross weight	51,000lb (23,134kg)
Powerplant	two RR Spey 101 11,030lb (49.0kN)
Maximum speed/height	Mach 0.95 or 668mph (1,075km/h) IAS clean
Weapon load	Normal 4,000lb (1,814kg) internal; bombs, Sea Eagle, Martel, RPs external

it comfortably filled the gap. Had the AW.168 been built it most likely would have served the Fleet Air Arm (FAA) well through the 1960s but it would not have been suitable to fill the RAF's tactical strike and reconnaissance requirements for the 1970s.

H. R. 'Hal' Watson, Chief Designer at AWA, was particularly disappointed at losing out having reached the 'semi-finals'. In fact, AWA produced a string of good designs between the late 1940s and the mid-1950s, all of which just missed being turned into a prototype. The AW.56 features in Chapter Two while *British Secret Projects: Jet Fighters* described how AWA's fighter projects were pushed out by the Lightning, Bristol 188 and Fairey 'Delta III'.

The Navy's new large carrier programme was abandoned in 1966 and a run-down in naval fixed-wing capability began with some FAA Buccaneers passing to RAF hands.

After the cancellation of the F-111K in January 1968 (Chapter Eight), an additional new-build order was placed to ASR.391 and the type served faithfully and successfully with the RAF until 1994. Early Buccaneer weapons included the American Bullpup air-to-surface missile (ASM) and Anglo–French Martel, a TV-guided ASM developed in the 1960s; both of these missiles were rocket powered. The longer-range British Aerospace Sea Eagle, developed from Martel, was a jet-powered ASM produced from the late 1970s against ASR.1226 as an over-the-horizon, fire-and-forget weapon; it had an active radar and sea-skimming capability.

BELOW The environment from which the Buccaneer was designed to operate. This white-painted S.Mk.1 is about to launch from HMS *Hermes* in 1962 during trials. Note the trailing edge flaps and, on the deck, the jet blast deflector in position.

Chapter Six
High-Level Finale

High-Altitude Reconnaissance Bombers: 1954 to 1957

ABOVE **Model made by John Hall of the Avro 730 in its final form.** *John Hall*

There was one last attempt to get another high-altitude bomber into RAF service. It began with a supersonic reconnaissance requirement that was intended to fill a vital gap in RAF capability against the Soviet Union. Had the winning Avro 730 been completed and flown it would have been a major achievement but, once again, significant advances in the development of defensive Soviet surface-to-air guided weapons quite literally brought everything down to earth and made the 730, at least in British eyes, an outdated and obsolete concept. The Avro 730 had much in common with the American Lockheed SR-71 Blackbird and pre-dated it by a year or two. Early American studies looked quite similar to some of the designs described in this chapter but America saw its programme through to fruition and the SR-71 served for many years. Whether Britain should have completed its machine, and would it have been worth the cost, are questions that most likely will never be answered.

R.156T (and OR.330)

The story of Avro 730 began on 23 July 1954 during Air Ministry discussions for a radar reconnaissance aeroplane. Britain's nuclear strike force was fully catered for by the V-bombers but the problem of providing reconnaissance for these aircraft when using stand-off bombs was very important to the Air Staff. A draft OR was proposed that was formally issued in August, the Air Staff having been advised that any attempt to combine both bombing and reconnaissance in one aeroplane might delay it for two years. A planned replacement bomber was, therefore, put in abeyance and the pure reconnaissance Tender Specification was completed on 27 October. It was the first of a new type written on the basis of the weapon system concept whereby the aircraft and its equipment were treated as a single entity. Tenders were invited in January 1955 and five companies submitted brochures in the summer for what was an incredibly advanced requirement (Britain's first supersonic fighter was still some years from entering service).

Specification R.156T requested a supersonic high-altitude reconnaissance aircraft to obtain radar and photographic information for conducting offensive operations and it was to be capable of operation by day or night and in any weather. This task would necessitate deep penetrations of enemy territory and success depended on the ability to maintain the highest possible cruising speed at the greatest possible altitude throughout a mission. Collecting satisfactory radar reconnaissance data was the more important role and performance was not to be compromised by including large and heavy photographic systems. Minimum still air range was 5,000nm (9,265km) and cruise ceiling was to be as high as possible but not less than 60,000ft (18,288m) when the aircraft was 1,000nm (1,853km) from base. The normal operational heights would occur between 45,000ft and 70,000ft (13,716m and 21,336m) and the top speed was to be as high as possible and in excess of Mach 2.5 at maximum cruise altitude.

A speedy development was vital and OR.330 asked for completion as soon as possible and as near to 1960 as was practicable. An early production date was to be a principal factor in the design selection and the Air Staff was prepared to consider slight reductions in performance (Mach 2.0 cruise and 4,000nm [7,412km] range) coupled with a promise of further development if this would substantially advance the service entry date. Kinetic heating of the airframe would be severe because of the high cruise speed and so the designers were expected to examine this thoroughly and prepare a comprehensive heat balance covering all probable conditions of operation, including the capability of all the

equipment to withstand such temperatures. The design configuration was left open and the resulting tenders brought forth layouts of great variety and technical interest.

Avro 730

Avro identified a big problem with OR.330 in that, for any powerplant currently promised by the engine manufacturers, the requirement would be difficult to meet within a weight of about 200,000lb (90,720kg). Consequently, the design had to ensure maximum efficiency, both in regard to its aerodynamic drag and structure weight. At the required height and Mach number the Avro 730 was designed to achieve a still air range of 4,500nm to 4,700nm (8,339km to 8,709km) and to obtain this some relaxation of present practice had been assumed including indirect vision for the pilot (a periscope would be used for landing though a raised canopy was available for early development flying). Flight refuelling was not fitted.

Consideration had been given to a reduced size and development time. At Mach 2.5 the skin temperature would be 190°C but at Mach 2.0 this fell to 100°C,

thereby permitting an aluminium alloy structure for the latter condition. However, Avro had based the 730's structure on high tensile steel since this permitted the specified Mach 2.5, arguing that its known and reliable properties offset the shorter development time of light alloy; it also offered possible development to even higher Mach numbers. Construction was to be in brazed honeycomb sandwich, tests to date having indicated that this gave the same advantages over conventional methods as a similar light alloy honeycomb had given the Avro 720 rocket fighter. The manufacture of sandwich panels was a straightforward technique that avoided the need for expensive machine tools to produce integrally stiffened skins.

A further consequence of aiming for Mach 2.5 was the chance to use an unswept rather than a highly swept wing. Although a wing leading edge swept behind the Mach lines would exhibit lower drag up to Mach 2.0, Avro's studies indicated clearly that the drag of an unswept wing was less at the Mach numbers required by R.156T. Furthermore, the unswept wing was suitable for development to any Mach number whereas the highly swept-back

BEOW Avro 730 (7.55).

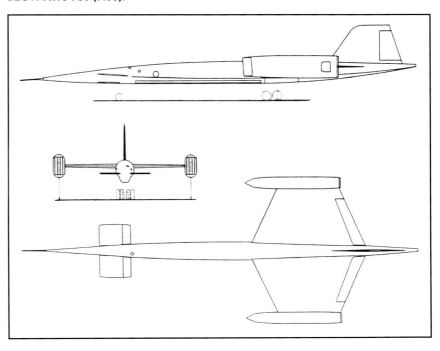

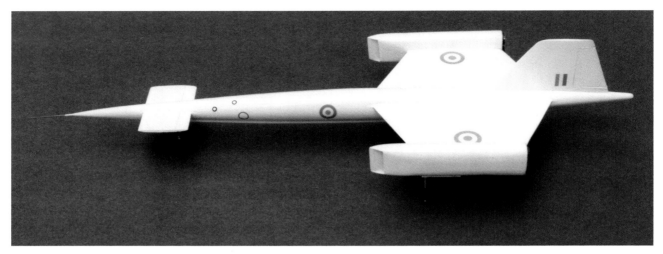

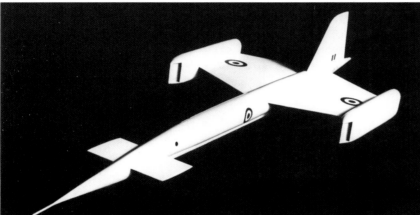

ABOVE AND LEFT Model of the Avro 730 as originally tendered. The first well-known picture shows an original manufacturer's model, the second a more recent example from John Hall.

BELOW The Avro 730's internal arrangement. Note the long Red Drover sideways-looking X-band aerial in the lower fuselage between the nose and main gears. *Avro Heritage*

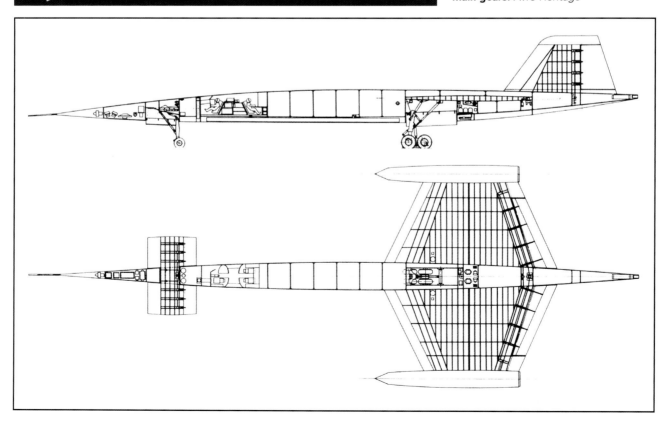

wing was limited to a Mach number somewhat below that at which its leading edge became supersonic. Other advantages of a straight wing were more lift at take-off and landing and the ability to place the whole of the powerplant at the wing tip, a structurally convenient move since the intakes were unaffected by the airflow around the aircraft and the nacelles acted as end-plates to improve lift at subsonic speeds.

Some felt that the optimum powerplant for supersonic aircraft should consist of a large number of relatively small engines, the plus factors being a low specific weight coupled with the shorter development time over a larger unit. But studies by Avro of nacelles housing various numbers of engines revealed that the small unit's lower weight was offset by the extra installation weight from the multiplicity of engine mountings, fuel systems and jet pipes. In addition, to obtain a good aerodynamic installation, the intake's leading edge should be ahead of the wing whereas the final nozzle must not be forward of the trailing edge, thus the total nacelle length had a minimum value that was dictated by the wing chord. Fitting two large engines to the 730's wing tip had shown that the minimum length of intake plus engine and propelling nozzle was little more than the wing tip chord, but for the same total thrust a nacelle with numerous small engines would have greater weight and drag.

Wing tip nacelles also presented the opportunity to introduce changes of engine and configuration with only minor effects. Comparative studies were continuing for aircraft with four, six, eight and sixteen engines but the brochure offered a design based on four Armstrong Siddeley P.159s along with two Armstrong Siddeley rocket motors underslung on the mainplane to assist with take-offs. Alternatives were four modified de Havilland Gyrons, four Bristol BE.36s, six Rolls-Royce RB.122s without reheat or sixteen of the new Rolls-Royce RB.121s; the thrust ratings were: RB.121 5,465lb (24.3kN), P.159 20,750lb (92.2kN), PS.48 Gyron 18,510lb (82.3kN), and BE.36 17,950lb (79.8kN). At Mach 2.5 the major part of the compression took place in the intake rather than the engine compressor. Therefore, intake efficiency would have a considerable effect on the overall performance and, in consequence, Avro proposed an intensive development programme to examine this area as a whole.

A supersonic aircraft would normally be designed to be statically stable longitudinally at subsonic speeds. The inevitable aft movement of aerodynamic centre at supersonic speeds led to excessive stability that, in the case of tailless or tail-aft aeroplanes, would give rise to trim drag. Hence, the 730 had been designed as a tail-first aircraft because this gave a big reduction in trim drag. This configuration also developed more lift at take-off and landing, the fuselage fitted very conveniently with the radar to give an aerial unobstructed by the wing and noseplane, and the all-moving noseplane could be mounted on the fuselage itself, which saved development time compared to an aft tailplane high on the fin. The canard's span was 21ft (6.40m) and its gross area 276sq ft (25.7sq m). (On all OR.330 canard submissions, the canard was not there so much for high lift but to assist with take-off rotation due to the very long, slender fuselage.)

Half the 730's take-off weight was fuel and a wing loading of about 100lb/sq ft (488kg/sq m) ensured that take-offs could be accomplished from normal aerodromes without resorting to special devices, except moderate RATO. The undercarriage had a single main leg positioned slightly aft of the centre of gravity and a conventional nosewheel, while the aircraft's lateral position at rest and slow speed was maintained by outriggers below each nacelle. To avoid distorting the fuselage shape, four of the eight main undercarriage wheels were to be jettisoned after leaving the ground. The primary equipment for OR.330 was the Red Drover sideways-looking X-band radar, for which two 52ft (15.85m) long aerials were provided in the lower fuselage between the nose and main gears.

Total fuel capacity was 14,320gal (65,112lit) of which 3,200gal (14,550lit) was housed in wing tanks with the remainder in the fuselage. At 222,660lb (100,999kg) weight the sea level rate of climb was predicted to be 12,300ft/min (3,749m/min); the maximum height

BELOW Wind tunnel model of the original Avro 730 proposal.

was 70,000ft (21,336m) but 93,000ft (28,346m) was possible in a zoom climb. A two-shock intake gave a Mach 2.5 cruise, a height of 60,600ft (18,471m) after flying 1,000nm (1,853km), a maximum height of 72,100ft (21,976m) and a still air range of 4,500nm (8,339km); the equivalent figures for a three-shock intake were Mach 2.6, 62,200ft (18,959m), 73,800ft (22,494m) and 4,740nm (8,783km). One pilot and two navigators formed the crew, but later on a second pilot was accepted.

Such a large aircraft built in steel honeycomb sandwich and employing a tail-first arrangement represented big departures from current practice. When the brochure was completed much low-speed wind tunnel testing had been accomplished that showed good results both longitudinally and laterally, but the supersonic tunnel work had yet to begin. It was intended that the first aircraft should fly in November 1959, three more would complete in 1960 and service entry would take place in the second quarter of 1964. The 730 was designed purely as a reconnaissance aircraft but Avro expected that a requirement would eventually arise for a bomber of similar performance to carry a ballistic bomb or, later on, a powered stand-off bomb. A 730 mock-up was built.

Avro 730	
Span	59ft 9in (18.21m)
Length	163ft 6in (49.83m)
Gross wing area	2,000sq ft (186.0sq m)
t/c ratio	3%
Gross weight	222,660lb (100,999kg)
Powerplant	four Armstrong Siddeley P.159 20,750lb (92.2kN) plus two rockets
Maximum speed/height	Mach 2.5 at 60,000ft (18,288m)

RIGHT English Electric P.10 (5.55). An outline of the tip tanks can be seen, plus in the half-underside elevation the outline for the starboard auxiliary jet engine. The half rear angle shows the jetpipe for this engine.

English Electric P.10

The EE P.10 was designed to cruise above 70,000ft (21,336m) at Mach 3.0. Again a canard, it had a ducted ramjet wing boosted by two turbojets in the rear wing root, a remarkable and novel feature. Propulsive power during cruise was supplied by the Napier ramjets burning at low fuel/air ratios with the turbojets acting mainly as auxiliary powerplants. The integration of the ramjet propulsive system with the wing necessitated an intimate relationship between its design as a load-carrying structure and as a system of bypass ramjets.

The wing was an integrated lifting and propulsive unit designed to give low supersonic cruising drag combined with large structural depth. To provide a sufficiently stiff and strong structure without interfering with the propulsive duct a 'Warren Girder continuum' was employed, consisting of a multiplicity of spanwise Warren girders with continuous chordwise 'ribs' along its diagonals, which defined the ducts laterally. Upper and lower wing skins and an integral tank in the diffuser completed the duct and a deep spar extended below the front face of the Warren continuum to increase the bending and torsional stiffness.

The flat wing panels were amenable to sandwich construction, either in steel or titanium, and the use of tip winglet extensions attached to the web of the spar to form subsonic drop tanks gave no significant weight penalty. These were to provide fuel for the take-off, acceleration and climb and, though handed, they were of constant subsonic aerofoil section; they would be jettisoned at near Mach 0.9 at 36,000ft (10,973m). In the region that formed the ramjet burner section a mesh insulation provided protection for the wing structure, which at no point passed through the gas stream. A simple two-dimensional nozzle was split into segments by vertical plates that served to brace the trailing-edge structure. Tunnel testing would determine if the outer segments of this nozzle flap could provide sufficient effect as low-speed ailerons and also see if the inner segments could act as landing flaps.

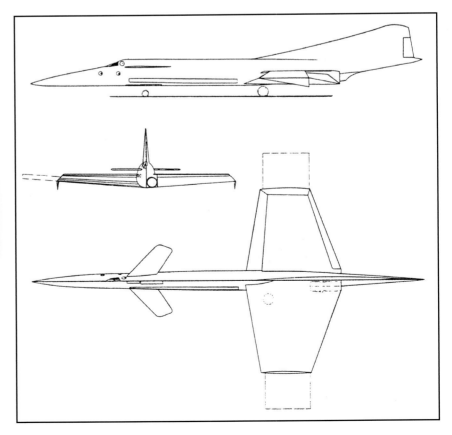

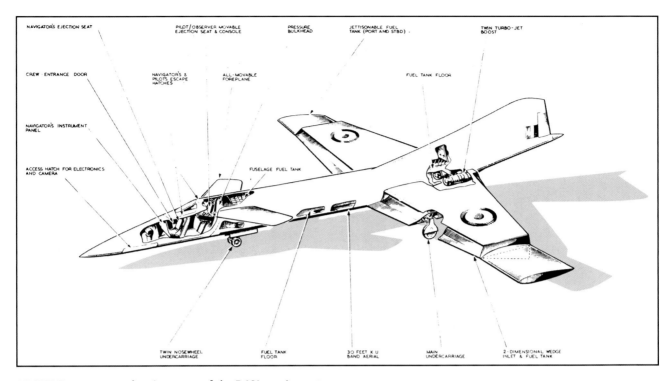

ABOVE Part cutaway showing some of the P.10's equipment.

Area rule was applied to the comparatively conventional fuselage that housed the fuel and equipment. Despite high surface temperatures (typically 240°C) on the nose section forward of the foreplane, a lack of loading (coming only from internal pressures) permitted the use of conventional light alloy skin-stringer construction in this region for a superior aerodynamic finish. Further aft, to combat the heavier fuselage loads experienced between the foreplane and the wing, alternative methods of construction comprised steel skin and stringers, or a double-skin sandwich with differing materials on the outer and inner skins to relieve the thermal stresses (both skins would be load carrying). A pear-shaped fuselage section would help to provide the critical level of stiffness required in the vertical plane.

The wing surfaces ran uncut through the lower fuselage and then the body deepened and narrowed into a low aspect ratio fin designed to eliminate the conventional couplings that gave wing flutter. A shallow 'egg box' construction replaced the fuselage shell as the fin became more wing-like. The swept foreplane panels spanned 19ft 6in (5.94m), their gross area was 128sq ft (11.9sq m) and they were mounted as all-moving surfaces. The undercarriage was a conventional tricycle form and a take-off with full fuel was considered practical only when the P.10 was mounted on a rocket-boosted trolley similar to the French Baroudeur fighter. However, a light fuel load take-off followed by in-flight refuelling presented no difficulties and was seen as the main method. P.10 had two crew, a pilot and an observer/navigator, two sideways-looking 30ft (9.14m) Red Drover aerials on 'KU Band' placed along the inside of the bottom of the centre fuselage and a Doppler aerial ahead of the nosewheel compartment.

In contrast to the turbojet, the ramjet lent itself very well to a wing-based installation since it had no moving parts and was not restricted to a circular cross-section, thus making full use of the flow area through the wing. And a great gain was that the powerplant weight was made up solely of sheet metal burners, exhaust nozzle and fuel system because the walls of the ramjet and its intake were wing structural items. The required cruise at supersonic speed was of such overriding importance that the propulsive system was designed essentially for this condition. Here air was compressed in an efficient multi-shock intake in the wing leading edge and then diffused to very low subsonic speed in a diffuser. At the end of the diffuser were the ramjet burners where the fuel was injected and the flame stabilised. In cruise the ramjets ran at very weak fuel/air ratios and only about one-sixth of the total air flow was actually used for combustion. Hence, during cruise at 70,000ft (21,336m) the ramjets were only producing about one quarter of their maximum thrust, so a huge margin was in hand for evasive manoeuvres. The rest of the air bypassed the burners and mixed downstream while, after leaving the combustion chamber, the gases were exhausted through a two-dimensional convergent–divergent nozzle. The drawing shows that the wing cross-section was divided into a number of triangular ducts, each with its own burner. By injecting extra fuel upstream of the cruise burners and using the variable nozzle, the ramjets were capable of developing a reasonable level of thrust for subsonic flight.

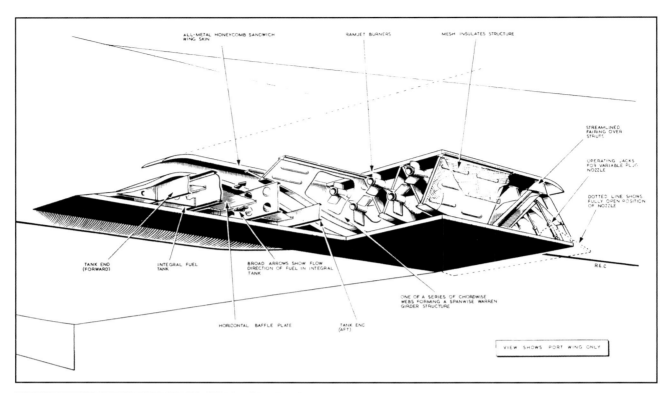

ABOVE Brochure view of the P.10's port wing structure with the integrated ramjets.

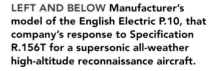

LEFT AND BELOW Manufacturer's model of the English Electric P.10, that company's response to Specification R.156T for a supersonic all-weather high-altitude reconnaissance aircraft.

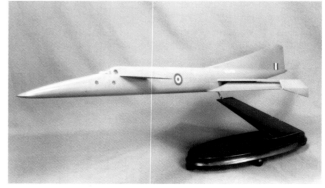

The point where thrust and drag were most likely to be critical came at near Mach 1.2 at 36,000ft (10,973m) and it was estimated that the ramjet thrust alone would equal the drag at this point; thus the extra thrust provided by the two turbojets was sufficient for providing acceleration at Mach 1.2. These auxiliary jets, developed Rolls-Royce RB.123s of 32in (813mm) diameter and mounted low in the rear fuselage, derived their air from wing ducts and they exhausted through the wing trailing edge. Their main role was to provide thrust for take-off but they were also available for low-altitude cruising after the mission had been completed. Immediately after refuelling the ramjets would be lit to continue a subsonic climb to 36,000ft (10,973m), the tip tanks providing all of the fuel used up to this point. The next stage was an acceleration to Mach 1.75 at 36,000ft (10,973m), before a climb and acceleration up to Mach 3.0 at 70,000ft (21,336m). After a full fuel load take-off it was just possible to accelerate to a speed at low level at which the ramjets could be lit (a ramjet cannot be used when the aircraft is at rest).

English Electric P.10	
Span	70ft 0in (21.34m)
Length	108ft 9in (33.15m) with tanks, 50ft 0in (15.24m) clean
Gross wing area	1,310sq ft (121.8sq m) with tanks, 1,050sq ft (97.65sq m) clean
t/c ratio	14.5% root, 12.5% tip
Gross weight	123,000lb (55,793kg)
Powerplant	twenty-four ramjet plus two RR RB.123 boosters
Maximum speed/height	Mach 3.0 at 70,000ft (21,336m)

EE predicted that, from an early contract date, a first flight could be expected in mid-1961 with service entry in the third quarter of 1964. The total internal fuel was 8,375gal (38,080lit), which EE felt was sufficient for the 5,000nm (9,265km) range, and the ceiling was 85,000ft (25,908m). R.156T had requested that no detail consideration be made for bomber applications, but EE did suggest some sketch bomber designs based on the P.10 that assessed the structural and performance penalties of carrying various sizes of ballistic bomb.

Handley Page HP.100

Handley Page's variation on the canard theme was the delta wing HP.100 designed to cruise at Mach 2.5 at a mid-range height of 65,000ft (19,812m). A detailed study of many different layouts showed that range performance remained substantially constant between Mach 2.0 and 2.5, but cruising above 60,000ft (18,288m) was essential to reduce the risk of interception. Existing light alloy structures were satisfactory for speeds up to Mach 1.8 or 2.0, but for Mach 2.5 steel or titanium was essential unless elaborate heat insulation and cooling was used. The HP.100 employed sheet steel construction but its development time would be cut to a minimum by applying the welded and riveted corrugated sandwich panel technique used so successfully on the Victor. Mach 2.5 cruise demanded a structure capable of functioning satisfactorily with skin temperatures of about 230°C; most of

BELOW Handley Page HP.100 (5.55). The Red Drover aerial is visible in the lower fuselage.

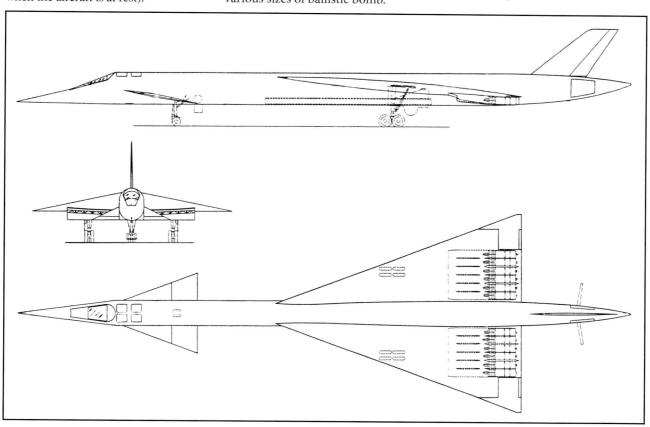

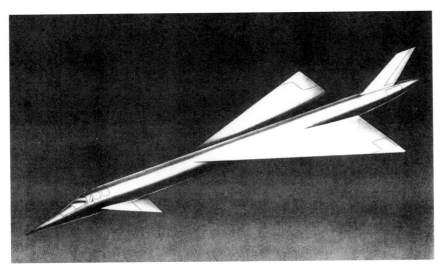

ABOVE **Original Handley Page sketch of the HP.100.**

the structure was designed for soak temperatures of 250°C to 270°C but items such as landing gears and power control units, containing materials or fluids unable to withstand such high temperatures, were to be located in cooled compartments.

The HP.100 was designed to fly in the early stages of its development programme with a range limit of 4,000nm (7,412km). The planned programme intended project design and tunnel testing to be completed in December 1956 and June 1957 respectively, aerodynamic design in June 1958 and detail design the following September. A first flight would take place in mid-1959 with service entry during the fourth quarter of 1964. Developments including more efficient engine intakes, a structural change from steel to titanium, and other changes would extend the range to 5,000nm (9,265km)

without flight refuelling. HP assumed there would eventually be a requirement to use this aircraft as a supersonic bomber with the ability to carry powered or ballistic missiles. A wide-spaced undercarriage and high ground clearance allowed carriage of both types beneath the fuselage, and powered missiles could also be carried above the fuselage. Operating as a bomber carrying a 12,000lb (5,443kg) external store, HP.100 had a range of 4,800nm (8,894km) at Mach 2.5 and a cruise height of 65,000ft (19,812m) over a target.

A detailed study of many arrangements including tail-first, tail-last and tailless, plus wings of various planforms, had showed that the tail-first slim delta of the HP.100 with an aspect ratio of 1.46 had an excellent range/load performance and good inherent handling characteristics; foreplane span was 24ft (7.32m) and

gross area 400sq ft (37.2sq m). The highly swept, sharp-nosed leading edges caused a flow pattern over the wing that remained substantially unchanged throughout the speed range, thereby ensuring no sudden changes in control and stability. A retractable visor was fitted that when lowered ensured that the pilot had an adequate view for take-off and landing, and when raised it gave a good aerodynamic shape at the fuselage nose for supersonic flight.

HP.100 had twelve RB.121 engines, but alternative studies had tried existing types such as the Gyron with which it had proved almost impossible to meet the demands of R.156T. Six RB.121s in three pairs were installed on each side of the aircraft in wide nacelles on the underside of the wing at the trailing edge – again alternatives such as fuselage installations, vertical banks at the wing tips and pods had been rejected. Vertical banks, in particular, were found to have adverse effects on stability and gave high drag; the HP.100's arrangement had low drag, no effect on stability and ensured a smooth airflow into the intakes at all usable wing incidences. A simple supersonic intake with fixed geometry had been chosen initially to help achieve an early flight date because this required no complex mechanical development and represented the type on which most work had been done both in the UK and USA. An alternative installation of four large Armstrong Siddeley P.159 units in the underwing nacelles had resulted in an extra 2,000lb (907kg) of weight plus an increase in nacelle drag.

BELOW **Views of John Hall's model of the Handley Page HP.100.**

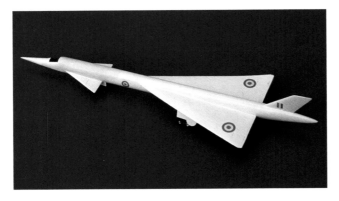

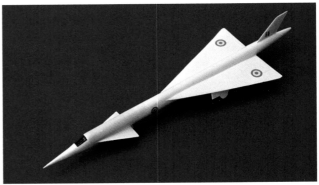

The radar fitting comprised two side-looking 50ft (15.24m) 'X-band' Red Drover linear array search installations with mirrors in the lower centre fuselage, plus a single Doppler system for ground speed and drift. The crew comprised two pilots and two rearward-facing navigators, and 16,875gal (76,729lit) of fuel was carried internally. Normal take-off wing loading at 205,000lb (92,988kg) weight was 82lb/sq ft (400.3kg/sq m) and the altitude when 1,000nm (1,853km) from base was expected to be 61,800ft (18,837m), or after a zoom climb from the cruise path 80,000ft (24,384m) with a speed of Mach 1.76; in fact, 100,000ft (30,480m) could be exceeded with a zoom climb. Range at altitude and Mach 2.5 was 4,050nm (7,505km), increasing after development to 6,020nm (11,155km) with air refuelling, and the range at sea level was 2,100nm (3,891km). An HP.100 mock-up was built.

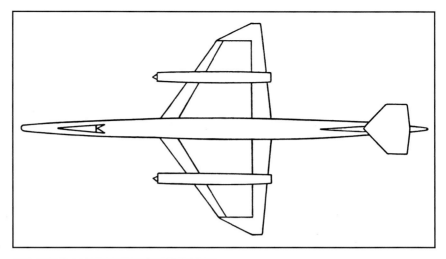

ABOVE Plan view of the Short P.D.12 (5.55).

Handley Page HP.100

Span	59ft 4in (18.08m)
Length	185ft 0in (56.39m)
Gross wing area	2,500sq ft (233.5sq m)
t/c ratio	4%
Gross weight	205,000lb (92,988kg)
Powerplant	twelve RR RB.121, 81,600lb (362.7kN) total
Maximum speed/height	Mach 0.95 at sea level, Mach 2.5 at 65,000ft (19,812m)

Short P.D.12

To the Ministry of Supply this project did not represent a formal tender; it was more of a study into the aspects and problems of flight at high supersonic speeds and appeared to present a design for a research aircraft to examine these problems. Presenting a relatively conventional layout, with engines in mid-wing nacelles and a T-tail, the brochure lacked detailed information and provided little, for example, on the equipment fittings; however, the X-band Red Drover aerial was 53ft (16.15m) long. Construction was to be in stainless steel with the main powerplant of four Bristol BE.36 engines housed in two nacelles, while two de Havilland Spectre rockets

Short P.D.12

Span	77ft 0in (23.47m)
Length	150ft 0in (45.72m)
Gross wing area	2,059sq ft (191.5sq m)
T/c ratio	?
Gross weight	175,000lb (79,380kg)
Powerplant	four Bristol BE.36 17,950lb (79.8kN) plus two DH Spectre rockets
Maximum speed/height	Mach 2.5 at c. 56,000ft (17,069m)

would provide extra thrust for take-off. Maximum height was 60,000ft (18,288m) with the cruise height when 1,000nm from base 57,000ft (17,374m), and maximum range 3,550nm (6,578km). Service entry would be the first quarter of 1963.

Vickers R.156T

The Vickers R.156T proposal employed conventional light alloy construction and would only require the development of existing plant for its manufacture, an approach that made possible a first flight by the end of 1960. Retaining light alloy was necessary because of the time, expense and education needed when using a new material. This had led to an aircraft designed to suit the temperature rise of a conventional structure, which gave a limiting speed of Mach 2.3 in the altitude band of 57,000ft to 74,300ft (17,374m to 22,647m), its maximum height. The project was the outcome of an exhaustive investigation into supersonic aeroplanes during which some fifty projects had been studied including unswept, delta, circular,

arrowhead and cranked-wing planforms. And performance comparisons of conventional and canard layouts in conjunction with different wing planforms had revealed that, in each case, the best canard configuration was capable of some 10% more range than the best conventional version.

Unless a very large tailplane was used a supersonic aircraft exhibited a nose-down pitching moment in the cruise condition due to the transonic rearward shift of aerodynamic centre. In a conventional layout this moment had to be balanced by a down load on the aft tailplane, the wing had to carry an extra load and the induced drag was thus increased. In a canard layout the balancing load of the foreplane was in an upward direction, relieving the wing and reducing the induced drag. So the choice was a canard layout giving a still air range without flight refuelling of 4,405nm (8,162km), rather better than the reduced specified minimum, and the standard 5,000nm (9,265km) would be possible with flight refuelling some 300nm (556m) from base. The chosen wing planform gave the following advantages:

a). A reasonable landing attitude, achieved by limiting the aspect ratio to a minimum of two.

b). Maximum range through a combination of low structure weight and low drag.

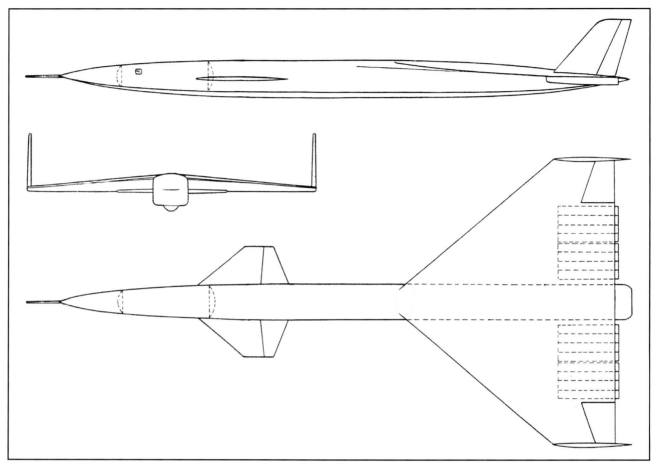

ABOVE Vickers R.156T (5.55).

c). A relatively large volume for stowage.

d). The smallest and smoothest movement of aerodynamic centre with Mach number.

e). Very low drag in the transonic speed range where the engine performance was poor, thus ensuring good acceleration and climb performance in this region.

Studies showed that a large increase in gross weight was required for a small increase in range; conversely, should a range of 3,500nm (6,486km) be considered satisfactory then a gross weight of only 123,000lb (55,793kg) was required, resulting in a cheaper aircraft that could be produced quickly and more easily. Low-speed models of this configuration had been tunnel tested and a series of rocket tests was in progress to obtain supersonic data. In addition, high-speed and supersonic wind tunnel testing would begin towards the end of 1955 with the engine intakes being tested at Rolls-Royce Derby. Twin fins, one above each wing tip, were preferred as the foreplane's wake would spoil the flow over a central fin. And no wing flaps were fitted since their provision would necessitate boundary layer control of the foreplane for trimming the aircraft with the flaps deflected. Foreplane span

BELOW Model made by John Hall of the Vickers R.156T. *John Hall*

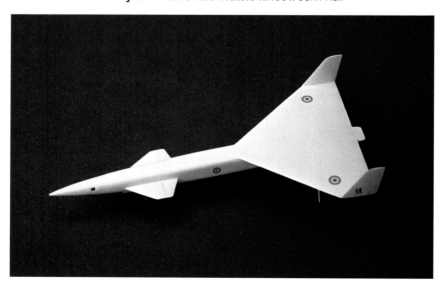

was 24ft 3in (7.39m) and gross area 367sq ft (34.1sq m).

Rolls-Royce RB.121 engines were to be used because they offered a low installation weight, low specific fuel consumption and made it possible to partially bury the engines in the wing for low installation drag. Napier's P.191, Bristol's BE.36, de Havilland's PS.38 and PS.48 and the Armstrong Siddeley P.159 had all been rejected. It was appreciated that using sixteen engines under the wing trailing edge brought complications but Vickers felt there were more gains from this format. The engine controls were simplified by dividing the powerplant into four banks, each bank comprising four engines, which allowed all the engines of a single bank to be operated as one unit. Investigations had shown that a two-dimensional 'letter box' intake with wedge-type centrebody was superior to the more widely known circular intake with a conical centrebody. A double-wedge type centrebody promised even better results since this required only three changes of angle for the second wedge throughout the Mach number range 0 to 2.3, thus avoiding the mechanical complexity of a continuously variable centrebody. The take-off would be conventional, but above an air temperature of 27°C RATOG would be employed in the form of two Spectre rockets.

The Red Drover aerial was 50ft (15.24m) long. For vision the pilot used a periscope but, in the event of its failure, a window on the port side could be opened out to 45° at speeds below 230mph (370km/h) as an emergency visual landing measure. Hiduminium RR.58 aluminium alloy was chosen as the principal structural material instead of titanium or steel. Problems with the supply of the new 'wonder-metal' titanium so early in its development were likely to prevent an early in-service date, while the difficulty of fabricating a large aircraft of this type in high-grade stainless steel remained formidable and would involve a thorough revision of tooling methods. Aluminium offered a lower structure weight and in fact a titanium alloy wing would be 18% heavier and a steel wing 30% heavier than a light alloy version, with an accompanying 'snowball' effect on the gross weight.

As far as possible machined integral panels were to be used for the main components and Vickers would gain experience in this type of construction with the Viscount replacement airliner before the manufacture of the R.156 had begun. A machined surface structural box would be built for the wing with multi-spanwise webs and

Vickers R.156T	
Span	63ft 3in (19.28m)
Length	133ft 0in (40.54m) with probe
Gross wing area	2,000sq ft (186.0sq m)
t/c ratio	4%
Gross weight	209,500lb (95,029kg)
Powerplant	sixteen RR RB.121 5,465lb (24.3kN) plus two DH Spectre rockets
Maximum speed/height	Mach 2.3 at 57,000ft (17,374m)

ribs, and this box was to be kept as large as possible in order to keep both the torsional stiffness and the fuel tankage at a maximum; the foreplane would use similar construction. The internal fuel totalled 14,550gal (66,157lit), no weapons were to be carried and the undercarriage used a four-wheel main bogie plus a nosewheel. A first flight was predicted for December 1960 with service entry in the first quarter of 1964.

Saunders-Roe P.188

Saunders-Roe undertook studies to R.156T under its P.188 project number and these embraced three preliminary layouts. Two of them utilised a total of sixteen Rolls-Royce RB.121 engines mounted either across the upper wing

BELOW Saunders-Roe P.188/1 preliminary general arrangement with sixteen RB.121s in tip nacelles (22.3.55). *Westland*

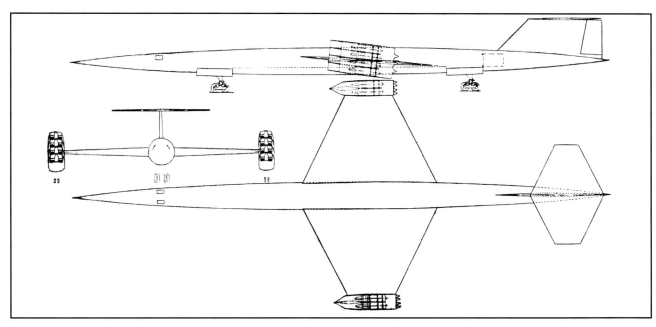

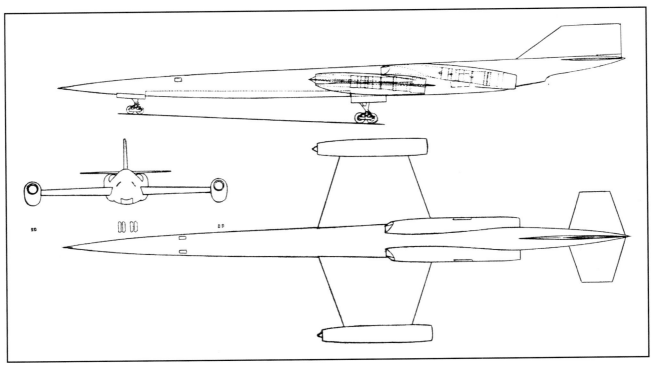

ABOVE Saunders-Roe P.188/2 preliminary general arrangement with four RB.122s in wing tip and upper fuselage nacelles and fairings (22.3.55). *Westland*

or in large wing tip nacelles, while an alternative configuration had four RB.122s, two of which were mounted on the fuselage and two at the wing tips. No brochure was tendered to the Ministry.

Several highly advanced British military aircraft programmes were under way during 1955 but R.156T/OR.330 was the most complex and potentially the most difficult of the lot. Throughout the summer a great deal of time, effort and

Saunders-Roe P.188-1	
Span	63ft 6in (19.35m)
Length	151ft 0in (45.72m)
Gross wing area	1,500sq ft (139.5sq m)
T/c ratio	?
Gross weight	170,000lb (77,112kg)
Powerplant	sixteen RR RB.121
Maximum speed/height	?

Saunders-Roe P.188-2	
Span	59ft 6in (18.14m)
Length	165ft 0in (50.29m)
Gross wing area	1,500sq ft (139.5sq m)
T/c ratio	?
Gross weight	180,000lb (81,648kg)
Powerplant	four RR RB.122
Maximum speed/height	?

paper was expended on assessing which of the tenders was best, and the final report totalled more than 250 pages. For example, in August the National Gas Turbine Establishment (NGTE) reported on EE's ramjet proposals.

NGTE explained that in terms of efficiency, for example in saving weight and drag, the possibilities of engine/airframe integration offered by the ramjet had been recognised even for short-range missiles, but until now had generally been avoided because other layouts offered apparently simpler development problems. The EE P.10 was a logical or even obvious way to use ramjets. The traditions and habits developed over many years with other types of engine would die hard and the fresh thinking so evident from EE was welcomed. However, despite the obvious attraction of the general principle, there was little practical evidence to support it and a careful detail study was needed to see if the possible gains were likely to be achieved. Here NGTE was disappointed by EE's brochure, which did not discuss the major technical and engineering

problems inherent with this system, problems that were novel, considerable and unpredictable.

More generally, the concept of the weapon system was apparently misunderstood by some companies. For example, choosing a canard was seen as a step taken by the aircraft industry primarily to overcome aerodynamic difficulties, rather than to provide the greatest benefit to the radar reconnaissance equipment. And only one company had given any thought as to how the aerial would be tested electrically and mechanically. From the radio aspect the HP.100 was most favoured because Handley Page had treated this area in far more detail and its arrangement offered the potential for improvement and development within the aircraft. Avro was a close second, having tackled the radar reconnaissance aspect fairly realistically, presumably because the company was fitting an experimental Red Drover into a Vulcan for the Royal Radar Establishment (RRE). However, the 730 offered slightly less room for development than the HP.100. Vickers got third place with English Electric and Shorts nowhere, but the assessor observed that 'it would appear that aircraft companies at present lack sufficient electronic knowledge'.

The Air Staff's operational analysis concluded that Vickers could be ruled out because it had chosen light alloy, thus restricting its speed to about Mach 2.0 and limiting the prospects for speed development. P.10 was ruled out because it would not be in service until 1965, while its low gross weight was achieved only by reducing the length of the aerial system below an acceptable limit and by making inadequate allowances for equipment. However, this design was most attractive and could form a suitable basis on which to meet a future requirement. Insufficient information was supplied by Short Brothers to assess the P.D.12 in detail, the company had failed to meet the range despite deleting 3,000lb (1,361kg) of equipment, and it was ruled out because there was no prospect of meeting the timescale. The Air Staff's estimates saw Avro and Handley Page competing for first place with a comparable speed and height performance. However, the 730 had the better range and met the 5,000nm (9,265km) limit in full without flight refuelling, when the HP.100 would only just meet the minimum 4,000nm (7,412km) until it was fully developed. Both could be modified to carry a bomb and their timescales were virtually the same, but past experience indicated that Avro was far more likely to meet the forecast date. On balance the Avro 730 appeared the more attractive.

The Tender Design Conference was held on 13 September 1955 and chaired by G. W. H. Gardner, DGTD(A). Short Brothers' P.D.12 was dropped immediately since it did not constitute a formal tender and failed to give the contractually required information. Air Commodore Kirkpatrick, DOR(A), said that the P.D.12 was not attractive to the Air Staff due to, among other things, its deficiency in range, while Nicholson of RAE felt that this was caused by an inadequate matching of

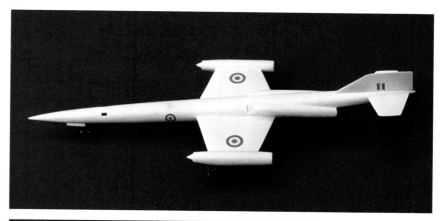

ABOVE **Privately made model of the Saro P.188/2.** *John Hall*

engines and airframe. P.D.12 had no outstanding technical or operational merits despite possibly employing experience gained with the Bristol 188. Kirkpatrick also reported that, due to its short range, the Air Staff had now ruled out the HP.100.

Morien Morgan of RAE explained that his team preferred the general configurations of the Avro 730 and Short P.D.12, although the wing plan of the HP.100 was of long-term interest. The 730's design was thought to be the best with its type of powerplant installation offering more flexibility. There was some opinion that canard layouts would present serious problems but Morgan thought that difficulties would be encountered whether the tailplane was at the back or the front. It was true that the Americans had run into troubles with canard guided weapons but these had largely cruciform configurations and the difficulties had been at higher incidences

than need be necessary on an aeroplane.

Morgan stressed that the relation between thrust and drag was extremely critical and any marginal inaccuracies would have a very large effect on range. The P.10 had interesting features but had achieved its small size only by omitting equipment; had it carried the full load, its weight and size would have been comparable with the others. Its main attraction was its propulsion system, rather than the basic design, but Morgan was not convinced that the two-dimensional array of ramjets was necessarily more efficient than having ramjets in pods. The development time for ramjets, and for a method of take-off, might be long and RAE considered it would be most unwise to rely solely on this design to meet OR.330. The OR involved technical advances that were not only substantially greater but also much more complex than had ever been undertaken in one step before.

Nicholson reported that the ranges, as estimated by RAE, were much less than those claimed by the companies – the Avro 730's was some 3,700nm (6,856km) but the HP.100 and Vickers designs came out at 2,400nm and 2,650nm (4,447km and 4,910km) respectively. With minor changes the 730 might achieve 4,000nm (7,412km) but neither the HP.100 nor Vickers were likely to reach even 3,000nm (5,559km), despite efforts to stretch the range including shifting the CofG in flight, overloading the aircraft and accepting lower flight factors, and also reducing the operating height (a reduction of 1,000ft to 2,000ft [305m to 610m] might improve the range by up to 10%). Beer and Turner of A&AEE, Boscombe Down, preferred some features on the HP.100 but confirmed that the 730's range was superior.

There was much discussion on whether to allow for weight increases from extra equipment or to freeze the design early on. For example, Air Commodore Evans said that no one firm had seriously catered for radar countermeasures (RCM) when, for operations in 1964 and beyond, such equipment would be more necessary than ever. However, Dr Robert Cockburn pointed out that these aircraft would be operated in ones and twos and their RCM could not saturate the enemy's defences without a prohibitive penalty. Controlling weight growth would clearly be a major development problem. From the reconnaissance and navigation aspect the P.10 was quite unacceptable because so much equipment had been omitted, but no firm had fully covered an integrated control system or paid any attention to an accurate alignment of the Red Drover, Doppler and Gyro system. By discarding so much equipment RRE questioned the attitude of English Electric to the weapon system concept, apparently regarding itself as an expert in the radar field when Avro was willing to be advised by specialists. Avro was the only company to cater for all the equipment.

Structurally Avro's 730 showed the simplest overall conception, but

production wise it introduced a new field. Low temperature brazing was seen as the right approach to steel sandwich construction and was probably an inevitable future technique, but of the designs submitted it posed the biggest problems. Finally, all the companies had made quite inadequate provision against the effects of kinetic heat and it was clear that considerable re-engineering would be necessary with an inevitable effect on weight. The preference was for the Avro 730 best meeting the specified requirements but the EE P.10 concept had attracted considerable interest because of its greater potential performance. It was felt that the P.10 could reinforce the 730 or be developed to future requirements or as a research aircraft.

The assessment had been confined wholly to the OR.330 reconnaissance role but on 6 April 1955 Air Marshal Pike, DCAS, had suggested the possibility of adapting the aircraft for bombing. Even during the original tendering period suspicion had grown that the OR.330 target date for operating with the V-bombers was unlikely to be met and the possibility of using the aircraft as the basis for a V-bomber successor was considered. For OR.330 Kirkpatrick said that the Air Staff had little option but to accept the Avro 730, although it fell short of the full requirement. Now bombing would also be required but the 730 had been selected without any actual reference to its ability to carry a bomb. G. W. H. Gardner, DGTD(A), explained that the primary requirement was changing from reconnaissance to bombing and Gp Capt H. N. G. Wheeler, DDOR, revealed that a bomber must be available not later than 1964 as a successor to the V class. The date now forecast for service release, 1964, disappointed the Air Staff and it was hoped that the time to first flight could be shortened by about six months. E. T. Jones, PDSR(A), said one of the first things Avro would wish to do would be to build some flying scale models, but whether they should be subsonic (with a short development time) or

supersonic (and therefore much longer) remained undecided.

Thoughts turned towards what to do with the P.10. Jones felt he could not support it as a research project since in present form it was too big, while its Mach 3 speed was much below the Mach 5 research aircraft for which he was seeking industry interest. Kirkpatrick said that the P.10 concept scaled up and carrying a powered bomb would go a long way towards meeting the new OR.336 (a follow-on requirement described shortly) and, if developed from now, would have the right three-year time separation from R.156. It was concluded that ministerial approval should be sought for separate contracts to Avro and EE to cover two years of research and development of a supersonic reconnaissance-bomber system. This followed American procedure for continuing designs for two years when the rate of expenditure was relatively low, to remove the difficulty of judging between them early on. In addition, a further contract would go to Avro to meet an amended OR.330 for bombing and another to EE to further pursue the advanced aspects of the P.10.

On 12 January 1956 EE reported how extensive tunnel testing had shown that the P.10's lateral and longitudinal stability characteristics were much better than had initially been found on the P.1 supersonic fighter and that little improvement was needed to make them as good as the P.1 today after several years' work. At low speeds there were no serious problems from the canard arrangement and the fish-tail fin shape had proved even better than expected. Bomber roles had not been considered in the original P.10 brochure but aspects of a bomber version had now been examined despite a lack of weight and geometric data being available for any new bomb. However, work on the P.10 would not progress much further.

A £25m contract was placed with Avro on 11 November 1955 for the preliminary design and supply of development aircraft to R.156T and the project received 'Superpriority' status to help it obtain the necessary raw materials. Work was under way on the prototype by the end of 1955 but design changes were soon necessary through the need for more powerful engines and to accommodate bombs. On 18 November A. E. Woodward-Nutt stated that no engine, either existing or already under development, satisfactorily matched the performance required of the aircraft. Hence, the competition to re-engine the 730 had by 24 January 1956 passed to the engine companies, who offered three possible alternatives:

i). A new 38.5in (978mm) diameter engine, the Armstrong Siddeley P.176/2.

ii). A new 37.5in (953mm) diameter engine, the Rolls-Royce RB.127.

iii). A 48in (1,219mm) diameter and heavily redesigned development of the de Havilland Gyron, the PS.26-4.

On 24 January 1956 the MoS's R. H. Weir concluded that there would be a substantial aircraft performance penalty if six PS.26-4s were used compared to eight P.176/2s or RB.127s, but there was little to choose between the performances of the latter pair. Unlike the others, it was also not possible to test the PS.26-4, complete with its air intake, under free-jet conditions in the new Engine Test Facility at NGTE Pystock. Therefore, despite the benefits of the prior existence of the basic Gyron and its development running to date, the decision favoured a smaller engine.

Weir continued: Rolls-Royce had been studying the supersonic engine for a long time and had gained much experience in intake and exhaust systems while being by far the most advanced company in the practical experience of the cooled turbine, an essential feature of the engine in question. But Armstrong Siddeley Motors (ASM) now had a lively appreciation of the problems involved and, although less advanced than Rolls-Royce in the practical experience of cooled turbines, its first Sapphire 8 had run some months ago and should rapidly supply experience through its

development for the Gloster Javelin fighter. Technically ASM had been in the unfortunate position of 'making the running' for the Avon with its Sapphire, but the only disappointment was that the company was rather late with a cooled turbine version of the Sapphire (which was in common with many companies on both sides of the Atlantic).

Weir felt both companies were capable of undertaking the design and development of the Avro 730's new engine. Technically, Rolls-Royce had the edge but two points favoured ASM:

a). The company's lower workload than Rolls, particularly now that Conway development up to Stage 4 was firmly established with the engine to be fitted into the Victor and/or Vulcan.

b). The company's close association with Avro through their common membership of the Hawker Siddeley Group.

On balance he recommended that ASM should be given contract cover to design and develop the P.176/2 for the Avro 730, and this was approved.

The P.176 was a single-shaft engine with a ten-stage axial flow compressor and a two-stage, high-temperature turbine with air-cooled rotor and stator blades. It was intended for use with a variable geometry supersonic intake and a variable area convergent–divergent propelling nozzle. Maximum sea level thrust was 14,000lb (62.2kN) and it was designed to give 4,500lb (20kN) thrust at 60,000ft (18,288m) when flying at Mach 2.5. The eight-stage compressor RB.127 was rated at 12,600lb (56kN) at sea level and 4,530lb (20.1kN) at Mach 2.5/60,000ft (18,288m); the seven-stage PS.26/4 Gyron had equivalent figures of 20,000lb and 6,055lb (88.9kN and 26.9kN). P.176 was the lightest at 2,757lb (1,251kg) and this was mainly through having a titanium compressor, the RB.127 weighed 2,942lb (1,334kg) and the PS.26-4 4,280lb (1,941kg).

By April 1956 it was hoped to fly a P.176 subsonically in a Vulcan at the end of 1958 and the 730 was expected to fly in December 1959. After the 730

was cancelled ASM looked at ways of keeping the engine project alive, including awarding a licence to Curtiss-Wright in America to which the Ministry did not object. However, the Ministry's support for the engine was cancelled in 1957 and its detail design was never finished.

Avro 730

In the ten months following contract award and the introduction of bomb-carrying capability Avro sought ways of reducing the 730's basic weight. For a supersonic aircraft with extended range the payload was about 5% of the gross weight (an increase in payload was reflected by a twenty-fold increase in gross weight), so the company concentrated on possible payload reductions. Avro now proposed a crew of two only, pilot and navigator seated side-by-side, which involved repositioning the navigational and blind bombing displays in a scheme that reduced the payload. This also eased the structural problems of providing an adequate escape hatch and it reduced the length of the crew compartment, thereby either reducing the fuselage length or making available more space for fuel.

It also became possible to carry a smaller bomb since the development of nuclear weapons had advanced to a short case megaton store for carriage in a reconnaissance-type aircraft. Hitherto, to fulfil the bomb-carrying part of the requirement the 730's design had been based on the experimental Blue Rosette store armed with a Green Bamboo warhead. A store weight of 7,000lb (3,175kg) was assumed, which itself had now dropped to nearer 6,000lb (2,722kg), but Avro had also learned of the existence of the Orange Herald A-bomb warhead that would give a store weight of 3,500lb (1,588kg). From now on the 730 would be based around the smaller weapon, but Avro felt it was wise to provide a bomb bay large enough to take the bigger store if required.

The size of the 730 was affected by the P.176's dimensions. With the changes to crew and bomb, Avro completed a full study of twenty-five different variations of the same basic layout before choosing a final form in December 1956. The first draft of RB.156D for what was now a reconnaissance bomber had been completed on 6 April 1956 (it was later renumbered B.156). For the 730 the height when 1,000nm (1,853km) out from base was now 60,800ft (18,532m) and its range with full internal fuel (take-off weight 292,000lb [132,451kg]) was 4,280nm (7,931km); the fuel capacity was 21,000gal (95,485lit) and maximum height 66,000ft (20,117m).

P.176 was finalised at 4,400lb (19.6kN) thrust at Mach 2.5 and 60,000ft (18,288m). Eight units were to be fitted, four per nacelle, and the wing shape was now much changed with sections added outboard of the nacelles. Since it had been possible to reduce Red Drover's length within an overall fatter fuselage of 9ft 4.2in (2.85m) maximum diameter (instead of 7ft 6in [2.29m]), a bomb bay had been added behind the aerials to take a 6,000lb (2,722kg) load comprising either the specially designed short-course weapon described above or the Red Beard tactical bomb. The canard's span was now 19ft 7in (5.97m) and its gross area 240sq ft (22.3sq m).

Avro 730 (Final form)

Span	65ft 7in (19.99m)
Length	159ft 0in (48.46m)
Gross wing area	2,100sq ft (195.3sq m)
t/c ratio	2.75%
Gross weight	292,000lb (132,451kg)
Powerplant	eight Armstrong Siddeley P.176 14,000lb (62.2kN)
Maximum speed/height	1,650mph (2,655km/h) between 55,000ft (16,764m) and 70,000ft (21,336m), Mach 2.0 over 45,000ft (13,716m)

Avro 731

Following suggestions for a flying model, Specification ER.180D was raised on 9 September 1956 around the proposed Avro 731 Scale Model Research Aircraft and it requested a speed of Mach 1.3 in level flight. The exacting performance requirements of

R.156 had demanded the adoption of a number of novel features – tail-first layout, thin unswept wing, tip-mounted nacelles and central main wheel with outriggers. Tunnel testing indicated that the 730 would have satisfactory flying characteristics but there was no flying experience with any aircraft having any of these features and, after judging whether the design and development effort devoted to a model at the expense of the operational machine would be too severe, Avro had concluded that such a model would be beneficial.

The Avro 731 design of December 1955 was a relatively simple three-eighths scale flying model that took every opportunity to use existing components and techniques in its construction. The manufacture of three aircraft was proposed:

a). The first to explore take-off, landing and low-speed behaviour with special attention paid to developing high lift; it would fly towards the end of 1957 with existing jet engines.

b). The second flying in mid-1958 with more powerful engines using simplified reheat and capable of extending level flight into the low supersonic region at around Mach 1.3.

c). The third also flying in mid-1958 with full reheat to allow short bursts up to Mach 1.8.

Two powerplants were considered – one Bristol Orpheus in each wing tip nacelle or two Rolls-Royce RB.108s per nacelle. Although basically designed for VTOL aircraft, Rolls-Royce was planning to develop its RB.108 for applications in training aircraft.

Direct flight evidence could be obtained in many areas, including the manoeuvrability at all speeds of the tail-first layout and general pilot familiarisation in the important low-speed phases of flight. The behaviour of a thin sharp-edged low aspect ratio wing at subsonic and transonic speeds would also be important. It was clear from tunnel testing that considerable regions of separated flow existed on

wings of this type and the association of flow separation with buffeting had been demonstrated on existing aircraft. It was vital to know the extent of the associated problems as soon as possible.

Aluminium alloy construction was to be used, the fuselage being built in honeycomb sandwich as employed in the Avro 720 fighter, and the 731's 'V' windscreen was a modified 720 type. The wing tip nacelles were to conform as near as possible to the 730's but here it was not achievable, with any of the suitable engines available, to make the nacelles exactly three-eighths scale. For the Orpheus the engine was mounted in a monocoque shell attached to the main wing torsion box and the nacelle was made long enough to accommodate the 6ft (1.83m) of jet pipe required when the 'Bristol Simplified Reheat', or full reheat, was fitted. With two Orpheus 3s the time needed to get to 36,000ft (10,973m) was predicted to be four minutes with the maximum level Mach number (using Simplified Reheat) reaching 1.4; four RB.108s gave figures of 6.5 minutes and Mach 0.99. Canard span was 9ft 3in (2.82m), gross area 53.8sq ft (5.0sq m) and 458gal (2,082lit) of fuel were to be carried.

By 7 April 1956 the MoS was proposing up to four 731s, with the first expected to fly in February 1958 and the others at three-monthly intervals – May, August and November; the Blackburn Buccaneer's Gyron Junior PS.43 engine was to be used. Avro also proposed PS.50 engines for the second and subsequent aircraft but this proved impossible because the special category engines to this standard would not be available before March 1959. PS.43s with moderate reheat would be as good and were to be developed as part of the PS.43 programme, except that the variable nozzle had to be deflected for the 731. The PS.43 was to fly for the first time during 1956 in an EE Canberra test bed, one year before the first engines were expected for the first Avro installation.

A separate high-speed research programme had begun with the Rolls-Royce Avon powered Bristol 188 to

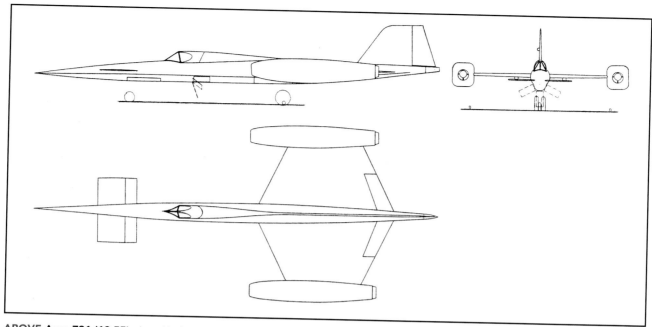

ABOVE Avro 731 (12.55). *Avro Heritage*

BELOW Artist's impression of the proposed Avro 731 flying scale model aircraft. *Avro Heritage*

ER.134D (described in *British Secret Projects: Jet Fighters since 1950*). With a supersonic successor to the Gloster Javelin fighter under way (to F.155T/OR.329), and the Avro 730, it was decided in September 1955 to order three additional Bristol 188 aircraft to accelerate these programmes. When it was established in February 1956 that the P.176's dimensions lent themselves to the 188's configuration, it was decided to adopt the engine for these additional aircraft so they could act as flying test beds for the 730 powerplant. Additionally, the 188 could assist the 730 with experience in steel manufacture and, to some extent, in aerodynamic control and kinetic heating, though it was realised that flight data would not be available in time to feed into the 730's design. In the end, delays to the Bristol 188, ironically from difficulties experienced in fabricating the stainless steel structure, prevented any data being made available to the Avro 730 programme.

Avro 731	
Span	25ft 7in (7.80m)
Length	59ft 0in (17.98m)
Gross wing area	338sq ft (31.4sq m)
t/c ratio	3%
Gross weight	14,310lb (6,409kg), or 14,246lb (6,462kg) with RB.108s
Powerplant	two Bristol Orpheus 3 or four RR RB.108
Maximum speed/height	Orpheus Mach 1.4, RB.108 Mach 0.99 at 36,000ft (10,973m)

OR.336

On 12 January 1956 Air Commodore Kirkpatrick wrote that 'from 1965 we may have to give the OR.330 an extended life with a power-guided missile as per the V-bombers, but OR.330 was not designed to carry such a thing'. But in June 1955 a Draft Operational Requirement OR.336 had been agreed at Staff level for a Medium Bomber System to replace the Avro 730. Further developments of the V-bomber force were expected to maintain its effectiveness over the next seven years, but improvements to Russian defences would prohibit their operation after that. These could include a possible active homing, long-range SAGW capable of use against supersonic targets by 1964 and the possible introduction of supersonic all-weather fighters by about 1960. It was evident that reliance on the V-bomber system and its improvements as the main support of Britain's deterrent policy would become progressively less acceptable after about 1960, and probably quite unjustifiable in the period 1962–65.

It was therefore essential to strengthen the country's offensive power for that period and studies had shown

that an effective long-range, high-altitude bombardment system could be produced within ten years. OR.336 was to define the broad outline of such a system. The effective radius of action was to be 2,500nm (4,633km) with the operational height at all times when in reach of the enemy's defences 60,000ft (18,288m), and then at least 70,000ft (21,336m) at the point of weapon release. Minimum top speed at altitude was to be Mach 3 and a ballistic nuclear weapon was to form one of two alternative loads along with an air-to-surface missile. It was against OR.336 that EE's P.10 had been seen as a possible candidate.

A Supersonic Bomber Discussion Group met regularly from 27 June 1956 to consider a successor to the Avro 730, having recognised that the very long development periods now needed for new aircraft meant such studies must start now. Despite the high-level requirement in the draft OR.336, the Group also analysed a possible low-altitude supersonic bomber and the delivery of nuclear weapons at low level; bombing techniques in general formed a major part of the discussions. The Group worked on the lines that a manned

aeroplane would continue to occupy an important role in the deterrent threat and much of this later crystallised into OR.339, a document that raised for the first time a small war capability to go with reconnaissance and bombing.

The Group concluded that there was a need for a manned system to supplement the deterrent effect of the missile and provide a more economical bombardment system for limited war purposes. But its paper expressed the view that the considerable improvement to SAGW defences in the period 1965 to 1975 would put the manned air-breathing vehicle at a disadvantage in the struggle to gain enough height, speed and manoeuvrability against a contemporary missile system.

In February 1957 the service entry for the Avro 730 was scheduled to be 1965 and the manufacture of the first test fuselage was well under way at Chadderton. But in March the Air Staff completed an examination of the contribution that manned fighter aircraft could make to the defence of the United Kingdom, concluding that the major threat to the country was changing fairly rapidly from aircraft carrying nuclear weapons to one of ballistic missiles with nuclear warheads. This, of course, formed the basis of the famous April 1957 Defence White Paper that stated that the contribution future manned fighters could make was insufficient to warrant their development. As a result the Saro SR.177 and Fairey F.155T were no longer required; only the Lightning survived to satisfy the short-term need.

At the same time the Air Staff examined the problem of maintaining the deterrent and, in view of the increasing capacity of the Russian defensive system (including surface-to-air guided weapons), it was now considered most unlikely that the Avro 730 could survive during the period it would be operational. On 11 March Air Commodore J. F. Roulston, now DOR(A), wrote: 'Since more certain methods of delivering nuclear weapons [missiles] are expected to be available in the same timescale, the Air Staff no

BELOW The Avro 730 in its final form to RB.156D (1956). *Avro Heritage*

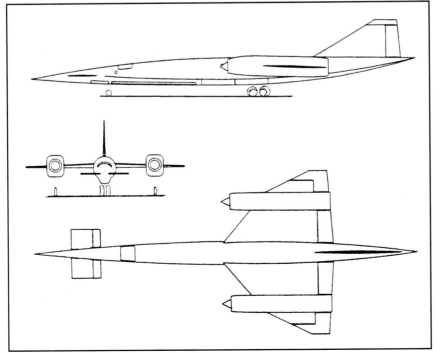

ABOVE John Hall's model showing how the Avro 730 would have looked had the prototype been completed. *John Hall*

longer requires the development of the aircraft to OR.330 nor any equipment peculiar to this aircraft'.

OR.336 was cancelled in April 1957 along with the Avro 730, the last meeting of the Discussion Group being held on 27 May. Roulston confirmed 'all that was required was an adequate deterrent, i.e. a threat to deliver thermo-nuclear bombs over long ranges. It was considered that ground-to-air missiles can always be developed to provide defence against aircraft at any time so that, after the present V-bombers, the threat would have to depend entirely on Intercontinental

Ballistic Missiles [ICBMs]. To maintain the threat reconnaissance would not be required, and in the event of a short global war we would not be interested in reconnaissance. For small wars OR.339 was the next step to provide both the required reconnaissance and bombing capability'.

In April 1957 H. J. Kirkpatrick, by now Air Vice-Marshal and ACAS(OR), wrote a paper explaining the future of manned bombers, doubts having been expressed as to the wisdom of cancelling the Avro 730. In fact, the decision was strongly influenced by new information on the

effectiveness of SAGWs with nuclear warheads. There had been concern all along about the chances of survival against missiles with conventional high-explosive warheads, but the possible availability of nuclear SAGWs in the timescale for which the 730 was expected to enter service had led the Air Staff to conclude that the aircraft would have a low chance of reaching its objective. Therefore, since more certain methods of delivering nuclear warheads were now available in the same timescale, the Air Staff no longer felt justified in continuing the OR.330 project.

ABOVE Additional Bristol 188 research aircraft were to be ordered as flying test beds for the Avro 730's P.176 engine, but they were never built. The second 188, XF926, is seen with a Hawker Hunter chase plane behind. *Bristol*

There was good reason to believe, however, that a low-altitude threat might be difficult to counter. Although low-altitude operation might not be readily compatible with the reconnaissance requirement, a low-altitude bombardment system offered attractive possibilities. In fact, the Air Staff now considered that it had tended to overrate the value of reconnaissance as a contribution to the main deterrent and there was no justification in proceeding with a project for a manned aircraft designed solely for this purpose in the 1965–1975 time period. The usefulness of a manned high-altitude bombardment system to supplement the deterrent threat of the Medium-Range Ballistic Missile was also considered and ruled out on the grounds of its vulnerability to a nuclear-

headed SAGW, and the enormous cost of developing such a system.

The manned high-altitude system might still have a limited war potential but its usefulness here could not on its own justify continuing with the project, especially when this work could be done rather better by the sort of Canberra replacement Tactical Strike Reconnaissance aircraft now under consideration. However, after a further study made on his behalf, Kirkpatrick felt that the Air Staff would not be justified in proceeding further with a project for a low-altitude bomber either. Actually, as the next chapter shows, that work was well under way and the first draft of General Operational Requirement GOR.339 had already been written.

Official records show that serial numbers were never allocated to either

the Avro 730 or 731 and it is most likely that the 731s were never ordered; they were to have been built by Armstrong Whitworth. Bristol's work on the 188 did continue but the three P.176-powered machines were also cancelled. Would the Avro 730 have been a success? The aeroplane was full of advanced systems and equipment and there was plenty of scope for problems. There were also concerns about how well the aircraft could fly if it was damaged (would it be able to return to base?) and whether there would be sufficient stiffness in such a long slim fuselage. Finally, the all-steel Bristol 188 itself proved very difficult to build, so would manufacturing the 730's structure have been an equally difficult task? The Avro 730 has left us with plenty of points to discuss.

Chapter Seven
Canberra Replacement

Tactical Strike Aircraft: 1951 to 1958

ABOVE **Model of the Bristol 204 proposal to GOR.339. The distinctive 'Gothic' wing and foreplane are well shown.**

It is now more than five decades since the TSR.2 was cancelled by the British Labour Government yet the arguments for or against that decision remain as strong as ever. The aircraft itself was a great technical achievement and one of the finest products of the British aircraft industry, taking its place alongside Concorde as the military and civil design peaks for the 1960s. The companion *British Secret Projects: Fighters* describes how the 1957 Defence White Paper closed almost all future development on manned fighters, a step that ensured there would be insufficient military work to occupy the whole industry. The only new project to survive was the 'Canberra Replacement' and most of

the companies fell over themselves to tender for it. In fact, work had been ongoing for six years.

It was often Air Ministry practice to consider a new type's replacement from the point it first entered service. When OR.302 was issued in September 1951 for a developed Canberra it was also thought to be an appropriate time to start looking at the type of aircraft that would be needed to replace it (the Air Staff would have been astonished to know that some Canberras would serve well into the twenty-first century). On 22 February 1952 Air Vice-Marshal Geoffrey Tuttle, ACAS(OR), wrote: 'Frankly, I do not believe that we will get much operational value out of the Canberra from 1955 onwards … the

aircraft is already out of date and I doubt its chances of survival in daylight against present MiG-15 opposition.' Air Cdr H. V. Satterly, DOR(A), felt Canberra was 'clearly incapable of further development to meet the light bomber task'. So a draft requirement for a new light bomber to attack targets beyond the range of fighter-bombers was circulated in March 1952 but, although the Air Staff accepted the general concept, at this stage it was not regarded as a project of first-level importance.

Throughout the history of the RAF larger and larger aircraft had been developed with greater bomb loads and ranges, but there had also been a continuing need for a bomber that was smaller, cheaper and easier to produce than its heavy contemporaries. Despite the fact that warfare was now conducted in greater depth than previously, the small bomber's primary role was still to attack enemy airfields, communications and troop concentrations, usually as part of the land/air battle. In addition, the recent wartime de Havilland Mosquito had been adapted to undertake further duties such as photo reconnaissance, night intruding and interdiction, target marking and shipping strikes. In an appreciation dated 27 May 1952, Sqn Ldr A. J. L. Craig concluded that guided missiles or a planned expendable bomber could only fulfil a limited part of the offensive short-range task; a light bomber was still required.

Gloster Thin Wing Javelin

Suggestions to adapt the Gloster Thin Wing Javelin fighter for the role were made in January 1953 and OR.328 was allocated to the project later in the year, but a lack of funding meant progress was slow. The Air Staff intended to exploit the potential low-level performance of the Thin Wing Javelin in the bomber role and its maximum range at high subsonic speed would be 1,000nm (1,852km). The great difficulties of defending against low-altitude attack should allow a Javelin bomber to have a useful low-altitude operational life until about 1966, but its high-level capability would be limited by the short range (250nm [463km]) of its ground-based blind bombing aid and its vulnerability to enemy defences during deep penetrations.

Gloster's approach was to adapt the fighter to OR.328 as closely as possible with minimal redesign, though meeting the full endurance proved difficult. Deleting the fighter equipment made space for 2,600gal (11,822lit) of internal fuel while drop tanks under the fuselage and one wing would increase this to 4,000gal (18,188lit). Olympus 6 engines were to be fitted and a 'light' atom bomb would go under the other wing, but the preferred 1959 in-service date would be missed by two years. However, in its 1955 annual review the

Defence Research Policy Committee (DRPC) recommended that OR.328 should be abandoned and so on 11 April 1956 the document was cancelled.

In early 1953 English Electric considered a replacement of its own (a supersonic mid-wing type with engines buried in the wing roots) but more serious study concerned Blackburn's naval B.103 (later the Buccaneer – Chapter Five). In October 1955 this was considered as an RAF tactical bomber but was rejected. Satterly, now ACAS(OR), stated that it was 'not much of an advance on the Canberra'. Since it was designed for low altitude and subsonic performance, its high-altitude performance was 'handicapped by either a lack of span or too early drag rise' while fitting new engines and modifying the existing wings would make a service entry in 1960 impossible. It was clear 'that to meet our requirements in full, a completely new design is necessary'. The B.103 was also thought to have an insufficient chance of surviving enemy defences and Gp Capt H. N. G. Wheeler added that it was 'simply not designed for the purpose and … barely exceeds in speed and target height the PR.Mk.9 Canberra; it seems quite wrong to introduce in 1960 a subsonic aircraft that stands no hope of being supersonic'.

Progress on the Canberra replacement was slow, principally because most of the ongoing effort was concentrated on developing the strategic bombers to provide a deterrent. During 1956, however, the absence of the tactical aircraft type from forward planning became increasingly marked, especially so during the Suez episode, and support for it became much stronger. By now the situation had been reached, bearing in mind the eight years or so needed to develop a new type, where a Canberra successor could not be expected in service before 1965.

On 28 November 1956 OR.339 was recorded for a tactical strike and reconnaissance aircraft and by February 1957 all the commands operating tactical air forces supported the low-altitude penetration concept. Only Bomber Command suggested that primary emphasis should be given to

high-level performance while the Army felt that the project represented a tremendous advance on anything it had had before. During this period adaptations of the Saunders-Roe F.177 and Fairey 'Delta III' fighters were examined, together with a VTOL low-level strike aircraft from Shorts. The B.103 was again rejected and one point raised by a joint RAF/MoS investigation was that a modified Supermarine Scimitar, costing only some £5m to develop, could meet the requirements of NA.39, for which Blackburn's aeroplane was being developed at a cost of £20m. The RAF really had it in for Blackburn's strike aircraft and in August 1957 the Admiralty had to fight off an attempt to stop developing it for the Navy.

The time-honoured practice for providing tactical strike/reconnaissance aircraft for the RAF had been to take a front-line interceptor and dress it up with ground attack weapons as a fighter-bomber. In July 1957 Tuttle noted that such practice in the jet era alone made dismal reading. Early Gloster Meteors with the 2nd Tactical Air Force in 1945, and Meteor F8s in Korea, had proved relatively ineffective in the ground attack role through a lack of range and flexibility while 'today our Swifts and Hunters are gravely restricted in the fighter reconnaissance and ground attack roles overseas. A developed F.23 [EE Lightning] would be no better'. During the recent action in Egypt the limited range of de Havilland Venoms had meant that they were operated on a sortie profile that gave maximum early warning to the enemy, and against even moderate opposition this could have had disastrous consequences. Tuttle concluded that a new and specialised aircraft was required to perform these functions (including tactical nuclear strike) with the ability to operate under any weather conditions at all ranges, day and night. And emphasis was placed on low-level capability since this posed the greatest defence problem to the enemy.

For the first time tentative features of a new type were set out in a General

Operational Requirement, GOR.339 dated March 1957, though intimations of its existence had reached EE and Hawker a year earlier. Delays and problems in developing previous military aeroplanes had led to a recommendation for a broad GOR to be raised for issue to industry at an early stage. It was intended to enlist the assistance of several companies to suggest improvements before completing a more detailed OR.339, so that advantages could be gained by getting industry involved much earlier than had been possible in the past. However, the White Paper delayed GOR.339's transmission to industry until September, and then it went to many companies, rather than to just the two or three whose advice it had been hoped to solicit. Meanwhile, in spring 1957 knowledge that the RAF needed a tactical aircraft prompted some companies to submit 'interim' variants of current types.

Blackburn B.103A

The B.103A was a simple modification of the NA.39 with integral fuel tanks inserted in the wings to replace the wing fold mechanism and a fuselage extension behind the rear cockpit for more fuel. It retained the in-flight refuelling capability and had modified Gyron Juniors providing 10% more thrust than the PS.43 but with the same cruise consumption. With the total fuel increased by 300gal (1,364lit) the take-off weight would be 48,000lb (21,773kg), radius of action 850nm (1,574km) and penetration speed Mach 0.85. The B.103A carried all the various loads of the B.103 plus two additional cameras and would be available in 1962 at the earliest.

de Havilland Christchurch DH.110

de Havilland's 'DH.110 Tactical Bomber' merged two separate RAF and Navy brochures that had been prepared during the autumn of 1956. Designed for both land and carrier operations, this aircraft made full use of the extensive experience already acquired from the standard DH.110 (Sea Vixen) with minimal changes. Tip tanks were now fitted permanently but the span was reduced by the tanks' width, which kept the overall span the same. Further underwing tanks were carried and a fuselage extension behind the cockpit made room for another 850gal (3,865lit), and so with the wing tanks the total fuel load came to 3,500gal (15,914lit). The aircraft would have a complete flight refuel system and act as a 'buddy' tanker to refuel other aircraft. Carrier operations would need a lower fuel load for take-off but flight refuelling afterwards would restore the full range.

To help the airfield performance flap blowing was installed along with extra droop on the leading edge inboard of the fence. The elevator area was increased as per the original DH.110 night fighter to F.4/48 and some wing structure was changed from DTD.683 aluminium to more fatigue-resistant 24S steel. Wing folding and the arrestor hook were retained on the land version. The extra fuel gave a 550nm (1,019km) sea level radius of action, the last

BELOW de Havilland DH.110 Tactical Bomber and Photo Reconnaissance Aircraft (3.57). *RAF Museum*

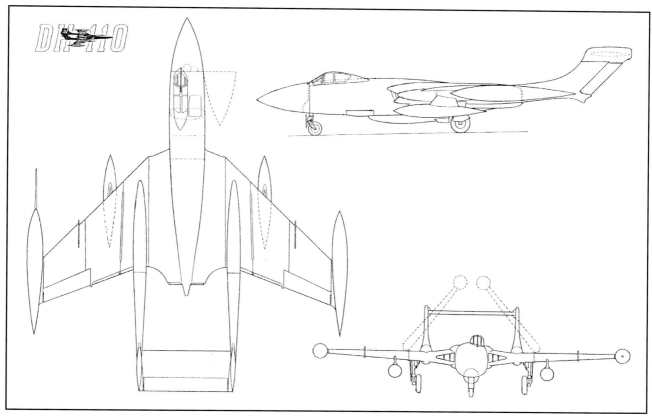

ABOVE Artist's impression of the 'interim' DH.110 with its fuselage extension. *BAE SYSTEMS*

LEFT AND BELOW Joe Cherrie's model of the DH.110 development. *Joe Cherrie*

200nm (370km) to and from a target being flown at Mach 0.87 (662mph [1,065km/h]); high altitude operation increased the radius to 1,575nm (2,917km). A burst at Mach 0.95 in a dive was planned over the target area and the dive speed limit was Mach 1.2 above 14,000ft (4,267m).

The Vixen's RA.24 Avons were replaced by Rolls-Royce RB.133s (a developed Avon) and an optional de Havilland Spectre rocket motor could be installed in a jettisonable pack between the two jets to assist take-offs. Maximum take-off weight with a TMB partly submerged in a bay in the aircraft's belly plus two drop tanks was 59,960lb (27,198kg) (wing loading 97.3lb/in2 [475kg/m2]), but four 1,000lb (454kg) bombs carried on two underwing hardpoints and in the fuselage position would increase this to 62,080lb (28,159kg). Alternative warloads comprised 24 3in (7.62cm) or 96 2in (5.08cm) rocket projectiles and reconnaissance cameras were installed in the nose alongside the radar. de Havilland intended building

de Havilland DH.110 Tactical Bomber	
Span	50ft (15.24m)
Length	59ft 6in (18.14m)
Gross wing area	611sq ft (56.8sq m)
t/c ratio	10%
Gross weight	See text
Powerplant	two RR RB.133 13,880lb (61.7kN) plus optional DH Spectre rocket
Maximum speed/height	Mach 0.87
Weapon load	See text

two prototypes during 1957 using standard Sea Vixen wings and engines to make possible an introduction into service in 1962.

BELOW **Supermarine Type 565 (2.57).**

Hawker P.1121

Hawker had put a great deal of effort into its single-engined P.1121 private venture fighter but little interest had been forthcoming from the Air Staff. A prototype was due to fly in mid-1958 and the proposal here was a tactical variant that Hawker claimed could serve both offensive and defensive functions. The company favoured the Rolls-Royce Conway 11R for offence rather than the fighter's de Havilland Gyron PS.26-6. The take-off weight with a TMB under the port wing, 1,500gal (6,820lit) of fuel and fifty 2in rockets in an internal retractable installation came to 43,700lb (19,822kg); and it became 48,200lb (21,863kg) when three more 150gal (682lit) drop tanks were carried to give a 700nm (1,296km) radius of action. Hawker stated that this aircraft would be available in 1962.

Vickers (Supermarine) Type 565

This tactical variant of the Supermarine Scimitar, begun on 21 February 1957, had a new nose to house a Blue Parrot search radar, two crew seated side-by-side, the guns and their ammunition replaced by fuel and an extra pylon under each wing, inboard of the undercarriage, which permitted a load of six 1,000lb (454kg) bombs to be carried. The wing folding and arrestor hooks had been deleted and 500gal (2,273lit) slipper tanks introduced to go with a flight refuelling capability. For nuclear delivery a single bomb was carried under the port wing balanced by a 200gal (909lit) drop tank on the starboard side. Improved Mk.2 RA.24 Avons were chosen with an optional 8,000lb (35.6kN) Spectre rocket to assist

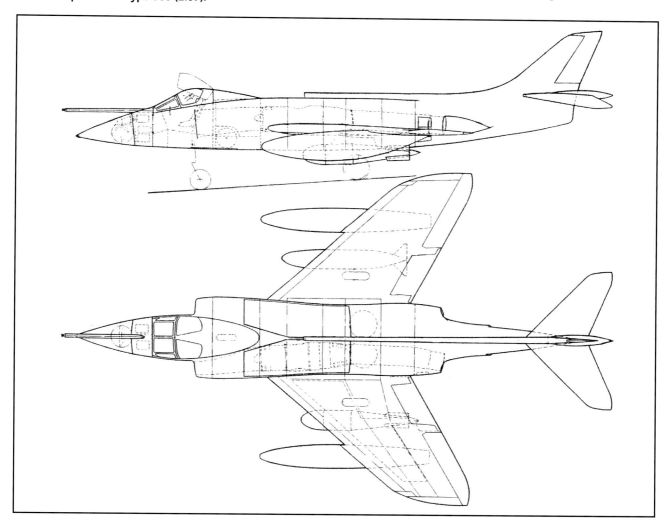

Vickers (Supermarine) Type 565	
Span	61ft 5½in (18.73m)
Length	37ft 2in (11.33m)
Gross wing area	?
t/c ratio	8%
Gross weight	See text
Powerplant	two RR RA.24 Avon Mk.2s plus optional DH Spectre rocket
Maximum speed/height	Mach 0.93
Weapon load	one TMB or six 1,000lb (454kg) bombs

on take-off. Take-off weight with one TMB, 1,548gal (7,039lit) of internal fuel, one 200gal (909lit) and two 500gal (2,273lit) drop tanks was 48,570lb (22,031kg), penetration speed Mach 0.83 with the maximum combat speed Mach 0.93, low-level range 670nm (1,241km) and high-level range 950nm (1,760km). Intended to be available in 1961, the Type 565 would have been too heavy for carrier operations.

These proposals were assessed in May 1957. All except perhaps the P.1121 would be available two years before GOR.339's required 1964 service entry, but their continuous operating speed and all-weather strike capacity fell far short of the requirement and only the modified DH.110 had the 1,000nm (1,852km) range. P.1121 was unacceptable through its single crew, external stores and short range and, indeed, it was quite different in concept to a strike aircraft. It would cost as much as an all-new design when the other 'interim' projects were intended to be a lot cheaper. The rest had a penetration speed of Mach 0.85, not GOR.339's 0.95, they lacked a short take-off capability and showed severe weaknesses in their ability to find a target; for example, the Sea Vixen development had a radar that was only really effective in good visibility. And neither the DH.110 nor the Type 565 offered solutions to the thermal problem of carrying nuclear stores externally (i.e. heat build-up from air friction).

There was also a query over 'early entry into service and low cost' since past experience had shown that such cases had produced serious

underestimates of the design work involved. Examples quoted were the swept wing on the third N.9/47 fighter prototype (Supermarine Type 508 conversion to Type 525) and the third prototype F.23/49 (English Electric Lightning P.1B), the latter taking 17,000 man weeks to produce compared to the 16,500 taken by the P.1A. The B.103A's wings and fuselage implied a large drawing office task while changes to the DH.110 and Type 565 would also need a heavy drawing effort; a 'conversion' often took as much work as the basic aircraft. Clearing the DH.110 for RAF duty would need six development machines including one for RB.133 testing, but none of these aircraft would maintain the viability of the RAF in the tactical strike/reconnaissance role beyond 1965. These aircraft would not be capable of penetrating the expected defensive systems to strike at inland targets and so all of them were rejected in July.

GOR.339

The requirement document noted that the advent of the hydrogen bomb had strengthened the deterrent enormously, and that decreased the likelihood of global war. However, limited wars were considered an increasing possibility and hence weapon systems in the tactical field should have the best possible limited war capability as well as meeting global war requirements. The Air Staff believed that the tactical strike/reconnaissance requirements could be met more adequately by a manned aircraft weapon system because the ballistic missile, though possessing several advantages, was unsuitable for meeting Cold War needs, it had no capacity for attacking unknown positions, nor a reconnaissance capability. In addition the missile was a most uneconomical method of delivering high explosive when required.

A self-contained all-weather bombing system was needed with an adequate range to permit operations from the UK's overseas bases or, in a global war, from outside the highly vulnerable tactical area. Actual independence from airfields was felt desirable, but if runways were

needed then the take-off and landing distances were to be kept to a minimum in order to facilitate operations from damaged or dispersed strips. The Canberra was to continue providing the tactical strike and reconnaissance force for some time to come but how long it would be effective in the tactical role was unknown. However, operated at low level, the Air Staff felt it could continue for limited war use at best to 1965 and in a global war until 1963. Thus, a tactical strike/reconnaissance aircraft to conduct the tactical offensive was defined with the following roles in order of priority:

a). Tactical nuclear weapon delivery from low altitudes up to the maximum range, by day or night, with minimum consideration of weather conditions.

b). Photographic reconnaissance, medium and low level in day, low level at night.

c). All-weather electronic reconnaissance without compromising the nuclear delivery role.

c). Effective delivery of tactical nuclear weapons by day or night from medium altitudes under visual conditions or with blind bombing.

d). Effective delivery of high-explosive bombs or rockets under visual conditions.

The majority of the mission had to be flown at 1,000ft (305m) or less above the ground. An alternative medium-altitude capability offered more flexibility, which was very desirable but was not to compromise the low-level requirement. The aircraft would have no defensive armament and be independent of long runways, operating from 3,000ft (914m) strips. A 1,000nm (1,852km) radius of action was stated without flight refuelling with the final 200nm (370km) to and first 200nm (370km) from the target flown at low level (the first draft of GOR.339 had requested a 600nm [1,111km] radius that still featured during the assessment). Penetration speed at sea level had to be a minimum Mach 0.95, ferry range 2,000nm

(3,704km) and in-flight refuelling would be available. An additional supersonic dash capability was preferred. The weaponry included the Red Beard Target Marker nuclear store developed to OR.1127 and alternative secondary loads of four or overload six 1,000lb (454kg) bombs, seventy-four 2in (5.08cm) or twelve 3in (7.62cm) rockets. Bomb delivery would use a loft manoeuvre at low level or a dive toss attack from medium height. Crew comfort was particularly important because some form of gust alleviation was needed to maintain tolerable conditions during long periods of high-speed, low-altitude flight.

By March 1958 further issues of GOR.339 had brought many changes, significantly some low-altitude flight at 150ft (46m) (500ft [152m] in blind conditions) and a minimum speed of Mach 1.7 at the tropopause. Part of the sortie profile now included 100nm (185km) at Mach 1.7+. The aircraft had to be in service in 1964 or as soon thereafter as possible.

A September 1957 meeting between the Ministry of Supply and the heads of all the major companies revealed that contracts would only go to groups of companies working together, the Government stating that this would be policy for any future aircraft plans (this was the first indication for a planned amalgamation of the individual companies). All submissions had to be made by 31 January 1958, eight companies plus the Hawker Siddeley Group being invited to tender. In the event some of the submitted brochures did not give clear details of their company's working partners, which counted against them during their assessment.

Avro 739

Avro's Type 739 studies were assisted by previous work on the Type 721 low-altitude and 730 supersonic high-altitude bombers, the latter providing knowledge in automatic stabilisation and control. The specified high sea level speed was a major influence on the design since it was essential to keep

aircraft response to atmospheric turbulence at a level where the crew could perform satisfactorily. Avro stated that for a given level of gustiness normal acceleration depended on forward speed, wing loading and some aerodynamic characteristics so, as the forward speed increased, the wing loading should increase accordingly to maintain the comfort level.

The 739 used conventional construction, mainly aluminium but with titanium in the hot regions near the engine. The need for an efficient structure led to the main load-carrying torsion box of the wing, constructed from panels machined integrally from slab, being taken right through the fuselage between the weapon bay and engines. An all-moving tail was mounted in the low position, which was essential for satisfactory longitudinal stability and control. Low-speed control came from the ailerons, rudder and tail, but at higher speeds the ailerons were locked so that roll control was provided by differential movement of the tailplane, which gave better rolling power at supersonic Mach numbers. Drooped leading edges

and supersonic blowing over the deflected leading and trailing edges provided lift augmentation and the wing loading was 142lb/sq ft (693kg/sq m), a figure set by the toss bomb manoeuvre. Type 739's fuselage was area-ruled, it used normal skin-stringer construction and housed the entire undercarriage because there was insufficient space in the thin wing.

GOR.339 requested a supersonic dash at sea level but the direct effect of this was to increase the structure weight. The defence against a GOR.339 type would be a radar-directed ground-to-air missile and both high aircraft speed and low aircraft altitude would reduce such a system's efficiency. It was expected that an increase in aircraft speed would, all other things being equal, lead to a rise in its height above the ground, which might nullify any reduction in vulnerability. Avro understood that recent studies had indicated how a speed of Mach 0.9 would give reasonable protection against ground-to-air defensive systems and the 739 was therefore based on a Mach 0.9 to 0.95 sea level cruise speed.

BELOW Avro 739 (1.58). *Avro Heritage*

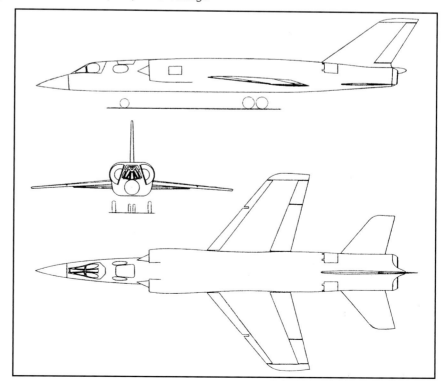

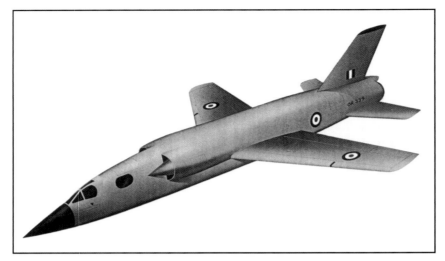

LEFT Manufacturer's model of the Avro 739. *Avro Heritage*

Fuel was housed in the wings, in large tanks above the bomb bay and in the lower rear fuselage, and two extra 600gal (2,728lit) underwing tanks or a flight refuelling pack were available if required. A 600nm (1,111km) mission radius with 100nm (185km) at Mach 2, or 1,000nm (1,852km) all subsonic, was possible on the internal fuel. The 1,000nm (1,852km) radius with a Mach 1.8 burst needed the drop tanks, which would be jettisoned prior to a supersonic acceleration. Sea level rate of climb at 70,000lb (31,752kg) weight was 10,950ft/min (3,338m/min) and at 90,000lb (40,824kg) this fell to 8,100ft/min (2,469m/min).

Six different engines had been considered: the Rolls-Royce Conway 11R/3B and 11R/3C, Bristol Olympus 14R, 15R and 21R and the Rolls-Royce RB.142. The latter was a reheated military derivative of the RB.141 Medway engine chosen for the de Havilland DH.121 airliner that had a two-spool

ABOVE AND LEFT Model made by John Hall of the Avro 739. *John Hall*

compressor and offered good cruise economy. Its initial ratings were 14,000lb (62.2kN) dry, 22,700lb (100.9kN) with reheat (RB.141 was an entirely new design based on the Conway that was later dropped and replaced by the smaller RB.163 Spey). The Ol.15R was an improved Ol.14R derived from the 200 Series production Olympus, it offered 24,700lb (109.8kN) in reheat and, having two shafts, high compression and a convergent–divergent nozzle, matched the GOR's requirements very well. For convenience the data table quotes the RB.142R because most rivals chose the same engine, but each of the engine types could take the 739 over Mach 2 at 36,000ft (10,973m). However, at that height there was an appreciable difference in performance at Mach 1 to 1.5. For example, the Conway 11R/3C (19,580lb [87.0kN] dry, 29,850lb [132.7kN] with reheat) and Olympus 21R (18,800lb [83.6kN] and 28,000lb [124.4kN]) gave 50% more acceleration, so the maximum Mach number at higher altitudes was correspondingly increased. Also, the 'small' Ol.15 and the RB.142 gave an aircraft up to 6,000lb (2,722kg) lighter than the 'heavy' Conway and Ol.21R.

The electronics included a nose-mounted 33in (838mm) radar dish and sideways navigational and reconnaissance aerials (X and Q-band), and four vertical cameras could be carried in a pack fitting. The weapon bay, placed beneath the intakes, was designed around the Red Beard store that, after a forced ejection, would be delivered by toss bombing, but Avro felt a winged stand-off bomb part buried in the lower fuselage would be more accurate. Variable sweep and VTO had been rejected because of longer development times and an alternative single-engine machine was discarded since engine failure away from base meant loss of aircraft (this would also need extra assistance on take-off). It was expected that the Type 739's first flight would be November 1961 and fifteen development aircraft would be completed during the following thirty-three months. A fighter derivative with Red Top missiles

Avro 739	
Span	41ft 3in (12.6m)
Length	80ft 9in (24.6m)
Gross wing area	568sq ft (52.8sq m)
t/c ratio	4.5% root
Gross weight	(600nm [1,111km]/1,000nm [1,852km] radius): 80,080lb (36,324kg), 90,760lb (41,169kg)
Powerplant	two RR RB.142R 'Medway' 14,590lb (64.8kN), 23,620lb (105.0kN) reheat
Maximum speed/height	Mach 0.95 at sea level, Mach 2+ at 36,000ft (10,973m)
Weapon load	Red Beard, three 1,000lb (454kg) bombs, twenty-four 3in (76.2mm) or ninety 2in (50.8mm) RPs internal; four 1,000lb (454kg) under wings, two thirty-seven 2in (50.8mm) RP pods on wing tips

was briefly outlined as a suitable long-range interceptor to succeed the English Electric P.1 (Lightning).

Blackburn B.108

The B.108 was a more extensive B.103 development from Blackburn than the B.103A, although the modifications were kept to a minimum. It departed in several ways from the GOR but the changes were felt to be acceptable when weighed against the cost, time and the greater certainty of a satisfactory product. The new operational concept of high-speed, low-level sorties introduced new problems in the

aerodynamic and aeroelastic fields while Blackburn's work on the naval B.103 had also revealed difficulties with control and structural fatigue due to the high levels of turbulence at low altitude. Consequently, the company felt its team had a unique understanding of these problems and the methods needed to overcome them.

Blackburn envisaged two stages of development, neither of which departed from the B.103's aerodynamics. Firstly, the basic airframe was increased in length by 18in (457mm) and in weight by 800lb (363kg) to accommodate a new two-seat cockpit, a new sideways-looking J-band navigation radar and a second forward-looking set for terrain following. The naval fittings were retained and photo reconnaissance gear was housed internally. With large drop tanks to supplement the internal fuel GOR.339's maximum ranges could all be met except for the 1,000nm (1,852km) limit, but in-flight refuelling was also available. Wing loading was 98lb/sq ft (478kg/sq m). These changes were offered as a low-cost alternative to an all-new supersonic design and were to be followed by a second stage offering considerable longer-term developments in speed and range. A B.108 Stage 2 would introduce a redesigned wing and reheated Gyron Junior D.GJ.12 engines.

BELOW Blackburn B.108 (1.58). *BAe Brough Heritage*

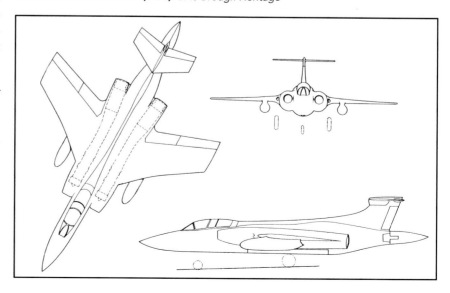

ABOVE Impression of the B.108. *BAe Brough Heritage*

The B.108's D.GJ.4 Gyron Juniors were the same as the B.103's D.GJ.1s except for the addition of cooled turbine blades. These gave the B.108 a top speed of Mach 0.95 at sea level, although Mach 0.85 was considered sufficient for penetration at low level. The climb and cruise would be made at Mach 0.85 and the dive at 748mph (1,204km/h) Mach 1.05. There was no supersonic capability in level flight since Blackburn felt the required service entry date effectively ruled this out. Supersonic performance would result in an aeroplane 50% larger than a transonic machine with a much increased development time and cost.

Several supersonic projects had been studied but it had been found that their general characteristics made them most unsatisfactory as high-explosive dive bombers and unsuitable as a limited war weapon. The first of four B.108 development aircraft (in fact the eleventh B.103 suitably modified) would be ready to fly in January 1960.

Bristol 204

Bristol's 'Gothic' wing Type 204 design was intended to have low bumpiness characteristics, it would meet the stringent take-off and landing limits without using direct lift and very high-blown flaps and have good supersonic performance without degrading its subsonic performance. Thus a relatively thick and lightly loaded (79lb/sq ft [386kg/m2]) wing was chosen with simple trailing-edge flaps trimmed by a foreplane. Recent work had revealed that the Gothic's flow pattern was more stable than that of a conventional narrow delta, especially at high incidences, and the induced drag was considerably lower than for a plain delta.

A 'Gothic' foreplane was mounted under the nose on a pylon, the front section having 10° of upward movement and the rear 40° downward. This was to be used as the primary longitudinal

control and to trim out the main wing's full-span, single-slotted trailing-edge flaps/ailerons; foreplane span was 8ft 5in (2.56m) and area 50sq ft (4.7sq m). The powerplant was integrated with the wing in having the intake on top and then burying the engines behind the combined frontal area of intake and wing. Bristol felt that the resulting configuration should give good subsonic performance, be free from major handling vices and be inherently good from a fatigue point of view. No new basic aerodynamic information would be required other than that currently being produced for the supersonic transport programme, where much theoretical and experimental work was under way.

The Type 204 used mainly conventional skin-stringer construction, primarily aluminium but with some titanium and stainless in the hot regions near the engines. These were Olympus 22s modified from the Ol.15R with simplified reheat to give 15% more thrust, the Ol.15R having been found to be a better engine than the Rolls-Royce RB.141. Two were placed side-by-side at the rear with convergent–divergent nozzles and an unusual 'letter box' two-shock wedge intake. Partially buried in the wing at the front, the engines broke through the bottom surface at the rear to form a complete nacelle. A central keel ran between the engines and through the intake while the nacelle's sides were carried forward as main ribs in the wing. The swept fin grew from the keel and had a conventional rudder, while the four-wheel main gears were placed well outboard but retracted inwards into the wing adjacent to the fuselage.

A mission radius of 875nm (1,621km) could be achieved on 4,334gal (19,706lit) of internal fuel but the specified 1,000nm (1,852km) figure required the use of drop tanks under the wings, though in-flight refuelling could be utilised. The front part of the wing outboard of the body formed the forward main fuel tank, the aft main tank coming behind the bomb cell under the wing. Radars comprised a forward-scanning 24in (610mm) X- or

Blackburn B.108	
Span	42ft 6in (12.95m)
Length	65ft 6in (19.96m)
Gross wing area	500sq ft (46.5sq m)
t/c ratio	7.5%
Gross weight	49,000lb (22,226kg) (600nm/1,111km range only)
Powerplant	two DH Gyron Junior D.GJ.4 7,700lb (34.2kN)
Maximum speed/height	723mph (1,164km/h) Mach 0.95 at sea level
Weapon load	Red Beard, four 1,000lb (454kg) bombs, thirty-six 3in (76.2mm) or seventy-four 2in (50.8mm) RPs internal; four 1,000lb (454kg) bombs external

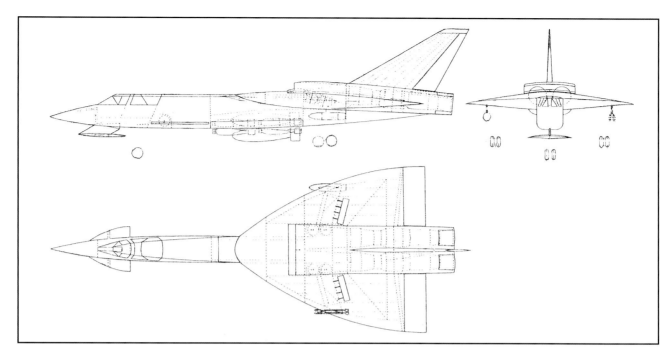

ABOVE Bristol Type 204 (14.1.58).
RAF Museum

J-band set plus a sideways J-band navigational aerial, and a photo reconnaissance pack was included. Red Beard or four 1,000lb (454kg) bombs were held in a mid-fuselage internal bay and these were to be lowered beneath the fuselage prior to release. No programme dates were given but a Type 204 fighter was also projected.

Bristol 204			
Span	32ft 0in (9.75m)	Maximum speed/height	Mach 0.95 at sea level, Mach 2.0
Length	79ft 6in (24.23m)		between 36,000ft (10,973m)
Gross wing area	820sq ft (76.3sq m)		and 55,000ft (16,764m)
t/c ratio	8.5%	Weapon load	Red Beard or four 1,000lb
Gross weight	(600nm [1,111km]/1,000nm		(454kg) bombs internal; two
	[1,852km]):		1,000lb (454kg) bombs, twelve
	65,050lb (29,507kg), 75,700lb		3in (76.2mm) or seventy-four 2in
	(34,338kg)		(50.8mm) RPs under wings
Powerplant	two Bristol Olympus Ol.22R		
	19,050lb (84.7kN), 22,520lb		
	(100.1kN) in reheat		

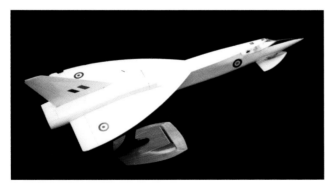

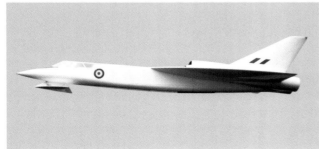

LEFT AND BELOW The Bristol 204 tactical strike/reconnaissance aircraft model.

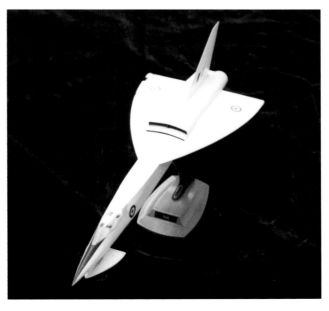

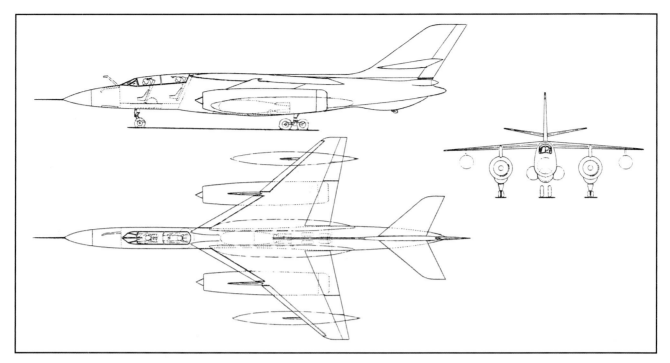

de Havilland Christchurch GOR.339

This was an unnumbered design from W. A. Tamblin's team at Christchurch and its most radical feature was a kinked 8° variable incidence wing with podded engines, the weight saving through the use of such a wing having been proved on the American F8U Crusader fighter. A moderately high loading of 110lb/sq ft (537kg/sq m) was chosen, mainly for the low-altitude sortie to help with crew comfort and structure fatigue. High-lift devices included plain blown flaps, drooping and blown ailerons and a full-span drooped leading edge. The tail and fin were conventional and a central undercarriage had a four-wheel main bogie with stabilisers under the engine pods.

The RB.142R was chosen from a selection of engines, its low specific consumption and high reheat thrust giving good flexibility. The engine nacelles had fixed centrebody intakes and continuously variable nozzles, and were far enough away from the aircraft centreline to avoid undue heat and noise effects on the rear fuselage structure; provision was made to fit a 15,000lb (66.7kN) Spectre rocket if

ABOVE de Havilland GOR.339 (first drawn 23.12.57). *RAF Museum*
BELOW Impression of de Havilland's GOR.339 aircraft. *BAE SYSTEMS*

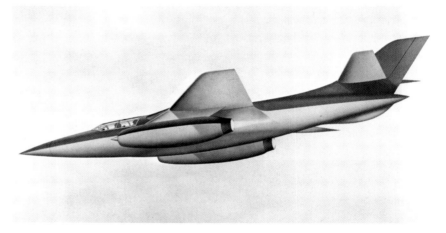

required. The wing incidence deflected the engines downwards to provide a significant vertical thrust component relative to the fuselage and tail. In reheat the climb from 1,500ft (457m) to 50,000ft (15,240m) would take 1.4 minutes with acceleration to Mach 2 on the way. Then, allowing the speed to fall off, the climb could continue until above 80,000ft (24,384m) had been reached in a total time of two and a half minutes, before the aircraft would fall back below its 1g ceiling of around 60,000ft (18,288m). Top speed with the reheat unlit was Mach 1.04 at sea level, Mach 1.30 at 36,000ft (10,973m).

Sufficient internal fuel (3,750gal [17,051lit] in the wing and in four fuselage tanks) was carried for the 600nm (1,111km) sortie but drop tanks, stressed for supersonic speed but jettisoned prior to the high-speed burst, were needed for the 1,000nm (1,852km) requirement. Studies suggested that a gross weight exceeding 70,000lb (31,752kg) was needed to carry enough internal fuel for the full mission, but this smaller aeroplane met most of GOR.339's limits and flight refuelling was available in the 'buddy' installation that had proved successful on the Sea Vixen and Scimitar. DH felt that the fuel reserves suggested in GOR.339 were unnecessarily stringent, studies with the Canberra and Javelin having indicated that they could be some 25% less. If the 100nm (185km) penetration at Mach 2.0 was done instead at Mach 0.9 at low level, the radius of action rose by some 120nm (222km).

The DH proposal had no forward-scanning radar (the nose could accommodate a 30in [762mm] dish), but sideways navigation and reconnaissance sets and photo reconnaissance equipment were fitted. Red Beard or two 1,000lb (454kg) bombs were housed internally and two more bombs were attached around the outside of the slightly protruding mid-fuselage weapon bay; two more could be carried on underwing pylons as overload and rockets, extra fuel or a reconnaissance pack could also go in the bay. A VTO option involved a wraparound belly fairing containing eight rockets that would allow the aircraft to lift off from its own pad. de Havilland stated that if contracts were placed in the autumn of 1958 it would be possible to have the

de Havilland GOR.339	
Span	34ft 0in (10.36m)
Length	67ft 6in (20.57m) without nose probe
Gross wing area	440sq ft (40.9sq m)
t/c ratio	5%
Gross weight	(600nm [1,111km]/1,000nm [1,852km]): 48,750lb (22,113kg), 60,400lb (27,397kg)
Powerplant	two RR RB.142R 14,000lb (62.2kN), 22,400lb (99.6kN) in reheat
Maximum speed/height	Mach 1.3 at sea level, Mach 2 at altitude
Weapon load	Red Beard, two 1,000lb (454kg) bombs, fourteen 3in (76.2mm) or eighty-four 2in (50.8mm) RPs internal; two 1,000lb (454kg) bombs under fuselage; two 1,000lb (454kg) bombs, twelve 3in (76.2mm) or seventy-four 2in (50.8mm) RPs under wings

type in service early in 1965. A brief examination had also been made into operating this aeroplane from Fleet Air Arm carriers and as a fighter, the high available thrust providing fighter-type performance.

English Electric P.17

EE's private venture studies for a 'Canberra replacement' began in mid-1956, well ahead of GOR.339, when it was necessary to guess the required performance. Discussions with the MoS had begun in October of that year and a figure of Mach 1.3 in the target area was quoted, along with thoughts of a P.1B (Lightning) variant. This was taken up with EE's new ideas coming under the P.17 label while the P.1B development was designated P.18. Through the winter a long series of projects were assessed within the P.17 studies, before in January 1957 the team apparently settled on a straight equi-tapered wing, twin side-by-side RB.133 engines, intakes below the wing and a low-set tail. However, work also continued on deltas and by the following October this planform's superiority had become clear, the configuration was set and tunnel tests now concentrated on refining it. The P.18 was dropped once it was clear that this type could not meet the RAF's range and airfield performance limits.

The favoured layout, a delta with a low-set, all-moving tail and a single fin,

BELOW This model of a DH GOR.339, shown 'on board' HMS *Ark Royal*, has its variable incidence wing in operation. *BAE SYSTEMS*

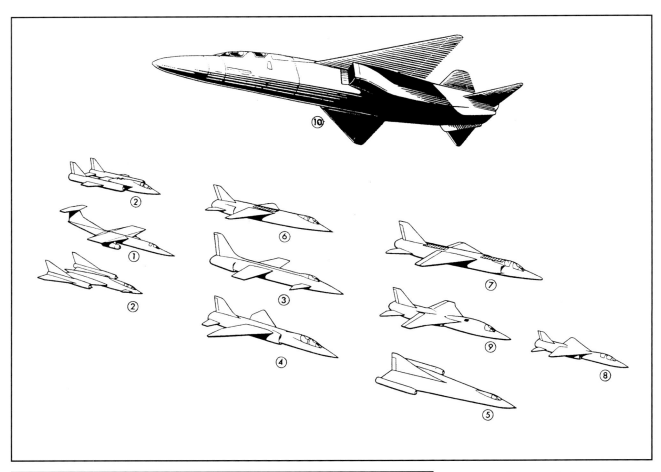

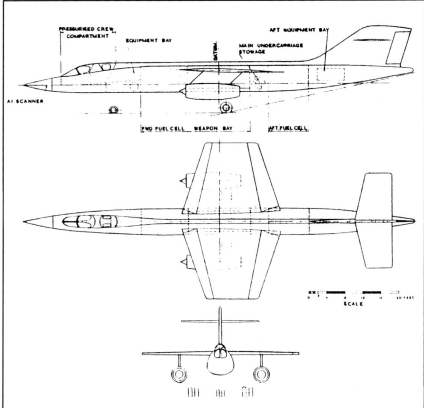

ABOVE To illustrate the level of work that can go into the design of a new aircraft type, these are just some of the designs considered by EE during 1956/57, before the team settled finally on the P.17A (top). None of them met GOR.339 in full.
North West Heritage Group

LEFT This version of the English Electric P.17 with a trapezoid wing and engines in nacelles was drawn in about October 1956. *North West Heritage Group*

was called the P.17A. At the time the firm's P.1B was the only aircraft under operational development with high supersonic experience and an integrated weapon system, which proved of great value to the P.17A. Most important of all, it was the only aircraft in the world known to have flown with good controllability up to Mach 1 at very low altitudes and in very rough air. Hence some P.1B features were carried over into the P.17A, in particular its low tail and leading-edge sweep. The favoured powerplant was the RB.142R, though with minor changes the aircraft could

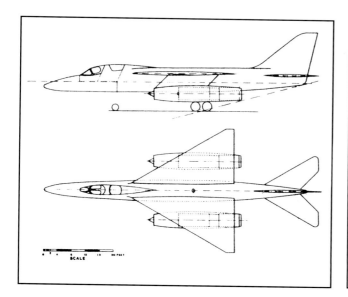

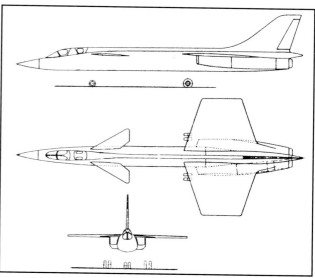

ABOVE Podded engine delta wing version of the P.17 from around November 1956. The engines are reheated Bristol Olympus Ol.21Rs. *North West Heritage Group*

ABOVE Early English Electric P.17 design that was tunnel tested during the period December 1956 to February 1957. *North West Heritage Group*

accommodate Olympus 14s or 15s. Each engine had an individual shock-controlled intake designed for efficient operation up to Mach 2.0 and a variable nozzle of convergent type.

P.17A's structure was made largely in aluminium. Its wing had full-span blown flaps with no ailerons, roll control being provided by differential movement of the tail; in fact, the entire trailing edge was hinged to form a blown plain flap that in normal flight would be locked rigidly to the wing to prevent flutter. The wing's primary box structure was formed by top and bottom skins reinforced by conventional stringers; wing loading was 108lb/sq ft (527kg/sq m). A large mid-fuselage armament bay had a rotating door to allow photo reconnaissance or ground attack rocket packs to be installed quickly, and it could accommodate the six 1,000lb (454kg) bomb overload with ease. No weapons were to be carried under the wings and the electronics included a terrain-following attack radar derived from the AI.23 intercept model plus sideways navigation and reconnaissance aerials. The tricycle undercarriage retracted into the fuselage, where the majority of the internal fuel, 4,300gal (19,552lit) in all, was also housed, which would be sufficient for the 1,000nm (1,852km) mission.

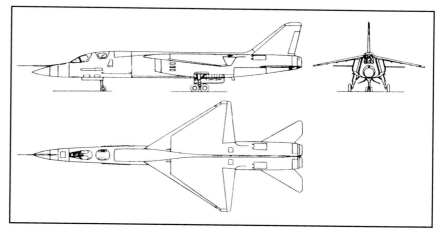

ABOVE Final English Electric P.17A configuration (1.58). *North West Heritage Group*
BELOW AND OVEREAF Model of the P.17A made by Joe Cherrie. *Joe Cherrie*

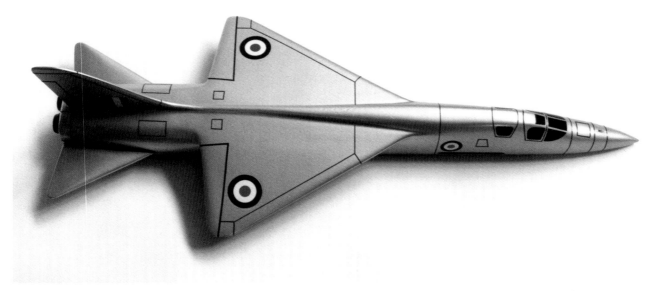

Over a number of years English Electric and Shorts had collaborated successfully on several programmes, including certain marks of Canberra and the S.B.5 low-speed development aircraft for the P.1; in addition Shorts had extensive VTOL experience. As a result the P.17 project brochure also detailed a P.17D lifting body that, rather confusingly, was labelled P.D.17 by Shorts. EE felt it was not possible to develop a pure VTOL type in time to fulfil GOR.339 and so instead had designed an aeroplane for use off conventional runways (the P.17A) while

LEFT Well-known manufacturer's artwork showing the P.17A strike aircraft being lifted into the air by the P.17D lifting body. *North West Heritage Group*

Shorts added a separate piloted lifting VTOL platform (the P.17D). This would act as a parent aircraft to take the P.17A aloft vertically and then accelerate it to its flying speed ready for release. The concept offered extra range or the advantage of surprise in making an attack from an unexpected direction.

The P.17D was a flying wing with tip extensions and fins at the tips. It would use no fewer than fifty-six Rolls-Royce RB.108 lift engines with two banks of eighteen mounted vertically along each leading edge, two groups of six either side of the rearwards cockpit that could tilt to assist with the transition to and from forward flight, and then another eight to provide the normal forward power. The P.17A was attached by a large hook and together they totalled 128,000lb (58,061kg) gross weight, with the P.17D weighing about 46,000lb (20,866kg). The combination's take-off procedure would be to ascend vertically to 2,000ft (610m) in forty seconds and then accelerate horizontally to 230mph (370km/h) before release. For retrieval the two would formate at 230mph (370km/h) and then engage before returning to base and setting down vertically. (One wonders about the maintenance job and the noise this astonishing idea would have brought with it!)

It was anticipated that the first relatively unequipped P.17A prototype would fly before the end of 1961 and ten development machines would be needed to get the type into service in late 1963. The composite system with the P.17D would enter service in mid-1965, the first of the lifting platforms itself flying in late 1962. P.17A's combat performance was felt to be similar to current supersonic fighters and so once again a fighter derivative was proposed. As the P.22 this replaced the terrain radar with air intercept equipment and it would carry Red Top AAMs. The P.17A itself was capable of development to speeds above Mach 2. In April 1958 Vickers approached EE about collaboration and copies of the P.17A and Vickers 571 brochures (below) were exchanged. As a result, Shorts gradually disappeared from the scene.

English Electric P.17A

Span	35ft 0in (10.67m)
Length	84ft 6in (25.76m)
Gross wing area	610sq ft (56.7sq m)
t/c ratio	4%
Gross weight	(600nm [1,111km]/1,000nm [1,852km]): 66,000lb (29,938kg), 73,400lb (33,294kg)
Powerplant	two RR RB.142R 13,300lb (59.1kN), 22,700lb (100.9kN) reheat
Maximum speed/height	Mach 0.95 at sea level, Mach 2.0 at altitude
Weapon load	Red Beard, six 1,000lb (454kg) bombs, twenty-four 3in (76.2mm) or 370 2in (50.8mm) RPs internal

Short P.D.17/2

The text goes out of alphabetical order here because an EE P.17A STOL variant called the P.17B had also been considered with twin RB.133s for forward propulsion and three RB.108s providing lift. The jet lift installation for this was designed by Shorts but it was found that the take-off distance would be reduced only at the expense of extra weight or less range. Shorts also produced its own GOR.339 study using jet lift under the P.D.17 designation. For more than three years, while the design, construction and development of the firm's S.C.1 experimental VTOL aircraft had proceeded, Shorts had been studying the application of powered lift to various strike aircraft. So when GOR.339 was issued it was clear that the company should study a VTOL

aircraft to meet the stated requirements. When the discussions with EE began it was found that the basic P.D.17 layout was similar to the much more thoroughly developed P.17A above, and so several features were incorporated into the Shorts' project to turn it into the P.D.17/2; for example the wing and tailplane planform and shape were exactly similar to the P.17 but larger.

P.D.17/2's brochure was dated April 1958 and the aircraft had a large battery of twenty-eight Rolls-Royce RB.108s for jet lift while the main propulsion units were two RB.142s (the RB.133 had been rejected because it was not powerful enough). A switch to two Olympus 14s or 15s along with 10 7,820lb (34.8kN) Bristol Orpheus lift engines could be made without fundamental changes. Several alternative layouts had been studied but the most promising had a 60° delta wing placed high on the fuselage with a low all-moving tailplane of similar planform. The propulsion engines were in the fuselage above the weapons bay and the lift units were positioned in two groups forward and aft of the main units. The thrust from the main engines could if required be made available for landing by the installation of thrust deflectors in the jet pipes immediately behind the engines to turn the exhaust through 70°, while the twenty-eight lift jets were the minimum required for a vertical landing and did not allow for engine failure. The main engines had side air intakes, the lift jets retractable scoop-type inlets fitted to each bay.

BELOW Shorts drawing of the preliminary general arrangement for the Shorts P.D.17 VTOL strike aircraft (early 1958).

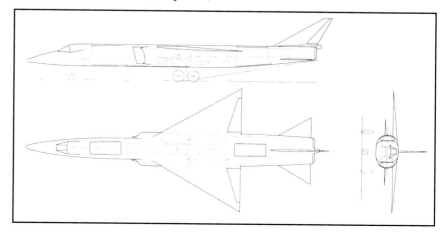

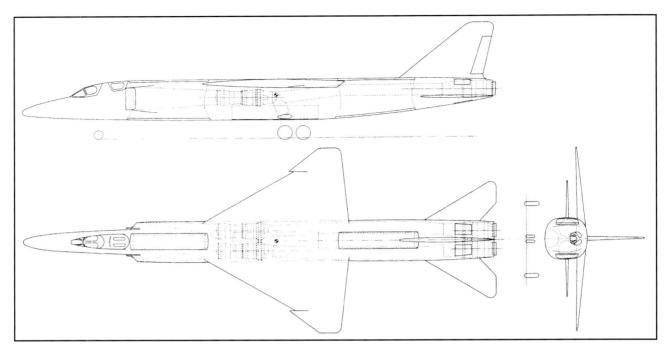

ABOVE The P.D.17/2 after the incorporation of features from the EE P.17A (4.58). This is in fact the 'Bristol' version with two reheated Olympus Ol.15R propulsion engines and ten VTOL Orpheus units. Span 41ft 4in (12.60m), length 102ft (31.09m), gross wing area 850sq ft (79.05sq m), wing t/c 5%, vertical take-off weight 87,200lb (39,554kg) and overload take-off weight 110,900lb (50,304kg). This aircraft was to carry 6,345gal (28,850lit) of internal fuel.

To save weight the wing had no control surfaces of any kind but there were air jet controls comprising six variable-area nozzles, two at each end of the fuselage and one at each wing tip, and all directed downwards. Asymmetric movement of the tailplane would provide lateral control in flight while the jet lift facility had removed the need for flaps. The airframe was primarily aluminium with a conventional sheet type fuselage supported by Z-section stiffeners and channel section frames. All three units of the tricycle undercarriage retracted into the fuselage and the bomb bay had a rotating door. Again, the alternative loads included reconnaissance cameras.

The two-seat P.D.17/2 could take off vertically at a weight of 83,300lb (45,282kg), which would allow an effective strike to be made at a radius of action of about 400nm (741km), but the aeroplane needed to be overloaded to 110,810lb (50,263kg) for the 1,000nm (1,852km) radius. At 70,000lb (31,752kg) weight the sea level rate of climb was given as 7,350ft/min (2,240m/min), while the design dive speed was to be the lesser of 850 knots (979mph/1,575km/h)

Short P.D.17/2	
Span	41ft 4in (12.60m)
Length	101ft 0in (30.78m)
Gross wing area	850sq ft (79.05sq m)
t/c ratio	5%
Gross weight	(600nm [1,111km]/1,000nm [1,852km]): 96,890lb (43,949kg), 110,810lb (50,263kg)
Powerplant	two RR RB.142R 13,300lb (59.1kN), 22,700lb (100.9kN) reheat, twenty-eight RR RB.108 2,500lb (11.1kN)
Maximum speed/height	c. Mach 2.0 at altitude
Weapon load	Red Beard, six 1,000lb (454kg) bombs or twenty-four 3in (76.2mm) or 370 2in (50.8mm) RPs internal

EAS or Mach 1.82. Although it offered some marginal advantages over the P.17A, P.D.17/2 was later in timescale and introduced new problems when the P.17A was already into detail design.

Fairey GOR.339

The structural and aerodynamic features that contributed so much to the success of the Fairey Delta 2 research aircraft were used again here for the firm's GOR.339 offering, the structure

itself having been based on the Delta 2's design and flight experience to cut down the necessary research and development time. Having rejected V/STOL, Fairey's preliminary studies embraced twin and four-engine layouts using conventional, tailless and canard configurations with podded or buried engines. The smallest possible aircraft would be a tailless delta but the limitations with this included rocket boost for short take-offs. A conventional tailed layout was also rejected because the best flight characteristics required a high wing position and a low tail. That also made podded engines unacceptable as the jet efflux impinged on the tailplane, while buried engines needed long intakes and pipes which increased weight. Fairey finally concluded that a 60° delta with a canard would best meet the GOR. Although having to accept that the foreplane might interfere with the intakes, this layout would give many inherent advantages.

The foreplane span was 18ft 7in (5.66m) and area 228sq ft (21.2sq m) and the surface gave an estimated

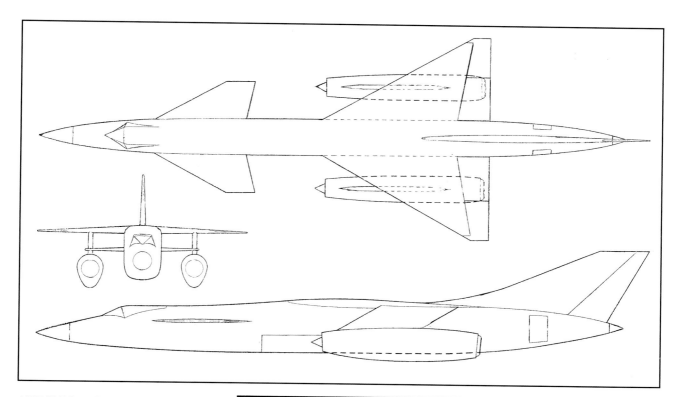

ABOVE Fairey GOR.339 (31.1.58).

**RIGHT AND OVERLEAF Fairey's
response to GOR.339 was a canard
design with a 60° delta wing, the
structural and aerodynamic features of
which owed much to experience gained
from the Delta II research aircraft. These
views show the original model made by
Fairey to accompany the project
brochure.**

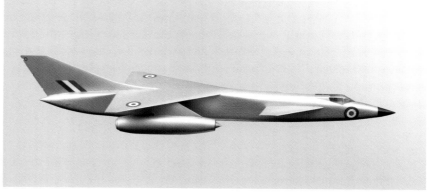

20% lift. Conventional light alloy
construction was used, the choice for
much of the structure being
Hiduminium RR.58 because this was
the best material for the flight
temperature range. The wing loading
was 92lb/sq ft (449kg/sq m), which
Fairey felt would be sufficient to give
acceptable flight conditions for the
crew when the airframe was hit by
low-altitude gusts. No form of
auxiliary lift system (suction or
blowing) was incorporated, bar
reheat and methanol/water, because
of the problems created if an engine
failed; this left just plain flaps and
ailerons. A deck hook was fitted and
a bicycle undercarriage was used with
outriggers in the engine nacelles.

The overall length was rather more
than that of an equivalent tailless delta so,

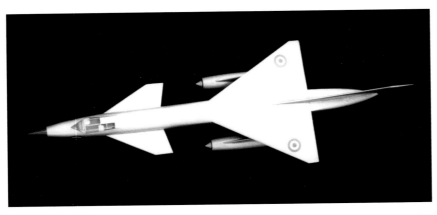

for the lightest and simplest installation, podded engines were used that had simple cone centrebody intakes with no moving parts. The brochure data described two RB.142Rs with variable reheat, but full interchangeability with the Olympus 15R had been designed in for a slightly higher weight. Two engines gave adequate power for the various performance criteria, and while more would raise the ceiling they would add to the weight by a vast amount. A very high sea level rate of climb with reheat lit added considerably to the type's escape potential and Fairey felt supersonic bursts should primarily be looked upon as a very temporary means of evasion or escape. With reheat lit the sea level rate of climb at 52,500lb (23,814kg) weight was 53,400ft/min (16,276m/ min), and at 62,500lb (28,350kg) this became 44,520ft/min (13,570m/min). Time to 30,000ft (9,144m) was 1.15 minutes and the maximum sea level speed with reheat unlit was Mach 1.0. An analysis of supersonic flight at low level had revealed a rough exchange rate that for every 10 miles (19km) flown at supersonic speed

Fairey GOR.339

Span	34ft 8in (10.57m)
Length	100ft 9in (30.71m)
Gross wing area	600sq ft (55.8sq m)
t/c ratio	4%
Gross weight	(600nm [1,111km]/1,000nm [1,852km]): 55,900lb (25,356kg), 65,900lb (29,892kg)
Powerplant	two RR RB.142R c. 14,000lb (62.2kN), 22,700lb (100.9kN) in reheat
Maximum speed/height	Mach 1.1+ at sea level, Mach 2.15 at 36,000ft (10,973m)
Weapon load	Red Beard, six 1,000lb (454kg) bombs, twelve 3in (76.2mm) or seventy-four 2in (50.8mm) RPs internal

this cut the overall radius of action by 55nm (102km). Consequently, Fairey had excluded any supersonic elements from the operational profile.

Designed around the 600nm (1,111km) sortie, the airframe had a central fuselage bay to take either Red Beard, six 1,000lb (454kg) bombs or the rocket packs, the narrow wing span preventing any carriage of underwing weapons. All of the fuel, 3,600gal

(16,369lit), was to be housed in fuselage and wing tanks and this was sufficient to fly the 1,000nm (1,852km) mission. The electronics included a forward-scanning X-band radar, and sideways-facing X-band navigation and Q-band reconnaissance equipment, while radar and photo reconnaissance packs and a flight refuel pack were available when needed. No details were given in regard to development aircraft.

Gloster Thin Wing Javelin

Gloster conducted an investigation into GOR.339 but never tendered a brochure; however, a report dated 10 December 1957 summarised the firm's study. As a basis it used the P.386 development of the Thin Wing Javelin fighter to Specification F.153D that, with 4,500gal (20,461lit) of fuel (3,540gal [16,096lit] of this internal), could meet the 600nm (1,111km) radius of action but not the 1,000nm (1,852km) limit. A level speed of Mach 2.0 was also not possible; a best of only Mach 1.13 was attained on the outward journey with the Red Beard store carried externally under the port wing, and Mach 1.41 on the inward leg. To correct this and meet the GOR more closely, an increase in the internal fuel and a reduction in supersonic drag were required.

More space for fuel was found by taking the engines out of the fuselage and installing them in underwing pods. And a fuselage redesign permitted the carriage of stores internally that, along with the deletion of the external tanks, helped to reduce supersonic and subsonic drag. The wing t/c ratio was cut from 7.5% to 5%, area ruling was applied and the resulting P.384 was faster, but it could still not reach Mach 2 and Gloster noted that more power was needed, which meant more engines. With 5,500gal (25,008lit) of internal fuel the P.384 could reach the 600nm (1,111km) limit and with 7,000gal (31,828lit) the 1,000nm (1,852km) figure. Take-off wing loadings for P.384 with these fuel loads were 81.4lb/sq ft (397kg/sq m) and 92.7lb/sq ft (453kg/sq m) respectively.

Gloster P.386

Span	60ft 8in (18.49m)
Length	72ft 0in (21.95m)
Gross wing area	1,235sq ft (114.9sq m)
t/c ratio	7.5%
Gross weight	83,050lb (37,671kg) (750nm/1,389km radius only)
Powerplant	two Bristol Olympus Ol.21R 17,270lb (76.8kN), 27,600lb (122.7kN) reheat
Maximum speed/height	Mach 0.95 at sea level, Mach 1.41 at altitude
Weapon load	Red Beard or high explosive bombs under wings

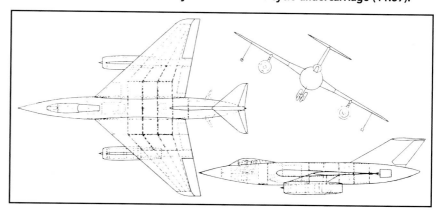

ABOVE Gloster P.386 Thin Wing Javelin development to GOR.339 with Red Beard under the port wing, a 200gal (909lit) tank under the starboard wing and twin 370gal (1,682lit) ventral drop tanks (11.11.57).

BELOW Gloster P.384 Thin Wing Javelin development with podded engines. Its fuel and weapons are housed internally and there is a bicycle undercarriage (11.57).

Gloster P.384

Span	60ft 8in (18.49m)
Length	77ft 0in (23.47m)
Gross wing area	not given
t/c ratio	5%
Gross weight	(600nm [1,111km]/1,000nm [1,852km]): 100,500lb (45,587kg), 114,500lb (51,937kg)
Powerplant	two Bristol Olympus Ol.21R 17,270lb (76.8kN), 27,600lb (122.7kN) reheat
Maximum speed/height	Mach 0.95 at sea level, Mach 1.58 at 36,000ft (10,973m)
Weapon load	Red Beard or high explosive bombs under wings

Handley Page Study

Another manufacturer that did not tender officially to GOR.339 was Handley Page but the firm did produce an outline study using a rough working shape. This had a butterfly tail and a 4% t/c 'delta' wing, with a rectangular centre section extending between two engine nacelles. Its span was 48ft (14.63m), length 75ft (22.86m) and wing area 924sq ft (85.9sq m). No optimisation was attempted since the objective was to find the effect of the GOR's requirements on the aircraft's size and gross weight. The report concluded that a 1,000nm (1,852km) radius might be possible with a take-off weight of around 60,000lb (27,216kg), with no supersonic burst, and provided that high-bypass ratio engines were used. The non-availability of such engines meant higher weights or less

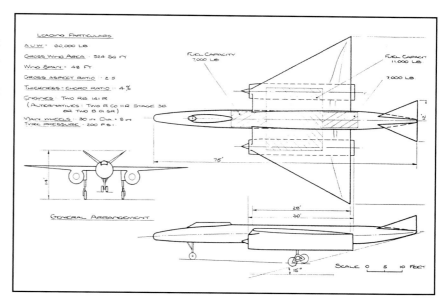

ABOVE The outline design for a Tactical Strike Aircraft drawn for the Handley-Page GOR.339 research (1.58).

range while the low-altitude supersonic burst near the target resulted in a large penalty in take-off weight. This layout's top speed came to about Mach 1.7 when using twin RB.142Rs giving 13,200lb (58.7kN) of thrust dry and 21,200lb (94.2kN) with reheat. Handley Page indicated no further interest in the requirement.

Hawker P.1123 and P.1125

Hawker Aircraft's submission to GOR.339 was the P.1129 below, but this was the culmination of earlier work that is worth looking at closely. Further developments of the P.1121 (above) brought the P.1123 tactical bomber and P.1125 strike aircraft. The P.1123 was probably only a brief study but represented a final two-seat development of the P.1121's chin intake arrangement. It used a single reheated Rolls-Royce Conway 31R, carried the nuclear bomb semi-recessed in the lower fuselage, 3,310gal (15,050lit) of fuel and had four-wheel main gears. It also cured a weakness of the P.1121 in that on the earlier aircraft the undercarriage and flaps had clashed where the flaps could not be lowered when the undercarriage

was down; P.1123 remedied this by housing the main gears in 'Küchemann type' fittings. The P.1123 was not a direct comparison to the P.1125, it was part of the process of development that had begun with the P.1103 fighter in 1954.

The P.1125 and P.1129 formed the main line of Hawker's research and received more attention than the P.1123. The P.1125 was another company response to the initial ideas for the forthcoming GOR.339 and the brochure, undated but thought to be from March 1957, described a long-range, two-seat development of the P.1121 project. Hawker considered the new design to be a logical development of the P.1121 with similar aerodynamic qualities. Its centre and rear fuselage had been redesigned to accommodate a twin-engine arrangement with Rolls-Royce RB.133 units and also an internal weapons bay. The basic wing, tail unit, flying controls system and undercarriage units were the same as the single-engine P.1121, while the fuselage forward of the wing was to be an interchangeable unit that could be equipped to suit the role.

The RB.133 was a supersonic development of the RA.24 Avon currently

in production and strengthened to permit speeds of Mach 1.3 at sea level and Mach 2.4 above 36,000ft (10,973m). Convergent/divergent nozzles were fitted and to accommodate these power units within the fuselage the P.1125's air intakes had semi-conical fixed centre bodies with after-spillage and suction relief. P.1125 was to have an internal fuel capacity of 2,000gal (9,094lit), plus provision for a further 900gal (4,092lit) in two 300gal (1,364lit) and two 150gal (682lit) tanks carried externally on underwing pylons inboard and outboard respectively. The wing was swept back to an angle of 36° on the quarter chord line and contained a continuous integral tank across the fuselage, while the forward and rear fuselage fuel was contained in lightweight bag tanks. A retractable flight refuelling probe was fitted ahead of the pilot's canopy and an additional 600gal (2,728lit) could be provided in the weapon bay for ferry flights. The weapons bay itself could accommodate conventional bombs or gun or rocket packs, while large stores such as the nuclear Target Marker Bomb were to be carried semi-recessed. Besides the fuel tanks the underwing pylon stations could also take bombs or rocket armament.

BELOW Hawker P.1123 Mach 2 Tactical Bomber (21.1.57). *Hawker Siddeley via Chris Farara*

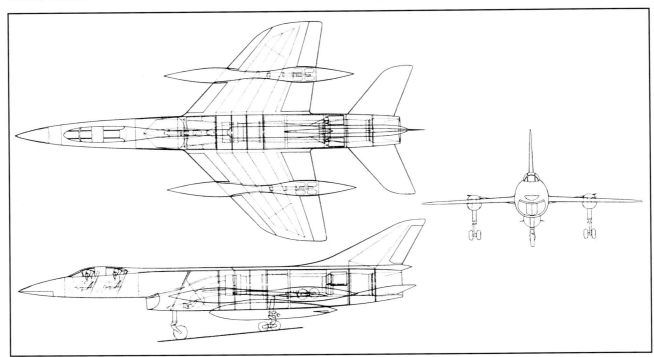

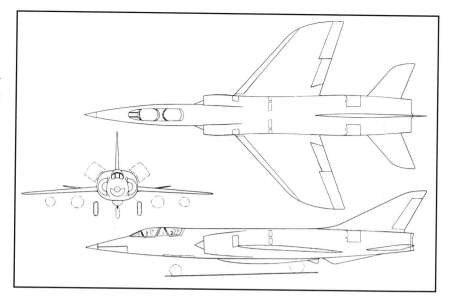

In order to complete its nuclear strike sortie, either in daylight or at night and in all weather conditions, the P.1125 was provided with a comprehensive radar mapping system, including a Doppler/inertia navigation aid, a sideways-looking radar with photographic display and moving map equipment, a forward-looking ground mapping radar and radar ranging. P.1125 was capable of cruising supersonically and the normal take-off weight with full internal fuel and internal armament only was 49,000lb (22,226kg). Sea level rate of climb at a start weight of 43,000lb (19,505kg) was estimated to be about 52,000ft/min (15,850m/min) and the ceiling at the engine thrust limit was given as 59,000ft (17,983m). Combat radius for a high/low level strike sortie with a Target Maker and 900gal (4,092lit) of external fuel was estimated to be 1,050 miles (1,690km). In the end the P.1125 proved to be an exploratory step and it would not meet the full GOR.

Hawker P.1123	
Span	38ft 0in (11.58m)
Length	70ft 0in (21.34m)
Gross wing area	?
t/c ratio	?
Gross weight	?
Powerplant	one RR Conway Co.31R
Maximum speed/height	Mach 2 at altitude
Weapon load	one nuclear weapon

Hawker P.1125	
Span	38ft 8in (11.79m)
Length	69ft 0in (21.03m)
Gross wing area	530sq ft (49.29sq m)
t/c ratio	5% root, 3.5% tip
Gross weight	59,300lb (26,898kg) with target marker bomb and 900gal (4,092lit) fuel in underwing tanks
Powerplant	two RR RB.133 13,000lb (57.8kN), 18,150lb (80.7kN) with reheat
Maximum speed/height	Mach 1.3 at sea level, Mach 2.32 at 36,000ft (10,973m)
Weapon load	Nuclear weapon, bombs, RPs, guns or guided missiles

Hawker P.1129

The Hawker Design Department's preliminary studies to the full GOR made in October 1957 suggested that a large aircraft of some 130,000lb (58,968kg) weight would be needed to meet the standard flight plan with supersonic burst. The Project Office then commenced investigations towards a 60,000lb (27,216kg) aircraft as a more likely compromise and the result was the P.1129. On 18 November Air Marshal Kyle, ACAS/OR, visited Kingston, where he expressed the opinion that the Air Staff would not be allowed to have a large aircraft, and he thought that the P.1129 appeared to be a good compromise.

The P.1129 had a take-off wing loading of 101lb/sq ft (493kg/sq m) as a balance between a value to satisfy the performance criteria (including the loft bombing manoeuvre) and a desirable figure for crew comfort and structural fatigue during high-speed, low-level operations. It was felt that the chosen value of 90lb/sq ft (439kg/sq m) over the target provided tolerable conditions for the crew but it was acknowledged that there was a general lack of practical evidence in this area and so an active investigation would begin using a two-seat Hunter. This would include testing the effectiveness of spring-mounted seats to eliminate resonant frequencies, which were known to be particularly distressing.

This was another project to use conventional light alloy construction and the airframe was considered to be the smallest possible to fulfil all the requirements. Full-span leading-edge droop and trailing-edge flaps with area suction were provided to augment the lift for take-off and landing and the aircraft had a slab all-moving tail and a tricycle undercarriage retracting into the body. More than 40% of the fuel, 1,600gal (7,275lit), was carried in external tanks as overload and Red Beard was to be housed semi-recessed under the fuselage; alternatively, four 1,000lb (454kg) bombs could be mounted internally on rotatable Martin doors. The internal fuel in wing tanks and three large fuselage tanks totalled 2,250gal (10,231lit), there was an optional tanker pack for in-flight refuelling and the 1,000nm (1,852km) radius could be achieved with the overload fuel.

The electronics were kept to a minimum but the P.1129 had a modified AI.23 set with an 18in (457mm) dish for its forward-facing radar plus sideways X-band navigation and Q-band reconnaissance equipment. The radar ranging and pilot attack sight doubled as a flying and navigation aid while specialised packs for all-weather reconnaissance were available as alternative loads to the bombs. Power came from a pair of RB.142Rs, which

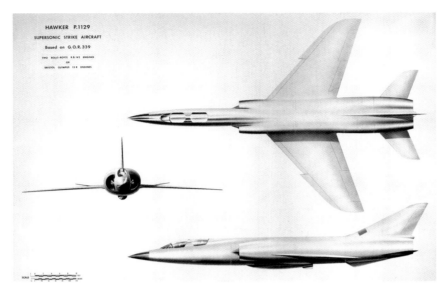

LEFT Shaded 3-view of the P.1129 (1.58). *Nick Stroud/The Aviation Historian*

BELOW Views of a manufacturer's model of the P.1129 that has unfortunately received some minor damage.

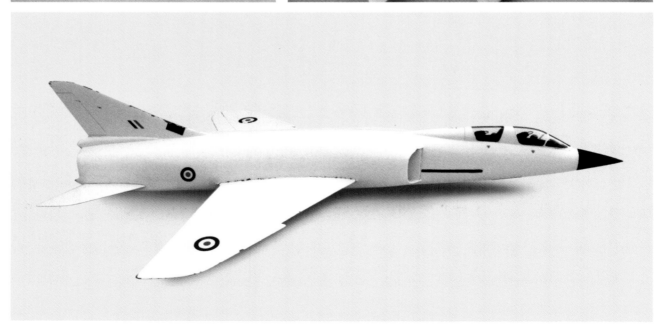

Hawker declared showed the best economy of any available engine (the Olympus 15R was considered a slightly less suitable alternative). The engines had individual intakes on the fuselage side with fixed two-shock half-cones and suction relief doors and the nozzles were fully convergent–divergent. Absolute ceiling was at least 60,000ft (18,288m) and the P.1129's small size bestowed fighter-type handling characteristics. Maximum speed with reheat unlit was Mach 1.05 at sea level and about Mach 1.2 at 36,000ft (10,973m).

The complete system could be in service in 1964 provided an ITP had been made by July 1958. A programme for three prototypes based on an April 1958 ITP was given as:

First Prototype – first flight mid-1960. This would be used for aerodynamic and performance development with Olympus 14R or 15R engines, since the RB.142 and parts of the weapon system would not be ready.

Second Prototype – first flight spring 1961. Used for engine and weapon development; this should receive RB.142 engines.

ABOVE **The P.1129 model seen alongside an original BAC model of TSR.2.**

Hawker P.1129	
Span	48ft 8in (14.83m)
Length	72ft 9in (22.17m)
Gross wing area	630sq ft (58.6sq m)
t/c ratio	6% at side of body, 4% at tip
Gross weight	(600nm [1,111km]/1,000nm [1,852km]): 63,825lb (28,951kg), 79,125lb (35,891kg)
Powerplant	two RR RB.142R 13,800lb (61.3kN), 22,500lb (100.0kN) in reheat
Maximum speed/height	Mach 1.28 at sea level, Mach 2.3 above 36,000ft (10,973m) = aircraft design limit
Weapon load	four 1,000lb (454kg) bombs or 2four 3in (76.2mm) or seventy-four 2in (50.8mm) RPs internal; Red Beard under fuselage; four 1,000lb (454kg) bombs, twenty-four 3in (76.2mm) or 148 2in (50.8mm) RPs external under wings

Third Prototype – first flight end 1961. This was to be as fully representative as possible to help prove the overall weapon system concept and the specialised weapon and reconnaissance packs.

Vickers (Supermarine) Type 571

The Vickers military aircraft division had been formed from the previous Supermarine division with some reinforcement from Weybridge. More than forty designs were studied, six in detail, before two were chosen to form the tender under the Type 571 designation. Variable geometry had been rejected and early investigations had shown that meeting the GOR in one combined role would need a very large aeroplane. Thus, a policy of miniaturisation and alternative packs had been adopted to keep all the military equipment to a minimum weight and size, which then allowed the basic aircraft to be much smaller. Most of the brochure was devoted to a small single-engined layout favoured by Vickers but a larger twin-engined version was also described.

Type 571 had a light alloy structure though titanium was employed in the engine bay for load-carrying heat shields. Construction was conventional with frames, skins and stringers in the fuselage and skins with multiple

webbing in the wing. Four ribs made up the complete wing box and the entire wing formed an integral fuel tank. More fuel was housed in the fuselage and provision was made for jettisonable tip and underwing tanks and flight refuelling. After studying those engines predicted to be available in 1964 it was concluded that the RB.142 would be the most satisfactory for these aeroplanes, although the Conway 11R/3C was also considered. On the single-engine layout the RB.142 was placed right aft in the fuselage where noise would not damage the structure, and both 571s had convergent–divergent nozzles and side intakes with raked-forward outer lips, an unusual feature in British designs.

Wing loading for the large 571 was 166lb/sq ft (810kg/sq m) while the smaller version had the high figure of 194lb/sq ft (947kg/sq m), which should solve the problem of severe turbulence frequency at low altitude. Compared to a Gloster Meteor flying at 460mph (741km/h), the small 571 showed a three-fold improvement in 0.5g gust response and a forty-fold improvement at 1.5g. An all-moving tail, all-moving fin and tricycle undercarriage folding into the fuselage were common to both proposals, the twin having tandem-wheel main gears, and the high-lift devices comprised full-span blown drooped flaps. On the small machine compressor air was blown over the

From a start date of June 1958 the development programme outlined for the small Type 571 was a first flight in February 1962, the first flight of a fully equipped aircraft in February 1963 and CA Release in May 1964. The required design effort was considered to be of similar magnitude to the Scimitar and the programme was based on the experience gained with that aircraft in addition to estimates for the Vanguard and VC10 civil airliners. Nine small Type 571s were planned for CA trials along with two static test airframes and choosing the larger aircraft was expected to extend the later stages of the programme by about six months. Production would be undertaken at the company's South Marston Works. Vickers noted that should a single-engined aircraft be unsuitable then the small design could be fitted with two smaller engines to give approximately the same performance, and in February 1958 a brochure was prepared around this idea. In May a further brochure described a naval strike fighter variant suitable for carrier operations.

Many of the GOR.339 brochures highlighted a particularly important point, i.e. a low-aspect ratio wing with a high wing loading was needed in order to achieve an acceptable gust ride for the crew. The problem was that aircraft response to gusts in flight (of which there are many at low level over

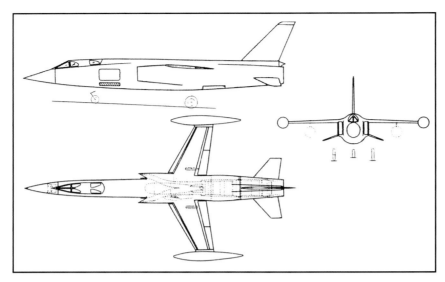

ABOVE Vickers (Supermarine) single-engine Type 571 (1.58). *RAF Museum*
BELOW Impression of the single-engine Type 571 taken from the project brochure.

wing surface at the junctions of the nose and trailing flaps and the ailerons. This developed the system in use on the Scimitar and reduced the approach speed by some 18mph (30km/h). A short take-off was possible using the 'Fire Hose' catapult system on the principle that it was better to have STOL apparatus on the ground than to carry it around on every sortie. The large 571's extra power reduced its take-off distance by 30%.

The design limit for both types was Mach 2.3 above 36,000ft (10,973m), the single-engine 571 being capable of Mach 2 up to 52,000ft (15,850m), the twin up to 54,000ft (16,459m). The small design could achieve the 600nm (1,111km) radius on 1,948gal (8,857lit) of internal fuel but needed small

external tanks for the 1,000nm (1,852km) limit, although the large machine could accomplish both roles on just internal fuel. With four 375gal (1,705lit) drop tanks the twin's maximum weight reached 94,075lb (42,672kg). Common avionics included a 22in (559mm) forward-scanning X-band radar dish and sideways J-band navigation and reconnaissance radar aerials, while identical weapon loads or alternative radar or photo reconnaissance packs were carried in mid-fuselage bays. Vickers felt the large version offered only marginal advantages over the smaller type and these needed to be weighed against the extra cost, so the bigger machine had been described in rather less detail.

Vickers (Supermarine) Type 571 (Small)	
Span	28ft 0in (8.53m)
Length	58ft 0in (17.68m)
Gross wing area	200sq ft (18.6sq m)
t/c ratio	5%
Gross weight	(600nm [1,111km]/1,000nm [1,852km]): 36,820lb (16,702kg), 45,400lb (20,593kg)
Powerplant	one RR RB.142R c. 14,000lb (62.2kN), 22,700lb (100.9kN) reheat
Maximum speed/height	835mph (1,343km/h) Mach 1.1 at sea level, 1,388mph (2,233km/h) Mach 2.1 at 36,000ft (10,973m)
Weapon load	Red Beard, four 1,000lb (454kg) bombs or 2four 3in (76.2mm) RPs internal; four 1,000lb (454kg) bombs under wings

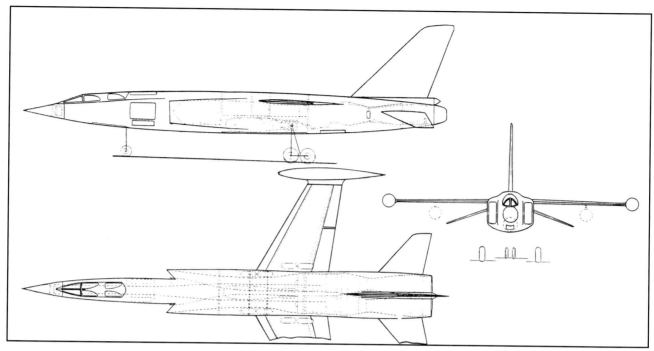

hilly terrain) increased with aspect
ratio (ratio of span to average chord)
and the inverse of wing loading (weight
divided by wing area). Keeping the size
and rate of the 'bumps' down at high
speed and low level required a small,
highly swept wing that would be
somewhat inefficient in cruise. This
then led to a large fuel weight and a big
fuselage and so, to enable the short
wing to provide short take-offs,
auxiliary high-lift devices such as
blown flaps were needed that were
complex, expensive and added more

**ABOVE Vickers
(Supermarine)
twin-engine Type
571 (1.58).**
RAF Museum

**RIGHT AND
BELOW
John Hall's model
of the twin-engine
Type 571.**

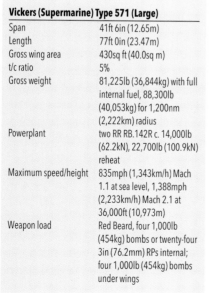

Vickers (Supermarine) Type 571 (Large)	
Span	41ft 6in (12.65m)
Length	77ft 0in (23.47m)
Gross wing area	430sq ft (40.0sq m)
t/c ratio	5%
Gross weight	81,225lb (36,844kg) with full internal fuel, 88,300lb (40,053kg) for 1,200nm (2,222km) radius
Powerplant	two RR RB.142R c. 14,000lb (62.2kN), 22,700lb (100.9kN) reheat
Maximum speed/height	835mph (1,343km/h) Mach 1.1 at sea level, 1,388mph (2,233km/h) Mach 2.1 at 36,000ft (10,973m)
Weapon load	Red Beard, four 1,000lb (454kg) bombs or twenty-four 3in (76.2mm) RPs internal; four 1,000lb (454kg) bombs under wings

weight. Weight escalation then became a factor. Today's fly-by-wire technology would have been a big help here.

Choosing a winner from this long list of proposals involved rather more than just assessing the designs, although the best features of each were recorded in an effort to produce an 'ideal' configuration. Never before had such an advanced aircraft, so complex to develop and construct, been proposed for the RAF. Consequently, studies of each company's capability to produce, its experience in the supersonic field, manufacturing and flight test facilities, management strength and technical and scientific manpower, formed a major part of the assessment by the MoS, its establishments and the Air Staff. For example, when reviewing the structural aspects consideration was given to specialist experience, flutter, fatigue and kinetic heat testing facilities, plus general experience of airworthiness and strength problems. Most weight was placed on the parent company, the supporting company (in parenthesis) being classed as subsidiary. The brochures were also taken as a measure of a company's ability to appreciate problems.

English Electric (partnered by Shorts and Vickers) was the most competent company from most aspects of structural design. Vickers-Armstrong (with EE) came next with the reservation that the pressure of civil work might have an adverse effect on a GOR.339 aircraft. Avro's flutter team (as the focal point of Hawker Siddeley) was weaker, but apart from this there was little to choose between the company and Vickers. Bristol (with Shorts) had a strong design team, especially on flutter and fatigue, with experience of high-speed research aircraft, but it was likely to take longer than the others to design the aircraft.

Of the rest Fairey (Blackburn) was weak on flutter and vibration and general design. Blackburn (Fairey) would have been low on the list even without the Buccaneer, while the de Havilland proposal did not promote confidence in the design team at Christchurch whom, it was felt, was unwise to rely on a support company with large civil commitments

(an agreement provided design assistance from Hunting and Fairey for the Hatfield division and its DH.121 civil aircraft, leaving a small contribution from Fairey for Christchurch's GOR.339). Their flight test organisations were also closely scrutinised, those at EE, Avro and Vickers being first class with DH Hatfield not far behind based on the evidence of Comet flight testing. But Christchurch, Blackburn, Bristol and Fairey were felt to be much poorer in quality. In fact, de Havilland's Christchurch division fell far below the standards of Hatfield in many areas.

Regarding the individual designs, Blackburn's B.108 was particularly disliked. An Air Staff memorandum dated 21 March 1958 described it as being much nearer to the original B.103 than the interim B.103A, thereby enlarging the deficiencies of that model. It was rejected because of an inferior radar and too great a take-off distance that would restrict the aircraft to V-bomber bases. Subsonic and with too short a range, the conclusion was that the B.103 and B.108 were no better than the Canberra, except in their speed, and it was unlikely that the RAF would ever require them. To purchase them as a replacement for Canberra would be unnecessary and outrageously expensive.

Unconventional solutions to GOR.339 were also discussed, in particular variable sweep wings. EE had dismissed them because of mechanical problems while Avro felt that the necessary changes of sweep immediately before and after a loft bombing attack impaired the chances of success. It was significant however that Vickers, the company employing the leading advocate of variable sweep in Barnes Wallis, made no mention of it in its brochure, so the device was rejected by the assessment group. VTOL had been dismissed by many companies on the grounds of increased development time and cost, while self-contained VTOL would reduce range. The EE/Short lifting platform approach, however, had much to commend it since it only needed to be used in areas where VTOL was desirable; in other areas the bomber

could operate from standard runways while by itself the platform could act as a freighter. The Assessment Group also concluded that a single RB.142 aircraft could not have GOR.339's radius of action unless it used runways that were 25% longer than specified.

It appeared that the more promising aircraft to meet GOR.339 was a twin-engine type of conventional pattern. All of the companies had described such an aeroplane, although Vickers put one as its second choice; the RB.142 was the most favoured engine. With the exception of EE and Vickers, the brochures presented contained little comment on the required instrument and electronic systems. It became clear that the choice lay between three groups – Hawker Siddeley, Vickers and English Electric. When GOR.339 was put out to tender Hawker Siddeley's initial bid had not been very powerful, but a revised and more promising technical approach was made subsequently that also included detailed proposals for a combined design and industrial team (this revision is described in Chapter Eight).

Vickers' and English Electric's work was considered to be of the highest quality, not least through some extensive preliminary studies that had given them a marked lead over their rivals. EE's experience with the P.1 would benefit GOR.339 directly and a combination of these two teams would command excellent technical resources; EE's design team was considered particularly valuable. The possibility of awarding two design study contracts was discussed, one to Vickers and EE and another to Hawker Siddeley, but this was rejected because the latter was six to nine months behind and such a move would delay the programme by another year; time was already short to achieve an in-service date of 1965. Hence, in July 1958 the Research and Development Board invited the Permanent Secretary to recommend that the development of the GOR.339 system should be allocated to a combined Vickers and English Electric team, with the former as leader.

Chapter Eight
TSR.2

Politics in Extremis: 1958 to 1968

ABOVE BAC TSR.2 prototype XR219 pictured in flight with undercarriage down. *Terry Panopalis*

The submissions to GOR.339 show how designers could create many different shapes to the same requirement. They also reveal the great waste of effort generated by such severe competition within the industry of a small country such as Britain, preparing and assessing so many designs to one requirement. Surely one of the better results of this story was the merging of most of the aircraft companies into two far more internationally competitive groups, Hawker Siddeley Aviation (HSA) and the British Aircraft Corporation (BAC), sad though it was to see so many famous names disappear. This step came into effect in February 1960 when the Blackburn group joined the other members of Hawker Siddeley (Avro,

AWA, Gloster and Hawker) and Bristol, EE and Vickers joined forces as BAC.

This chapter looks at the resulting aeroplane from GOR.339, the TSR.2, but first let us close Hawker Siddeley's part in the story. Chapter Seven noted that Hawker Siddeley's GOR.339 submissions came from Avro and Hawker (a covering letter stated that Avro's 739 was at the time the main submission and represented the thinking of the group). Thin Wing Javelin studies were also made by Gloster and the three companies met regularly to examine their designs and consider joint development, but the group as a whole was criticised for its confused submissions. One problem was that Avro, having lost the 730, considered GOR.339 as its natural field of interest

and this resulted in some internal competition.

On 21 October 1957 the chief designers at Avro, Gloster and Hawker, J. R. Ewans, Richard Walker and Sydney Camm respectively, attended a Hawker Siddeley Group meeting chaired by Sir Arnold Hall to discuss GOR.339. On 13 November it was agreed that each company would submit its own proposals, though by mid-December it was realised that Avro's 739 approached Hawker's P.1129 very closely indeed. On 11 December 1957 Walker had visited Hawker Aircraft, where the Kingston design team told him that the Javelin configuration was very inappropriate to the GOR's concept, a move that effectively finished that project.

A group meeting between Sir Frank Spriggs, Sir Roy Dobson and J. R. Ewans on 27 January 1958 revealed a certain reluctance to officially submit the P.1129, but clearance was given on the evening of the 31st. In late February Ewans told Hawker that he was worried about the lack of co-operation within the group and that might affect its chances in the competition, but on 19 March Morien Morgan, Deputy Director at RAE, reported that the P.1129 brochure had been well received at his establishment. In late June Sir Arnold Hall was told that the P.1129 was second favourite to English Electric's P.17A.

The policy changed on 4 July with a move to resubmit a single group project to OR.339 and Sir Sydney Camm was put in overall charge of the design team. Four days later it was agreed to use the P.1129 as the basic design with certain improvements from the Avro 739. Joint investigations between Hawker and Avro were intended to produce an aircraft taking in the best features of the 739 while retaining the original P.1129 design features, in particular its small size, operational flexibility and relatively low cost. On 23 July brief details of this 'P.1129 Development' went to the MoS, which agreed to give serious consideration to this 'promising design'. A full compromise design had evolved by 27 October 1958 that satisfied the main differences of opinion and a brochure was issued on 28 November by Avro under the heading of the Hawker Siddeley Group.

Hawker Siddeley Supersonic Strike Aircraft

This unnumbered project closely resembled the July layout but had improved supersonic capability thanks to a reduced wing thickness, wing area and close attention to 'area rule', thereby giving minimum drag at Mach 1.34. It basically retained the wings, tail and fin of the P.1129 but had a redesigned fuselage. The P.1129's performance and effectiveness as a weapon system were improved and, without changing the overall size, the internal fuel load was increased. The all-moving tail, with no dihedral, could now be used for supersonic speed roll control while the small low-speed ailerons were placed further outboard than previously, which permitted larger-span flaps and reduced the wing structure weight.

The 739 and P.1129 represented two approaches to the same problem and had differed mainly in their size and wing load. On the P.1129 emphasis had been given to airfield performance and subsonic cruise at altitude, while the 739 was designed around the low-level and supersonic phases of the flight plan. Following the original submissions a series of intake configurations had been studied that resulted in a change from external to internal compression to give better thrust minus drag at supersonic speeds. Low-speed wind tunnel testing on the 739 had confirmed its basic stability and control, while RAE had tested a 739 radar echo model and its recommendations were also incorporated in this new project. Flap blowing was available on both leading and trailing edges.

Performance breakdowns were given for two RB.142/3 or Olympus B.Ol.22R engines for the standard 1,000nm (1,852km) sortie, including 100nm (185km) at Mach 1.7; the respective gross weights for this mission were 73,700lb (33,430kg) and 74,850lb (33,952kg) and take-off wing loadings 123lb/sq ft and 125lb/sq ft (600kg/m2 and 610kg/sq m). The maximum speed was probably around Mach 2 (no figure

BELOW Hawker Siddeley Group's joint submission to GOR.339 was based a good deal around the Hawker P.1129 and Avro 739 and featured improvements such as an 'area rule' fuselage (11.58). The drawing shows the design with four 1,000lb (454kg) bombs, wing tip rocket packs and 250gal (1,137lit) tanks. *Avro Heritage Centre*

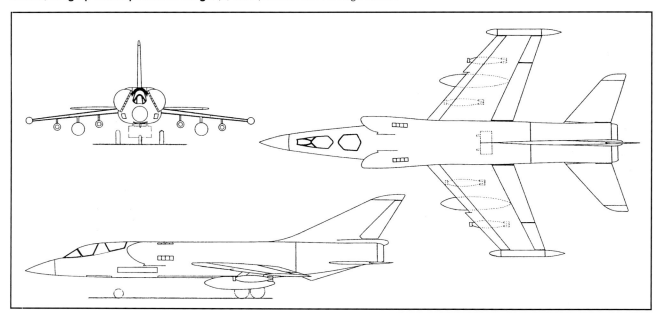

ABOVE **Model of Hawker Siddeley's joint project.** *Avro Heritage Centre*

was given) but the Olympus-powered aircraft had the better supersonic performance. Internal fuel, carried in fuselage and wing tanks, totalled 3,536gal (16,078lit), which was sufficient for the 1,000nm (1,852km) requirement, but two 250gal (1,137lit) underwing drop tanks would increase the flight plan radius to 1,200nm (2,224km).

The radar and reconnaissance equipment comprised a forward-looking modified Blue Parrot radar with a 28.3in (719mm) scanner in the nose and twin, 7ft (2.13m) long, sideways-looking X-band aerials mounted at the sides of the nosewheel bay. In addition there were Q-band aerials, linescan and various cameras carried as a separate pack in the mid-fuselage weapon bay. The weapon bay itself had been redesigned so that two

Bullpup guided missiles could be carried as an alternative load to either Red Beard, conventional bombs or rockets, or a flight refuelling pack.

A development programme envisaged thirty-four months between ITP (assumed January 1959) and first flight, ITP covering mock-ups, test rigs and tunnel testing; a full weapon system contract would follow later in the year. Twelve development aircraft and two static test airframes were planned with the first four flight articles receiving minimum equipment. The next five would be partially equipped and the final three fully fitted and, after completion of development flying, would be delivered to the RAF. Initial CA release was estimated to be end 1963, with full release in mid-1964. The analogy with the combined English

Electric and Vickers designs that produced TSR.2 is notable and the author considers this project to be the 'cup finalist' with that aircraft.

HSA Combined Strike Aircraft	
Span	45ft 10in (13.97m)
Length	74ft 3in (22.63m)
Gross wing area	600sq ft (55.8sq m)
t/c ratio	5% root, 4% tip
Gross weight	74,870lb (33,961kg) for the 1,000nm (1,852km) radius
Powerplant	two Bristol Olympus Ol.22R
Maximum speed/height	Mach 1+(?) at sea level, Mach 2(?) at altitude
Weapon load	Red Beard, two Bullpup, three 1,000lb (454kg) bombs, twenty-four 3in (76.2mm) or ninety 2in (50.8mm) RPs internal; four 1,000lb (454kg) bombs under wings, two thirty-seven 2in (50.8mm) RP pods at wing tips

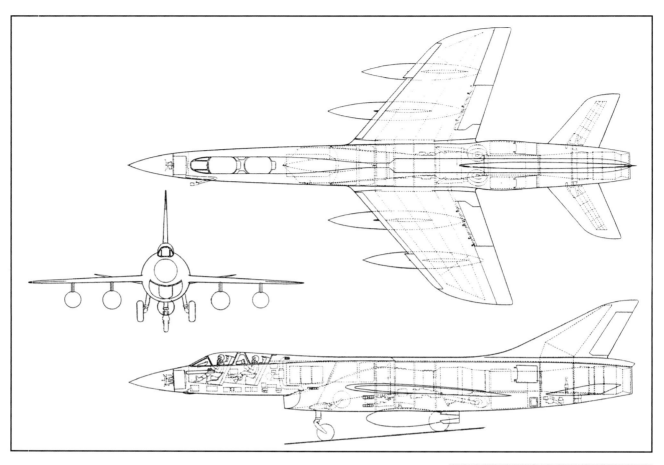

ABOVE Hawker P.1121 in its final form as a supersonic two-seat strike aircraft (1.7.58). On some earlier P.1121 drawings there was a spot where the undercarriage and flaps appeared to clash, but here the flap has been cut away to remove this problem. *Hawker Siddeley via Chris Farara*

Hawker P.1121 (7.58)	
Span	37ft 0in (11.28m)
Length	67ft 8in (20.63m)
Gross wing area	474sq ft (44.1sq m)
t/c ratio	?
Gross weight	50,710lb (23,002kg) normal with two drop tanks
Powerplant	one Bristol Olympus Ol.21R 29,000lb (128.9kN) reheat
Maximum speed/height	Mach 1.3 979mph (1,575km/h) at sea level, Mach 2.2 above 36,000ft (10,973m) (engine limit)
Weapon load	Red Beard or 2 1,000lb (454kg) bombs under fuselage, four 1,000lb (454kg) bombs, thirty-six 3in (76.2mm) or 148 2in (50.8mm) RPs under wings

Hawker P.1121

Concurrently Hawker continued its studies to adapt the P.1121 into a two-seat all-weather strike reconnaissance aircraft as a cheaper alternative to GOR.339, and as such the firm completed a brochure on 1 July 1958. The design retained Mach 2 performance at high altitude but introduced ground attack strength factors and supersonic capability at sea level. Its Olympus 21R combined good supersonic performance and economical cruise consumption, and both leading and trailing edges had flap blowing. Red Beard, two 1,000lb (454kg) bombs or a reconnaissance pack were carried partly recessed under the fuselage, while four underwing pylons could each take a bomb, rocket battery or a drop tank.

The overload weight (two 300gal [1,364lit] tanks inboard, two 200gal [909lit] outboard) came to 54,590lb (24,762kg) and the internal fuel totalled 1,500gal (6,820lit). The 600nm (1,111km) radius could be achieved but 1,000nm (1,852km) needed flight refuelling. Consideration of the P.1121 in this role continued into October 1958.

In the meantime, although the Vickers single-engine 571 had been considered very promising, in August 1958 the company looked at the merits of one or two engines and produced a 'condensed twin' proposal that offered both airfield and speed performance. On 17 December 1958 a House of Commons statement noted that

GOR.339 had been approved and design contracts were about to be issued. This was the first public acknowledgement of the project's existence and it became a hot topic with both the press and MPs; indeed much of the content of the draft OR was disclosed by Government officials with a surprising lack of reticence and security. Internally it was stressed that this was a different aircraft to the Avro 730 so the same excuses could not be used to stop it. Then on 1 January 1959 the Minister of Supply, Aubrey Jones, announced that Vickers-Armstrong and English Electric were to develop a new strike aircraft, called for the first time TSR.2, using the Olympus engine. Sir George Edwards of Vickers would head the project (this was also a deliberate move towards reorganising the aircraft industry).

Air Chief Marshal Sir Claude Pelly, Controller Aircraft, told Sydney Camm on 8 January 1959 that the decision to use Vickers and EE had been made in the summer of 1958, which confirmed suspicions that Hawker Siddeley's later OR.339 work had been a waste of time (a Ministry document described it as a 'going through the motions' effort). Missing out on orders for its P.1129-type aeroplanes was a great disappointment to HSA and from now on Avro concentrated on civil types while Hawker moved on to the VTOL P.1127 discussed in Chapter Ten.

Originally the TSR.2 was to have been known as the OR.339, but in 1958 a comparison had been made between the as yet unnamed NA.39 Buccaneer, the OR.339 aircraft and the Hawker P.1127 vertical take-off aircraft in Chapter Ten, for which purpose the three types were called TSR.1, TSR.2 and TSR.3. When Aubrey Jones publicly announced the existence of the new strike aircraft he called it TSR.2 in error and the title stuck. Government circles in fact became rather fussy about the publication of just a number for the type but TSR.2 was never given a name. However, on 1 January 1959 an interesting memo on this matter came from P. Humphrey Davies, Deputy Secretary to the Minister of Defence. In it he wrote: 'There seems to be security objections to meeting the Minister of Defence's wish to publish a number for this aeroplane. Is not the solution to name it here and now? I suggest "Velvet". Apart from the pleasant associations with mailed fist, it of course stands for Vickers English

Electric Various Explosives Transporter. It will annoy the Air Ministry to name the thing at this stage but it is their own fault for being so fussy about the number.' Vickers liked the suggested name but EE did not and instead offered 'Thunder' as an alternative.

OR.343

A new, more advanced requirement called OR.343 replaced OR.339 in May. The original GOR had essentially been a 'feeler' or preliminary target designed to stimulate reaction from the MoS and industry; OR.343 was much more precise, being written against the background of technical advice from these sources. In some areas it was more exacting, the more significant differences being a minimum height of 200ft (61m) or less instead of 1,000ft (305m), Mach 2 at altitude (which would require some air intake development and the introduction of ECM) and operations from lower-grade airfield surfaces. Development costs to initial CA release were estimated to be £62m with the first release for nuclear strike in December 1965.

TSR.2 was essentially moulded out of the P.17 and Type 571, EE's wing and blown flaps, tail and rear fuselage being combined into a datum design with the Vickers long fuselage. EE's team was the only one to have extensive experience of Mach numbers up to 2 and it accordingly centred upon the aerodynamic, stability and control aspects of the design. Vickers had instituted a far-reaching study into electronic systems and airborne equipment and in consequence had a more refined fuselage in its Type 571. The aircraft was split cleanly near the trailing edge of the wing box and Vickers was to make everything in front of this line while EE was responsible for the wing, rear fuselage, powerplant installation and tail. This arrangement satisfied the 50/50 split between the two companies and for administration the position was greatly simplified by the formation of BAC. The engine would be developed by Bristol Siddeley Engines (BSE), which

was formed by the merger of Bristol and Armstrong Siddeley. During 1959 the Netherlands and Australia showed strong interest in the aircraft.

Vickers-English Electric Type 571 (TSR.2)

A Preliminary Brochure describing the agreed datum design was produced in late July 1959. It was still known as the Type 571 and a growth of 12.5% on the dry weight had been made to cover the additional performance requested in OR.343. P.17's delta wing was picked ahead of Vickers' swept wing because it had offered a better gust response and transonic handling characteristics, though both were suitable aerodynamically. Revised data had been received for the Olympus 22R that, compared to the de Havilland PS.55/3, affected adversely the range and take-off distance, giving values that at this stage were unsatisfactory. To restore the performance the wing area had been increased by 10% with a consequent increase in the size and weight of the whole aircraft.

Using blown flaps increased lift at low airspeeds quite dramatically – high-pressure, high-temperature air was bled from the engine compressors and piped to the wing trailing edge where it was blown over the extended flaps to re-energise the 'tired' airflow. Without blowing the upper surface airflow over both the wing and flaps could begin to break up and become turbulent at low airspeeds, thereby leading to a loss of lift and more drag. Selecting blowing kept the airflow in contact with the upper surfaces and prevented it from breaking away, thus increasing the lift. The datum aircraft had an all-moving fin, all-moving tail, part-span trailing-edge flaps, a wing with a notched leading edge and a sawtooth and, at this stage, square air intakes (variable half-cone intakes were adopted in 1960).

In December 1959 the MoA sought Treasury approval for a full development contract to initial CA release but only limited approval was given while the

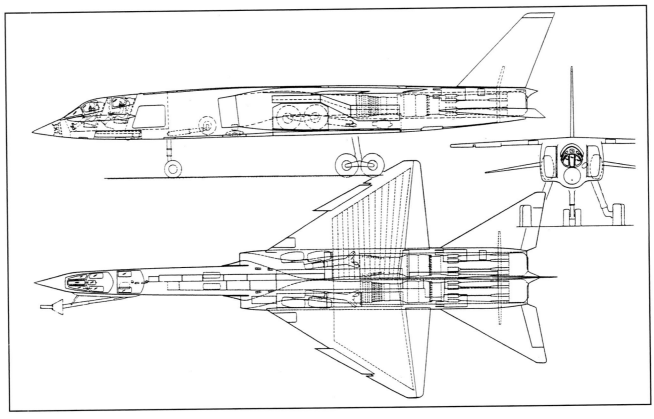

ABOVE The combined BAC Type 571 datum design (7.59). *North West Heritage Group*

BAC Type 571 (TSR.2 Datum) (7.59)	
Span	37ft 1in (11.30m)
Length	84ft 1in (25.63m)
Gross wing area	697sq ft (64.8sq m)
t/c ratio	3.6% root
Gross weight	85,070lb (38,588kg)
Powerplant	two Bristol Olympus Ol.22R 16,600lb (73.8kN), 30,600lb (136.0kN) reheat
Maximum speed/height	Mach 1+ at sea level, Mach 2+ at altitude
Weapon load	(Specification RB.192D) one Tactical Nuclear Weapon, six 1,000lb (454kg) bombs internal; two Tactical Nuclear Weapon, four 1,000lb (454kg) bombs, four Bullpup, twenty-four 3in (76.2mm) or 148 2in (50.8mm) RPs external

whole matter was reviewed, and this included a further assessment of the Buccaneer (the 'inadequacies' of which were stressed once again). Three months later the Minister of Defence, Harold Watkinson, asked the Chiefs of Staff to advise him on the necessity of TSR.2 and a full study was set in motion. A cockpit mock-up was officially viewed at Weybridge on 14 January 1960 and in May the Minister asked for a study to

give TSR.2 a strategic capability with the carriage of a stand-off missile such as Blue Steel. This work included assessing the effectiveness of nuclear and high-explosive warheads against representative targets and the aiming accuracy that would be required with this aircraft to meet those levels of effectiveness. The need for TSR.2 was agreed on 29 July, but a month later Prime Minister Harold Macmillan reopened the whole issue and another assessment was begun.

On 11 September 1960 Sir Solly Zuckerman, Chief Scientific Advisor to the Minister of Defence, compared TSR.2 against the Buccaneer and noted that 'there can be no doubt that the TSR.2 specification is up to the performance demanded of the aircraft and that there is no other that can meet it. The very best technical brains have bent themselves on this issue.' TSR.2 was expected to be in service as a strike aircraft in 1966 but it would not be perfected as a blind, all-weather

reconnaissance aircraft, able to follow contours at 200ft (61m) altitude, until about two years later. However, Zuckerman had learnt that TSR.2's capacity to fly very fast and low, thereby exploiting a height range in which current defence systems could not operate, did not give it special merit in terms of vulnerability. The MoA and his own staff informed him that a speed of Mach 1.1 or 1.2 at low level gave no advantage over a speed of Mach 0.9. Even the Buccaneer, which could achieve the latter, would be to all intents and purposes invulnerable at low level unless the target had a standing supersonic fighter patrol. But TSR.2 would give a better ride and when the 'black boxes' were ready it would be a much better contour follower.

TSR.2's ability to fly at Mach 2 at height was acknowledged but this might not mean so much by the 1970s when Soviet SAGW defences would have improved, although such speed would be a major advantage in any other theatre of operations. The Buccaneer could not go supersonic, but Brough's B.112 development would put that aircraft's speed at altitude up to Mach 1.6 (the B.112 was a variant proposed in 1958 as a naval combat air patrol fighter). TSR.2's size was also important because the Buccaneer could not house the sideways-looking radar that was essential for critically accurate navigation. Zuckerman appears to have favoured both aircraft but he noted that if the OR was relaxed, which he felt was a valid point, then the RAF's needs could be met by an improved Buccaneer, which would save a lot of money.

Four days later Watkinson confirmed and supported the need for TSR.2. He wrote, 'the whole history of air warfare had conclusively shown that performance was absolutely vital; only an aircraft with the requirements stated for TSR.2 could hope to survive and to fulfil its functions in the period under discussion, namely the late 1960s to the end of the 1970s'. There was no possible compromise, the Buccaneer could not be developed to approach the OR and the specified limits could not be reduced. As a result a full contract was placed in October 1960 for nine development aircraft with a first flight planned for March 1963.

However, from the moment Watkinson raised the issue of a strategic nuclear role TSR.2's performance requirements were gradually expanded (instead of simplifying the aircraft's systems to keep down the cost) and in 1961 the conventional and tactical nuclear load was increased, the latter being doubled to two bombs. In April 1959 Republic Aviation of America approached the Parliamentary Secretary with a view to influence the UK to order its F-105 Thunderchief as the RAF's strike and reconnaissance aircraft. In fact, the F-105 had been considered in 1958 but it did not meet any RAF requirement and particularly OR.339 as it then was. The outcome was the passing of information to Republic on the Olympus, Conway and large de Havilland Gyron engines to assess their use in the F-105. This contact also

established that the USAF had no light bomber of its own and the British Government considered it might be interested in TSR.2. However, the US aircraft industry would in due course create the F-111 (below) as a lethal rival.

Specification RB.192D, written around OR.343, was issued in August 1960 and instead of Red Beard a tactical nuclear 'lay-down' weapon for low-level use was now planned to ASR.1177. This was to become the WE.177, which joined the RAF's inventory in 1966 and stayed until 1998. OR.343 Issue 2 was accepted in May 1961 and this introduced a performance ceiling of 56,000ft (17,069m) and increased the number of 1,000lb (454kg) HE bombs carried internally to six. The internal carriage of rockets and air-to-surface guided weapons was also now deleted and these changes were considered practicable without significantly increasing cost.

BAC felt that the airframe would not present any problems and BSE was satisfied that the powerplant would meet the timescale. It was thought that the nav/attack system, a new area in electronics, would be the weak link. TSR.2 would have a comprehensive electronics suite, much of which broke new ground, and delays in developing such advanced equipment were thought to be inevitable. As it happened, the airframe took longer to design and construct than had originally been expected and the engine suffered a sequence of mechanical faults. By June 1961 progress was about three months behind schedule and two months later the gross weight had risen to 93,283lb (42,313kg).

By now, however, powerful forces were lobbying against the project. One group believed that most of TSR.2's tasks could be performed by a ground-to-ground missile such as the BAC Blue Water, while another saw no reason why the RAF's needs could not be met by the Buccaneer. Politicians were naturally concerned about the programme's eventual cost and to the Government in general it was hard to disguise the fact that the new aircraft meant a complete reversal to the policy that was stated in

April 1957 – that 'the Government has decided not to go on with the development of a supersonic manned bomber' (the Avro 730 in Chapter Six). Other problems were the often less than cordial relationship between Vickers and EE and the co-ordination between the many companies across the country, contracted or subcontracted into the programme, via a large committee system. In practice this impeded rather than helped the process of making decisions. In early summer 1962 the Ministry met George Edwards to consider cancelling the project because of its cost, but Edwards commented that this would make 1,100 design staff redundant and 'shake the industry to its roots'. It was agreed, however, that the cost estimates should be reduced and a great deal of effort was put into this, unfortunately without success because a further increase in BAC's estimate followed within six months.

On 11 January 1963 the Ministry told Edwards of its dissatisfaction over BAC's programme management, which he acknowledged as a 'substantial failure'. Apart from increased labour and material costs, BAC admitted that it had failed to make valid estimates of the effort necessary to complete TSR.2's development and to exercise sufficient control over its sub-contractors. Analysis showed that the failure not only applied to those parts of the project that broke new ground (mainly the systems), but also to those that were of advanced but conventional design (such as the airframe) where BAC's experience should have stood it in good stead. BSE was also criticised for its method of estimating and financial control.

Two severe in-house critics of TSR.2 were Admiral of the Fleet Lord Mountbatten, Chief of the Defence Staff, and now Solly Zuckerman, both of whom favoured the Buccaneer. And the hostility to the project by Harold Wilson's Labour Party, prior to its taking office as the new Government in 1965, is well documented. But from 1962 serious doubts also existed within the Conservative Government. In late January 1963 Macmillan asked how the

ABOVE In-flight view looking down upon XR219 with the aircraft at low speed and undercarriage deployed. *BAC via Terry Panopalis*

project was progressing and for details of cost estimates. Julian Amery, the Minister of Aviation, replied that the estimated cost for R&D had risen from £90m in December 1959 and £137m in March 1962 to a present £175m minimum, £3.5m of this representing 'improvements resulting from changes since the programme was approved (e.g. modifications asked for by the Air Ministry)'. Taking away increases in wages and material costs, the net or true increase was at least £65m.

Amery thought this was 'very serious' and put it down to two reasons:

i. The firms and the Ministry greatly underestimated the difficulty of the job and hence the time it would take. We were, of course, attempting something quite new and there was little or no past experience to guide us. In a project of this kind delay in R&D involves a direct and steep increase in cost. It is the men's time and the daily overheads of the firm that are expensive.

ii. Until very recently management control of the airframe was in practice split between Vickers and English Electric.'

As a result work at both factories had been brought under unified control with a single man responsible. Amery had no doubt about the project's technical validity but there were clear worries. (Watkinson has written by hand on this document 'Minister: This is a terrible story. I suppose we are prisoners to our decisions. When will all this come out?')

One factor behind TSR.2's high cost compared to previous projects was the use of more expensive materials such as titanium alloys, high-grade steels and aluminium-lithium alloy sheet. In mid-February 1963 the Defence Research Policy Committee (DRPC) approved the continuation of the project but with much reservation, criticism and suggestion for economies. On the 7th ACAS(OR), Air Vice-Marshal C. H. Hartley, questioned 'the competence of

the MoA … either to manage a major project or to offer any valid advice about it'. There was plenty of dispute between the ministries over TSR.2.

TSR.2 could not fulfil a full strategic role because it lacked the V-Force's range, and it had never been intended to undertake this task anyway. Yet the aircraft was now considered as such to fill the gap between the V-bombers and the Polaris deterrent bought by Macmillan in 1963 after the American Douglas Skybolt had been abandoned. The Lockheed Polaris was a submarine-launched ballistic missile and its acquisition brought the momentous decision to transfer the responsibility for the British nuclear deterrent from the RAF to the Royal Navy. That transfer was made on 30 June 1969.

On 15 November 1963 Alec Douglas-Home, Macmillan's replacement, minuted his Minister of Defence, Peter Thorneycroft, with the words: 'I am rather troubled about this project. It seems to be turning out to be considerably more expensive than we thought; and its military value is also being called into question. Ought we to have a new look at the whole venture and satisfy ourselves that it is still an integral element in our defence programme.' Thorneycroft's reply noted that: 'Unless we find a replacement for the Canberra of a quality which will enable it to live in a hostile environment of the sophistication which will be inevitable in the 1970s, we will cease to be an effective air power. By 1968 the Canberra will be worn out and in any event could not survive even against second class opposition. Our ability to hit targets behind the immediate battle area will have gone.' This conclusion was reinforced by the 'very serious fall-off that will occur in our conventional air capability with the phasing out of the V-Force in the early 1970s'.

In March 1963 the first flight was due in January 1964, but by April 1964 this had slipped to mid-1964 due to some engine failures suffered during bench testing. Beyond nine development and eleven pre-production machines (the latter approved in June 1963) a total of 138 TSR.2s were planned for the RAF with their production to be completed in 1973 (there had been suggestions for 320 examples in all). Aircraft 1 to 9 were to be used for development, 10 to 14 would go to A&AEE Boscombe Down and 15 to 20 were earmarked for the RAF's TSR.2 Development Squadron (No 237 OCU) at Coningsby. The Air Staff wanted the nuclear strike role to get first priority and a CA Release to clear the twenty-first aircraft to drop a nuclear weapon 'by single means' was expected in January 1967. Materials for thirty production TSR.2s were ordered in March 1964.

On 21 August 1963 it was finally decided to drop the 2,000lb (907kg) Red Beard nuclear store because of the difficulties in carrying it plus the confidence that the new WE.177 would be ready within TSR.2's timescale. TSR.2 would now carry two versions of WE.177 (Types A and B), 1,000lb (454kg) HE bombs, 1,000lb (454kg) retarded HE bombs to AST.1194, 2in (51mm) rockets, both versions of a new

air-to-surface tactical missile to ASR.1168 and bomblet dispensers to AST.1197. The salient features of TSR.2 were released to the national press on 28 October 1963 and a month later the Germans showed some interest in the aircraft as a replacement for the F-104G. Federal Minister of Defence Kai-Uwe von Hassel and his party saw the prototype at Weybridge in May 1964, but there were concerns in the British Cabinet about repercussions in the UK if the Germans were allowed to buy an aircraft capable of delivering nuclear bombs, despite the fact they were still under United States custodial arrangements.

A big blow was Australia's decision in October 1963 to buy the American TFX (which became the F-111) instead of the TSR.2. On the 30th G. McD Wilks noted that 'Australia's choice of TFX abandoned their usual insistence for a proven aircraft and they have chosen an aircraft much further away from service than TSR.2. [Robert] Menzies stated that the RAAF *did* recommend a proven aircraft (the American RA-5C Vigilante) and that it was the Australian Cabinet which, for financial reasons, selected the TFX out of the two unproved aircraft. Their Canberras are wearing out quickly and the Australians could undoubtedly get TSR.2 more quickly into service ... I think [the] Australians have basically taken a political decision.' TFX (F-111) was now a very serious rival to TSR.2, although the Ministry felt its planned in-service date of 1967 was 'decidedly optimistic'. It was known that General Dynamics, the TFX's manufacturer, was having problems and sections of the USAF's Headquarters were impressed by the way Vickers had overcome some of its difficulties. The feeling was that Vickers was doing a better job in certain areas than General Dynamics.

But the costs still rose. TSR.2 was the only combat aircraft for eight years to undergo a full-scale development in Britain and so it carried the burden of supporting the basic R&D that would be required for any advanced national aviation programme. Hence the Air Staff

felt justified in ensuring that it was capable of many different tasks, an essential feature in modern strategy. The resultant aircraft, though complex and heavy, could, according to the Air Staff, be applied effectively to any of Britain's many defence commitments. The F-111 did not have nearly such a diverse operational capability. However, between 1963 and 1965 there were proposals for economy, such as deleting particular roles and equipment, but only small savings could be achieved and then only by disproportionate losses in capability. For example, it was concluded in 1964 that if the top speed was reduced from Mach 2.05 to 1.7, the saving in R&D expenditure would only be £3m.

The first aircraft, XR219, finally made a successful first flight on 27 September 1964. The wait had been a particular worry and on the 28th Geoffrey Tuttle told Amery: 'It is a great weight off everyone's mind and I am encouraged to hear how satisfied Beamont [the pilot] was with the aircraft on the trip.' But in the following month the General Election returned a Labour Government and numerous comparison studies were begun immediately between TSR.2, the American F-4 Phantom and the F-111, a new Mk.2* Buccaneer and the Hawker P.1154 supersonic VTOL aircraft (Chapter Ten). Their costs, together with future defence strategy as a whole, was analysed closely to see if they were affordable and justified; Polaris, however, was retained.

A report published in November by the Treasury noted that Britain had a relatively small defence industry and armed forces compared to America's much greater resources, plus a faltering economy, and so it could not afford to develop a wide range of weaponry. In recent years many projects had been cancelled by the Conservatives, while estimates suggested that the huge amounts of money invested in defence R&D had produced just 2.5% of Britain's exports. Many experts felt that acquiring American weaponry would be a good move, while many Members of Parliament and journalists in the media felt TSR.2 was just over-ambitious.

Between 13 and 19 December 1964 a team led by Air Marshal Sir Christopher Hartley visited Washington and Fort Worth on a fact-finding mission for the F-111 (the first prototype flew on 21 December), the McDonnell F-4C Phantom and some transport aircraft. Around this time the Air Ministry moved in favour of replacing TSR.2 with the F-111 (though it was still against the Buccaneer) and on 7 January 1965 there were strong rumours in the national press forecasting the TSR.2's cancellation. Eight days later aircraft industry chiefs and the Aviation Minister (Roy Jenkins) dined with Prime Minister Harold Wilson to discuss the future shape of the industry. On 2 February Wilson announced the cancellation of the Hawker P.1154 but he deferred a decision on TSR.2, principally to allow further studies to be made regarding the industrial and social consequences of cancellation.

ABOVE TSR.2's characteristic wing tip vortices seen just after XR219 had taken off for a test flight. *North West Heritage Group*

BELOW This view shows the size of TSR.2's all-moving fin and how 'clean' the aircraft appeared when the undercarriage had been retracted.

ABOVE **A sad sight – one of the incomplete TSR.2 airframes (XR226) being cut up at Warton in 1965.** *North West Heritage Group*

By now the debate surrounding TSR.2 in Whitehall and the media had become very bitter. By February 1965 the estimates had risen to between £252m and £272m for R&D, £55m for the eleven pre-production aeroplanes and £410m for a quoted production run of 147 aircraft. CA Release for the nuclear role was now to be the fourth quarter of 1967 and for other roles it was fourth quarter 1968. Another MoD/MoA party visited America in March 1965 to learn more about the F-111's avionics, while on the 19th of that month the Air Staff issued a paper that identified the requirement for either TSR.2 or F-111 while laying the Buccaneer Mk.2* and the F-4C Phantom to rest.

Amidst this mess the TSR.2's superb flying and engineering qualities were reported by Wg Cdr Beamont and in mid-March 1965 he completed a full appraisal of its handling characteristics, which was sent to Jenkins. George Edwards added: 'In my 30 years of designing and making aeroplanes I have learnt that by one means or another they can all be made to work. Every now and

again the basic design conditions are met, or exceeded, right through the whole aeroplane. When this happens (and my only previous experience of this was with the [civil] Viscount) then there is very little alteration from the prototype to the production aircraft. All the available evidence points to this being the case with TSR.2.' However, the end was close.

The Cabinet decided to cancel TSR.2 on the evening of 1 April 1965 after two long meetings held during the day and this was to be announced on 6 April during that year's Budget speech. Denis Healey had pressed hard to replace the aircraft with the F-111 but others, including Roy Jenkins, favoured cancellation without taking an option on the American aircraft. The discussions were heated and Straw and Young (see Bibliography) reported that Wilson eventually presented the Cabinet with three alternatives: 'postpone a decision on TSR.2 even longer, cancel the aircraft without an F-111 option, or cancel and take the American offer' (the F-111 had been offered at very favourable terms). A 'substantial

minority of about 10 ministers (against 12) argued for TSR.2's retention' on the grounds that if we eventually needed a bomber of this type, 'we would be forced to buy the F-111 and thus become unduly dependent on the United States'. In the end Healey's proposal was accepted but Straw's and Young's in-depth article shows the decision was taken neither hastily nor easily. Work also now began on a collaborative project with France called the Anglo–French Variable Geometry Aircraft or AFVG (see Chapter Fourteen).

Cancellation was a huge step to take and brought both praise and criticism. Controller Aircraft (now Morien Morgan) was aghast at the implications of the 'surgical excision – rapid and complete – of the TSR.2'. He described the machine as 'the spearhead of advanced technology in this country. With its complex weapon system … it is the big spur to progress. Retaining our position as a force in the World aeronautical design scene means that we must undertake really advanced work – pedestrian projects would lead to steady decay'. On 7 April he sent

ABOVE TSR.2 pictured over a snowy Wiltshire landscape during its seventh flight made on 22 January 1965.
BAE SYSTEMS Heritage

George Edwards a telegram: 'Regret no further flying of TSR.2 is to take place. In the meantime both aircraft should be kept serviceable.'

On 25 April 1965 a survey began looking into the possibility of utilising the existing TSR.2s for research. To do so, however, it would be necessary to extend the flight envelope before any serious work could be done on an engine programme and this would need some fifty hours of flying. Then a full programme could use two or three aircraft for 150 hours flying until the end of 1967 at a cost of £2–3m. This was expected to benefit the development of the Concorde SST's version of the Olympus and the areas analysed would include subsonic and supersonic engine handling and behaviour, intake configuration and effects, engine performance in subsonic and supersonic conditions, kinetic heating (TSR.2's long

endurance would enable more data to be collected than would be possible with any other research aircraft), extending the flight envelope to Mach 2.05 between 40,000ft and 55,000ft (12,192m to 16,764m), aerodynamic stability at high Mach numbers, flutter characteristics and supersonic drag.

Controller Aircraft noted that the results would benefit the whole of our future aircraft programme, including Concorde and AFVG. But the Defence and Overseas Policy Committee decided on 1 June 1965 against further flights, noting that the money it required could be substantially more if any minor snags held up the flying programme 'which are almost inevitable on an aircraft of this performance and capability'. The flying so far completed by TSR.2 had been achieved only by the immense efforts of a large and enthusiastic team. Jenkins advised that the risks of failure were 'very

high. Spending £2–3m to get some return for an investment approaching £200m may at first seem an attractive proposition, but the information may not be indispensable'. James Callaghan, Chancellor of the Exchequer, felt it could prove to be 'a very costly business indeed. To embark upon such a programme would seem to run directly counter to the decision to cut our losses on this project and to release resources for more productive use'. He felt it was not worth contemplating such a programme.

So that was the end and the subsequent destruction of most TSR.2 hardware, with great haste, was considered in industrial circles to be totally unforgivable. Only the first prototype ever flew but the second was ready to fly, several more were nearly complete and manufacture had reached a point where components for many more airframes had been made. The author's

BAC TSR.2 (Flown)	
Span	37ft 1¾in (11.32m)
Length	89ft ½in (27.14m)
Gross wing area	703sq ft (65.4sq m)
t/c ratio	c. 3.6%
Gross weight	95,900lb (43,500kg) normal, 105,000lb (47,628kg) overload
Powerplant	two Bristol Olympus Ol.22R 19,600lb (87.1kN), 30,610lb (136.0kN) reheat
Maximum speed/height	c. Mach 1.1 at sea level, Mach 2.05 at 36,000ft (10,973m); best achieved Mach 1.13 at 30,000ft (9,144m)
Weapon load	two WE.177 or six 1,000lb (454kg) bombs internal; two WE.177, four 1,000lb (454kg) bombs, four AS.30 air-to-ground missiles or 148 2in (50.8mm) RPs under wings

ABOVE Artist's impression of the General Dynamics F-111K equipped with 600gal (2,728lit) wing tanks and 1,000lb (454kg) bombs. *General Dynamics via Joe Cherrie*

former employer, for example, High Duty Alloys Ltd, had forged many different parts in aluminium, titanium and steel and each of these required planning, metal production, forging, heat-treatment, machining and testing. One large component, the 'tailplane frame', involved hand forging and machining a huge slab of RR.58 aluminium alloy into a fuselage rib to fit around the engines. It was 119in (302cm) wide, 46in (117cm) tall and more than 9in (23cm) thick and there would be one per airframe. At cancellation sixty-five had been made only to become so much scrap metal. Most aircraft cancellations bring plenty of waste but fortunately much of TSR.2's technology did find its way into the Tornado (Chapter Fourteen).

General Dynamics F-111K

To replace the TSR.2 the Government went for the F-111K, the designation for the British version of the General Dynamics aircraft, and through the summer of 1965 ASR.343 was drafted around the type. In February 1966 the Defence White Paper established a need for fifty F-111s while rejecting a developed version of the Buccaneer Mk.2, and on 22 March the UK signed the Letter of Offer for the first ten aircraft. In September the avionics and all major areas of the British F-111 configuration were fixed and a

Preliminary Design Review, attended by a Ministry team, was held in the USA on 6 November 1965. Basically the F-111K was a standard American F-111A with a higher gross weight take-off capability, some updated systems, some specific British systems and the capacity to carry British weapons. Two versions were to be delivered, a strike reconnaissance variant and a trainer strike type, and structurally their airframes were to be near identical. Each of the two prototypes would be configured to one form, No.1 acting as the strike/recce prototype and 'wired' to carry and launch the Martel ASM.

The option for the remaining forty aircraft was exercised on 29 March 1967 and the first F-111K entered final assembly on 18 September. However, revised estimates received from America in early October 1967 indicated a significant degradation in the aircraft's strike radius and altitude performance. Then on 25 November, as a result of a devaluation of the British Pound, it was announced that the unit cost of the F-111K had risen to £3.02 million. On 16 January 1968 the F-111K was cancelled, ASR.343 being held in abeyance from the 31st. During May 1969 it was decided to dismantle the two part-built F-111Ks for spares and this process was completed by the end of September.

In 1967 the British Government, faced with a major economic crisis, abandoned Britain's commitment 'east of Suez', a move that rendered one of the main roles envisaged for TSR.2 as no longer necessary. Hence, the F-111K followed it down the cancellation road to be replaced by the loathed Buccaneer, discussions beginning almost immediately in regard to the type's existing capability and the modifications that would be needed for RAF service. Former FAA Buccaneers began transferring to the RAF in 1969. The Air Staff did not rate the Buccaneer but it had, over the years, assessed the type perhaps more than any other aeroplane. Their opinion was supported by some of Britain's allies and on 12 April 1965 the *Daily Telegraph* quoted one US general commenting: 'If the RAF operates the Buccaneer in the 1970s it will give its opponents the hysterics and earn the pity of its friends. The US Air Force discarded aircraft of the Buccaneer's performance a decade ago.'

Dassault/BAC Mirage IV

In 1965 a French Dassault Mirage IV fitted with Rolls-Royce Speys rather than the usual SNECMA Atar 09K jets was proposed as a substitute for the F-111K, and in July an MoD/MoA team visited Dassault to evaluate the concept. A detailed joint study by BAC and Dassault,

ABOVE The first two UK F-111Ks seen in quarantine on 20 March 1968 at the point of maximum assembly, and pending a decision on their future. 'K2' was to have been completed to the planned dual control trainer configuration. These airframes were eventually reduced to spares. *General Dynamics via Joe Cherrie*

ABOVE A version of the Dassault Mirage IV fitted with Rolls-Royce Spey engines came under consideration during 1965.
Dassault via Wolfgang Muehlbauer

completed in November, postulated that a significant improvement in range could be achieved by using the Spey's better fuel consumption. The modifications necessary to accommodate the Spey would include a longer fuselage (which permitted extra internal fuel), a redesign of the majority of the rear fuselage and larger intake ducts, but there were no major structural changes. However, the Mirage IV offered only an 870nm (1,611km) range rather than ASR.343's 1,000nm (1,852km) and, having been specifically designed for the high-altitude nuclear strike role, fitting British equipment for long-range strike/recce operations could make it as expensive as the F-111K. It was well into 1966 before the idea was officially rejected.

Back in the 1950s the role of the strategic bomber was clear and so was that of the close support aircraft such as the wartime Hawker Typhoon fighter-bomber. But the gap in the middle was often more difficult to define. The wartime light bomber, represented by types such as the North American B-25 Mitchell in RAF service, faded away after 1945 but a very light 'multi-role' bomber such as the Mosquito, 'the maid of all work', was still needed to hit tactical targets and airfields. The Canberra was really a jet Mosquito but improved defences

meant a replacement might be needed from the mid-1950s. The 1956 Suez crisis showed that it was, but this presented big problems since no one could really decide just what form it should take and how much money should be spent on it.

A Foreign Office telegram sent on 10 April 1963 noted that TSR.2 was not, and was never intended to be, the basis of a British deterrent. TSR.2 would have delivered nuclear bombs very well but it was a very expensive way of carrying iron bombs. The type was first seen as a relatively simple aircraft but from the late 1950s the concept became progressively more complex. As a result TSR.2 outgrew its original tactical duties and eventually nuclear weapons became its primary armament to fulfil a strategic role as well, an idea that at first was never intended. The weapon bay was designed around two standard UK nuclear bombs, although it could also carry six 1,000lb (454kg) conventional bombs. This moved TSR.2 up from secondary system level but providing the capability to penetrate Soviet airspace increased the price and brought rows over range. Fortunately, Britain did not get involved in a major war with the Soviet Union and so the TSR.2 was not really missed by the service. In the end, after all the

criticism given to the Buccaneer, the RAF received that aircraft, and then the Tornado, and both have done the service proud. TSR.2 was in many ways ahead of its time but Tornado benefited from the design work undertaken on it.

Way back in April 1953, the Operational Requirements Branch was grappling with the replacement for the Canberra and in particular a requirement for Mach 1.4 speed, together with the weight problem that this created. On 28 April, P. Broad, DDOR1, noted: 'We will not be able to afford a new light bomber if it is going to be larger than 60,000lb (27,216kg) gross weight when carrying a bomb load of not more than 10,000lb (4,536kg).' He felt that the solution was a cruising speed of between Mach 0.8 and 0.9 with the capability of short bursts at more than Mach 1. His words were very prophetic since the type he described resembled the Buccaneer rather than TSR.2, and he knew we could not afford a large aeroplane. The fighter-bomber eventually evolved into the Harrier and Jaguar light ground attack and tactical support types, while the light bomber became the heavier interdictor strike aircraft represented by Tornado, carrying weapons designed to hit bigger targets such as airfields and bridges.

Chapter Nine
VG and OR.346

Swing Wings and Multi-Role: 1959 to 1964

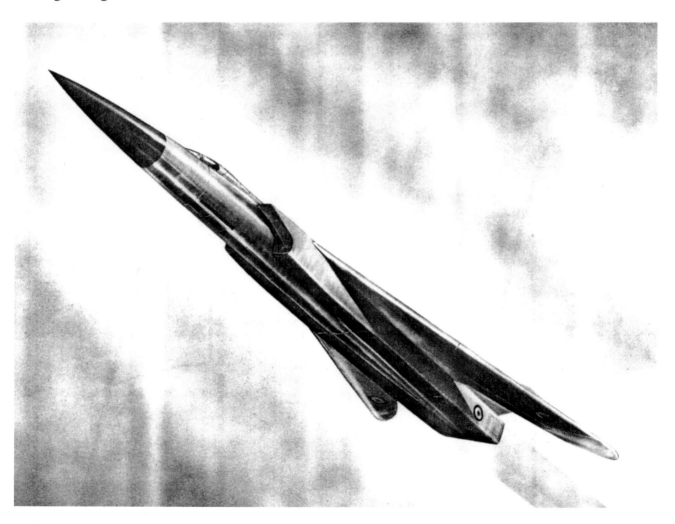

ABOVE Artist's impression of the Vickers Type 581 ER.206/3 (3.60).

Despite the policy presented to the British aircraft industry by the 1957 Defence White Paper, two years later work began on another advanced military aeroplane. This was covered by Operational Requirement OR.346 and was intended primarily to assess the application of some variable sweep work by Vickers to a strike fighter. However, the Hawker Siddeley Group also produced its own ideas to OR.346.

Vickers-Armstrong Swallow

In the 1950s Vickers' R&D Department at Weybridge became involved with variable geometry swing-wing aeroplanes through the work of designer Barnes Wallis. Wallis' first thoughts on the subject, using jet propulsion, dated back to the start of the Second World War and in 1943 he realised that ranges and speeds might be obtained far

beyond anything hitherto achieved. After working on a VG wing project called Wild Goose, his studies came under the all-embracing title of Swallow. These initially covered civil applications but the need to continue to find funding ensured some military variants appeared as well. Vickers patented the Swallow principle in January 1954 and the construction of a radio-controlled, subsonic, free-flying model began in

April. In September the first flight was made of a direct-controlled flying model at Predannack airfield and the following year saw the start of subsonic tunnel tests and then supersonic free-flight trails at Larkhill.

Alongside the theoretical study, tunnel testing and the use of large-scale models, several aircraft project studies were made and some mechanical parts associated with sweeping wings were manufactured and tested, the latter including an oil-lubricated pivot bearing in August 1956 and a dry bearing wing pivot in May 1958. In October 1955 a design study was prepared to R.156T and a second four months later was based on OR.330, and then in 1957 two research aircraft were proposed of 10,000lb (4,536kg) and 25,000lb (11,340kg) weight respectively. The MoS was actively engaged throughout this period, but after the 1957 White Paper all financial support was withdrawn and the work at Predannack ceased in June.

In April 1958 Wallis completed a brochure for a Swallow bomber based on the requirements of OR.339.

Wallis claimed that the Swallow configuration was pre-eminently suited to combine the smallest possible gross weight with high performance, very long range and low take-off and landing speeds. Its dimensions, and those of a long-range supersonic fighter, were identical to a planned research aircraft. Various studies had revealed the advantages of the highly swept arrowhead configuration for supersonic flight but it was incapable of take-off and landing, so the wings would have to be swept forward for those actions to take place. The engines, four Bristol BE.38 'Supersonic' Orpheus units, were mounted in nacelles above and below the outer wing and one Red Beard store was to be carried in a rear fuselage housing. The official assessment of this proposal suggested that developing a Swallow bomber from ITP to CA Release would

take a minimum of ten years, and perhaps fourteen, which was far too long.

Vickers continued alone until joint discussions on a VG programme were held in the spring of 1958 between the MoA, Vickers and the United States Mutual Weapons Development Programme (MWDP). The American finance was vital but they USA had also flown two experimental VG prototypes in the early 1950s, the Bell X-5 and the

Vickers/BAC Swallow (OR.339)	
Span	117ft 5in (35.79m) forward, 30ft 8in (9.35m) swept
Length	77ft 0in (23.47m) forward, 95ft 7in (29.13m) swept
Gross wing area	537sq ft (49.9sq m) forward, 900sq ft (83.7sq m) swept
t/c ratio	13.1% forward, 3.6% swept
Gross weight	50,000lb (22,680kg), 33,000lb (14,969kg) as research aircraft
Powerplant	four Bristol BE.38 Orpheus 3
Maximum speed/height	Supersonic at height
Weapon load	Red Beard, five 1,000lb (454kg) bombs, seventy-four 2in (50.8mm) or twelve 3in (76.2mm) RPs

BELOW AND OVERLEAF Vickers Wallis Swallow project adapted to OR.339 (4.58). The first view shows the wings spread, the second fully swept.

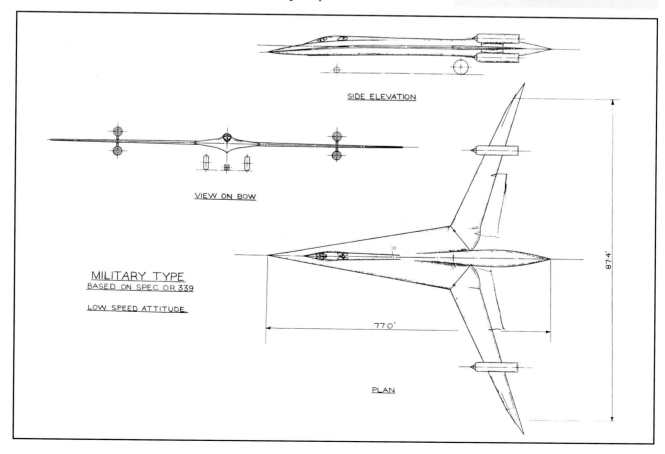

SIDE ELEVATION

VIEW ON BOW

MILITARY TYPE
BASED ON SPEC. OR.339

LOW SPEED ATTITUDE.

87.4'

77.0'

PLAN

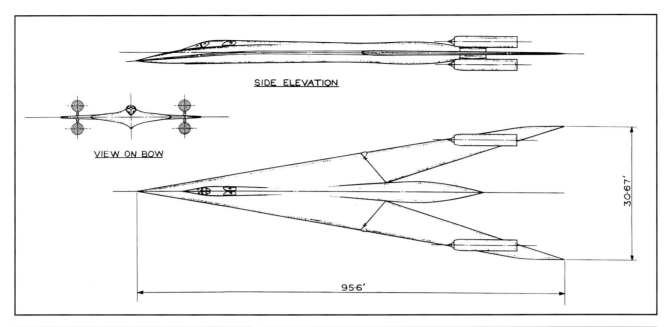

SIDE ELEVATION

VIEW ON BOW

30·67'

95·6'

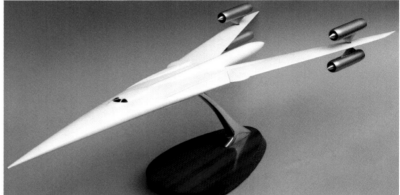

ABOVE This Vickers model of the original Wallis Swallow design has recently been restored. The OR.339 study was based on this project. *George Cox*

ABOVE AND OPPOSITE TOP An early swing wing/VG research aircraft flown in America was the Bell X-5, which made its maiden flight in 20 June 1951. No equivalent aircraft was ever flown in the UK.

Grumman XF10F Jaguar. In November 1958 a joint Ministry/Vickers team visited NASA's Langley Field to discuss the areas to be covered by each party. An agreement was reached between MoA and MWDP in February 1959 for a one-year joint research programme to assess the feasibility for operational applications of the Swallow variable geometry principle. Vickers received a contract in May and the programme was split into two parts – further research and then a project study to a service requirement, for which an interim brochure was to be ready by 31 October 1959 and a more complete proposal by 31 January 1960.

OR.346 and ER.206

On 17 March 1959 a new Naval Staff Target outlined a multi-purpose strike fighter and reconnaissance aircraft to enter service in 1970, and on 3 April discussions began between the Ministry and the Air and Naval Staffs that led to the issue of Joint Naval/Air Staff Target OR.346 as the basis for a research programme. The Navy amplified this with a draft OR for a carrier-based aircraft of 50,000lb (22,680kg) maximum gross weight. In the primary tactical strike role this would take

6,000lb (2,722kg) of bombs over a 1,000nm (1,852km) radius of action (with the last 200nm [370km] to the target flown at low level) and as an interceptor it would carry four AAMs to intercept and destroy an intruder flying at Mach 2.0 at 80,000ft (24,384m) off a combat air patrol of four hours. In addition, low take-off and approach speeds of the order of 80 knots (92mph [148km/h]) were desirable.

High supersonic speed (Mach 2.5+), long range at high subsonic speed, a 'low-altitude capability' and a reconnaissance capability were also requested. The ability to switch from one role to another at fairly short notice (twelve to twenty-four hours) was also important. The draft naval OR was subsequently used for a variable sweep design study under experimental research specification ER.206. The primary task for all of these projects was strike.

In June 1959 John Stack at Langley presented the results of NASA's wind tunnel tests on the original Swallow with engines on the wings and a submerged body. They were not good! The arrow wing did not give the expected high value of lift/drag ratio while inherent pitch-up instability was experienced at

low speeds. NASA had made a series of alterations to cure this and eventually arrived at an arrangement that departed from the arrowhead tailless Swallow to a more conventional aircraft with fuselage-mounted engines and a low horizontal tail. Stack described this alternative VG strike aircraft concept (which was now under comprehensive test by NASA) and it would eventually lead to the F-111. These changes to the VG layout brought an end to Barnes Wallis's involvement with the project.

Vickers-Armstrong ER.206 Projects (Type 581)

ER.206/1

Vickers' work to the Joint OR commenced on 1 May 1959. Since the naval strike sortie was very similar to that laid down for TSR.2 (but with a bigger bomb load), it was felt useful to see to what extent a TSR.2 type could be adapted by scaling it down in size, and three versions of this were assessed. These could be in service in 1966 but they used light alloy as their main structural material, which limited the usable Mach number to about 2.5.

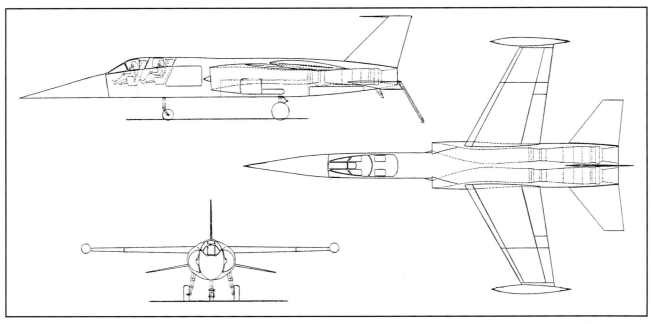

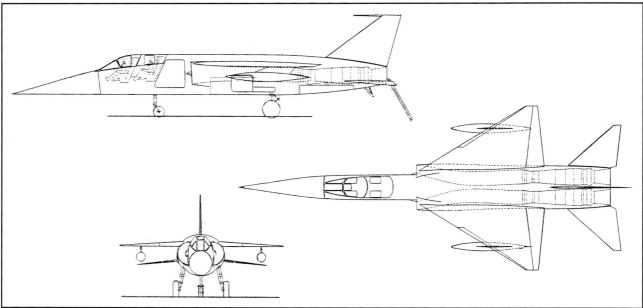

ABOVE Vickers Scheme C TSR.2 adaptation with delta wing (mid-1959).

ABOVE TOP Vickers Scheme B adaptation of TSR.2 to ER.206 with 25° swept wing (mid-1959). Scheme A was similar but had a smaller wing and tail surfaces.

LEFT Impression of the TSR.2 adapted to ER.206.

Schemes A and B had near-identical fuselages but with high-mounted wings of different area, while Scheme C had a TSR.2-style delta. Air was bled from the compressors to both leading edge and trailing-edge flaps to reduce the take-off and landing speeds and each design had an all-moving tail and fin. However, the 25° sweep versions had ailerons while the delta, like TSR.2, achieved roll control by differential movement of the port and starboard halves of the tailplane. A and B had tip tanks that would be jettisoned before going into action.

Alternative engines were twin Bristol BE.61 bypass units, Rolls-Royce RB.142/4 bypass units scaled to half thrust or four RB.153 straight jet engines. The half-scale RB.142/4 showed up best and was used in the performance presentation. For strike the electronics were based closely on TSR.2 and the weapons were carried internally and on external pylons. For interception two new 12ft (3.66m) long semi-active AAMs were housed in the weapon bay, while the forward-looking terrain clearance and the sideways-

Vickers-Armstrong ER.206/1 (TSR.2 Developments)	
Span	Scheme A 41ft 0in (12.50m) with tip tanks, Scheme B 43ft 8in (13.31m) with tip tanks, Scheme C 28ft 3in (8.61m)
Length	All 66ft 7in (20.30m)
Gross wing area	Scheme A 284sq ft (26.4sq m) without tanks, Scheme B 400sq ft (37.2sq m) without tanks, Scheme C 410sq ft (38.1sq m)
t/c ratio	Scheme A 5%, Scheme B 5%, Scheme C 3.6%
Gross weight	All 48,800lb (22,136kg) in strike role, 48,000lb (21,773kg) as interceptor
Powerplant	All two RR RB.142/4 8,000lb (35.6kN), 13,000lb (57.8kN) reheat
Maximum speed/height	All Mach 2+ at altitude
Weapon load	All Strike: Red Beard, six 1,000lb (454kg) bombs or two Bullpup missiles internal, Bullpup, RPs or bombs under wings; Interceptor: two 750lb (340kg) AAMs internal

BELOW The first configuration for the Vickers Interim Type 581 ER.206/2 derived from the Swallow (10.59). Note how the arrow wing stretches as far as the cockpit.

looking radar were replaced by an AI set with a 36in (0.91m) dish. None of these arrangements fulfilled the OR completely but this was to be expected since the 50,000lb (22,680kg) maximum weight was around 60% of TSR.2's while OR.346's task was more exacting. The efforts to meet the more severe deck requirements by conventional means had led to an inferior sortie performance.

ER.206/2

A fairly direct derivative of the arrow-wing Swallow was evaluated in the October Interim Report. The biggest change had been to put the engines, crew and equipment into a fuselage and the report indicated that the OR could be met by a variable geometry aircraft of about 50,000lb (22,680kg) take-off weight; however, it was not yet possible to state the best configuration, principally through a lack of knowledge in regard to low-speed longitudinal stability.

This aircraft had four RB.153s arranged in a four-square block on the upper rear fuselage that formed an

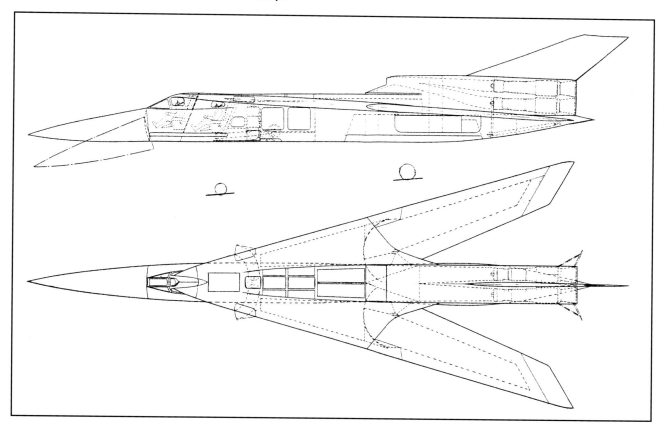

ABOVE Artist's impression of the Vickers ER.206/2 study.

ABOVE The naval ER.206/2 shown with everything down and about to land on board a carrier. Note the small retractable intake near to the cockpit and the extensive flap arrangement.

independent unit from the main structure; air was supplied from intakes above the wing. Blown flaps were used for low-speed landing and the resulting nose-down moment was offset by two Rolls-Royce lift engines placed behind the pilot (their intakes would fold into the wing leading edge). The largest practical forward-looking radar with a 36in (0.91m) dish was housed in the nose, while the other equipment was arranged along the lines of TSR.2 with the sideways-looking navigation radar stowed under the pilot's floor. The bomb bay occupied the fuselage beneath the wing centre section and would house all the weapons, including semi-active AAMs; nothing was carried externally. A conventional structure was used except for the wing centre section, the wing itself consisting of a highly swept delta forewing and two afterwings pivoted so that they could be swept from 25° to 75°. Both forewing and centre section were mounted on top of a fuselage of circular cross-section. Maximum speed was Mach 3.0 subject to the limits of the materials used. An alternative layout had four side-by-side engines fed by large side intakes.

BELOW The ER.206/2 brochure also included a revised configuration with the four engines placed side-by-side and fed by side intakes (10.59).

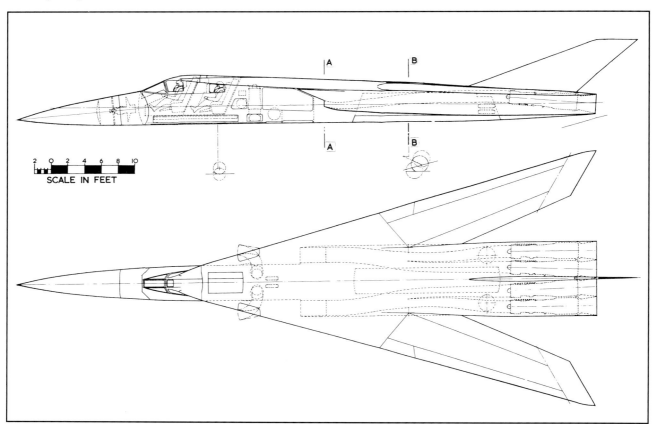

SCALE IN FEET

Vickers-Armstrong ER.206/2 (10.59)	
Span	57ft 6in (17.53m) forward, 31ft 0in (9.45m) swept
Length	76ft 4in (23.27m)
Gross wing area	554sq ft (51.5sq m) forward, 552sq ft (51.4sq m) swept
t/c ratio	11.5% forward, 4.19% swept
Gross weight	50,000lb (22,680kg) strike role, 48,000lb (21,773kg) interceptor
Powerplant	four RR RB.153 plus two RR lift engines
Maximum speed/height	Mach 3.0 between 43,000ft (13,106m) and 70,000ft (21,336m)
Weapon load	Strike: Red Beard, six 1,000lb (454kg) bombs or three Bullpup missiles, 2in (50.8mm) or 3in (76.2mm) RP packs. Interceptor three 600lb (272kg) AAMs

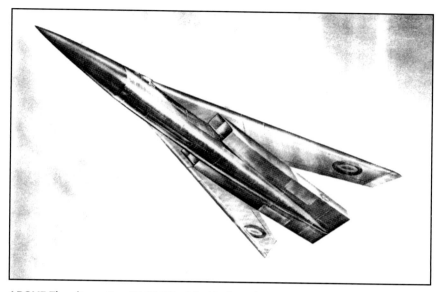

ABOVE The alternative ER.206/2 with side-by-side engines as shown in company artwork.

ER.206/3

The deadline to complete the full feasibility study was extended to March 1960. Vickers reported that VG offered a very considerable advance in aircraft capability and, except for a reduction in weapon load and provided that engines scaled from existing types to match the OR were available, OR.346's 1970 in-service date could be met at a gross weight not exceeding 50,000lb (22,680kg). There was, however, disagreement as to whether the stability and control problems could be met with a tailless aircraft. Here NASA supported a fairly conventional layout with a tail, the MoA had an open mind but tended to favour a tail, while Vickers felt that on the strength of the work so far nothing had come to light to show that a tailplane was essential from a control and stability point of view. The penalty for fitting a tail would be an increased structure weight and a lower lift/drag ratio, which needed more fuel and thus gave a heavier aeroplane. Hence, the Vickers brochure discussed a tailless configuration, which again was designed primarily around the naval requirement.

The ER.206/2's sweep angles and all-moving fin were retained and control was affected by wing tip elevons. Again,

RIGHT The layout of Vickers Type 581 (ER.206/3) with the wing leading edge blended into the intake sides (3.60).

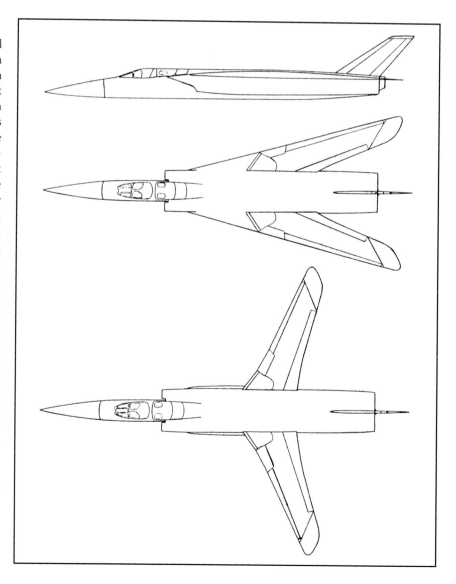

ABOVE Artist's impressions of the Vickers Type 581 ER.206/3.

LEFT A Vickers ER.206/3 takes off.

in the absence of a tailplane, the flaps produced a nose-down pitching movement that had to be balanced by duplicated lightweight lift engines placed just aft of the navigator seat bulkhead, control of which would be automatic and coupled to the elevons. The trimming engines only ran during take-off and landing and their folding intakes and exhaust doors lay respectively on the top and bottom of the fuselage, the exhaust gases being directed away from the surrounding structure and the nosewheel. Tunnel tests supported the use of elevons for longitudinal and lateral control while the addition of under-fuselage strakes together with the central fin gave acceptable directional stability. The elevons could be inclined so that useful control was available at all angles of sweep.

LEFT AND BELOW Model of the ER.206/3 showing different sweep angles.

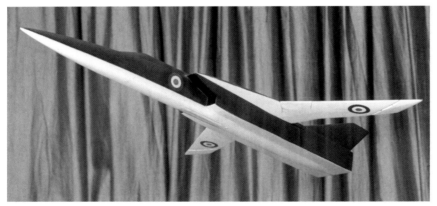

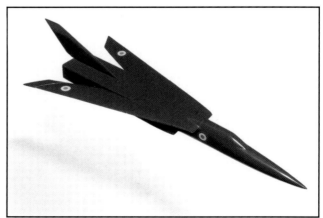

Leading-edge and trailing-edge flaps with boundary layer control were proposed. Exploratory tests had found a method whereby the inherent pitch-up instability detected by NASA in the Swallow was delayed to a point where a sufficient safety margin could be allowed. This was achieved by getting rid of the forewing as a lift producer at low speeds by either folding it along the intake duct side (the favoured alternative) or retracting it into the fuselage as the afterwings moved forward. Leading-edge slats or a blown drooped leading edge plus blown flaps could be fitted. The fuselage was the minimum size to take the crew, equipment and stores, while fuel was carried in the forewing, afterwings and fuselage. The nose could be drooped in flight to provide a good forward view for landing.

Studies between a simple jet, a bypass engine and a reheated aft fan engine had shown that the medium bypass unit was generally the best. Two 0.7-scale reheated RB.163s placed either side of the weapons bay had horizontal variable geometry wedge intakes, a fully variable integral reheat system and aerodynamic ejector-type nozzles. Weapons were carried internally in the large bay beneath the wing (which could also take auxiliary fuel tanks) and the naval version would have high-pressure wheels on a conventional undercarriage, catapulting hooks and an arrestor sting. (Most naval OR.346 projects were given folding wings and noses.)

There were two crew and the interceptor's 36in (0.91m) radar dish, which had a search range of about 70nm (130km), was again housed in the nose. The forward-looking radar's primary functions were terrain following, radar ranging for attack, airfield homing and blind approach. These could be performed by a much smaller radar than was necessary for long-range interception, so in the strike role the set was replaced by a TSR.2-type radar within the same radome. A Doppler and inertial platform produced data for the computing system (i.e. ground speed and drift and reference of azimuth, elevation and roll). The sideways-looking radar

ABOVE An ER.206/3 comes in to land. Note how the forward portion of the wing leading edge has folded downwards to permit the rest of the wing to move forward.

provided fix information in blind conditions at low and high altitude (which enabled corrections to be made to the Doppler/inertial platform/computer system) and also supplied reconnaissance information to go with an optional self-contained recce pack.

The weights quoted were for an aircraft capable of continuous operation at Mach 2 with short bursts at Mach 2.5. Range with a 4,000lb (1,814kg) load was given as 1,000nm (1,852km) and the internal fuel totalled 12,700lb (5,761kg). To meet the 1970 in-service date it was essential that

work on the VG aircraft should not be allowed to run down and so Vickers outlined a future programme based on the first flight of a pre-development aircraft in mid-1964.

ER.206/4

Vickers felt that removing the naval aircraft's severe weight restriction could make for a very attractive RAF version and the company completed a study for this in May 1960. The main differences between the Navy and RAF requirements were that the former needed *slow* take-off and landing speeds, low gross weight and small size while the RAF wanted a *short* take-off and landing capability from semi-prepared strips. Otherwise the performance limits were similar. A 'denavalised' RAF version would have low-pressure tyres and be suitable to operate from semi-prepared airfields, and without the limits of carrier landing it could carry the full six 1,000lb (454kg) bomb load and more fuel. A 3,000lb (1,361kg) weapon load was assumed for the interceptor role and it was noted that the ability to loiter subsonically, coupled with efficient flight at supersonic speeds, was one advantage of VG. The design diving speed was 800 knots (921mph/1,482km/h) EAS or Mach 1.21 at sea level. Two RB.165 engines were fitted that had the same characteristics as the 0.8-scale RB.163.

Vickers-Armstrong ER.206/3 (3.60)	
Span	58ft 0in (17.68m) forward, 31ft 0in (9.45m) swept
Length	71ft 6in (21.79m)
Gross wing area	528sq ft (49.1sq m) forward, 526sq ft (49.0sq m) swept
t/c ratio	4.1% swept
Gross weight	45,114lb (20,464kg) strike role with four 1,000lb/454kg load, 44,574lb (20,219kg) interceptor
Powerplant	two 0.7 scale RR RB.163 7,740lb (34.4kN), 13,480lb (59.9kN) reheat
Maximum speed/height	Mach 2.5 between 60,000ft (18,288m) and 75,000ft (22,860m)
Weapon load	Strike: one 2,000lb (907kg) TMB, six 1,000lb (454kg) bombs or three Bullpup. Interceptor: four AAMs

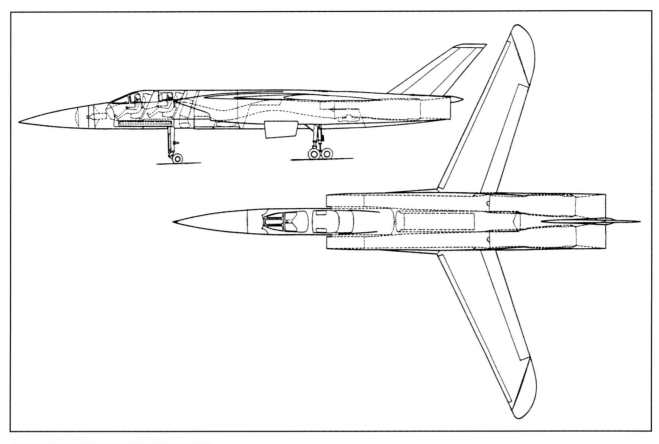

ABOVE **Vickers ER.206/4 for the RAF with four-wheel main gears and two-wheel nose gear (5.60).**

Vickers-Armstrong ER.206/4 (5.60)	
Span	59ft 10in (18.24m) forward, 32ft 6in (9.94m) swept
Length	66ft 1in (20.14m)
Gross wing area	430sq ft (40.0sq m) forward, 600sq ft (55.8sq m) swept
t/c ratio	11.5% forward, 4.1% swept
Gross weight	47,850lb (21,705kg)
Powerplant	two RR RB.165 8,850lb (39.3kN), 15,400lb (68.4kN) reheat
Maximum speed/height	Mach 2.5 at height
Weapon load	Strike: one 2,000lb (907kg) TMB, six 1,000lb (454kg) bombs or three Bullpup. Interceptor: four AAMs

Vickers Type 582

The adapted TSR.2 layouts produced as alternatives to the Swallow had proved inadequate to meet OR.346, the preferred alternative having no potential for weight growth. After considering other possibilities Vickers made a detailed study of a more advanced alternative design called the Type 582 in which the power installation was integrated with the wing structure. The report concluded

that a total military load of 8,000lb (3,629kg) could be carried within the 50,000lb (22,680kg) limit. With a twin fuselage and a structure consisting mainly of FV520 steel honeycomb this aircraft was capable of very high Mach numbers; in addition, thanks to the use of the jet flap principle where the exhaust gases were blown out of the wing trailing edge, it could also take off and land at low speeds (this idea was tested on the Hunting H.126 research aircraft from March 1963 but only at low speeds). To meet the 1970 in-service date a development batch of Type 582s would be required by 1966; new engines were an important feature but the RB.153 could be used for early development flying.

Eight reheated 1,800lb (8kN) dry thrust engines of similar design to the RB.163 were housed in the wing centre section. Flaps on the upper and lower surfaces of the wing leading edge and trailing edge would vary the intake and

exhaust geometry to cover the range of flight speeds, including deflecting the exhaust downwards for take-off and landing. The outer wing panels were equipped with blown leading-edge and trailing-edge flaps and folded downwards for carrier stowage, while the two fins were connected by an all-moving tailplane equipped with a blown flap for use during slow flying. The crew was located in the port fuselage, the radar and other electronics in the starboard fuselage. Fuel and weapons were shared between the two with enough provided for a strike radius of 1,200nm (2,224km) when carrying a tactical atomic weapon. Alternative low- and medium-altitude reconnaissance packs were available and an airborne early warning (AEW) version of the Type 582 was also proposed.

A four-leg undercarriage was fitted that on the naval version had single main and nosewheels; the RAF version

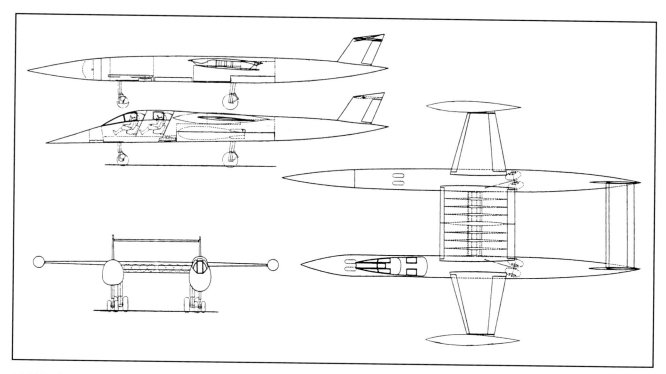

ABOVE The RAF version of the Vickers Integrated Power Type 582 design in its strike role with a TMB housed in the weapon bay (3.60). The naval version was identical bar having single wheels on each leg plus wing and nose folding.

RIGHT Impression of the Royal Navy version of the Vickers integrated power Type 582 in its strike configuration.

had a pair of wheels on each leg with low-pressure tyres and also two 200gal (909lit) wing tip tanks that on a strike mission were to be jettisoned before descending to low altitude. A four-hour patrol endurance was provided for the interceptor role together with four semi-active AAMs, their guidance being derived from the large AI radar in the starboard nose. This aircraft was especially suited for 'off the deck' interception and with the jet flap operating the estimated speeds were 100 knots (115mph/185km/h) EAS at take-off and 106 knots (122mph/196km/h) on the approach. Mach 2.5 ceiling was 60,000ft (18,288m) at 40,000lb (18,144kg) weight and 65,000ft (19,812m) at 31,000lb (14,062kg). However, rather less structural analysis and tunnel testing was carried out on the 582 compared with the Vickers VG designs.

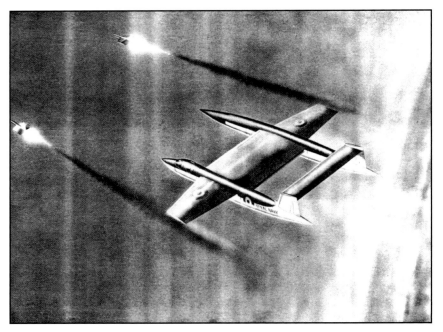

LEFT Impression of the naval Type 582 shown here operating as a high-altitude interceptor and releasing two air-to-air missiles.

An alternative, single-fuselage layout was studied briefly but this gave more drag than the twin, which forced an increase in fuel and hence the total weight. However, the smaller strike radar and radome removed the need for a drooping nose and the single fuselage also presented some advantages in sideways view over the twin. It retained the good carrier performance of the twin-fuselage 582 but for the same total weight the sortie performance was not quite as good. However, without the take-off weight limit Vickers felt the single fuselage presented the better choice for the RAF.

Vickers Type 582 (twin fuselage)	
Span	45ft 0in (13.72m) with wingtip AAMs, 40ft 0in (12.19m) without
Length	65ft 4in (19.91m)
Gross wing area	405sq ft (37.7sq m)
t/c ratio	12.6% in centre section
Gross weight	46,230lb (20,970kg) in strike role
Powerplant	eight scaled RR RB.163 1,800lb (8.0kN) dry
Maximum speed/height	Mach 2 at height (Interceptor: Mach 2.5)
Weapon load	Strike: one tactical atomic weapon, six 1,000lb (454kg), four Bullpup. Interceptor: four AAMs

Vickers Type 582 (single fuselage)	
Span	45ft 0in (13.72m) with wingtip AAMs, 40ft 0in (12.19m) without
Length	65ft 8in (20.02m)
Gross wing area	408sq ft (37.9sq m)
t/c ratio	12.6% in centre section
Gross weight	46,087lb (20,905kg)
Powerplant	eight scaled RR RB.163 1,800lb (8.0kN) dry
Maximum speed/height	Mach 2(?)
Weapon load	Strike: 1 tactical atomic weapon, six 1,000lb (454kg), four Bullpup. Interceptor: four AAMs

LEFT The RAF version of the Type 582 takes off.

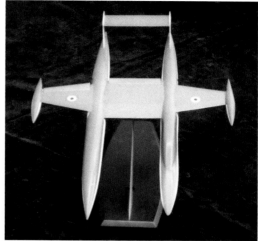

ABOVE Model of the extraordinary twin-fuselage Vickers Type 582.
ABOVE The single fuselage version of the Type 582 in its strike configuration armed with Bullpup missiles (3.60).

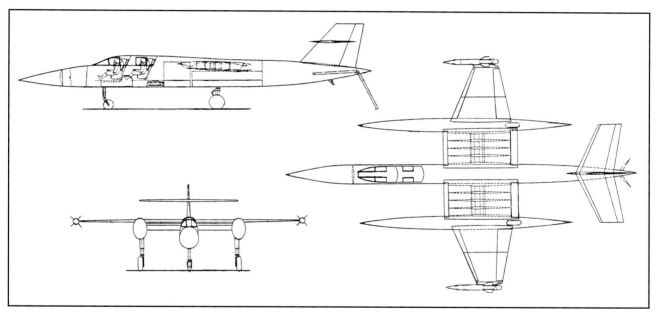

RIGHT Although of poor quality, this unique illustration depicts the single-fuselage version of the Vickers Type 582 as it might have appeared in RAF service. The engines were mounted within the inner wings in two batches of four. With the size of the wing nacelles to house the undercarriage and much of the equipment, one could almost say that this configuration really represents a triple fuselage aircraft.

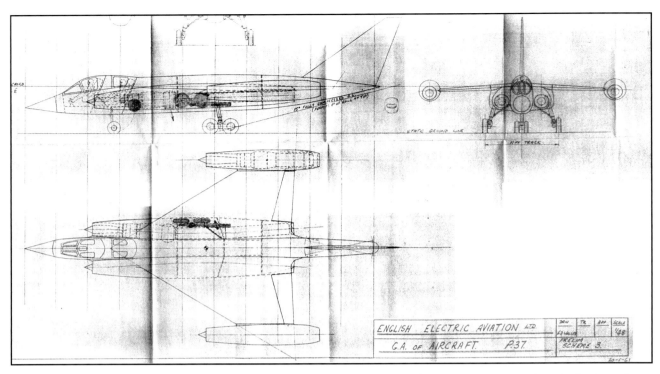

ABOVE In early 1961 BAC (EE) produced a set of STOL strike fighter designs under its P.37 project number. At the time of writing it has not been established if these were related in any way to OR.346 but they were aimed at both the RAF and Navy. This is Preliminary Scheme 3 dated 20 January 1961, which had a wing area of 500sq ft (46.5sq m) and a gross weight of 40,000lb (18,144kg). The powerplant was four Bristol Orpheus engines with the inboard pair scaled down to 5,610lb (24.9kN) thrust and the outboard pair to 7,770lb (34.5kN). *North West Heritage Group*

BELOW BAC P.37 Preliminary Scheme 5. The wing span here was 31ft 3.5in (31.29m), wing t/c 4%, all up weight 40,000lb (18,144kg) and powerplant two Bristol Siddeley Olympus 591/2 units scaled to 0.805. The drawing is dated 30 January 1961. *North West Heritage Group*

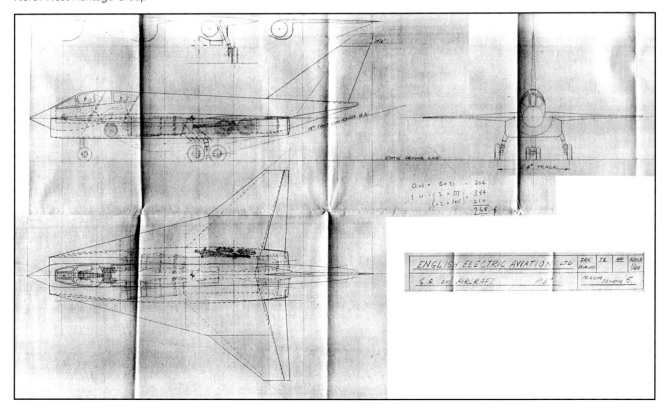

The MoA assessed Vickers' results in June 1960 and acknowledged that the VG types offered considerable advantages over conventional fixed-wing aircraft, particularly in terms of approach speed. All of these projects were capable of cruising supersonically at the expense of range. The Type 582 had a lighter combined structure and installed powerplant weight but inferior cruise aerodynamics and gust response (the VG's gust response was itself slightly worse than TSR.2's). Nevertheless, it was felt that Vickers had produced a potential competitor to variable sweep that might take less time to develop, but its success would depend on the new small engines having the assumed performance, while their introduction might take too long. RRE thought Vickers' approach to the many problems of designing a weapons system was very naive but the twin-fuselage Integrated Power airframe did offer big advantages to the radar designer in that it allowed the use of a large aerial.

The results of the Vickers VG work were summarised as follows:

1. The proposed Swallow configuration was found to present so many problems, especially in regard to safety in flight, control and aerodynamics, it was not considered feasible to adopt it and so no further work was carried out.

2. The joint research programme, however, had demonstrated that the application of variable sweep wings for certain military uses gave considerable improvements in performance, in particular the approach speeds on landing.

3. The ingenious spherical pivot (covered by a Vickers patent) that Dr Wallis had designed for a variable sweeping wing might well be found to be an important feature, certainly as regards the application of VG to UK military types.

A further programme of VG work by Vickers, financed by the MoA without American participation, began on 1 August 1960 and covered the construction and testing of more tunnel

models, the structural testing of a sweep mechanism and an engineering assessment of the variable sweep part of an aircraft. This suggested that the potential advantages of VG without a tailplane could represent the most attractive advanced solution in the strike fighter field. In October discussions between the Air Staff and MoA began for a new Air Staff Target (AST) to cover the application of VG to a wide range of future requirements. Three months later the R&D Board turned down an MoA submission to further extend Vickers' research because it felt that the next step should be to build a VG aeroplane – both the services and the Aeronautical Research Council pressed strongly for a research aircraft programme.

Adequate funds were allocated in the 1962–63 and 1963–64 estimates for VG research and the Ministry's R&D Board agreed in principle to a programme of two experimental aircraft (much of Vickers' work had been self-financed). On 1 April 1962 a design study contract was placed with Vickers for an experimental VG aircraft (the Type 589), a step confirmed in the House of Commons on 9 July by Mr Woodhouse, Minister of Aviation. In fact, the company was to put together a family of VG projects, which is described shortly.

OR.346 was to influence aircraft design for some time to come but by 1961 the Navy's need to replace several of its aircraft had also become a factor. In May discussions began for replacing the de Havilland Sea Vixen fighter and the Buccaneer by an OR.346 type in the 1970 to 1972 period. Gp Capt T. Witt, DDOR1, noted on 13 July 1961 that the Naval Staff was still fairly wedded to the OR.346 concept and the development of a special naval aircraft, while the Admiralty had designed a new carrier around the Vickers VG aircraft to OR.346. The Ministry of Aviation was an ally because it was 'desperate to go ahead with a VG aircraft'.

In the meantime, the RAF was looking at a TSR.2 replacement and in the summer of 1961, after a request from Controller Aircraft who wanted a

focus point, the Air Staff hurriedly raised OR.354, which called for an in-service date of about 1975. However, when it was realised that the Buccaneer successor was not required until 1974, then OR.354 was substituted by OR.355 (first draft October 1961), which detailed a TSR.2 and Buccaneer replacement; by August 1964 this had been succeeded by AST.355. Handley Page completed a brief study to OR.354 in December 1961 and designer Godfrey Lee reported that it had compared a 60,000lb (27,216kg) slim delta wing, a straight-wing type, a swept wing and a VG aircraft. Calculations showed that the first two were non-starters because of an impossibly low percentage structure weight but, despite a 5% weight increase from the swing-wing mechanism, the VG arrangement was on the whole the best solution.

BAC (Vickers) Type 583

The Type 583 project was more of a fighter than a bomber and is described in *British Secret Projects: Jet Fighters since 1950* but it also acted as a pre-development research aircraft to OR.346. In July 1964 Vickers (now BAC) noted that, whereas OR.346 could only operate from new carriers, in its current form the 583 provided the required multi-role capability and could also be flown from existing carriers fitted with BS4 (151ft [46.02m]) catapults and uprated Mk.13 arrestor gear. This claim was made after the Royal Navy had announced its intention to order the American McDonnell F-4 Phantom and a comparison between the two types indicated that the Type 583 would be superior. A Type 583 version with lift jets was also suggested for OR.355.

BAC (Vickers) Type 585

The Type 585 began as a naval derivative of the Type 584 NATO NBMR.3 proposal (see Chapter Ten) but it eventually settled down into a single-engine close support aircraft. It carried 7,000lb (3,175kg) of internal fuel and its supersonic cruise duration totalled ten minutes at Mach 2.0, but this study was relatively brief.

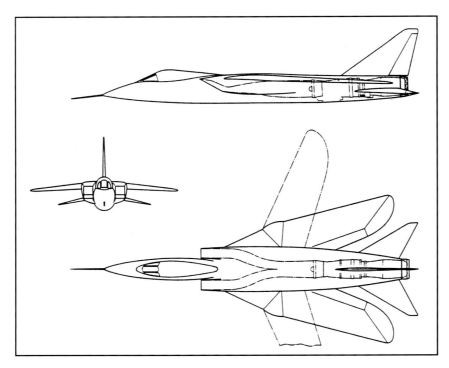

Vickers Type 585

Span	46ft 8in (14.23m) forward,
	24ft 8in (7.52m) swept
Length	58ft 4in (17.78m)
Gross wing area	300sq ft (27.9sq m) forward
t/c ratio	not given
Gross weight	26,000lb (11,974kg) (take-off
	weight)
Powerplant	one RR Avon with reheat
Maximum speed/height	Mach 2.2 at height
Weapon load	?

ABOVE BAC (Vickers) Type 585 (mid-1961).

BELOW BAC (Vickers) Type 588 VG version of the English Electric Lightning (1961).

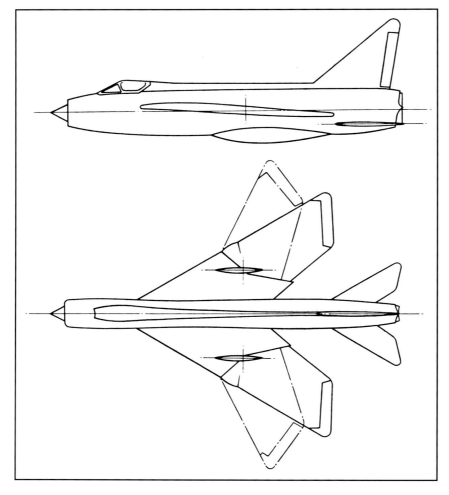

BAC (Vickers) Type 588

As part of the work to the NBMR.3 strike reconnaissance competition draft proposals were submitted at the request of the MoA for two research aeroplanes. One would be based on current fighters but fitted with VG wings under the Type 588 heading, the other was a new aircraft resembling the OR.346 design called the Type 589. Because of its proven supersonic capability, the great majority of the Type 588 work centred on modifying the English Electric P.1B Lightning, though in June 1961 a brief study was also made towards converting the Supermarine Swift. Changes were confined to the P.1B's wings with the hinge position about one-third of the span out from the root. Preliminary tunnel tests confirmed the feasibility of part-span variable sweep wings as applied to the Lightning and part-span flaps and slats gave satisfactory results, with a strong pitch down at the stall with the slats extended. However, the MoA considered that to ask for money for a VG Lightning would jeopardise the financial support for an all-new research aircraft, despite the fact that it would cost about one-tenth of the price of the new type, so from January 1962 Vickers pushed for financial sanction for the Type 589. Type 588 VG Lightning work ended on 3 February 1962.

BAC (Vickers) Type 589

Type 589 covered a pair of all-new prototype variable sweep research aircraft intended to extend the data collected by the Type 588 and a preliminary brochure was completed in February 1963. Since the Type 589 was projected against future RAF and RN requirements for the 1970s it could also be readily developed into an operational aeroplane. Although emphasis was placed on pure research, the Type 589 had two engines and two crew and the general layout of a typical strike aircraft. As such, these would be expensive machines and so the twin engine layout was considered justified on the grounds of reliability. In an effort to keep down costs existing components were to be used where possible and these included TSR.2's cockpit hood, a high percentage of TSR.2 system components and a nose undercarriage fitted complete from a Scimitar naval fighter.

Vickers had pressed for a contract to build a VG aeroplane and the American move to order a production aircraft based on the work done by Vickers in this field (the TFX/F-111) substantiated the company's faith in this system. The Americans too had taken a long time in deciding to proceed with a VG aircraft and it was felt that if Britain wished to do the same it was essential that it obtained the necessary design experience now; variable sweep could then be applied to future projects. Type 589's objectives would include proof of the engineering design, development of VG aerodynamics, the reliability of those systems peculiar to a VG configuration, understanding of the weight penalties and the aeroelastic and stability problems over a wide speed range, and the analysis of structural loads.

Three wing positions would cover the aircraft's flight range, although it could be flown at any intermediate angle of sweep. The forward position would be used for take-off, landing and subsonic cruise, a higher sweep angle would be employed for transonic flight and then maximum sweep for supersonic flight at Mach 1.4+. Two Rolls-Royce Avon engines similar to those used in the EE Lightning would power the Type 589 but, owing to the greater air bleed demands, the compressor casing would be changed for one dimensionally similar to the Scimitar's Avon RA.24 (RB.168s were also under consideration). The air

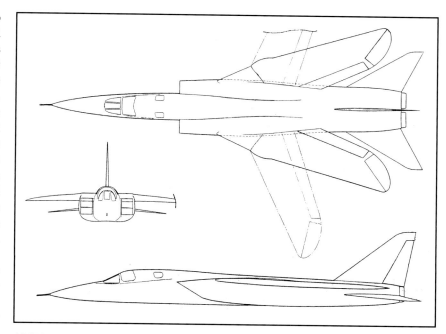

ABOVE **BAC (Vickers) Type 589 (28.1.63).**
BELOW **Sketches of the Types 589 and 585.**

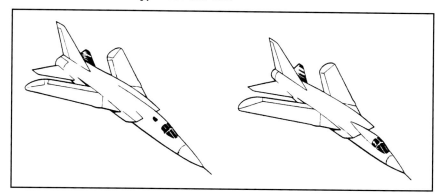

intakes were of the horizontal wedge type with a variable throat, while variable exhausts were fitted to the reheat pipes. Type 589 carried 14,900lb (6,759kg) of internal fuel and experimental equipment only, but allowances had been made to fit more advanced equipment at a later date.

The wings were swept by two mechanically interconnected hydraulic jacks, the sweep position could be varied automatically with Mach number and height, but the pilot could override the automatic variation. Control features included leading-edge slats and blown trailing-edge flaps (to give a high lift coefficient for take-off and landing), wing tip ailerons, an all-moving tail and a rudder mounted on a fixed fin. The undercarriage had

single-wheel main gears and was designed for operation from both aircraft carriers and concrete runways; launching hooks and arrestor gear were also fitted. The basic structure was in light alloy except those areas experiencing extreme conditions and the use of special light alloys and steels had been avoided. Maximum sea level rate of climb was 30,000ft/min (9,144m/min), the absolute ceiling was 55,400ft (16,886m) and the supersonic cruise duration was given as 15 minutes at Mach 2.0.

The Type 590 was intended to be a production strike version of the Type 589 aimed at OR.346 and it formed the naval objective of the 589's research. By 31 October 1962 the 590's take-off weight in the strike role stood at

ABOVE Type 589 model with the wings swept forward.

BELOW AND RIGHT Model of the BAC (Vickers) Type 589 showing the wings **swept back.** *North West Heritage Group*

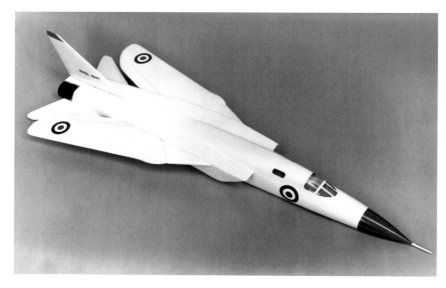

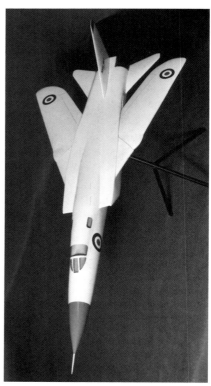

RIGHT AND ABOVE During the early 1960s Vickers drew many projects with VG wings. This model may be an early version of the Type 589 but it features side intakes with conical centrebodies.
George Cox

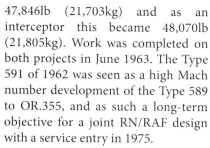

BAC (Vickers) Type 589 (research aircraft)	
Span	49ft 9in (15.16m) forward, 27ft 6in (8.38m) swept
Length	64ft 3in (19.58m)
Gross wing area	355sq ft (33.0sq m) forward
t/c ratio	not given
Gross weight	48,900lb (22,181kg) normal take-off
Powerplant	two RR RB.146 Avon reheated
Maximum speed/height	Mach 2.2 above 38,000ft (11,582m)
Weapon load	None

47,846lb (21,703kg) and as an interceptor this became 48,070lb (21,805kg). Work was completed on both projects in June 1963. The Type 591 of 1962 was seen as a high Mach number development of the Type 589 to OR.355, and as such a long-term objective for a joint RN/RAF design with a service entry in 1975.

Eventually the Navy split its Sea Vixen replacement into a separate document, AW.406/OR.356 (this is described in *British Secret Projects: Jet Fighters since 1950*). It was also agreed that the RAF's tactical requirements to the end of the 1970s could be settled by the TSR.2 and the P.1154 (see Chapter Ten) and so it was too soon to start work on a successor. When the 1962

project study was awarded to Vickers it was hoped that after twelve months the Ministry would be in a position to proceed with the design of an experimental VG aircraft whose characteristics would be based firmly on those of a foreseen military type. However, on 25 January 1963 the Defence Research Policy Committee reported that the changed circumstances regarding the development of military aircraft types meant that the case for building an experimental variable sweep aircraft as a lead-in had diminished.

It was still generally agreed that a research type would help the development of an operational aircraft, but the experiment would be very

costly (£10m to £20m) and its value would be much less if the final operational aircraft differed markedly from the experimental type, or if it was delayed considerably. Both of these circumstances were now likely to arise and so the committee had concluded that this stage of development must be deferred. However, work could continue on the engineering, structural and aerodynamic problems of VG while studies could be extended to embrace transport and maritime reconnaissance designs. This meant that the Type 589 would not be built. By April 1964 Weybridge was working on a smaller research aeroplane that it called the Type 593, but later that year the company's VG work was

ABOVE This Vickers model shows an aircraft fitted out in fighter configuration with a large radar and four air-to-air missiles. *George Cox*

BELOW The same aircraft design now in strike configuration with air-to-ground weapons and a smaller radar. *George Cox*

OR.346. On 13 December 1960 the Admiralty gave a presentation to Hawker Siddeley representatives on the future of naval air operations. New carriers that were to be in service in 1970 would require the OR.346 multi-purpose Mach 2 interceptor strike aircraft that Hawker noted was, in effect, a TSR.2 limited to 50,000lb (22,680kg) gross weight. In February 1961 a meeting between Blackburn, de Havilland (DH) and Hawker, chaired by S. D. Davies, discussed the 'new combined OR.346'. Here it was agreed that, as DH had progressed further on OR.346 than any other member of the Hawker Siddeley Group, it should be allowed to concentrate on this project while still using the experience of the other companies. An OR.346 Group team was therefore formed under de Havilland's W. A. 'Bill' Tamblin and meetings began on 16 June 1961. However, separate investigations into OR.346 were initiated at Brough, Hatfield and Kingston, although these were also looked upon as alternative layouts to the P.1154 supersonic VTOL aircraft described in Chapter Ten.

transferred to its sister company within BAC at Warton (formerly English Electric), a move that eventually brought forth the Tornado. This story is continued in Chapters Thirteen and Fourteen. (Note: although Vickers became part of BAC in 1960 it was still called Vickers, even in Government documents, for several years afterwards.)

Vickers was not the only company to produce designs to the joint Bi-Service

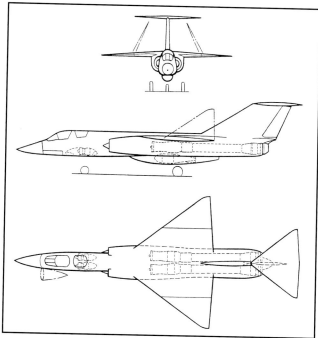

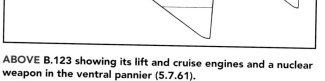

ABOVE B.123 showing its lift and cruise engines and a nuclear weapon in the ventral pannier (5.7.61). *BAe Brough Heritage Centre*

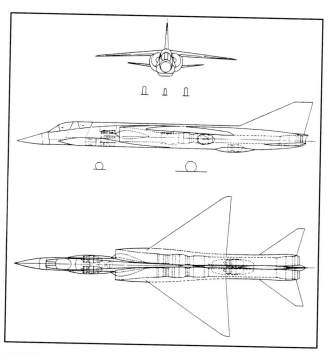

ABOVE HSA (Blackburn) B.123 with the tail now moved to a low position (9.61). *BAe Brough Heritage Centre*

HSA (Blackburn) B.123

Hawker Siddeley (Blackburn) at Brough specialised, of course, in naval aircraft and its first thoughts towards the B.123 strike/interceptor, which could be considered as a successor to the Buccaneer for the early 1970s, were based broadly on OR.346's naval elements. The main objectives included a take-off weight as near to 50,000lb (22,680kg) as possible, a strike radius of 1,000nm (1,853km) at Mach 0.95 (with 100nm/185km of this both into and away from the target flown at low level), a top speed for the 'clean' aircraft of greater than Mach 2, and a low approach speed (80 to 100 knots [92mph to 115mph/148km/h to 185km/h]). VG was rejected because of the Vickers efforts in this field, so for the present a delta was adopted for cruising at altitude at Mach 0.95. The best powerplant was two Rolls-Royce Speys and by arranging to deflect some of the thrust downwards behind the CofG, and to balance it by further downward thrust from lightweight vertical lift units placed ahead of the CofG, a substantial contribution to lift could be obtained for the low approach speed.

It was apparent that the next-generation strike aircraft would have to fly to and from the target through missile-defended areas, so it would make maximum use of natural cover by keeping very near to the ground. In the company's view the high longitudinal response and damping in pitch necessary to follow the terrain accurately were extremely difficult to obtain on a delta wing without using a tailplane or a foreplane. The latter gave some advantages since it contributed lift when a gain in height was needed, but the total drag, trim difficulties and layout problems had led to the choice of a conventional tail.

The B.123's structure used aluminium-copper alloys, although some steel would be employed for highly stressed components. Because the small t/c ratio gave high spanwise loads when the aerodynamics required accurate contours and a long fatigue life, the wing skins would be machined from solid billets of stretched material. The wings inboard of the fold joints would form large integral fuel tanks and the choice of a delta instead of a

trapezium planform gave much-reduced loads across the wing fold hinge and a much lighter wing in general. Fuselage structure would be conventional and the forward-looking radar had a 36in (0.91m) dish. In the strike role the 2,000lb (907kg) nuclear bomb would be carried in a ventral pannier, while for conventional sorties a larger and longer pannier could hold eleven 1,000lb (454kg) bombs with four more being carried on underwing pylons, two per wing in tandem just inside the fold position.

The brochure also included a version with a low tail, a lower gross weight and its overall length reduced to 72ft 6in (22.10m). It was unlikely that an aircraft meeting OR.346 would have a take-off weight of below 55,000lb to 56,000lb (24,948kg to 25,402kg) and so some thought was also given to a separate light strike aircraft of about 40,000lb (18,144kg) weight having a reduced load and range and powered by a single reheated Rolls-Royce Medway.

Two months later Brough completed a second B.123 brochure, although the method of construction was unchanged.

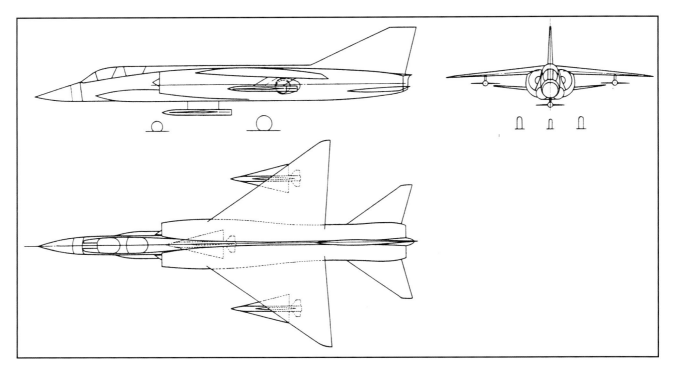

ABOVE The B.123 shown armed with a new type of delta-wing air-to-air missile. Air-to-ground missiles would have been carried on the same pylons. *BAe Brough Heritage Centre*

The low tail was now preferred but it was realised that in many respects the requirements of the two services were incompatible and attempting to reconcile them within a single design would fail to satisfy either in full; once again, however, this design stressed the naval side. The RB.168s had two stages of reheat, the first immediately following the rearmost turbine section with the second at the jet pipe outlet. Stage 1 gave a total of 18,000lb (80kN) thrust, at which stage the whole of the engine throughput could be diverted downwards to provide vertical lift. The Stage 2 reheat unit had a variable area exit nozzle, while two horizontally mounted RB.162s were installed behind the cockpit and these had deflectors to divert the thrust vertically downwards to provide trimming and additional lift. Fuel was carried in the wing and in two fuselage tanks.

All the weaponry was now carried externally, fairings being provided for those stores that needed to be housed in conditioned compartments while the underfuselage items were partially submerged and faired as necessary to

reduce drag. Six 1,000lb (454kg) bombs could be loaded under the fuselage in three rows of two, while the 2,000lb (907kg) nuclear store when carried would go under the centre fuselage. In addition, three Bullpup missiles could each go beneath the fuselage in a one and two arrangement and there could be one more Bullpup under each wing, or one AAM (of a projected delta wing type) or an RG.10 ASM were under the fuselage with one more under each wing.

Cruise at altitude was now made at Mach 0.9 and, with 22,100lb (10,025kg) of internal fuel, targets could be attacked with 4,000lb (1,814kg) of bombs at up to 1,000nm (1,853km) from base (the maximum internal fuel totalled 24,100lb [10,932kg]). A two-and-a-half-hour Combat Air Patrol could be made with the three AAMs aboard. At 50,000lb (22,680kg) weight the sea level rate of climb was 42,000ft/min (12,802m/min) with reheat lit and 17,500ft/min (5,334m/min) with reheat unlit, while the service ceiling at 55,000lb (24,948kg) weight was 54,000ft (16,459m) with reheat on, 45,000ft (13,716m) with reheat off. The maximum carrier weight

was 61,380lb (27,842kg) regardless of the weapon load, the fuel volume being amended to compensate, and at 40,000lb (18,144kg) weight the approach speed for landing was 100 knots (115mph [185km/h]). A forward-looking aerial was used for search, lock-on and weapon release purposes (and air-interception) and a sideways-looking aerial was installed for reconnaissance.

A preliminary study was also made for the RAF. This had four more RB.162 lift jets, two in a pack under the propulsion jet pipes and two placed vertically in a forward housing behind

Blackburn B.123 (7.61, T-tail)	
Span	37ft 0in (11.28m)
Length	81ft 0in (24.69m)
Gross wing area	550sq ft (51.2sq m)
t/c ratio	5%
Gross weight	56,500lb (25,628kg) = maximum deck weight with 2,000lb (907kg) nuclear bomb
Powerplant	two RR Spey reheated
Maximum speed/height	Clean: Mach 2+ at height
Weapon load	Strike: one 2,000lb (907kg) nuclear weapon, six 1,000lb (454kg) bombs, Bullpup missiles; Interceptor: AAMs

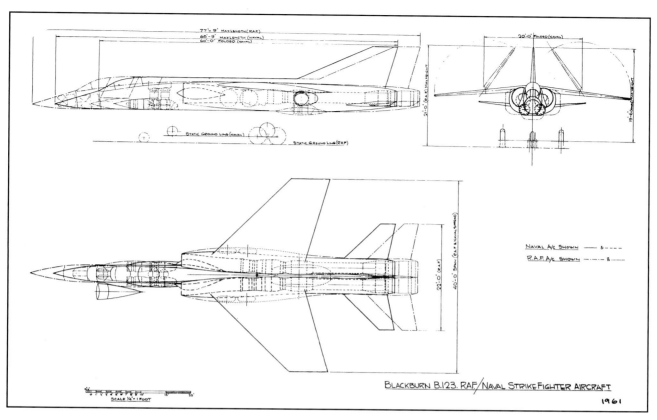

BLACKBURN B.123. RAF/NAVAL STRIKEFIGHTER AIRCRAFT

1961

ABOVE This version of the B.123 has a tapered swept wing instead of the delta, the solid lines showing the naval version, the broken lines the longer RAF version. Span 40ft 0in (12.19m), length RAF 77ft 9in (23.70m) and Navy 68ft 9in (20.955m). This drawing comes from a company review compiled in 1961 of military V/STOL design studies made across the entire Hawker Siddeley Group.
National Aerospace Library

Blackburn B.123 (9.61, low tail)	
Span	40ft 0in (12.19m)
Length	73ft 9in (22.48m)
Gross wing area	600sq ft (55.8sq m)
t/c ratio	5%
Gross weight	61,380lb (27,842kg) for naval strike or with AAMs
Powerplant	two RR RB.168-1R 15,000lb (66.7kN), 25,500lb (113.3kN) reheat and two RR RB.162 lift units 5,000lb (22.2kN)
Maximum speed/height	Clean: Mach 1.4 at sea level, Mach 2.5+ at 36,000ft (10,973m)
Weapon load	Strike: one 2,000lb (907kg) nuclear weapon, six 1,000lb (454kg) bombs, five Bullpup or three RG.10 ASMs; Interceptor: three AAMs

the naval version's trim-lift units. To accommodate them the fuselage length was increased by 10ft (3.05m) and this machine could carry 6,000lb (2,722kg) of bombs over 1,000nm (1,853km). Its normal take-off weight was 72,090lb (32,700kg) and the maximum speeds were unchanged.

HSA (de Havilland) DH.127

The DH.127 was a tailless delta designed to meet OR.346 at a minimum size and cost and to operate from *Ark Royal* size aircraft carriers. It utilised jet lift assistance in the form of deflected thrust, together with twin RB.162 lift engines for trim, to provide STOL characteristics and low launch and approach speeds. A particular emphasis was placed on a very large internal fuel capacity to give long range and endurance and the DH.127 could carry the 2,000lb (907kg) nuclear weapon over a 1,390nm (2,576km) radius of action (or 1,500nm [2,780km] with drop tanks). It could also deliver eight 1,000lb (454kg) bombs on a 900nm (1,668km) radius of action and on each of these missions the sea level cruise speed would be Mach 0.9. This 8,000lb

(3,629kg) load could also be deployed on a 'cab rank' sortie of 200nm (371km) radius coupled with a stand-off endurance in the target area of up to 2.7 hours. Readily converted to a fighter, off the deck at a light load the DH.127 could intercept a Mach 3.0 target at 80,000ft (24,384m) and 100nm (185km) from the carrier. Finally, at its maximum take-off weight it could stay on patrol for nearly four hours.

DH considered that the delta offered certain advantages over VG, including the absence of structural complication, a 'fail-safe' wing structure not dependent on a single joint, and the ability to carry external loads on the wings. Hawker Kingston's jet lift experience on the P.1127 (Chapter Ten) would be directly applicable here, as would Avro's work on deltas. Deflecting the propulsive engine's thrust downwards at a small distance behind the CofG to give a vertical thrust

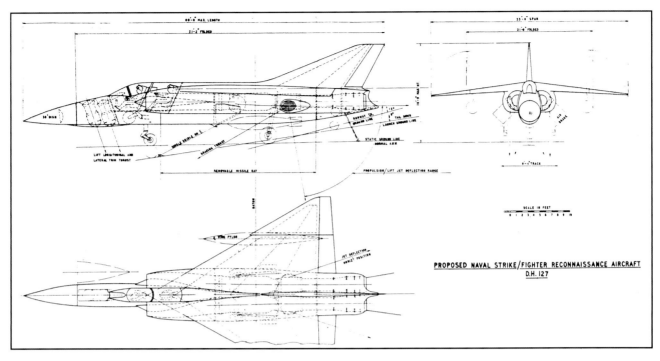

ABOVE HSA (de Havilland) DH.127 (mid-1961).

component would provide substantial lift and a minimum approach speed of just 85 knots (98mph [157km/h]). This thrust lift moment together with the nose-down moment from the wing produced by the flaps was balanced by the two lift engines situated in the front fuselage. A single jet deflection nozzle per engine penetrated through the side of the cowling, which in turn was slightly recessed to give clearance for the jet – in normal wing-borne flight the compartment would be closed by upper and lower doors to form a smooth contour. The RB.168s had inlets with

variable geometry conical centre bodies and fully variable convergent nozzles and, by using reheat and the forward trim thrust, a 'free take-off' at 40,000lb (18,144kg) weight would be possible from a carrier moving at speed (31mph [50km/h]) in zero natural wind.

The DH.127 was given a simple continuous wing, to which were attached the fuselage, engines, undercarriage and a single fin with its rudder. It would be made of machined skins with comparatively few internal ribs and spanwise members and it had elevon/flap controls. The absence of

high-lift devices and freedom from cut-outs enabled a simple structure to be maintained throughout and allowed fuel to be stowed in six integral tanks that, apart from a small space in the leading edge, filled the wing completely from fold to fold. Aluminium-copper alloys were employed for the primary structure because they produced the lowest weight commensurate with the effects of kinetic heating and fatigue damage.

An underfuselage bay could take (semi-submerged) most of the weapons envisaged for the DH.127's different roles, a strong point was also provided under each wing for tanks or bombs, and the fuselage's contours would be preserved by fairings peculiar to the weapons carried. The bay could hold four 1,000lb (454kg) bombs, the 2,000lb (907kg) nuclear weapon or four AAMs (either Red Top or its successor) and another 1,000lb (454kg) would go under each wing. The wing tanks, a fin tank and front and rear fuselage tanks housed 2,390gal (10,867lit) of internal fuel while two 250gal (1,137lit) wing pylon tanks and either a 300gal (1,364lit) or 1,050gal (4,774lit) weapon bay tank could also be carried. An alternative recce pack could be housed

BELOW The DH.127 tailless delta multi-purpose strike fighter would have operated from *Ark Royal*-size aircraft carriers. This aircraft could stay on combat air patrol for up to four hours but is shown here carrying Bullpup air-to-ground missiles.

in the weapons bay. The DH.127 was later renumbered DH.128.

The brochure also observed that the problems associated with the accurate delivery of a high-explosive attack were well known and no adequate solution had yet been proposed. Indeed, analysis of attacks with free-fall bombs had shown this method to be most uncertain and uneconomic. Air-to-ground guided missiles now coming into service were a considerable improvement, but they suffered from the fact that the target must be accurately pinpointed before launch and that the launch aircraft had to make a diving attack, during which it was highly vulnerable. There was a clear requirement for a new weapon and de Havilland's Weapons Research Group was at the time tackling the design of an air-to-ground missile that could be guided with great accuracy through cloud and other weather conditions, while permitting the launch aircraft to take evasive action immediately after despatch. This weapon was designated RG.10 and it used television guidance with a head containing an optical system and a camera. Preliminary studies had suggested a weight of about 1,000lb (454kg), a length of 12ft (3.66m), launch at speeds up to Mach 1.5 and a firing range of 9nm (16.7km). This effort appears subsequently to have become part of the Anglo–French Martel programme, the development of which started in 1964.

ABOVE **Model of the DH.127.**
George Cox

de Havilland DH.127	
Span	33ft 0in (10.06m)
Length	60ft 0in (18.29m)
Gross wing area	560sq ft (52.1sq m)
t/c ratio	5%
Gross weight	49,100lb (22,272kg) when standard to OR.346, 56,000lb (25,402kg) overload
Powerplant	two RR RB.156-1R 11,065lb (49.2kN), 18,650lb (82.9kN) reheat and two RR RB.162 lift units 4,400lb (19.6kN)
Maximum speed/height	Mach 2.5 at height
Weapon load	Strike: one 2,000lb (907kg) TMB, eight 1,000lb (454kg) bombs, four Bullpup or RG.10 missiles; Interceptor: four Red Top AAMs

Hawker (Siddeley) P.1149 and P.1151

On 16 June 1961 a team from Rolls-Royce's Projects Department visited Kingston to discuss Hawker's P.1149 design, which was virtually a Canberra/Buccaneer replacement. This had six lift engines and two vectored thrust propulsive engines but fell considerably short of OR.346 in that its weapon and range capabilities had been sacrificed to a certain extent to achieve a vertical take-off at light loads.

All of Kingston's projects to OR.346 were large and complex affairs. P.1151 was a supersonic jet flap type with four reheated RB.153s stacked in pairs along the fuselage sides, the jet flap being fed by air tapped from the compressor.

Hawker (Siddeley) P.1152

This V/STOL strike fighter appears to have been examined in a little more depth than the P.1151 and another design below called the P.1153. Four RB.162 lift jets with aft vectoring nozzles were placed individually near the four corners of the wing roots and a single reheated clang-box RB.177 cruise engine with deflected vectorable exhaust was used for hover lift. The RB.177 had two vectoring nozzles under the wing and a tail jet pipe with a variable area reheat nozzle. A high variable incidence wing was employed with three-piece leading-edge flaps, plain flaps, two-piece ailerons and two-

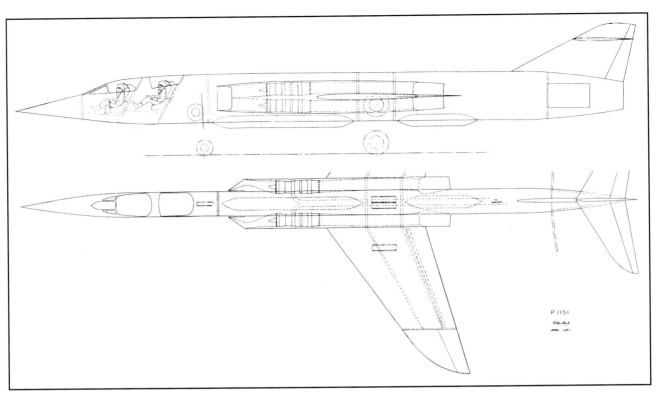

ABOVE Hawker (Siddeley) P.1151 (4.61). *Hawker Siddeley via Chris Farara*
BELOW Hawker (Siddeley) P.1152 (mid-1961). *Hawker Siddeley via Chris Farara*

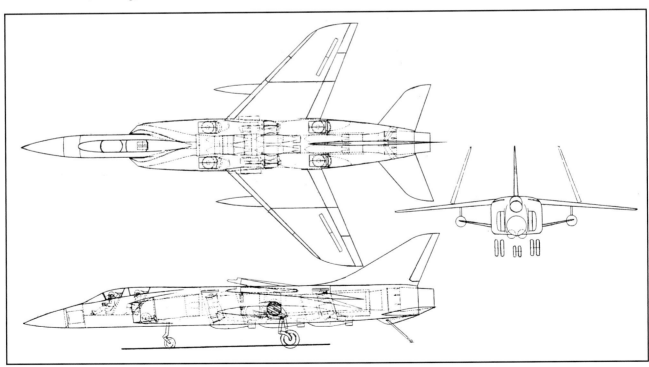

piece outboard spoilers. A low-position all-moving slab tail was fitted, each leg of the tricycle undercarriage had two wheels and the lower rear fuselage carried an underfin with a tail hook.

Three tandem pairs of semi-submerged 1,000lb (454kg) bombs could be carried along the underfuselage inside the line of the RB.162s.

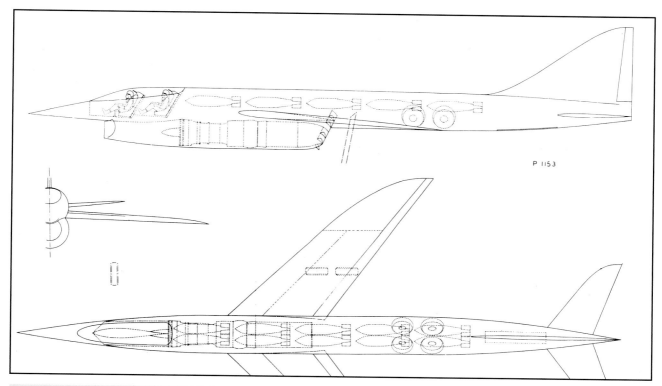

ABOVE **Hawker (Siddeley) P.1153 (4.61).** *Hawker Siddeley via Chris Farara*

Hawker (Siddeley) P.1152	
Span	45ft 0in (13.72m) for RAF, 40ft 0in (12.19m) Royal Navy
Length	68ft 6in (20.88m)
Gross wing area	?
T/c ratio	?
Gross weight	50,000lb (22,680kg)?
Powerplant	one RR RB.177 lift/cruise engine, four RB.162 lift engines
Maximum speed/height	Mach 2
Weapon load	Strike: Includes one nuclear weapon, six 1,000lb (454kg) bombs; Interceptor: AAMs

Hawker (Siddeley) P.1153

This large supersonic strike aircraft to OR.346 had one reheated Olympus 22R engine in a ventral housing beneath the forward fuselage that was fed by a chin intake. It also had deflected thrust that was activated by a cascade deflector with two vanes that slid down behind the jet pipe orifice, plus a rotating vane at the bottom of the jet pipe. This was a brief study only.

With the arrival of the NBMR.3 competition (Chapter Ten), the Admiralty was directed by the Government to look into the prospects for agreeing to a common version of the winning aircraft to cover both RAF and RN requirements. The Navy rejected this idea in February 1962, despite showing interest in the Hawker P.1154, because the requirement's range and weapon-carrying capability were inadequate, and the problems of low-altitude strike and all-weather interception demanded a crew of two (NBMR.3 was to be a single-seater). Also, giving the NBMR.3 an adequate interceptor capability would make it so similar to the OR.346 fighter mode that this additional and separate development was not justified.

However, after the P.1154 had 'won' NBMR.3 the Navy had to take a version of it, which brought an end to its ambitions for an OR.346 type aircraft. None of the studies in this chapter were turned into real aeroplanes, but they did lay down much of the groundwork for Tornado.

Chapter Ten
Vertical Take-Off

Harrier and NBMR.3: 1957 to 1985

ABOVE **One of the Hawker Siddeley Kestrel evaluation aircraft, serial XS695.**

Hawker Aircraft at Kingston will be forever remembered for the Second World War Hurricane, the beautiful Hunter jet fighter and the Harrier vertical and short take-off and landing (V/STOL) attack aircraft. Endowed with that V/STOL capability, the Harrier has to be one of the most remarkable aircraft to have been produced anywhere in the world. Many developments and variants were proposed, either privately or to official requirements, before the Kingston factory closed in 1992.

Hawker P.1127

The concept of a combined lift/thrust engine, based on the principle of vectored thrust, emerged in 1956 as a result of studies by Bristol Aero Engines and the subsequent co-operation between Bristol and Hawker resulted in

the P.1127 of 1957. Hawker's interest in developing a VTOL aircraft using this novel engine, the BE.53 (Pegasus), came to the fore as a private venture in the middle of June 1957. The company's P.1121 supersonic strike fighter had been declared unacceptable for the RAF on 30 May and designer Sydney Camm knew his team needed more work.

The BE.53 was essentially a ducted fan driven by the free turbine stage of a conventional gas turbine. The fan air was collected into ducts, which were rotated to direct the jet rearwards or downwards, and by August 1957 the fan gave an estimated sea level static thrust of 7,350lb (32.7kN) and the turbine exhaust another 4,000lb (17.8kN). In early P.1127 studies it was assumed that the hot jet gases would not be deflected but instead the aircraft would sit nose-up at a high angle when hovering so that approximately half of

the BE.53's thrust would be available as lift. The fan nozzles were directed slightly forward of vertical so that the horizontal components of fan and jet were cancelled out. In this configuration, however, a VTO was not possible with a useful military load and other methods of hot gas deflection were investigated. Eventually the jet outlet was bifurcated behind the turbine in the manner employed on the Hawker Sea Hawk fighter and ducted to nozzles on either side of the fuselage so that deflection was accomplished by nozzle rotation in the form still used today.

The P.1127 project was finalised in August 1957 as a single-seat subsonic strike and reconnaissance aircraft and presented to Supreme Headquarters Allied Powers in Europe (SHAPE). The brochure showed a very basic aircraft that could take off vertically in 'clean' condition with full fuel (270gal [1,228lit] in a single wing tank) or lift off with 2,000lb (907kg) of external stores after a ground run of only 600ft (183m). It could be regarded as a minimum airframe capable of VTO for short-range duties and able to lift off with a range of external stores from any main road or average-size field; in addition this was achieved without sacrificing a high subsonic top speed of Mach 0.94. The duties envisaged for P.1127 did not need transonic speeds so the flying surfaces were swept only moderately. All its weapons or two 100gal (455lit) drop tanks were carried externally and the sea level rate of climb at half fuel weight (7,500lb [3,402kg]) was 35,300ft/min (10,759m/min).

During the September Farnborough Show SHAPE's Colonel Chapman visited Hawker and commented favourably on the design, but he suggested that the radius should be doubled to around 250nm (463km) and that VTO was not necessary at higher weights, especially when carrying a nuclear weapon. By the end of the month the P.1127 had been altered to carry a 2,000lb (907kg) atomic weapon under the fuselage. The design was generally similar but for a

ABOVE Prior to the Hawker P.1127 jet-powered vertical take-off in the UK had been investigated using another research aircraft, the Short S.C.1 built in 1956. *David Birch, The Rolls-Royce Heritage Trust*

bigger span (24ft [7.3m]), the internal fuel had been increased to 500gal (2,273lit) and water-methanol injection had been added to the BE.53, which increased the total thrust to 13,000lb (57.8kN); this would permit a VTO at 10,250lb (4,649kg) weight. In the absence of any firm requirement leading to a specialist role for the P.1127, Hawker's aim had been to provide the most generally useful airframe that could take advantage of the new possibilities opened up by direct lift.

This new brochure was delivered to SHAPE Headquarters in Paris on 8 October 1957 by Hawker Managing Director Frank Spriggs, Chief Designer Sydney Camm, Ralph Hooper (P.1127 Project Engineer responsible for the aircraft's design) and Bob Marsh (Head of the Project Office). Great interest was shown and while the performance and range appeared to be of the right order, it was considered that more equipment was needed, including radar ranging for ground attack and a form of Doppler navigation. The recently completed

BELOW P.1127 prototype XP831 pictured in the snow of winter 1963. *Hawker Siddeley via Chris Farara*

NATO 'light fighter' competition won by the Fiat G.91 (Chapter Twelve) had shown that the competing aircraft suffered severely through a lack of such equipment. Hawker asked SHAPE for some financial support because none was forthcoming from the MoS, although the Controller Aircraft had praised the design.

In January 1958 it was confirmed that American MWDP support would be available for the BE.53 and that NATO interest in a VTO tactical fighter was growing. For P.1127 the emphasis moved back to VTO and ultra-short take-off at the expense of equipment, and within a month Hawker had finalised two approaches – one virtually the existing P.1127 with a nuclear weapon and moderately sophisticated electronics, the other reduced in size and carrying underwing RPs and minimal military equipment. On 11 March Sir Thomas Pike, Head of Fighter Command, saw the P.1127 and was much impressed. A few days later Wg Cdr Nelson-Edwards from Operational Requirements also showed great interest but he expressed the opinion that, in order for it to receive any serious consideration, the P.1127 should have supersonic interception in addition to its strike capabilities.

A full-scale meeting at Hawker on 5 August 1958 included General Boyd and John Stack of NACA, Chapman and Colonel Klein from MWDP, Sir Arnold Hall (Hawker Siddeley Group Technical Director) and all the company's directors. The Americans were very impressed with the design and its progress (but they were also interested in the P.1121 strike fighter, which they considered was a better proposition for the RAF to consider now rather than OR.339 in some five years' time). Seven weeks later Camm was told by Air Marshal Sir Geoffrey Tuttle, DCAS, that the Air Ministry was considering 'target' requirements for a VTO transport and a light fighter and in January 1959, thanks to increasing Air Staff interest, the MoS began to consider ordering two prototype P.1127s. The Air Staff, having 'triumphed' on OR.339, felt freer to take

an active interest in other projects and they intended to ask for a P.1127 type to replace Hawker Hunters in the tactical ground support role. However, no MWDP money was available because the Vickers Swallow had used up all its funds for the last financial period.

On 27 November 1959 the Minister of Aviation, Duncan Sandys, the architect of the 1957 Defence White Paper and its 'no more manned fighter' policy, visited Kingston to learn about the P.1127. He was treated to a full presentation but the Hawker diary notes that he 'generally did not appear to be very receptive'. There were opponents to the P.1127 concept, including a Wg Cdr Chamberlain, who often displayed a critical and discouraging pose; on one occasion Hawker's representatives noted that he and Gp Capt T. Witt had both received 'the anti-P.1127 treatment from Rolls-Royce'. Rolls-Royce preferred the individual lift jet concept and that company's Adrian Lombard and Ronnie Harker visited Kingston in March 1960 to discuss an alternative VTO powerplant for a P.1127 type, but Hawker told them that the separate lifting engine technique gave no weight advantage over a single lift/thrust powerplant.

In 1959 the MoA issued a contract for the development and manufacture of two P.1127s for research into V/STOL operations – up to now the aircraft had been a private venture. At the same time the Air Staff thought the P.1127 would be suitable for 'Colonial Policing' and, under MoA pressure, issued a draft Staff Requirement in February for a tactical ground attack fighter. In June 1960 this was officially issued as GOR.345 (with Specification ER.204D) for a short-range V/STOL ground attack reconnaissance aircraft for close support in a limited war. The first prototype, XP831, made its initial hovering flight on 21 October 1960, four more prototypes were ordered in November, XP831 made its first conventional flight on 13 March 1961 and full transitions from vertical to horizontal flight and back were achieved on 12 September.

Hawker P.1127 (19.8.57)

Span	20ft 0in (6.10m)
Length	34ft 0in (10.36m)
Gross wing area	154sq ft (14.3sq m)
t/c ratio	9%
Gross weight	11,000lb (4,990kg)
Powerplant	one Bristol BE.53 11,350lb (50.4kN)
Maximum speed/height	706mph (1,136km/h) at sea level, 639mph (1,028km/h) at 30,000ft (9,144m)
Weapon load	1,000lb (454kg) bombs, RP dispensers, napalm tanks

Hawker P.1127 (flown)

Span	24ft 4in (7.42m)
Length	49ft 0in (14.94m) with probe
Gross wing area	185sq ft (17.2sq m)
T/c ratio	?
Gross weight	Initially approx. 11,800lb (5,352kg)
Powerplant	one Bristol BE.53/3 Pegasus 2 initially 11,300kb (50.2kN)
Maximum speed/height	720mph (1,158km/h) at sea level, Mach 0.97 at 36,000ft (10,973m)
Weapon load	None

During the early stages of its VTO research Hawker examined several alternative designs and engine arrangements, which included the following:

Hawker P.1126

The very early P.1126 double-delta wing strike VTOL aircraft project had twelve Rolls-Royce RB.108 lift jets and twin Bristol propulsion units. To reduce storage volume and drag the 'pop-out' RB.108s retracted outwards to lie sideways in the inner wing, the increase in powerplant weight being offset by the adoption of a light helicopter-type skid undercarriage with very small wheels (the P.1126 had no STOL capability). Using two separate banks of lift engines avoided the suck-down problem experienced in types such as the Short S.C.1 research aircraft, while the jet 'fountain' created at the fuselage centreline gave a positive cushion near the ground. Span was 32ft (9.75m), length 53ft (16.15m), wing area 640sq ft (59.5sq m), fuel capacity 740gal (3,365lit) and the aircraft was to carry strike weapons only. The P.1127

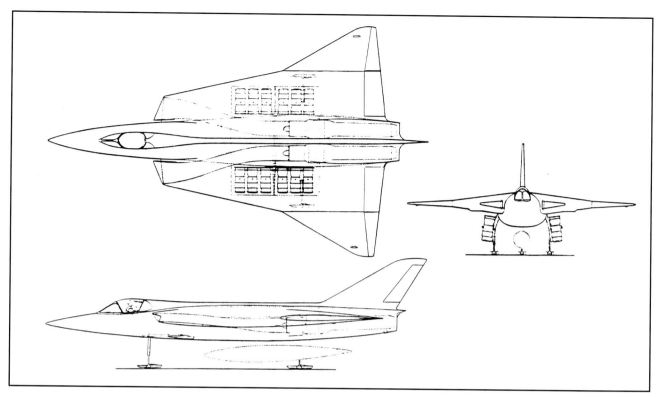

ABOVE Hawker P.1126 (6.57). *HSA via Chris Farara*

BELOW Hawker P.1126 with its twelve RB.108 lift jets deployed.

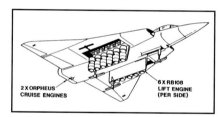

2 X ORPHEUS CRUISE ENGINES

6 X RB108 LIFT ENGINE (PER SIDE)

arrangement was an altogether simpler and cheaper approach.

Hawker P.1132

The Hawker P.1132 was designed as a subsonic VTOL strike aircraft to perform tactical duties over land and sea. It had twin BE.53s housed side-by-side in the fuselage, a large centre fuselage and intakes and a delta wing. The P.1132 itself of 18 April 1958 had twin booms, tip tanks, a single forward nozzle on each side and rear nozzles turned inwards to the rear of the centre fuselage. Its span was 37ft (11.28m),

RIGHT The twin-boom version of the Hawker P.1132 (18.4.58).
HSA via Chris Farara

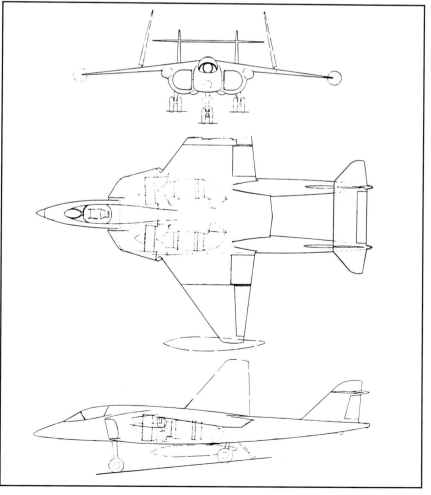

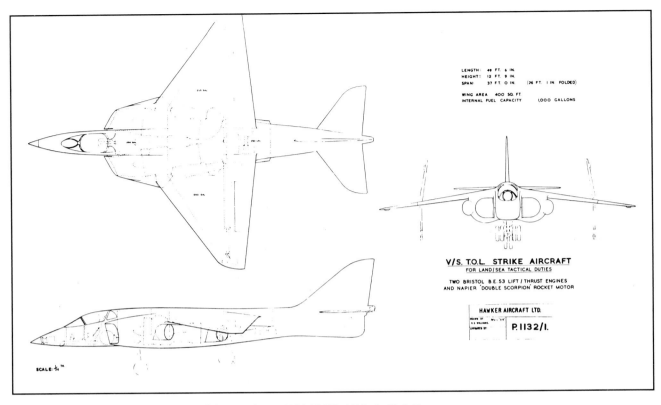

LENGTH: 49 FT. 6 IN.
HEIGHT: 12 FT. 9 IN.
SPAN: 37 FT. 0 IN.   (26 FT. 1 IN. FOLDED)

WING AREA   400 SQ. FT.
INTERNAL FUEL CAPACITY   1,000 GALLONS

V/S. T.O.L. STRIKE AIRCRAFT
FOR LAND / SEA TACTICAL DUTIES

TWO BRISTOL B.E.53 LIFT / THRUST ENGINES
AND NAPIER 'DOUBLE SCORPION' ROCKET MOTOR

HAWKER AIRCRAFT LTD.

P.1132/1.

SCALE: 1/48

ABOVE The central fuselage version of the Hawker P.1132 (4.58). *HSA via Chris Farara*

length 48ft 6in (14.78m), wing area 400sq ft (37.2sq m) and 1,200gal (5,456lit) of internal fuel was to be carried. The P.1132-1 (April 1958) had a P.1127-style tail unit, Napier Double Scorpion rocket motor and four side nozzles (two from each engine), with the BE.53s angled inwards towards the rear to make room for the rear nozzles. Span was 37ft (11.28m), length 49ft 6in (15.09m), wing area 400sq ft (37.2sq m) and internal fuel 1,000gal (4,547lit).

Engine-out asymmetry would have been a problem with these designs because the lack of crossover ducting between the BE.53s would create a rolling moment. The only response to the loss of thrust when hovering, and the consequent rapid downward acceleration, would be an immediate ejection. After an engine failure the twin-boom P.1132 would have three-quarters of its remaining thrust close to the centreline but, much worse, the single fuselage type would have half the remaining thrust well offset.

NBMR.3

In August 1961 the Air Ministry reported that the subsonic P.1127 would not meet its needs but it was prepared to take up to thirty aircraft if that would help a foreign sale; they could also provide a constructive 'lead-in' to later supersonic versions. For its Hunter replacement the Air Staff really wanted a supersonic type such as the Dassault Mirage IIIV. This policy was officially stated in November and the MoD was tasked to submit proposals for developing a supersonic close support aircraft that took both Navy and Air Force requirements into consideration. The result was Hawker's supersonic P.1150 with plenum chamber burning (PCB), but Chapman felt this aircraft was too pedestrian and was not large enough to meet a new SHAPE requirement that had also appeared.

That document was NATO Basic Military Requirement 3 (NBMR.3) for an all-weather supersonic VTO strike, reconnaissance and tactical support aircraft. This was circulated to European industry in June 1961 with designs to be submitted by year's end. Project NBMR.3 was to consist of two phases: the first would cover further development and testing of the P.1127; the second would see the production of a supersonic aircraft capable of speeds above Mach 1, even possibly at ground level. It would be able to deliver 2,000lb (907kg) of stores, including nuclear, over a 250nm (463km) radius of action and fly at a minimum of Mach 0.92 at sea level with its medium-altitude speed as high as possible. The operating altitude would be between 500ft (152m) and 40,000ft (12,192m). Service entry was expected four years after the selected prototype first flew.

Before looking at the direct NBMR.3 proposals, there was some alternative research also under way at BAC Warton.

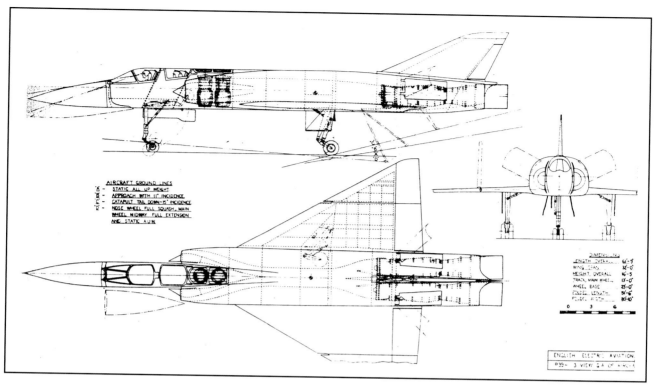

BAC (English Electric) P.39

ABOVE A drawing of the BAC (EE) P.39 development of the Dassault Mirage IIIV that shows the engine positions (2.63). *North West Heritage Group*

BAC (English Electric) at Preston and Warton also became involved in these studies with developments of the French Mirage IIIV. The resulting P.39 project was basically an Anglicised IIIV and work started on the idea in October 1961. In February 1963 a variant was proposed as an all-weather interceptor, strike and reconnaissance aircraft for the Royal Navy, but it was also aimed at Air Staff requirements for a type with virtually the same performance capability as that stated in NBMR.3.

The P.39 retained the same basic shape as the Mirage IIIV to minimise the necessary development flying and to prove the basic aerodynamics. A naval version would not require any built-in VTOL capability since the carrier's normal catapult and arrestor gear would suffice, so the Mirage IIIV's original eight lifting engines were now superfluous and had been removed.

RIGHT BAC P.39 armed with four AST.1168 air-to-surface missiles. This drawing is especially interesting because they show how the missile looked before it became Martel.

The aircraft's low delta wing was swept 60° 35' at the leading edge and, to obtain the maximum advantage from the take-off and landing speeds available on a carrier, high lift flaps (giving drooped blown elevons) were incorporated to increase considerably the aerodynamic lift from the wing. The resultant nose-down pitching moment was to be balanced by the thrust of two RB.162 lift engines situated in tandem on the aircraft centreline aft of the cockpit. The cruise powerplant was a pair of RB.153s placed side-by-side in the rear fuselage, these having been selected after a study of several different engines. For example, both this type and the Rolls-Royce RB.168 had very acceptable thrust characteristics for a supersonic acceleration, but the SNECMA TF106 failed in this respect.

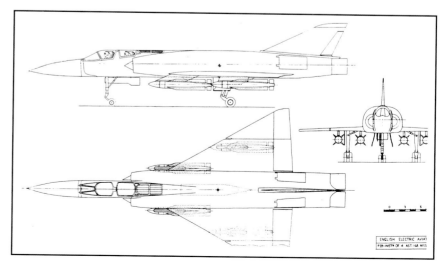

The P.39's nose could be drooped, and also folded through 180° for stowage aboard carriers. All the aircraft's stores were to be carried externally, either on wing mounted pylons or on the underside of the fuselage centre section – there was no internal bay. In the interceptor role the P.39 would carry four Red Top AAMs in external streamlined faired packs or pods to reduce drag, while in the strike role a load of 4,000lb (1,814kg) of stores could be carried over a radius of action of 800nm (1,482km). The bulk of the fuel (15,000lb/6,804kg) was housed in the fuselage but the inboard wing also formed two integral tanks with a capacity of 1,250lb (567kg) per side. P.39 had a design dive speed of 800 knots (1,482km/h) and a Mach 2.5 ceiling of about 60,000ft (18,288m).

BAC (EE) P.39	
Span	32ft 0in (9.75m), 20ft 10in (6.35m) wing folded
Length	61ft 9in (18.82m), 51ft 6in (15.70m) folded
Gross wing area	526sq ft (48.9sq m)
t/c ratio	3.5%
Gross weight	38,896lb (17,643kg) as interceptor with four AAMs (2.5 hours Combat Air Patrol)
Powerplant	two RR RB.153-61C cruise engines, two RR RB.162 lift units
Maximum speed/height	At least Mach 0.95 at sea level, Mach 2.5 at height
Weapon load	Interceptor: four Red Top AAMs; Strike: four 2,000lb (907kg), four 1,000lb (454kg) bombs or four AST.1168 (Martel) ASMs under wings, two 1,000lb (454kg) bombs under fuselage

Eleven designs were tendered to NBMR.3, including three all-British projects and the Breguet Br 1115, Dassault Mirage IIIV (with Sud and Rolls-Royce), Fiat G.95/6, Focke-Wulf FW.1262, Fokker/Republic D.24 Alliance, Lockheed/Short CL-704 and Nord 4210. The British contenders to NBMR.3 were as follows:

RIGHT BAC (Vickers) Type 584 to NBMR.3 showing three different sweep angles for the wing (12.61).

BAC (Vickers) Type 584

The Type 584 drew on Vickers' TSR.2 and VG experience and its comprehensive range of equipment would enable the single crewman to carry out tactical duties under any weather conditions. BAC's accumulated experience with the Swift and Scimitar in high-speed low-level flight, and high supersonic speed with the Lightning, formed the background to the project. Furthermore, during the design and development of TSR.2 the company had made further intensive studies of high-speed, low-level flight and high supersonic performance at medium and high level, all combined with advanced all-weather attack/navigation systems.

Type 584 could deliver a 1,250lb (567kg) nuclear bomb on a target 300nm (556km) from base, reconnaissance information being acquired on the same sortie by high-definition, sideways-looking radar. Its variable sweep mainplane would reduce the gust response and give minimum subsonic drag while the overall dimensions were probably the smallest that could fully meet NBMR.3. A single Rolls-Royce RB.177 bypass engine (known in May 1962 as the Medway) supplied the propulsive thrust while eight RB.162 lift jets were located in two groups, one forward between the RB.177's intakes, the other aft alongside its jet pipe. On take-off the fuselage would be inclined 15° nose up so that the thrust's vertical component would augment the lift, and a device for spoiling or reversing the propulsive thrust was located in the fuselage tail cone. BAC reported that using separate engines offered rapid acceleration, and thus a short transition time, while keeping the frontal area to a minimum.

Two weapon bays were located either side of the lower centre fuselage while the terrain-following radar and target ranging equipment were in the nose. The 584 had wing tip ailerons and an all-moving tail but no leading-edge or trailing-edge flaps, and during the VTOL phase control was provided by jet reaction nozzles fed with air bled from the lift and propulsion engines. These nozzles were coupled with the aerodynamic control surfaces, which would become fully effective by the time wing-borne flight had been

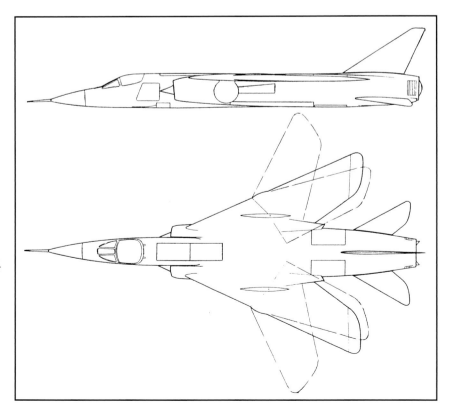

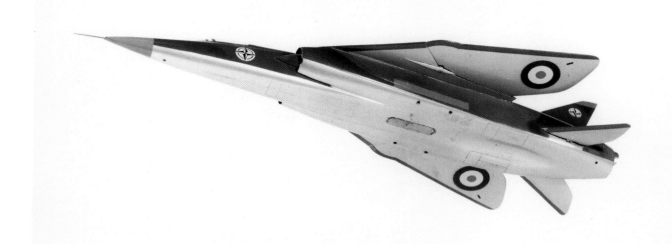

ABOVE AND RIGHT Views of the Type 584 model with its wings both fully swept and fully forward. *BAE SYSTEMS*

BAC (Vickers) Type 584	
Span	41ft 2in (12.55m) forward, 25ft 5in (7.75m) swept
Length	56ft 3in (17.15m)
Gross wing area	397sq ft (36.9sq m) forward, 382sq ft (35.5sq m) swept
t/c ratio	c. 10% forward, c. 5% swept
Gross weight	36,000lb (16,330kg), 44,000lb (19,958kg) for naval version
Powerplant	one RR RB.177-1R Medway 27,300lb (121.3kN) in reheat plus eight RB.162-6 4,400lb (19.6kN)
Maximum speed/height	NBMR.3: Mach 1.1 at sea level, Mach 2.16 above 40,000ft (12,192m); Navy: Mach 2.49 at 55,000ft (16,764m)
Weapon load	Minimum 3,000lb (1,361kg) of stores

BELOW The Type 584 in the hover. *BAE SYSTEMS*

BELOW Manufacturer's artworks showing the Type 584 during flight with the wings in the forward position. *BAE SYSTEMS*

achieved. Vickers declared that if an ITP was received in early 1963 then the Type 584 would enter service in mid-1968. Both RN and RAF variants were proposed but work on the project was stopped on 29 June 1962 after the design had been rejected. Rolls-Royce declared that the Type 584 had a greater capability than the Mirage IIIV.

Short P.D.56

The P.D.56 was designed for low-level tactical strike and reconnaissance with high-speed interception as a secondary role. A bank of four RB.162 lift units was placed either side of the centre fuselage, elevons were installed along the delta wing's trailing edge and conventional power was supplied by a single Rolls-Royce RB.168. Shorts felt that multiple lifting engines provided the maximum degree of safety in jet-borne flight and the P.D.56 could continue its take-off transition, complete its mission and then return to base even after the total failure of one lift engine at any point in the take-off. The radius of action with a 1,000lb (454kg) load flown at low-level was

given as 280nm (519km), at medium altitude and subsonic speed this became 540nm (1,000km), and with a supersonic dash from half distance 220nm (407km). Internal fuel totalled 7,750lb (3,515kg) and P.D.56's ceiling was more than 50,000ft (15,240m).

Short P.D.56

Span	28ft 0in (8.53m)
Length	54ft 6in (16.61m)
Gross wing area	?
t/c ratio	?
Gross weight	29,700lb (13,472kg) VTO maximum
Powerplant	one RR RB.168-1R reheated Spey, eight RB.162-2 4,400lb (19.6kN)
Maximum speed/height	Mach 1.08 at sea level, Mach 1.95 at 40,000ft (12,192m) with 1,000lb (454kg) load
Weapon load	Maximum 2,400lb (1,087kg) of stores including Bullpup, 1,000lb (454kg) bombs and nuclear

Hawker (Siddeley) P.1150-1

The companion volume *British Secret Projects: Jet Fighters since 1950* has already described the P.1154's 'career', but a version was proposed to the NATO specification (the overlap between fighter and bomber is never closer than in this particular story). However, Hawker's supersonic P.1150-1 of January 1961 powered by a Bristol BE.53-6 with 800°K PCB was the company's first suggestion to NBMR.3 (plenum chamber burning, or PCB, incorporated fuel burning in the normally unheated cold bypass airstream to the front nozzles). This had a span of 26ft (7.92m), length 53ft (16.15m), wing area 244sq ft (22.7sq m) and internal fuel load 850gal (3,865lit). When the requirements were upgraded the P.1150-1 became too small and a modified version called the P.1150-3 was drawn, which was redesignated P.1154. Hawker's full P.1154 submission to NBMR.3 was delivered to the MoA on 8 January 1962 for transmission to NATO.

BELOW Short P.D.56 to NBMR.3 (1961).

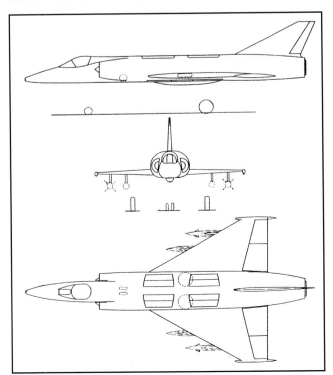

BELOW Model of the P.D.56.

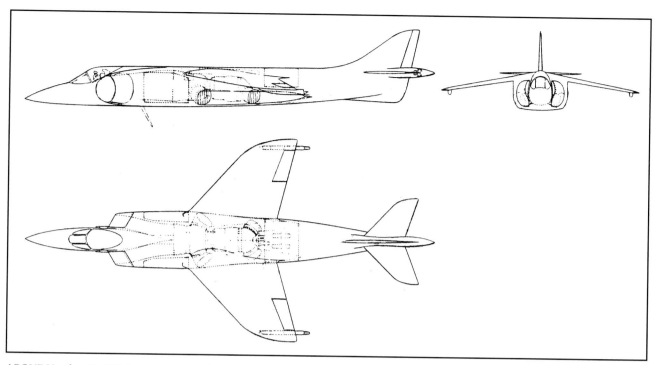

ABOVE Hawker P.1150-1 supersonic strike aircraft (29.1.61). *HSA via Chris Farara*
BELOW Model of the P.1150-1.

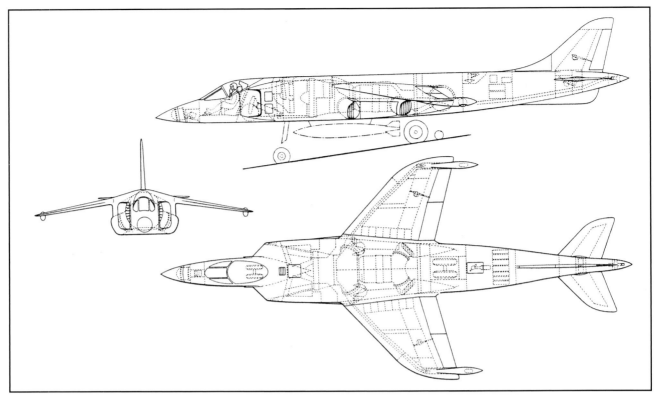

ABOVE Hawker P.1154 to NATO Specification NBMR.3 with a nuclear weapon under the fuselage (1.62). *HSA via Chris Farara*

Hawker (Siddeley) P.1154

Hawker described its NBMR.3 P.1154 as a second generation V/STOL fighter and the natural supersonic development of the P.1127. It used an enlarged BE.53 type lift/thrust engine called the BS.100/9 along with PCB. From a VTO this offered a larger military payload for the high-speed, low-level strike mission and Mach 2.0 performance at altitude. BS.100/9 was a scaled down version of the BS.100/3 considered by Fokker/Republic and Breguet in their NBMR.3 designs, it gave 17% less thrust but offered a performance that still exceeded NBMR.3.

Hawker observed that what NBMR.3 really requested was an aircraft that combined the airfield performance of a helicopter with the combat performance of the latest supersonic fighters and that a speed range of this order of magnitude had not previously been attempted even by a research aircraft, let alone a fully operational weapon system. During the preliminary design study phase Hawker considered many different configurations and powerplant combinations but concluded that the single-engined

lift/thrust concept demonstrated by the P.1127 was the type that met NBMR.3 most completely. Other powerplants such as multiple lift engines along with a separate propulsive unit might offer slight advantages in certain specialised areas, but they failed in the overriding case of providing a practical operational system. The experience gained from flying the P.1127 had put Hawker Siddeley in a unique position in that no other high-performance aircraft had undertaken transitions from both vertical and short take-offs, and this with a representative military aircraft.

For NBMR.3 the P.1154 had a lightweight forward-looking radar that formed the basis of a simple automatic system for terrain-following and a blind approach to a vertical landing, as well as for target ranging in attack. One nuclear weapon or two 1,000lb (454kg) bombs could be carried under the fuselage along with ASMs, AAMs, more 1,000lb (454kg) bombs or RPs on four underwing pylons. A nose camera or special pods under the fuselage would be used for reconnaissance, the internal fuel totalled

1,150gal (5,229lit) and the normal weapon load was 2,000lb (907kg). With a pitot intake P.1154 had a maximum speed at altitude of Mach 2.0 and a radius of action in the primary low-altitude mission of 295nm (545km); an alternative variable-wedge intake offered Mach 2.4 and 265nm (491km) but the airspeed design limit was 864mph (1,390km/h) IAS and Mach 2.3. From ITP it was estimated that a squadron of twelve aircraft could be produced within four years and the subsequent production rates could meet NATO's requirements in full.

Hawker P.1154	
Span	26ft 0in (7.92m)
Length	55ft 4in (16.86m)
Gross wing area	244sq ft (22.7sq m)
t/c ratio	not given
Gross weight	28,795lb (13,061kg) normal
Powerplant	one Bristol Siddeley BS.100/9 33,150lb (147.3kN) reheat
Maximum speed/height	Mach 2.4 at 36,000ft (10,973m)
Weapon load	one nuclear or two 1,000lb (454kg) bombs under fuselage, ASMs, AAMs, bombs or RPs under wings

ABOVE AND RIGHT **Model of the NBMR.3 P.1154.**
BELOW **The RAF single-seat strike variant of P.1154.**

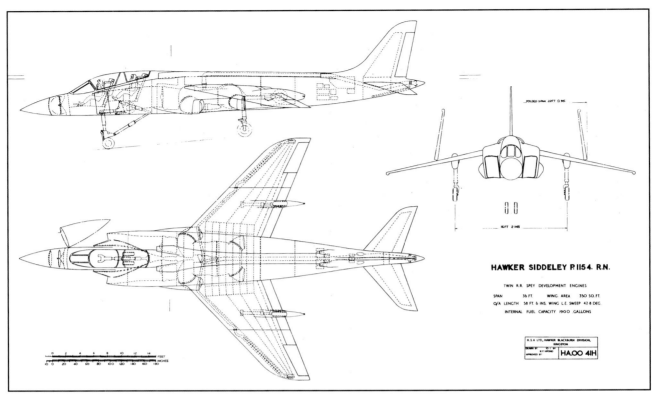

HAWKER SIDDELEY P.1154. R.N.

TWIN R.R. SPEY DEVELOPMENT ENGINES

SPAN   36 FT.   WING AREA   350 SQ.FT.
O/A LENGTH 58 FT. 6 INS. WING L.E. SWEEP 42.8 DEG.
INTERNAL FUEL CAPACITY 190.0 GALLONS

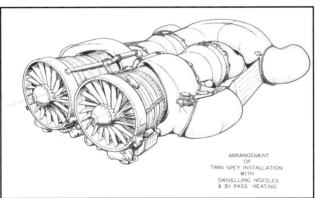

ARRANGEMENT
OF
TWIN SPEY INSTALLATION
WITH
SWIVELLING NOZZLES
& BY-PASS HEATING

ABOVE A version of the P.1154, the P.1154-34, showed a Navy version with a twin Rolls-Royce Spey powerplant (drawing dated 10.1.64). First proposed in December 1962, the two Speys were placed side-by-side and fitted with PCB and cross-over pipes. The Kingston team was not happy with this arrangement and work in the Experimental Design Office was halted in mid-February 1964. This Spey P.1154 had a span of 36ft 0in (10.97m), overall length 58ft 6in (17.83m) and wing area 350sq ft (32.55sq m). Internal fuel totalled 1,900gal (8,639lit). *BAe via Chris Farara*

LEFT The arrangement of the twin-RR Spey installation for the P.1154 variant with swivelling nozzles and by-pass heating. *Copyright Rolls-Royce plc*

Hawker (Siddeley) P.1155

The P.1155 was a three-engine NBMR.3 alternative to Kingston's P.1154. It originated from a February 1962 request made by DGSR for the design team to investigate using the existing Pegasus engine (augmented by separate lift units) instead of the BS.100 should that engine's development not proceed (there were doubts concerning the BS.100's availability due to its development costs). P.1155 was first presented to DGSR on 24 April 1962 and it used substantially the same airframe as P.1154, having begun life as the P.1150-2. The big difference was the

BE.53 Pegasus 5 with PCB and two RB.162 lift units, one behind the cockpit between the intakes and one behind the main undercarriage bay; intake doors were visible on the upper fuselage. On 6 December 1961 the Defence Committee had authorised the official consideration of a supersonic development of the P.1127 and this was the type of aircraft it had in mind, the MoA regarding it as a most promising development. The powerplant arrangement, however, did not find favour with the Ministry's Technical Branch but it was financially more

acceptable since the engines themselves were already being funded. Internal fuel totalled 1,150gal (5,229lit) and the nuclear weapon was still carried beneath the fuselage.

Hawker concluded that the P.1155 after a VTO would have a radius of action of about 20 miles (32km) less than the P.1154, and about 40 miles (64km) less with the aircraft loaded to clear a height of 50ft (15.2m) after a 500ft (152m) take-off run. The total weights for the two types were substantially the same but P.1155's top speed was about Mach 0.1 less at

36,000ft (10,973m). Because of its greater propulsive thrust the P.1154 would, in getting up to high speeds, have about 50% more acceleration.

In general Hawker expressed strong opinions against the three-engined concept on the grounds of safety, complexity, ground erosion and debris ingestion problems. The Ministry acknowledged that any engine failure in a three-engine type during a large part of its take-off manoeuvre was likely to lead to a major accident because of the loss of a substantial portion of its thrust. Additionally, if a lift engine failed, unless the other lift unit was cut very quickly (presumably by automatic devices) then very rapid changes in pitch would take place. This suggested that the three-engined aircraft was not as safe as the single-engined version, though in any situation other than a take-off the loss of the propulsion engine was just as likely as for the P.1154. It was felt that the P.1155 was in many respects the ideal technical solution for a supersonic P.1127 but these studies had also revealed serious operational and logistical drawbacks. The idea was not attractive to the services and P.1155 was therefore not submitted to NBMR.3.

Hawker P.1155	
Span	26ft 0in (7.92m)
Length	54ft 8in (16.66m)
Gross wing area	244sq ft (22.7sq m)
T/c ratio	not given
Gross weight	c. 28,800lb (13,064kg)
Powerplant	one Bristol Siddeley BS.53/5, two RR RB.162
Maximum speed/height	Mach 2.3 at 36,000ft (10,973m)
Weapon load	one nuclear or two 1,000lb (454kg) bombs under fuselage, ASMs, AAMs, bombs or RPs under wings

By late April 1962 five NBMR.3 submissions were still in the running but Short's P.D.56 solution had been one of those eliminated. The NATO assessment body felt that the BAC 584 was attractive technically but it was heavier, more complex, more expensive

and later in timescale than envisaged for NBMR.3, and so as a consequence this too would be rejected. The Fokker/Republic project was likely to be ruled out and the Breguet design was not expected to win, but the P.1154, a private venture from Hawker, and the French Mirage IIIV stood a good chance of winning. In addition there was a desire by the Ministry to put UK requirements in line with NBMR.3, although they were not identical.

The Air Staff felt that NBMR.3 could result in a decision that P.1154 was the winner or – more likely – the winner in all but French eyes, but the Mirage's prospects had improved because that programme was going full speed ahead with official support while P.1154's airframe had no such backing and the engine had only limited financial assistance. Consequently, there was some debate as to whether the British would buy the Mirage IIIV if it was declared the winner, when it was believed that no non-British aircraft could meet the needs of both services.

It seemed vital to preserve Britain's freedom of action in these activities and one solution could be to have no undisputed winner (if the P.1154 did not become the undisputed winner). That meant, if necessary, entering a minority report on behalf of P.1154 and seeking to make that minority greater than one by getting support from other nations; for example the Italians 'owed us a favour for our help with the Fiat G.95/6'. And it was agreed in April 1962 that the P.1154's engine and airframe development should now receive full and immediate Government support to maintain its competitive position within NBMR.3. Eventually the P.1154 was adjudged the technical winner, but then France announced it intended to pursue the Mirage IIIV anyway. Such national considerations, plus the technical unknowns stemming from the need to combine VTO and supersonic capability, made it virtually impossible to solve this dispute and so NATO's requirement was withdrawn in the autumn of 1962. NBMR.3 had been

a very political affair and perhaps Europe was not quite ready for it.

In January 1962 the first draft of NASR(OR).356 was issued in place of GOR.345 and this eventually covered the P.1154 after it was chosen to serve with both the RAF and Royal Navy. In November this was amended to a two-stage development – a single-seat V/STOL strike/reconnaissance aircraft for the RAF by 1968 (the P.1154A) and a two-seat all-weather version, primarily a fighter, for the Navy by 1970 (P.1154B). Specification F.242 covered the requirement but was later replaced by SR.250D first drafted in July 1964. As the developments proceeded it was found that the required level of 'commonality' compromised each service's aircraft and accordingly the specification was revised to give more scope to specialised designs for each role. Gradually the two versions grew apart and in February 1964 the Royal Navy was allowed to drop the P.1154 and buy the McDonnell F-4 Phantom from America instead. Just the RAF P.1154 remained and some 'serious' engineering was completed towards this design only for it to be cancelled in February 1965 for economic reasons, at which point the first prototypes were 33% complete.

Hawker Siddeley Kestrel

During the 'P.1154' period the P.1127 kept a relatively low profile, though the prototypes flew well. In February 1963, after a full year of discussions, a joint agreement was reached between Britain, West Germany and the United States to build nine improved aircraft to perform a service evaluation of the V/STOL concept. The first aircraft (XS688 built to Specification FGA.236D&P) made its first flight on 7 March 1964 and in July the name Kestrel FGA.Mk.1 was accepted by the Air Staff, appropriate since 'this was a hovering Hawk/Falcon type bird'. The Tripartite Kestrel Evaluation Squadron (involving the RAF, US Air Force, US Navy, US Army and the German Luftwaffe) carried out its assessment through the first half of 1965 and this proved a total success, with

226

ABOVE Hawker Siddeley Kestrel XS692 pictured during what appears to be a rolling take-off. *Crown Copyright*
BELOW Official photo showing RAF Harrier development aircraft XV276 in the hover. *Crown Copyright*

ABOVE The Harrier's strength – operations from grass and other unprepared surfaces!
BELOW A Harrier GR.Mk.1 and GR.Mk.3 (nearest) fly together. The later mark had a modified nose housing a laser ranging and marked target seeker.

the RAF in particular pleased with the results. The Kestrel was the first jet V/STOL aircraft in the world to be granted a release for use by service pilots.

Hawker Siddeley Harrier

By January 1965, and with the end of the P.1154 in sight, there was considerable activity in Kingston's Project Office looking into a proposed P.1127 Development. The Ministry had decided that, since V/STOL and supersonic performance could not be found together in any other aircraft, the tasks required of the Hunter replacement should be met by a mix of F-4 Phantoms and a developed version of the Tripartite Kestrel. The indications were that if the P.1127 was fitted with more a powerful engine and with the equipment proposed for the P.1154 (except for the

Harrier GR.Mk.1 (flown)	
Span	25ft 3in (7.70m)
Length	45ft 6in (13.87m)
Gross wing area	201sq ft (18.7sq m)
t/c ratio	10.07% centreline, 3.90% tip
Gross weight	24,200lb (10,977kg) = loaded (short take-off)
Powerplant	one Bristol Siddeley Mk.101 Pegasus 6 19,000lb (84.4kN)
Maximum speed/height	740mph (1,191km/h) at sea level, Mach 1.3 in dive at altitude
Weapon load	two detachable 30mm Aden gun pods, maximum 5,000lb (2,268kg) of stores

radar), in the strike role its performance would not be greatly inferior to the P.1154's. As such the P.1127 could be regarded as a reasonable substitute in the low-level strike role. During the following month a draft requirement, ASR.384, was circulated for an operational aircraft to be called the P.1127(RAF) and this was covered by Specification SR.255D&P. A period of twelve months of project definition and preliminary design study was then started on 1 April 1965.

The initial brochure noted that the changes from the Kestrel would include a Pegasus 6, the addition of comprehensive military equipment and a stronger undercarriage and structure. On 8 July 1965 Wg Cdr Bairsto informed Kingston that 'he would like to place on record how pleased MoD were that the company were able to go so far towards meeting the exacting ASR, starting from an existing aircraft'. The main arguments against the P.1127(RAF) were a poor VTOL weapon load (1,000lb/454kg) and a low cost-effectiveness in the VTOL mode when compared with the Phantom and Buccaneer (which were both incapable of VTO). In its favour the type would keep Britain in the forefront of V/STOL technology, it could operate intimately with the Army and off almost any available site, it would give a rapid response

capability, and could often be used in the STOL mode with a greater weapon load. It would also be capable of further development (a P.1127 with PCB was, for example, proposed in June 1966).

Full development was authorised on 9 March 1966, and on 22 December the Cabinet decided to place a firm order for sixty aircraft. Names considered earlier for the P.1154 had been Falcon, Peregrine and Harrier favoured in that order, but the production P.1127 was allocated Harrier on 17 March 1967. The first of six development aircraft, XV276, flew on 31 August 1966 and the first production Harrier GR.Mk.1, XV738, became airborne on 28 December 1967. Deliveries of seventy-eight Mk.1s to the RAF began in April 1969 and most of these were later upgraded to GR.Mk.3 standard with an uprated Pegasus 11 plus a laser ranging and marked target seeker (LRMTS). Harrier's primary role was to be close air support and the aircraft proved to be an immense success with the RAF and the US Marine Corps (as the AV-8A).

If the P.1154 had not been cancelled then the P.1127(RAF) Harrier would not have been developed. And although the latter looked quite similar to the original P.1127 prototypes their airframes were nothing like the same.

Hawker (Siddeley) P.1156

Over the years Kingston produced numerous Harrier development proposals and the P.1156 was a V/STOL strike fighter similar to the P.1127. It was to be powered by a Pegasus 5 with anhedral multi-vane nozzles like the P.1154, which would allow the engine to be removed with the wing still in place. Span was 23ft 4in (7.11m), length 42ft 0in (12.80m), wing area 186.4sq ft (17.3sq m) and internal fuel capacity 600gal (2,728lit).

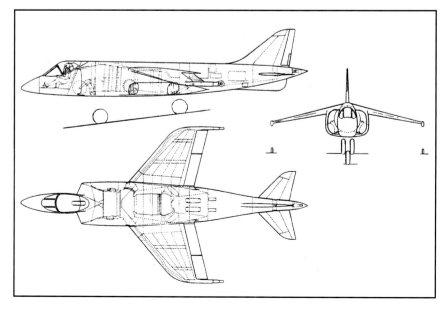

LEFT Hawker P.1156 V/STOL strike aircraft (12.61). *HSA via Chris Farara*

Hawker (Siddeley) HS.1175

Hawker/Hawker Siddeley Kingston invented, developed and proved the single-engine vectored thrust fighter-attack configuration but the company was never complacent about it. The Harrier had its faults and weaknesses and the Kingston design team (and later Warton when the companies had merged as part of British Aerospace) strove constantly to find alternative solutions. Other V/STOL and STOVL configurations were assessed and some of these showed advantages, but they proved inadequate when judged against the four-nozzle vectored thrust format. (Author's note – from about the HS.1170 onwards some of the future project studies embraced many different layouts.)

The HS.1175 was proposed privately in 1967 as the first 'second-generation' V/STOL subsonic strike aircraft, having much of its structure and systems in common with the Harrier. However, the Pegasus used a two-nozzle arrangement (with the fan and core engine exhaust mixed) and was supplemented by a single vertically-mounted Rolls-Royce-Allison XJ.99 lift jet (an Anglo–American engine

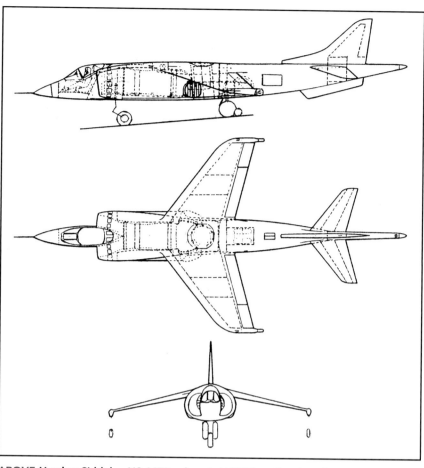

ABOVE Hawker Siddeley HS.1175 subsonic V/STOL strike aircraft (1967). *BAe*
BELOW The HS.1175 variant that had the main undercarriage moved to wing pods (18.2.67). Its dimensions were the same as the bicycle undercarriage version except for a length of 54ft 0in (16.46m).

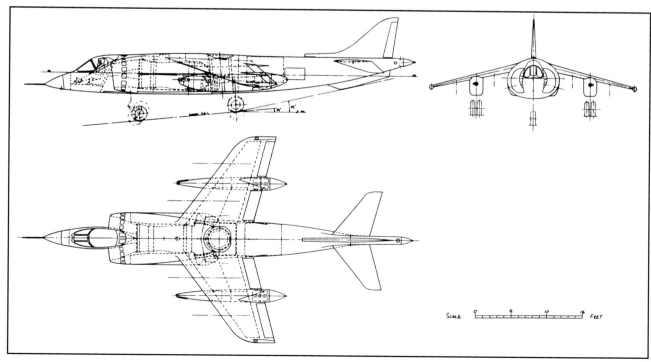

developed jointly under the US/UK Advanced Lift Jet Engine Demonstrator Programme that, at the time, had no production application, but it had been bench tested). This extra VTO thrust and a new large-span wing with three pylons per side would enable the aircraft to take much larger weapon loads on VTOL missions. And the nozzles were positioned around the CofG with the XJ.99 in between, so if an engine did fail there should not be a rapid change in attitude and the pilot would have time to regain control (or at least to eject). A second version had the main undercarriage moved to wing pods to keep it away from the lift engine.

HS.1175's timing was flexible and dependent upon the progress of Harrier developments. Most of the funded Harrier improvements (increases in Pegasus thrust, improved systems, etc.) could be used on the HS.1175, which would then follow on naturally as the Harrier's development tailed off. Its low-level radius of action from a VTO with full internal fuel (875gal [3,979lit]) and 3,000lb (1,361kg) of weapons was 225nm (417km), while an 800ft (244m) ground run plus two 200gal (909lit) external tanks would push this up to 310nm (574km). High-level flight followed by low level over the target increased these figures again to 460nm and 600nm (852km and 1,111km) respectively. The maximum VTO weight was 24,500lb (11,113kg) and the Mach number limit 1.30. Work on the HS.1175 had ceased by April 1969.

Hawker Siddeley HS.1175	
Span	29ft 0in (8.84m)
Length	56ft 6in (17.22m)
Gross wing area	237sq ft (22.0sq m)
t/c ratio	not given
Gross weight	31,550lb (14,311kg)
Powerplant	one Bristol Siddeley Pegasus BE.53/103 21,000lb (93.3kN), one XJ-99 8,200lb (36.4kN)
Maximum speed/height	Mach 0.90 685mph (1,102km/h) at sea level, Mach 0.94 622mph (1,001km/h) at 36,000ft (10,973m)
Weapon load	Maximum 10,000lb (4,536kg) of stores

Hawker (Siddeley) HS.1176

In its basic version the HS.1176 was externally similar to the Harrier but had its intake area enlarged by some 10% to accept the greater airflow of the 24,500lb (108.9kN) Pegasus 9D. The design was proposed to the US Department of Defense in partnership with Allied Systems for possible use by the USAF as a rapid response strike aircraft. It also formed the basis of a joint UK/USA cost-effectiveness study in which V/STOL strike aircraft (typified by the HS.1176) were compared with current and future conventional strike aircraft. Strengthened pylons offered an external weapon load of 6,000lb (2,722kg), and at overload this rose to 10,000lb (4,536kg) for a maximum take-off weight of 27,300lb (12,383kg). More advanced versions were also suggested.

Hawker (Siddeley) HS.1179

This designation covered a substantial private venture study by both HSA Kingston and Brough and which embraced more than twenty strike fighter projects. They were aimed at the requirements for the MRCA (Chapter Fourteen) then being drafted for the RAF, Dutch, Italian and German Air Forces as a UK and European Advanced Combat Aircraft, with a prospective market of around 800 aeroplanes. In general, vectored thrust designs were investigated by Kingston (HS.1179A to

BELOW The single-seat HS.1179H study was powered by a single reheated RB.199 with PCB and reheat. Its span was 30ft 6in (9.30m), length 51ft 0in (15.54m) and wing area 300sq ft (27.9sq m). *HSA via Chris Farara*

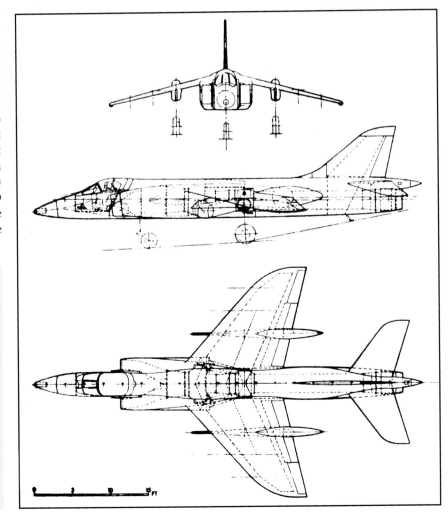

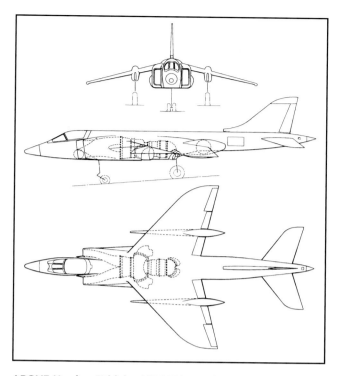

ABOVE Hawker Siddeley HS.1179L single-seat V/STOL strike aircraft (mid-1968). *HSA via Chris Farara*

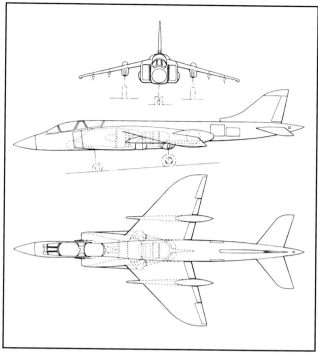

ABOVE Hawker Siddeley HS.1179M two-seat V/STOL strike aircraft (mid-1968). *HSA via Chris Farara*

M), while projects using VG or boundary layer control (BLC) came from Brough (HS.1179S to Z). Recent work at both sites had concentrated on a vectored thrust layout using a Pegasus 9D-03, a PCB derivative of the unit proposed for the HS.1176.

Kingston's HS.1179 studies included Turbo-Union RB.199 engines (Bristol Siddeley had been purchased by Rolls-Royce in 1968 and Turbo-Union was a joint venture between Rolls, MTU and FiatAvio to build the RB.199 for the MRCA Tornado). The HS.1179E had twin reheated RB.199s and PCB in the side nozzles, while the single-seat HS.1179H used a single reheated RB.199 with PCB. The latter's span was 30ft 6in (9.30m), length 51ft 0in (15.54m) and wing area 300sq ft (27.9sq m), but the HS.1179J was a bigger two-seat twin-RB.199 version with a near-identical wing. The ultimate Kingston projects appear to have been the HS.1179L and M, again single and two-seat versions of the same aircraft. At low level with full fuel (10,900lb and 11,600lb [4,944kg and 5,262kg] respectively) and 4,000lb (1,814kg) of

weapons their radius of action was given as 225nm (417km); these designs were limited to Mach 2.1.

On 30 July 1969 Hawker Siddeley's Ralph Hooper, P.1127 Project Engineer from 1961 and Assistant Chief Designer (Projects) from 1963, told the MoD's Lt Cdr J. O. F. Billingham that the 'L and M proposals, particularly the former, aim to be sensible engineering offers which do not invoke a brand new powerplant, which was perhaps the Achilles Heel of the 1154'. Some of the lessons learnt from the P.1154 effort had been absorbed into the proposed layouts:

a). There was no fuselage bending structure beneath the engine, which was, therefore, simply withdrawn beneath the fuselage.

b). The rear nozzles were close together and mounted in a hemispherical termination of the engine rear face. In this way the gas generator efflux was liberated beneath the fuselage close to the aircraft centreline, which should avoid the buffet pick-up by the tailplane that the company had experienced on the Harrier.

c). HSA advised against demands for a higher top speed than was strictly necessary since the intake's variable geometry mechanisms began to escalate in weight and complexity above about Mach 1.8.

Hooper added that 'all of us on the engineering side at Kingston look forward to working on a second-generation V/STOL aircraft, by comparison with which a conventional aeroplane seems a very dull device'. He hoped that the worst excesses of 'multi-roleism' could be averted because that had contributed strongly to the death of the P.1154.

Brough's work was undertaken between July 1968 and February 1970 and compared the vectored thrust type with a conventional aircraft designed for a similar role. To begin with comprehensive parametric studies were made of fixed thrust line aircraft with boundary layer control (BLC) high-lift systems. These were then backed up by small design studies aimed at producing the smallest, lightest aircraft to meet the requirements. A variable sweep aircraft received similar

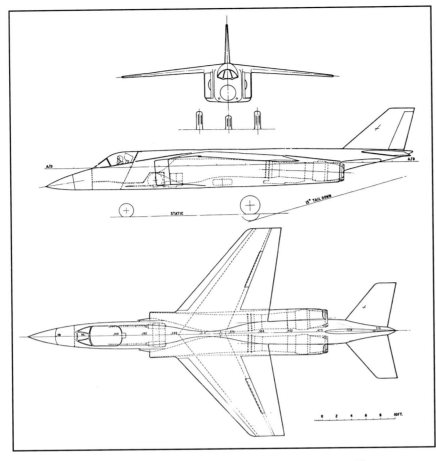

Hawker Siddeley Kingston HS.1179L (1969)	
Span	30ft 6in (9.30m)
Length	51ft 6in (15.70m)
Gross wing area	300sq ft (27.9sq m)
t/c ratio	not given
Gross weight	39,200lb (17,781kg)
Powerplant	one RR Bristol Pegasus 9D-03 34,000lb (151.1kN)
Maximum speed/height	Mach 1.15 875mph (1,408km/h) at sea level, Mach 2.1 1,382mph (2,223km/h) at 36,000ft (10,973m)
Weapon load	Maximum 10,000lb (4,536kg) of stores

Hawker Siddeley Kingston HS.1179M (1969)	
Span	30ft 6in (9.30m)
Length	55ft 9in (17.00m)
Gross wing area	300sq ft (27.9sq m)
t/c ratio	not given
Gross weight	43,800lb (19,868kg)
Powerplant	one RR Bristol Pegasus 9D-03 34,000lb (151.1kN)
Maximum speed/height	Mach 1.13 860mph (1,384km/h) at sea level, Mach 1.9 1,255mph (2,020km/h) at 36,000ft (10,973m)
Weapon load	Maximum 10,000lb (4,536kg) of stores

Hawker Siddeley Brough HS.1179X (c. 1969)	
Span	31ft 0in (9.45m)
Length	51ft 0in (15.54m)
Gross wing area	309sq ft (28.74sq m)
t/c ratio	not given
Gross weight	31,340lb (14,216kg) strike role, 28,400lb (12,882kg) interceptor
Powerplant	two Turbo-Union RB.199 30,510lb (135.6kN)
Maximum speed/height	Not given but supersonic
Weapon load	Two cannon under cockpit. No details for stores

ABOVE The Hawker Siddeley Brough HS.1179X project used a BLC lift system.

treatment and some characteristics of vectored thrust, such as structural design, were also examined using the HS.1179M as a basis (since this layout was most likely to provide the best comparison with the aircraft the RAF expected to get out of the MRCA programme).

It so happened that an aircraft conforming roughly to some of the MRCA requirements could be designed around a Pegasus 15-03 engine, and so Brough felt that it would be sensible to see how much 'better', or how different, an aircraft could be designed using an aerodynamic approach to the high lift problem and using engines based about the RB.199. It was found that the weight penalty for variable sweep outweighed its advantages and so the 'datum' aircraft then became the BLC layouts. In the end the designs labelled HS.1179X and T proved to be the best BLC high lift

solutions to the single- and twin-seat aircraft types respectively. Brough's conclusions suggested that a VG aeroplane should not be a contender for the MRCA and that a BLC fixed sweep type produced the best aircraft except in the case of landing performance. It was also established that a supersonic V/STOL proposal could not be considered against the MRCA requirements.

Hawker (Siddeley) HS.1185 and AV-16

Work on the HS.1185 began in 1970 while a short-lived Anglo–US study led to an aircraft called the AV-16 Advanced Harrier. A total of 110 AV-8A Harriers had been procured by the US Marine Corps (USMC) between 1971 and 1976 and a licence agreement was established between HSA and McDonnell Aircraft (McAir) that also covered joint studies for future developments. On 12 April

1973, following several months of close collaboration between Government agencies and UK and US industry, the go-ahead was given for an eight-month Programme Definition Phase for the jointly funded development of the AV-16 powered by a 24,500lb (108.9kN) Pegasus 15.

The preferred minimum change aeroplane was a subsonic attack aircraft and Phase 1 development was concluded in the closing weeks of 1973 and presented to the US and UK Governments. This was agreed and by spring 1974 further proposals had been completed. Essentially the aircraft would be similar to the Harrier but with double the payload or combat radius. AV-16A had a broader fuselage to accommodate the larger diameter Pegasus 15 fan (for which reason the engine could not be retrofitted to existing aircraft), enlarged air intakes, a new wing of greater span and more area, a raised cockpit, strengthened structure and undercarriage and new or revised avionics. A V-tail had also been considered. The maximum VTO weight was 21,100lb (9,571kg), internal fuel totalled 6,500lb (2,948kg) and 300gal (1,364lit) drop tanks could be carried. The exhaust nozzles were to be strengthened and two alternative wing designs were available, developed by HSA and McAir. The former was based on the so-called 'sonic rooftop' wing, the latter on supercritical work done by NASA, and both were similar in sweepback and planform.

The RAF's aircraft would have seven stores points, a 30mm Aden cannon and an undernose sensor. Both RN and US Navy aircraft (the latter for the new Sea Control Ship) would have nose-mounted radar with the American machines carrying Sidewinder or Sparrow AAMs and Harpoon, Maverick or Condor ASMs. The first of two YAV-16A prototypes was expected to fly in America at the start of 1977 and the first AV-16A would also fly in America in mid-1979. The US Marine Corps was expected to take 342 aircraft but the aircraft's development costs (especially for the new engine) proved to be unacceptable, particularly against a background of worldwide increases in inflation, and Britain pulled out in March 1975. This precipitated the AV-16's demise and the two countries went their separate ways, Kingston replacing it with new wing investigations for Harrier (see below).

Some supersonic versions were also drawn. One, the HS.1185-6 (AV-16S-6), showed the first steps taken to move the jet streams away from the rear fuselage and empennage (the jet streams that brushed the flanks of the

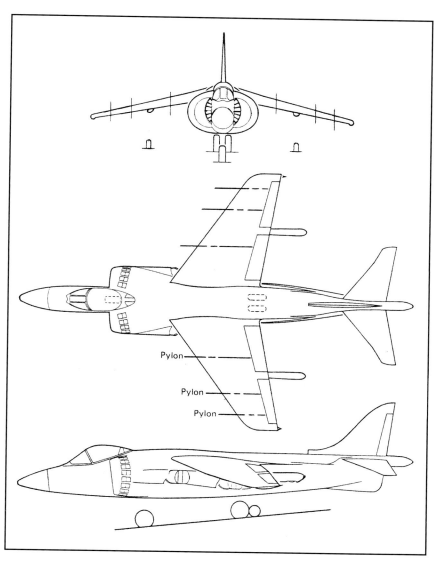

ABOVE Hawker Siddeley AV-16A (5.12.73).

rear fuselage and passed closely under the wing and tailplane were one of the less desirable features of the Harrier configuration). The later P.1205 series of fighters (described in the companion volume covering fighters) then took the separation of the engine nozzles and the rear portions of the airframe as far as was possible within the constraints imposed by a conventional layout. Further versions of the HS.1185 were proposed against AST.396 (Chapter Fifteen).

Hawker Siddeley HS.1185 and AV-16	
Span	30ft 4in (9.24m)
Length	46ft 6in (14.17m)
Gross wing area	230sq ft (21.4sq m)
t/c ratio	11.5% root, 7.5% tip
Gross weight	28,000lb (12,701kg)
Powerplant	one RR Pegasus 15 (Mk.201/F402-RF-403) 24,500lb (108.9kN)
Maximum speed/height	combat speed 720mph (1,158km/h)
Weapon load	See text

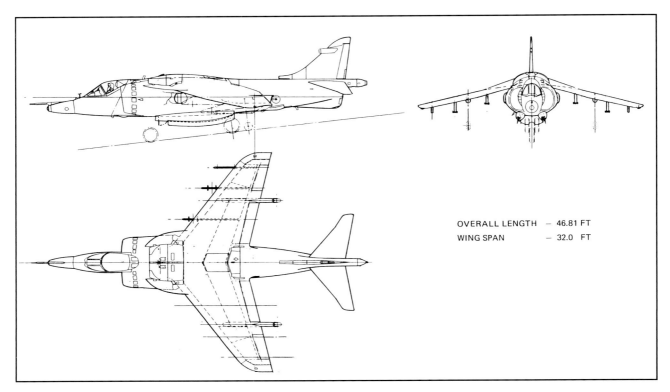

OVERALL LENGTH — 46.81 FT
WING SPAN — 32.0 FT

ABOVE The original Big Wing Harrier proposal (brochure dated 8.78).
HSA via Chris Farara

Hawker Siddeley Big Wing Harrier

In the mid-1970s HSA Kingston realised that before the end of the decade a new version of the Harrier would be needed to supplement and later supplant the original RAF 'Jump-Jets' and so the Big Wing concept was started with informal talks between the MoD and HSA. The basic theme was that present Harriers were effective in their main role of ground attack and reconnaissance but they lacked a self-defence capability. A new wing giving increased lift and carrying AAMs would improve this without reducing the offensive load. More internal fuel was also needed so, in short, what was required was a bigger and better wing with six pylons that could be retrofitted to existing aircraft. An MoD-funded programme had also investigated the fitting of leading-edge root extensions (LERX) to the Harrier and the resulting wind tunnel data and flight trials indicated that this gave useful increases in usable lift at high angles of attack.

Prior to this, however, the near total lack of interest shown by the UK Government through the late 1960s and

early 1970s towards developing the Harrier had led to the initiative crossing the Atlantic. In 1974/75 McDonnell Douglas proposed to the US Government a modified AV-8A that would provide increased capability, including twice the original's bombload radius, while importantly using the same basic engine. The result was the AV-8B Harrier II. Changes were principally a new carbon fibre composite wing of greater area that incorporated large slotted flaps for improved STO performance, six pylons, underfuselage strakes and a cross-dam for better VTO performance, and an improved efficiency engine intake. This was a joint McDonnell/HSA design for which Kingston had a big team of designers based at St Louis.

The first of two prototype YAV-8Bs, converted from AV-8As, flew on 9 November 1978. The American wing had many of the features desired for the UK's aircraft but it was unsuited for retrofit. A UK evaluation team tested a prototype in 1980 and found that, while it performed well in

its design role as a close air support 'bomb truck', it had two notable deficiencies. First, the top speed at low altitude was more than 57mph (92km/h) slower than existing RAF Harriers and, second, while the manoeuvring performance was better than the Harrier's, the rate of turn was still less than required (but production AV-8Bs were expected to be better).

In October 1977 Kingston received a contract for a feasibility study to replace the existing wings on GR.Mk.3 or T.Mk.4 aircraft with what was now officially called the Big Wing. This had a greater span and area, carried three pylons per side and its aerodynamic design used the latest supercritical technology, and it would fit on to the existing marks of Harrier with the minimum of modification. The leading-edge sweep angle was 37.5° compared to the GR.Mk.3's 40.4°, but LERX were to be fitted that contributed to a much better air-to-air combat capability. In addition, the Harrier's plain flap had been replaced with a single-slotted flap of increased

ABOVE AND LEFT Model of the Hawker Siddeley Big Wing 'Harrier GR.Mk.5' (13.7.78). *BAE SYSTEMS*

span to improve the STO and combat manoeuvring performance. The Big Wing was constructed in light alloy, not carbon fibre, though carbon was to be used in due course for new-build aircraft with a saving of 300lb (136kg) in weight. The internal fuel load rose to 880gal (4,001lit) from the GR.Mk.3's 632gal

(2,874lit) and (according to one company report) the fuselage would be based on the Royal Navy's Sea Harrier fighter with a raised cockpit and more space for sensors and equipment.

When hovering at less than 10ft (3.0m) above the ground the Harrier experienced a strong up-flow due to the

mutual interference of the four jets spreading over and being reflected by the ground. The pressure recovery of this up-flow beneath the aircraft's belly was enhanced on the Big Wing Harrier by large strakes and a retractable 'cross-dam' mounted respectively on and between the gun pods; these features were called

BELOW One of the American AV-8B prototypes pictured in 1978.

ABOVE RAF Harrier GR.Mk.5 flying with a full weapon load for publicity pictures made in 1988.

Underfuselage Cushion Augmentation Devices. This idea had been patented in the early days of the P.1127 and further developed by McDonnell Douglas for the AV-8B. The aircraft could now lift off vertically with nearly 1,500lb (680kg) more fuel or external stores than the GR.Mk.3, or with an extra 3,000lb (1,361kg) from a 1,000ft (305m) ground run. Other performance figures, particularly the low-level turn rate, were also much improved.

The resulting configuration came to be referred to as the GR.Mk.5 and it was expected that a five-year development programme could be met with a service entry in 1985. Kingston stressed that the choice was the Big Wing Harrier or the AV-8B, which was a 1974/75 concept and which would not enter service itself until 1985, after ten years of development. BAe feared that if the MoD ordered the AV-8B it would be re-importing original British technology in an inferior product, when BAe itself was a world leader in the V/STOL field. However, an MoU was signed in August 1981 to buy AV-8Bs modified significantly to the ASR.409 requirement as the Harrier GR.Mk.5 and with two extra dedicated pylons for Sidewinder AAMs. The MoD's choice was based on cost. The first development aircraft flew on 30 April 1985 and the type entered RAF service in 1988; they were later upgraded to GR.Mk.7 and then GR.Mk.9 standard. All AV-8Bs and GR.Mk.5s were built jointly by McDonnell Douglas and BAe on a 50/50 work-split basis.

Alongside the Big Wing and Advanced Harrier studies, Kingston continued its research into more advanced V/STOL ideas. The HS.1205, P.1212, P.1214 and P.1216 series is described in *British Secret Projects: Jet Fighters* but there were others, including the following:

BAe Kingston P.1208

The P.1208 was a 1978 project, produced after the formation of British Aerospace, for a survivable ground attack type with air combat capability. A meeting held at Kingston on 30 May 1978 agreed that the aircraft was to be based on 'the essentials of the Harrier but it would be a totally new STOVL airframe'. P.1208 was considered as a replacement for Harrier and as a 'fallback' option to the very much more expensive supersonic vectored thrust P.1205 (ex-HS.1205) fighter to AST.403. How the P.1208 would compare with the various big wing developments of the Harrier would have to be defined carefully otherwise its advantages would not be clear. The engine was based on the existing Pegasus and there would be four nozzles, although a three-nozzle arrangement would be

considered after tests. PCB would not be fitted and the engine rating would emphasise combat thrust, say 23,000lb (102.2kN), rather than take-off thrust.

The aircraft had to be able to sustain high 'g' at low speed and low altitude and STOVL was required with a soft field capability superior to the Harrier. P.1208's carbon fibre composite construction was identical to the P.1205's with its wing loading slightly above the level of the conventional P.1202 (ex-HS.1202) fighter design. Leading-edge and trailing-edge flaps, and leading-edge strakes, were fitted and two Sidewinder AAMs were to be carried as standard with two inboard-mounted guns and six wing pylons for other stores. The aircraft was seen as a single-seat design and clamours for two seats were to be resisted. The P.1208-1 layout had side intakes and a conventional swept wing. The P.1208-2, dated 15 September 1978, introduced a chin intake, a canard and forward sweep wings.

Hawker Siddeley Big Wing Harrier	
Span	32ft 0in (9.75m)
Length	46ft 10in (14.27m)
Gross wing area	250sq ft (23.25sq m)
t/c ratio	9.22% tip, 12.54% centreline
Gross weight	25,592lb (11,609kg) with four BL755 and two AIM-9L
Powerplant	one RR Pegasus 11-35 22,700lb (100.9kN)
Maximum speed/height	c. 740mph (1,191km/h) at sea level
Weapon load	two Sidewinder AAMs, two 30mm Aden cannon, free fall bombs, BL755 cluster bombs or RP launchers

BELOW BAe P.1208-2 with cannon in the wing roots and tip-mounted Sidewinder missiles (15.9.78).
HSA via Chris Farara

BAe P.1208-2	
Span	29ft 0in (8.84m)
Length	44ft 5½in (13.55m)
Gross wing area	290sq ft (27.0sq m)
t/c ratio	not given
Gross weight	?
Powerplant	one RR Pegasus 11-35
Maximum speed/height	Mach 0.95
Weapon load	two AAMs, two cannon, six bombs

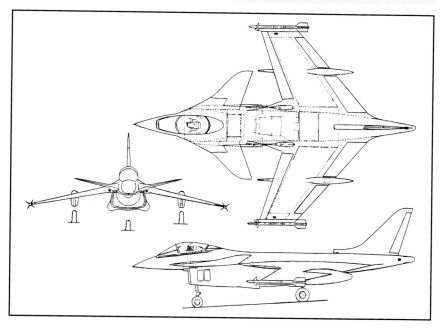

BAe Kingston P.1209

By 1979 the original P.1127 subsonic demonstrator had led to a still-growing family of operational aircraft projects right up to the ASR.409 'Advanced Harrier'. Without the P.1127, and the establishment of operational concepts using the Kestrel, it was unlikely that the Harrier would have appeared. With the P.1154 Kingston had recognised the possibility for supersonic V/STOL and since then had studied virtually every possible supersonic STOVL configuration, but found repeatedly that the single-engined vectored thrust with PCB concept gave the best cost-effectiveness compatible with acceptable pilot safety. However, a lack of flight evidence was a weakness and, with a long-term programme for further subsonic V/STOL aircraft in place (ASR.409), Kingston felt a market for a supersonic type would be unlikely before 1990. The company realised that a UK-only supersonic V/STOL demonstrator would be an important step and defined the idea in its P.1209 brochure of 30 March 1979.

This would look at the interaction between the jets and airframe, the optimum nozzle shape and their location on the fuselage, and the balancing of the centres of thrust, lift and mass. Calculations and tunnel tests could in part resolve these issues but, as at the time of the P.1127, this would be inadequate to ensure a design that was satisfactory in all respects. Although the initial P.1127 design proved substantially correct, improvements in performance, control and safety did result from the aircraft's early flight trials. Differences between a supersonic V/STOL aircraft with PCB and the Harrier included the need for larger front nozzles with an efflux of higher temperature and velocity, plus a proportionately greater fuel load due to the PCB's higher fuel consumption. Larger nozzles had already been model tested.

Although a supersonic V/STOL aircraft would in some respects operate quite similarly to the Harrier, in others it would differ. Its missions, equipment and operational systems would not be the same and PCB, with its higher

temperature and fuel consumption, would need special handling techniques. The choice of what demonstrator to build centred either on an elaborate ground rig or 'bedstead', fitting PCB into a standard Harrier, designing a simple metal airframe around a PCB engine using as many existing parts as possible, designing a new metal airframe with Mach 1.6 potential (the P.1209), or producing the P.1205 with all its other technical innovations. The brochure suggested that the 'bedstead' and converted Harrier could test V/STOL but not the correct airframe representation, so their results would be a useful guide but not proof of feasibility. The simple airframe could not test the supersonic potential but would cost nearly as much as the P.1209 (since the major expense was the development of PCB), while the P.1205 would commit everyone to far greater spending before proof of feasibility. On balance the P.1209 represented a minimum cost airframe that would be capable of demonstrating PCB both in V/STOL and in supersonic operations.

The chosen configuration, the P.1209-2, had a Pegasus 11F-33C engine (the AV-8B's 11-35 fitted with PCB) and was shaped so that the aerodynamic flows were very similar to those expected for the operational P.1205. Conventional metal skin and stringer construction was to be used and active control technology (ACT) was not included. The extra weight from not using carbon fibre in the airframe was more than compensated for by the absence of operational equipment, such as radar and guns, and the reduced flight envelope conditions selected. Its wing, fuselage and tail would be very similar to the P.1205-11 but the rear nozzle area had been increased by 7% and the front nozzles were slightly smaller; the nominal PCB temperature was 1,600°K and the fuel capacity was expected to be 9,000lb (4,082kg). Every opportunity was to be taken to use existing hardware and provision would be made for the trial carriage of dummy wing tip Sidewinder AAMs and dummy tanks or stores on undercarriage and

inboard wing pylons. With PCB off the maximum level speed in the clean condition would be about Mach 0.96, with PCB on Mach 1.54, but having wing tip AAMs in place dropped these figures to Mach 0.95 and 1.48 respectively (with tip-mounted AAMs the P.1205-11 could reach Mach 1.54).

BAe P.1209

Span	30ft 10in (9.40m)
Length	52ft 9in (16.08m)
Gross wing area	300sq ft (27.9sq m)
t/c ratio	not given
Gross weight	27,443lb (12,448kg)
Powerplant	one RR Pegasus 11F-33C 22,840lb (101.5kN) PCB off, 32,220lb (143.2kN) PCB on
Maximum speed/height	Mach 1.15 at sea level, Mach 1.54 at 36,000ft (10,973m)
Weapon load	Dummy AAMs and bombs only

BAe Kingston P.1226

The P.1226 project looked at proposals for a third-generation V/STOL aircraft. P.1226-1 was essentially a subsonic version of the P.1216 twin-boom fighter, while the P.1226-2 had a Harrier-type fuselage but with a canard and forward-swept wings. The fuselage had been stretched by inserting an 18in (457mm) plug behind the pilot and another 36in (914mm) plug to the rear of the Pegasus. Two of the latest Sidewinder AAMs were carried on the wing tips, two gun packs were mounted under the fuselage, the inner undercarriage pylons could each carry two bombs or other stores and there were two more underwing pylons per wing. Span was 30ft (9.14m), length 50ft 10in (15.49m) and wing area 269.7sq ft (25.1sq m).

The key to Harrier's success, apart from its simple basic configuration, has been the vectored thrust Bristol Pegasus turbofan, which was designed specifically for V/STOL applications as the BE.53 and first run in August 1959. Thrust vectoring was achieved by using four rotatable nozzles simultaneously operated and symmetrically positioned on the sides of the engine, outside the aircraft's fuselage. The front nozzles discharged bypass air while the rear nozzles discharged the turbine efflux. To minimise control problems in the aircraft the resultant total thrust from the four nozzles passed through a fixed point, the thrust centre, regardless of the nozzle angle, while high-pressure compressor bleed air was used to control and stabilise the aircraft in jet-borne flight. The Pegasus has been progressively improved and uprated, allowing developments from the P.1127 through to the Harrier II and beyond; the engine always led and Kingston designed the airframes to the thrust available from the engine as it was developed. However, anything powered by a dry Pegasus would be subsonic because, like all turbofans, it had a low jet velocity; supersonics needed PCB or reheat.

Bristol Siddeley's BS.100 for the P.1154 was a larger turbofan engine in which, to boost the thrust for take-off, climb and supersonic flight, the fan flow to the front nozzles passed through a duct (or plenum chamber) incorporating fuel injectors and combustion stabilisers. This method was termed plenum chamber burning and was very efficient because, unlike afterburning in the already very hot turbine exhaust, burning was taking place in a relatively cold gas stream. In fact, compared with a dry Pegasus the boost in thrust in the powered lift mode came to 35% to 40%, and at high altitude 300%.

Bristol's vectored thrust engines proved to be a thorn in the flesh of Rolls-Royce, which favoured separate vertically mounted lift jets. On 30 May 1962 Rolls' Adrian Lombard wrote that it was 'significant that all future combat aircraft will call for V/STOL characteristics which we pioneered through the [Gloster] Meteor deflected thrust, Ryan Vertijet, [Rolls-Royce] Flying Bedstead and Short S.C.1 research aircraft, and we have done more than any other establishment to publicise the technical and tactical advantages of VTOL by direct jet reaction. Perhaps the most important military business is associated with future NATO projects such as the NBMR.3 strike reconnaissance project and a major issue will be which of the two alternative VTOL powerplant systems will be selected. A factor of major concern is the British Government's

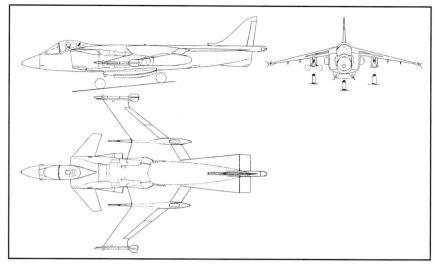

ABOVE BAe P.1226-1 with all-moving canards (1.8.84).
HSA via Chris Farara

RIGHT Manufacturer's sketch of the P.1226-1.
HSA via Chris Farara

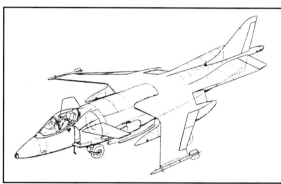

support of the Hawker P.1154 with its BS lift/thrust engine (presumably because of their earlier support of the STOL Hawker P.1127) without regard to the fact that the majority of aircraft designers have confirmed our powerplant solution'. Most NBMR.3 projects had lift jets, but the fact that the only non-Soviet V/STOL aircraft to enter service used a single lift/thrust engine tells its own story.

The Harrier eventually beat all its competitors, but it needed luck. The late Dr John Fozard, Chief Designer, Harrier, from 1965 to 1978, wrote that 'the energy release of the P.1154 in V/STOL would have constrained the choice of surfaces and sites very much more than has proved acceptable with the "softer" non-PCB Pegasus in the subsonic Harrier which replaced this cancelled project. It is possible that such a difficult and limiting experience with the first Service use of jet V/STOL might well have led to the supporting air arm, as well as all others, to turn away from off-base jet STOVL, convinced of its impracticability.

Thus, by a turn of politics and of history, we are fortunate that the modest-energy, modest-footprint, subsonic Harrier became the first in service, so providing the RAF with demonstrable practicality and hence ensuring a positive future destiny for jet V/STOL in the field'. Dr Fozard was sure that the P.1154 could have been developed satisfactorily but he felt that, viewed with hindsight, in 1965 it was 'an aircraft whose time had not yet come'. Its cancellation was a big disappointment but it would not have sold as well as the P.1127.

Today the future of western V/STOL combat aircraft is the F-35B variant of the Lockheed Martin Lightning II, developed in America with British assistance. In the UK these will replace the Tornado and already retired Harrier and the type is set to become operational with the RAF in 2018.

Chapter Eleven
Over the Sea

Anti-Submarine Aircraft: 1945 to 1969

ABOVE Avro Shackleton MR.Mk.2 WG531 pictured during transit to the SBAC Farnborough Display in September 1952.

The term 'bomber' embraces all manner of aircraft types designed to deliver bombs, missiles or other weapons at targets on or in the ground or sea. The aeroplane may have been produced specifically to convey bombs to a target, or instead bombing may be just one of a number of roles allocated to it. One of the more unsung types is the anti-submarine (A/S) aircraft based either on land or aboard aircraft carriers. This type's ability to undertake long-endurance patrol flights over water will probably mean that it will be quite different to the high-performance types described in most of the rest of this book. It will need to be relatively slow and economic to fly so, as a result, it may well be piston or turboprop powered. But over the years the anti-submarine aircraft has been called upon to perform a vital role.

Land-Based Maritime Patrol Aircraft

During the Second World War the Allied anti-submarine aeroplanes operating from coast or land bases encompassed flying boats such as the Short Sunderland or adapted long-

range bombers such as the American Consolidated B-24 Liberator. The Short Shetland flying boat, a successor to the Sunderland that flew in December 1944, was intended to continue this trend but it never entered service. Even as late as November 1948 a specification was issued for a maritime reconnaissance flying boat to replace the Sunderland; R.2/48 called for a bomb load of up to 8,000lb (3,629kg) and the projects tendered to it included the Saro P.162 Duchess, Blackburn B.78, Short P.D.2 and Supermarine Type 524. In early 1950 Shorts was informed that

ABOVE Shackleton anti-submarine capability is displayed by MR.2 WR966.

it was likely to win the contract for R.2/48 (which was to be renumbered R.112D) but by 1952 it was clear that a flying boat was no longer required to patrol the Atlantic and the aircraft was never built. The Avro Shackleton, operating from conventional runways, was seen as the way forward.

Avro Shackleton

Derived from the Avro Lincoln heavy bomber, the Avro Type 696 Shackleton MR.Mk.1 was essentially a wartime design produced to specification R.5/46 and OR.200 and the first prototype flew on 9 March 1949. There appears to have been no competition to the Type 696 from other British aircraft companies. The type entered service in April 1951 and seventy-seven Mk.1s or Mk.1As were built, followed by another sixty-nine Mk.2s. In due course OR.320 appeared for an improved long-range

Avro 696 Shackleton MR.Mk.1 (flown)	
Span	120ft 0in (36.58m)
Length	77ft 6in (23.62m)
Gross wing area	1,421sq ft (132.2sq m)
Gross weight	86,000lb (39,010kg) (Mk.2)
Powerplant	two RR Griffon 57 plus two Griffon 57A 2,450hp (1,827kW)
Maximum speed/height	274mph (441km/h)
Weapon load	two 20mm cannon, large bay for A/S bombs, DCs and other stores

maritime reconnaissance aircraft to fill the gap left by the withdrawal of the last Sunderlands. The leading competitor was a Shackleton Mk.3 but the Saro P.162 and Canadair CL.28 (a Canadian development of the Bristol 175 Britannia airliner, which became the Argus) were, for a period, also in the picture.

Avro 716 Shackleton Mk.3

By October 1950 Avro felt that the Shackleton Mk.2 with its existing Rolls-Royce Griffon engines represented the limit of development for the aircraft in its present form. The Type 716, a direct development of the Mk.2, offered an increased radius of action and a higher cruise speed, which would cut the duration of the outward and return flights, while its slow flying qualities would allow a maximum search time over the target area. Avro wanted an engine with the lowest possible specific fuel consumption, even at the expense of extra weight, so the Griffons were replaced by Napier Nomad turbo-compound diesel engines that, compared to current supercharged piston units, offered more flexibility of operation between sea level and 20,000ft (6,096m). In addition, the Nomad exhaust system would be extremely quiet, noise having been a major problem with both the Shackleton Mks.1 and 2.

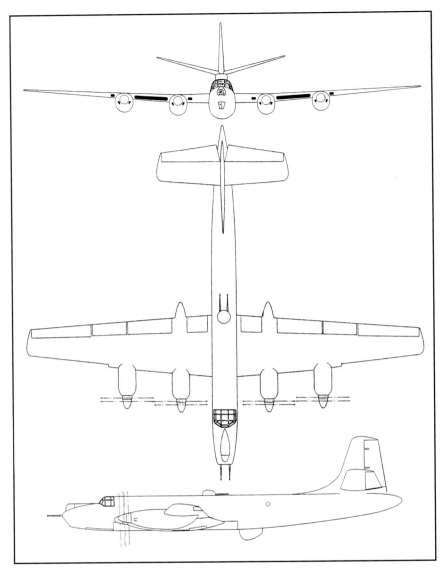

ABOVE Avro Type 716 (19.10.50). *Avro Heritage Centre*

Avro 716 (at 4.50)	
Span	120ft 0in (36.58m)
Length	106ft 6in (32.46m)
Gross wing area	1,600sq ft (148.8sq m)
Gross weight	113,314lb (51,399kg)
Powerplant	four Napier Nomad N.NM.3 3,000shp (2,237kW)
Maximum speed/height	342mph (550km/h)
Weapon load	four 20mm cannon, large bay for A/S bombs, DCs and other stores

(1,524m) 3,580nm (6,630km) (Mk.1 figures were 18,600ft [5,669m] and 2,620nm [4,852km] respectively). An Appendix gave brief details of an alternative and completely new proposal that had a wider circular fuselage, a more compact bomb compartment to accommodate two 'Pentane' weapons side by side and a new stressed-skin wing. By December Avro favoured this later project more than the original proposal.

Avro 719

The Avro Type 717 test bed was intended to fly with two Napier Nomad engines in the outer nacelles. The Type 719 was another Mk.3 proposal from January 1952 with a new fuselage and four Nomads on standard outer wings. Coastal Command's draft requirements were now looking at eight hours' search time at an operating radius of 1,000nm (1,852km) together with good manoeuvrability and minimum noise and vibration. Thanks to the need for economy in the design and manufacturing effort the Type 719 offered an alternative to the 'final' 716 based on the present Mk.1 and 2 wing. The outer wing was unchanged but a new centre section of increased span was introduced that offered greater fuel capacity and aerodynamic efficiency. Existing jigs could be used for its construction and the new aircraft could follow the Mk.2 Shackleton production line.

It was proposed to modify the wing structure aft of the rear spar to incorporate ailerons of increased power at the outboard end and high-lift

A new wing would carry the necessary extra fuel (for a total capacity of 4,400gal [20,006lit]) and improve the aircraft's aerodynamic efficiency. High-lift double-slotted flaps would give a marked improvement in the take-off and landing characteristics and it was proposed to fit multi-wheel main units and dual nosewheels so that the runway loadings might be considerably reduced when compared with the Shackleton Mk.2, despite a much higher take-off weight. Experience from the Mk.1 relating to the influence of the slipstream on longitudinal stability and trim meant that the 716's tailplane was now attached to the base of a single fin and rudder. However,

this was raised by dihedral to a sufficiently high position to alleviate the reduction in longitudinal stability usually associated with the 'power-on' condition. In addition, the size of the tail had been increased to accommodate the large changes in trim experienced when lowering and raising the high-lift flaps.

The Type 716 used all-metal construction and reintroduced the twin 20mm nose cannon, while the Nomads were fitted with co-axial propellers. Sea level rate of climb was estimated to be 970ft/min (296m/min), compared to the Mk.1's 730ft/min (223m/min), service ceiling 24,600ft (7,498m) and still air range at 5,000ft

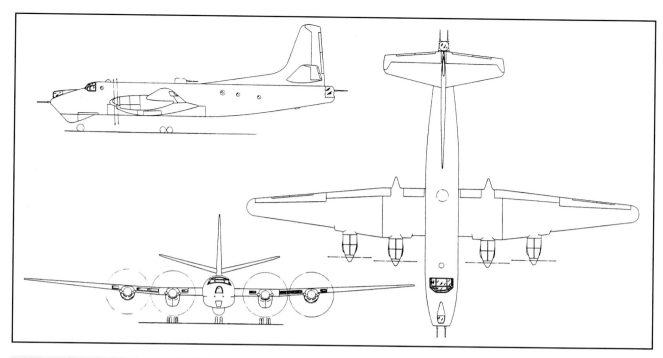

Avro 719

Span	132ft 0in (40.23m)
Length	102ft 8in (31.29m)
Gross wing area	1,615sq ft (150.2sq m)
Gross weight	114,693lb (52,025kg) with Centaurus, 114,843lb (52,093kg) with E.145
Powerplant	four Bristol Centaurus 660 or Napier Nomad E.145 (Nomad 3,050shp/2,274kW)
Maximum speed/height	Centaurus: 324mph (521km/h) at 14,000ft (4,267m); E.145: 354mph (570km/h) at 13,000ft (3,962m)
Weapon load	six 20mm cannon, large bay for A/S bombs, DCs and other stores

flaps over the inboard and centre sections. The former would give increased rolling power and the latter short take-off and landing distances in spite of a higher gross weight. The chosen powerplant was the Napier Nomad compound engine but, pending its development to a standard suitable for service use, it was proposed initially to fit four Bristol Centaurus 660 radials. The installation was designed so that it was possible to convert from Centaurus to Nomad with the minimum of work. To keep down the runway loading the main undercarriage would use four-wheel,

eight-tyre bogie units that were substantially the same as those on the Avro 698 (Vulcan). The fuel capacity was 4,710gal (21,416lit) and a rear turret was introduced. Avro believed that if an order was placed in May or June of 1952 then the first aircraft could be flying in August 1954.

Bristol 175 Development

In October 1951 Bristol submitted a proposal for a maritime reconnaissance variant of its Type 175 Britannia airliner, which the company then revised in January 1952 with four 3,150shp (2,349kW) Napier Nomad N.Nm.6 engines. The later variant's estimated weight was 147,000lb (66,679kg) and it would carry up to 8,000lb (3,629kg) of offensive stores, patrol at 173mph (278km/h) between sea level and 5,000ft (1,524m) and provide an endurance of 12 hours for a 1,000nm (1,852km) radius of action.

By now a draft requirement was in place for a Shackleton replacement but, because the companies knew little about it, the Avro 719 and Bristol 175 development had both been prepared based on a guess of what might be

required. They were assessed together from February 1952 and both had front, mid-upper and tail turrets each armed with two cannon, the specification suggesting two Adens in the front and rear turrets, 20mm in the dorsal position. Some within the Ministry felt that the 175 offered the best solution because the Avro 719 would not give a reasonable combination of range and endurance. Despite being a new design, the 719 was thought to be too small to give an acceptable patrol time and it had no development future.

At 135,000lb (61,236kg) gross weight, the 175 offered around twice the patrol time of the 719. As a variant of a civil aircraft its development and production costs should also be lower and it would benefit from subsequent increases in power from the Nomad. However, neither project could operate from a 2,000-yard (1,830m) runway at high enough weights to give a suitable endurance, partly because the take-off power of the Nomad during the early stages of development would be 3,050shp (2,274kW). Some thought was given, therefore, to fitting rockets for take-off assistance but this would rob both proposals of their main attraction, i.e. the use of wings or part wings already developed for other aircraft. In tropical conditions the 175 would need a considerable weight of rockets to get off in under 2,000 yards (1,830m) and the Ministry doubted if the Nomad would provide its full power in time (the expected fully developed figure of 3,500shp [2,610kW] would be sufficient to meet the runway limits). Coastal Command felt that the 719 had many good features but it wanted any new very long-range MR aircraft to be a flying boat rather than a landplane.

In September 1952 Avro submitted its Shackleton Mk.IIA brochure, a more conservative design compared to the 719 with four Griffon 57s. Despite lacking the crew comfort of both of the above projects it offered a slightly longer patrol time (the Shackleton III/719 gave higher drag) and, after being confirmed as acceptable to the RAF in January 1953, it was eventually ordered as the MR.Mk.3. The aircraft

retained the twin fins but introduced a tricycle undercarriage, more wing fuel, a different cockpit canopy and better interior sound-proofing. A total of thirty-four were built for the RAF, with the first flying on 2 September 1955.

Bristol 175MR

In 1953 Bristol took its development of the Britannia airliner a stage further with the Type 175MR project. The Britannia's Bristol Proteus turboprops were replaced by American Wright R3350-32W radials with 15ft 6in (4.72m) diameter Curtiss Electric three-blade propellers, there was a Bristol Type N nose turret with two 20mm cannon and (provisionally) a Bristol B.17 dorsal turret with two more. A large lower fuselage bomb bay could hold a mix of anti-submarine weapons, while rocket projectiles and other missiles could be fired from positions beneath the outer wing. Span with tip tanks was 144ft (43.89m), length with nose guns 123ft (37.49m)

and wing area 2,060sq ft (191.6sq m). The Bristol Type 189 was a similar project powered by Napier Nomads.

By 1958 thoughts had moved on towards a medium-range replacement for the Avro Shackleton. In addition, in 1957 NATO had opened a competition between European aircraft manufacturers for a maritime patrol aircraft to replace the American Lockheed Neptune in European air forces (during the 1950s the Neptune served with Coastal Command as a stopgap). This was NBMR.2 and the required aircraft would carry about 6,000lb (2,722kg) of search equipment and offensive armament on a basic mission consisting of either a four-hour search period at a 1,000nm (1,852km) radius from base or an eight-hour search period at 600nm (1,111km). The search was to be undertaken at sea level and a transit speed of 300 knots (345mph/559km/h) was required. A number of competing designs were

BELOW Bristol 175MR (22.4.53).

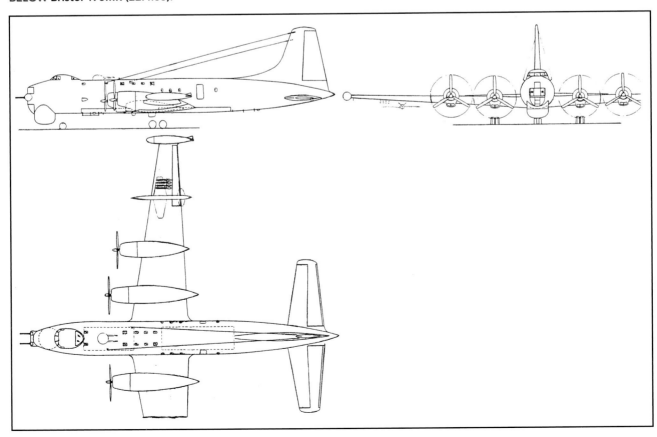

submitted before the French Breguet 1150 Atlantic was chosen as the winner. Others came from France, Germany and Italy and the following from British manufacturers. There was also the Armstrong Whitworth AW.651 and Saunders-Roe P.208, both of which were to be powered by Rolls-Royce Tyne turboprops. For more illustrations and details of these designs the reader is advised to consult *Nimrod's Genesis: RAF Maritime Patrol Projects and Weapons Since 1945* by Chris Gibson, published by Hikoki in 2014.

Bristol 206 and 207

The Bristol Type 206 carried 4,410gal (20,052lit) of fuel and was to be powered by two Rolls-Royce Tyne turboprops with 16ft (4.88m) diameter propellers. Besides the standard A/S stores in the weapon bay it could also carry one Bullpup ASM on a pylon under each wing placed midway between the engine nacelle and tip pod. A retractable ECM radome was housed in the lower fuselage level with the propellers, the port wing tip pod contained a searchlight and the starboard wing tip pod housed missile electronics. Bristol also produced the Type 207 version with two Mamba engines and one BE.53, but both the 206 and 207 were dropped early on in the competition.

Bristol Type 206	
Span	107ft 0in (32.61m)
Length	77ft 0in (23.47m)
Gross wing area	1,150sq ft (107.0sq m)
Gross weight	83,200lb (37,740kg)
Powerplant	two RR Tyne R.Ty.11 5,030shp (3,751kW) + 1,290lb (5.7kN) thrust
Maximum speed/height	?
Weapon load	At least 6,000lb (2,722kg) of stores in bay, 2 Bullpup ASMs under wings

Fairey Project 83 Maritime Patrol Aircraft

Since primary cost and economy of operation were of fundamental importance to this requirement, Fairey had made a number of preliminary studies to determine the minimum size of aircraft that would comply with the required operational characteristics. And, like the other competitors described here, the company had concluded that a twin-engined, land-based aircraft represented the most suitable solution. At the required speeds the propeller-turbine was superior in efficiency to the pure jet, while ease of maintenance had ruled out any mixed powerplants, the very sophisticated compound engine or coupled versions of existing single engines. Fortunately an existing turboprop, the Tyne, was available and two Mk.11 units were fitted with 16ft (4.88m) propellers. Semi-monocoque (predominantly aluminium) skin construction was used throughout and a multi-spar wing was fitted. The maximum continuous cruising speed at the 81,000lb (36,742kg) take-off weight was 355mph (571km/h) at 30,000ft (9,144m) and 350mph (563km/h) at sea level. Rate of climb was 2,190ft/min (668m/min) and service ceiling 34,500ft (10,516m); at 75,000lb (34,020kg) weight the service ceiling became 36,600ft (10,973m), when the specification had requested 20,000ft (6,096m). Total fuel load was 31,200lb (14,152kg).

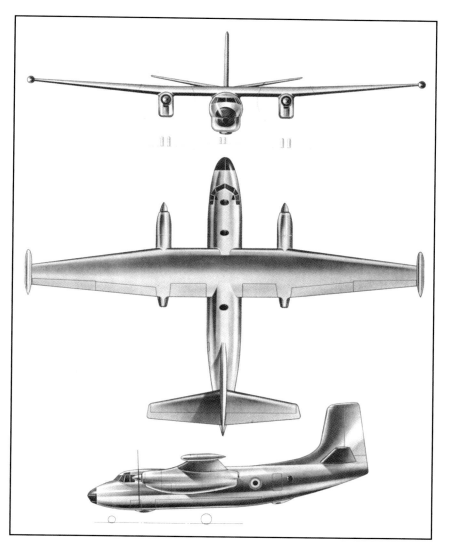

RIGHT Bristol 206 (2.5.58).

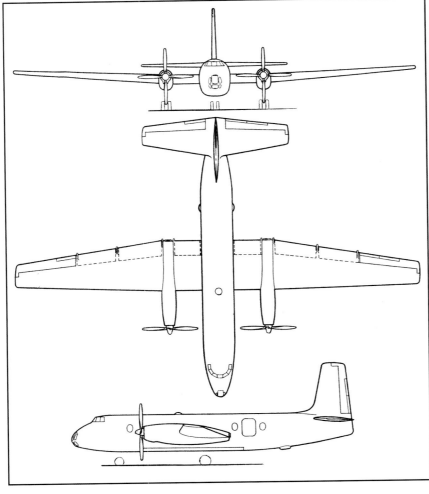

ABOVE Fairey Project 83 Maritime Patrol Aircraft (21.6.58).
BELOW Artist's impression of Fairey's Project 83 Maritime Patrol Aircraft.

Fairey Project 83	
Span	115ft 0in (35.05m)
Length	80ft 0in (24.38m)
Gross wing area	1,286sq ft (119.6sq m)
Gross weight	81,000lb (36,742kg)
Powerplant	two RR Tyne R.Ty.11 5,030shp (3,751kW) + 1,290lb (5.7kN) thrust
Maximum speed/height	371mph (597km/h) at 20,000ft (6,096m)
Weapon load	Various stores in internal bomb bay

Avro 745

Avro felt that the high transit speed could best be met by cruising at medium altitude and using gas turbines, once again Tyne turboprops driving 16ft (4.88m) four-bladed de Havilland propellers. A twin-Tyne aircraft would meet all the specification requirements but a four-engined aircraft could be powered by Rolls-Royce Dart 10s or the proposed Bristol Siddeley Mamba 10. The Dart aircraft would be appreciably heavier, while the twin-Tyne and four-Mamba versions would have similar weights. The Tyne, already under development for the Vickers Vanguard airliner, was preferred.

To obtain an efficient wing structure the complete torsion box had to pass through the fuselage and, since the 745's wing was located below the fuselage floor, this resulted in a split bomb bay with one part forward and the other aft of the wing centre section. Any required store could be carried in either bay, while the low wing offered the best characteristics in the event of ditching. The wing structure was of the fail-safe type, the main torsion box consisting of front and rear webs with skins stiffened by Z-section stringers. Most of the wing torsion box formed an integral fuel tank, while high-lift Fowler-type flaps and conventional sealed balance ailerons occupied the wing trailing edge. The fuselage structure was conventional, consisting of formers and stringers attached to the skin. An ASV.21 search scanner was located in the forward end of the fuselage ahead of the bomb bay and could retract within the fuselage

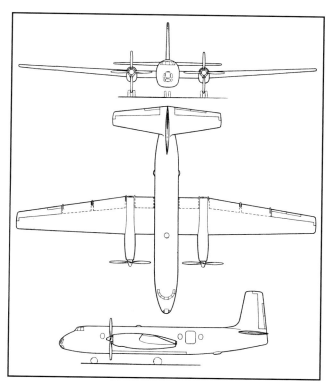

ABOVE Avro 745 (6.58).
Avro Heritage Centre

RIGHT **Views of an original Avro 745 model.**
Avro Heritage Centre

contours to give minimum drag when cruising; the whole scanner could be jettisoned to open the forward parachute exit.

A complete cabin mock-up of the 745 was constructed at Avro's Manchester headquarters. The design's fuel capacity was 3,860gal (17,551lit), estimated sea level rate of climb 2,280ft/min (695m/min), service ceiling 32,200ft (9,815m) and patrol speed 196mph (315km/h). The eight-

Avro 745	
Span	112ft 3in (34.21m)
Length	82ft 9in (25.22m)
Gross wing area	1,050sq ft (97.7sq m)
Gross weight	79,400lb (36,016kg)
Powerplant	two RR Tyne R.Ty.11 5,030shp (3,751kW) + 1,290lb (5.7kN) thrust
Maximum speed/height	Cruise at 65,000lb (29,484kg) mean weight 382mph (615km/h) at sea level, 397mph (639km/h) at optimum height
Weapon load	six DCs or 1,000lb (454kg) mines, ten 1,000lb (454kg), twenty-one 500lb (227kg) or thirty-five 250lb (113kg) bombs

hour/600nm (1,111km) radius requirement was achieved but the 745's patrol time at 1,000nm (1,852km) was higher at 5.4 hours. The three finalists in the competition were the Avro 745, a design from Nord and the Breguet 1150, and the latter was chosen as the winner in October 1958.

ABOVE The NBMR.2 competition was won by the Breguet 1150 Atlantic.

Hawker Siddeley HS.801 Nimrod

During the early 1960s the search for a Shackleton replacement continued under OR.350 and specification MR.218, to which competing Hawker Siddeley designs were a version of the Comet airliner with four RB.168 jet engines, the Avro 776 project with three Medway jets, a version of the Trident airliner, a Shackleton development (which did not meet the specification) and the Breguet Atlantic; BAC's offers were versions of the Vanguard and VC10 airliners. This was succeeded by AST.357, which again brought forth numerous proposals including the P.D.69 from Shorts and further versions of current British airliners. The Shackleton Mk.2 was to be replaced by the AST.357 aircraft in about 1970 but a reappraisal in 1964 indicated that the latter would not be available until about 1978 and noted that it would be unwise to keep the Shackleton 2s in service until then.

As a result, ASR.381 and MR.254 for an interim maritime reconnaissance aircraft were written around the Breguet Atlantic specification since that aircraft was the contender with the minimum acceptable performance. The requirement was issued on 19 June 1964 and further contenders were examined by the MoA and industry. Final proposals were due on 14

LEFT Lovely view of Nimrod MR.Mk.1 XV230 taken during a patrol.

Hawker Siddeley HS.801 Nimrod (flown)	
Span	114ft 10in (34.75m)
Length	126ft 9in (38.63m)
Gross wing area	2,121sq ft (197.3sq m)
Gross weight	178,000lb (80,741kg)
Powerplant	four RR Spey 250 12,140lb (54.0kN)
Maximum speed/height	582mph (936km/h) maximum operating speed
Weapon load	A/S torpedoes, mines, DCs and bombs

December and the winner was the HS.801 Nimrod, an extensive redesign of the Comet airliner, which beat a variant of the Trident called the HS.800. A careful assessment was also made of the Atlantic and the American Lockheed P-3 Orion but, in terms of the radii of action and weapons loads needed for Britain's worldwide task, neither was considered by the Air Staff to be cost-effective compared to the HS.801.

The aircraft's configuration was agreed on 30 September 1965 and two Comets were flown to Woodford for conversion to HS.801s; the first of these flew on 23 May 1967, the same month that the new type was named Nimrod. On 19 January 1966 a contract was signed for thirty-eight production aircraft and the type entered RAF service in 1969. On 25 July 1996 the

Government announced that the BAe Nimrod 2000 had won the Replacement Maritime Patrol Aircraft (RMPA) contract with state-of-the-art systems and BMW 710 engines. However, as the Nimrod MRA.Mk.4 this programme was cancelled in 2010.

Carrier-Based Anti-Submarine

In 1945 preliminary discussions began to find a replacement for the wartime Fairey Swordfish and Barracuda with an aircraft that would operate from escort carriers. The MoS was asked to prepare a specification to meet a Naval Staff requirement and this became

GR.17/45 coupled with OR.220. Westland responded with a twin-engined aeroplane but prototypes of both Blackburn and Fairey's proposals were first ordered in April 1946.

Fairey Type Q

Fairey's first GR.17/45 brochure was completed on 14 December 1945 and showed two designs, Schemes A and C. On 12 March 1946 a follow-up described Schemes D and E, which differed principally from the first pair in having their wing area increased from 445sq ft (41.4sq m) to 475sq ft (44.2sq m). This allowed a full overload take-off in low wind speeds (around

RIGHT **Fairey GR.17/45 Scheme E (6.3.46).**

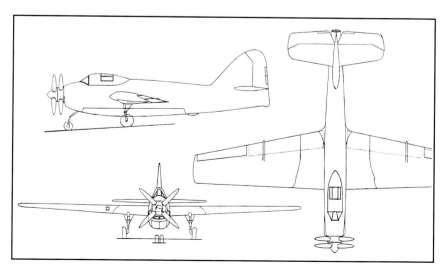

ABOVE Unusual and splendid photo of a Fairey Gannet flying with part of the powerplant shut down.

21mph [34km/h]) to be effected with a run of 420ft (128m), while the approach speed with a full strike load and two hours' of fuel still aboard had been reduced to the extremely low figure of 76mph (122km/h). The improvements in D and E's low-speed performance were achieved at the cost of a very small reduction in top speed, while a saving in fuel balanced the increase in structure weight from the bigger wing area; the overload weights were 18,200lb (8,256kg) and 17,610lb (7,988kg) respectively.

Scheme D was powered by a single Rolls-Royce AP.25 double-propeller-turbine (later called the Tweed) and E by coupled twin Armstrong Siddeley Mamba turboprops. After about eighteen months of design work Rolls-Royce discontinued the Tweed so Fairey stayed with the Armstrong Siddeley engine, which became the Double Mamba. Redesignated the Fairey 17, the first prototype flew on 19 September 1949 and differed considerably from the early Type Q drawings; by October 1951 it had been named Gannet.

Fairey GR.17/45 (Schemes D & E)	
Span	55ft 0in (16.76m)
Length	43ft 0in (13.11m)
Gross wing area	475sq ft (44.2sq m)
Gross weight	D: 16,750lb (7,598kg), E: 16,550lb (7,507kg)
Powerplant	D: one RR AP.25 2,500shp (1,864kW), E: two AS coupled Mamba
Maximum speed/height	D: 306mph (492km/h) at sea level, 316mph (508km/h) at 15,000ft (4,572m); E: 316mph (508km/h) at sea level, 305mph (491km/h) at 15,000ft (4,572m)
Weapon load	one A/S torpedo, six DCs or bombs, sixteen RPs

BELOW Fairey Gannet T.Mk.2 prototype WN365 pictured at Farnborough in 1954.
Terry Panopalis collection

ABOVE The third Fairey Gannet prototype WE488 seen on public display at Farnborough in September 1951. *Terry Panopalis collection*

BELOW This very similar view of Blackburn Y.B.1 prototype WB797 was also taken at Farnborough and permits the Blackburn and Fairey rivals to be compared. *Terry Panopalis collection*

Blackburn B.54 (Y.A.5)

Blackburn's first GR.17/45 proposal was a development of the earlier B.48 'Firecrest' torpedo bomber with a chin radome and powered by either an Armstrong Siddeley Python or Napier Double Naiad propeller-turbine with large diameter contra-rotating airscrews. A model was exhibited at the September 1948 Farnborough Show but again, as built, the B.54 was to look quite different. Initially it was called the Y.A.5 and three prototypes were ordered.

Comparing the two rival designs, Blackburn had taken the line of providing high engine power, either from a coupled Naiad or single Tweed, while accepting a fairly high wing loading. On the other hand, Fairey had proposed using a lower-powered engine, the twin Mamba, and had adopted a lower wing loading. On balance Fairey's scheme, thanks to its higher structure weight, came out at about 500lb (227kg) heavier but neither design came within the gross weight requirement of 16,500lb (7,484kg). It was eventually agreed to raise the specified normal gross weight to 17,500lb (7,938kg) and in May 1948 the B.54's weight was expected to be 17,100lb (7,757kg).

Blackburn Y.A.7/8 and Y.B.1

By mid-1947 it was clear that the B.54 would be delayed and that the coupled Naiad would be much later than first thought. It was therefore agreed to fit a Griffon engine in the first prototype, with an installation similar to the Shackleton's, to test the airframe aerodynamics. A year later the estimated first flight of the Naiad machine had dropped back to December 1949 at the earliest, so Blackburn proposed fitting a Double Mamba in the second aircraft to ensure that the company could have a turbine-propeller aeroplane flying at the same time as Fairey's. In the event the first two prototype B.54s flew with Griffons as the Blackburn Y.A.7 and Y.A.8 respectively, the first taking to the air on 20 September 1949, while the third flew with a Double Mamba on 19 July 1950 having been redesignated B.88 (SBAC designation Y.B.1). The aircraft's take-off performance with flaps down proved to be poor, which counted against it during official assessment.

Blackburn B.88/Y.B.1 (flown)	
Span	44ft 2in (13.46m)
Length	42ft 8in (13.01m)
Gross wing area	?
Gross weight	13,091lb (5,938kg)
Powerplant	one AS Double Mamba 2,950ehp (2,200kW)
Maximum speed/height	320mph (515km/h)
Weapon load	one A/S TT, six DCs or bombs, underwing RPs

OPPOSITE **Y.B.1 WB797 pictured during flying displays at Farnborough. The first view was taken on 5 September 1950.**

ABOVE The S.B.3 makes a fast pass at Farnborough in 1950 with one engine shut down. *Terry Panopalis collection*

Short S.B.3 Sturgeon

At around the end of 1947 it was stated that the need to operate from escort carriers was now unlikely, and soon afterwards the Staff requested that GR.17/45 should be a three-seat aircraft because its search radar needed a dedicated operator. Consequently, the entire situation was re-examined, GR.17/45 was upgraded and a third aeroplane came into the picture. This was an A/S version of the wartime Short Sturgeon torpedo bomber (and later target tug) suggested as a possible interim aircraft, although it would probably only be suitable to operate from large carriers. At an MoS conference on 8 March 1949 it was agreed to convert two Sturgeons from the production line as quickly and as cheaply as possible (in fact the last production airframe was turned into the first prototype while the second was begun from scratch). Specification M.6/49 and OR.275 were written around the project, which was called the Short S.B.3.

BELOW The Shorts S.B.3 runs up its engines in August 1950, possibly on the day of its first flight. Note that the aircraft has not yet been painted.

It was soon obvious that the S.B.3 would not be ready quickly enough to make it an interim type, but there was still a good case for building it since it would help to develop the best equipment and tactical methods for finding and killing submarines, areas in which there was general ignorance. It could also be a long-term insurance against the complete failure of the Blackburn and Fairey designs. Most of the S.B.3 was similar to the Sturgeon TT.Mk.2 target tug but the forward fuselage was redesigned extensively and bulged to accommodate a search radar under the floor, while two Mamba turboprops replaced the original Merlin engines. However, delays were caused by an excessive number of design defects and also by Shorts' move from Rochester to Belfast, so the S.B.3 did not fly until 12 August 1950. Early trials showed deficiencies in longitudinal and directional stability at slow speeds. The second machine was delayed by the non-delivery of its powerplants and in fact never flew at all, because on 11 April 1951 it was decided that work on the S.B.3 should cease.

Short S.B.3 (flown)

Span	59ft 9in (18.21m)
Length	44ft 8in (13.62m)
Gross wing area	560.4sq ft (52.1sq m)
Gross weight	23,600lb (10,705kg)
Powerplant	two AS Mamba 1,475shp (1,100kW)
Maximum speed/height	c. 320mph (515km/h)
Weapon load	one A/S TT, six DCs or bombs, RPs

Competitive trials between the anti-submarine contenders were held in 1950. Initially the Fairey 17 was found to have some flight problems, and in regard to its maintenance and accessibility the machine compared unfavourably against Blackburn's machine. However, Fairey won the competition and a hundred production Gannets were ordered to Specification GR.117P; there was no production order for Blackburn. The Gannet was now intended to replace A/S versions of the piston-engined Fairey Firefly developed since the war but the

Double Mamba turboprop, designed so that the aircraft could cruise on half power only, incorporated many innovations. Its slow development resulted in a gap in the Navy's A/S capability and in June 1950 there was even a proposal to fit a Griffon 57 instead. In addition, the production Gannet had so many changes from the prototypes that it was virtually a new aircraft. Therefore, as a stopgap, a hundred Grumman Avengers were acquired from America and these began to arrive in Britain in March 1953.

Fairey Gannet

The first production Gannet AS.Mk.1 flew on 9 June 1953 and the type entered operational service in 1955. Eventually nearly 350 were built in six versions, including the very extensively redesigned AEW Mk.3 flown in 1958. Other developments considered but not built included another A/S version from June 1953. This was substantially the same as the Mk.1 but had an ASV.20 radar, Blue Silk Doppler navigation equipment and the ability to carry a 3,300lb (1,497kg) Blue Boar-type anti-submarine radar-homing bomb.

Fairey Gannet AS.Mk.1 (flown)

Span	54ft 4in (16.56m)
Length	43ft 0in (13.11m)
Gross wing area	482.8sq ft (44.9sq m)
Gross weight	19,600lb (8,891kg) at take-off
Powerplant	one AS Double Mamba 100 2,950ehp (2,200kW)
Maximum speed/height	310mph (499km/h) at sea level
Weapon load	two 1,000lb (454kg) or four 500lb (227kg) bombs, two TTs, six DCs, one 2,000lb (907kg) or two 1,000lb (454kg) mines

Lightweight Anti-Submarine

The GR.17/45 Gannet type would represent the backbone of the Navy's air anti-submarine forces and become the service's standard A/S aircraft. It was large, expensive and fitted with comprehensive electronic equipment,

and was expected to be outstanding in its role, but it could only operate from carriers of the later light fleet size or above and not from escort carriers. A smaller, lightweight anti-submarine aircraft would be ideal to complement it and NR/A.32 with Specification M.123 was raised to cover this. This project and the Gannet broke with tradition because both were designed as dedicated anti-submarine aircraft when, previously, the job had been given to converted types such as the Fairey Firefly.

Blackburn B.83 and B.91

Blackburn's first design was the B.83 project of July 1950 with a Rolls-Royce Merlin 35 piston engine, 250gal (1,137lit) of internal fuel (125gal/568lit in each wing), a bomb bay housing an A/S torpedo and underwing pylons for smaller weapons. Span was 45ft 0in (13.7m), folded span 27ft 10in (8.48m) and length with tail up 41ft 7in (12.7m) and in 1951 this was followed by the Mamba-powered B.91. Blackburn did not tender to M.123 once the design team had realised that a low wing loading would be undesirable in the turbulent conditions expected with rough seas, and in addition using the powerful flaps that were needed to give sufficient high lift would make it very difficult to achieve adequate lateral control.

Short S.B.6 (P.D.4)

When first proposed in September 1950 this project had a tricycle undercarriage and three crew. The project proved to be the winning design but as built it had a tailwheel undercarriage and the crew had been cut to two to reduce the fuselage size and the weight.

Westland Light A/S aircraft

The Westland project covered two designs, one with a retractable undercarriage, the other with fixed legs; the wing, fin and T-tail were essentially the same but their fuselages differed somewhat, as did the seating arrangements for the three crew. The

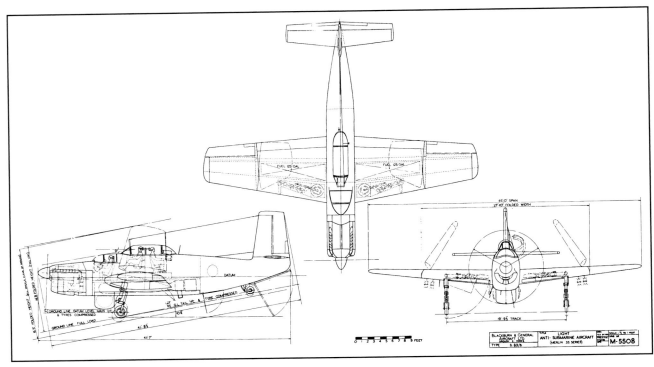

ABOVE Blackburn B.83 (24.7.50). Note the torpedo in the weapon bay.
BAe Brough Heritage

Westland Light A/S Aircraft

Span	55ft 0in (16.76m)
Length	42ft 0in (12.80m)
Gross wing area	500sq ft (46.5sq m)
Gross weight	13,320lb (6,042kg) with retractable u/c, 13,240lb (6,006kg) with fixed u/c
Powerplant	one AS Mamba AS.Ma.3 1,400shp (1,044kW) or one RR Dart R.Da.3 1,320shp (984kW)
Maximum speed/height	?
Weapon load	one A/S torpedo or bombs, DCs

Mamba could be replaced by a Rolls-Royce R.Da.3 Dart turboprop. Internal fuel totalled 270gal (1,228lit) and the homing torpedo was carried in a lower fuselage bay.

BELOW Westland light anti-submarine aircraft with fixed undercarriage (mid-1950).

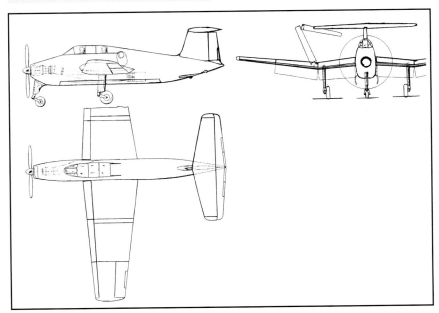

In October 1951 Fairey offered a cut-down Gannet with a single Mamba and a new nose but with the rest of the aircraft essentially unchanged. Fairey felt this conversion offered many advantages over an all-new design and one of the GR.17/45 prototypes could be converted, which would save time. And since the aircraft differed only superficially from the original GR.17/45 its flight development programme would be much reduced. However, the Short S.B.6 was chosen and three prototypes were ordered in March 1952, the aircraft being named Seamew. It was felt that the Gannet was rather too elaborate an aircraft to equip RNVR A/S squadrons, but the Seamew would be ideal since it would cost about half of the Gannet's price and be simple to operate and maintain. Australia and France were also potential customers.

ABOVE Nose of the Short Seamew prototype at Farnborough. *Terry Panopalis collection*

ABOVE Nose, forward fuselage and wing of a production Short Seamew at Farnborough in September 1955. *Terry Panopalis collection*

Short Seamew

The first Seamew flew on 23 August 1953 and revealed some vicious handling characteristics, but an initial batch of forty-one aircraft was ordered in 1955 covering AS.Mk.1s for the Navy and MR.Mk.2s for RAF Coastal Command. A year later the RAF machines were cancelled and then the 1957 Defence White Paper disbanded the RNVR's Air Branch altogether, cancelling the Seamew order with it. By that stage twenty-four production machines had flown and several had been accepted by the Royal Navy.

Short Seamew AS.Mk.1 (flown)	
Span	55ft 0in (16.76m)
Length	41ft 0in (12.50m)
Gross wing area	585sq ft (54.4sq m)
Gross weight	14,400lb (6,532kg)
Powerplant	one AS Mamba AS.Ma.6 1,590shp (1,186kW)
Maximum speed/height	235mph (378km/h) at sea level
Weapon load	Maximum 1,844lb (836kg) of stores

BELOW Seamew prototype XA209 at Farnborough in September 1954. *Terry Panopalis collection*

Chapter Twelve
Variations on a Theme

ABOVE **Model of the P.1233-1.**

This chapter covers items that were essentially peripheral to the general course of bomber developments. However, because they were studied in some detail it is felt that they demand deeper coverage than that normally addressed in Appendix One.

Supermarine Scimitar

An entire chapter of the companion *British Secret Projects: Jet Fighters since 1950* is devoted to the Supermarine Type 544 Scimitar but, during the course of its service with the Fleet Air Arm, the de Havilland Sea Vixen took most of the Navy's interception duties, leaving the Scimitar for bombing and strike operations. The main weapon for what was to become the aircraft's primary role was a tactical nuclear

bomb to be delivered at low altitude, but other roles included ground attack with Bullpup ASMs, RPs or 1,000lb (454kg) bombs. It is not surprising, therefore, that there were several proposed developments dedicated to strike or bombing, including two based on the Scimitar's ancestors, the Types 508 and 525.

Supermarine Type 522

In 1947 the Naval Staff raised a new requirement NR/A.19 for a single-seat strike aircraft. Various designs were considered to meet it, including a version of Fairey's N.40/46 all-weather fighter, before the Staff settled on a conversion of Supermarine's Type 508 day fighter to N.9/47. This project, the Type 522, had been requested by the MoS on 7 July

1948. There was to be minimal alteration to the 508's existing structure and twin 6,500lb (28.9kN) Rolls-Royce Avon installation, no changes to the overall dimensions and no modifications to the wings and tail. Space was available in the lower fuselage between the engines for a weapon bay and removing the guns gave a bit more room. The bay was enclosed by doors that when closed formed a shallow blister on the fuselage underside forward of the wheel wells; a second 'bomb cell' aft of the wheel wells also formed a shallow blister.

The 'bomb cells' had to be split because moving the main undercarriage would have resulted in major modifications. If large CofG shifts were to be avoided a large weapon such as a 2,000lb (907kg) bomb had to be housed at or about the CofG. Unfortunately the 508's main wheels retracted into the fuselage just aft of the CofG and almost met on the centreline. The solution was to carry the 2,000lb (907kg) bomb, or two 1,050lb (476kg) Red Angel rockets, externally under the wings in place of one of the drop tanks. Most of the other specified stores (two 1,000lb [454kg], four 500lb [227kg] bombs or various mines) would be carried internally but eight 60lb (27kg) RPs had to be carried externally on an underfuselage point just above the bomb bay door hinges. These arrangements were hampered by the fact that some established weapons were undergoing dimensional changes while the size of the newer weapons had not yet been frozen.

The performance requirements were severe, particularly the dive braking limits, which would necessitate considerable modification to the 508's wings. The strike requirements had also led to a heavier aircraft than the 508, which reduced the Type 522's manoeuvrability, but the level was still expected to be adequate. Internal fuel totalled 600gal (2,728lit) and the 522 could also carry two 200gal (909lit)

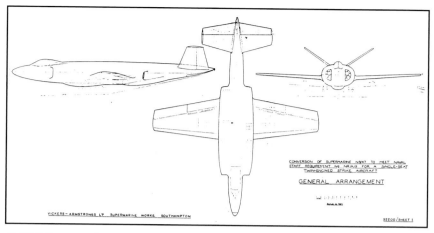

ABOVE Supermarine Type 522 (10.48).

external tanks, the top speed at sea level for a clean aircraft was 622mph (1,000km/h) and with drop tanks 535mph (862km/h), and the gross weight was 24,775lb (11,238kg). A reconnaissance role was also envisaged for this aircraft.

Supermarine Type 537

The Type 508 fighter was succeeded by an all-swept version called the Type 525 so the Naval Staff began to discuss a swept wing type for NR/A.19 (at this time the 525 was thought to be the

aircraft that would go into service). A proposal submission was requested on 10 January 1950 and the result was the Type 537 completed in April. This was a pure strike conversion of the Type 525 complete with its swept V-tail (when flown the 525 had a conventional tail) and the biggest change was a long ventral bulge beneath the fuselage stretching from the rear cockpit to just ahead of the tail. This single bomb cell had replaced the 522's separate cells and would house all of the weapons internally except for the 60lb (27kg) RP

BELOW Supermarine Type 537 (4.50).

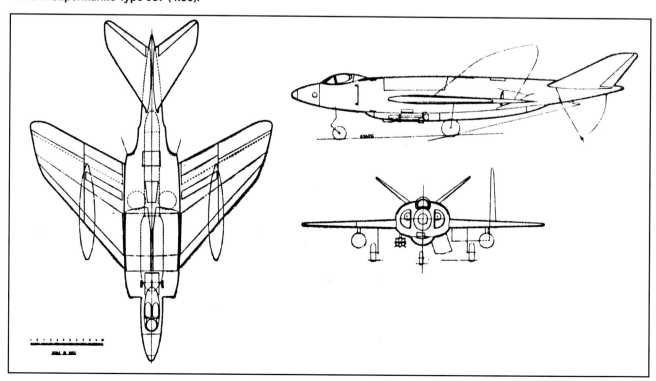

pylons placed to the sides of the fuselage (the weaponry was unchanged from the 522); the wings themselves and the tail had more area than the 522. However, plans to build prototypes of the Type 537 were suspended on 18 April 1950 because of a lack of money.

Supermarine Type 537	
Span	37ft 6in (11.43m)
Length	54ft 0in (16.46m)
Gross weight	23,950lb (10,864kg), overload 27,830lb (12,624kg)
Powerplant	two RR Avon
Maximum speed/height	678mph (1,091km/h) 'clean', 570mph (917km/h) with drop tanks

Supermarine Type 561

The Type 561 was planned as a de-navalised Scimitar adapted for the RAF as a low-level nuclear bomber. It was discussed through the summer of 1956 and received considerable interest from the Air Staff as an interim type. One tactical nuclear bomb would be carried and the Type 561 would cruise to its target at low level and high subsonic speed, but successful navigation at low level without a second crewman was thought to be a difficult problem to overcome.

Supermarine Types 562 and 564

Work on the Type 562 interceptor and strike aircraft began in January 1956, brochures were sent to the MoS in mid-July and Supermarine claimed that deliveries could start in 1959 directly after Scimitar production had been completed. This design is covered in more detail in *British Secret Projects: Jet Fighters since 1950*, but a revised strike version called the Type 564 was offered on 10 February 1957 with Avon RA.24s or de Havilland Gyron Juniors. With one TMB, one 200gal (909lit) and two 500gal (2,273lit) drop tanks the respective weights with these two engines were 47,438lb (21,518kg) and 48,764lb (22,119kg). The smaller Gyron Juniors had extra fuel to fill the space that they saved, while 'blow' would be extended across half the ailerons. Work on the project appears to have ceased in March 1957.

Supermarine Type 567

The Naval Staff had forecast a gap between the Westland Wyvern strike fighter's retirement in 1957/58 and the Blackburn Buccaneer's introduction in 1961/62, and the NR/A.19 type was thought to be the most suited to fill it. The result was the single and two-seat Supermarine Type 567 of April 1957, which was prepared to, and expected to meet, the major items of the NR/A.39 M.148 (Buccaneer) requirement; the two-seater appears to have been the more important. (At this time Scimitar itself had completed more than 400 hours flying on three prototypes and six production machines.) The main differences from the Scimitar, other than two seats and M.148 equipment, were the deletion of guns, provision of part-span aileron blowing, increased internal fuel from 1,064gal (4,838lit) to 1,374gal (6,247lit), strengthened wings and an extra store station near each wing root. In zero wind a radius of 420nm (778km) was possible at a 42,000lb (19,051kg) take-off weight but flight refuelling would push this up to 915nm (1,695km). The two-seater's span was

BELOW All the Supermarine designs described here were based around the company's straight wing Type 508 or swept wing Type 525 fighter prototypes, or the Scimitar itself. This view shows Scimitar XD215 while in the hands of A&AEE Boscombe Down.

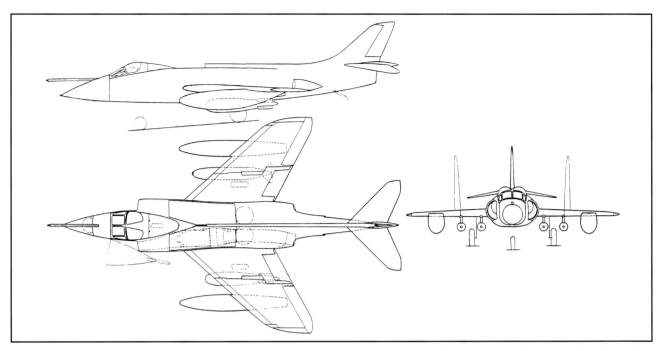

ABOVE The two-seat version of the Supermarine Type 567 (4.57). The head-on view shows four 1,000lb (454kg) bombs and two 500gal (2,273lit) drop tanks.

37ft 2in (11.33m), length 61ft 10.5in (18.86m), gross weight with one TMB, one 200gal (909lit) and two 500gal (2,273lit) tanks 50,220lb (22,780kg), and with four 1,000lb (454kg) bombs and two 500gal (2,273lit) tanks 50,460lb (22,889kg). Work continued throughout the year and in October wing tip tanks were suggested to improve the range.

Supermarine Type 576

The Type 576, a supersonic Scimitar development, was first proposed on 5 December 1958 as a strike aircraft and its bulkier fuselage, which housed dorsal fuel tanks, brought a substantial change in appearance. The RA.24 Avons were replaced by non-reheated 13,220lb (58.8kN) Rolls-Royce RB.146s and a single-seat version had more fuel and extra pylons to carry either a six 1,000lb (454kg) external load or four bombs with two tanks. A Ferranti Airpass I search radar, as fitted to the EE Lightning, gave a ship search facility of 60nm (111km) and provided a much closer approach to all-weather capability in both strike and fighter roles. And the extension of 'blow' or 'supercirculation' over the outer as well as the inner wing had reduced the catapult wind requirement by about

9mph (14.5km/h). With these improvements, the maximum strike radius in the M.148 low attack sortie when carrying a TMB at a weight of 47,425lb (21,512kg) was 665nm (1,232km). Span was 37ft 2in (11.33m) and length 61ft 0in (18.59m).

A two-seater was intended to meet M.148 more closely. The dorsal tanks held 600gal (2,728lit) of fuel, the fuselage tankage was increased by another 302gal (1,373lit) and a further two 1,000lb (454kg) bombs were housed internally so that six bombs could be carried in addition to the nacelle tanks. Here the strike radius with the TMB was 788nm (1,459km) and a typical launch weight was 53,000lb (24,041kg). This aircraft was intended to be available for delivery to service in 1962. (Type 576 fighter developments are covered in *British Secret Projects: Jet Fighters since 1950.*)

Further proposals made on 15 April 1959 indicated a host of possible retrospective modifications to current Scimitar airframes to convert them to supersonic Type 576 standards (with lower development costs than would be expected for a completely new aircraft design). In summary, the improvements offered by the Type 576 over the current

Scimitar were the removal of the limitation to fair weather operations in both strike and fighter roles, twice the effective strike radius and, when the Red Top AAM was available, the ability to attack targets flying at Mach 2 and 65,000ft (19,812m).

NATO Light Strike

In 1954 NATO formulated a requirement called NBMR.1 for a daylight ground attack type with the ability to also perform as a fighter. This called for Mach 0.95 at low altitudes, the carriage of two 500lb (227kg) bombs and twelve 3in (7.6cm) RPs and the ability to take off from a grass strip. Emphasis was placed on simplicity because the increasing complexity of modern combat aircraft was causing concern. Contenders included Italy's Fiat G.91, from France the Breguet Br 1001, Dassault Mystère XXVI (alias the Etendard VI) and the Sud-Ouest SO 6150, and from Britain the Avro 727 and a version of the Folland Gnat fighter. Several of the competitors were built, and then in January 1958 the G.91 was chosen as the winner and this aircraft went on to serve with both the Italian and West German Air Forces.

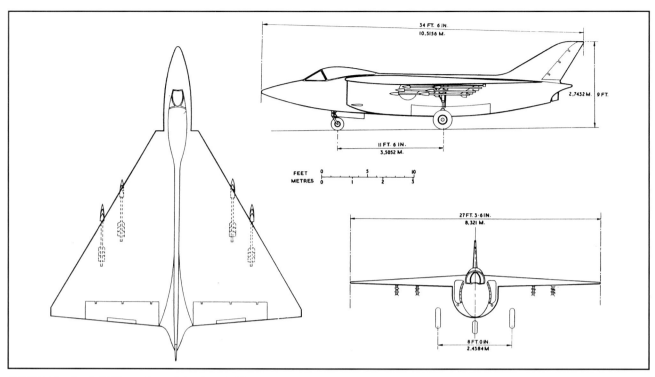

34 FT. 6 IN.
10,5156 M.

2,7432 M. 9 FT.

11 FT. 6 IN.
3,5052 M.

FEET
METRES

0   5   10
0   1   2   3

27 FT. 3·6 IN.
8,321 M.

8 FT. 0 IN.
2,4384 M.

ABOVE The April 1954 version of the Avro 727.

BELOW Model of the Avro 727 in April 1954 form carrying underwing rockets.

Avro 727

When first drawn in January 1954 the Avro 727 was essentially the firm's 726 fighter powered by an 8,000lb (35.6kN) unreheated jet and fitted to carry RPs or two 1,000lb (454kg) bombs (the 726 itself was a supersonic jet-powered version of the Avro 720 rocket fighter). By April, when work began on the NATO study, the aircraft had changed and side intakes and a higher wing had been introduced. Power came from a single Bristol BE.26 Orpheus jet of 3,750lb (16.7kN) sea level static thrust,

BELOW Avro 727 in its final form of September 1954, though it differs little from when it was first designed to NATO's requirements. Here the span was the same at 27ft 3.6in (8.32m) but the length was 35ft 9½in (10.91m).
Avro Heritage Centre

BELOW Impression of the final Avro 727 configuration.
Avro Heritage Centre

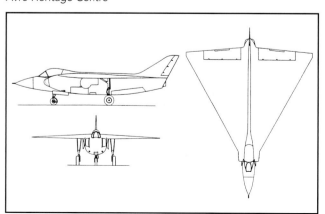

but this figure was to be increased eventually to 4,850lb (21.6kN). Armament was two 30mm Aden cannon or four 0.5in (12.7mm) Browning guns in the lower front fuselage plus twelve 3in (7.6cm) air-to-ground rockets; alternatively, two 500lb (227kg) or 1,000lb (454kg) bombs or two napalm tanks could be carried with the guns. The gross weight came to more than 10,000lb (4,536kg), rather more than the desired 8,000lb (3,629kg), but Avro stated that this would not affect the aircraft's handling or operation from poor surfaces. The extra size meant there was also great development potential within the design.

The 727 used the same wing as the 720 (with minor modifications) and Avro felt that this configuration offered an 'unequalled combination of flying qualities'. A low wing loading, the stiff wing and the large, power-operated elevons gave great manoeuvrability at both high and low speeds while the thin, highly swept wing postponed the effects of compressibility; indeed, no adverse behaviour was expected over the speed range up to Mach 1.0. Except for its fuselage the 727's aerodynamic configuration was the same as the Avro 720's so its behaviour should have been proved before it flew (in fact the Avro 720 was cancelled in 1955 before completion). Its structure consisted mainly of metal honeycomb sandwich.

After delivering its ground ordnance the 727 could switch to its fighter role. With the low engine power rating the maximum level speed in the 'clean' condition was Mach 0.95, with twelve rockets Mach 0.89, the sea level rate of climb with rockets was 6,000ft/min (1,829m/min) and service ceiling 40,000ft (12,192m); with the extra power

these figures became Mach 0.97, Mach 0.92, 9,100ft/min (2,774m/min) and 46,000ft (14,021m) respectively. Internal fuel was 360gal (1,637lit). The 727 was still a live project in September 1954.

BAe Kingston SABA

This project presents something of an oddity since the SABA (Small Agile Battlefield Aircraft) does not really fit into the category of either bomber or fighter. Judged solely on weapon load (AAMs and no bombs) it could be classified as a fighter but, because it was designed to destroy helicopters, tilt-rotor aircraft and ground targets such as tanks and trucks, it perhaps fits more comfortably in a bomber book. It certainly was not intended to tangle with fighters and the concept really needed air superiority to make it work.

By the 1980s a number of new threats had begun to emerge, particularly in Europe, which included heavily armed high-performance helicopters, unmanned air vehicles, tilt-rotor aircraft and very mobile ground forces. It appeared to BAe that no suitable air counter was available to assist thinly spread friendly ground forces threatened by such opposition. The principal needs for an effective battlefield counter-air and ground forces suppression aircraft would include low cost, low vulnerability, very high agility, carefree handling, soft field operation, long endurance and all-weather day and night operation. The key markets were seen to be NATO Europe and the US Army (in the

autumn of 1986 the latter had solicited US industry proposals for an 'Advanced Counter-Air Fighter' optimised for the anti-helicopter role).

SABA possessed outstanding agility and turn performance to allow it to take out enemy attack helicopters. Its rate of turn was intended to be 180° in five seconds, which was considered essential to guarantee a kill opportunity against nap-of-the-earth targets, with a maximum turn radius of 410ft (125m) at combat speeds. Current 'extremely agile' combat aircraft had lower turn rates, which they achieved at high speeds, and a large radius owing to their high wing loadings. The maximum speed was intended to be 460mph to 520mph (741km/h to 837km/h) to enable this aircraft to make a rapid transit to threatened areas at very low altitude while also enhancing its survivability in a dash across the battle zone. SABA could loiter with AAMs and a gun at low level over the battle area for at least four hours, the number of weapons reflecting the fact that its targets usually operated in substantial groups.

This concept was essentially a BAe private venture and it came together in a combined brochure in May 1987. Several configurations were studied. Meeting the agility limits demanded an aircraft with a good lift/drag ratio in the high-lift condition, while a variety of powerplants was considered ranging from propfans (offering exceptional fuel economy and high static thrust) to low-bypass turbofans (which had a superior dash performance).

Avro 727 (at April 1954)

Span	27ft 3.6in (8.32m)
Length	34ft 6in (10.52m)
Gross wing area	approx. 360sq ft (33.5sq m)
Gross weight	10,344lb (4,692kg) with bombs
Powerplant	one Bristol BE.26 Orpheus 3,750lb (16.7kN)
Maximum speed/height	Mach 0.95
Weapon load	See text

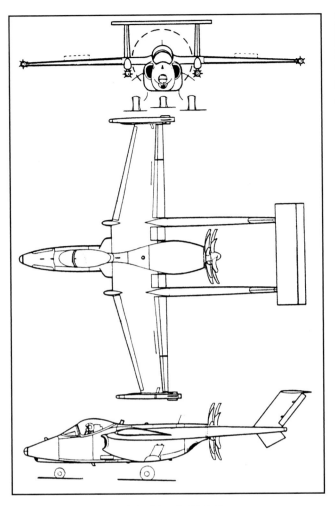

ABOVE **BAe P.1238 (5.87).** *BAe via Chris Farara*

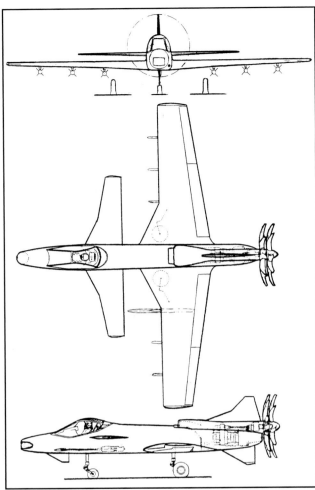

ABOVE **BAe P.1233-1 (5.87).** *BAe via Chris Farara*

BAe P.1238

The P.1238 was a twin-tail boom pusher type intended to be fitted with simple systems and manual control. It was armed with six ASRAAM missiles mounted at the wing tips and on the booms and one fuselage-mounted 25mm cannon. This was the low-technology approach and was powered by a 4,502hp (3,357kW) Avco Lycoming T-55 propfan. Span 36ft (10.97m), length 37ft 11in (11.6m), wing area 200sq ft (18.6sq m), maximum take-off weight 11,098lb (5,034kg).

BAe P.1233-1

P.1233-1 was considered to be a 'state-of-the-art' approach. An aft T-55 pusher propfan could provide directional stability but it would reduce the effectiveness from a rear-mounted rudder, so a nose rudder had been used instead. The canard enhanced the manoeuvrability since the foreplane load required to increase the angle of attack would act in the same direction as the wing lift. Obtaining the best performance from the combination of wing and foreplane, with flaps on the former, and

while avoiding departure in manoeuvres, would be helped by a fly-by-wire control system in pitch. Six ASRAAMs were carried on pylons. Span 36ft (10.97m), length 31ft 4in (9.55m), wing area 219sq ft (20.4sq m), maximum take-off weight 11,000lb (4,989kg).

ABOVE There appears to be only manufacturer's artwork and a model for this version of the SABA, the P.1233-1.

ABOVE **Impression of the P.1233-1 showing the aircraft just after it had attacked and shot down an 'enemy' helicopter.** *BAe via Chris Farara*

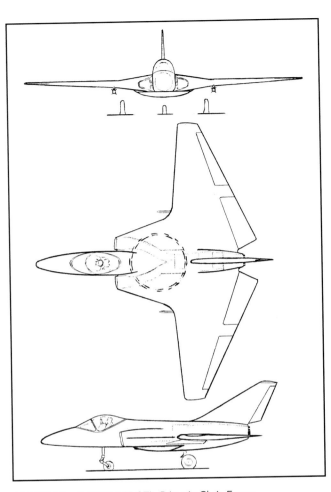

ABOVE **BAe P.1234-1 (5.87).** *BAe via Chris Farara*

BAe P.1234

The P.1234 number covered three separate projects:

P.1234-1

This was a novel idea schemed to investigate the integration of a gun turret into a manoeuvrable aircraft, since the combination of a helmet-mounted sight and a powerful cannon with a wide field of fire offered great flexibility against targets of opportunity. The large turret dictated a blended-body wing and a 5,715lb (25.4kN) thrust Rolls-Royce Adour RT-172-871 powered the aircraft, the low bypass ratio minimising the size of the intake. Two ASRAAMs were carried for self-defence while static instability and active controls were essential to obtain maximum manoeuvring from the large

wing. Span 36ft (10.97m), length 31ft 6in (9.60m), wing area 387sq ft (36.0sq m), maximum take-off weight 12,685lb (5,754kg).

P.1234-2

To compare the constraints of propfan and turbofan layouts the P.1234-2 was drawn with a 7,515lb (33.4kN) Avco Lycoming ALF.502, which essentially used the T-55 as its core. The wing geometry was equivalent to the P.1233-1 and P.1238 and full-span flaperons and spoilers were suggested for low-speed roll control. To maximise the manoeuvrability the P.1234-2 needed static longitudinal instability and active controls, though simple manual controls could be used but with a penalty in performance. The engine

installation meant that the fuselage design was compromised markedly and the intake duct dominated the layout. Armament was the same as the P.1233-1. Span 36ft (10.97m), length 29ft 8in (9.04m), wing area 200sq ft (18.6sq m), maximum take-off weight 12,396lb (5,623kg).

P.1234-3

An alternative to the P.1234-1's gun system shortcomings was a guided hypervelocity missile system. The twin-tube launcher could rotate to allow a launch at any angle to the aircraft's direction of flight, the extraordinary acceleration of a hypervelocity missile preventing any appreciable disturbance; reloads were contained in a feed mechanism in the fuselage and twelve

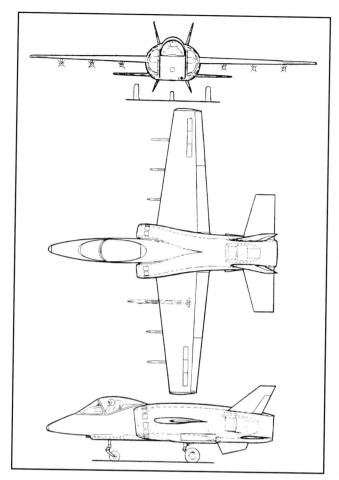

ABOVE BAe P.1234-2 (5.87). *BAe via Chris Farara*

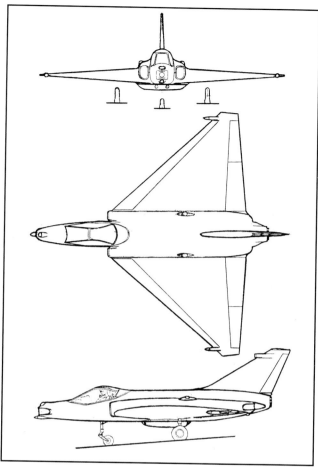

ABOVE BAe P.1234-3 (5.87). *BAe via Chris Farara*

rounds were carried. To gain the full benefit of the missile's destructive power a highly capable acquisition, tracking and engagement system was needed with its optical or infra-red components contained in seeker turrets in the nose and on either side of the rear wing root fairing; further infra-red and radar receivers were placed around the airframe. Combining the launch turret's 360° azimuth coverage with a high rate of roll allowed the pilot to engage targets in any position within range and this freedom reduced the need for extreme aircraft agility. Fly-by-wire was essential and the Adour installation was similar to the P.1234-1. A 12.7mm

machine gun was also available to attack targets for which missiles were unsuitable or wasteful. Span 30ft (9.14m), length 31ft 3in (9.53m), wing area 331sq ft (30.7sq m), maximum take-off weight 12,747lb (5,782kg).

SABA was produced at a time when aircraft companies were seeking new markets and it appeared that the canard propfan P.1233 would meet the requirements. Some felt that the NATO market was potentially massive but as a whole British Aerospace was doubtful about this idea. In the event the SABA did not progress much further than this brochure.

Chapter Thirteen
Strike Trainers

Background to Jaguar: 1962 to 1970

ABOVE Jaguar GR.Mk.1 XZ356 of No. 14 Squadron pictured in 1985. *North West Heritage Group*

In 1960 the RAF held the view that a supersonic advanced trainer would not be necessary as a lead-in to contemporary supersonic fighters such as the English Electric Lightning. The USAF disagreed and adopted the Northrop T-38 as its advanced trainer but the capability of this aircraft to fly at Mach 1.3 made it expensive. Some European air forces felt that costs could be reduced by eliminating the advanced trainer altogether, so that the pupil passed directly from his basic trainer to a dual version of an operational aircraft. But the gap between the two types was really too wide and a two-seat operational aircraft was far more expensive to buy and operate than an advanced trainer. The solution was an advanced trainer

that could also be marketed as a front-line light strike export aircraft for those countries that could not afford a more sophisticated bomber. Several manufacturers examined this idea, which was eventually to lead to one of the RAF's most successful attack aircraft, Jaguar.

Folland Fo.147

In October 1960 Folland proposed, as a successor to its Gnat advanced trainer, a single-engined variable geometry trainer called the Fo.146, and in January 1962 followed it up with an armed version powered by two Rolls-Royce RB.153 engines. Between the two versions came the Fo.147 swing-wing aircraft designed to demonstrate the proposed uses of VG in the air,

which Folland thought needed to be done using an operational aircraft and not merely a 'flying model'. The company had long felt that there was a requirement for a comparatively small supersonic (Mach 2+) aircraft in the interceptor and ground attack class and had proposed the twin-engine Gnat Mk.5 as just such a type.

The brochure suggested that the application of VG to such a simple and inexpensive aircraft as the Gnat Mk.5 could increase the top speed by 50% to Mach 3 and, while retaining the Gnat Mk.1's low-speed performance, could also provide a higher ceiling and greater radius of action and military load. The Fo.147 was based on the Gnat Mk.5 fighter-trainer and would use wing sweep angles between 0° and 25°

ABOVE Model of the Fo.147 with its wings swept back to 70° at the leading edge. *John Nineham Collection*

BELOW Model of the Fo.147 with the wings swept forward (20° at the leading edge) and foreplane deployed. *John Nineham Collection*

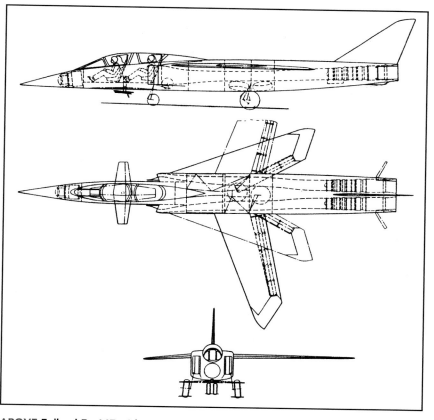

ABOVE Folland Fo.147 with retractable foreplane (4.61). *John Nineham Collection*

Folland Fo.147	
Span	36ft 6in (11.13m) forward, 18ft 0in (5.49m) swept
Length	51ft 0in (15.54m)
Gross wing area	186sq ft (17.3sq m) forward, 195sq ft (18.1sq m) swept
t/c ratio	not given
Gross weight	18,500lb (8,392kg)
Powerplant	two RR RB.153 reheated
Maximum speed/height	Mach 2.2 initially
Weapon load	None

for low speeds (where maximum use could be made of high-lift devices) and angles between 60° to 70° for flight at Mach 2+. Two reheated RB.153s were used, initially limited to Mach 2.2, the internal fuel capacity was 610gal (2,774lit) and the design diving speed 835mph (1,343km/h) EAS. The main

proposal had a rotating retractable foreplane and no tail but an alternative dispensed with the foreplane and introduced tail surfaces and modified wing tips.

Folland Fo.148

This work came together in May 1962 as the Fo.148 advanced supersonic weapons and operations trainer and strike aircraft, which was offered in three forms. Firstly, it could be produced as a primary trainer operating with its VG wings fixed forward and without radar, Stage 2 (which would replace the Gnat trainer) had VG wings but no operational equipment or reheat, and Stage 3 would include the full range of wing sweep, a reheated engine, nose radar and full equipment. Hence, one basic airframe could perform primary, advanced and operational training and also be comfortably afforded by overseas countries (it was the export version that was intended to undertake any attack operations).

Developed from the Gnat Mk.1 trainer, the Fo.148 had a single reheated RB.153-61 bypass engine fitted with a thrust reverser to reduce its landing run. It could fly as a tactical ground attack trainer or interceptor and carry the navigation and fire control equipment used in the TSR.2, Buccaneer or Lightning (all these aircraft used variants of the same Ferranti search and weapon-aiming radar). The VG mechanism comprised a neat fuselage-mounted 'pivot and shoe' arrangement without any retracting parts positioned in front of the wing, which itself had full-span leading-edge flaps and slotted trailing-edge flaps. Stores, including Bullpup ASMs or Red Top AAMs, could be carried on two pylons fixed to the side of the fuselage level with the main wheels. The ceiling was 60,000ft (18,288m) and the estimated radius of action as a trainer was 330nm (611m), as an interceptor 200nm (371km), as a strike aircraft on a high-altitude mission 255nm (473km) and on a low-altitude sortie 180nm (334km). The Fo.148 may have been a

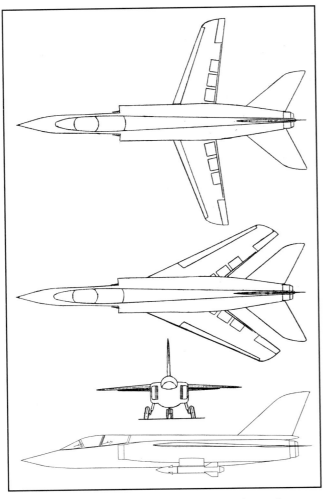

ABOVE Folland Fo.148 (1962). The side view shows the aircraft carrying a Bullpup missile.

TOP AND MIDDLE RIGHT Model of the Fo.148 with its wings in the forward position. *Philip Norman Collection*

ABOVE AND BELOW Model of the Fo.148 with its wings swept back. *Philip Norman Collection*

sensible idea and was expected to fly in 1963/64 but it never happened. This was the last Folland designation to be used after the company had joined Hawker Siddeley in 1960.

Folland Fo.148	
Span	35ft 0in (10.67m) forward
Length	47ft 0in (14.33m)
Gross wing area	?
t/c ratio	?
Gross weight	16,500lb (7,484kg) armed version
Powerplant	one RR RB.153-61 6,720lb (29.9kN), 11,750lb (52.2kN) reheat
Maximum speed/height	Mach 2.05
Weapon load	2,000lb (907kg) of stores including two Bullpup ASMs or Red Top AAMs

BAC (Vickers) Type 593

In April 1964 BAC Weybridge proposed the experimental Type 593 to confirm by flight test the company's claims for, and solve the problems posed by, variable sweep; it would also determine the handling characteristics and drag of a VG aircraft. In the absence of any immediate military or civil requirement the 593 would be the next step forward after the company's many years of VG study and it would keep together and maintain the skills of a design team that had acquired so much VG knowledge. In Chief Designer Alan Clifton's opinion 'much valuable time had already been lost in the argument associated with settling a service type' (in recent years his company had made six variable sweep proposals). Minimum cost was a primary objective and so the 593 would, for example, use current production engines.

This aircraft would be the founder member of, and a scale model for, a family of possible military VG types up to about 80,000lb (36,288kg) in weight. Both twin and single-engined versions were drawn, the bulk of the study and information being devoted to the former (Aircraft A) but performance, weight and cost variations were also given for a single-engine Aircraft B. Both were single-seaters with variable sweep available at wing angles of between 25° and 65°. The structural design was conventional using aluminium and steel and the wing would pivot at the side of the fuselage on a single pin, this simple mounting having already been tested on the Type 999 variable sweep test specimen (a ground-based test apparatus, not an aircraft) but with the difference that all bending moments and shear were reacted by the pin alone. The wings had ailerons at the tip and a split trailing-edge flap, there was an all-moving tail and the undercarriage came essentially from the Folland Gnat.

The powerplant was served by fixed semi-circular intakes with a fixed cone. Type 593A used the American General Electric J85, which was the only production unit available of a size suitable for a twin-engine layout of

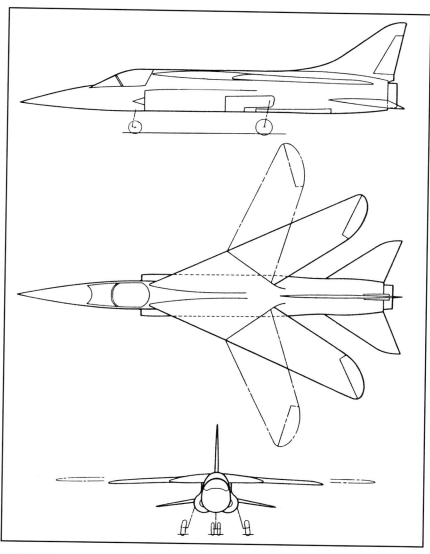

ABOVE Single-engine BAC Type 593 Aircraft B (4.64).

supersonic capability. Aircraft B had an RB.153-61, which at the time was in limited production against a German requirement. The RB.145 had been considered for Aircraft A but this was a heavier engine giving slightly less thrust. Aircraft A was thrust-limited to Mach

1.6 and B structure-limited to Mach 1.75, and their maximum time at Mach 1.6 would be 5.2 and 15.0 minutes respectively. Both carried 3,000lb (1,361kg) of internal fuel and 400lb (181kg) of instrumentation. A first flight would be made in about 1967.

BAC Type 593 Aircraft A	
Span	33ft 5in (10.18m) forward, 22ft 2in (6.76m) swept
Length	37ft 8in (11.48m)
Gross wing area	160sq ft (14.9sq m) not including fixed forewing
t/c ratio	10%
Gross weight	11,140lb (5,053kg)
Powerplant	two Gen. Elec. J85-GE-13 8,140lb (36.2kN) reheat
Maximum speed/height	Mach 1.6
Weapon load	None

BAC Type 593 Aircraft B	
Span	35ft 7in (10.85m) forward, 23ft 7in (7.19m) swept
Length	40ft 4in (12.29m)
Gross wing area	180sq ft (16.7sq m) not including fixed forewing
t/c ratio	10%
Gross weight	12,490lb (5,665kg)
Powerplant	one RR RB.153-61 11,750lb (52.2kN) reheat
Maximum speed/height	Mach 1.75
Weapon load	None

At the same time the Weybridge Military Project Office was helping BAC Warton's Project Office with AST.362 (below). Three families of aircraft were being studied to this requirement and they embraced numerous designs fitted with and without reheat:

a). Variable sweep aircraft with two engines.

b). Variable sweep aircraft with a single engine.

c). Fixed-wing aircraft with one and two engines.

Item b) used an RB.168 and was the variant examined by Weybridge. This work was covered by Warton's P.45 designation (which appears to have overtaken the Type 593) and picks up the story of British VG development left off in Chapter Nine.

AST.362

In June 1963 the Air Staff began studying a new advanced pilot trainer to AST.362 to replace the Gnat/Hunter sequence. This would be used for preliminary conversion training and squadron continuation training along with a secondary minor operational role. By the end of the year the final draft was specifying a target date of 1975, but then the document was put on hold after a similar requirement appeared in France in February 1964. The British and French Staffs now discussed their respective needs and in March a combined Anglo–French provisional requirement was produced and issued by the MoA to British industry. This noted that the Royal Navy, RAF and French Air Force needed a dual-purpose, advanced two-seat pilot training/light strike aircraft. Although the French were more interested in the operational aspects of the aircraft when British interest centred on the training side, the two requirements could be compatible. A joint project could lead to material savings in cost and effort in both countries while providing a more useful aircraft all-round, which might also prove attractive to other air forces.

In-depth discussions over a possible joint project began two months later. Early problems centred on a difference in weight, the French industry's assessment of an aeroplane to meet its home requirements only coming out much lighter than the MoA's figure for a combined type. The French Air Staff primarily required fairly large numbers of an inexpensive light tactical strike aircraft with a first-class, low-level capability but, although secondary in importance, its advanced pilot and crew trainer had to be the first version delivered (by 1970). The British side wanted its advanced trainer to be supersonic at altitude but also suitable for low-level training; a strike/reconnaissance version was a secondary requirement.

During the summer of 1964 studies using AST.362 as a basis were undertaken by BAC and HSA that drew on previous trainer proposals and the two firm's research into variable sweep and vectored thrust respectively. The aircraft assessed were two twin-engine versions of BAC Warton's P.45, one with a VG wing, the other with a delta wing and elevon tailplane derived aerodynamically from TSR.2 (but with the wing loading reduced to suit the AST), and then the supersonic single-engine Hawker Siddeley HS.1170B with deflected thrust and plenum chamber burning (PCB).

BAC (English Electric) P.45

The wings of the VG version of the P.45 pivoted about vertical hinge-pins built into the fuselage sides and could be swept from 25° for economic subsonic cruise and good airfield performance back to 68° for high-altitude supersonic

BELOW Model of one version of the BAC P.45. *BAE SYSTEMS*

flight and high subsonic flight near the ground. Full-span Fowler flaps and leading-edge slats were incorporated to take full advantage of the low sweep angle during take-off and landing. An all-moving tailplane was fitted, fuel was housed in the wing and fuselage and the intakes were of a fixed ramp, single wedge type; reheat would be used for take-off and supersonic flight only. Except for the wing, at this stage the non-VG version was virtually identical and used the same engine (the small Rolls-Royce RB.172 bypass unit, which also permitted versions with twin power units to be drawn). Part-span blown flaps were fitted for high lift but the fixed 58° sweep wing carried no controls.

BAC had recognised that the UK was now behind the USA (with its F-111) in the practical development of the variable sweep technique first proposed in Britain. Hence, the P.45 brochure advocated the immediate design and construction of prototypes of this design and a full experimental flight trials programme. The project was seen as a multi-role VG aircraft capable of acting as an advanced trainer, an air defence fighter (with particular application for overseas duties) and a light strike and reconnaissance aircraft. Low cost was a big attraction but the company's investigations had also shown that this type could be very effective in the air-to-air role when compared to air defence systems of much greater maximum weights. The normal gross weight was about half that of the Type 583 strike fighter and BAC felt that the P.45 offered great export potential.

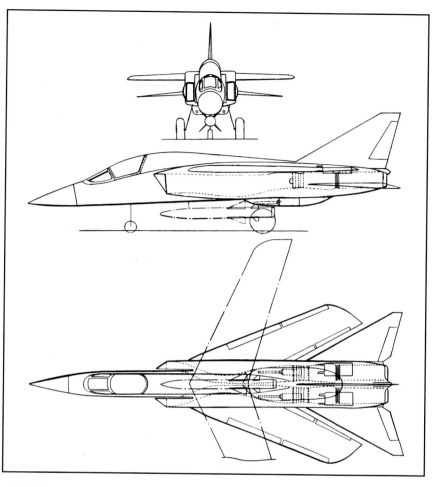

ABOVE Drawing of the twin-engine BAC P.45 taken from the brochure showing the type in strike aircraft mode (6.64). *North West Heritage Group*

Hawker Siddeley HS.1179 and HS.1170B

The HS.1170B resembled the P.1154 and started life as the P.1163 with a single Rolls-Royce RB.163 and PCB. Developed into the HS.1170 by Kingston and now with a vectored thrust Bristol BS.94/5 and PCB, it was proposed in 1964 as a subsonic aircraft to a German nuclear strike fighter requirement called VAK.191, which was intended to replace the Fiat G.91. The HS.1170 would have been a joint programme with Focke-Wulf with the aircraft operating purely in the VTOL mode. It would have flown in 1966 and entered service in 1969 but it was never built and instead the German manufacturer produced and flew its FW 1262 design as the VAK.191B.

The HS.1170B was a larger strike/trainer version proposed to AST.362 in May 1964 by HSA (Folland) at Hamble. The fixed wing had 40° leading-edge sweepback, full-span slotted flaps and leading-edge slats for

Brochure BAC P.45 (VG)

Span	35ft 0in (10.67m) forward, 21ft 0in (6.40m) swept
Length	50ft 0in (15.24m)
Gross wing area	200sq ft (19.6sq m) forward, 240sq ft (22.3sq m) swept
t/c ratio	12% forward, 5.75% swept
Gross weight	20,500lb (9,299kg)
Powerplant	two RR RB.172-49R 7,710lb (34.3kN), 13,050lb (58.0kN) reheat
Maximum speed/height	Mach 1.1 at sea level, Mach 2.2 at 36,000ft (10,973m)
Weapon load	ASMs and bombs

Brochure BAC P.45 (fixed wing)

Span	25ft 0in (7.62m)
Length	50ft 0in (15.24m)
Gross wing area	300sq ft (27.9sq m)
t/c ratio	4%
Gross weight	20,000lb (9,072kg)
Powerplant	two RR RB.172-49R 7,710lb (34.3kN), 13,050lb (58.0kN) reheat
Maximum speed/height	Mach 1.1 at sea level, Mach 2.2 at 36,000ft (10,973m)
Weapon load	ASMs and bombs

Hawker Siddeley HS.1170B	
Span	25ft 0in (7.62m)
Length	50ft 0in (15.24m)
Gross wing area	200sq ft (18.6sq m)
t/c ratio	6%
Gross weight	20,850lb (9,458kg)
Powerplant	one Bristol Siddeley BS.94/5 13,500lb (60.0kN), 19,000lb (84.4kN) PCB
Maximum speed/height	Mach 1.1 at sea level, Mach 1.7 at 36,000ft (10,973m)
Weapon load	ASMs and bombs

high lift, and conventional ailerons. The all-moving tail had a similar planform to the wing and the usual P.1127-style bicycle undercarriage was employed with outriggers. A pitot type intake located either side of the fuselage just ahead of the wing was used since the aircraft's subsonic performance did not require anything more sophisticated. Fuel was accommodated in integral wing and fuselage tanks. HS.1170B's engine thrust was adequate for the AST's take-off requirement but its relatively low 'reheat' (PCB) temperature meant that its supersonic performance was less than that of either variant of the P.45.

These projects were reviewed by the Ministry's A. T. Jarrett and K. W. Clark on 24 September 1964. Each project came in trainer and strike versions that shared identical airframes and engines,

the only difference being the additional equipment and armament required for the strike role installed in place of the trainer's rear cockpit. The quoted data covers the strike variants, all of which had a 270nm (500km) radius of action, and each of the trainers would have been over 2,100lb (953kg) lighter. Jarrett and Clark noted that variable sweep granted the ability to vary the handling characteristics of the aircraft in step with a pupil's progress from the basic to the final operational trainer, thereby giving the ability to cover a wider range in the training programme than present advanced trainers. Each design had five weapon stations, four under the wings and one under the fuselage on the fixed-wing types, two under the moving wings and three under the fuselage for the VG P.45; sea level top speed for each design when carrying five stores was about Mach 0.7.

The authors concluded that in terms of weight and general performance there was little difference between these projects, so an AST.362 strike aircraft would weigh in at about 20,000lb (9,072kg) and the advanced trainer at 18,000lb (8,165kg). The two roles seemed fairly compatible within one airframe. More specifically the VG P.45, at an extra cost of some 9%, offered advantages in performance and greater flexibility that should increase its export potential. The

vectored thrust HS.1170B did not offer enough advantages in this context to offset its greater cost and the absence of engine-out safety. All the trainer versions could be in service in 1970, the VG striker in 1972 and the others in 1971.

Speaking recently to ex-Warton staff, there are strong opinions regarding variable sweep wings. Some felt that Barnes Wallis' Swallow concept was not good and essentially wasted effort. It could only have been made to work using fly-by-wire (FBW), a system first perfected more than twenty years later. Many published works have criticised the abandonment of the Swallow and the decision not to build the P.45, but the latter was too small for a VG wing, the penalties for using VG far outweighing its benefits. The main problem was the extra weight of a VG wing's pivot and actuating assemblies and the space that this mechanism absorbed, particularly if the pivot was housed in the fuselage.

The pivot itself was heavy while the wing needed a slot in the fuselage side into which it could fit when fully swept, and this slot used up valuable space. The result was that VG wings forced a trade between weight and space against aerodynamic advantage – the benefits were that the same aircraft could fly at high supersonic speed (Mach 1.5+) and yet operate from short strips. As the sweep angle decreased it effectively thickened the wing and reduced the stalling speed so that the aircraft could take off and land at much slower airspeeds. There was no point in fitting VG for a Mach 1.1 maximum speed because this could be achieved in other ways; serious supersonic speed was the key. VG was fashionable in the 1960s but it only really proved practical and useful for an aircraft of Tornado size upwards (see Chapter Fourteen). And the AA-107 described shortly would have been too small for VG.

Hawker (Siddeley) HS.1173

Alongside the HS.1170B Hawker Siddeley Hamble also proposed its HS.1171 VG project to AST.362 which

BELOW Hawker Siddeley HS.1173 (1964/65).

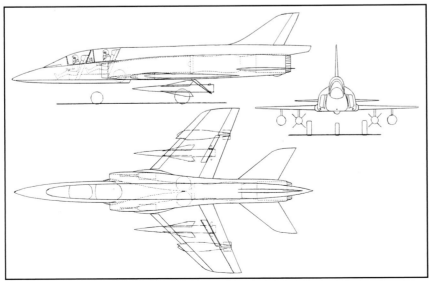

weighed about 20,000lb (9,072kg) and had two Rolls-Royce RB.172 engines. Another private proposal was Kingston's HS.1173. Kingston was very interested in the idea of a supersonic Hawker Hunter/de Havilland Vampire replacement that was affordable, flexible and quite the opposite of the P.1154. HS.1173 was a conventional Mach 2 design but it had no load-carrying structure below the cockpit floor. A large internal fuel volume was thought to be essential if the aircraft was to have a worthwhile supersonic endurance, and if the four underwing pylon stations were to be left free for ordnance. To this end the normal dorsal spine had been enlarged to form a tank running from cabin to fin that contained more than half the internal fuel. Fuel was also housed around the intake ducts and the single-seater had an additional tank in the front fuselage that increased the capacity from 580gal (2,637lit) to 700gal (3,183lit).

Double-slotted area-increasing flaps were provided together with a leading edge that drooped in two sections. Due to the large span of the trailing-edge flaps the ailerons were relatively small and at high speeds these would be augmented by spoilers. Rectangular two-shock intakes had been chosen and the HS.1173 carried twin 30mm cannon beneath these solely for ground attack. Two ASMs or 1,000lb (454kg) bombs were carried on the inner underwing pylons and two 100gal (455lit) drop tanks on the outer pylons. As a single-seat strike aircraft in 'clean' condition (internal fuel plus loaded cannon) the HS.1173 weighed 16,250lb (7,371kg), while as an advanced trainer the 'clean'

weight was 15,000lb (6,804kg). The range with external tanks and two 1,000lb (454kg) bombs was given as 250nm (463km) at Mach 0.85. This study was terminated in March 1965.

SEPECAT Jaguar

By September 1964 the British/French weight discrepancy had narrowed and on 5 November Naval and Air Staff Requirement (NASR) 362 for an advanced trainer was endorsed by the British Operational Requirements Committee as the basis for a joint study. High-level staff discussions with the French resumed on 5 February 1965 and late in the month agreement was reached for HMG and the French Government to co-operate in developing a fixed-wing supersonic strike trainer, and to collaborate on other VG studies. On 26 March it was confirmed that an advanced training aircraft that would meet both countries' needs could not be developed economically from a VG operational aircraft. Separate discussions on VG aircraft now followed that were to crystallise into the Anglo–French Variable Geometry Aircraft described in Chapter Fourteen, but VG for the trainer was dead.

France's original requirement had been for an essentially simple aircraft called the ECAT (*Ecole et d'Appui Tactique*) and the Breguet Br 121, owing much to its manufacturer's earlier Br 1001 Taon prototype, was favoured in a competition that included the Potez P.92 and Dassault Cavalier. The protocol covering Anglo–French co-operation on the strike/trainer (and other projects) was agreed on 17 May 1965 when it was announced that an MoU had been signed between Britain and France for the mutual development of a trainer and ground attack aircraft. BAC and Rolls-Royce were nominated as the British contractors.

Nine days later a combined MoD/MoA/BAC team visited Villacoublay for a presentation on Breguet's Br 121. The project was to be evaluated to see if it could meet the joint requirement and in mid-September cockpit mock-ups of the 121's basic design and an improved droop nose version were examined at Warton by RAF/RN specialists and French representatives. A nose with a downward view of 8.5° was accepted by both parties and discussions looked at alternative engines before the company's proposals

Hawker Siddeley HS.1173	
Span	25ft 0in (7.62m)
Length	45ft 0in (13.72m)
Gross wing area	210sq ft (19.5sq m)
t/c ratio	6% root, 4% tip
Gross weight	20,250lb (9,185kg)
Powerplant	one RR RB.172-57AR 13,000lb (57.8kN) reheat
Maximum speed/height	Mach 1.4 at sea level, Mach 2.4 at 36,000ft (10,973m)
Weapon load	two 30mm cannon; two 1,000lb (454kg) bombs or two ASM

BELOW Breguet Br 121 (1965).

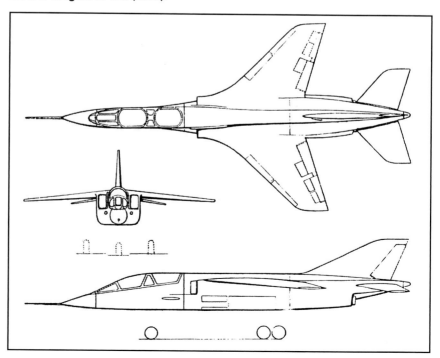

ABOVE Manufacturer's model of the Jaguar strike aircraft from about 1967.

BELOW The second British Jaguar S strike prototype XW563 releases a bomb during a test flight.
North West Heritage Group

ABOVE **Group photo showing British single-seat Jaguar S/GR.Mk.1 and two-seat Jaguar B/T.Mk.2 prototypes. The aircraft right front is XW560.** *North West Heritage Group*

and provisional specification were completed on 3 December 1965. A wing thickness redesign would be needed to ensure a high-altitude supersonic performance of Mach 1.3 in a 1.5g turn and this was agreed in January 1966. (Essentially BAC's part in the programme was to design and fit a supersonic wing to the Br 121.)

In January 1966 there were indications that a British tactical version might also now be required. The prototype specification was finalised in March and the requirement for a British tactical version was endorsed on 19 May. By now the Royal Navy had withdrawn so the requirement became Air Staff Requirement ASR.362 with the 'N' omitted. The aircraft was named Jaguar in June 1966 and was to be built by joint BAC/Breguet organisation called SEPECAT (Société Européenne de Production de l'Avion ECAT). During August good progress was made in harmonising the layouts of all the versions and the specification for the British S attack prototype was agreed in February 1967.

The versions ordered were the French Jaguar E trainer, which became the first prototype to fly on 8 September 1968, the French tactical support Jaguar A flown on 23 March 1969, the British tactical support Jaguar S which first flew on 12 October 1969 (and became the GR.Mk.1 in RAF service), and the

British Jaguar B trainer (T.Mk.2) flown on 30 August 1971. Their differences came mainly in equipment but a variant for the French Navy called the Jaguar M was abandoned in 1973 having flown in 1969. The engine used in these aircraft was the Rolls-Royce/Turboméca Adour, which was based on and developed from the RB.172 and had run for the first time on 10 May 1967.

On 19 May 1970 VCAS noted that the RAF's requirement for Jaguar S was currently ninety-six aircraft, to replace seventy McDonnell Douglas Phantom FGR.Mk.2s in the ground attack and reconnaissance roles in 1974/5. The total buy of trainers was put at 130. The Air Staff had long been aware that the number of aircraft available for close support was inadequate and well below that necessary to meet the task. And recent changes to NATO strategy had accentuated this shortage (this was the switch to Flexible Response, which required NATO forces to continue to maintain a deterrent posture and yet, at the same time, put more emphasis on conventional forces to avoid early recourse to nuclear weapons). At the same time, it had become increasingly evident that introducing Jaguar to the Advanced Flying School would increase the costs of flying training very substantially. Clearly the

proportion of single-seat operational to two-seat trainer Jaguars had to be altered, with a less sophisticated and much cheaper aircraft found for advanced training.

As a result the RAF eventually received 165 GR.Mk.1s and 35 two-seat conversion aircraft (deliveries began in 1973) and the original need for an advanced trainer was met by the Hawker Siddeley HS.1182 Hawk. So by a roundabout method, starting with a trainer requirement, the RAF acquired an outstanding attack machine. Another 200 were bought by France, many more Jaguar Internationals built by BAC were sold overseas and a licence build was established in India.

SEPECAT Jaguar GR.Mk.1	
Span	28ft 6in (8.69m)
Length	55ft 2½in (16.83m) with probe
Gross wing area	260.3sq ft (24.2sq m)
t/c ratio	?
Gross weight	c. 34,000lb (15,422kg)
Powerplant	two RR/Turboméca Adour 102 5,115lb (22.7kN), 7,305lb (32.5kN) reheat
Maximum speed/height	Mach 1.1 839mph (1,351km/h) at sea level, Mach 1.6 1,056mph (1,699km/h) at 36,000ft (10,973m)
Weapon load	two 30mm Aden cannon, two AAMs, 10,000lb (4,536kg) of stores including bombs, ASMs & RPs

ABOVE Model of the Commonwealth Aircraft/BAC AA-107 strike trainer (9.68). *North West Heritage Group*

BELOW The fixed-wing BAC P.61 F3 design (6.70).
North West Heritage Group

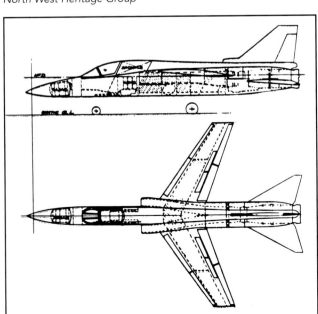

BELOW VG wing BAC P.61 V3 (6.70).
North West Heritage Group

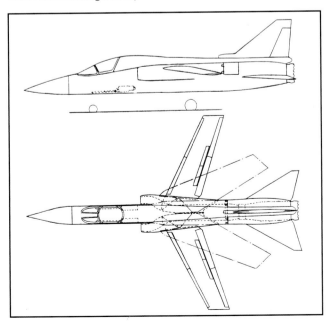

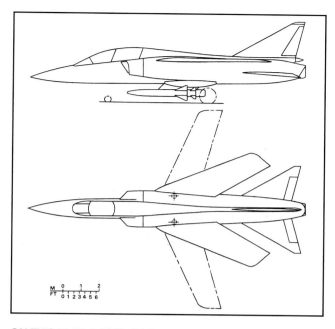

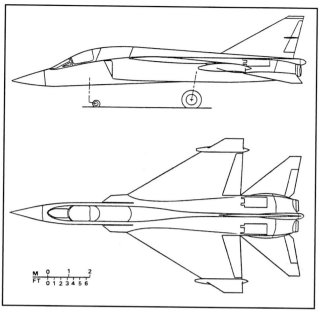

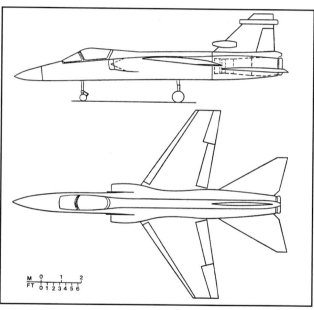

ON THIS PAGE A 1970s BAC Warton report describing its work to the AST.403 fighter requirements began with a short review of earlier studies. This included these drawings, which it is assumed show the P.45 and PANNAP designs in later forms.

AA-107 and BAC P.60 and P.61

In September 1968 a collaborative supersonic VG strike trainer design study was undertaken by Commonwealth Aircraft of Australia and BAC Warton with the designation (Anglo–Australian) AA-107. This advanced trainer, with an appreciable close support capability, was to be powered by one reheated Adour engine and possess a moderate supersonic performance of the order of Mach 1.45. There was some interest but the RAAF reached the same conclusion as did the RAF in that its specialised training aircraft would not need supersonic capability. With no overseas orders the project died in 1970, but from it BAC acquired background knowledge on the development of, and the markets for, a small relatively simple sub-Jaguar type of aircraft with two seats, adequate avionics for close support, a reheated engine and a reasonable payload.

The AA-107 work was eventually split into two distinct lines of study. One was the P.59/P.62 series of trainer designs to RAF requirements, the other

ABOVE LEFT Arrangement of the BAC P.45 with VG wing and RR Spey engine. *North West Heritage Group*

ABOVE RIGHT The BAC P.45 with a fixed wing and two Spey engines. *North West Heritage Group*

ABOVE The PANNAP aircraft powered by an RB.199 engine. *North West Heritage Group*

investigated both fixed and variable sweep wings for air superiority and close air support missions using the Adour engine and also an advanced engine proposal which eventually became the RB.199. These studies were reported in 1970 under the heading of 'The BAC 107 Family'. This work then provided the nucleus for further studies under the P.61 designation made in association with Messerschmitt-Bolkow-Blohm [MBB] and Aeritalia (i.e. Panavia, the joint company

responsible for the MRCA Tornado) which prompted the name PANNAP (for Panavia New Aircraft Project). In some respects this was a minor study to keep Panavia's design staff at work. Considerable emphasis was placed on a good thrust/weight ratio and combat manoeuvrability, and the requirements for air superiority as distinct from battlefield interdictor were to be catered for by a common airframe fitted with different weapons and equipment.

The resulting family of designs

within the P.60 and P.61 series had a definite geometric resemblance but the more combat-capable P.61 series powered by the 'advanced engine' (the RB.199) required a larger duct and reheat pipe and a deeper fuselage to accommodate the increased mass flow. The range encompassed trainers through close support to machines with a performance sufficient to be classified as air superiority and interceptor. The family was divided into two branches, one with a thin fixed 35° sweep wing, the other pivoted at the fuselage side for VG between 27° and 69°; the latter also needed a large slot in the fuselage which had to be sealed at all conditions of wing sweep. Both groups shared a very similar fuselage, full-span flaps and slats on the wing, spoilers and an all-moving differential tail, although the fixed wing offered a simpler proposition. External stores were mounted tangentially under the fuselage and on wing pylons and fuel was carried in the centre fuselage and, in some cases, in the wing. Switching from the Adour to a RB.199 would add structural and mechanical complication so the fixed wing was intended to retain around the same level of airfield, range and supersonic performance, but to compensate it removed the complexity of the VG wing. By June 1970 the two groups comprised the following, all of which looked similar except for their wing:

P.60 F1 – A basic/advanced trainer powered by an unreheated Adour.

P.60 F2 – A close support aircraft with advanced/applied trainer capability powered by a reheated Adour. One DEFA cannon was mounted under the second cockpit, external stores could be carried on wing pylons (two per wing) and on four hardpoints under the fuselage (two rows of two), while another centre fuselage store point would normally be used for an external tank. The internal fuel in wing and fuselage tanks totalled 3,200lb (1,452kg).

P.61 F1 – Advanced/applied trainer with close support capability powered by one unreheated RB.199. The DEFA cannon and stores arrangement were identical to the P.60 F2 but the weapon pylons would not be used in the trainer role. Internal fuel 3,750lb (1,701kg).

P.61 F2 – Close support aircraft near identical to the P.61 F1 but with a reheated RB.199.

P.61 F3 – Interceptor/close support/air superiority aircraft identical in layout to the P.61 F2 but with the rear cockpit replaced by avionics and gun ammunition, leaving the nose free for a search radar. Two DEFA cannon were mounted under the 'rear' cockpit position. At a take-off weight of 15,000lb (6,804kg), both the P.61 F2 and P.61 F3 could reach 30,000ft (9,144m) in 1.4 minutes and had a low-level and high-level range of 690nm (1,278km) and 1,500nm (2,778km) respectively. Their ceiling was 57,000ft (17,374m).

P.60 V1 – A basic/advanced trainer powered by an unreheated Adour with the VG wing modified over the inboard section to convert it to a fixed wing.

P.60 V2 – Advanced/applied trainer with close support facility, reheated Adour and wing and centre fuselage identical with the P.60 V1. Armament as per P.60 F2, internal fuel 3,588lb (1,628kg).

P.60 V3 – The aircraft was previously the AA-107 and was identical to the P.60 V2 except that the wing was now VG pivoted, which meant that the wing pylons must now swivel. Internal fuel 3,500lb (1,588kg).

P.61 V1 – This was the VG version of the P.61 F1 trainer, internal fuel 3,500lb (1,588kg).

P.61 V2 – Close support aircraft near identical to the P.61 V1 but with a reheated RB.199.

P.61 V3 – Interceptor/close support/air superiority aircraft identical in layout to the P.61 V2 and which was the VG version of the P.61 F3.

These designs essentially formed a study to see what could be done within the concept of an aircraft family but they also provided a useful comparison to the MRCA (Chapter Fourteen). The fixed-wing P.61 F3 with a single RB.199 weighed in at 15,109lb (6,853kg) when the MRCA was estimated to be 35,277lb (16,002kg), but its simple pitot intake still allowed a maximum Mach 1.85 and a ceiling of 57,000ft (17,374m). There was probably little likelihood that a P.60/P.61 type of aircraft would ever have been built.

BAC P.61 F3	
Span	26ft 10in (8.18m)
Length	40ft 0in (12.19m)
Gross wing area	160sq ft (14.9sq m)
t/c ratio	5%
Gross weight	15,109lb (6,853kg), 17,745lb (8,049kg) with Taildog missiles
Powerplant	one RR RB.199 8,394lb (37.3kN), 14,997lb (66.6kN) reheat
Maximum speed/height	Clean Mach 1.85 at 36,000ft (10,973m); with six AAM Mach 1.64 at 36,000ft (10,973m)
Weapon load	two 30mm DEFA cannon, eight pylons for bombs, RPs, ASMs and AAMs

BAC P.61 V3	
Span	28ft 0in (8.53m) forward, 16ft 6in (5.03m) swept
Length	40ft 0in (12.19m)
Gross wing area	not given
t/c ratio	10%
Gross weight	15,428lb (6,998kg)
Powerplant	one RR RB.199 8,394lb (37.3kN), 14,997lb (66.6kN) reheat
Maximum speed/height	Clean with 69° sweep Mach 1.95 at 36,000ft (10,973m)
Weapon load	two 30mm DEFA cannon, eight pylons for bombs, RPs, ASMs and AAMs

Chapter Fourteen
A Destructive Localised Storm

Background to Tornado: 1964 to 1982

ABOVE Panavia Tornado of No. 15 Squadron RAF pictured in 1987. *North West Heritage Group*

After the cancellation of TSR.2 (Chapter Eight) the intention was to replace this aeroplane with two different strike aircraft types, the American F-111K and a collaborative project to go with it called the Anglo–French Variable Geometry Aircraft, or AFVG. The latter would also help Great Britain to retain its capability to develop advanced combat aircraft and, like the Jaguar, it was to be an Anglo–French product, although here BAC would be in company with Dassault rather than Breguet. Eventually this too was cancelled and replaced by a programme that was to give the RAF the Tornado, a bomber that since 1990 has been to war on numerous occasions.

Anglo–French Variable Geometry Aircraft (AFVG)

Parametric studies made during 1964/65 for an interceptor with strike capability concluded that a requirement could be met by a VG aircraft weighing about 40,000lb (18,144kg). The Anglo–French discussions of February to April 1965 (see Chapter Thirteen) also embraced possible VG projects and when the MoU was signed on 17 May it included the decision to collaborate on a VG aircraft. The UK Air Staff's main interest was for an interceptor to replace the EE Lightning but the RAF, Royal Navy, French Air Force and French Navy were all interested in this AFVG project, the French specifically for intercept and strike. It would use SNECMA/Bristol Siddeley M.45G bypass engines and on 13 July Specification 260 and ASR.388 were issued to define the British version. The documents requested a 2,500lb (1,134kg) weapon load, a maximum 920mph (1,480km/h) at sea level and Mach 2.5 at altitude, a sustained ceiling of 60,000ft (18,288m), 400nm (741km) radius of action in the strike/reconnaissance role, a ferry range of 3,500nm (6,482km) and a three-hour Combat Air Patrol.

British AFVG would be an aircraft optimised for conventional strike/reconnaissance operations to complement the General Dynamics F-111K when the V-bombers were phased out from 1975; any resultant interceptor capability was considered incidental and secondary.

In March 1966 the RB.153 was proposed as an alternative to M.45G and in May ministers noted that both countries needed the aircraft by 1974, although the timescale for beginning the prototype had slipped. At this time the datum aircraft had semi-circular intakes with conical centre-bodies, full-span leading-edge slats and double-slotted extending trailing-edge flaps, spoilers for low-speed flight and all-moving tailerons (where both sides of the tail were used as primary control surfaces in both pitch and roll). The wings pivoted on bearings inside the fuselage and carried 330gal (1,500lit) of internal fuel, while another 990gal (4,501lit) was housed in the fuselage and 55gal (250lit) in the fin. One French 2,500lb (1,134kg) 'special (nuclear) weapon' could be carried below and partly within the fuselage and there were three underfuselage air-to-air missile stations semi-recessed to reduce drag. The datum AFVG could take four 1,000lb (454kg) bombs under the fuselage and still retain its supersonic performance, but larger loads under both fuselage and wings (up to eighteen 1,000lb/454kg bombs) would keep the maximum speed subsonic; in this full load condition the aircraft's wings would stay in the forward position. Two 30mm cannon could be loaded into the fuselage aft of the intake by removing the auxiliary fuel tanks.

For the strike role a forward-looking radar with an 800mm to 900mm dish would be used for terrain following, ground mapping and radar ranging and an inertial platform (possibly Doppler monitored) would also be carried. The design dive speed with wings swept was 920mph (1,480km/h) Mach 2.3 for short periods, and with the wings forward 518mph (834km/h)

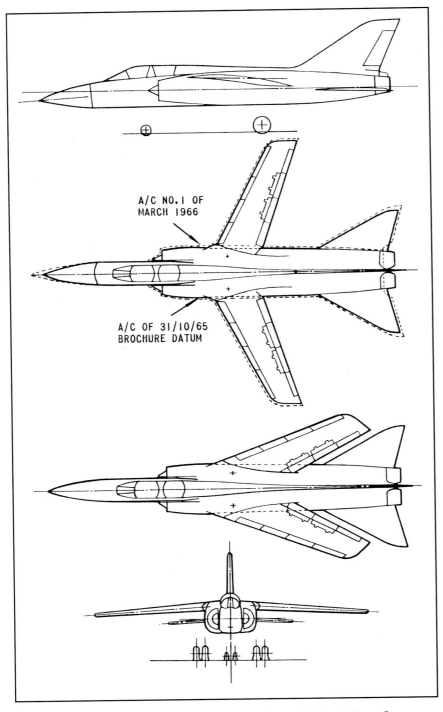

ABOVE Drawing showing the AFVG datum aircraft. *North West Heritage Group*

A feasibility study began on 1 August 1965 and quickly revealed some disappointing features with the M.45G, which meant some critical aspects of the performance had to be based on a smaller, hypothetical engine. Designs were studied at gross weights of 30,000lb, 40,000lb and 50,000lb (13,608kg, 18,144kg and 22,680kg) and at 16,000lb (7,258kg) for the French Navy's carriers. From November much of the work centred on securing a better engine/airframe match within the French aircraft carrier limits but, as an outcome of the February 1966 Defence Review that ended Britain's new large carrier programme, RN interest in the AFVG ceased. Now the

RIGHT Model of the AFVG datum aircraft (3.66).
North West Heritage Group

Mach 0.8. Time to climb to Mach 2.2 at 50,000ft (15,240m) with 1,500lb (680kg) of missiles was 4.95 minutes (the requirement was 5 minutes), acceleration from Mach 0.7 to 2.2 at 36,090ft (11,000m) was 2.25 minutes, ferry range 3,780nm (7,000km), land-based strike range (four 1,000lb/454kg bombs released) was 785nm (1,454km), or 1,220nm (2,260km) with wing tanks, and supersonic radius of action 360nm (667km). The first prototype flight was to be made during the first half of 1968 and a detailed AFVG mock-up was built at Warton.

Due to the apparent cost of the datum AFVG studies were requested in July 1966 for alternatives, but a smaller design demonstrated that a significant reduction in unit cost could only be achieved by an aircraft with insufficient performance to meet the ASR, while a single-engine type offered only a small cost saving. Neither was acceptable and it was agreed by Anglo–French ministers on 7 November that only the datum aircraft merited further study. In September 1968 it had been recommended that should France withdraw a UK variable geometry aircraft should continue as a fallback. The French still had to decide on their

ABOVE Further views of the AFVG model showing the wings set at their extreme limits of sweep. *BAE SYSTEMS*
BELOW Well-known photo of the AFVG mock-up. *North West Heritage Group*

budget before AFVG's future could be clarified but they rejected the RB.153, insisting on the performance being met by one of the M.45 family. However, the M.45G9 (an RB.172 derivative) showed an imbalance between the strike and air defence roles so a further type, the M.45G10, was proposed by the engine manufacturers.

A revised timetable (airframe Project Study to start 1 April 1967, completed 30 September and evaluated by the end of December so that the Prototype Stage could begin on 1 January 1968) was accepted by ministers on 16 January 1967. Aircraft with alternative versions of the M.45 were now examined but by March 1967 the latest estimates indicated that an initial in-service date, with limited CA Release, could not be expected before January 1975. On 8 May the French Air Staff target was confirmed, which requested a maximum speed at altitude of Mach 2.2 and a low-level strike radius of 700km (435 miles) on internal fuel. Both countries agreed to go ahead with a Project Study to meet these limits and BAC would lead on the

AFVG (Datum 3.66)	
Span	42ft 8in (13.01m) forward, 23ft 3½in (7.10m) swept
Length	53ft 10in (16.41m)
Gross wing area	198sq ft (18.4sq m) forward (net), 169.6sq ft (15.8sq m) swept (net)
t/c ratio	12% forward, 5.7% swept
Gross weight	38,107lb (17,285kg)
Powerplant	two 'Assumed' jet engines 6,940lb (30.8kN), 12,120lb (53.9kN) reheat
Maximum speed/height	Mach 2.2 at height
Weapon load	two 30mm cannon, three AAMs, one nuclear weapon, eighteen 1,000lb (454kg) bombs or two (four ?) Martel missiles

airframe, SNECMA on the engine, but a 50/50 principle was to be maintained. The M.45G10 engine was now accepted by both countries.

However, when the Conseil de Defense met on 15 and 16 June 1967 the French Government's ratification of the ministers' agreement of 8 May was not given and further progress now depended on the political outcome (as a consequence the UK's fallback position was re-examined). On 29 June

1967 the French withdrew from the joint AFVG project for 'financial' reasons, French Defence Minister Pierre Messmer notifying UK Defence Secretary Denis Healey of the decision even though both countries had at last successfully reconciled their differing operational requirements into the one aircraft. In fact, France had in general been very lukewarm towards the AFVG, while Dassault was hostile and had even developed a VG aircraft of its own that it called the Mirage G. No secret was made of the G's existence, which clearly conflicted with the AFVG and threatened the programme. The British AFVG requirement had primarily been 'east of Suez'. (Some in industry said that Healey had been mesmerised by Messmer throughout the whole affair.)

United Kingdom Variable Geometry Project (UKVG)

The UK did continue its VG work and during July 1967 a Ministry of Technology (MinTech) Project Study

ABOVE **The BAC UKVG design, seen here heavily laden with bombs (11.67).** *North West Heritage Group*

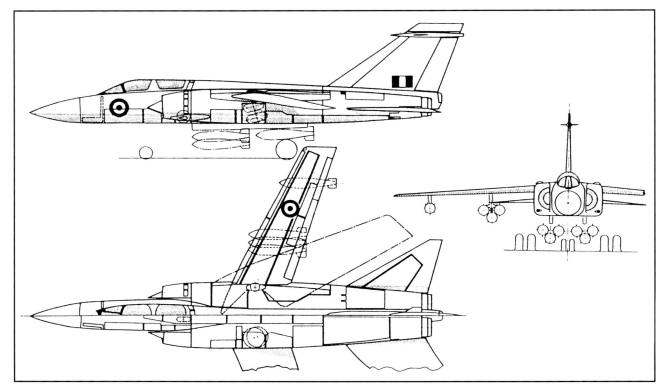

was proposed to look into the cost and feasibility of a UKVG aircraft (with a similar strike performance to the AFVG) and also into collaboration with other countries. BAC Warton was asked to undertake a four-month Project Definition to ASR.388 beginning on 1 August. The parameters were a low-level dash at Mach 0.9, at high altitude with reheat Mach 2 to 2.2, ferry range 2,800nm (5,186km), high-level range (low level over the target) with external fuel and four 1,000lb (454kg) bombs up to 1,000nm (1,852km), and low-level range (internal fuel only and four 1,000lb/454kg bombs) up to 400nm (741km).

An early BAC drawing, dated 5 September 1967 and called P.51, showed an aircraft with two RB.153-67-02 bypass engines. A UKVG brochure for a near-identical aircraft was completed in November 1967 with figures based on the RB.153-02, but an alternative was the BS.143, a new unit of 8,122lb (36.1kN) thrust dry and 13,998lb (62.2kN) reheated that used a scaled RB.193 IP compressor and fan and the M.45H HP spool (no decision was in fact to be made on the UKVG's engine). BAC noted how, despite variations in requirements during the period, the VG aircraft's basic layout had remained substantially the same for more than three years. Consequently BAC had great confidence in the design, which was backed up by more than a million wind tunnel data and pressure points plus engineering rig tests on the wing hinge and its associated structure. And the design work needed to find a suitable VG pivot bearing with a sufficient fatigue life had developed into a major research programme.

The UKVG had low-mounted, all-moving tailerons (which permitted the use of full-span wing trailing-edge flaps) and again the wings pivoted just inside the fuselage contours; this pivot position eliminated the need for leading-edge gloves, which improved the take-off and landing characteristics. It was discovered fairly early in the

feasibility phase that overall cost-effectiveness was best secured by fitting full-span leading-edge and trailing-edge high-lift devices on the wing for take-off and landing. Having no leading-edge glove meant that full-span leading-edge slats were possible and beneficial in contributing to the maximum lift coefficient. It was also proposed to use these devices, partly extended, to enhance the subsonic manoeuvrability.

The aircraft had translating conical centre-body intakes situated well forward of the wing (box intakes would have been simpler and easier but slightly heavier and not so effective). Their location, compared to an underwing intake, greatly reduced any boundary layer bleed and diverter problems and gave a long settling length between the intake throat and the engine face to help damp out any fluctuations in airflow, an important feature for bypass engines, which were more sensitive to flow fluctuations than a straight turbojet. All the stores were mounted on external pylons beneath the fuselage and wings. Eight attachment points were available under the fuselage for pylons and a ventral fuel tank and there were two more on each wing. In addition, the inboard wing store locations were capable of swivelling, which allowed the wing to be swept when carrying stores. Two cannon were to be carried internally but this armament was not specified in the definitive mission performance estimations.

The tailerons were the primary source of roll control when the wings were fully swept and these were set well below the wing plane since aerodynamically this was found to be the best practicable position. When the wings were in their forward position primary roll control came from spoilers on the wing, though there was still a limited amount from the tailerons. Most of the structure was semi-monocoque with the use of machined frames and forgings kept to a minimum. Aluminium-copper alloys were used for most of the airframe to give good fatigue, stress corrosion and high-temperature properties. Steel was

used only in regions of high stress such as the wing root diffusion member, the lugs of the wing centre section and the tailplane spigots. Titanium was restricted to the firewalls and frames around the brake parachute and flap supports. The avionics were housed immediately behind the nose radar scanner and beneath the pilot's floor. Design dive speed was 920mph (1,480km/h), unswept Mach number limit about 0.8, 1g ceiling about Mach 1.4 to 1.8 at 58,000ft (17,678m) and in a zoom climb the UKVG could reach about Mach 1.47 at 78,000ft (23,774m).

On 25 October 1967 BAC presented a UKVG variant to West German representatives in Bonn that was designed to meet their requirements for a Heavy Airborne Weapon System, but the response was disappointing. Possible collaboration was again explored but West Germany's in-house NKF studies (a VG project of its own replacing the defunct German/American AVS V/STOL strike fighter project) ensured that little interest was forthcoming for a UKVG type. In early December MinTech asked BAC to investigate a fighter application and the use of advanced technology in the engine and airframe because, although the RAF still wanted a strike/reconnaissance aircraft, an air defence type would be needed later on.

UKVG	
Span	45ft 10in (13.97m) forward, 27ft 0in (8.23m) swept
Length	57ft 5in (17.50m)
Gross wing area	300sq ft (27.9sq m) forward, 374sq ft (34.8sq m) swept
t/c ratio	12% forward, 5.7% swept
Gross weight	58,344lb (26,465kg) with 1eight 1,000lb/454kg bombs, 45,937lb (20,837kg) with 4 Martel
Powerplant	two RR RB153-02 7,674lb (34.1kN), 12,972lb (57.7kN) reheat
Maximum speed/height	Mach 2.3 between 36,000ft (10,973m) and 45,000ft (13,716m)
Weapon load	two 30mm cannon, 1eight 1,000lb (454kg) bombs or four Martel ASMs under wing/fuselage

BAC Advanced Combat Aircraft

Advanced Combat Aircraft studies continued throughout the first half of 1968, primarily against the all-weather low-level strike and reconnaissance role but also including single-engine and single-crew variants. The Advanced Combat Aircraft concept (with a set of missions of generally shorter range) replaced the UKVG, although steps continued towards possible collaboration with Canada and the 'F-104 Consortium'. The latter, comprising Germany, Italy, Belgium and the Netherlands in a single group, had been set up to replace their Lockheed F-104 Starfighters with a common aircraft.

After a meeting in Rome held on 16 and 17 May 1968 between the Chiefs of Staff of the 'F-104 Consortium' countries, Britain was invited to join a Working Group with the intention of finalising an operational requirement by December 1968. In July 1968 ASR.388 was superseded by AST.392 for an Advanced Combat Aircraft and an MoU was signed by Britain, Canada and the 'F-104 Consortium' to define an aircraft to meet the needs of the member countries. This was to be called the Multi-Role Combat Aircraft, or MRCA, and was to be in service by 1975. Back in January the F-111K's cancellation had brought the end of the old 'OR.339/TSR.2 requirements'. Now the RAF MRCA's first-priority targets would be East German airfields from which enemy close support might be operating; interdiction and targets deeper into Warsaw Pact territory would be less important.

Panavia MRCA (Tornado)

By November 1968 studies had advanced sufficiently to suggest there was a good chance of meeting the requirements of Germany, Italy, the Netherlands and the UK (Belgium and Canada had by then dropped out and the Netherlands would follow in July 1969). Using parameters agreed by the Chiefs of Air Staff on 17 December, a Feasibility Study for MRCA was conducted by a joint company, Panavia Aircraft GmbH, and presented on 31 January 1969. Officially registered in Germany on 26 March 1969 and formally established in September, Panavia was formed by BAC, Messerschmitt-Bolkow-Blohm [MBB], Fiat and Fokker and based in Munich. BAC and MBB were at the time still working separately on different layouts, but were exchanging views.

The Feasibility Study reported that a viable collaborative project was possible based on a twin-engine VG design having good manoeuvrability and the capacity to operate from short airstrips. Handel Davies of the Steering Committee noted that there were 'grounds for being more hopeful about the outcome of the exercise than we have been at any time in the past'. A number of important compromises had to be made to reconcile differing national requirements, and in particular the RAF had to accept a reduction in range below what it would have preferred. A decision on the engine was also still to be made but the Feasibility Study was conducted using the characteristics of the RB.199.

Panavia's baseline aircraft was presented on 14 March 1969 with the RB.199-33R, but this was quickly overtaken by a modified design incorporating an advanced technology three-shaft engine with a higher thrust/weight ratio that was based on early RB.199-34R data. This offered a substantial performance improvement and reduced the aircraft's size, but Germany insisted on a competition between engines from Rolls-Royce and Pratt & Whitney. This became one of the few sticking points since Germany wished to press ahead using the Pratt & Whitney JTF-16 (TF-30), but information on this was denied to the Netherlands and Italy.

At this stage Germany and Italy required a single-seater for close air support and as an air superiority fighter respectively; the RAF needed a two-seater for strike and reconnaissance but with the potential for development into a fighter later on. According to the Air Staff, Britain's MRCA would fill three major roles:

a). Strike and Reconnaissance. Following the collapse of successive plans to replace the Canberra, the measures taken to provide a stop-gap and to meet, in part, Britain's NATO obligations included prolonging the Vulcan's life, using

LEFT The first MRCA model to be seen in public. However, when this appeared at the Paris Air Show in 1969 the quite different final configuration had already been agreed for some time. This model has blended intakes, an undersize canopy and wing pivots well inboard, when MRCA's were further out.
North West Heritage Group

ABOVE Another manufacturer's model, which in fact is recorded as showing a version of the BAC P.45 described in Chapter 13. However, it appears quite close to the MRCA Tornado as built. *BAE SYSTEMS Heritage*

ABOVE This model provides a little more detail in terms of engine intakes, etc. for the early MRCA studies. *BAE SYSTEMS Heritage*

Buccaneer Mk.2s in the overland strike role, and extending the operational life of the Canberra PR.Mk.9 to compensate for the inadequacies of the Buccaneer Mk.2 in the reconnaissance role. The relatively slow Vulcan was expected to become increasingly vulnerable to Warsaw Pact defences, the Buccaneer lacked terrain-following radar and a blind nav/attack capability and so would also become increasingly vulnerable during the

late 1970s, and the Canberra was an old design restricted by limited performance. Each of them needed replacing and an initial CA Release to the service was required by the first quarter of 1976.

b). Air Defence. A new aircraft would be needed to replace the Phantom from 1979.

c). Maritime Strike. A replacement for the Buccaneer Mk.2 would be needed for maritime operations from about 1982.

In May 1969 Britain agreed to participate in the Project Definition Phase, which was concluded in spring 1970. Shortly before it was complete the Germans, having long campaigned for the single-seat Panavia 100, announced their decision not to proceed with it but to adopt the twin-seat Panavia 200, which was virtually identical to the RAF aircraft. This would cut the development costs but it was a blow to the Italians who could not continue with the single-seat MRCA in isolation, and there was some

BELOW The second MRCA prototype P.02 (serial XX946) shown here was built by BAC and first flown on 30 October 1974. *BAE SYSTEMS*

ABOVE An RAF Tornado seen in flight with its wings in the forward position. *BAe*

concern that they might drop out. As a minority partner, Italy was extremely vulnerable to any changes made by the two majority partners. At this point Germany stated a requirement for 600 aircraft (later cut to 420), Italy 200 and the UK 385. The Air Staff noted that the MRCA was 'an advanced aircraft but less ambitious, in relation to the current state of the art, than TSR.2'.

In June 1969 a tri-national company called Turbo-Union Ltd, embracing Rolls-Royce, MTU and Fiat, was set up at Bristol to produce the MRCA's supersonic lightweight RB.199-34R reheated bypass turbofan. The decision to use this 'paper' engine instead of the American JTF-16 was not announced until September, but eventually the RB.199 was to become the largest single-engine production project carried out in Europe. It was a three-shaft augmented turbofan of extremely advanced design that used modular construction to assist rapid stripping and rebuilding, and it was first bench tested on 29 September 1971. A detailed airframe work share was finalised in February 1970, Britain being allocated the nose and tail with Germany having to do the centre fuselage and Italy the wings, and the development phase, essentially the go-ahead for the MRCA programme, began on 22 July.

The first prototype flew on 14 August 1974, in the process becoming the first British-participation VG aircraft to fly,

LEFT And a spectacular view of another Tornado in high-speed mode with the wings fully swept. *BAe*

and in September the MRCA was named Tornado (rather than Panther as had been suggested by Panavia). A total of 992 aircraft were eventually built for the three participating countries and for Saudi Arabia. The RAF received 228 interdictor/strike (IDS) aircraft (allocated Warton project number P.67 in 1971), most of which were GR.Mk.1s covered by ASR.392, and the type entered RAF service in 1982. ASR.395 described the Tornado F.Mk.2 and Mk.3 air defence fighter variants designed at British expense for the RAF (the ADV was Warton's P.68) and the first of these flew in October 1979. This was a modified IDS with a longer fuselage and politically was the right direction to take since it could be done as a UK-only aircraft (because the parts affected were all made in the UK – altering German-made parts would have been a more sensitive and difficult option). A mid-life update under SR(A).417 saw 142 RAF GR.Mk.1s upgraded and extensively re-manufactured to GR.Mk.4 standard with more advanced weapons and equipment. The first Tornado GR.Mk.4 flew on 29 May 1993.

In the 1970s it became declared UK policy that major new national defence projects could not be funded alone and it was the MRCA Tornado that set the pattern for collaboration. Generally the programme ran very smoothly and it was never acrimonious. When the Tornado IDS arrived in Germany it gave the RAF a true low-level day/night and all-weather aircraft and enabled the service to make a major contribution to NATO. Since then it has racked up an impressive record of action and service and has been

ABOVE The Tornado GR.Mk.4 upgrade 'prototype' seen over the sort of country one has always expected to see these aircraft flying. *BAe*

involved in a number of conflicts. It proved to be the right aircraft to develop at the time and yet the flight envelope is similar to TSR.2 cancelled so long ago.

Panavia Tornado (IDS flown)

Span	45ft 7½in (13.91m) forward, 28ft 2½in (8.60m) swept
Length	54ft 10in (16.71m)
Gross wing area	286.3sq ft (26.6sq m) with 25° sweep
t/c ratio	?
Gross weight	61,620lb (27,951kg)
Powerplant	two Turbo-Union RB.199 Mk.103 9,100lb (40.4kN), 16,075lb (71.4kN) reheat
Maximum speed/height	Over 920mph (1,480km/h) at low level, Mach 2.2 at height
Weapon load	two 27mm cannon, more than 19,840lb (9,000kg) of external stores

THIS PAGE AND OPPOSITE These models reportedly show versions of Tornado that were offered to America, it is thought against the multi-role strike fighter (Enhanced Tactical Fighter) requirements that in 1984 were satisfied by the McDonnell Douglas F-15E Strike Eagle (another competitor had been the General Dynamics F-16XL). Here, however, both models show Tornados in Wild Weasel configuration armed with radar-seeking missiles to destroy enemy radar and defence systems.
Allison Vought

Because Tornado is so complex there was little chance that it could have been produced as a single-seat aircraft in the way Germany and Italy had wished; those countries had judged their needs on F-104 experience. Today Eurofighter Typhoon has a much-simplified cockpit and the pilot's workload is reduced, so now it should be possible to design a large single-seat strike aircraft (or even a machine without a pilot). Tornado was something of an old-fashioned

design in that it lacked fly-by-wire and other advanced electronics, the time delay needed to mature such new technologies would have delayed the aircraft's entry into service, and so they were not employed.

Tornado benefits fully from its swing wings. To make the pilot's ride comfortable during high-speed flight at low level in turbulent conditions the wing loading needed to be high. A small highly swept wing is a great help

in reducing gust effects and when a VG wing is swept back the increase in lift from gusts (i.e. bumps) is much less, which gives an increased fatigue life. However, Tornado also needed to get out of short airfields from runways around 3,000ft (914m) in length but it could not do this with a normal swept wing. The VG wing in its forward position does the job and this capability was fundamental in achieving Tornado's major goals; in fact it made

VG practical and almost necessary for a strike aircraft.

Matching the development of complex low-level strike aircraft such as TSR.2 and Tornado came developments in weaponry and systems. Terrain-following radar was vital for low-level flight in all weathers, while the introduction of laser-guided bombs and advanced ASMs allowed aircraft to hit targets far more accurately. The BAe ALARM air-launched anti-radiation missile to AST.1228 was one of a new breed of ASMs designed to lock on to the emissions from enemy ground radars and then destroy them. Tornado can apparently carry more than seventy different kinds of store, all externally except for its guns (there is no internal bay) and including the now withdrawn WE.177B freefall nuclear bomb. One piece of ordnance specifically designed for Tornado was the Hunting JP.233 airfield denial weapon, which dispensed sixty runway cratering munitions and in addition area-denial mines that were intended to hamper follow-up repair operations. Each Tornado GR.Mk.1 could take two JP.233s, but the GR.Mk.4 does not carry it or any nuclear weapons. The GR.Mk.4 was intended to use stand-off weapons as its primary store.

The last of the RAF's nuclear weapons, the WE.177, was withdrawn at the end of March 1998, a move that signified the end of the service's nuclear strike role after more than forty years. The responsibility for providing Great Britain's nuclear deterrent now rests with the Royal Navy and its submarine-launched Trident missiles.

Chapter Fifteen
AST.396

A Battlefield Aircraft: 1970 to 1975

ABOVE **One of the aircraft types intended for replacement by the AST.396 designs was the SEPECAT Jaguar, an example of which is seen here in an RAF publicity photo from 1997.** *Crown Copyright*

In 1970 the Air Staff was expecting the RAF combat force's close support/short-range reconnaissance component to be composed exclusively of Harriers and Jaguars. The former was scheduled to be withdrawn from service during 1980 and the Jaguar in 1984, so a replacement would be needed some time during 1980–85 and the first draft of Air Staff Target AST.396 to cover this was prepared in July 1970. Studies to the AST were to be conducted around an operational scenario foreseen essentially within a European war. Such a conflict was expected to see many thousands of Warsaw Pact tanks moving *en masse* across the European countryside.

NATO could not afford to build the vast number of tanks needed to counter this threat but aircraft could stop the procession and it was hoped that AST.396 might clarify the types that would be best suited for the job.

AST.396

To meet the full threat, including enemy ground forces operating at night and in poor weather, a close support aircraft that could operate effectively in such conditions must inevitably be equipped with comprehensive and advanced avionics. This was likely to be technically complex and expensive and the Government might not be able to afford to provide a worthwhile force of

such aircraft. The Air Staff hoped to resolve this problem by creating a composite close support force comprising a relatively small number of complex aircraft capable of operating at night and in adverse weather plus a larger number of less complicated and relatively inexpensive machines capable of visual attack and reconnaissance only. It was intended that the former could be met by MRCA (Tornado) while the simpler machine would probably be a new design.

This second type should be a single-seat, single-engine layout, although a cost-effective multi-engine installation would be considered. Simplicity was paramount and all possible steps were to be taken to ensure that cost and complexity were minimised. The aircraft would serve primarily in the NATO area (i.e. Europe) and should also be capable of effectively performing a secondary role of battlefield air defence to destroy enemy strike, reconnaissance, close air support and fighter aircraft operating at low altitude in the battle area. The basic AST mission called for a battlefield interdiction sortie 60 miles (96km) behind enemy lines with six cluster bombs or Matra pods, two Sidewinder or Taildog missiles and two internal cannon. A dash Mach number of 0.9 on the level without reheat was requested and also the ability to sustain a turn at 7.5g at Mach 0.8 with reheat lit, while the take-off had to be achieved in a ground run of between 2,000ft and 3,000ft (610m and 915m). An initial CA Release for in-service use was required by the last quarter of 1980, with full CA Release a maximum of one year later. The first issue of AST.396 was endorsed on 21 May 1971.

Studies to AST.396 occupied both BAC and HSA throughout the first half of the 1970s and the proposals show there was some doubt as to just how simple the aircraft should be. A certain amount of advanced avionics would still be needed, together with some sophisticated weapons (including air-to-air) and, most probably, a STOVL or STOL capability. Even the possibility of using remotely piloted vehicles (RPVs) was considered and extensive studies of these types were made at HSA Brough, and at BAC Warton under project numbers P.75 and P.80 to P.85. The general research also studied in more detail the application of composite structures using carbon fibre, while supporting contracts were also placed on Rolls-Royce during 1972 to supply information to BAC and HSA on a wide variety of existing and postulated engines. The types of aircraft considered by industry covered a wide range, from developments of the HS.1182 Hawk trainer to the MRCA and new supersonic types.

British Aircraft Corporation Proposals to AST.396 (Report dated March 1972)

BAC P.69 (Jaguar Developments)

The P.69 project number covered conventional Jaguar developments in the 30,000lb to 35,000lb (13,608g to 15,876kg) weight range with increased thrust and improved high lift. Work began with comparatively simple, relatively short-term modifications that, while not meeting all of the AST's limits in full, might well offer a cost-effective solution. More extensive changes were also studied since the conversion of existing airframes into 'boiler plate' prototypes was expected to be a fairly quick and cheap process. There were five variants of the P.69:

1. The existing Jaguar with modified avionics to cater for AST.396 missions. Take-off weight 29,258lb (13,271kg).

2. The existing Jaguar with uprated Adour Stage 1 or 2 engines and a take-off weight of 31,782lb (14,416kg). Considerable importance was attached to uprating the propulsion system and there was great scope to increase the Adour's thrust, in stages, to a maximum reheat figure of 9,430lb (41.9kN).

3. Adour Stage 2 engines plus more substantial airframe developments directed at the AST. Rockets could provide a short burst of up to 10,000lb (44.4kN) of additional thrust. Span 29ft 0in (8.84m), length 52ft 3.5in (15.94m).

4. A further development of version 3 featuring a redesigned wing of 5% t/c ratio and a straight trailing edge; gross weight 36,402lb (16,512kg), internal fuel 8,690lb (3,942kg).

5. A tentative development featuring two RB.199-34R or American General Electric YJ-101 engines of about 15,000lb (66.7kN) and

14,300lb (63.6kN) reheated thrust respectively. In both cases the fuselage needed widening and deepening to accommodate the larger intakes and engines, the engine installation itself would need considerable redesign, a stronger undercarriage was essential and variant 4's wing would be used. The RB.199 variant's gross weight was 35,476lb (16,092kg) and internal fuel 10,180lb (4,618lit).

The 1972 Warton report concluded that the Jaguar's life could be extended well into the 1980s by fitting composite fibre components and introducing other advances, but the most worthy improvement was an increase in thrust that completely transformed the aircraft's performance up to the levels of AST.396.

BAC P.70 (Pegasus Engine Solutions)

The P.70 series utilised a vectored thrust Pegasus engine for lift and forward propulsion. The designs offered a much simpler approach than multi-engine types but there were penalties including extra drag and a higher fuel consumption. The studies used the Pegasus 15-03 with PCB but an alternative engine was the RB.422-04 with PCB, an entirely new proposal based on 1980 technology, smaller than the 15-03 but similar in layout. Installation problems and drag penalties were such that the aircraft was only just supersonic when using PCB and could not be supersonic without it. PCB also brought problems with the airframe design and meant that the front nozzles now formed an integral part of the engine change unit, whereas on non-PCB Pegasus marks these had been airframe mounted. To ensure that the engine could be 'dropped-out' as requested in AST.396, all the structure in line with or below the nozzles had to be removable, which left just two relatively shallow fuselage sides and the wing slot floor to carry primary loads. Therefore, load-carrying cowl doors were also provided.

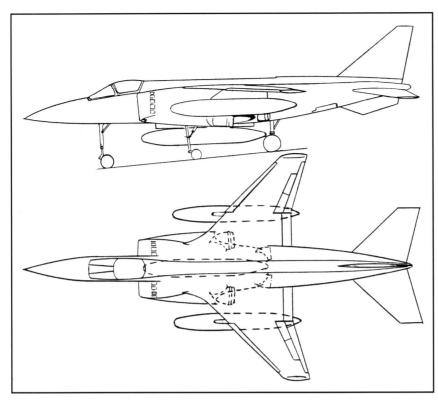

ABOVE **The first BAC P.70 sketch (drawing EAG.8404), which formed a basis for detailed design (drawing at 3.72). For the ferry mission seen here the aircraft carried three 265gal (1,205lit) long-range fuel tanks mounted on inboard wing pylons and on a centreline pylon. Note the gun port just beneath the air intake lip.** *North West Heritage Group*

BELOW **Twin-boom BAC P.70 (EAG.8436 21.1.72).** *North West Heritage Group*

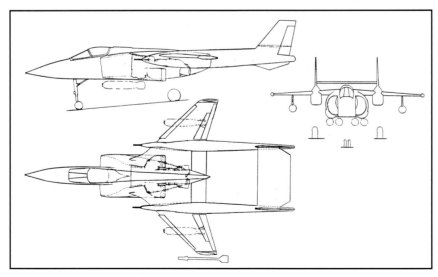

The first P.70 drawing (EAG.8404) used many Jaguar or modified Jaguar parts and formed the basis for a detailed design. It had a Jaguar S nose and front fuselage (with some internal redesign) and a French Jaguar M nose leg. A new centre fuselage had large Harrier-style intakes and outrigger undercarriage legs located in fairings forward of the PCB nozzles (which avoided long tip-mounted outriggers). Two developed Aden guns were available and stores could be carried up to four abreast aft of the nosewheel bay

and on underwing pylons. The rear fuselage spine, wings, fin and tailplane were similar to Jaguar (although the wing t/c was increased to 7%) and a '1980 technology level' aircraft would make extensive use of composite materials and fly-by-wire (computer-controlled flight). A naval version (EAG.8472) carried two Martel ASMs on the inboard wing pylons and sported a longer nose that housed a 27in (0.69m) diameter radar dish instead of the laser.

To overcome the engineering problems associated with installing a Pegasus within a conventional fuselage, the most promising alternative configuration was a twin-boom layout (EAG.8436). The advantages included keeping the rear exhaust nozzles closer together, the fuselage structural loads were drastically changed and were more compatible with the engine bay shape and size, and a conventional undercarriage could be used that eased considerably the problems of exhaust gas impingement and debris deposition. Changes from the basic P.70 included a centre fuselage modified so that the fuselage and engine loads were carried directly to the wing box, and a centre wing section that had a straight trailing edge and rear spar. The booms were area-ruled and housed the main wheels, fuel tanks and guns, and the fins carried a slab all-moving tailplane. Four stores could be carried across the fuselage aft of the nosewheel bay, singles could be loaded on the outboard pylons and the aircraft had tip-mounted AAMs.

BAC P.70 (Basic Configuration EAG.8404)	
Span	29ft 6in (8.99m)
Length	51ft 6in (15.70m)
Gross wing area	not given
t/c ratio	7%
Gross weight	37,100lb (16,829kg)
Powerplant	one RR Pegasus 15-03 with PCB
Maximum speed/height	Mach 1+
Weapon load	two 30mm Aden cannon, various stores including Martel ASM

BAC P.70 (Twin Boom EAG.8436)	
Span	29ft 2in (8.89m)
Length	51ft 0in (15.54m)
Gross wing area	not given
t/c ratio	7%
Gross weight	c. 36,000lb (16,330kg)
Powerplant	one RR Pegasus 15-03 with PCB
Maximum speed/height	Mach 1+
Weapon load	two 30mm Aden cannon, six bombs or other stores, two Sidewinder AAMs

BAC P.71 (Lift Engine Solutions)

It was felt that the technical feasibility of the aircraft type that used separate lift engines had been well established by experience accumulated from the Short S.C.1, Dassault Mirage IIIV and VFW Fokker 191B research aeroplanes, but the economic and operational factors had still to be clarified. The economics had been made more attractive by progressive developments in engine technology, particularly with reductions in lift engine weight, while the Kestrel and Harrier (which did not use lift engines) had helped to clarify a good deal of the operational aspects.

The jet lift vehicle introduced some special design factors; for example a low-speed control system was needed

that, by necessity, had to be a reaction system of some kind. And a critical aspect of all jet lift V/STOL projects was the nozzle location, with the factors involved including jet-induced interaction effects, airframe and undercarriage heating (particularly near the ground), re-ingestion of the efflux (again particularly near the ground), vulnerability to battle damage, thrust balance to minimise pitching, noise and vibration levels, ground erosion and debris scatter, and the consequences of engine failure. The P.71 studies were specifically aimed at reducing jet-induced lift losses, re-ingestion and heating effects, and BAC Warton preferred this solution rather than the single vectored thrust engine since 'greater freedom and adaptability is possible which can be used to considerable advantage'.

Rolls-Allison XJ.99 lift units were used although an alternative engine offering '1980' standards was the new advanced Rolls-Royce RB.227-01 proposal. The lift and propulsive engines were located respectively well forward and well aft of the aircraft's CofG, which gave some advantages – the centre fuselage was left free for fuel, main wheels, stores, ventral packs and guns while this also helped the aircraft's weight balance. The datum P.71

(drawing EAG.8413) was a long-term Jaguar development fitted with two RB.199-34Rs and two XJ.99s to give an gross weight of 37,749lb (17,123kg). This resembled the Jaguar quite closely but included the nose, wing, fin, tail and Jaguar M undercarriage of the Pegasus-powered P.70.

However, the centre fuselage and lift engine bay contained little Jaguar. This had been lengthened by 30in (0.76m) and almost completely redesigned to accommodate two lift engines inclined 15° from the vertical and fitted with blade deflectors. Both intakes and ducts were 50% larger than Jaguar's to allow for the increased mass flow of the RB.199s (the fixed pitot intakes had splitter plates), the internal fuel had been increased and a modified M-type undercarriage kept the belly free for weapons or reconnaissance packs. The reaction control system used air bled from the lift engines. The rear fuselage was similar to Jaguar but it was broader and deeper to accommodate the larger engines with their rotating cascades, the latter supplying the main engines' vertical thrust.

There were some smaller alternatives. One had a single Pratt & Whitney F.100 engine with twin cascades and twin XJ.99s, while an even lighter arrangement (drawing

BELOW The datum P.71 was drawing EAG.8413, a long-term development of the Jaguar (at 3.72). *North West Heritage Group*

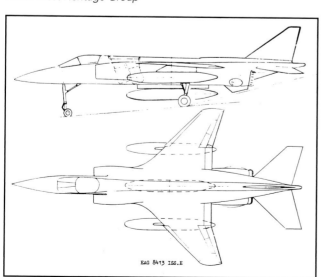

EAG 8413 ISS.E

BELOW Drawing EAG.8461 was a smaller version of the P.71 (at 3.72). *North West Heritage Group*

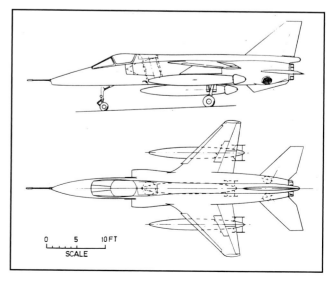

0   5   10 FT
SCALE

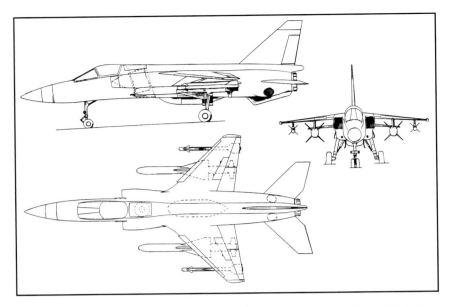

ABOVE Variant of the BAC P.71 for the Royal Navy (EAG.8471) with one RB.228 lift engine and one RB.199 propulsive engine (late 1971). Note the cascades around the lower rear fuselage. *North West Heritage Group*

EAG.8447) had a single YJ-101, two XJ.99s or RB.227s and a simplified structure and systems for an gross weight of 26,892lb (12,198kg). Another design (EAG.8461) had an even smaller wing, its fuselage length reduced by 3ft (0.91m), one RB.199-42R (the engine developed for the MRCA fighter) and one RB.228-02 with a central blade deflector (a scaled-

up RB.227 to retain the thrust balance). The centre and rear fuselage could accommodate large ventral packs and, after the load-carrying access doors had been removed, the complete engine and cascades could be 'dropped out'. The wings were based on Jaguar developments and the project had a Jaguar-style nose with its laser; the gross weight was given as 25,324lb

BELOW P.71 drawing EAG.8447 showed a design for both the RAF and Royal Navy with a radar, a single General Electric YJ-101 engine, two XJ.99 (in 1972) or RB.227 (1980) lift units, four cluster bombs in a belly pack and underwing AAMs and tanks. The RAF version had a length of 45ft 7in (13.90m), Navy version 46ft 8.5in (14.24m), and both had a span of 25ft 2.5in (7.68m). *North West Heritage Group*

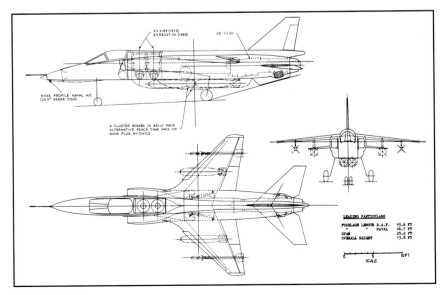

BAC P.71 (Small Naval version EAG.8471)

Span	22ft 11in (6.98m)
Length	43ft 7in (13.29m)
Gross wing area	not given
t/c ratio	7%
Gross weight	c. 26,000lb (11,794kg)
Powerplant	one RR RB.199-42R, one RR RB.228
Maximum speed/height	Mach 1+
Weapon load	two 30mm Aden cannon, six bombs, two Harpoon ASMs, two Sidewinder AAMs

(11,487kg). A naval version of this aircraft (EAG.8471) would have a different nose to take a 24in (0.61m) diameter radar dish. This final aircraft was small enough to do without wing folding and could carry two Harpoon ASMs on the inboard pylons and two Sidewinder AAMs outboard.

Other Possibilities and BAC P.66

Here the 1971 PANNAP P.61 family (Chapter Thirteen) formed a datum before the three basic designs, the P.66/1, P.66/2 and P.66/3, were split into a range of parametric studies. P.66/1 had an unreheated Adour RT.172-06, an appropriately reshaped fuselage and intake plus a set of avionics that generally met the needs of AST.396. The supersonic P.66/2 had an Adour Stage 2 of 9,550lb (42.4kN) reheated thrust, the same avionics and an gross weight of 20,287lb (9,202kg). P.66/3 used a single MRCA RB.199-34 engine but here there was no chance of this aircraft being sized to meet all the AST's limits. Hence the parameter examined most closely was the take-off weight and a figure of 25,000lb (11,340kg) was calculated to meet the interdiction mission 60 miles (96km) behind enemy lines.

BAC P.66/3

Span	31ft 8in (9.65m)
Length	43ft 0in (13.11m)
Gross wing area	not given
t/c ratio	not given
Gross weight	21,780lb (9,879kg)
Powerplant	one RR RB.199-34 c. 15,000lb (66.7kN) reheat
Maximum speed/height	Mach 1+
Weapon load	?

BAC P.72, P.73 and P.74

Warton also undertook numerous
alternative studies to AST.396 Issue 1.
These included the P.72 series of all-
new designs (some with delta wings),
the P.73 lightweight aircraft with
variable geometry swing wings, and
further Jaguar developments fitted with
new engines (the P.74). Versions of the
MRCA were also considered.

Hawker Siddeley Aviation Proposals to AST.396 (Report dated March 1972)

Hawker Siddeley's report, which covered
the first six months of research, embraced
versions of its Harrier and the Hawk
trainer, BAC's Jaguar and also the French
Dassault Mirage F.1 and Sweden's SAAB
37 Viggen. For reasons of space the two
overseas studies have been ignored, but
they were simply re-engined versions of
the basic aircraft. In addition, the Jaguar
studies, using the Jaguar S as a baseline
'Candidate Aircraft', saw the type refitted
with two of the uprated 9,550lb (42.4kN)
thrust Adour RB.172-19R engines or in a
more extensive development with two
16,900lb (75.1kN) RB.199-42Rs. This
was an attempt to provide much more
power but it resulted in a reduced combat
radius.

Different versions of the basic
'Candidate' airframes below accounted
for variations in engine and avionics
standards, fuel loads and other
significant parameters, and the studies
came both from Brough and Kingston.
Gross weights relate to 100% fuel plus
4,000lb (1,814kg) of weapons.

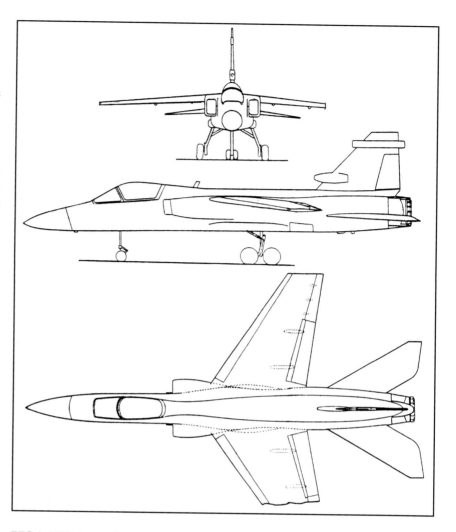

HSA HS.1182 Variants

The 'Candidate Aircraft' here was the
HS.1182 AJS two-seat strike version of
what became the Hawk jet trainer with
six weapon pylons, a detachable 30mm
gun pod and simple avionics. There
was also the single-seat HS.1182-50
development of the AJS with an avionic
system designed for clear night and
other low-level operations, the

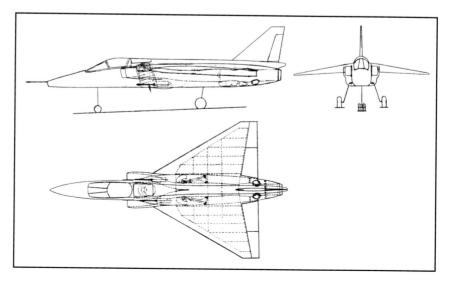

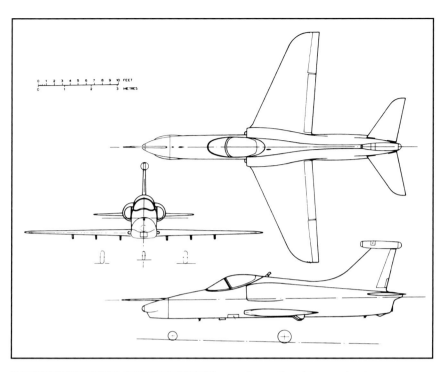

ABOVE HS.1182-50 at 3.72.
HSA via Chris Farara

HS.1182-52 (Version of HS.1182-50)	
Span	30ft 10in (9.40m)
Length	33ft 11in (10.33m)
Gross wing area	179.8sq ft (16.7sq m)
t/c ratio (mean)	10.5%
Gross weight	16,923lb (7,676kg)
Powerplant	one RB.172-19 Adour 6,480lb (28.8kN)
Maximum escape speed	Mach 0.80
Weapon load	4,000lb (1,814kg) of stores, two guns in wing roots

additional weight of the avionics being more than counter-balanced by the omission of the second crew member. There were four more versions of the single-seater and three of the two-seat AJS with changes based almost entirely around different versions of the Adour engine, some with reheat.

BELOW HS.1189-1 (c1970). *HSA via Chris Farara*

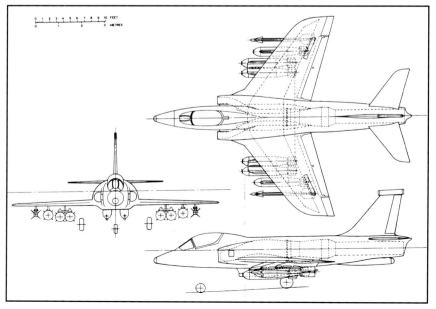

HSA HS.1189 Variants

Originally conceived in 1969 as a low-cost, close-support single-seater, the HS.1189-1 was intended to fill the gap between trainer/strike aircraft such as the HS.1182 and larger types such as the Hunter. A low-wing aircraft with 37° of sweep at the leading edge, it was powered by a non-reheat and non-thrust-reversing version of the MRCA engine, the RB.199-36. Three other versions were offered including the HS.1189-3 with a 9,550lb (42.4kN) Adour RB.172-19R and a reduced wing sweep angle of 24°.

The HS.1189-5 had an uprated RB.199-41 of 9,800lb (43.6kN) thrust appropriate to a 1982 timescale. It required slightly more fuel and had wing and tail surfaces of increased area so as to maintain the wing loading. This was likely to prove the most competitive HS.1189 variant with a useful mission performance. Despite its combat and airfield performance falling well below the target figures, the cost was low enough to make the type an attractive and cost-effective answer to operational tasks less demanding than those posed by AST.396.

HS.1189-1	
Span	28ft 9in (8.76m)
Length	37ft 0in (11.28m)
Gross wing area	240sq ft (22.3sq m)
t/c ratio (mean)	8.5%
Gross weight	17,150lb (7,779kg)
Powerplant	one RB.199-36 8,600lb (38.2kN)
Maximum escape speed	Mach 0.85
Weapon load	At least 4,000lb (1,814kg) of stores (up to six bombs), two guns in underfuselage pods, two Sidewinder AAM
Internal fuel	324gal (1,473lit)

HS.1189-5	
Span	31ft 3.5in (9.54m)
Length	39ft 0in (11.89m)
Gross wing area	218sq ft (20.3sq m)
t/c ratio (mean)	10%
Gross weight	19,213lb (8,715kg)
Powerplant	one RB.199-41 9,800lb (43.6kN)
Maximum escape speed	Mach 0.84
Weapon load	At least 4,000lb (1,814kg) of stores (up to six bombs), two guns in lower fuselage, two Sidewinder AAM at wingtips
Internal fuel	575gal (2,614lit)

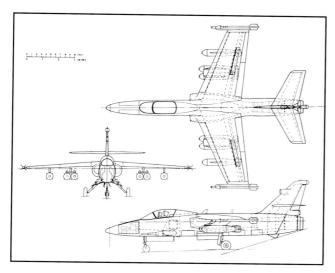

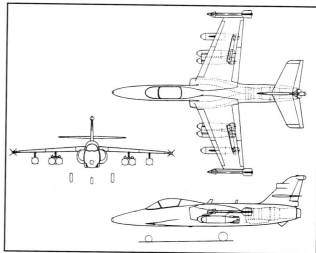

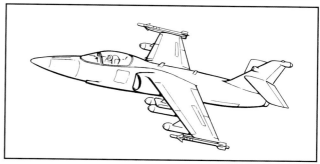

ABOVE The HS.1189-3 project was powered by an Adour RB.172-19R engine (2.72). Span 32ft 0.5in (9.76m), length 40ft 0in (12.19m), wing area 228sq ft (21.2sq m), gross weight 20,344lb (9,228kg), maximum escape speed Mach 0.85. *HSA via Chris Farara*

ABOVE RIGHT HS.1189-5 (26.2.72). *BAe Brough Heritage Centre*

RIGHT Sketch showing the HS.1189-5. *BAe Brough Heritage Centre*

HSA HS.1190 Variants

The HS.1190 was originally conceived as the HSA Brough P.153 interceptor project of 1969/70 (below). The basic candidate version of the HS.1190 used a single MRCA engine, the reheated RB.199-34R, which provided genuine supersonic potential. The airframe, however, required advanced technology features in order to reduce its size and weight and to keep the performance to a level competitive with other designs of similar size and price. Thus it was envisaged that the structure would use some 7% of titanium plus (potentially) carbon fibre-reinforced plastics, while

BELOW HS.1190 variant of Brough P.153 to AST.396 (1971/72). *BAe Brough Heritage Centre*

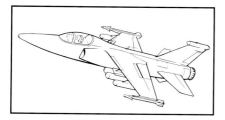

installing the baseline avionics meant that this was the smallest aircraft to be considered with the full AST.396 system. Blown flaps at the leading and trailing

edges (with the aid of a reverse thrust system) gave an airfield performance competitive with the best 'conventional' non-lifting-thrust aircraft, but this still

BELOW HS.1190-2 at 3.72. *BAe Brough Heritage Centre*

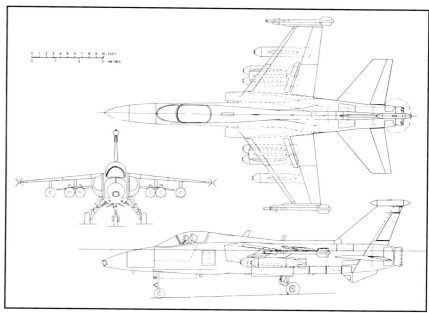

HS.1190-2	
Span	26ft 7in (8.71m)
Length	42ft 9in (13.03m)
Gross wing area	214sq ft (19.9sq m)
t/c ratio (mean)	5.5%
Gross weight	24,965lb (11,324kg)
Powerplant	one RB.199-34R 15,000lb (66.7kN)
Maximum escape speed	<Mach 1.1
Weapon load	At least 4,000lb (1,814kg) of stores (up to six bombs), two guns in lower fuselage, two Sidewinder AAM at wingtips

fell short of the AST figures. The HS.1190-1 and -2 had an uprated engine and an increased wing area respectively (by 15%), the latter with more fuel giving a total of 826gal (3,756lit); both had leading-edge sweep angles of 36°. However, because it could achieve the required 110nm (177km) radius of action the HS.1190-2 was regarded by HSA as the major contender.

HSA HS.1191 Variants

The candidate aircraft in the HS.1191 series was a two-seat canard design powered by a pair of RB.199-34R engines at the MRCA rating of 15,000lb (66.7kN) thrust each and with base burning applied to the large area between the engines. Base burning, effectively a third engine of poor

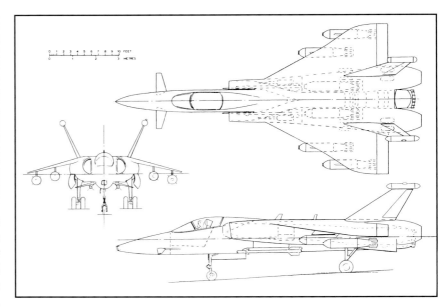

ABOVE **HS.1191-1 at 3.72.** *HSA via Chris Farara*

efficiency but light weight and common to the HS.1191 series, would involve high research and development costs but offered potential benefits, principally with the high penetration and escape speeds obtainable at low level. There was also the extra fuselage volume ahead of the base available for internal stores carriage. The candidate HS.1191 had first been designed by HSA in 1970 as a base-burning solution to the MRCA requirement (Chapter

Fourteen) and it used advanced systems, including the full two-seat avionics system. Its structure made extensive use (up to 15%) of titanium and nickel alloys with the nickel required in the base-burning areas. Consequently, the size and cost of this aircraft were incompatible with the aims of AST.396 but the HS.1191 did provide a useful check on the benefits of size. The mission radius and escape speed requirements would be met, but the take-off and landing distances were some three times the target figures. Base burning was considered further for the HS.1192 below.

The HS.1191-1 used the same base-burning principles as the candidate HS.1191 but within a smaller airframe fitted with a delta wing and a single RB.199-42R, the base areas at which burning would be used being positioned on either side. The structure would again use up to 15% titanium and (in base-burning areas) Nimonic alloy or steel, or even ceramic. Two internal bomb bays were provided, each capable of taking a BL.755 cluster weapon, and the remainder of the nominal weapon load was mounted on the wing. The Mach 1.1 escape speed should be

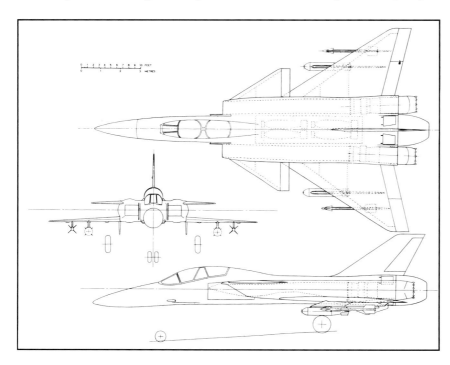

LEFT The original HS.1191 project (1970). *HSA via Chris Farara*

HS.1191

Span	35ft 0.5in (10.68m)
Length	56ft 2.5in (17.13m)
Gross wing area	514sq ft (47.8sq m)
t/c ratio (mean)	4%
Leading edge sweep	57°
Gross weight	45,453lb (20,617kg)
Powerplant	two RB.199-34R 15,000lb (66.7kN)
Maximum escape speed	Mach 1.1+
Weapon load	Drawing shows four bombs in weapon bay plus two under wings, two Sidewinder AAM
Internal Fuel	1,660gal (7,548lit)

HS.1191-1

Span	23ft 9.5in (7.25m)
Length	44ft 6in (13.56m)
Gross wing area	333sq ft (31.0sq m)
t/c ratio (mean)	4%
Leading edge sweep	60°
Gross weight	25,994lb (11,791kg)
Powerplant	one RB.199-42R 16,900lb (75.1kN)
Maximum escape speed	Mach 1.1
Weapon load	Drawing shows six bombs, two Sidewinder AAM
Internal Fuel	842gal (3,828lit)

attainable with the use of base burning.

The HS.1191-2 was externally similar to the -1 version but used the extra fuselage volume ahead of the base for the installation of four scaled 6,250lb (27.8kN) Rolls-Royce RB.227-01 lift engines rather than the internal bomb bays. The HS.1191-3 was generally similar to the -1 but featured a low-mounted wing with a canard foreplane instead of the high-mounted delta. Its basic weight with the canard layout was some 1,600lb (726kg) greater but the take-off distance was improved by 500ft (152m). This section of the report ended by saying that 'on balance, these preliminary investigations have failed to show sufficient performance advantages to offset the extra cost of the canard layout. Stores carriage (vital to the close support role) was also more difficult with the canard layout. The HS.1191-3 has therefore not been taken beyond the preliminary project stage'.

RIGHT Hawker Siddeley's HS.1184-1 subsonic Harrier development (7.70). Sidewinder AAMs are carried above the wing. *HSA via Chris Farara*

HSA HS.1184 Variants

Moving on now to proposed developments of the Harrier concept, the current first generation of this in-service V/STOL type was a natural precursor to the AST.396 aircraft. Any developments to the AST would form a second generation and the HS.1184-1 would be the natural and logical development of the Harrier series. Its nose had been lengthened to accommodate infra-red warning and laser units and the rear fuselage was extended to provide the necessary CofG balance and reaction control power. The wing was derived from the Harrier wing with a slightly extended and drooped leading edge and the Harrier ferry tip shape adopted as a permanent fixture. In this candidate form the HS.1184-1 assumed virtually no increase in technology standards beyond the Harrier itself. It had only slightly more fuel volume than the Harrier and therefore was still very short of fuel for the AST.396 mission, but it did have an improved take-off performance with 3,000lb (13.3kN) of thrust increase counterbalancing the 1,218lb (552kg) increase in basic weight. If required the HS.1184-1 could enter service in 1977.

A further version described in detail in the report was the HS.1184-7, which had been studied both with the advanced RB.422-06 engine at a thrust rating of 26,000lb (115.6kN) and also with the uprated Pegasus 15-02 engine installed at 28,600lb (127.1kN). These alternative powerplants were housed in a larger and almost entirely new airframe that incorporated the lessons learnt from Harrier experience. Thus, drooped nozzles were used, and the nozzles were moved further from the wing and integrated more fully with the fuselage, steps that would reduce interference drag and jet-induced suction losses. The internal fuel was increased by 242gal (1,100lit) relative to the HS.1184-1, so the mission radius could be flown with a more generous combat and deviation allowance than for the smaller version. The wing was larger and of a completely new design that used a supercritical section to delay the drag rise and permit higher dash speeds to be flown. Leading-edge sweep was 42° compared to the -1's 40°, the main undercarriage was wing-mounted and two 30mm Aden guns were mounted internally in the wing shoulders. HS.1184-7's structure was

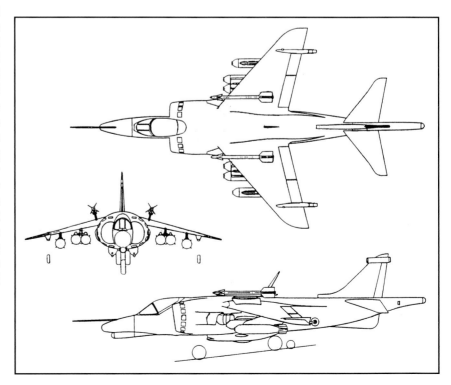

ABOVE Model of the HS.1184-1. *Chris Farara*

basically conventional and the baseline AST avionic system was assumed. Though still subsonic the HS.1184-7 was otherwise considered well suited to the AST requirements and seemed likely to prove the most attractive variant of the HS.1184 series.

A further six versions of the HS.1184-1 were all described briefly, each of them fitted with uprated engines or receiving other specific changes. And beyond AST.396 further designs were drawn over the next four years under the HS.1184 banner. These

studies did much to lay the ground for the AV-16 described in Chapter Ten.

BELOW HS.1184-7 at 3.72. *HSA via Chris Farara*

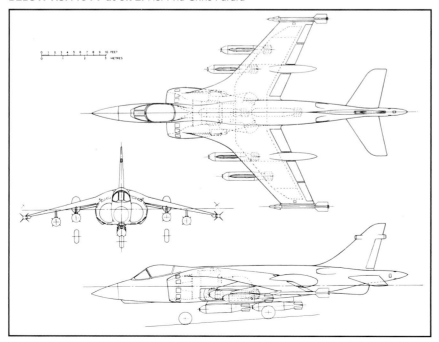

HS.1184-1	
Span	29ft 2in (8.89m)
Length	48ft 7in (14.81m)
Gross wing area	220.36sq ft (20.5sq m)
t/c ratio (mean)	8.3%
Gross weight	24,585lb (11,152kg)
Powerplant	one Pegasus 15-02 24,500lb (108.9kN)
Maximum escape speed	Mach 0.925
Weapon load	two Sidewinder AAM above wing, six bombs on four underwing pylons or four Taildog ASM, 2 cannon packs beneath fuselage
Internal fuel	665gal (3,024lit)

HS.1184-7	
Span	29ft 2.5in (8.90m)
Length	49ft 2.5in (15.00m)
Gross wing area	250.35sq ft (23.3sq m)
t/c ratio (mean)	10.6%
Gross weight	27,000lb (12,247kg)
Powerplant	See text
Maximum escape speed	Mach 0.94
Weapon load	two Sidewinder AAM at wingtips, six bombs on underwing and underfuselage pylons or four Taildog ASM, two cannon in wing roots
Internal fuel	907gal (4,124lit)

HSA HS.1185 Variants

The candidate HS.1185-9 benefited from all of the project studies, model tests, detail design work and indeed prototype construction carried out since 1961 on the P.1154 and HS.1179 supersonic V/STOL projects. It was to be powered by a Pegasus 15-03 engine of 34,850lb (154.9kN) thrust with PCB being used to give a 42% static thrust boost relative to the 'dry' Pegasus 15-02 rating. The use of PCB would complicate the installation problems and require a comprehensive research programme. The airframe had been deliberately left to low risk levels of technology, the baseline avionics only were fitted and the airframe structure was described as 'conservative', though with substantial areas of titanium skinning in those regions affected principally by the high temperature and energy of the jet exhausts. Here the wing leading-edge sweep was set at 41°. Further versions (the HS.1185-15 and HS.1185-16) featured more advanced avionic systems or advanced composite structures respectively, and to meet the airfield and combat performance requirements the HS.1185-9 would require more thrust. A twin-finned version was also drawn as the HS.1185-13 to illustrate the implications of the avionic system suggested by the AST, while the HS.1185-14 had an uprated 39,600lb (176.0kN) thrust Pegasus 15-03 with PCB. Further versions up to HS.1185-23 looked at more comprehensive composite structures, a smaller airframe or more fuel.

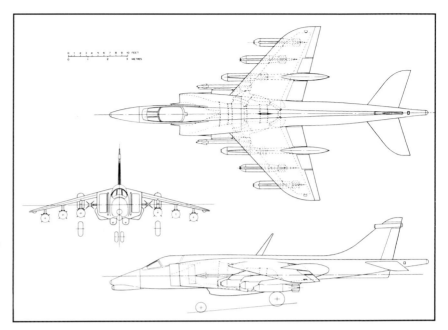

ABOVE HS.1185-9 at 3.72. *HSA via Chris Farara*
BELOW The HS.1185-13 had twin fins (3.72). *HSA via Chris Farara*

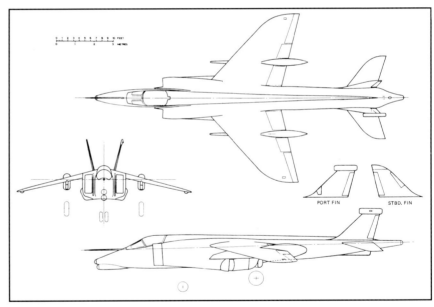

HS.1185-9	
Span	30ft 6in (9.30m)
Length	53ft 9.5in (16.40m)
Gross wing area	300sq ft (27.9sq m)
t/c ratio (mean)	6.4%
Gross weight	35,055lb (15,901kg)
Powerplant	one Pegasus 15-03 34,850lb (154.9kN)
Maximum escape speed	Mach 1.05
Weapon load	two Sidewinder AAM on fuselage sides, six bombs on underwing pylons, two cannon packs beneath fuselage
Internal fuel	1,317gal (5,988lit)

HSA HS.1186 Variants

The candidate HS.1186-1 was a four-nozzle vectored-thrust aircraft again incorporating lessons learnt from Harrier experience, but in an entirely new airframe. A Pegasus 16-02 engine was installed without plenum chamber burning. This powerplant incorporated a number of technological improvements relative to earlier engines in the Pegasus series and would require a protracted and expensive development, although a service entry would be possible in 1981 (i.e. well in line with the AST.396 timescale). The wing, swept 38.5° at the leading edge, was a totally new design using supercritical design techniques to a greater extent than for the Harrier and HS.1184-1. Conventional structural materials with titanium skinning over the rear fuselage were assumed for this candidate version, but an HS.1186-2 was also referred to that would make

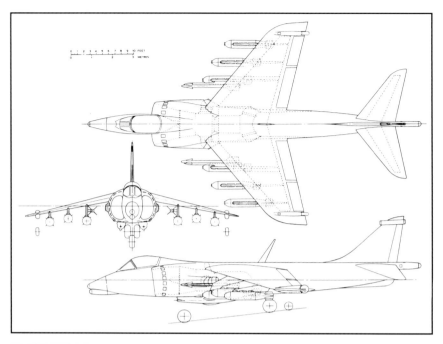

allow the HS.1187-5 to carry sufficient fuel for the full low level mission profile and to meet most of the other AST requirements. Wing leading-edge sweep angle was 41° and the structure was similar to that of the HS.1185. Baseline avionics were used, but once again more advanced airframe systems and composite were considered in three other versions. The review concluded, however, that 'the protracted and intensive development necessary for the Pegasus 16-13 engine, and the size of the airframe necessary to install it, together result in an aircraft price too close to that of MRCA to provide a sensible answer to the AST.396 concept'.

ABOVE HS.1186-1 at 3.72.
HSA via Chris Farara

13, a PCB version of the Pegasus 16 used in the HS.1186. The weights and performance data given for this aircraft had assumed a four-nozzle layout with moveable inter-nozzle ramps, but an alternative three-nozzle scheme was illustrated (and included here), which was under investigation at the time of writing. The engine's high thrust would

BELOW HS.1187-5 at 3.72.
HSA via Chris Farara

HS.1186-1

Span	33ft 11in (10.33m)
Length	53ft 6in (16.31m)
Gross wing area	330sq ft (30.7sq m)
t/c ratio (mean)	8.5%
Gross weight	32,168lb (14,591kg)
Powerplant	one Pegasus 16-02 35,500lb (157.8kN)
Maximum escape speed	Mach 0.95
Weapon load	two Sidewinder AAM and six bombs on underwing pylons, two cannon packs beneath fuselage
Internal fuel	1,190gal (5,411lit)

HS.1187-5

Span	35ft 2in (10.71m)
Length	59ft 11in (18.26m)
Gross wing area	400sq ft (37.2sq m)
t/c ratio (mean)	6.4%
Gross weight	43,417lb (19,694kg)
Powerplant	one Pegasus 16-13 with PCB 46,650lb (207.3kN)
Maximum escape speed	Mach 1.1
Weapon load	two Sidewinder AAM on fuselage sides, six bombs on underwing pylons, two cannon packs beneath fuselage
Internal Fuel	1,823gal (8,289lit)

extensive use of composite materials, while the -3 and -4 versions would have more extensive avionics beyond the basic AST requirement included in the -1. The report declared that 'the HS.1186-1 is a possible contender to AST.396 if the need for supersonic performance and other power parameters were relaxed; in other words it is well matched to the AST'. Curiously, the two Sidewinder air-to-air missiles were to be carried on mounts fitted to the inside walls of the innermost wing pylons.

HSA HS.1187 Variants

The HS.1187-5 was the largest single-engined vectored-thrust candidate included in this Hawker Siddeley study. It was to be powered by the Pegasus 16-

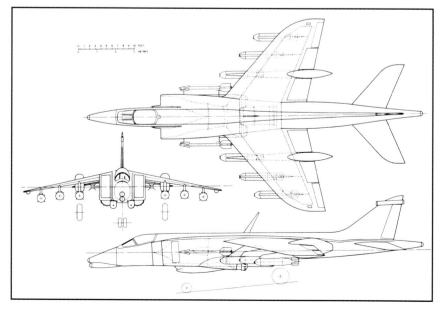

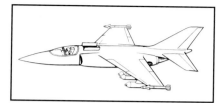

ABOVE Sketch of the HS.1192-1. Note the open lift engine doors.
BAe Brough Heritage Centre

RIGHT HS.1192-1 at 3.72.
HSA via Chris Farara

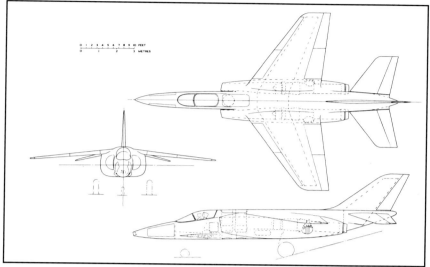

HSA HS.1192-1

The HS.1192-1 revived a powerplant arrangement previously considered in Kingston's P.1137, P.1140 and other projects, i.e. a combination of lift jets with reheated propulsion engines in which 'clangboxes' allowed the *unreheated* propulsion engine thrust to be deflected to provide lifting thrust at take-off and landing. Those early project investigations had proved that such layouts gave the optimum performance in terms of aircraft weight for a given capability, but they tended to be unreliable, vulnerable, difficult to operate and expensive to purchase.

The supersonic HS.1192 met all the AST requirements in full. However, it had this very complex powerplant with two propulsive engines similar in characteristics to the Rolls-Royce RB.231-02 but scaled to 19,000lb (84.4kN) thrust, with twin tailpipes and a pair of cascade nozzles with diverters behind, plus two RB.228-03 lift units scaled to 8,750lb (38.9kN) positioned behind the cockpit. (A cascade was a deflector made from several parallel aerofoil-shaped vanes that was placed inside the nozzle to give a smooth, redirected airflow. In contrast, a diverter was a door that closed across the jet pipe to divert the gas flow from one direction to another – it worked a bit like a thrust reverser and blocked the jet pipe so that the exhaust was diverted to the nozzle.) These engines were more advanced in technological standard than any others installed in aircraft within this study, but currently they were only at very preliminary design stages and so some

of the listed performance data was conjectural (later the HS.1192-1's lift engine type was designated RB.277). The aircraft's main wing was swept 36° at the leading edge.

The operation of aircraft such as the HS.1192-1 posed problems that were avoided by simpler designs. Apart from those stemming from the sheer complexity of the aircraft (such as extended starting sequences and pre-take-off and landing checks), with four separate engines the likelihood of failure was much greater (but no less catastrophic) than that for the single-engine types under the HS.1184, HS.1185, HS.1186 and HS.1187 numbers. Overall, the HS.1192-1 offered a performance that met the essential AST requirements but at a cost close to the MRCA. It also assumed technology levels (particularly in respect of the powerplant) that might not be achievable within the required 1982 timescale, and was thus scarcely comparable to the rest of the aircraft described in this study. Finally, the design had been optimised so definitely for the AST.396 missions and other requirements that it was likely to be less than ideal, and far too expensive, for certain other operational scenarios and roles.

An official review of this extraordinary array of designs reported that HSA's HS.1187-5 and HS.1191-1, and BAC drawings EAG.8404, 8413 and 8461

HS.1192-1	
Span	34ft 8in (10.57m)
Length	49ft 6in (15.09m)
Gross wing area	365sq ft (33.9sq m)
t/c ratio (mean)	5.5%
Gross weight	43,766lb (19,852kg)
Powerplant	See text
Maximum escape speed	Mach 1.1+
Weapon load	Two lower fuselage cannon, gross weight figure quoted 4,000lb (kg) of stores
Internal Fuel	1,850gal (8,412lit)

were the offerings that approached all the AST.396 performance requirements most closely.

AST.396 Issue 1 had been intended to provide guidelines for wide-ranging parametric studies that were aimed at defining the broad characteristics of an aircraft to replace both Harrier and Jaguar in the 1980s. These essentially revealed that, while technically feasible, the cost of developing an aircraft to meet the AST in full could be unacceptably high and this would preclude the purchase of substantial numbers of airframes. Moreover, parallel analytical studies showed that further increases over the speeds and manoeuvrability then current were of doubtful value in very low-level operations, and that the pursuance of much improved speed and manoeuvrability was no longer justified. It was also established that the new aircraft must have a priority requirement to operate at night and in poor visibility conditions, but otherwise it appeared that its performance need only be similar to Harrier and Jaguar. A re-assessment of the main features of the AST and their relative priorities was accordingly carried out and this indicated that operating from main bases and adopting a very low-level profile, thereby reducing the vulnerability and relaxing the aircraft performance criteria, would provide a more cost-effective solution.

Consequently AST.396 Issue 2, dated 6 December 1973 and endorsed on 18 April 1974, looked at exploiting the development potential of either the Harrier or Jaguar while concentrating on night and poor-vision capability. A CA Release for in-service use was required by 1987 and a maximum speed of 450 knots (518mph/834km/h) at 100ft (30.5m) was requested. The maximum speed at height was left open and most of the other limitations were unchanged from Issue 1; the armament was to be six BL.755 cluster weapons, a total of 6,000lb (2,722kg) of external stores plus two short-range infra-red homing AAMs. The resulting feasibility studies took place during 1974/75 and the number of airframe options to be considered was expanded to include types such as the Buccaneer.

Rather less detail is available for most of the BAC and HSA designs to AST.396 Issue 2. Warton suggested variants of the MRCA Tornado (covered by the P.76 designation and including a single-seat aircraft), yet more variants of Jaguar ranging from minimum-change versions (P.77) to designs with new wings including VG (P.78), or with a new fuselage and the existing Jaguar wing (P.79). Later, the P.86 long-term Jaguar development was suggested to AST.396 Issue 3. Hawker Siddeley's efforts included a version of the Buccaneer and the HS.1195.

HSA Kingston HS.1195

Several versions of this project were drawn from June 1974 and a modification of the HS.1195-4 was intended for AST.396 Issue 2. It had side-by-side sensors beneath the radome, one cannon each side beneath the cockpit, three-piece slats and flaps, tip-mounted Sidewinders, three underwing BL.755s per side, two tandem BL.755s beneath the fuselage and twin-wheel main legs. Its span was 34ft (10.36m) and length 47ft (14.33m) and the powerplant was an RB.238-10.

HSA Brough HS.1197

In 1974, following a request from the MoD, HSA Brough assessed the S.Mk.2B (RAF) Buccaneer against AST.396 Issue 2. The AST also desired that the battlefield/short-range interdiction and reconnaissance roles might be performed at longer ranges and the assessment indicated that relatively few modifications were needed to enable the Buccaneer to meet the AST in full. The most essential changes were a better take-off and landing performance and an improved navigation/attack system. The candidate aircraft was designated HS.1197-1 and with an early start it could be put into service in 1981. Dimensions were standard Buccaneer and the project was very similar to Brough's P.157.

BELOW The original HS.1195-4 shown here and drawn in about August 1974 was adapted with modifications to AST.396 Issue 2. *HSA via Chris Farara*

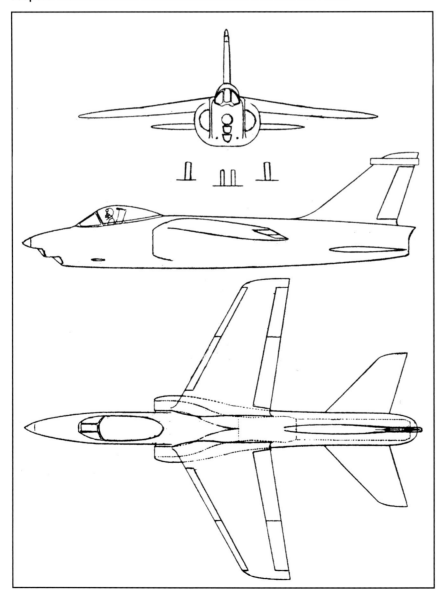

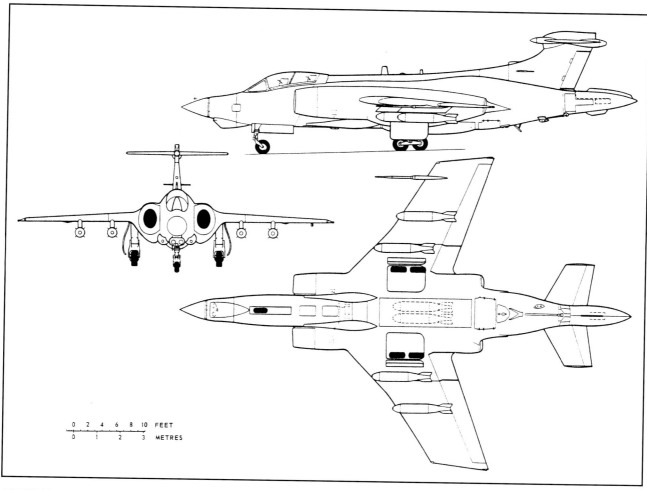

0 2 4 6 8 10 FEET
0 1 2 3 METRES

ABOVE The HS.1197-1 was a version of the Buccaneer offered against AST.396 Issue 2 in 1974.
BAe Brough Heritage Centre

HSA HS.1197-1	
Span	44ft 0in (13.41m)
Length	63ft 5in (19.32m)
Gross wing area	508.5sq ft (47.3sq m)
t/c ratio	9.25% to 6%
Gross weight	49,075lb (22,260kg)
Powerplant	two RR RB.168-78 11,560lb (51.4kN)
Maximum speed/height	670mph (1,078km/h) at sea level
Weapon load	two cannon, six BL755 or other stores

For a take-off and landing roll distance of under 3,000ft (914m) Brough felt that the most cost-effective solution was to utilise quick-acting blow for take-off and install a braking parachute for landing. No problems were envisaged with this because a number of quick-acting blow take-offs had already been performed with encouraging results, while a brake parachute had been fitted to some early Buccaneer prototypes. Buccaneer was probably large enough to accommodate all the possible night sensors for nav/attack including both FLIR and LLTV. Two gun packs were fitted to the lower fuselage beneath the intakes and to accommodate the heavier loads a tandem two-wheel main undercarriage was introduced. Radius of

action was given as 240nm (444km), penetration speed Mach 0.68 and escape speed Mach 0.88. This aircraft was intended to operate in conjunction with the very light HS.1182-74 or P.154 class of aircraft and to deal with the more extreme parts of AST.396. As before, further variations of the candidate design were described, including the HS.1197-3 which introduced a single RB.162-81 lift jet to complement the Spey engines.

An official report from April 1976 on the Industry and MoD studies stated that these had shown it was feasible to meet the AST.396 aerodynamic criteria by the development and modification of several existing aircraft types. The design that would virtually meet the AST at the lowest gross weight (and probably cost) was a Jaguar variant with a single RB.199-34R engine and a modified wing. If V/STOL performance was required then the only aircraft of those considered that approached the AST performance would be one of the Harrier variants, probably developed a stage beyond the AV-16 (Chapter Ten). Only the Panavia MRCA met the performance targets without any major modifications, though there were reservations on its structural strength and the weight and cost would be high. The Buccaneer met the AST with minor modifications but it was marginal on the airfield performance requirements and was also heavy, relatively expensive and

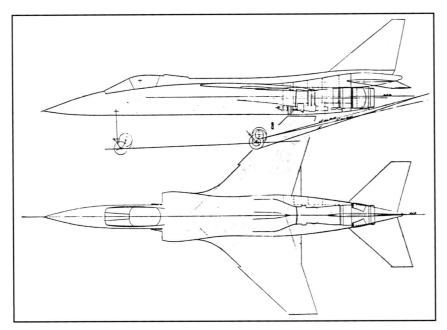

ABOVE A 1976 Ministry report declared that the design that would virtually meet the AST at the lowest gross weight was a Jaguar variant with a single RB.199-34R engine and a modified wing. This is the only single-engine Jaguar drawing to have been found so far (EAG.8522) and it is dated early 1974. There are no further details. *North West Heritage Group*

shortly going out of production. Variants of the Hawk, considered as a lightweight alternative, fell well short of most of the requirements (including range, take-off roll and speed) while the HS.1190 did not show up well in either the air combat or attack role, despite being an attempt to combine the two. A similar design study, the larger HS.1195, had been included at HSA's request and this benefited from being tailored specifically at AST.396's requirements. The report suggested that the HS.1195 could be competitive with single-engine Jaguar variants.

The feasibility studies emphasised that the difficulties in satisfying Issue 2 of AST.396 lay predominantly in the avionics requirements. Indeed, the avionic and ergonomic problem areas exposed were sufficient to raise major doubts about the fundamental feasibility of the Issue 2 target. It could also be said with reasonable certainty that a solution to the AST would require an aircraft of considerable complexity, size and cost, and that the complexity of such a weapon system would significantly exceed the concept of an aircraft complementary to, and cheaper than, the MRCA. Consequently, these

considerations led to the withdrawal of AST.396 Issue 2 and the termination of any further studies related to it. A new AST number (403) was allocated to the project as the operational concepts were developed further (although, as noted, further proposals appear to have been made against an AST.396 Issue 3).

HSA Brough's Roy Boot wrote in his book *From Spitfire to Eurofighter* that 'there was a good deal of alarm in the industry that the requirement [AST.396] was too restricted in the scope of the roles specified, and that it was too ambitious in some of the technological solutions needed to fulfil the envisaged operations'. He felt that a go-ahead for such a project might prove financially disastrous and, despite the wished-for low-cost option, some significant advances in technology would still be needed to accomplish the job. The AST.396 designs ranged from the most simple to quite complex aeroplanes. Boot reported that 'it was with considerable relief that we learned of the withdrawal of AST.396, with the subsequent issue of AST.403 which placed the primary emphasis on the air-to-air role'.

So the outcome of these considerations was a redefined concept calling for the combination of the roles of air combat and ground attack in an aircraft considerably smaller and cheaper than the MRCA Tornado. This concept was embodied in a new Air Staff Target AST.403 first issued in 1975 and which became the starting point for the Eurofighter Typhoon (the rest of the story is described in the companion *British Secret Projects: Jet Fighters since 1950*). In fact, until around 1985 the heavy drain on the Air Vote by variants of Tornado meant that little money would be available for any other new manned fixed-wing air projects. In this climate the Air Force Department OR Branch could do little with AST.396 other than assign BAC and HSA with small exploratory tasks designed to investigate new technology and equipment, such as fly-by-wire or incorporating the 1553B data-bus.

HSA Brough P.153

Reference was made earlier to the P.153 small combat aircraft project from Hawker Siddeley Brough that was begun in 1969. This design is worthy of a full description and it was intended to be more of a fighter than a strike aircraft. Results from actual and simulated air combat had led Brough to conclude that the majority of combat would be in the subsonic or low supersonic speed regime at low to moderate altitudes. P.153 used a single RB.199 engine while the application and extension of techniques in boundary layer control over full-span leading-edge and trailing-edge flaps for high lift, as developed for the Buccaneer and Phantom, provided good STOL capability (the BLC air was taken from the RB.199's low pressure compressor). To suit the size and scale of the P.153, and to reduce weight, AI radar had been excluded and so the proposed AI system was based on an infra-red sensor. A laser ranger would be used for ground attack.

The advanced technology RB.199 and simple pitot intake made possible a 33% reduction in aircraft size compared to previous-generation engines, and reheat and a thrust reverser were provided. Great attention was given to combat manoeuvrability but, apart from its BLC system, P.153 was fairly conventional and utilised current materials and manufacturing techniques. The mid/high wing position helped to minimise transonic drag and the 5,500lb (2,495kg) of internal fuel permitted an interception to be made 130nm (241km) from base, while two 100gal (455lit) drop tanks would increase the range to more than 220nm (407km). With fighter armament (six Sidewinder AAMs or SRAAM 100s) and fuel for combat at 100nm (185km) radius the P.153 weighed 19,084lb (8,657kg); as a ground attack aircraft with four 1,000lb (454kg) bombs and the same fuel it weighed 23,568lb (10,690kg). Two cannon were placed in the lower forward fuselage and there were seven weapon stations, comprising two wing tip mounts and five main pylons for bombs, missiles or drop tanks (two under each wing and one beneath the mid-fuselage point). Expected RB.199 developments would increase the available thrust to 20,000lb (88.9kN) and push the top speed at altitude up to Mach 1.8; a variable geometry intake would have permitted Mach 2 but at the expense of low-speed and transonic performance. The low-level penetration speed would be Mach 0.75 and the escape speed in reheat Mach 1.1.

By February 1972 the P.153 was considered to be a separate project from AST.396 since it was essentially a fighter with close air support capability. It was thought that a 1972 start date could bring a prototype first flight late in 1976 and put the aircraft in squadron service by 1981. Six pre-production machines would be needed for the bulk of the development and clearance work, which would take place from a first flight in 1978 until 1981. P.153 was pushed by Brough for several years but the British Government did not take it up because at that stage there was no fighter requirement. The project was eventually abandoned but in 1975 was succeeded by the pure fighter P.159 that,

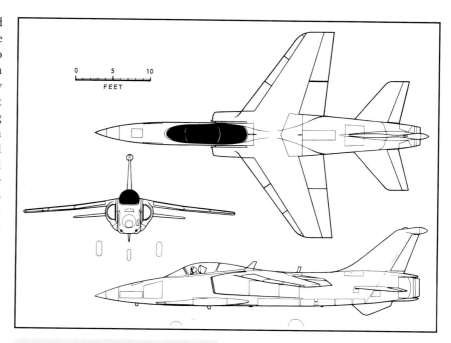

HSA P.153

Span	24ft 8in (7.52m)
Length	43ft 8in (13.31m)
Gross wing area	185sq ft (17.2sq m)
t/c ratio	not given
Gross weight	23,500lb (10,660kg)
Powerplant	one RB199-34R 15,300lb (68.0kN) reheat
Maximum speed/height	Mach 1.2 at low level, Mach 1.6 at height (both with AAM)
Weapon load	two 30mm Aden or DEFA cannon, five 1,000lb (454kg) bombs, seven 540lb (245kg) or BL755 cluster bombs, eight RP launchers

ABOVE HSA Brough P.153 project as it looked in June 1974.
BAe Brough Heritage Centre

apart from an increase in wing area, looked very similar. This, as the HS.1204, was proposed to AST.396's replacement, AST.403.

Future Offensive Air System (FOAS)

When the author completed the first edition of this book the future of the British bomber in terms of new developments was seen to be the Future Offensive Air System or FOAS. An initial operational capability was expected in around 2017 (right now), but in fact the FOAS was cancelled in June 2005.

At the end of 1995 initial studies were completed for a Future Offensive Aircraft (FOA) to a guideline requirement SR(A).425. In 1996 the

MoD and BAe completed a Pre-Feasibility study that looked at 'a range of aircraft-based weapon system concepts to determine their capability, cost timescale and technical risk'. In 1997 the MoD launched a full Feasibility study, the project having in late 1996 been redesignated the Future Offensive Air System to embrace non-piloted aircraft (Uninhabited Air Vehicles or UAVs flown by 'pilots' on the ground) and missiles. Options included an enhanced Eurofighter with a thicker wing to increase the fuel capacity, a new off-the-shelf single or two-seat stealth combat aircraft, a UAV, or conventional air-launched cruise missiles released at long range from a transport aircraft. Contracts were placed with industry and the Defence Evaluation and Research Agency (DERA) while the French Defence Ministry contributed to a Technology Demonstration Programme that covered the computer modelling of weapon systems. But, as stated, the FOAS was dropped in 2005 and its replacement, the Deep and Persistent Offensive Capability or DPOC requirement, was cancelled by the 2010 Strategic Defence review.

The latest research again refers to uninhabited bombers with their 'pilots' safely on the ground at their bases, but it is always unwise to try to predict the future of aerospace. The very day this was written there was growing tension between the Americans and Russians over Syria, which may loosen purse strings for new bombers. In fact, America has a contract in place for the Long Range Strike Bomber or LRS-B, but at the time of writing the hard-worked Tornado is hanging on in the UK, though it is gradually being replaced by the Eurofighter Typhoon as that aircraft is further adapted to carry air-to-ground stores. Only time will tell if the RAF will one day get a new Tornado replacement.

ABOVE Impressions of the P.153 small combat aircraft. *BAe Brough Heritage Centre*

Appendix One
British Bomber Projects Summary

ABOVE Model of the Blackburn B.109 interceptor strike project prepared for Canada (1958). *George Cox*

During their years of independence many of Britain's aircraft manufacturers became wedded to certain types of aeroplane or areas of manufacture. Hawker, for example, was a fighter specialist while Avro, Bristol, Handley Page and Vickers were usually inclined towards bigger game and built, or at least designed, many heavy bombers. Blackburn was just one manufacturer to supply aircraft regularly to the Fleet Air Arm and this was a major influence on its lines of development.

The following lists jet and turboprop-powered heavy bombers, light bombers, interdictors, strike aircraft, anti-submarine and close support aircraft, plus research types developed primarily to advance the bomber designer's art. To hold the list to manageable proportions, pure trainer and reconnaissance developments are omitted (with a few exceptions) although some designs produced as combined strike trainers do get in. In theory, all projects are 'official', despite some schemes lasting for such a brief lifetime (perhaps just a day or two) that they really have no right to be here, but sneak in as one cannot always determine which they are. For some projects little or no information is known to have survived and has probably been lost forever. Others, of course, are still secret. Designs produced at Brough, Kingston and Warton from about the early 1960s onwards would often cover a selection of different layouts and, from a publishing point of view, this makes life difficult since one cannot include every drawing. Hence, in such cases, only the most suitable or representative drawing is reproduced; perhaps one that has been examined in some depth or used as a baseline for other variations.

AIRSPEED

AS.69   Maritime reconnaissance variant of AS.57 Ambassador airliner, 1951. Had AS.57's high wing. AS.69A similar but wing in low position, 1951. AS.69A span 115ft (35.05m), length 82ft 6in (25.15m), gross weight with bomb load 60,000lb (27,216kg). Fitted with ASV radar and two gun turrets on upper fuselage.

ARMSTRONG WHITWORTH

AW.50   Flying wing jet bomber design study tendered to MAP mid-12.42. Designer 'Jimmy' Lloyd deleted fuselage to gain maximum benefit of laminar flow wing (recently developed in USA) and reduce drag; led to flying wing concept used by AWA for some years. Need for ultra-smooth surface met by construction using fairly thick light alloy skin supported by rolled corrugations of thinner gauge – skin and corrugations acted as spar flanges for taking bend and torsion and together with the webs formed a box spar that was lighter than conventional construction but with high degree of stiffness to maintain accurate profile shape. Only projections outside wing profile were crew cabin and remotely controlled twin 20mm turret behind. Design featured two fixed forward-firing 20mm cannon in wings between engines, four 4,000lb (17.8kN) MetroVick F.3 turbojets in pairs just outside each side of centre cockpit, split flaps, 'elevators' on the trailing edge near the tip, wing tip fins and rudders. Outboard movement of rudders greater through differential gearing. Estimated top speed 470mph (756km/h) at sea level, Mach 0.7 480mph (772km/h) at 30,000ft (9,144m), sea level rate of climb 3,340ft/min (1,018m/min), time to 30,000ft fourteen minutes, range 1,500 miles (2,414km), gross weight 49,765lb (22,573kg), wing loading 27lb/sq ft (132kg/sq m), bomb load 12,000lb (5,443kg). Span 120ft (36.58m), wing area 2,000sq ft (186sq m), t/c 23.5%. Revision with span 112ft 6in (34.29) and t/c 15% sent to MAP 1.44. Turret deleted but thinner wing forced introduction of fuselage for crew. Length 45ft (13.72m), gross weight 54,183lb (24,577kg), top speed 460mph (740km/h). Project soon abandoned.

AW.51 One-third scale wood glider to test aerodynamics of highly experimental AW.50, 1943.

AW.52 Experimental tailless aircraft to E.9/44 to test flying wing concept (with large-chord, low-drag wings) for large aircraft – bombers and civil. AW.52G scale glider flew 2.3.45. First of two AW.52 prototypes flew 13.11.47.

AW.56 Medium bomber to B.35/46 with five engines, 4.47; revised form with four engines late 47.

AW.168 Naval strike aircraft to M.148T, 9.54.

AW.171 Slim delta flying wing aircraft 'A' to ER.161T, 1955. Aerodynamic research aircraft to test flight problems created by very narrow delta or diamond-shaped (lozenge) planforms, for possible long-range bomber or transport. Span 17ft 7in (5.4m), length with probe 75ft 4in (23.0m), wing area (lozenge) 553sq ft (51.4sq m), leading-edge sweep angle 83°, t/c ratio 6%, two tip-mounted reheated 4,850lb (21.6kN) Bristol Orpheus for forward propulsion, ten vertically mounted 2,100lb (9.3kN) Rolls-Royce RB.108s for VTOL capability, gross weight 17,500lb (7,938kg). Pilot in prone position.

AW.172 Slim delta aircraft 'B' to ER.161T, 1955. As per AW.171 but smaller. Span 21ft (6.40m), length 50ft (15.24m), wing area (lozenge) 490sq ft (45.6sq m), LE sweep 76°, t/c ratio 3%, single fuselage-mounted de Havilland PS.53 Gyron Junior with reheat, no VTOL capability, conventional pilot seat. AWA preferred AW.171 because felt it was more suited for development into larger aircraft than AW.172.

AW.651 Twin-boom maritime patrol aircraft development of AW.650 freighter submitted to NBMR.2, mid-1958.

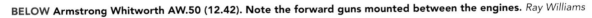

BELOW Armstrong Whitworth AW.50 (12.42). Note the forward guns mounted between the engines. *Ray Williams*

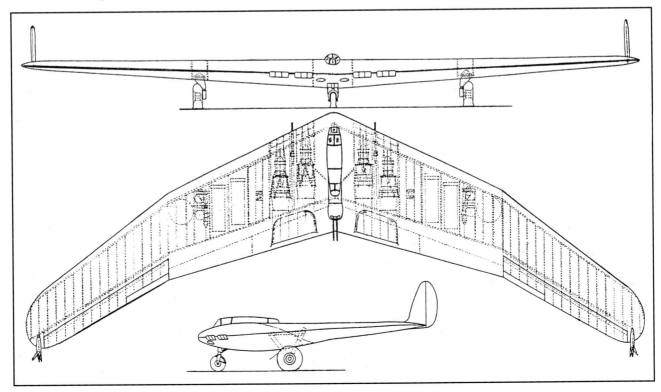

AVRO/HAWKER SIDDELEY/BRITISH AEROSPACE, MANCHESTER

A bomber specialist, but after the late 1950s Canberra Replacement programme the factory concentrated on civil aircraft.

696 Anti-submarine aircraft to R.5/46. Became Shackleton, first flown 9.3.49.

698 Medium bomber to B.35/46, 5.47. Became Vulcan, first flown 30.8.52. Numerous advanced developments followed.

Long Range Bomber Study based on scaled up version of Type 698. Covering report completed 7.47.

707 One-third scale 698 to E.15/48 to examine low-speed problems, 1948.

710 Half-scale 698 to test high-speed characteristics, 1948.

716 Shackleton Mk.3 proposal, direct development of the Mk.2, 19.10.50.

719 Shackleton Mk.3 proposal, new fuselage and engines on normal outer wings, 1.52.

721 Low-level bomber to B.126T, 12.52.

727 Light ground attack aircraft to NATO requirement, 1954.

730 High-speed high-altitude reconnaissance aircraft to R.156T, 7.55. Construction of modified design with bombing capability begun but cancelled 3.57.

731 Three-eighths scale model test aircraft for 730 to ER.180D, 12.55. Never built.

732 Delta-wing supersonic bomber studies, 7.56 onwards. Designs based on Vulcan.

738 Designs for a weapon system, 1957. No information available.

739 Low-level strike aircraft to GOR.339, 1.58. Design blended with Hawker P.1129 as combined Hawker Siddeley submission against BAC TSR.2, 11.58.

745 Medium-range replacement for Shackleton to NBMR.2, 6.58.

752 VTOL assault aircraft, 3.58. No information available.

762 Advanced weapons system, 11.58. No information available.

769 VTOL weapons system (Vulcan), early 1960s. No information available.

774 Long-endurance weapon system, early 1960s. No information available.

775 Maritime reconnaissance aircraft to replace Shackleton, 1960s. Two RR Tyne plus one rear-mounted RR RB.168.

776 Variant of Type 775 with three RB.178s. Span 135ft 8in (41.35m). Length 129ft 4in (39.42m).

784 Maritime reconnaissance aircraft with four turboprop engines, 1960s.

HS.801 Anti-submarine aircraft to MR.254. Became Nimrod, prototype first flew 23.5.67.

BLACKBURN/HAWKER SIDDELEY/ BRITISH AEROSPACE, BROUGH

This company designed new aircraft right through to the 1980s and some of its later projects are still classified; the last design was the P.183. With the total integration of Blackburn into the Hawker Siddeley organisation the B prefix was changed to P, although some brochures actually used an HS prefix, e.g. HS.146.

B.54 Anti-submarine aircraft to GR.17/45. Became Y.A.5, Y.A.7 and Y.A.8. First example flew 20.9.49.

B.61 Design study for naval strike aircraft, 1.4.46.

B.66 Transonic four-jet delta wing bomber, 10.9.46. 'Delta' Model 1 (tunnel model?) drawn 26.9.46 had wing/fin arrangement quite similar to German Lippisch DM-1 glider of 1944/45. Unknown if B.66 to be similar as design never progressed beyond Project Office. Designer George Petty felt B.66 was good proposal but company lacked resources to follow it through. Delta chosen for aerodynamic reasons but no decision reached to fit or omit tailplane.

Y.B.2 Designation of HP.88 scale model aircraft, 4.48. First flew 21.6.51.

B.79 Anti-submarine aircraft to replace B.54, 26.1.49.

B.83 Light anti-submarine aircraft powered by Rolls-Royce Merlin 35 engine, 24.7.50.

B.88 AEW adaptation of B.54 as Y.B.1, 1950.

B.91 Light anti-submarine aircraft, 1951.

B.96 B.54 with Napier E.141, 1952.

BELOW 'Working shape' for Hawker Siddeley Brough P.141 study as at 4.67. *BAE SYSTEMS*

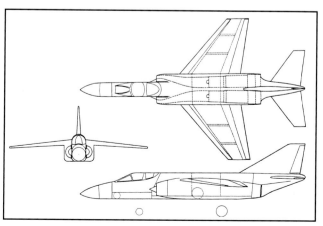

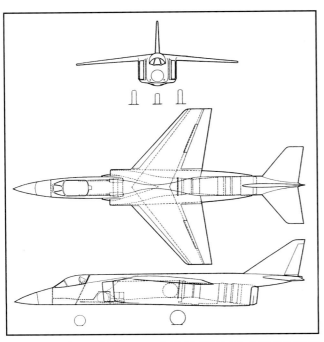

ABOVE Hawker Siddeley Brough 'HS.146' (4.69). *BAE SYSTEMS*

B.103 Naval strike aircraft to M.148T, 9.54. First preliminary drawings 1.12.52. Became Buccaneer S.Mk.1 first flown 30.4.58. S.Mk.2 developed later with RR Speys.

B.103A RAF version to embryonic GOR.339, 6.57.

B.108 Buccaneer development to GOR.339, 1.58.

B.109 Interceptor strike Buccaneer for Canada, 1958. Unsolicited proposal, lengthened nose and tail, non-folding wings, reduced t/c outboard of mid-wing; twin RR RB.146 engines, 13,000lb (57.8kN) dry, 18,000lb (80kN) with reheat. Span 42ft 6in (12.95m), length 71ft 8in (21.85m), top speed Mach 1.65. No interest from Canada.

ABOVE Artwork for the HSA Brough P.154 taken from the company brochure. *BAe Brough Heritage Centre*

B.111 Buccaneer proposal for RAF, 2.60. First Buccaneer with RR Spey (reheated to 18,000lb [80kN]). Various modifications from S.Mk.1, take-off weight normal fuel 46,988lb (21,314kg), with tanks 54,200lb (24,585kg). Estimated maximum Mach 0.85 at low level, Mach 1.25 at height (doubted by Air Staff); radius of action normal fuel 840nm (1,557km), with drop tanks 1,000nm (1,853km).

B.113 Variant of B.111 offered to Australia, 5.60.

B.116 Spey-powered Buccaneer offered to West German Navy, 6.60.

B.123 Advanced strike aircraft to OR.346, two brochures: 5.7.61 and 9.61.

B.124 Buccaneer development, 1961.

B.126 Land-based Buccaneer development, 1961.

B.127 Variable geometry Buccaneer, 1961.

B.128 Buccaneer Mk.2 with reheated RB.168R Speys for better take-off and manoeuvrability, 1962.

B.130 Advanced strike aircraft, 1962. Details unavailable.

P.131 Subsonic low-level strike aircraft, 1962. Details unavailable.

P.132 Buccaneer S.Mk.1 with RATOG, 1962.

P.133 Buccaneer S.Mk.2 with RATOG, 1962.

P.134 Buccaneer with improved weapon system, 1962. Became unofficially the Mk.2*.

P.135 Variable sweep strike-fighter proposed as Buccaneer successor, 1962. Two reheated Speys, both pivoting and translating wing swing mechanisms investigated for angles between 63° and 25°. Span limits 30ft and 60ft (9.14 and 18.29m), length 59ft (17.98m), maximum take-off weight 60,000lb (27,216kg). Project to fulfil requirements outlined for B.123; company considered P.135 as far more practical proposition.

P.136 Initial Buccaneer proposals to South Africa, 1962. Became S.Mk.50.

P.138 Counter-insurgency strike fighter, 1962.

P.141 Next Generation Tactical Aircraft, 1964–67. Studied type likely to replace Buccaneer, Phantom and Lightning. Identified need for major advance in aircraft survivability due to great increase in type's complexity. Fixed and VG investigations but, through drag considerations, main work on compact and efficient fixed sweep layout. With two crew, four 1,000lb (454kg) bombs semi-buried in fuselage and internal fuel for 1,000nm (1,853km) high-level range, minimum take-off weight calculated to be 38,000lb (17,239kg). Four wing pylons could take another twelve 1,000lb bombs or mix of weapons for ground attack role. Secondary interceptor capability built in with semi-buried

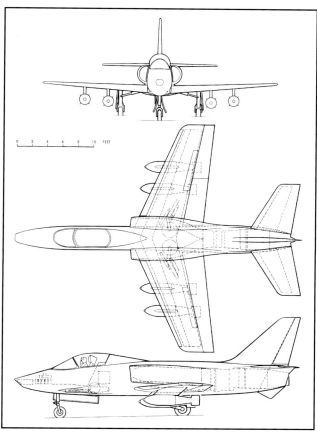

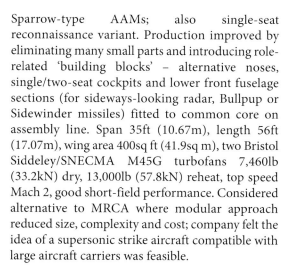

ABOVE HSA P.154 with low wing (9.71).
BAe Brough Heritage Centre

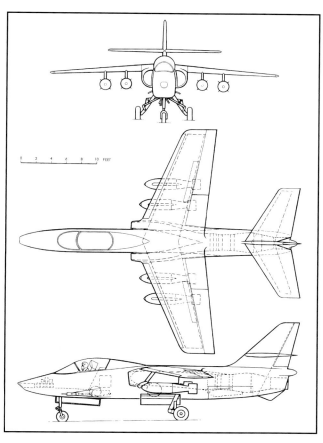

ABOVE HSA P.154 with high wing (9.71).
BAe Brough Heritage Centre

Sparrow-type AAMs; also single-seat reconnaissance variant. Production improved by eliminating many small parts and introducing role-related 'building blocks' – alternative noses, single/two-seat cockpits and lower front fuselage sections (for sideways-looking radar, Bullpup or Sidewinder missiles) fitted to common core on assembly line. Span 35ft (10.67m), length 56ft (17.07m), wing area 400sq ft (41.9sq m), two Bristol Siddeley/SNECMA M45G turbofans 7,460lb (33.2kN) dry, 13,000lb (57.8kN) reheat, top speed Mach 2, good short-field performance. Considered alternative to MRCA where modular approach reduced size, complexity and cost; company felt the idea of a supersonic strike aircraft compatible with large aircraft carriers was feasible.

P.142 Supersonic Buccaneer, 1965.

P.145 Land-based Buccaneer development, 10.66. Major improvements to standard aircraft plus additional large reconnaissance pack and substantial bomb-carrying capacity. Maximum take-off weight 62,000lb (28,123kg). RAF committed to F-111K so did not take up.

P.146 Private venture light ground attack aircraft, 1967–71. First in series of lightweight designs. Utilised Brough's Buccaneer experience in LE and TE flap blowing to give good STOL capability but idea fell away when Harrier VTOL concept was proved. RR Turboméca Adour or RB.199 alternative powerplants. At 4.69 'HS.146' had become carrier-based low-level interceptor and strike type of different configuration for operation with Brough P.139 AEW aircraft. Accent now on manoeuvrability in Mach 0.5 to 1.2 range, simple weapons system with visual acquisition of target after guidance from P.139. Two 30mm guns, two heat-seeking Taildog missiles. Visual strike capability now secondary but delivery of 4,000lb (1,814kg) bombs over 200nm (370km) radius available. One reheated Spey 5R 12,500lb (55.6kN) dry, 21,000lb (93.3kN) reheat (serving with RN Phantoms) or RB.199 14,130lb (62.8kN) dry, 24,700lb (109.8kN) reheat. Span 28ft 6in (8.69m), length 51ft 0in (15.54m), wing area 272sq ft (25.3sq m), gross weight 23,125lb (10,490kg), Mach 1.1 at sea level, Mach 1.8 at 36,000ft (10,973m).

P.148 Retrofit of Spey into Buccaneer S.Mk.1, 1967.

P.149 Buccaneer for RAF, 3.69. Development centred on redesigned nav/attack system for all-weather capability, bomb bay door with integral fuel tank and RR RB.162 or Rolls/Allison XJ.99 take-off boost engine in rear of fuselage. Existing aircraft to be modified. Max gross weight (twin 430gal [1,955lit] tanks, six 1,000lb [454kg] bombs) 62,889lb (28,526kg).

P.150 Supersonic Buccaneer for RAF, 1968. Response to Air Staff request for version with reheated Spey 202s. Used variable geometry intakes with translating cones and fitted with thrust reverser. Was 6ft (1.82m) longer than standard aircraft thus eliminating area rule bulge, had non-folding 6% thick wing, new tail unit and bogie main wheels to deal with extra weight. Maximum speed Mach 1.8, basic weight 7,000lb (3,175kg) above standard S.Mk.2.

P.151 Semi-strategic strike aircraft, 1969. Details unavailable but possibly tied in with HS.1179 studies.

P.152 Light tactical aircraft, 1971.

P.153 Lightweight strike fighter, 1969 to 1975. HS.1190 variant to AST.396, 1971.

P.154 Continuation of lightweight studies begun with P.146; Initial Feasibility Study, 9.71. Both low- and high-wing versions but latter would carry stores more easily and offer better aerodynamics. Wing and fuselage essentially the same. Alternative versions with twin Adours. All designs carried four 1,000lb (454kg) bombs under wings and two cannon in lower front fuselage. Span 30ft 0in (9.14m), length 37ft 6in (11.43m), wing area 194sq ft (18.0sq m), gross weight 15,692lb (7,118kg) with low wing, 16,065lb (7,287kg) with high wing, one non-reheat RB.199 engine.

P.155 Base-burning aircraft, 1971.

P.157 Close air support and strike variant of Buccaneer, 5.74. Final proposal for major development of the type. As HS.1197 proposed to AST.396.

P.165 Supersonic vectored thrust aircraft, 8.80.

P.167 New-generation V/STOL aircraft, 7.81.

P.168 Active control technology studies.

P.169 Stealth penetration aircraft.

P.170 Light attack aircraft, 11.82.

P.177 F-4 Phantom developments.

P.178 Harrier developments.

P.181 ASTOVL developments, 1.87.

BOULTON PAUL

P.111 Prototype for general delta wing research to E.27/46, first flown 10.10.50.

P.120 Delta wing research aircraft developed from P.111, first flown 6.8.52.

P.133 Dart-shaped fighter and strike aircraft for RAF and Navy evolved from Government-sponsored research on potential use of VTOL fan lift principle. First fighter P.133 (6.56), then smaller P.133A (8.56). Larger P.133B (submitted 12.56) pure naval strike aircraft based on NR/A.39 requirements but designed for catapult launch in zero relative wind conditions. Fan lift system would enable fully loaded aircraft to fly off at 115mph (185km/h). Landing approach speed dependent on weight (at 36,000lb [16,330kg] relative air speed of 63mph [101km/h] required); at lower weights approach speed set by controllability, not by lift (recommended minimum 58mph [93km/h]). Normal gross weight 40,120lb (18,198kg) but possible to operate P.133B at 45,000lb (20,412kg) with catapult take-off executed in 28mph (45km/h) relative wind. Two 10,000lb (44.4kN) Gyron Juniors for forward flight. For take-off and landing, jet efflux redirected to two two-stage turbines with total output of 25,000hp (18,643kW) that drove four 32in (81.3cm) diameter lifting fans. Fan lift forces varied by movable inlet guide vanes and at low forward speeds the normal control surfaces were assisted in pitch and roll by differential thrust from the fans. Total lift force of fans and turbines 34,000lb (151.1kN) and system's centre of lift set behind the CofG to offset the nose-up pitching moment generated by the wing when fans operated in forward flight. Large centreline bomb bay to accommodate two 2,000lb (907kg), four 1,000lb (454kg) or TMB. Span 28ft 0in (8.53m), length 57ft 0in (17.37m), wing area 841sq ft (78.2sq m), t/c ratio 8%, Maximum Mach 1.34 at sea level.

P.136 Research aircraft, 8.57. Part of extensive VTOL research programme with P.133, P.135 and P.137.

P.137 Definitive fan lift NR/A.39 proposal (though really a research aircraft), 11.57. Layout very similar to P.133B; two mid-span 10,000lb (44.4kN) Gyron Juniors plus ten lift fans converted from RB.108s giving 40,000lb (177.8kN) total thrust in two rows of five each between engines and bomb bay. Ducted fan system to support 86% of aircraft's weight, fully loaded aircraft to be flown off at 115mph (185km/h). Central bomb bay for same load as P.133B. Span 31ft (9.45m), length 56ft (17.07m), wing area 900sq ft (83.7sq m), t/c 11%, Maximum speed 946mph (1,523km/h) at sea level, internal fuel 1,570gal (7,139lit), gross weight 46,465lb (21,077kg).

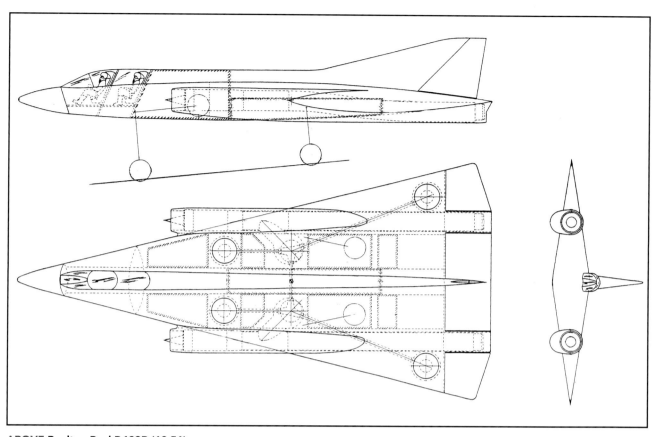

ABOVE Boulton Paul P.133B (12.56).
BELOW Boulton Paul P.137 'Naval Search and Strike Aircraft' (11.57).

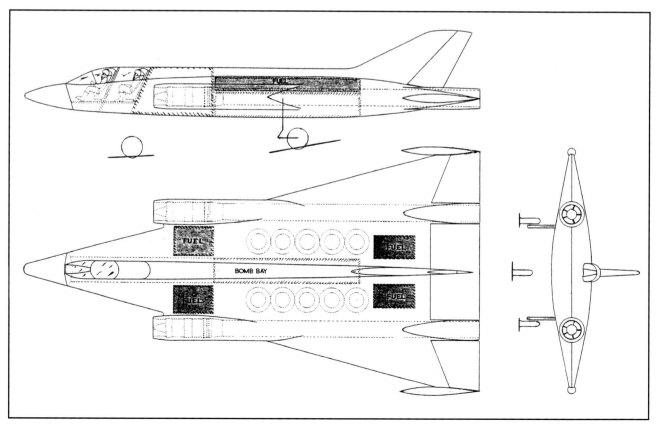

BRISTOL

172 Long-range bomber to unnumbered Air Staff requirement, 5.46 and 10.46.

174 Four-tenths scale model of Type 172 to E.8/47, 10.46 onwards.

Reconnaissance Aircraft and Target Marker Small twin-engine recce aircraft for locating and accurate visual marking of target at extreme range, 4.50. High speed over target (582mph [936km/h]) up to 7,000nm (12,964km) away, ceiling 42,000ft (12,802m), gross take-off weight with drop tanks 53,850lb (24,426kg), droppable marking load 1,275lb (578kg), total fuel including drop tanks 31,500lb (14,288kg). One crew aided by automatic navigation, no defensive weapons, new engine required, outer main wheels and RATO units jettisoned after take-off, drop tanks after climb. Span 63ft 0in (19.20m), length 65ft 0in (19.81m), gross wing area 565sq ft (52.5sq m), t/c 8.5. DMARD (A. E. Woodward Nutt) noted 'project of great interest technically but Air Staff not interested'.

Jet Bomber Unnumbered design with twin 12,150lb (54.0kN) Olympus Ol.3s, 1.5.51. Long-range recce aircraft (above) had showed promise so performance for follow-on bomber of similar form now examined. Very high speed (Mach 0.92) and good manoeuvrability at low level in target area, high cruise speed (500 knots, 576mph [926km/h]), height over target with 2,000lb (907kg) load 47,000ft (14,326m) and range 5,600nm (10,371km). Mass balancing effect of wing-mounted engines helped avoid flutter during high-speed, low-level flight; tunnel test showed good results for close-mounted wing nacelles but stalk-mounted alternatives to be assessed. Wing had modified high-lift Fowler flaps between body and nacelles, small span ailerons outside nacelles for rolling power at low level and high speed, large span ailerons extending inwards from tips. All-metal construction, bicycle undercarriage with two-wheel nose, four-wheel main gear and outriggers in nacelles, three crew in nose, provision in tail for one radar-guided 30mm cannon. Span 83ft 6in (25.45m), length 100ft (30.48m), wing area 1,000sq ft (93sq m), t/c 8.0, internal fuel 6,100gal (27,736lit), gross take-off weight 86,600lb (39,282kg), one 10,000lb (4,536kg), one 5,000lb (2,268kg), two 4,000lb (1,814kg) or six 1,000lb (454kg) bombs in bomb bay.

175 Maritime reconnaissance development of Type 175 Britannia airliner, 10.51.

175MR Further maritime reconnaissance development of Type 175 Britannia airliner, 22.4.53.

176 Three-tenths scale model of Type 172 to E.8/47 Issue 2, 1.48.

186 Low-level bomber to B.126T, 19.12.52.

189 Development of Type 175MR with Nomad engines, c. 1953.

196 Expendable unmanned bomber variant of Type 188 high-speed research aircraft, 1955. Twin RR Avon or Bristol BE.36 jets. BE.36 single-spool turbojet rated at 17,730lb (78.9kN) designed for Mach 2.5 performance.

BELOW Bristol long-range reconnaissance aircraft (4.50).

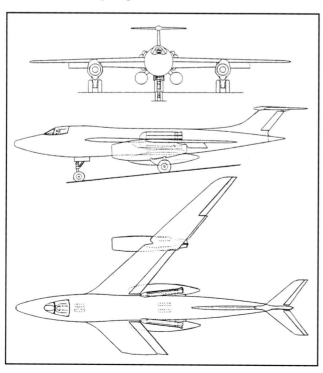

BELOW Bristol jet bomber (1.5.51).

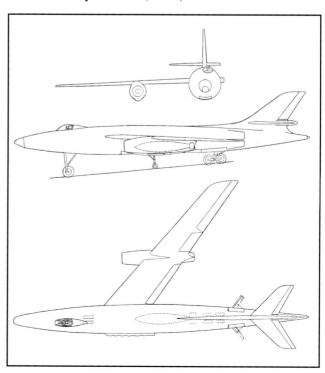

202 Medium-range low-altitude bomber with twin Olympus, 1957.

204 Low-level strike aircraft to GOR.339, 14.1.58.

206 NATO Maritime Patrol Aircraft to NBMR.2, 5.58.

207 NATO Maritime Patrol Aircraft to NBMR.2, 1958.

217 Supersonic strike reconnaissance project, 1959. Single vectored thrust 18,000lb (80kN) Bristol BE.53 and single seat. From side design resembled Hawker Harrier but had tiny wing. Span 13ft 6in (4.11m), length 50ft (15.24m), wing area 107sq ft (10.0sq m), gross weight 13,900lb (6,305kg), top speed 800mph (1,287km/h).

DE HAVILLAND

For a period in the 1950s there were two de Havilland aircraft design teams: the original Hatfield group and the former Airspeed factory at Christchurch. The latter was mainly responsible for modifying fighters already in production and did not allocate new project numbers, but it did produce two bomber projects.

DH.108 Swallow tailless research aircraft to E.18/45, flown 15.5.46. Based on Vampire fuselage. Designed primarily to probe unknowns of transonic flight for Comet airliner but results benefited aviation in general.

DH.110 Christchurch development of DH.110 fighter as tactical bomber for RAF (26.9.56) and for Navy (23.11.56). Combined for both land or carrier-based operation 3.57.

DH.111 Hatfield adaptation of DH.106 Comet airliner to B.35/46, 27.5.48.

GOR.339 Unnumbered Christchurch low-level strike aircraft to GOR.339, 23.12.57.

DH.127 Hatfield supersonic naval strike fighter and reconnaissance to OR.346, mid-1961.

DH.128 Derivative of DH.127.

ENGLISH ELECTRIC/BRITISH AIRCRAFT CORPORATION / BRITISH AEROSPACE, WARTON

This is probably the only project list with new items added in recent years, but there are gaps because of security considerations. How far the series has gone is unknown but some of the work will remain secret for years to come. Latterly depth of project investigation has depended on whether the work was undertaken to an MoD order or an internal study only.

A.1 High-altitude bomber project leading to Canberra. Unnumbered proposal with fuselage engines, 1.6.45. First proposal with wing root-mounted engines, 7.45; became A.1 on award of contract. First flew (as Canberra) 13.5.49.

B.35/46 Unnumbered medium- and long-range bomber to B.35/46, 7.4.47. Revised design with modified wing completed 2.48.

P.2 Intruder variant of Canberra, 18.5.50.

P.4 Canberra bomber development with redesigned nose, 2.5.51.

P.10 Supersonic reconnaissance aircraft to R.156T, 30.5.55. Bomber variant considered.

P.17 Low-level strike aircraft to GOR.339, 1.58. First studies from mid-1956, blended with Vickers (Supermarine) Type 571 to produce TSR.2, first flown 27.9.64.

P.18 Development of Lightning fighter in tactical bombing role, late 1956. Viewed as counterpart to more complex P.17 but unable to meet operational demands. Work ceased 1.57. Single store carried beneath centre fuselage.

P.28 Canberra low-level subsonic strike with clipped wings, 1958. Based on B(I).Mk.8 airframe with fighter-type canopy. P.28A span 52ft (15.85m), P.28B 41ft (12.50m), bomb load 10,000lb (4,536kg), 500gal (2,274lit) tip tanks. In April 1965 (same week TSR.2 dropped) BAC produced P.28MOD – major revision of project with Spey engines, TSR.2's forward-looking, terrain-following radar and large mix of underwing weapons including anti-shipping and air-to-air missiles. Span 57ft (17.37m), length 72ft (21.95m), maximum take-off weight 60,000lb (27,216kg), bomb load 10,000lb. Both refurbished and new-build aircraft planned.

P.31 VTOL strike reconnaissance aircraft to GOR.2, 17.12.59.

P.34 Ground attack variant of Lightning for RAF, 7.60. Proposed to convert Mk.1, 2 and 3 aircraft by fitting weapons pack with alternative twin Nord AS.30 missiles, 1,000lb (454kg) bombs, napalm tanks or Zuni rocket launchers.

P.37 STOL strike fighter studies for both RAF and Navy, early 1961.

P.39 VTOL strike fighter, 19.10.61 onwards. Much of work based on developing an Anglicised Dassault Mirage IIIV.

P.42 Hypersonic research aircraft, 1962 onwards.

P.45 Comparative fixed-wing and variable sweep strike fighter and advanced trainer design studies, 19.2.63 onwards.

P.46 Jones Committee aircraft studies (many projects, including interceptors), c. 1964. Was first Warton project with parametric studies but were done by hand, not with computers.

P.47 STOL Canberra study, 1965/66.

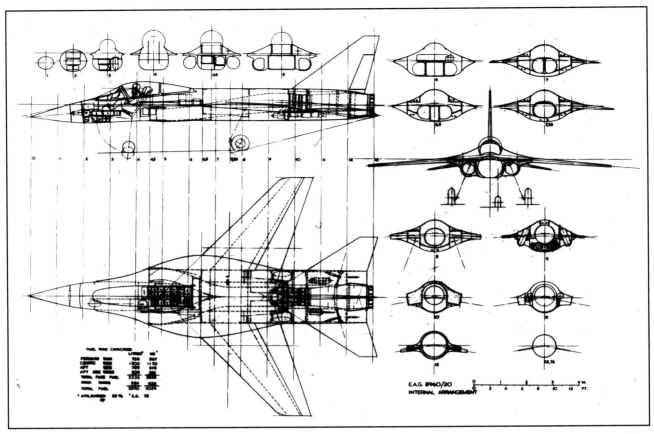

ABOVE Drawing EAG.8960 represents one of BAC's P.88 designs for a blended-body, fixed-wing aircraft (10.75). This aircraft would have carried 853gal (3,880lit) of fuel. *North West Heritage Group*

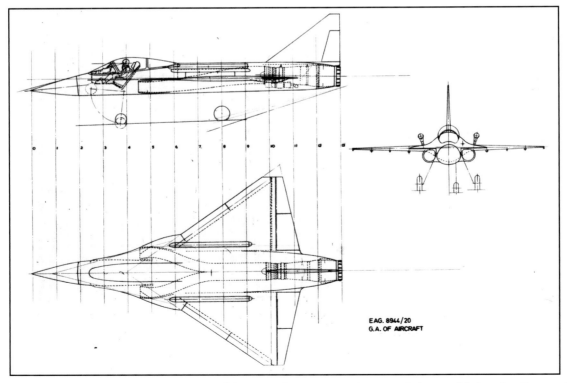

LEFT EAG.8944-20 shows a version of the BAC P.89 blended-body delta wing project (1.76). It was to have been powered by a single RB.199-52R engine. *North West Heritage Group*

ABOVE AND OPPOSITE TOP This group of drawings show some BAC Warton fighter and fighter/bomber studies that followed AST.396. They were produced before the full AST.403 studies described in the companion fighter volume.

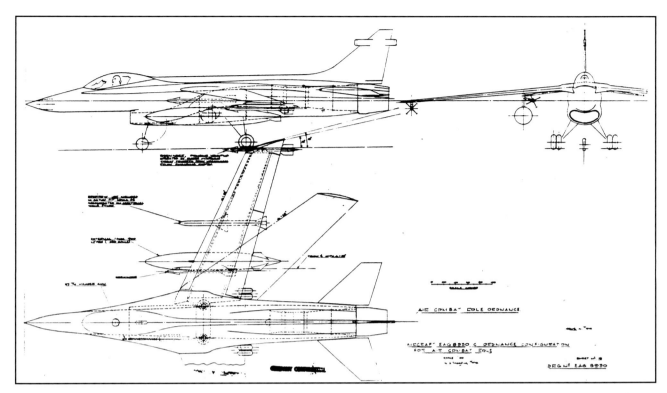

ABOVE The non-blended VG aircraft research under BAC project P.90 included drawing EAG.8930 (10.9.75). This multi-role design is shown here configured for the air combat role with air-to-air missiles and external tanks, plus a 27mm Mauser cannon in the port side leading edge extension. Note the twin main wheels. *North West Heritage Group*

AFVG Anglo–French Variable Geometry Aircraft, 5.65 onwards. Joint project between BAC and Dassault of France. Abandoned 6.67.

Jaguar Joint project between BAC and Breguet of France, 5.65 onwards. Begun as new pilot trainer for RAF to AST.362, 6.63. As SEPECAT Jaguar first flew 8.9.68.

P.49 Light strike/trainer with twin podded engines, 12.12.67.

P.51 VG strike aircraft, 5.9.67. Became United Kingdom Variable Geometry Aircraft (UKVG), 11.67. Studies continued in 1968 as part of Advanced Combat Aircraft.

P.53 Fixed-wing version of UKVG/MRCA aircraft, 26.11.68.

AA-107 Collaborative venture with Australia for small VG advanced trainer and close support aircraft, 9.68 to mid-1970.

P.57 'Package' aeroplane with fixed wing through to VG AA.107 type, 12.6.69.

P.60 Proposed family of aircraft – trainer and close support, 1969/70. Included AA-107.

P.61 PANNAP (Panavia New Aircraft Project) family, 1969/70 onwards. Series of trainer, close support and air superiority aircraft from Panavia design team to complement P.60.

BELOW BAC Warton wind tunnel model from 1976 with a delta wing. This may be a version of the P.89 and on the model the LERX could be replaced by alternative shapes – smaller, larger, more curved or straight edged.
North West Heritage Group

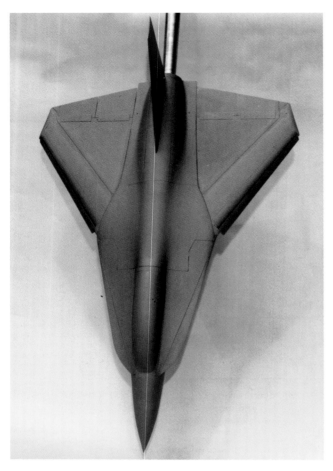

ABOVE BAC Warton wind tunnel model from 1976 with a delta wing. This may be a version of the P.89 and on the model the LERX could be replaced by alternative shapes – smaller, larger, more curved or straight edged.
North West Heritage Group

P.63 Jaguar developments to AST.396, early studies, 18.3.71.

P.64 New aircraft designs to AST.396, early studies, 18.3.71.

P.65 GAC/BAC new aircraft (US/UK), 6.10.71.

P.66 PANNAP variant, in part to AST.396 Issue 1, 1971.

P.67 Panavia MRCA (Tornado) Interdictor Strike IDS variant. Collaborative project between BAC, MBB (West Germany) and Aeritalia (Italy). First flew 14.8.74.

P.69 Jaguar developments to AST.396 Issue 1, 24.1.72.

P.70 VTOL aircraft to AST.396 Issue 1, 24.5.71. Jaguar and new components, RR Pegasus engine.

P.71 Lift + lift cruise variants to AST.396 Issue 1 using Jaguar and new components, 30.9.71.

P.72 Delta and other aircraft studies to AST.396 Issue 1, 1.12.71.

P.73 Lightweight VG studies to AST.396 Issue 1, 20.8.72.

P.74 Jaguar developments with new engines to AST.396 Issue 1, 20.3.73.

Note: *Project Nos. P.75 and P.80 to P.85 relate to RPV studies*

P.76 MRCA variants to AST.396 Issue 2, 1973. Includes single-seat aircraft.

P.77 Minimal change Jaguar variants to AST.396 Issue 2, 13.4.73.

P.78 Jaguar variants with new wings to AST.396 Issue 2, 27.6.73. Includes VG wings.

P.79 Jaguar variants with new fuselage and existing wings to AST.396 Issue 2, 6.12.73.

P.86 Long-term Jaguar developments to AST.396 Issue 3 and AST.403, 1975.

P.87 Jaguar short and medium-term developments, 4.8.75.

P.88 Blended body fixed-wing aircraft, 30.10.75.

P.89 Blended body delta-wing aircraft, 26.1.76.

P.90 Non-blended VG aircraft, 21.10.75.

P.98 Delta wing aircraft, 1.8.77.

P.100 RR Pegasus-powered tilt-wing aircraft.

P.101 Blitz fighter gunship Strikemaster development, 3.7.78.

P.102 Tilt-wing vectored thrust aircraft, 25.2.80.

P.140 Supersonic Harrier, c. 1990.

FOA Studies for a Future Offensive Aircraft to replace Tornado, 1994/95 onwards. Redesignated Future Offensive Air System (FOAS) but cancelled 6.05 and replaced by Deep and Persistent Offensive Capability (DPOC) requirement. DPOC cancelled 2010.

FAIREY

Fairey did not make full use of project numbers. Consequently, this list comprises those bomber-related projects known to have been undertaken.

Gannet Various studies for anti-submarine aircraft to GR.17/45. First brochure 14.12.45. As Type Q became Gannet, first flew 19.9.49.

Project 45 Cut-down version of GR.17/45 as light A/S aircraft with single Mamba replacing Double Mamba power unit, 12.10.51. Fuselage structure forward of front spar frame redesigned, ASV.19 scanner relocated to front end of bomb bay. Lightest version gross weight 14,500lb (6,577kg), top speed 241mph (388km/h) at 5,000ft (1,524m). Span 54ft 4in (16.56m), length 42ft (12.80m), wing area 471.5sq ft (43.8sq m).

M.148 Naval strike aircraft to M.148T, 9.54.

'Delta III' Fighter-bomber variant of all-weather fighter to F.155T, 1.57. Powerful engines coupled with delta wing gave flexible aircraft well suited to offensive and recce roles. Interceptor's Rolls-Royce RB.128 engines replaced by Bristol Olympus 21Rs for better low-altitude fuel consumption (engine still well suited for medium-altitude interception), massive ventral drop tank for much-improved range, radar replaced by low-altitude bomb sight. Two underwing pylons for TMB, armour-piercing bombs or RPs. For supersonic flight weapons held in special underwing containers cooled by air from aircraft's system to reduce temperature effects (prolonged supersonic flight would normally take temperature above point at which spontaneous explosion occurs). With TMB and fuel for 630nm (1,167km) sea level radius of action, gross weight 73,100lb (33,158kg). Fairey felt that with suitable AAMs the aircraft could still intercept bombers at medium altitude which, with Mach 2 capability, made this 'one of the most powerful fighter-bombers ever conceived'.

GOR.339 Low-level strike aircraft to GOR.339, 1.58.

Project 83 Maritime Patrol Aircraft project to NATO requirement NBMR.2, 21.6.58.

FOLLAND

(See HS.1170 and HS.1171 for additional projects)

Gnat Light ground attack variant of fighter to NATO requirement, 1954.

Fo.147 Twin-engined VG aircraft as basis for strike trainer, 4.61.

Fo.148 Advanced supersonic weapons and operations trainer and strike/recce aircraft with single RB.153-61R, late 1961 onwards.

GLOSTER

A fighter specialist that just occasionally dealt with bombers. The P numbers list drawings, not projects.

P.109 First 'Gloster Jet Bomber' proposal with four Whittle W2B jets in individual pods, 12.8.41. Modified P.109 proposed 24.11.41 with engines podded in pairs. Not intended as formal project, rather first examination of how the new jet engine could be used in a bomber. Span 100ft (30.48m), length 72ft (21.95m), gross weight 36,000lb (16,330kg), speed over target 405mph (652km/h) at 40,000ft (12,192m).

P.303/ Ground attack variant of Meteor F.Mk.8 with four 1,000lb (454kg) bombs, 2.50. Flown as private venture 4.9.50. Unofficially called Reaper; P.304 carried RPs, P.306 had long-span wings.

P.317 Long-range fighter-bomber development of F.4/48 (Javelin), 5.50. Four 1,000lb (454kg) bombs in two streamlined ventral panniers, one each side of aircraft's centreline.

P.324 Long-range fighter-bomber version of P.322 F.4/48 interceptor variant, 7.50.

Thin Wing Javelin Proposed developments as 'Canberra Replacement' to OR.328, 1953.

P.384 Development of Thin Wing Javelin fighter to GOR.339, 11.57. Podded engines.

P.386 Development of Thin Wing Javelin to GOR.339, 11.57. Engines in fuselage.

HANDLEY PAGE

A company that from a warplane point of view concentrated entirely on bombers.

HP.72A Long range bomber project, early 1946. Developed into HP.80 by mid-1946.

HP.75A Long range bomber with front 'rider-plane', 1946.

HP.80 Medium bomber to B.35/46, 5.47. Became Victor, first flown 24.12.52.

HP.87 One-third scale model glider of HP.80, 1947.

HP.88 Four-ninths-scale HP.80 wing and tail on fuselage of Supermarine Attacker fighter to E.6/48, 4.48. Also called Supermarine Type 521 and, by Blackburn who built it, YB.2. First flew 21.6.51.

HP.98 Target marker variant of HP.80, four RR Conway engines, 11.51.

HP.99 Low-level bomber 'Daisy Cutter' to B.126T, 1.53.

Victor III Enlarged version of Victor, 7.54.

HP.100 High-speed high-altitude reconnaissance aircraft to R.156T, 5.55. Designed also to carry ballistic missiles.

– Victor Phase 2, spring 1955.

HP.104 Victor Phase 3 with four Bristol Olympus Ol.7s, 28.4.55.

HP.106 Cruise missile to OR.1149, 24.11.55. HP.106M of 8.57 had eight RB.93/4 jets with reheat, offered Mach 3.0 speed and 1,200nm (2,224km) range.

HP.107 Supersonic bomber project, five Olympus engines, 24.11.55. Believed to have 60° delta wing, engines either in rear fuselage or under wing. Uncertainty surrounding position of horizontal stabilising surfaces and switched to 'canard' and back several times as difficulties arose with HP.107's balance. Believed that conventional rear surface was final choice.

– Victor Phase 4 supersonic development, 10.56.

GOR.339 Outline study only for tactical strike aircraft to GOR.339, 1.58.

HP.114 Victor Phase 6 missile carrier, 14.8.58.

OR.354 Firm completed brief study 12.61 for TSR.2 replacement.

HAWKER/HAWKER SIDDELEY/BRITISH AEROSPACE, KINGSTON

One of the most famous of fighter manufacturers but which rarely forayed into bomber development until the lead-up to the 'Canberra Replacement'. However, once the vertical take-off P.1127 and Harrier were flying, much of Kingston's effort centred on advanced versions that predominantly fit into the attack aircraft category. The prefix reverted to 'P' after the formation of British Aerospace in 1977.

P.1041 Mosquito replacement, 1944/45.

P.1044 Naval fighter-bomber, 1945.

P.1051 Naval medium bomber, 8.4.46. Twin RR AJ.65 (Avon), span 58ft 0in (17.68m), length 58ft 0in (17.68m), gross wing area including intakes 660sq ft (61.4sq m), 800gal (3,638lit) fuel all in fuselage, bomb bay for large missile.

P.1099 Hunter F.Mk.6 fighter – later developed into successful ground attack FGA.Mk.9. First conversion flew 3.7.59. Could carry Nord AS.30 or Bullpup missiles, RPs and 1,000lb (454kg) bombs.

P.1108 Naval strike aircraft to M.148T, 30.9.54.

P.1121 Version of strike fighter offered as tactical bomber for RAF, 10.3.57. Final proposal for two-seat, all-weather strike reconnaissance variant 1.7.58.

P.1123 Enlarged two-seat P.1121 as Mach 2 tactical bomber, 21.1.57.

P.1125 Supersonic strike aircraft project for RAF, 3.57.

P.1126 VTO double-delta strike aircraft with twelve RR RB.108 lift jets and twin Bristol Siddeley propulsion units, 6.57.

P.1127 Vertical take-off research aircraft to ER.204D, first flown 13.3.61. Developed into Kestrel and Harrier close support aircraft.

P.1129 Low-level strike aircraft to GOR.339, 1.58. Design blended with Avro 739 as combined Hawker Siddeley submission against BAC TSR.2, 11.58.

P.1132 Subsonic VTOL strike aircraft, 4.58.

P.1134 Mach 3 to Mach 4 research aircraft, 1958 onwards.

P.1136 Canard V/STOL aircraft, four RB.108 lift units, one reheated cruise engine, 4.59.

P.1137 Straight-wing supersonic tactical V/STOL aircraft, alternative to subsonic P.1127, 7.59. Seven RR RB.153 lift engines, three for lift in forward fuselage, two lift-cruise units with diverters and reheat in rear fuselage, one each with reheat in tilting wing tip pods. RB.153 was latest lightweight lift and propulsion engine but mass of power units gave high wing loading (feature common to most V/TOL designs) and study concluded that supersonic capability 'would nearly double the take-off mass of V/STOL tactical aircraft' (a long-term problem). Span 32ft 2in (9.81m), length 53ft (16.15m), gross wing area 250sq ft (23.25sq m), internal fuel 1,100gal (5,002lit).

P.1138 VTOL naval aircraft with canard and RB.153 lift and lift/cruise engine, 1959.

P.1139 Subsonic V/STOL strike fighter, 17.2.60. Two RB.153 lift units in forward fuselage, one reheated RB.163-1 clang-box lift/cruise unit in mid-fuselage with tail jet pipe plus diverter in bottom fuselage just beyond wing trailing edge. Span 25ft (7.62m), length 50ft 6in (15.39m), wing area 219sq ft (20.4sq m), internal fuel 600gal (2,728lit), wing t/c 7%. For hover thrust the diverter deflected gases away from tail pipe down through bottom fuselage exit, thus balancing the forward vertically mounted engines.

BELOW Hawker P.1051 (8.4.46). *BAe Farnborough*

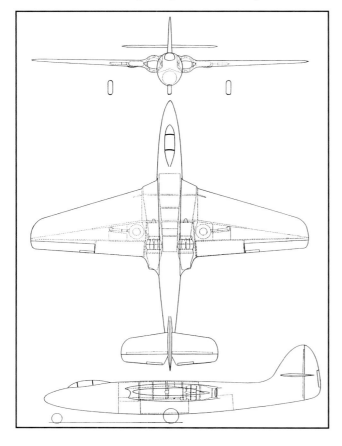

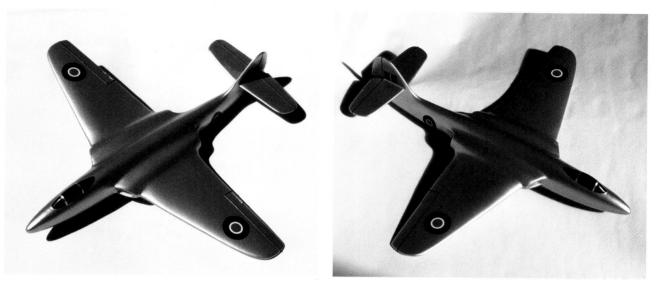

ABOVE This model of the Hawker P.1051 project was made by Joe Cherrie. *Joe Cherrie*

P.1140 Supersonic V/STOL strike fighter similar to and developed from P.1139, 4.3.60. Larger aircraft with three RB.153 lift units in forward fuselage; reheated RB.163-1 clang-box cruise engine had supersonic intakes. Span 26ft (7.92m), length 57ft 7in (17.62m), wing area 25sq ft (20.9sq ft), internal fuel 700gal (3,183lit), wing t/c 5%.

P.1141 Supersonic V/STOL strike fighter, 5.60. Single reheated BE.53/11, forward pair of thrust vectoring nozzles plus tail jet pipe, span 25ft (7.62m), length 49ft (14.94m). Second version had VG wing.

BELOW Hawker P.1137 (7.59). *Chris Farara*

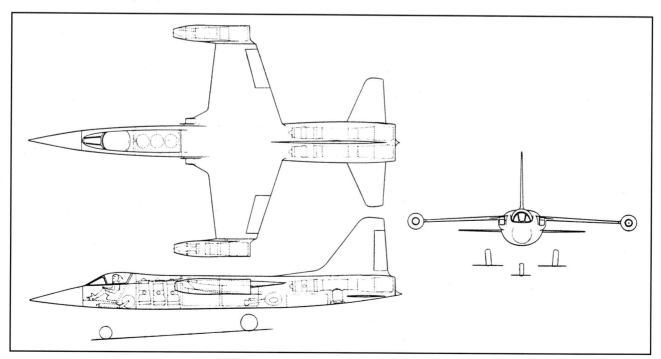

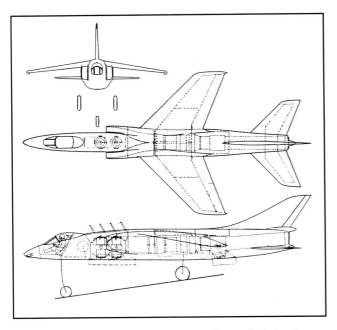

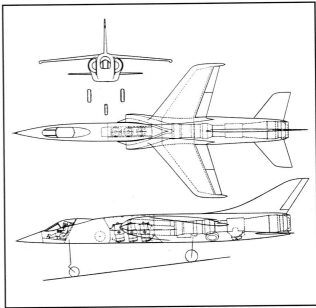

ABOVE Hawker P.1139 (17.2.60). Note forward lift jet doors on upper fuselage. *Chris Farara*

ABOVE Hawker P.1140 (4.3.60). Note the very long nosewheel leg on both the P.1139 and P.1140. *Chris Farara*

P.1143 Large supersonic strike fighter, ten RB.153s, 7.60. Long slim fuselage with six vertical RB.153s for lift only (three between cockpit and wing, three alongside wing trailing edge) and two pairs in swivelling wing tip nozzles (one above the other) for propulsion and VTOL lift. Straight-wing leading edge, trailing edge swept forward as per P.1137.

P.1144 Supersonic V/STOL strike fighter, 10.60. Multi-engined using RB.163 with PCB. Gross weight 30,000 to 40,000lb (13,608 to 18,144kg).

P.1146 Supersonic V/STOL aircraft, 1960.

BELOW Hawker P.1141 (5.60). *Chris Farara*

BELOW Hawker P.1149 (2.61). *Chris Farara*

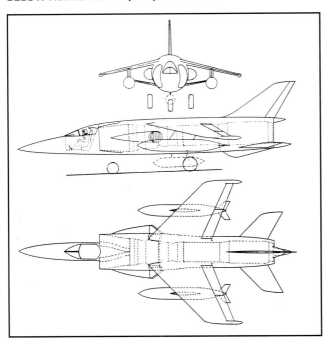

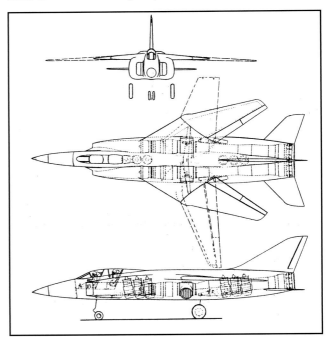

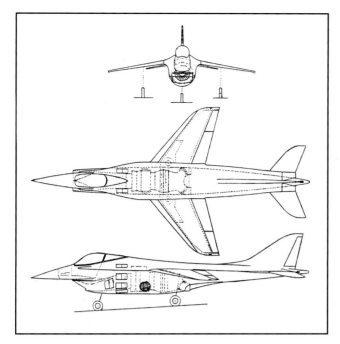

ABOVE Hawker Siddeley HS.1198-1 (13.1.75). *Chris Farara*

ABOVE BAe P.1213-1 (1979). *Chris Farara*

P.1149   Supersonic V/STOL strike aircraft, 2.61. Twin reheated RB.168R Spey for cruise, six RB.162 lift engines in two banks of three (one set forward, the other to rear) with both sets placed between main engines and exhaust pipes. Each RB.168 had single vectoring nozzle directly beneath VG wing for extra lift in hover. Two seats, span spread 47ft (14.33m), span swept 26ft (7.92m), length 62ft (18.90m), wing area spread 442sq ft (41.1sq m) swept 390sq ft (36.3sq m).

P.1150   Supersonic V/STOL strike fighter, 1.61 onwards. Developed into P.1154.

P.1151   Supersonic jet flap strike aircraft to OR.346, 4.61.

P.1152   Supersonic RAF/Naval V/STOL strike fighter to OR.346, mid-1961.

P.1153   Supersonic strike aircraft to OR.346, 4.61.

P.1154   (Originally P.1150/3) Supersonic V/STOL ground attack fighter with BS.100 PCB vectored thrust turbofan to NATO requirement NBMR.3, and AW.406/OR.356, 10.61 onwards. Prototype construction begun, but project cancelled 2.65.

P.1155   (Originally P.1150/2) Supersonic V/STOL strike aircraft to NBMR.3, 4.62. Alternative to P.1154.

P.1156   V/STOL strike aircraft, 12.61.

P.1158   Supersonic V/STOL aircraft derived from P.1155 with two Bristol Siddeley Pegasus 6 and PCB, 1962.

P.1159   V/STOL aircraft designed as replacement for Fiat G.91 with BS.94/4 and twin RB.162s, 1963.

P.1163   Fiat G.91 replacement with RB.168 and PCB, 1963.

Note: *Project Nos. P.1161, P.1162 and P.1164 to P.1169 not allocated*

HS.1170   Lightweight V/STOL strike reconnaissance aircraft developed from P.1163 to NATO VAK.191 competition ('191' indicated G.91 successor) with BS.94/5 PCB vectored thrust engine, 1964. Joint project with Focke-Wulf. Small aircraft with appearance similar to early Kestrel but rear fuselage considerably slimmer. Span 18ft (5.49m), length 38ft (11.58m). Also HS.1170B Folland Hamble strike/trainer variant to AST.362, 5.64.

HS.1171   Folland Hamble VG aircraft with twin RB.172 engines to AST.362, 5.64.

HS.1173   Light advanced trainer to AST.362, twin RB.172s, 1964/65. Single-seat, single reheated engine ground attack variant also drawn.

HS.1175   Second-generation subsonic V/STOL strike aircraft, 1966 onwards.

HS.1176   Subsonic V/STOL strike aircraft proposed to United States, late 1966 onwards. Similar externally to Harrier.

HS.1177   Supersonic V/STOL strike and recce aircraft, 1966 onwards. First variant (28.7.67) had single reheated BS.53/103 Pegasus cruise/lift engine plus one RR/Allison XJ-99-RA-1 lift unit, second (5.8.67) had twin reheated RR Spey 5Rs and an XJ-99-RA-1, third (18.8.67) had twin RB.168-31Ds only.

HS.1178   Subsonic V/STOL strike aircraft with PCB Pegasus, 1967.

HS.1179   Supersonic strike aircraft studies to MRCA standards, mid-1968 to 2.70.

HS.1180   RR Spey-powered version of P.1154, 1965-68.

HS.1181   V/STOL wide speed range aircraft with BS Pegasus 9D and 'pop-out' RR RB.202-10 lift fans, 1968. Appearance similar to Harrier family.

HS.1182   Developments of Hawk trainer to AST.396 Issue 1, 1971/72.

HS.1184   Long series of subsonic Harrier developments, 7.70 through 1974. Some versions to AST.396 Issue 1.

HS.1185 & AV-16   Subsonic and supersonic V/STOL strike aircraft, 1970 to 1975. Some versions to AST.396 Issue 1. Anglo/US study from 1973 planned for service use as AV-16; cancelled 1975. Both HS.1184 and HS.1185 popularly known as Super Harrier.

HS.1186   Advanced Harrier with Pegasus 16 to AST.396 Issue 1, 9.71.

HS.1187   Supersonic V/STOL strike fighter with PCB Pegasus 16, 1970 onwards. Some versions to AST.396 Issue 1. One variant had cranked delta wing and twin fins.

HS.1188   HSA/McDonnell Douglas advanced Harrier with Pegasus 16, 1970/71.

HS.1189   Kingston/Brough simple strike aircraft to AST.396 Issue 1, 1971/72.

HS.1190   Kingston/Brough (P.153) light strike to AST.396 Issues 1 and 2, 1971/73.

HS.1191   Kingston/Brough (P.155?) base-burning aircraft to AST.396 Issue 1, 1970 onwards.

HS.1192   Kingston/Brough supersonic V/STOL strike aircraft, AST.396 Issue 1, 1972.

HS.1193   Supersonic V/STOL with PCB Pegasus 15 and 'nawar' delta wing, 29.6.73.

HS.1194   Lightweight supersonic STOL with RB.199, 1972/73.

HS.1195   STOL strike aircraft with RR Spey developments, 1973/74. Several designs, one to AST.396 Issue 2.

HS.1196   MINICAS very small close air support type, 1973/74. Submerged cockpit, engine in pod on back of fuselage, various engines including RB.401, weapons included anti-tank missiles.

HS.1197   Buccaneer development to AST.396 Issue 2, 1974.

HS.1198   Variable cycle vectored thrust research aircraft, single RR RB.406, 13.1.75. Span 28ft (8.53m), length 53ft (16.15m), wing area 250sq ft (23.3sq m). Also version with side intakes.

Big Wing Harrier   Study to fit big wing to Harrier aircraft as GR.Mk.5, 1976 to 1978. Replaced by HSA/McDonnell Douglas AV-8B, prototype of which first flew 9.11.78.

P.1208   Ground attack type with air combat capability, 5.78 onwards. P.1208-1: side intakes and conventional swept wing; P.1208-2 (15.9.78): chin intake, canard and forward sweep.

P.1209   Supersonic V/STOL demonstration aircraft, test bed for PCB Pegasus, 1978/79. P.1209-2 dated 5.1.79.

P.1213   V/STOL canard design with Pegasus engine, 1979.

P.1218   F-14 Tomcat/A-6 Intruder replacement for USN, 1981.

P.1222   V/STOL with RR Bristol tandem fan engine, 1983.

P.1226   Initially subsonic variant of P.1216 fighter layout, 1984. Later P.1226-2 (1.8.84) essentially forward sweep version of Harrier II.

P.1228   Supersonic naval V/STOL with PCB and canard, 1985. Strike and interceptor capability.

P.1229   Supersonic naval V/STOL with dry engine, P.1184 configuration, 1985.

P.1230   Supersonic naval V/STOL with PCB, P.1205 configuration, 1985.

P.1231   Supersonic V/STOL with four-nozzle engine, AV-16-S4 revived, 1985.

P.1232   Sea Harrier FRS.Mk.2 front fuselage with 8in (20.3cm) plug, Sea Harrier wing, Harrier GR.Mk.5 rear fuselage, 10.9.85.

P.1233   Small Agile Battlefield Aircraft (SABA), 1987.

P.1234   Three layouts for SABA, 1987.

P.1236   SABA studies not in final brochure.

P.1237   ASTOVL aircraft with advanced RALS (Remote Augmentation Lift System) powerplant, 1986.

P.1238   Simple 'low technology' SABA, 1987.

P.1239   SABA versatile, 1987.

PERCIVAL

Renamed Hunting Percival Aircraft in 1954, the company became part of BAC in 1960.

P.61   Swept-back research aircraft, c. 1948.

P.70   Naval anti-submarine aircraft, c. 1949.

P.97   Naval strike aircraft (possibly to M.148T, 1954).

H.128   Single-seat ground attack aircraft utilising Jet Provost trainer's wings, rear fuselage and empennage, RB.145 engine.

BAC.167   Strikemaster ground attack variant of Jet Provost T.Mk.5 trainer developed specifically for small overseas air forces. Uprated RR Viper engine and increased weapon capability. First example flew 26.10.67; type proved very successful.

H.168   Ground attack derivative of Jet Provost with larger military load over greater distance. RB.172/T.260 engine.

H.171   Ground attack Jet Provost with RB.153-61.

SAUNDERS-ROE

Saro had long experience designing flying boats but in the 1950s it also produced the odd bomber project.

P.176   Flying boat A/S patrol aircraft with two Napier E.151 Eland turboprops, 1953.

P.178   Swept-wing naval strike aircraft designs, 1.54 and 4.54.

P.188   Schemes for high-speed high-altitude reconnaissance aircraft to R.156T, 7.55. Not known if designs adapted to carry bombs. No official tender to specification.

P.208   Updated version of P.176 flying boat patrol aircraft submitted to NBMR.2, mid-1958. Gross weight 73,000lb (33,113kg).

SHORT BROTHERS & HARLAND

This company's main number sequence, the S series, embraced projects from Rochester and Belfast over many years. The P.D. series applied to Belfast preliminary designs originating from 1947 onwards as schemes or tenders. If the latter progressed beyond this stage, a number was allocated in the SBAC designation system.

S.42/S.A.4 Sperrin First S.A.4 six-engine bomber, 11.45, followed by similar four-engine design 26.4.46. Developed into Sperrin, first flown 10.8.51.

S.B.1 (P.D.1)
          Medium bomber to B.35/46, 5.47. One-third scale glider also called S.B.1 built to test aero-isoclinic wing. First flew 14.7.51.

S.B.3   Anti-submarine development of Sturgeon naval aircraft to M.6/49. Prototype first flew 12.8.50.

S.B.4   Rebuild of S.B.1 glider with Blackburn-Turboméca Palas jets. First flew 4.10.53. Named Sherpa.

S.B.6 (P.D.4) Seamew Anti-submarine aircraft to M.123D. First flew 23.8.53.

S.C.1   VTOL research aircraft to ER.143T. First flew 2.4.57.

S.C.2   Proposed Seamew Mk.2 for Coastal Command.

P.D.6   S.A.4 Sperrin test bed for DH Gyron engine. First flew 7.7.55.

P.D.9   Low-level bomber to B.126T, 12.52.

P.D.10   Supermarine Swift fighter fuselage fitted with 'aero-isoclinic' wing for high speed research to ER.145, 7.53. Follow-on to S.B.1/S.B.4 but not built.

P.D.12   High-speed, high-altitude reconnaissance aircraft to R.156T, 5.55.

P.D.13   Naval strike aircraft to M.148T, 9.54.

P.D.17   Projects to GOR.339 along with English Electric, 1958. Included lifting body.

P.D.23   Four schemes for VTOL naval strike aircraft, 12.56. During late 1950s Shorts undertook much research into VTOL using any number of lift engines. P.D.23 was a large project but example shown had small wing. Two crew, span 28ft 0in (8.53m), length 72ft 6in (22.10m), wing area 300sq ft (27.9sq m), t/c 6%, operating weight 36,955lb (16,763kg), gross weight 62,000lb (28,123kg), maximum wing loading 207lb/sq ft (1,011kg/sq m), fuel 2,783gal (12,652lit), large bomb. Two Avon RA.29 propulsive engines, twenty RB.108 lift units in two banks in front of and behind wing. Maximum Mach 1.0, cruise Mach 0.9, range 450 miles (724km).

P.D.25   Five schemes for VTOL ground attack aircraft, late 1950s into 1960. Delta wing, delta canard on nose, propulsive engines in (swivelling?) wing tip pods, lift engines in fuselage behind cockpit.

ABOVE Artist's impressions of two unnumbered Shorts bomber projects (10.53 and 11.53). No details are available. *Both Shorts*

ABOVE AND LEFT Views of the Short P.D.49 model in its early form with double-delta wing (11.60). The black-lined box over the upper fuselage presumably indicates the lift engine position. *Shorts*

BELOW Short P.D.23 (12.56).

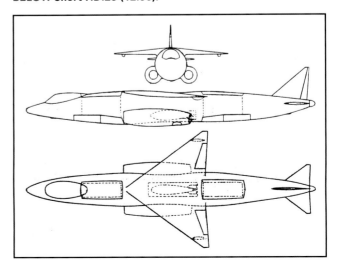

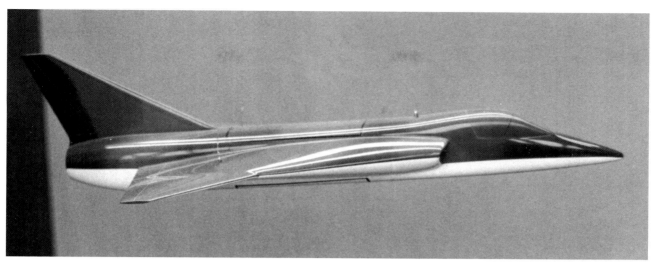

ABOVE Another P.D.49 model (11.60). *Shorts*

RIGHT Late version Short P.D.49 with pure delta wing and two separate groups of four lift jets in the centre fuselage (6.61).

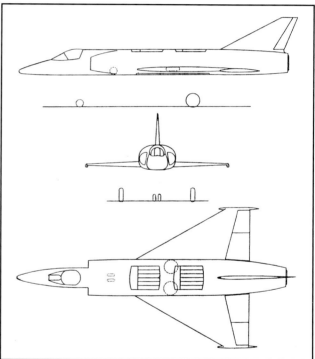

BELOW An unnumbered model of a Shorts VTOL lightweight strike fighter for ground attack described by its accompanying paperwork as 'hypothetical'. It was to follow the basic principles of the SC.1 VTOL research aircraft. Lift would be provided by eight vertically mounted engines in two batteries of four with propulsion affected by a turbofan with afterburner. This aircraft would have a speed of about Mach 0.98 at sea level and would be supersonic at altitude, and it would be capable of carrying a one ton payload over a radius of action of 250 miles (402km), operating at low altitude all the way. This is almost certainly another version of the P.D.49. *Shorts*

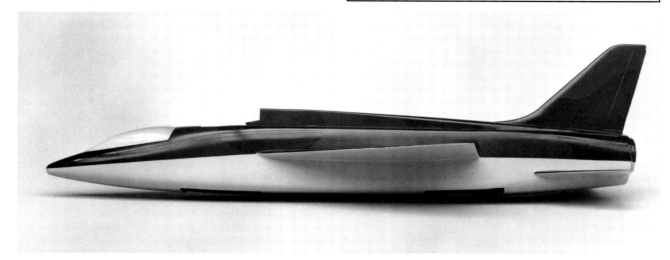

BRITISH SECRET PROJECTS: JET BOMBERS SINCE 1949

VOLUME 2

P.D.33   Proposal for Canberra with increased span.

P.D.44   Naval strike aircraft, 1960/61.

P.D.45   VTOL low-level strike aircraft, 1960/61.

P.D.49   VTOL light strike reconnaissance to NATO limits (250nm [463km] sea level range with 2,000lb [907kg] load), 1960/61. First studies (9.60) show double delta; by 6.61 had pure delta with eight RB.162 lift units (two groups of four in centre fuselage) and one propulsive reheated RB.168-1R. Maximum Mach 1.73 at 36,000ft (10,973m) at 26,000lb (11,794kg) weight but airframe could go faster with more power. Lift engines close to CofG to minimise offset moment resulting from a failure during jet-borne flight – effect of failure counteracted by nozzle control system. Central lift engines meant propulsion installation in rear fuselage, longitudinal balance achieved by placing all equipment in forward fuselage forward and aft of cockpit. Lower ends of lift engines tilted outwards to allow semi-submerged bomb stowage on centreline (one tactical nuclear or 1,000lb [454kg]) with minimum additional drag. Lift nozzles tiltable so horizontal component of lift thrust could be generated for acceleration or deceleration in transitional flight. Main engine fed by air passing either side of lift units joining up in front of main engine – duct walls integrated with fuselage structure to save weight. For jet-borne control, hovering control system similar to S.C.1's. Weapons included Bullpup or Nord AA.20 missiles, RP packs, 1,000lb (454kg) bombs or Firestreak AAMs on four underwing pylons, twin 30mm Aden cannon and retractable 2in (5.1cm) air-to-air RP launcher in bay forward of lift units between main intake ducts. Span 28ft (8.53m), length 53ft 6in (16.31m), VTO weight 23,000lb (10,433kg). Provision for Ferranti Airpass IIC multi-purpose radar. Alternative design had twin RR RB.179 main units.

P.D.56   VTOL strike fighter to NBMR.3, 1961/62.

P.D.69   Anti-submarine aircraft to AST.357, c. 1963.

VICKERS-ARMSTRONG

After 1960 Weybridge combat aircraft projects were listed as a continuation of the old Supermarine list (below).

Jet Bomber High-altitude bomber, 3.45. Four 8,000lb (35.6kN) RR jets stacked in pairs forward of wing, air fed from nose intake, individual very long jet pipes (would have been two-thirds shorter if discharged through fuselage sides just aft of wing, but rejected by structural problem of holes in side and thrust loss when turned 7° to side, 10° down). Engine nacelles rejected through drag and effects on laminar flow. Three crew in nose, tricycle undercarriage with six-wheel nose and four six-wheel main units. Sideways wheel retraction rejected through difficulty

providing sufficient torsional stiffness in wing – chassis nacelles estimated to increase thrust required for specified cruise by 6% only and shaped such that laminar flow preserved along whole span. Recovery dive flaps fitted, landing flaps omitted, structure metal covered throughout bar control surfaces. Stowage for two 22,450lb (10,183kg) 'Grand Slam', four 13,000lb (5,897kg) 'Tallboy' bombs or combinations of smaller, no defensive weapons since thought difficult to intercept at planned speed and height. Maximum bomb load 52,000lb (23,587kg), normal 24,000lb (10,886kg), normal gross weight 102,000lb (46,267kg), overload 120,000lb (54,432kg), 4,000gal (18,188lit) internal fuel. Cruise 475mph (764km/h) at 45,000ft (13,716m) and 102,000lb weight, maximum 530+mph (853+km/h) in light condition above 35,000ft (10,668m), sea level climb 3,400ft/min (1,036km/min), range 1,250 miles (2,011km) at overload, 2,000 miles (3,218km) at normal load. Span 169 ft (51.51m), length 122ft (37.19m), wing area 2,860sq ft (266sq m), t/c 15%.

B.35/46   Medium bomber project to specification, 5.47. Revised version 3.11.47.

660   Medium bomber to B.9/48. Covers first prototype WB210, first flew 18.5.51.

Long Range Bomber Three schemes based on Valiant 8.49, updating initial work of 5.49. Scheme 1 basis was development of B.9/48 but with 45° continuous sweep instead of 'crank' plan form, longer fuselage, bicycle undercarriage (thin wing could not house conventional gear) and five 9,700lb (43.1kN) RB.80/1s – four in wing roots, one in fuselage tail. Was described by Vickers as 'fairly representative of the British approach' and cruised over target at 576mph (926km/h) and 49,000ft (14,935m). Span 128ft 0in (39.01m), length 134ft 8in (41.05m), gross wing area 3,200sq ft (297.6sq m), t/c ratio root 12%, tip 8%, total take-off weight 163,600lb (74,209kg), full load service ceiling 49,800ft (15,179m). Max speed at mean weight of 123,560lb (56,047kg) 618mph (995km/h) at sea level, 629mph (1,012km/h) at 30,000ft (9,144m); full load rate of climb 4,680ft/min (1,426m/min) at sea level, 2,450ft/min (747m/min) at 30,000ft. After examining American practice Vickers felt it would be worthwhile to look at alternatives based on American concept of higher wing loads and aspect ratios. Scheme 1 aspect ratio 5.12 and take-off wing loading 51.1lb/sq ft (249.5kg.sq m); Schemes 2 and 3 loadings and aspect ratios progressively higher and both had engines in external nacelles because insufficient depth to fit them in wing. Aspect ratio of 2 and 3 = 6.82 and 8.58 respectively, wing area 2,405sq ft and 1,910sq ft (223.7m2 and 177.6sq m), total take-off weight 165,500lb and

167,150lb (75,071kg and 75,819kg), take-off wing loading 68.8 and 87.5lb/sq ft (335.9 and 427.2kg.sq m), over target cruise 567mph (912km/h) at 49,800ft (15,179m) and 580mph (934km/h) at 50,000ft (15,240m), full load service ceiling 48,800ft (14,874m) and 49,000ft (14,935m) respectively. Scheme 2 used 10,000lb (44.4kN) of rocket thrust to get off at full load, Scheme 3 needed 20,000lb (88.9kN). Scheme 2 span 128ft 0in (39.01m), length 116ft 0in (35.36m), t/c ratio 12% to 10%, max speed at a mean weight of 121,350lb (55,044kg) 623mph (1,002km/h) at sea level, 628mph (1,010km/h) at 30,000ft, full load rate of climb 4,670ft/min (1,423m/min) at sea level, 2,400ft/min (732m/min) at 30,000ft. Scheme 3 span 128ft 0in (39.01m), length 109ft 6in (33.38m), t/c ratio 12% to 10%, maximum speed at mean weight of 123,860lb (56,183kg) 654mph (1,053km/h) at sea level, 632mph (1,017km/h) at 30,000ft, full load rate of climb 5,000ft/min (1,524m/min) at sea level, 2,580ft/min (786m/min) at 30,000ft. All achieved 5,000nm (9,265km) range with 10,000lb (4,536kg) bomb; load included one 10,000lb 'special' or HC, two 5,000lb (2,268kg) HC or 15 1,000lb (454kg) MC. Concluded that RATOG essential for Schemes 2 and 3 and both showed high take-off and landing speeds, poor margin of excess 'g' for manoeuvre and increase in profile drag of about 15%. Scheme 1 was 'best solution', bearing in mind British aerodrome limits and that design could manoeuvre at minimum of 2'g'.

667   Second Valiant prototype WB215 (Sapphires instead of Avons).

673   Valiant B.Mk.2 prototype WJ954, first flew 4.9.53. Unofficially called Pathfinder.

674   Early production Valiant B.Mk.1.

706   Main production Valiant B.Mk.1.

710   Valiant B(PR).Mk.1 production.

711   First studies for Red Rapier flying bomb, 1951.

712   Proposed conversion of Valiant B.Mk.2 with RR Conway engines, 1951.

718   Proposal for Valiant Pathfinder with Conway engines, 1951.

–   Combined brochure for separate low-level and supersonic Valiant developments, 1.52.

719   One-third scale model of Red Rapier flying bomb, 1951.

722   Proposed Valiant Mk.3, 5.52.

–   Supersonic bomber, 2.54. Preliminary investigation into suitable aircraft for high-altitude, long-range supersonic bomber role. To carry 5,000lb (2,268kg) bombs internally for still air range of 4,315nm (7,991km) with over target height of 70,000ft (21,336m); cruise at Mach 2.2 to 2.5 throughout flight. Used all-moving foreplane and light alloy construction (Hiduminium RR.58 suitable for use up to 190°C, the temperature experienced at Mach 2.5) and six non-reheated Rolls-Royce turbojets designed specifically for supersonic cruise (current engines unsuited to long-range cruise between Mach 1.5 and 3.0). High power and low landing wing loading enabled flaps to be dispensed with. Used single crewman. Top speed Mach 0.53 404mph (650km/h) at sea level, Mach 1.12 740mph (1,191km/h) at 36,000ft (10,973m), Mach 2.5 1,651mph (2,656km/h) at 70,000ft. Span 60ft 10in (18.54m), length 101ft 6in (30.94m), gross wing area 1,850sq ft (172.1sq m), t/c ratio 3.5%, foreplane span 25ft 10in (7.87m), area 416sq ft (38.7sq m), gross weight 175,000lb (79,380kg).

799   High-speed high-altitude reconnaissance aircraft to R.156T, 5.55.

Swallow   Studies from 1954 by Barnes Wallis into arrow-wing VG aircraft. Military proposals based on requirements of R.156T (10.55) and OR.339 (4.58).

BELOW Vickers supersonic bomber (2.54).

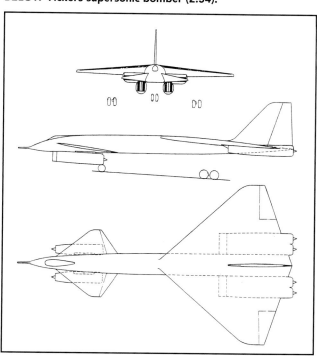

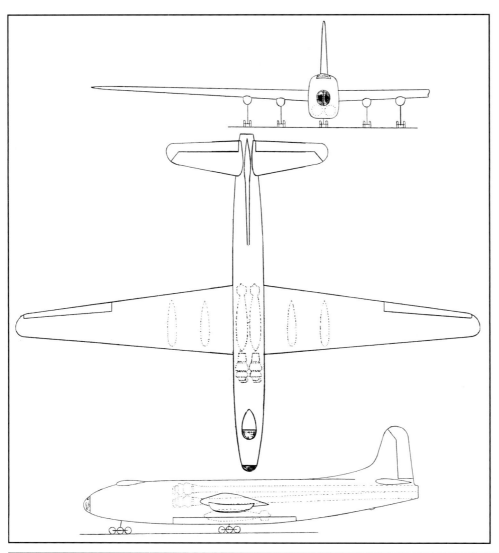

LEFT The massive Vickers jet bomber designed at the end of the Second World War (14.3.45). Two 10-ton 'Grand Slam' bombs fit snugly into the bomb bay.

BELOW AND OPPOSITE The three versions of the proposed Vickers Long-Range Bomber of August 1948; Schemes 1, 2 and 3 respectively.

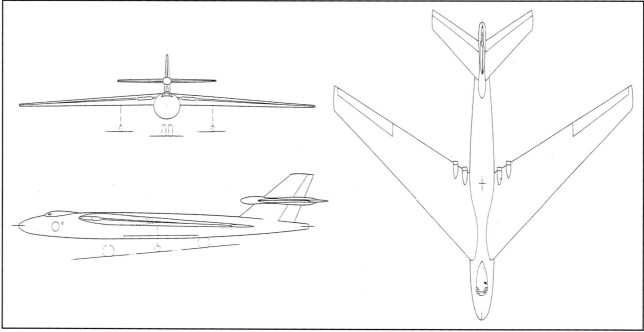

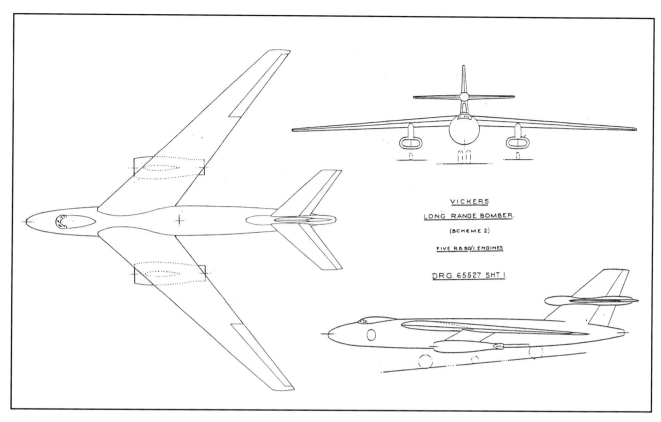

VICKERS

LONG RANGE BOMBER.

(SCHEME 2)

FIVE R.B.80/1 ENGINES

DRG. 65527 SHT. 1

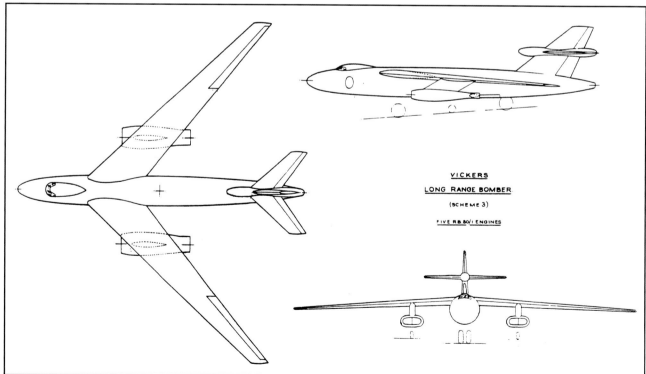

VICKERS

LONG RANGE BOMBER.

(SCHEME 3)

FIVE R.B.80/1 ENGINES

ABOVE Model by John Hall of the Vickers supersonic bomber.
John Hall

VICKERS SUPERMARINE

Accurate dates for many of these projects are unavailable since brochures were often undated. Designs from 1960 onwards originate from the Vickers/BAC Weybridge team, which continued the old Supermarine project number series.

521	Designation for HP.88, 4.48.
522	Conversion of Type 508 N.9/47 fighter into strike aircraft to NR/A.19, 10.48.
537	Strike conversion of Type 525 N.9/47 fighter to NR/A.19, 4.50.
544	Scimitar jet fighter to N.113D, first flew 19.1.56. In FAA service role switched to strike prior to introduction of Buccaneer.
561	Scimitar low-level nuclear bomber development for RAF, 1956.
562	Interceptor and strike development of Scimitar, 1.56 to 3.57.
564	Revision of Type 562 as naval strike aircraft, 1956/57.
565	Scimitar tactical bomber development for RAF, 2.57.
566	Scimitar strike variant for Navy, Sperry Integrated Flight Control System, 2.57.
567	Scimitar single and two-seat strike developments for Navy, 4.57.
569	Guided powered bomb for carriage by V-bombers, 1957. Powered by four RB.93/4 Soar motors.
571	Low-level strike aircraft to GOR.339, 1.58. Result of studies undertaken during 1957. Blended with English Electric P.17 as TSR.2, first flew 27.9.64.
572	Denavalised tactical reconnaissance Scimitar for RAF, 1958.
574	Scimitar project, 1958.
576	Supersonic Scimitar developments, 12.58 onwards.

577	Various projects for supersonic strike aircraft, 1959/60. Early study (26.6.59) showed high delta wing and all-moving low-set tail. Twin 7,250lb (32.2kN) thrust BE.61 ducted fan engines, wing area 410sq ft (38.1sq m), fuel 1,800gal (8,184lit) in fuselage, 180gal (818lit) in wings, 400gal (1,819lit) in two drop tanks. By 18.1.60, three versions of same basic layout – all 66ft 7in (20.29m) long, 29ft (8.84m) folded span. Span with drop tanks: 'A' 41ft (12.50m), 'B' 43ft 6in (13.26m), 'D' 44ft (13.41m); wing area with tanks: 'A' 312sq ft (29.0sq m), 'B' 419sq ft (39.0sq m), 'D' 399sq ft (37.1sq m); basic equipped weight: 'A' 28,624lb (12,984kg), 'B' 30,288lb (13,739kg), 'D' 26,581lb (12,057kg): take-off weight in strike and interceptor roles: 'A' and 'B' both 48,000lb (21,773kg), 'D' as interceptor 47,860lb (21,709kg). To carry Bullpup. Draft brochure expected 26.2.60.
579	Number allocated to English Electric-built TSR.2s.
581	A series of naval and RAF strike aircraft designs to specification ER.206 and OR.346 including adaptations of TSR.2, 1959/60.
582	Twin-fuselage strike aircraft to OR.346, first quarter 1960.
583	VG naval strike fighter to AW.406, mid-1961 onwards. Also acted as pre-development aircraft for OR.346.
584	V/STOL strike aircraft to NBMR.3, 12.61. Tri-service aircraft (NATO, RAF, RN), also to OR.345.
585	Begun as naval derivative of Type 584, mid-1961. Became single-engine close support aircraft.

Note: Types 586 and 587 were Mach 2 VG airliner studies as part of all-embracing research by the company into swing wings

588	VG research aircraft – Lightning (and Swift) with VG wings, mid-1961 onwards.
589	VG research aircraft, all-new airframe, demilitarised Type 590. Also formed part of work to NBMR.3, 2.62.
590	Strike aircraft to OR.346, mid-1962 onwards. Also covered naval side of research needs. Was production version of Type 589.
591	High Mach number development of Type 589 to OR.355, mid-1962 onwards.
592	No information
593	Small experimental VG aircraft, 4.64.
594	Believed allocated to Preston TSR.2 production.

WESTLAND

A company that never actually built a pure jet bomber (production Wyverns were turboprop powered), but it was designing jet aircraft by the middle of the Second World War. This work came under W. E. W. Petter and gave him experience prior to his move to English Electric, where it was put to good use on the Canberra.

P.1056, P.1057 & P.1061 Fighter-bomber projects, early 1944. Similar configurations with twin MetroVick F.2/4 jets in centre fuselage.

W.34 Wyvern long-range strike to N.11/44. RR Eagle piston engine. First flew 12.12.46.

W.35 Wyvern with RR Clyde or AS Python turboprop to N.12/45, first flew 18.1.49. Other developments to specification had Napier Nomad compound engine or Napier E.141 Eland double turboprop.

W.36 Wyvern development with either 6,500lb (28.9kN) RR AJ.65 or 7,000lb (31.1kN) MetroVick F.9 jets to N.12/45. Span 44ft (13.41m), wing area 360sq ft (33.5sq m), gross weight AJ.65 19,000lb (8,618kg), F.9 20,000lb (9,072kg). Fuselage and tail basically as W.34, tricycle undercarriage. Four 30mm Aden.

GR.17/45 Twin-engine anti-submarine patrol aircraft, competitor to Fairey Gannet, 1946.

NR/A.32 Light anti-submarine aircraft to NR/A.32, two layouts, mid-1950.

M.148T Naval strike aircraft to M.148T, 9.54.

BELOW Early version of Vickers Type 577 strike interceptor (for the Royal Navy) shown with twin 200gal (909lit) drop tanks (26.6.59).

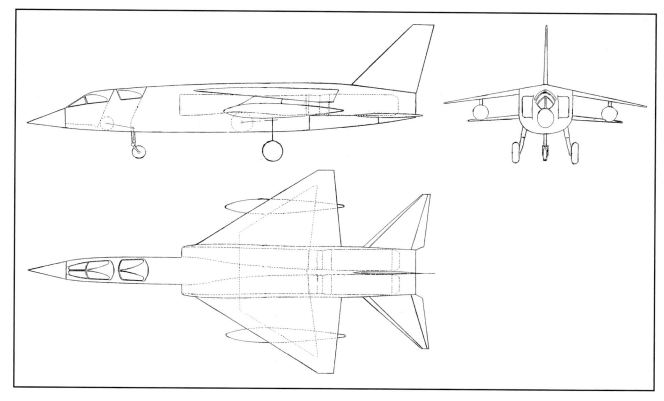

Appendix Two
Post-War British Bomber Project Specifications

The Air Ministry (the main functions of which were absorbed into a reconstituted Ministry of Defence in April 1964) has traditionally signalled expected future requirements to the British aircraft industry via a series of specifications against which tenders were invited. Until the end of 1949 the sequential system used to issue these specifications was a letter/number/year arrangement. A typical example is B.9/48 for a Medium-Range Bomber (in fact what became the Vickers Valiant): B stood for bomber and '9' indicated it was the 9th specification issued in that year, which was 1948. Alternative prefix letters included F (fighter), E (experimental) or N (naval).

From 1950 the system changed and at the same time was declared 'Secret' in an effort to prevent any public insight into the thoughts of the Air Council and Admiralty. The new specifications were also prefixed by letters that again indicated the intended role of the aircraft, e.g. B, F, N, plus ER (experimental research), FGA (fighter ground attack), GAR or GR (ground attack, reconnaissance), M (maritime), MR (maritime reconnaissance), SR (strike reconnaissance), T (trainer) or UB (unmanned bomber). The second element was a number in a series that began at 100 and which by the 1980s

had passed 300. A suffix letter, for example T (for tender), D (development) or P (prototype), usually completed the specification. There was no longer any reference to indicate the year of issue. B.104D was one of the first of these new-style specifications to be issued and was written for the Vickers Type 673 Valiant Mk.2 Pathfinder. In the case of B.126T, the suffix 'T' indicated that this was the basic document to which industry would tender for a planned low-level bomber, and if one of the tendered designs had been ordered then a more detailed B.126D would have been written around it.

Specifications for an aircraft required for military service were usually accompanied by an Operational Requirement with its own 'OR' number, for example OR.314 in the case of B.126. In later years the 'OR' was substituted by AST (Air Staff Target), ASR (Air Staff Requirement), NAST or NASR (Naval Air Staff Target/Requirement) or SR/A (Staff Requirement/Air). Separate naval requirements were covered by NR/As, e.g. NR/A.39 for M.148 (Blackburn Buccaneer), although many books and papers prefer to write this as NA.39. Further details of pre-1950 specifications can be found in *The British Aircraft Specifications File* by Meekcoms and Morgan.

Spec	Aircraft
B.3/45 (OR.199)	English Electric A.1 Canberra.
GR.17/45 (OR.220)	Blackburn B.54 (Y.A.5), Fairey Type Q (later Type 17 and then Gannet), Westland GR.17/45.
R.5/46 (OR.200)	Avro Shackleton.
R.5/46/Iss. III (OR.320)	Avro Shackleton Mk.3, Canadair CL.28, Saro P.162.
(OR.230)	Bristol Type 172, Short S.A.4, Handley Page HP.72A/HP.80.
B.14/46 (OR.239)	Short S.A.4 Sperrin.
B.35/46 (OR.229)	Armstrong Whitworth AW.56, Avro 698, English Electric B.35/46, Handley Page HP.80, Short S.B.1, Vickers B.35/46; *Also:* de Havilland DH.111.
B.5/47 (OR.235)	English Electric Canberra B.Mk.2.
E.8/47 (OR.250)	Bristol Type 174.
E.8/47/II	Bristol Type 176.
R.2/48 (OR.231)	Blackburn B.78, Saro P.162, Short P.D.2, Supermarine Type 524.
E.6/48	Handley Page HP.88.
B.9/48 (OR.229)	Vickers Type 660 Valiant.
E.15/48	Avro 707.
B.22/48 (OR.263 & OR.302)	English Electric Canberra B.Mk.5.
M.6/49 (NR/A.9 & OR.275)	Short S.B.3.
(NR/A.18)	Variant of de Havilland N.40/46 fighter (?).
(NR/A.19)	Variant of Fairey N.40/46 fighter, Supermarine Types 522 & 537.
E.10/49	Avro 707B.
E.11/49	Avro 698 'flying shell' or Avro 710.

B.104D (OR.285)	Vickers Type 673 Valiant Pathfinder.
GR.117P (OR.220)	Fairey Gannet AS.Mk.1.
M.123D & P (NR/A.32)	Blackburn B.83 & B.91, Short P.D.4 (S.B.6) Seamew, Westland M.123.
B.126 (OR.314 & OR.324)	Avro 721, Bristol Type 186, Handley Page HP.99, Short P.D.9.
B.128P	Handley Page Victor B.Mk.1
B.129P	Avro Vulcan B.Mk.1.
M.148T (NR/A.39)	Armstrong Whitworth AW.168, Blackburn B.103, Fairey M.148, Hawker P.1108, Short P.D.13, Westland M.148; *Also*(?): Saro P.178.
(OR.328 Draft only)	Gloster Thin Wing Javelin.
R.156 (OR.330)	Avro 730, English Electric P.10, Handley Page HP.100, Short P.D.12, Vickers R.156; *Also*: Saro P.188.
(OR.336)	Long-range high-altitude bomber – studies only.
(GOR.339)	*Interim*: Blackburn B.103A, de Havilland DH.110, Hawker P.1121, Vickers (Supermarine) Type 565. *Full*: Avro 739, Blackburn B.108, Bristol Type 204, de Havilland GOR.339, English Electric P.17, Fairey GOR.339, Hawker P.1129, Vickers (Supermarine) Type 571 (two designs); *Also*: Gloster Thin Wing Javelin, Handley Page study, Combined Avro 739/Hawker P.1129 project.
ER.180D	Avro 731.
RB.192D (OR.343)	BAC TSR.2.
(ASR.343)	General Dynamics F-111K.
ER.204D (GOR.345)	Hawker P.1127.
ER.206 (OR.346)	Blackburn B.123, de Havilland DH.127, Hawker P.1151, P.1152 & P.1153, Vickers (Supermarine) Types 581, 582, 583, 589 & 590.
GAR.214D (OR.345)	Ground attack aircraft. 'In hand' 1960–63 but abandoned.
MR.218 (OR.350)	Avro 776, Avro Shackleton development, Breguet Atlantic, versions of the BAC Vanguard and VC.10 airliners, versions of the Hawker Siddeley Comet and Trident airliners.
B.222P	Avro Vulcan Mk.2 with Skybolt.
M.232D & P	Hawker Siddeley Buccaneer Mk.2 (1963).
FGA.236D & P	Hawker Siddeley Kestrel.
(OR.354)	TSR.2 replacement – studies only.
(OR.355 & AST.355)	TSR.2 and Buccaneer replacement – studies only.
F.242 (later SR.250D & P) (NASR[OR].356)	Hawker Siddeley P.1154, RAF & RN.
(AST.357)	Various including Short P.D.69.
(AST.362)	BAC P.45 variants, Hawker Siddeley HS.1170B, HS.1171, HS.1173.
(ASR.362)	SEPECAT Jaguar.
(ASR.380)	Low-level V-bomber operations.
MR.254 (ASR.381)	Hawker Siddeley HS.800, Hawker Siddeley HS.801 Nimrod.
SR.255D & P (ASR.384)	Hawker Siddeley Harrier GR.Mk.1.
M.258D & P	Hawker Siddeley Buccaneer Mk.2 (1965).
260 (ASR.388)	Anglo–French Variable Geometry Aircraft (AFVG); *Also*: BAC UK Variable Geometry Aircraft (UKVG).
(ASR.392)	Panavia Tornado GR.Mk.1.
(AST.396 Iss. 1)	BAC P.66, P.69, P.70, P.71, P.72, P.73 & P.74, Hawker Siddeley HS.1182 developments, HS.1184, HS.1185, HS.1186. HS.1187, HS.1189, HS.1190, HS.1191 & HS.1192.
(AST.396 Iss. 2)	BAC P.76, P.77, P.78 & P.79, Hawker Siddeley HS.1195 & HS.1197.
GR.297 (ASR.409)	BAe Harrier GR.Mk.5.
(SR/A.417)	Panavia Tornado GR.Mk.4.
(SR/A.420)	BAe Nimrod 2000.
(SR/A.425)	Future Offensive Air System (FOAS).

Appendix Three
Post-War British Bomber Contracts

Type	Serials	Contract	(Date)
AFVG	No serials allotted		
Avro 698	VX770, VX777	6/Acft/1942/CB.6(a)	(22.6.48)
Avro 707	VX784, VX790	6/Acft/2205/CB.6(b)	(22.6.48)
Avro 707A	WD280	6/Acft/3395/CB.6(b)	(6.5.49)
Avro 707A & C	WZ736, WZ739, WZ744	6/Acft/7470/CB.6(a)	(13.11.51)
Avro 710	VX799, VX808	6/Acft/2626/CB.6(b)	(22.6.48)
Avro Shackleton	VP253-268, VP281-294	Acft/6062/C.4(a)	(9.3.46)
	VW126, VW131, VW135	6/Acft/1077/CB.6(a)	(17.7.47)
Avro 730/731	No serials allotted		
BAC TSR.2	XR219–227	KD/2L/02/CB.42(a)	(10.10.60)
	XS660–670	KD/2L/13/CB.42(a)	(14.6.63)
Blackburn Y.A.7 etc	WB781, WB788, WB797	6/Acft/822/......	(14.3.49)
Blackburn B.103	XK486–491, XK523–536	6/Acft/11790/CB.9(a)	(2.6.55)
Bristol Type 174	VX317, VX323	6/Acft/1308/CB.6(b)	(5.4.48)
EE Canberra B.Mk.1	VN799, VN813, VN828, VN850	Acft/5841/CB.6(b)	(10.12.45)
EE Canberra B.Mk.2/5	VX165, VX169, VX173, VX177, VX181, VX185	6/Acft/2000/......	(22.1.48)
Fairey Gannet	VR546, VR557	6/Acft/494/CB.9(b)	(31.7.46)
	WE488	6/Acft/3874/CB.9(a)	(19.7.49)
General Dynamics F-111K	XV884–887, XV902–947		(8.8.67)
Handley Page HP.80	WB771, WB775	6/Acft/1875/CB.6(a)	(11.3.49)
Handley Page HP.88	VX330, VX337	6/Acft/2243/CB.6(b)	(5.4.48)
Hawker P.1127	XP831, XP836	KD/2Q/02/CB.9(c)	(14.6.60)
	XP972, XP976, XP980, XP984	KC/2Q/02/CB.9(c)	(12.8.60)
Hawker P.1154	No serials allotted		
HSA Kestrel	XS688–696	KC/2Q/016/CB.9(b)	(2.7.63)
HSA Harrier	XV276–281	KC/3G/02/CB.9(b)	(8.3.66)
HSA Nimrod	XV147, XV148	KD/G/64/CB.6(b)	(17.9.65)
Panavia MRCA/ Tornado GR.Mk.1	XX946–948, XX950	NAMMO/BCI/C/3100/71/NU	(19.7.73)
SEPECAT Jaguar	XW560, XW563, XW566	'Av. Sec. 2A'	(15.10.68)
Short S.A.4 Sperrin	VX158, VX161	6/Acft/656/CB.6(b)	(19.1.48)
Short S.B.3	WF632, WF636	6/Acft/3955/......	(6.4.50)
Short S.B.1/S.B.4	No known official contract		
Short S.B.6 Seamew	XA209, XA213, XA216	6/Acft/7762/CB.9(a)	(3.52)
Vickers B.9/48	WB210, WB215	6/Acft/2339/......	(10.12.48)
Vickers Valiant B.Mk.2	WJ954	6/Acft/5957/CB.6(b)	(1.11.50)

Glossary

A&AEE	Aeroplane & Armament Experimental Establishment, Boscombe Down (in 1995 became part of DERA, the Defence Evaluation and Research Agency, and in 2001 part of the commercial QinetiQ organisation).
AAM	Air-to-air missile.
ACAS(OR)	Assistant Chief of the Air Staff (Operational Requirements) [Air Ministry post].
ACAS(TR)	Assistant Chief of the Air Staff (Technical Requirements) [Air Ministry post].
ACM	Air Chief Marshal.
ACT	Active control technology.
ADARD	Assistant Director of Aircraft Research and Development [Ministry of Supply post].
AI	Air Interception.
ALARM	Air-launched anti-radiation missile.
AMRAAM	Advanced medium-range air-to-air missile.
Anhedral	Downward slope of wing from root to tip.
AoA	Angle of attack, the angle at which the wing is inclined relative to the airflow.
AP	Armour piercing.
Area rule	The optimisation of longitudinal cross-section area distribution for minimum wave drag.
AS	Armstrong Siddeley.
A/S	Anti-submarine.
ASM	Air-to-surface missile.
Aspect ratio	Ratio of wing span to mean chord, calculated by dividing the square of the span by the wing area.
ASR	Air Staff Requirement.
ASRAAM	Advanced short-range air-to-air missile.
AST	Air Staff Target.
ASTOVL	Advanced short take-off and vertical landing.
ASV	Anti-surface vessel.
AVM	Air Vice-Marshal.
AWA	Armstrong Whitworth Aircraft Ltd.
BAC	British Aircraft Corporation.
BAe	British Aerospace (today BAE Systems).
Boundary layer control	Control of the layer of air that is in immediate contact with the aircraft's surface to increase lift, reduce drag and/or improve control under extreme flight conditions.
BP	Boulton Paul Aircraft.
BSE	Bristol Siddeley.
CA	Controller of Aircraft (UK).
CAD	Computer-aided design.
CAP	Combat air patrol.
CAS	Chief of the Air Staff [Air Ministry post].
CCV	Control-configured vehicle.
CinC	Commander in Chief.
Chord	Distance between centres of curvature of wing leading and trailing edges when measured parallel to the longitudinal axis.
CofG	Centre of gravity.
Critical mach number	Mach number at which an aircraft's controllability is first affected by compressibility, i.e. the point at which shock waves first appear.
CS(A)	Controller of Supplies (Air).
CTOL	Conventional take-off and landing.
DARD	Director of Aircraft Research and Development [MoS post].
DC	Depth charge.
DCAS	Deputy Chief of the Air Staff [Air Ministry post].
DCNR	Deputy Chief Naval Representative (Air) [MoS post].
DDARD(S)	Deputy Director of Aircraft Research and Development (Supply). [MoS post].
DDGSR(A)	Deputy Director General of Scientific Research (Air) [MoS post].
DDOR	Deputy Director of Operational Requirements.
DGSR	Director General of Scientific Research [MoS post].
DGTD(A)	Director General of Technical Development (Air) [MoS post].
DH	de Havilland.
Dihedral	Upward slope of wing from root to tip.
DMARD	Director of Military Aircraft Research and Development [MoS post].

DOR(A)	Director of Operational Requirements (Air).
DTD	Director of Technical Development [MoS post].
EAP	Experimental Aircraft Programme.
EAS	Equivalent airspeed (a rectified figure incorporating a compressibility correction).
ECM	Electronic countermeasures.
EE	English Electric.
FAA	Fleet Air Arm.
FBW	Fly-by-wire.
FLIR	Forward-looking infra-red.
HAL	Hawker Aircraft Limited.
HC	High-capacity bomb.
HE	High explosive.
HMG	His/Her Majesty's Government.
HP	Handley Page.
HSA	Hawker Siddeley Aviation.
HSG	Hawker Siddeley Group.
HTP	High-test peroxide (rocket fuel).
IAS	Indicated airspeed.
Incidence	Angle at which the wing (or tail) is set relative to the fuselage.
IR	Infra-red.
ISA	International Standard Atmosphere.
ITP	Instruction to Proceed.
Jet flap	An air jet placed at the wing trailing edge where the flow is induced around a strongly curved path to give very large lift coefficients.
Kinetic	heating of the airframe by friction created by its passage through the air. This can take the surface temperature towards the heat-resisting limit of the constructional materials.
LE	Leading edge.
LERX	Leading-edge root extensions.
LLTV	Low-light television.
LRMTS	Laser ranging and marked target seeker.
MAP	Ministry of Aircraft Production – created May 1940 to relieve the Air Ministry of its role of procuring aircraft and the equipment and supplies associated with them. Functions transferred to the Ministry of Supply in 1946.
MBB	Messerschmitt-Bolkow-Blohm.
MC	Medium-capacity bomb.
MetroVick	Metropolitan Vickers.

MinTech	Ministry of Technology – created in 1964 to cover computers, telecommunications and machines tools. Extended in 1966 to embrace other industries including merchant shipbuilding. In 1967 it merged with the MoA but a few years later the military aviation side was removed to be covered by the MoD Procurement Executive (MOD[PE]).
MoA	Ministry of Aviation – created October 1959 when the civil aviation functions of the Minister of Transport and Civil Aviation were transferred to the Ministry of Supply and merged.
MoD	Ministry of Defence – created late 1940s to co-ordinate the policy of the three armed services. In April 1964 the MoD was reconstituted to absorb the functions of the Air Ministry, Admiralty and War Office, the Air Ministry (the civilian body that had governed the RAF) ceasing to exist.
MoS	Ministry of Supply – created August 1939 to provide stores used by the RAF (and Army and Navy). Disbanded and reconstituted as the Ministry of Aviation in 1959.
MoU	Memorandum of Understanding.
MRCA	Multi-Role Combat Aircraft (later Tornado).
MWDP	United States Mutual Weapons Development Programme.
NACA	National Advisory Committee for Aeronautics (in America). Today is NASA, the National Aeronautics and Space Administration.
NASR	Naval Air Staff Requirement.
NAST	Naval Air Staff Target.
NATO	North Atlantic Treaty Organisation.
NBMR	NATO Basic Military Requirement.
NGTE	National Gas Turbine Establishment (merged with RAE in 1983).
nm	Nautical mile.
OR	Operational Requirement.
PCB	Plenum chamber burning.
PDRD(A)	Principal Director of Research and Development (Air) [MoS post].
PDSR(A)	Principal Director of Scientific Research (Air) [MoS post].
PDTD(A)	Principal Director of Technical Development (Air) [MoS post].

PR	Photo reconnaissance.
R&D	Research and Development.
RAAF	Royal Australian Air Force.
RAE	Royal Aircraft Establishment, Farnborough (in 1995 became part of DERA, the Defence Evaluation and Research Agency, and in 2001 part of the commercial QinetiQ organisation).
RATO	Rocket assisted take-off.
RN	Royal Navy.
RNVR	Royal Naval Volunteer Reserve.
RP	Rocket projectile.
rpm	Revolutions per minute.
RPV	Remotely piloted vehicle.
RR	Rolls-Royce.
RRE	Radar Research Establishment/Royal Radar Establishment (became part of DERA, the Defence Evaluation and Research Agency, and in 2001 part of the commercial QinetiQ organisation).
RSS	Relaxed static stability.
RTO	Resident Technical Officer.
SAGW	Surface-to-air guided weapons.
SAM	Surface-to-air missile.
SBAC	Society of British Aircraft Constructors, the UK's national trade association, which represented companies that supplied military and civil aircraft and their equipment and space. It later became the Society of British Aerospace Companies and today forms part of the ADS Group.
SR(A)	Staff Requirement (Air).
SST	Supersonic Transport.

STOL	Short take-off and landing.
STOVL	Short take-off and vertical landing.
TAS	True airspeed.
t/c	Thickness/chord ratio.
TE	Trailing edge.
TMB	Target Marker Bomb (= tactical nuclear weapon).
Transonic flight	The speed range either side of Mach 1.0 where an aircraft has both subsonic and supersonic airflow passing over it at the same time.
TRE	Telecommunications Research Establishment, Malvern. In 1953 TRE was combined with the Radar Research and Development Establishment to form the Radar Research Establishment (RRE). In 1957 it was renamed Royal Radar Establishment and in 1976 became RSRE for Royal Signals and Radar Establishment. Became part of DERA, the Defence Evaluation and Research Agency, and today comes within QinetiQ.
TT	Torpedo.
US(Air)	The Under Secretary of State for Air.
USAAF	United States Army Air Force.
USAF	United States Air Force.
USN	United States Navy.
VCAS	Vice Chief of the Air Staff [Air Ministry post].
VG	Variable geometry.
VIFF	Vectoring in forward flight.
V/STOL	Vertical and short take-off and landing.
V/TOL	Vertical take-off and landing.

Useful Conversion Factors

x 0.093	square feet (sq ft) to square metres (sq m)
x 0.3048	feet (ft) to metres (m)
x 0.4536	pounds (lb) to kilograms (kg)
x 1.2	Imperial (UK) gallons to US gallons
x 1.609	miles to kilometres (km) also miles per hour (mph) to kilometres per hour (km/h)
x 1.852	knots to kilometres/hour (km/h)
x 2.54	inches (in) to centimetres (cm)
x 4.5469	Imperial/UK gallons (gal) to litres (lit)
÷ 225	pounds (lb) to kilonewton (kN)

Bibliography and Source Notes

During the research for this book a great deal of primary source material was consulted including original documents held by the National Archives (in Record Groups AVIA 53, AVIA 54, AVIA 65 and AIR 20) and with museums, heritage centres, groups and individuals, as per the acknowledgements. Important secondary source material helped to get things started and fill gaps:

Armstrong Whitworth Paper Planes: Ray Williams; *Air Enthusiast* No 43, 1991.

Avro Aircraft since 1908: A. J. Jackson; Putnam, 1965.

The Avro Type 698 Vulcan: The Secrets Behind Its Design and Development: David W. Fildes; Pen & Sword, 2011.

Blackburn Aircraft since 1909: A. J. Jackson; Putnam, 1968.

The Bomber Role 1945 to 1970: Humphrey Wynn; Unpublished MoD Air Historical Branch review, 1984.

Boulton Paul Aircraft since 1915: Alec Brew; Putnam, 1993.

Bristol Aircraft since 1910: C. H. Barnes; Putnam, 1964.

The British Aircraft Specifications File: K. J. Meekcoms & E. B. Morgan; Air-Britain, 1994.

Choosing a Pirate for the Navy: Tony Buttler; *Air Pictorial* March & April 1997.

Comet Bomber Project: Michael J. F. Bowyer, *Air Pictorial* September 1987.

de Havilland Aircraft since 1909: A. J. Jackson; Putnam, 1962.

English Electric Aircraft and their Predecessors: Stephen Ransom & Robert Fairclough; Putnam, 1987.

Fairey Aircraft since 1915: H. A. Taylor, Putnam, 1974.

From Sea to Air – The Heritage of Sam Saunders: A. E. Tagg & R. L. Wheeler; Crossprint, 1989.

From Spitfire to Eurofighter: Roy Boot; Airlife, 1990.

Gloster Aircraft since 1917: Derek James; Putnam, 1971.

Hawker Aircraft since 1920: Francis K. Mason; Putnam, 1971.

Kingston's Fighters – The Jet Age: Ralph S. Hooper; (40th R. K. Pierson Lecture – text unpublished) 1992.

Low Level to Moscow – A Cold War Concept: Tony Buttler; *Air Pictorial* July 1996.

Operational Requirements: Ray Sturtivant; *Aeromilitaria* Issue 4 1996 & Issue 1 1997.

Planemakers 2 – Westland: David Mondey; Jane's, 1982.

Project Cancelled: Derek Wood; Jane's, 1986.

Red Rapier – Britain's Flying Bomb: Eric Morgan; *Air Enthusiast* Nos 70 & 71, 1997.

Seamew – A White Paper victim: Keith Saunders; *Air Pictorial* January 1999.

Short S.A.4 Sperrin: Clive Richards; *Wings of Fame* Issue 19, 2000.

Shorts Aircraft since 1900: C. H. Barnes; Putnam, 1967.

Strike Rivals: Tony Buttler; *Air Enthusiast* No 59, 1995.

Supermarine Aircraft since 1914: C. F. Andrews & E. B. Morgan; Putnam 1981.

Sydney Camm and the Hurricane: John Fozard (ed); Airlife, 1991.

Tactical Jet V/STOL – Its Future in a CTOL World: John Fozard; British Aerospace publication, 1985.

The Ten-Year Gap: Bill Gunston; *Flight International* 19th December 1963.

Tornado – Multi-Role Combat Aircraft: John Lake & Mike Crutch; Midland, 2000.

The TSR.2 Programme 1957–1965: Technological Innovation vs Economic Reality?: Clive Richards; *Airstream* 1997.

TSR.2 with Hindsight: Conference proceedings; RAF Historical Society, 1998.

Vital Bombers: Tony Buttler; *Air Enthusiast* No 79, 1999.

Westland Aircraft since 1915: Derek James; Putnam, 1991.

Wilfred Freeman: Anthony Furse; Spellmount, 2000.

The Wilson Government and the Demise of TSR.2, October 1964–April 1965: Sean Straw & John W. Young; *Journal of Strategic Studies* Vol 20 No 4, December 1997.

Index

INDEX OF PEOPLE

British Secret Projects Volume 1

Jet Fighters Since 1950

The original version of this book described the development work from the end of the Second World War to build the new generation of British jet fighters, in doing so it lifted the lid on many projects and 'dead-ends' which had never been publically discussed. This was the book that launched the hugely successful 'Secret Projects' series and the writing career of renowned historian and author Tony Buttler.

This completely revised and redesigned second edition takes the original primary source material and adds to it much new material that has come to life in the decades since the original edition was published. Particular emphasis is placed on the tender design competitions and the decisions at the Air Ministry to reject many promising projects, yet allow others to be built and flown. Aircraft types covered include the Hawker P.1103/P.1116/P.1121 series, the extraordinary jet and rocket mixed power-plant interceptors from Saunders-Roe, the equally impressive Fairey 'Delta III' and the origins of today's Hawk and Eurofighter.

The book includes appendices that list all the British fighter projects and specifications for this period. There are also a number of specially commissioned colour renditions of 'might-have-been' types in contemporary markings, plus photographs and general arrangement 3-view drawings – over 400 illustrations in total.

The result is a unique insight into the secret world of British jet fighter projects through the 'golden years' of the British aerospace industry, while also presenting a coherent picture of British fighter development and evolution.

Tony Buttler
Hardback, 224 pages
ISBN 9 781910 809051
£27.50 US $44.95

American Secret Projects Volume 1
Fighters, Bombers and Attack Aircraft 1937-1945

With all that has been written about the United States' combat aircraft of WWII, it is astounding how little has been published about the dozens of aircraft designs that were rejected before reaching production.

By December 7, 1941 almost all the major American combat aircraft of WWII had been designed, selected and in many cases were under production – everything from the P-40 fighter to the huge B-36 'Peacemaker'. Even so, the war years to 1945 saw a dizzying array of new aircraft designs and types being proposed. For example, between 1942 and 1944 Boeing alone submitted no fewer than eight multiengine, intercontinental bomber designs for consideration by the USAAF – every one of which had a wingspan of over 200ft; one had a span of a whopping 277ft! The Navy competition that resulted in the F7F Tigercat carrier fighter received more than a dozen different design submissions from at least half a dozen manufacturers. Then there are the virtually unknown Vought 'flying flapjack' series of designs, including one fighter and one attack aircraft for the USAAF.

In researching *American Secret Projects vol 1*, internationally-renowned aviation authors Tony Buttler and Alan Griffith have uncovered hundreds of previously classified files to provide specifications, histories, artist illustrations and 3-view drawings – many redrawn for clarity from the original factory submissions specifically for this book. The result is an unparalleled and fascinating record of the creative genius of American aircraft designers, from material which has lain hidden and forgotten for over 70 years. *American Secret Projects vol 1* is filled not only with aircraft that most historians, aircraft enthusiasts and modellers have never heard of, but many more that no-one but their designers could ever have dreamt up

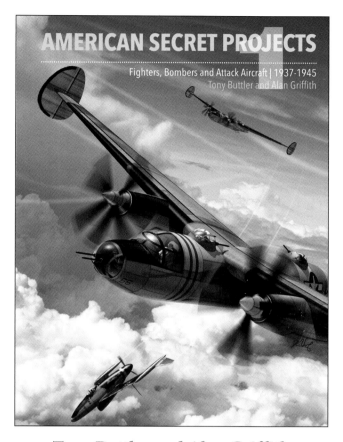

Tony Buttler and Alan Griffith

Hardback, 192 pages
ISBN 9 781906 537487
£27.50 US $44.95

French Secret Projects Volume 1
Post War Fighters

Following World War II France made determined efforts to catch-up with other countries in developing high-performance aircraft and designed successful machines to fulfil the needs of the Armée de l'Air, the Marine Nationale and compete in export markets.

For the next twenty years they were the only aircraft manufacturers to investigate with equal effort, turbojet, ramjet and rocket propulsion for manned fighters, either taking advantage of German 'war-booty' technology or using national pre-war research. A few, such as the Leduc and Griffon ramjet-powered fighters, reached prototype form, the Trident rocket-interceptor advanced to the experimental series (pre-production) stage and the Ouragan, Mystère, Super-Mystère, Mirage III and Etendard were produced in quantity and went on to win export orders.

Later, many attempts were made to design variable-geometry aircraft (including the Mirage G series) and VTOL types (the SNECMA Coléoptère and Dassault Mirage IIIV), and there were even a few flying boat interceptor studies. In the late sixties, in the pursuit of ever-higher speeds, Nord Aviation, Sud Aviation and primarily Avions Marcel Dassault also produced many Mach 3+ proposals.

Period drawings, promotional art, photographs of prototype aircraft, mock-ups, wind tunnel and promotional models are all combined to present, for the first time in the English language, a complete view of French military aircraft design from the Liberation of France to the late twentieth-century.

J-C Carbonel
Hardback, 280 pages
ISBN 9 781910 809006
£27.50 US $44.95

All titles from Crécy Publishing Ltd,
1a Ringway Trading Est, Shadowmoss Rd, Manchester M22 5LH
Tel 0161 499 0024
www.crecy.co.uk

Distributed in the USA by Specialty Press,
39966 Grand Ave, North Branch, MN 55056 USA.
Tel (651) 277-1400 / (800), 895-4585
www.specialtypress.com